# The Housebu... Bible

## An Insider's Guide to the Construction Jungle

## 5th Edition — 2002

## Mark Brinkley

Published July 2002

ISBN 0-9524852-4-9

### Ovolo Publishing Ltd

| | |
|---|---|
| Post | Orchard House |
| | Heath Road |
| | Warboys PE28 2UW |
| Phone | 01487 824704 |
| Fax | 01487 823186 |
| URL | www.ovolopublishing.co.uk |
| E-mail | info@ovolopublishing.co.uk |

**We run a mail order book service. Phone for details.**

Printed by
Burlington Press
Foxton
Cambridge

# Table of Contents

# Tables and Diagrams

# Preface

The Housebuilder's Bible first saw the light of day in 1994. It has always been my brainchild and over the past eight years it's success has transformed my life from being that of a working builder into that of a full-time writer. How did it come about?

From 1980 to 1994, I worked as a carpenter, small builder and developer in and around my home town of Cambridge, fifty miles north of London. That is what I would probably still be doing had it not been for the economic downturn in the early 90s. This book is very much a by-product of that recession.

In 1986, I went into partnership with Robin Gomm, a designer builder, and together we began buying up expensive plots and development opportunities, borrowing money to finance the bulk of the deals. In common with tens of thousands of small builders and developers (and millions of homeowners) we were caught out when the property market turned sour at the end of 1988. During that fateful year, we were building a four bedroomed house a few miles outside Cambridge and we had lots of interest. I remember turning down a cash offer of £180,000 on the house in the summer, deciding to hold off till we were completely finished in the hope of netting £200,000. But by the time we had finished, the market sentiment had turned and all deals were off. We ended up selling it for £154,000, virtually cost price, eight months later. At least we sold. Many developers refused to sell at these apparently knockdown prices and hung on far too long. They mostly went under.

Among the other bits of land we had accumulated was a building plot in Weston Colville, a small village east of Cambridge. We'd picked it up for £45,000 in 1986, seen its value double and then halve again. We decided that rather than try and build a house there for resale in this climate, we would just sell the plot. But in 1989 there were no takers, not even at £40,000. After a year on the market without an offer, it became obvious that it was time for a rethink. For during this period I had also married my wife, Charlotte, and together we were in the process of having three children in four years. A family house in the country suddenly seemed quite an appealing prospect. And whilst there was no market for rural building plots, even in 1990 it wouldn't take too long to sell a terraced house in central Cambridge. Thus we decided to go and build a house for ourselves on this unsaleable plot.

My partner, Robin, was meanwhile winning quite a bit of work from some farming contacts we had. A large new house, a series of barn conversions, some renovation work. It wasn't developing, it was design and build, but it kept us busy and paid the bills. My project took a back seat for a couple of years whilst we cracked on with the jobs in hand. It enabled us to spend a little time thinking about what we would build, how we would build it and how much we would hope to build it for. It was also during this time that the genesis of the Housebuilder's Bible occurred: initially just a little furtive note taking.

Work started on the house in Weston Colville in 1992, after the planners had had their say and re-worked many of our original thoughts. It was a sloping site, unusual for Cambridgeshire, and I was unprepared for just how much spoil we had to shift off site to get a level footprint. More note taking, plus a few calculations — the origins of Brinkley's Slope Law that features in Chapter 6. I took an active part in the groundworks and drainage, I serviced the brickies for a month and then worked as part of the carpentry team erecting the timber frame upper storey. After fourteen weeks we had the superstructure built and covered in. I then had to stop work whilst we negotiated a sale on the terraced house, whilst simultaneously helping my wife with the arrival of our third child in July. Finally we threw a whole mass of people at the house for eight weeks to enable us to move in before Christmas 1992.

Despite being the sixth house I had been directly involved in commissioning, I had found the process of housebuilding for myself and my family an amazingly rushed and frustrating experience. There simply wasn't anywhere to go to get a handle on the choices to be made, their costs and their pros and cons. There was at the time just one major book on selfbuild, Murray Armor's *Building Your Own Home*, which had sold in vast quantities since it first came out in the 1970s. It was and remains an excellent book, currently in its 17th edition, but it doesn't really deal with the technicalities of building. My idea was to put together a book which more or less started where Murray Armor's book left off — actually analysing the process of housebuilding from a builder's point of view.

The analogy of travel guides kept coming to mind. Imagine being dumped in a foreign city where you don't speak the language. You want to see the sights but you have no idea where they are or how to get to them. You have three days. You rush around like a whirling dervish, checking out likely looking buildings, catching buses all over the place and generally being pretty frantic. When the time comes to leave, you know you've "done" Rome or Barcelona or wherever it was you went, but you really don't have a clue whether you've seen the best bits or not. That was what it was like building a house in 1992. And so I figured there must be a market for guide book which would list the attractions, the admission prices, and the directions. That is more or less what the Housebuilder's Bible sets out to do.

I started the project by approaching a couple of publishers to see if there was any interest in such an idea. "Absolutely no way," said the first, "it's far too specialised." "Absolutely no way," said the second, "anything with prices in will date far too quickly." If anything, these responses just strengthened my resolve. I react well to being told I am crazy. I decided I would self-publish and concentrate on selling the book directly by mail order and at selfbuild exhibitions. First I had to write it.

All I had was a series of notes on an Amstrad PCW plus masses and masses of price data in the office. It seemed a mammoth task to turn it into a readable book, especially with a young family to look after, a new house to finish off and an existing business to keep going. Looking back on it, I am not too sure how I got it all from an idea to a physical book in just 18 months with all that going on in the background. As I said, this book is a by-product of recession and recessions make you work that much harder. A key figure in all this was undoubtedly my mother who believed me when I said I was going to write a book and who kept us afloat during 1994 when I was taking three days a week off from the building business to get the first draft completed. I couldn't really work at home because of the distractions of three pre-school boys padding about the house. So I took a leaf out of the notebook of one of my heroes, singer songwriter Randy Newman, who, whenever he had to produce a new album, went and hired an office, put a piano in it and shut himself away in it for eight hours a day until the work was complete. Like Randy, I found a room in a village office complex and shut myself away. It worked. That is where I cracked it.

Come November 1994, I had something worth putting down on paper. I had bought an Apple Mac and taught myself how to use PageMaker and Photoshop, the tools of the desktop publisher. I had the costs all worked into one unwieldy Excel spreadsheet. It wasn't going to be glossy but I was sure it would be useful. My first print-run was tentative, a few hundred run out on a DocuTech machine, a sort of upmarket photocopier. Had they sat around for ages, I would have written off the whole project to experience and gone back to join Robin in the building business. But the first edition sold. They sold off the page in the selfbuild mags and the sold by the hundred at the selfbuild exhibitions. Within a couple of months I had to do a reprint and the Housebuilder's Bible was on its way.

And ever since then there has been what I would describe as a very slow snowball effect going on. Each year has seen on average around 30% more Bibles sold than the year before. For the first couple of years I tried to get a presence in the major bookshops, making several appeals to WH Smith and Waterstones to stock my baby. But they were not in the least interested in such an amateurish product without a major publisher or a TV series behind it. Despite this, the sales kept climbing and the book sold very well through the selfbuild magazines and also through some professional titles as well. It surprises many who think of it primarily as a selfbuild title that around half the sales are made to 'professionals' - small builders and tradesmen, architects, surveyors, even estate agents. The fourth edition, the Millennium one, finally broke through into the retail market albeit via amazon.co.uk, the internet bookseller, whose sales depend to a large part on customer reviews. The Bible had some good

ones — and no, I didn't write them myself! By 2002, the Millennium edition was regularly appearing in the top 100 of all Amazon's book sales and was frequently one of their top five Home and DIY titles. I believe that the Housebuilder's Bible has become their biggest selling independent (i.e. self-published) title, something that surprises them almost as much as me.

During this period, I have also turned my hand to a little journalism. Michael Holmes, the long time editor of the leading selfbuild magazine Homebuilding & Renovating, was an early fan. He asked me to write for his magazine in 1996 and I have been contributing pieces to it ever since. And David Birkbeck and Jo Smit, editors of Building Homes, were also very supportive. Thanks to them I have published over 200 articles, many of them deepening and expanding areas I had covered in the Bible. Journalism has also improved my skills as a writer — I don't waffle as much — and in 2001 I picked up my first ever gong, Residential Property Writer of the Year, at the Halifax Laing Homes Press awards.

So much for me. What about this new edition, the 5th?

New editions seem to last between two and three years. The prices change, the regs change, the names change, the internet arrives, the range of products gets larger and the guide keeps gently expanding to reflect all this. I must admit that I am finding it an increasingly difficult subject to stay abreast of. Back in the early 90s, housebuilding seemed a much simpler task than it does now. In recession, value for money was king and all I needed to do really was point out how not to get ripped off and how to design in value. Today, there is a whole lot more money sloshing about and people are regularly specifying stuff like Jacuzzis, granite worktops and gyms, things that really didn't feature ten years ago. There are stacks of products around that didn't exist back then — sunpipes, SIPS panels, photovoltaic cells, rainwater harvesters, CAT 5 cabling, I beams, self placing concrete, to name but seven. The first edition of the Housebuilder's Bible was very much a hands-on book. This edition is much more the work of a jobbing journalist and I recognise that as a weakness but also probably an inevitability. The market as a whole has expanded to such an extent that it would be almost impossible to have worked with everything that's now regularly used in housebuilding.

The agenda has also moved on. Whilst material costs haven't really changed a great deal in ten years, labour rates have rocketed and,

to make matters more difficult, they are now very variable across the country where once they were more nearly uniform. One of the key benchmark rates in housebuilding is how much bricklayers charge for laying a thousand bricks. Back in 94, it was more or less £180/thousand across the country. Today it varies between a little over £200/thousand in some of our quieter backwaters to over £500/thousand in and around London. Such is the pressure of these price rises that developers are beginning to abandon brickwork in favour of cheaper solutions. In fact two of the stories I covered in the early part of 2002 involved building houses with what are called brick slips, not a million miles away from stone cladding. There is a huge and growing interest in housing solutions that remove as much as possible of the (expensive) sitework and replace it with semi-automated factory procedures, something the Japanese have been quietly doing for the past forty years. It's a very interesting time for housebuilders, large and small and it's been fascinating to watch it develop and change over these past few years. My hunch is that the technological changes will hasten if house prices continue to rise but will come juddering to a halt if the market takes another tumble.

In order to cover the innovation aspects more thoroughly, I plan to expand the editorial output of the Housebuilder's Bible. During the lifespan of this edition, expect to see occasional supplements appearing. I am not sure how often yet — plans are still formulating — but these digests will be able to keep abreast of the regulation changes — there are more happening today than at any previous time in our history — price movements, market trends and innovations. If you want to see one of these supplements, we will of course need to have your contact details — see the very last page of this book to find out more.

Housebuilding is a vast topic and no one can hope to know everything there is to know about it. I am no exception and I am aware that in some areas I am barely doing more than skating over the surface, handing out a few pointers. The value of a book like this derives in great part from pooling other peoples' expertise into one accessible source. Every edition of this book improves on the one before and many of these improvements are as a direct result of readers contacting me about little things which are unclear, misleading or just plain wrong. So I will finish with an offer of thanks to the many hundreds of people who have helped me with this project over the years and a plea to keep the feedback rolling in.

Mark Brinkley May 2002

## Acknowledgements

*Benchmark House* ..................................... *Andrew and Roger Allen, AB Homes*

*Intial editing* ............................................... *Sean McSweeney*

*Proof Reading* .......................................... *Anne Bragg*

*Book design* ............................................... *Nick Ellis*

*Cover design* .............................................. *GDA Associates*

*Front cover illustration* ............................ *Adam Brinkley*

*Primary Reference Sources* ................... *NHBC, Building Research Establishment, Financial Times, Hutchins' Priced Schedules, Centre for Alternative Technology, Which?, National Home Energy Ratings, Building and Building Homes, Zurich*

*Not forgetting* ........................................... *Robin Gomm, Norman Cox, Andrew Bailey, David Birkbeck, Jo Smit, Michael Holmes, David Snell, Bob Matthews, David Olivier, Jeremy Pembrey, Phil Ayton, Rick Hughes, Tim Crump, Steve Mattick, Nick Jones, Brian Belton and a multitude of others*

*Project management* ............................. *Charlotte Brinkley*

*Impossible without* ................................. *Diana Brinkley*

*General thank you to numerous tradesmen and businesses which have taken the time and trouble to provide informations and quotations. Good prices and useful information will frequently have resulted in a mention and I hope this somehow repays the trouble you have all taken.*

*Also to the many people who have mailed, rung, faxed or e-mailed me with new information and corrections on current data.*

*Dedication: to David Thomas, a fine writer and a close friend since schooldays. His untimely death in a car crash in Kuwait, where he was reporting on the aftermath of the war in 1991, provided me with the inspiration to get cracking on this project.*

# Chapter 1
# Background

## The Builders Dilemma

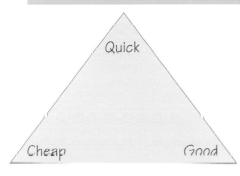

This triangle represents the age-old conundrum for all builders and would-be builders. It is said that you can have any two of these points in a building job but only at the expense of the third. Thus you can have a good, cheap job but it won't be quick, or a cheap, quick job that won't be any good.

So when you hear claims — as you may — of people having built (or more likely "put up") a house in just eight weeks you can reply, confidently, "Ah, but how much did it cost you?" And, similarly, if you meet someone who claims to have built a house for £17/ft², you can look them in the eye and exclaim "I bet it took you years" — and you'll be right. So before you set out to build a new house, first examine your motives and see where you fit into the triangle.

### The Cheap House
The average new house is constructed entirely by builders; it takes about 6-8 months to complete and costs around £50/ft² (that's £540/m²). It is built to standards that meet — and do not exceed — the current building regulations.

If you want to maximise the financial return on your new house — in all but the most upmarket areas — it pays to keep it dead simple. Whether you plan to actually be a hands-on builder or not, the following advice should be carried out to the letter.

Dispense with any notions of individual design. Aim for a four-square box drawn up by a technician or a surveyor or better still from some already existing book of house plans — in fact anyone except an architect.

- Avoid all of the following:
a) Layouts with any more than four external corners
b) Anything round or curved
c) Anything poking out through the roof (dormers, chimneys)
d) Anything other than large format concrete tiles on the roof
e) Anything other than face brickwork on external walls
f) Anything other than straight stairs
g) Complicated sites (unless bought for bargain price)
h) Fancy Continental plumbing systems
i) Timber frame (except in Scotland where it's cheaper)
j) Trying to build an "Eco" house
k) Underfloor heating
l) Central vacuum cleaning systems
m) Kitchens that don't come from MFI
n) Bathrooms that don't come from Plumb Center
o) Anything but Magnet casement windows
p) Home cinema rooms
q) Handmade anything at all (bricks, tiles, pavings)
r) Agas
s) Garages — especially ones with remote-controlled doors
t) Porches and entrance canopies
u) Conservatories
v) Built-in cupboards
w) Hardwood floors
x) Data cabling
y) Any lighting that doesn't hang from a pendant in the middle of each room — especially if it's got the word halogen in it
z) Almost everything second-hand — it's only been salvaged because it's worth more than the new replacements.

Your sole remaining decision will be whether to paint or stain your woodwork. Received wisdom is divided on this topic; stain is quicker and easier to apply but it's more expensive to buy and the joinery needs more careful preparation. What you will end up with will have all the charm of a 50s council house. But if space for bucks is your main motive in taking on a construction project, then you'll be very happy. Much of the book that follows is concerned with the options that might turn a cheap house into a good house and therefore much of the book will be of little relevance to you. I have, however, always tried to indicate what the cheapest option is in each element of the house.

### The Quick House
The quick house will almost certainly be a kit house, which is largely prefabricated in a workshop or factory. It will also, very likely,

be a timber framed house. They are rarely cheap; even the simplest box-type designs are likely to add a little to construction costs, though with some blocklayers now charging their labour out at over £1 per block this is no longer a universal truth. But neither are framed houses necessarily that much quicker to build. What really takes up a builder's time is the finishing tasks and these are pretty much the same whatever your chosen building methods.

## The Good House

Most would-be individual housebuilders are not hard up nor in a hurry — at least they're not when they're just planning it all; they might beg to differ when they're halfway through building. They can afford to browse and contemplate and research. They will look at many different options before embarking and will probably be keen that the finished product should somehow be an expression of their personality as well as a way of meeting their individual needs in a way that an off-the-peg house couldn't hope to. Even if you are building for resale rather than personal occupation, you are more than likely to want to build an attractive house that

passers-by will come to admire and occupants will love to call home. After all, the house is likely to be standing long after any transient profit is banked and spent, and may well still be there when they are burying your grandchildren. To build well, you have to know what's going on and not just rely on experts: the more you are involved in the design, the more you will appreciate the outcome, and the more you are involved in the building, the better that outcome will be.

## Is this book for you?

What follows is housebuilding's first bodice ripper, a warts 'n' all rough guide. It is not a DIY manual (there are enough of those) and it is not a disguised advertisement (I'm not selling anything apart from this book). Although primarily concerned with new housebuilding, there is also much information specifically tailored for people converting or restoring existing properties. Many of the tricks and tips described I have learnt the hard way since I started as a selfbuilder in 1980. As the old saw goes, experience is the best education but it is also the most expensive. My hope is that some of my "experience" and research will help you avoid expensive pitfalls, many

of which I've had the doubtful pleasure of falling victim to myself. In short, the aim of this book is to enable you to build a good house cheaply and quickly. Now hang on a minute, I thought that wasn't possible.

# Housebuilding in the UK

Housebuilding in Britain has always been a boom or bust activity, and this has never been more clearly illustrated than in the last few years. The early 80s saw a huge surge in private housebuilding caused partly by the postwar baby boomers entering the housing market for the first time and partly by people choosing to live in smaller groups. This increased demand also led to a huge increase in house prices which, in turn, encouraged more and more people to jump onto the bandwagon of home ownership, encouraged by the Thatcher Government which made the supposed benefits of property owning a key plank of its programme.

## The Slump

This particular bandwagon came juddering to a halt on August 1st, 1988 when Nigel Lawson, then our Chancellor of the Exchequer but now better known as Nigella's Dad, stopped a tax perk known as double mortgage tax relief. I remember the day well. I was property developing at the time, owed the bank about

a quarter of a million and had just learned that I was about to become a father for the first time. It was also the day we completed on a rather large barn for conversion in a village just outside Cambridge. The timing was about as bad as it can get.

Double mortgage tax relief sounds like rather an obscure tax perk as indeed it was; these days we have no tax relief of any description on mortgages but back in 1988 both halves of an unmarried couple could claim tax relief on a mortgage which was worth a few bob. It was an anomaly and Chancellor Lawson strove to eliminate anomalies. The problem was that he announced his intention to do so in his budget speech in March, telling us all that the elimination of this particular anomaly would take place at midnight on the 31st of July. People who, in more normal times, would never have considered house purchase together were suddenly bounced into it by a fear that it was now or never for the housing ladder. The housing market, al-

ready toppy, duly went ballistic for four and a half months in the rush to get sales completed before the Chancellor's cut off point. In Cambridge, average house prices jumped by nearly 25% virtually overnight. Many of the 'Lawson couples' lived to regret the unwarranted emotional entanglement caused by this feverish speculation. All of them lived to regret the financial chaos brought on by the price bubble bursting on August 1st. For almost all of them, it would be ten years before the houses they bought at ridiculous prices in 1988 would be worth as much again.

For us property developers, it was more painful still but then, as a group, we have never elicited much sympathy. What happened on August 1st was distinctly eerie. The housing market just came to a standstill. Viewing stopped. Offers to buy were withdrawn. People just lost interest in buying homes altogether. Prices didn't fall overnight. But then with hardly any house sales happening, it was hard to know what house prices were really doing. However, during 1989 it became apparent that all the estate agents' talk of the market "just taking a breather" was bull and, as the number of sales continued to decline, the rout set in. Things weren't helped at all by another of Nigel Lawson's foibles, the decision to peg the pound to the deutchmark (remember that currency?) which led to interest rates going up and up — the base rate was 15% from October 1989 to October 1990. As you can imagine, housebuilders took a bath. It wasn't until 1993 that house prices stopped falling. Even then, the recovery was painfully slow. Rather than being a return to the good old days before Lawson's bubble where house prices gently rose year on year (or so it seemed), everything seemed to remain frozen. Newspapers were full of stories of families stuck in "negative equity" and unhappy young homeowners just handing their keys back to the mortgage lenders and going back to live with Mum and Dad.

The climate all changed once again with the election of New Labour in 1997. Strange to think of a supposedly left wing government riding to the rescue of the property owning classes but then life was ever full of these little ironics. The fact is that average house prices were back to exactly the same level in May 1997 as they had been on that fateful day back in March 1988 when Nigel Lawson delivered his budget speech. Since 1997, house prices have begun to behave exactly as they did from the 1950s through till 1988 — in Cambridge, they have increased by an average of nearly 15% each year, equivalent to doubling every five years. The Brits love this state of affairs. Never mind that the NHS is crumbling, the schools are appalling and that the trains keep crashing — just see how much our homes are worth. It contributes in no small way to the national feelgood factor. A semi in Reading is worth the same as a small chateau in the Limoges. It's a moot point as to who is really better off with this state of affairs but there is no doubt that somehow it makes us feel important. We could as a nation, if we wanted to, just about buy the whole of France and still have change for a couple of Spanish Costas and a Greek Island or two. It's also been a major factor in keeping Labour in power. It's the Tories who are remembered for messing with house prices — New Labour has returned us to the status quo ante. Whether there will be a Gordon Brown bubble to rival Nigel Lawson's remains to be seen but the longer the good times roll in property, the bigger the hangover.

## Mini-markets

It's a fact that, although commentators love to talk about "the housing market", in reality there is no such entity. The painful bubble ef-

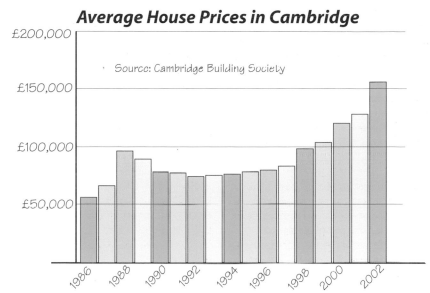

### Average House Prices in Cambridge

Source: Cambridge Building Society

Looked at over a 17-year period, the Lawson Bubble of 1988 looks insignificant. But the pain was real enough. Let's hope there isn't another one lurking in wait for us, but the chart doesn't look promising.

fect of 1988 was largely restricted to Southern England. Generally speaking, the further away from London you travelled the less spectacular the effect. Price rises had been much more muted in the 80s and sales activity far less frenetic; consequently, the market didn't fall off a cliff in 1989. In Northern England and, in particular, Scotland, prices continued to rise gently for some time after that date — it is the idle boast of some Edinburgh estate agents that house prices have never fallen in that city, ever.

Statistics published in the media about the housing market are, therefore, usually next to useless because they tend to conceal the different trends going on in the various regional markets. To really get the feel for a market, it must be studied at a local level.

## How we build houses

There are other interesting aspects to the British housebuilding scene besides the topsy turvy nature of the housing market. Particularly pertinent to this book is the way we go about building homes — more particularly who builds them. Because it turns out that we are pretty unusual in this respect too. If you were to imagine a pie chart representing the total number of houses built each year in the UK — around 180,000 — there would be three slices in it marked

• Speculative housebuilders (80%)
• Social housing (12%)
• Others (8%)

What do these descriptions mean? Starting with the middle one, social housing. This is mostly homes built by housing associations

for rent or shared ownership. This has more or less taken over from the council housing schemes which were such a feature of the middle years of the 20th century. Some fascinating and innovative schemes have been put together in the past few years, notably by Peabody Trust in and around London. But by and large these schemes are for multiple units, not really the essence of what this book is about.

Now let's move on to the first category. Speculative housebuilders. First thing to note is just how big this section is, accounting for over 140,000 new homes every year. In most other countries, speculative housebuilding is an also-ran. But in Britain not only is it by far the most common method of delivering new homes, but this huge market is dominated by comparatively few names. In fact, the top twenty speculative housebuilders knock out around 90,000 homes between them. They are almost all national concerns, almost all quoted on the stockmarket which, incidentally, treats them as though they have all just been diagnosed with leprosy. Beneath them are several dozen regional housebuilders accounting for around 30,000 homes in total, each of them building a few hundred homes each year. And beneath this are the small housebuilders doing anything from one site of maybe twenty at any one time right down to the general builders who occasionally do a spec build.

And then there are the others. Sorry if I make it appear as though we are constantly sliding down the pyramid towards the bottom of the heap. Because this book is primarily intended for the builders down here at the bottom of the housebuilding heap. The small builders and the others. Particularly the others.

In many ways, this *others* grouping is by far the most interesting. Although it may account for less than 10% or so of new homes, that still amounts to between 15,000 and 20,000 each year. And the great bulk of these are built by individuals for their own occupation — what the media and everyone else has learned to call Selfbuild. The crucial, defining distinction between selfbuild and spec building is that selfbuilding is done for your own occupation and is, consequently, out of the tax net. It's not being carried out as a trade and therefore there is no profit being made and no income tax to pay. And additionally there is no

capital gains tax to pay because principal residences are tax exempt - always have been.

In the next section (and indeed throughout the book) I will be looking in greater detail at some of the pros and cons of selfbuild but before getting stuck into that I think it's important to point out that there is a huge grey blanket of an area spread out between the sort of selfbuild featured in Channel 4's *Grand Designs* and the output of a small spec builder who builds a house or two for sale every year and every so often builds a new one for himself, that way netting a nice little tax free earner. I have often heard of builders referring to odd plots of land they own as "their

pension" and all good pensions should be tax free, shouldn't they?

Many good people, academics amongst them, have tried to assess the size of the UK selfbuild market and they get into all sorts of difficulties because selfbuild is not a clearly defined entity. The first 10,000 selfbuilds are easy to spot — they show up on the VAT returns — but the next 10,000 get murkier and murkier the higher the total gets. Hence I quite like the term *others*. It covers a lot of nefarious undertakings.

# Selfbuild

Not that long ago, back in the 1970s and 80s, selfbuild had a decidedly alternative flavour to it. Selfbuild was usually group selfbuild. This typically involved a number of individuals or families pooling their labour to build homes for themselves in a little estate. Group selfbuild enjoyed a boom in the 80s but came horribly unstuck when the Lawson bubble burst in 1988 (see previous section for more on this). Groups were left with homes worth less than they had paid for them and some of these schemes were abandoned half built. Private group selfbuild all but disappeared off the radar screens after this, though a couple of the original organisers continue, notably Wadsworths. But group selfbuild also existed in another guise where the schemes were done for rent rather than ownership — it's now known as Community Selfbuild — and this small sector continues to flourish though it rarely accounts for more than a dozen schemes each year. In order to form a Community Selfbuild group, you need to have identified a number of people living in the same area who are in genuine housing need. Whereas the country is stuffed full of people in genuine housing need, not many of them have the time or inclination to go about meeting it by building a house which they then have to rent. So it remains a bit of a niche. The emphasis is often on building cheaply, simply and in an environmentally sound way, which often means building the Walter Segal way. Walter Segal (1907 - 1985) was an innovative architect who designed and promoted a very simple method of building timber frame houses which could be easily mastered by novices. The Segal Trust continues to pro-

mote his vision and should be a first port of call for anyone interested in pursuing these options. Another useful contact is the Community Self Build Agency who keep abreast of up-and-coming schemes all over the country and can act as a sort of dating service for would-be community self builders.

Whilst this specialised niche is alive and thriving, it is now dwarfed by the mainstream selfbuild market which consists of people acting as, what the Americans call, paper contractors — do-it-yourself property developers. This group tend to be fairly well-off and tend to build relatively high spec houses; some estimates reckon that over a third of all detached housing in the UK is now selfbuilt. For many of this new breed of selfbuilder there will be little or no physical involvement in the construction of their homes; they are instead providing the nous (and money) to get a plot of land purchased and to build a new home on it. Throughout the postwar years, this group was typically buying and doing up old wrecks of houses, but as the wrecks with the most potential have mostly been snapped up now, their attention has moved on to building from scratch. Now it is recognised that there is such a thing as a selfbuild industry which supports many specialist businesses, three national magazines — Build It, Selfbuild & Design and Homebuilding & Renovating — and various exhibitions up and down the land.

Selfbuild has experienced something of a boomlet against a background of a house-building sector generally with no growth whatsoever. It would have experienced a full

scale boom if only it wasn't so hard to buy land to build on: for every successful self-builder, there are four or five who give up the dream and go and do something else instead.

Much of the sales literature which is used to attract individuals to build their own homes is based on the fact that there is a large, tax-free profit to be had. Whilst the responsible end of the market likes to rein in such claims, you still come across examples of this hype. Typical of these is one that appeared in July 95 in the magazine Nationwide Properties:

*Interested in a management activity for your spare time which should gain you more in a year than your regular salary? With the benefits completely tax free? If so, you are looking at selfbuild. It is all based on the fact that the cost of a serviced building plot added to the cost of building a house on it using subcontractors is significantly less than the finished value of the property. Typically the savings will be around 25% and on a £160,000 home this can be £40,000.*

Sounds too good to be true? You guessed it. I've already described the slump that followed the last housing boom. As we reach the start of the new century, large tracts of the nation are back in the grip of another boom with prices rising almost as dramatically as they did in the 80s. Painless paper profits are being made on house sales and London dinner parties are once again being burdened with tales of gazumping and thieving estate agents. Property development is once again highly profitable. In fact the above quote looks to be just about spot on. But (and it's a big but) the profits flowing towards today's selfbuilders and property developers are the result of the broad swell of a friendly economic tide, not of any brilliant ruse of making money out of the banks and the building trade. When the tide turns (as it did in 1988) you'd better watch out.

## Land Costs are the Key

The way in which prices for building plots are set is based on subtracting the building costs from the estimated value of the completed house. For example, if the estate agent or surveyor marketing a plot reckons that a nicely finished house there might fetch £200,000 and that it might cost around £100,000 to build, then he will probably recommend that the plot be sold for around £80,000, maybe more, leaving a small element of profit for the builder. There is obviously a return here but the problem is that there are many more costs involved than just the plot price and the building costs. If house prices increase by 15% during the time it takes you to build, all appears well and good and you do appear to get a fantastic return on your efforts; but if house prices don't go up you'll have to throw an almighty number of hours at your building project if you are to keep costs down to a level at which you appear to make a profit of more than a few per cent.

The bulk of the profit in a greenfield housing site tends to go to the landowner who succeeded in getting planning permission to turn whatever was there before into building land. In most places in the UK, agricultural land is worth around £2000/acre; in contrast, in SE England, half acre building plots are currently fetching over £300,000. One effect of this relationship between land costs and finished housing costs is that building plots tend to go up in value faster than house prices when house prices are rising; conversely, plot prices fall further than house prices when house prices slump. And recently, we have been seeing the phenomenon of land prices being bid up to unrealistic levels because the competition is so fierce.

## Understanding the Costs

Table 1a compares the development costs for a professional developer and a selfbuilder using a timber frame kit house on an averagely profitable site. The costings reflect something akin to our standard house — see Chapter 2 The Benchmark. If you just add plot costs and building costs together you'd see a 20-30% profit (this is the margin that the press get so excited about), but a more thorough analysis reveals that the figure is nowhere near this amount. In particular, the finance costs eat into the gross profit at an alarming rate and the effect of a) interest rates going up and b)

failure to obtain a quick sale are disastrous. Anyone who borrows to finance a project as large as a new house is extremely vulnerable to changes in interest rates — see Table 1b to see just how catastrophic these effects were for developers at the end of the 80s. Table 1b assumes that around £80,000 is borrowed in four stages to finance the building of a house, fairly typical of this kind of development deal. When interest rates start to rise, professional developers tend to get squeezed not just by the extra cost of this finance but also by the fact that the level of sales tends to decline, sometimes accompanied by the dreaded fall in house prices. Housebuilders are very vulnerable in these circumstances and what looks like a healthy profit on a house can evaporate within a matter of weeks. A selfbuilder is in a subtly different situation to a speculative developer and this may mean that they are able to hang on to more of this gross profit margin. The selfbuilder doesn't need to find a buyer and therefore has no selling costs; also the selfbuilder can keep construction costs down by carrying out supervision and some construction work. Against this, however, it is unlikely that they can build as cheaply as a professional developer, whatever construction methods they use.

## The DIY Approach

DIYers are, in any event, a race apart from the conventional building client; they are drawn to take on challenges like a moth to a flame and will use any handy facts and figures to back up what is really an emotional decision. The majority of building projects are designed and commissioned along the time-honoured lines of sending out the plans for quotation to a number of builders and then selecting the best option from them. DIY builders are very unlikely to use this macro approach (although they will keenly search for best material and subcontract prices) because they will assume that their endeavours will produce a cheaper and probably a better job. Maybe they will, but how could one ever tell?

*Richard and Valerie Dring: one of the 15,000-odd self builders who graduated in 1997. Their project involved lots of hands-on work from both of them and from other family members. What's so special about the Drings? Mrs. Dring just happens to be my bank manager.*

Common sense dictates that selfbuilding, whether just project management or carrying out some of the work as well, should achieve some savings on employing a main contractor for the whole job. But if you value your labour at all, you will probably find that you are worth a depressingly small amount per hour worked: I would anticipate around £2-3/hr for a beginner, rising to double or at most treble for an experienced builder/ speculator when house prices are stable.

## Real Savings

The costs of the average residential building job are made up of around 50% on-site labour and 50% materials. (Obviously this varies from project to project but is almost always within the 60:40 and 40:60 ratios). In theory, you could therefore achieve savings of around 50% on construction costs if you carried out all the labour yourself — but here we have to look at some rather complex actuarial calculations about the value of your time and the cost of borrowed money. Only if you are both rich and unemployed can you afford to ignore these calculations.

## 1a: Comparison of Costs: Developer v Kit Home Selfbuilder

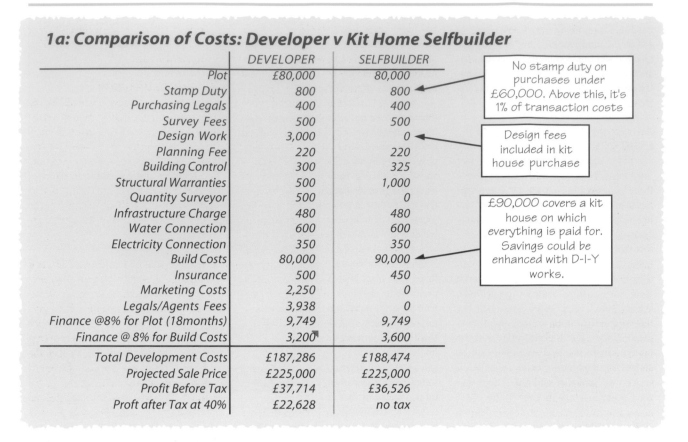

|  | DEVELOPER | SELFBUILDER |
|---|---|---|
| Plot | £80,000 | 80,000 |
| Stamp Duty | 800 | 800 |
| Purchasing Legals | 400 | 400 |
| Survey Fees | 500 | 500 |
| Design Work | 3,000 | 0 |
| Planning Fee | 220 | 220 |
| Building Control | 300 | 325 |
| Structural Warranties | 500 | 1,000 |
| Quantity Surveyor | 500 | 0 |
| Infrastructure Charge | 480 | 480 |
| Water Connection | 600 | 600 |
| Electricity Connection | 350 | 350 |
| Build Costs | 80,000 | 90,000 |
| Insurance | 500 | 450 |
| Marketing Costs | 2,250 | 0 |
| Legals/Agents Fees | 3,938 | 0 |
| Finance @8% for Plot (18months) | 9,749 | 9,749 |
| Finance @ 8% for Build Costs | 3,200 | 3,600 |
| Total Development Costs | £187,286 | £188,474 |
| Projected Sale Price | £225,000 | £225,000 |
| Profit Before Tax | £37,714 | £36,526 |
| Profit after Tax at 40% | £22,628 | no tax |

Note boxes:
- No stamp duty on purchases under £60,000. Above this, it's 1% of transaction costs
- Design fees included in kit house purchase
- £90,000 covers a kit house on which everything is paid for. Savings could be enhanced with D-I-Y works.

Most DIY projects are of low value (say, less than £1000) and have little effect on house values. They are carried out because the occupants appreciate their amenity value. However, larger building projects — extensions, conversions, rehabilitations and especially new housebuilding — call for much closer assessment of your labour input. By taking on even part of the work yourself, you are in effect becoming a speculative builder whose work will be rewarded by enjoying an increase in the value of your property. The more work you carry out yourself, the less you pay to others and the greater your eventual profit (in theory). The problem with this sort of work is that your labours are far more likely to be rewarded in line with property price movements rather than with how hard or well you yourself work. In boom times your rate per hour may appear to be enormous (and you'd probably think yourself very clever for embarking on this nice little tax-free earner); however, building through a slump puts all that into a new perspective, and many DIY builders will have found that they have actually lost money — and the more masochistic will have converted that into a loss per hour which begins to make slavery look like an attractive alternative.

Most people would not consider carrying out all the work themselves. In fact, the vast majority of people would have no more wish to take on such a task than they would choose to educate their children at home; life simply isn't that long. There are, however, many people who find their work is seasonal, intermittent or out of normal working hours, to whom a high level of involvement in a building project makes good sense. They will tend to be practical and experienced in problem solving and those that are already running their own business will have much of the organisational backup in place already. The extra costs involved will not be enormous and even if their work only nets them £2.50/hr, that's still more than they'd get doing nothing.

However, for many people selfbuilding may just prove to be a lousy option. They will be committing themselves to 2-3000 hours work — often very hard and dirty work — putting up an overpriced structure to a design that isn't very good in the vague hope of making a "dream home" and a "fantastic windfall profit" to boot. Ask yourself two questions:
- If it is that easy to make money, why don't more selfbuilders turn into professional property developers?
- If builders' profits are so exorbitant high, how come so many of them keep going bust?

I started as a selfbuilder (albeit with a renovation not a new build) and went on to become a "professional" (in that other people paid me for my labours), often working alongside selfbuilders. It'll come as no surprise when I report that the hours are long, the work is backbreaking and the pay is crap. Actually, when I started building in 1980 the pay was quite good: a good builder would earn more than most manual workers and as much as many professionals like teachers and junior doctors. However builders have tended to fall way down the list though the reignited boom in SE England has tended to balance things up again. For much of the 1990s, most tradesmen reck-

## 1b: Effect of Interest Rates

| BORROWING RATES | 8% | 12% | 16% |
|---|---|---|---|
| Stage 1: £20k for 8 months | £1,067 | £1,600 | £2,133 |
| Stage 2: £20k for 6 months | 800 | 1,200 | 1,600 |
| Stage 3: £20k for 4 months | 533 | 800 | 1,067 |
| Stage 4: £20k for 2 months | 267 | 400 | 533 |
| Total interest after 8 months | £2,667 | £4,000 | £5,333 |
| Interest for each extra month | £533 | £800 | £1,067 |

oned they were doing well if they pulled in £15,000/annum; however, the skills shortage has caused a significant hike in rates and in areas like London, tradesmen are now regularly netting £150/day, equivalent to £30,000 a year.

## Management with a Broom

For every seven or eight hours spent on construction, one hour has to be put into servicing the site. This can involve any and everything from sweeping up and unloading lorries to meeting building inspectors and buying materials. Many selfbuilders take on this "management with a broom" role thinking that they may not be able to plaster a wall or fit a staircase, but they had no trouble organising the school run, therefore... Be warned. You'd be right to think that the organisational skills are not in themselves exceptional, but their efficient execution is very dependent on a thorough working knowledge of the building trades and the local building practices and prices. After three or four projects, you'll start to get halfway good; if it's your first time, you'll find it an almighty struggle and you'll be unlikely to do it well. Your subcontractors will very quickly realise they are working for a novice and the less scrupulous ones may be very tempted to take advantage of this and to cut corners or to bodge, particularly if you've negotiated "keen" labour prices. Whilst your building inspector should ensure that the structure is adequate, very little professional checking takes place above foundation level and, in any event, most of the finishing trades are not covered by building regulations.

Furthermore, don't kid yourself that you're doing away with the overheads of employing a main contractor by managing the project yourself. Your phone bill will be up by £100-£200/quarter; your mileage will increase two or three fold, even if you are living on site; you will need site insurance; you will suffer damage to materials which will have to be replaced at your own expense; you will end up with leftovers that you cannot easily get rid of, and at the end of the job, you'll have to chase yourself to get all those little snags finished. Over half of a main contractor's mark-up goes on paying overheads that would be common to professionals and amateurs alike. And, as the pie chart opposite hopefully makes clear, there is still the tricky little matter of finance to pay. There are many other costs besides plot and building costs, and they are all conspiring to eat away your paper profit.

## Still Wanna Selfbuild?

Having got all that off my chest, I will also readily point out that I have met many selfbuilders who have made a tidy packet out of their dealings. Nevertheless, I would argue that the rewards of selfbuilding are not chiefly financial. What it really allows people to do is to have the freedom of choice to design and build a new house to their specifications, something that you will not be able to do by any other route. For many people it represents one of the great challenges in life. The more they are involved in the project, the more they get out of it and the whole attraction of self-build is the pure adventure of it all. If this is your motivation then more power to your elbow and all that. You'll may well end up just a little disappointed by the outcome and will perhaps be haunted by a whole host of "what ifs" and "if onlys." Fear not, this is an experience common to all designers and builders. You'll just have to do it all again.

However, if your motivation is mainly financial then I warn you to look very carefully at the sums involved.
- Yes, you can save money selfbuilding but it may not be as much as you might first expect.
- Don't ignore the well-trodden route of hiring a designer (who in turn manages the job for you) just because you think it is bound to be expensive.
- Never forget that property developing (for that is what you are doing) is a very risky business. Unlike many financial products which are now sold with warnings attached, building plots and the houses that go on them are sold on the understanding that the buyer knows the

risks involved. You are assumed to be a sophisticated investor; make sure that you actually are.

## American Viewpoint

In the States, the concept of selfbuilding (or owner build as they call it) is more established than it is in the UK. There are many people who build this way primarily to save money but the expectations are generally much more realistic. I am indebted to several US builders and owner builders who have e-mailed me about selfbuild in the USA and here are two of the typical responses.

Clay Thompson of Minnesota: *There is a strong contingent of people who act as their own general contractor here in the States. This practice, to the uninitiated, is a frightening experience at best. The problem for most is that they find there is no way to keep the small details from slipping through the net. They do boast a cost savings of about 10 percent. I think they are lying, though the ones who have some business savvy and the time to work out the details do okay.*

Denis Hathaway: *I'm a general contractor in Los Angeles, and I've heard (and seen) various horrors visited upon homeowners who undertook to act as their own contractors. My advice is to forget about it unless you've got a lot of time and energy to put into selecting and supervising subcontractors. You've got to make sure they're properly licensed and insured, you've got to make sure they'll do the work to your satisfaction at a fair price, you've got to know how to schedule them if you don't want the job to take forever. Hav-*

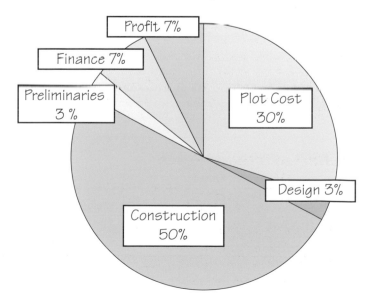

## Where the Money Goes

Profit 7%
Finance 7%
Preliminaries 3 %
Plot Cost 30%
Design 3%
Construction 50%

*ing been in the building business now for 15 years, I can tell you that proper supervision is the key to the successful completion of any project, and that this supervision requires a significant investment of time and energy.*

This last sentence hits the nail on the head. Houses don't build themselves and the subcontractors that build them don't all gell together like a well-oiled machine; they need a huge amount of chivvying, chasing and challenging.

In fairness to the other side of the argument, I should point out that there are American owner-builders who claim to have saved a whole stack of money by organising it themselves. But I suspect that what is really going on here is a variation on the old saying that an optimist sees a glass as being half full whilst a pessimist sees it as being half empty. The selfbuilder has an emotional investment in their project and really wants to believe that all that work actually made sense financially; on the other side, the professional builder has good financial reasons for not wanting to exaggerate the profitability of any scheme they undertake — to do so would be to hand money over to the taxman. Thus the professional builder will account for every cost they possibly can whereas the selfbuilder will be inclined to overlook many of the legitimate overheads in order to make the final sum look more pleasing to their eyes.

Nowhere is this discrepancy greater than in the area of finance. To a developer, finance is just another job cost, essentially no different than the cost of the land or the building costs. When the house is sold on, they will total up all the loan interest they have paid and add it in as a legitimate business cost. The selfbuilder is in a rather different position. They may — probably will — already have a mortgage before they even think of taking on a major project like a new house or a major renovation. By transferring this mortgage from an existing house to a building plot they are not necessarily altering their cashflow at all and do not have to add this cost into their calculations. What they are doing is exchanging a year or two's hardship (such as living with the in-laws or in a caravan on site) for the opportunity to live in a bigger or better house than they could otherwise afford. Whilst a cost accountant would probably say that the selfbuilders are deceiving themselves, it seems to me to be a perfectly legitimate approach to things.

If there is a danger for the selfbuilder in all this, it is that they will tend to get greedy and to overreach themselves. It is notoriously difficult to accurately predict building costs and the world is full of people with a vested interest in making building costs look cheaper than they actually are. Getting prices out of builders and subcontractors is often much easier said than done and the chances are that most selfbuilders will have to commit themselves to a building project before they have a clear idea of the actual costs of the project. Often people realise at a comparatively late stage that they can't afford the scheme they have embarked on and desperately start seeking ways of reducing the costs. Many will complain bitterly just how expensive builders are when the root of the problem is that they always had inflated expectations of what they could achieve with the money at their disposal. Many people are bounced into becoming project managers because they think it is bound to be cheaper to build directly with subcontractors. This is not the way to become a selfbuilder, it's the way to become a headless chicken. Even hard-bitten professionals have problems reconciling their dreams with their budgets and it is essentially in response to this problem that I wrote this book — to help put you, the person paying all the bills, back in control of the situation.

## Postscript

The bulk of this section appeared in the first edition of this book, published at the end of 1994. Several people have commented to me since that it's too gloomy in tone and that selfbuild isn't quite as bad, or as impoverishing, as I make out. Indeed since that time a number of selfbuilders have made a small tax free fortune out of their dealings. Perhaps the gloomy tone was affected by the times, when recession was still very present and the property market was mired in slump conditions. I did think of completely rewriting this section to reflect the more upbeat spirit of the age but then I figured that it served as a useful reminder to people that selfbuild is not a licence to print money. If the property market turns sour in the next few years, I will be able to say "Told you so!" — not that it will do me much good. The chief reason I haven't changed the tone is because I have had feedback from others who are grateful for a counterblast, a view from the other side so to speak. A few have even said it encouraged them to take on some large building project because it enabled them to make a decent stab at evaluating the risks involved.

## 1c: How Big is that House?

| | m² | ft² | Range of building costs |
|---|---|---|---|
| One-bedroom flat | 40 | 430 | £20,000-£30,000 |
| Terraced two-bedroom house | 60 | 650 | £30,000-£50,000 |
| Semi-detached, 3 bedrooms | 90 | 970 | £50,000-£75,000 |
| Detached 3/4 bedrooms, integral single garage | 130 | 1,400 | £70,000-£120,000 |
| Large detached 4/5 bedrooms, detached double garage | 200 | 2,150 | £100,000-£200,000 |

# Chapter 2
# The Benchmark

*AB Homes' Great Gidding, Newborough, Cambs 2002*

This is what the developers, AB Homes, chose to say about this house. It's an interesting bullet list if only because it shows you what they thought would most appeal to their potential buyers.

- Four bedrooms plus converted loftspace - 160m² floor space
- En-suite shower room to master bedroom
- Separate lounge and dining room
- Efficient kitchen and ample cupboards and worktops
- Oven, hob and cooker hood included
- Breakfast room off kitchen via archway
- Utility linking kitchen and garage
- Separate study off hallway overlooking front garden
- Bedroom 2 has a 'character' walk-in bay window
- Walk-in bay window to lounge
- Gas central heating via system boiler and thermostatically controlled radiators
- Mains pressure hot water cylinder — good hot water pressure with no tanks or pipes in loft
- Solid masonry construction including bedroom and bathroom partitions
- uPVC double glazing with 20mm air gap
- Plaster coving throughout
- Hardwood front door with stained glass panel
- Additional telephone and TV aerial point
- Separate garage with garage loft for light storage
- Wide frontage and garden

Since the Housebuilder's Bible first appeared (in 1994), it has based itself around a newly built house which is used as a benchmark for both costing purposes and as a comparison with the many alternative ways of building homes. For this edition, I have selected a house — more accurately a house type — built by a small developer in Newborough, near Peterborough in Cambridgeshire. Serial readers will maybe recognise both the house type and the builders as they featured in the previous edition as well but three years on they are still being built so the choice remains pertinent. The builders are two brothers, Andy and Roger Allen, and their cousin, Peter Allen, who have been working away in and around the Peterborough area for 25 years and their business, known as AB Homes, spent most of 2001 and the first half of 2002 constructing 21 detached houses on a small estate now known as Waterfall Gardens in Newborough.

The Allens are very experienced housebuilders. They were born into a building family: they run a tight ship. Waterfall Gardens was built largely by subcontract labour. The brothers use one of the houses as a show house and they use the garage in this show house as their office from which they supervise the labour on site. Besides a secretary, they have just two other people on the books, one driving the forklift and one clearing up. Their construction programme was phased over an eighteen month period so that a house is finished at the rate of one every three or four weeks and, at any one time, there will be about ten or twelve houses being built. This steady build pace is typical of multi-unit sites: it allows a good spread of trades to be kept busy all the time so that, for instance, an electrician could probably have a steady supply of work from the first house to the 21st. Subbies naturally like such an arrangement and this enables the Allens to shave costs and to keep within tight cashflow limits.

A final build cost of just under £500 per square metre is an outcome that most people building one-off houses can only dream about, though partly this figure looks so low because the extra space in the roof (more on this in a moment) is a little cheaper to build than comparable space in a two-storey house. If you're are planning to build a one-off house or convert something into a home, don't assume you will be able to get anywhere close to the unit costs that AB Homes achieve.

Andy Allen is unusual for a housebuilder because he has trained as an architect and he consequently designs the houses that they build. Architects, as a rule, tend to steer clear of speculatively built housing, or is it the housebuilders who give architects a wide berth? Either way, before qualifying Andy spent several years as an estimator and surveyor and this is reflected in the largely mainstream designs which they are building. The 21 homes are all for private sale and they are typical of what you might currently see on a new housing estate almost anywhere in the UK. Newborough is hardly an upmarket location and there is a great deal of competition from both local and national housebuilders in the area so any deviation from traditional forms and detailing has to be both subtle and justifiable.

At the upper end of the price range there is a house type which the Allens have called Gidding — after a nearby village. There is a variation called the Great Gidding, which moves the integral garage outside the basic footprint to form an attached garage and it's this variation, the Great Gidding, which is the benchmark house. In many ways, the Giddings are typical of the output of volume housebuilders but there is one critical difference which makes them ever-so slightly remarkable — AB Homes build the Great Gidding with the loftspace converted to make two bonus rooms. It's only remarkable because so few new homes currently offer this feature, despite a demand for larger houses and a shortage of land on which to build them.

In searching out potential benchmark houses, I am not actually looking for unusual homes and were it not for these lofts, the Gidding range would be very close to the standard detached developer home in terms of both size and amenity. Without converted loftspace, the Great Gidding is 122m$^2$ internal floor area. This provides four bedrooms, two bathrooms, a kitchen with utility area, a lounge cum dining rooms (divided by a pair of glazed doors) and a small study.

Adding the fully converted loft provides an additional 38m$^2$ of living space, consisting of two rooms opening off each side of a central staircase. On their previous site, AB Homes offered the Great Gidding with an open loftspace option. For an extra £5,000 the housebuyers could convert their loft at a later date. But at Newborough, they decided to finish out the bonus rooms . They would have built more but the parish council objected, saying that six bedrooms was "too upmarket" for Newborough!

In order to build a Great Gidding with habitable loftspace, the Allens make four specific changes to the standard specification.

- The roof trusses are changed from the normal closed fink style to open attic trusses. There are also some double trusses placed in the roof to facilitate the placing of a staircase — it is always imperative that trussed roofs shouldn't be altered once in place. This adds around £800 to the costs plus the added cost of hiring a crane to get them up onto the roof.
- The roof shape is changed from hips to gables in order to get usable space inside the loft. There are some savings on roofing costs in using a gable design but these are more than offset by the added cost of having to build two gable walls. All in all, this switch costs around £2000.
- At first floor level, the window lintels need to be upgraded in order to take the extra load — this adds £80 to costs.
- The ridge needs to be ventilated — adding £200 to costs.

In the loft itself, they install six Velux rooflights and all the insulation and partitioning work, as well as upgrading the electrics and the plumbing. The houses all have mains pressure hot water systems in any event, so moving tanks in the loft would not be an issue. And all the houses in Waterfall Gardens have been designed with 45° roof pitches which make much more usable loft space on small footprint designs.

## 2a: Benchmark House Building Costs: Table 1 (of 3)

| Item | Quantity | | Rates per m² or item | | | Totals | | | Costs |
|---|---|---|---|---|---|---|---|---|---|
| | | | Mats | Labour | Plant | Material | Labour | Plant | |
| Clearing Oversite | 25 m³ | | 0.50 | 2.00 | 14.00 | 13 | 50 | 350 | 413 |
| Setting Out Foundations | 86 m² | | 0.25 | 2.80 | | 21 | 239 | 0 | 261 |
| Excavating Foundations | 22 m³ | | 0.50 | 1.40 | 14.00 | 11 | 31 | 308 | 350 |
| Trenchfilled Concrete | 21 m³ | | 50.00 | 7.00 | | 1,050 | 147 | 0 | 1,197 |
| Footings | 26 m² | | 11.00 | 21.00 | | 290 | 554 | 0 | 845 |
| House Floor Slab | 71 m² | | 11.00 | 10.00 | 2.00 | 777 | 706 | 141 | 1,624 |
| 100mm Underfloor Insulation | 71 m² | | 4.60 | 1.40 | | 327 | 99 | | 426 |
| Garage Floor Slab | 15 m² | | 11.00 | 10.00 | | 164 | 149 | 0 | 313 |
| Foul Drains | 15 m | | 18.00 | 16.80 | | 270 | 252 | 0 | 522 |
| Rainwater Drains | 30 m | | 13.00 | 14.00 | 2.00 | 390 | 420 | 60 | 870 |
| Main Drain Connection | proportion for each house on esate | | | | | 1,500 | 2,000 | 500 | 4,000 |
| Service Trenching/Ducting | 15 m | | 2.00 | 10.50 | 2.00 | 30 | 158 | 30 | 218 |
| **GROUNDWORKS** | | | | | | **4,843** | **4,806** | **1,389** | **£11,038** |
| Inner Skin Blockwork | 162 m² | | 6.00 | 8.40 | | 970 | 1,357 | 150 | 2,477 |
| Outer Skin Brickwork | 162 m² | | 19.00 | 20.00 | | 3,079 | 3,241 | 150 | 6,471 |
| Extra for Gables | | | | | | | 400 | 50 | 450 |
| Garage Blockwork | 11 m² | | 6.00 | 8.40 | | 68 | 96 | | 164 |
| Garage Brickwork | 29 m² | | 19.00 | 20.00 | | 555 | 584 | | 1,138 |
| Downstairs Blockwork | 45 m² | | 6.00 | 8.40 | | 271 | 379 | | 649 |
| Upstairs blockwork | 47 m² | | 6.00 | 8.40 | | 279 | 391 | 50 | 720 |
| Regular Lintels | 30 No. | | | | | 560 | 130 | | 690 |
| Steel Beams | 3 No. | | | | | 150 | 150 | | 300 |
| 100mm Cavity Wall Insulation | 162 m² | | 3.00 | | | 485 | | | 485 |
| **MASONRY** | | | | | | **6,416** | **6,728** | **400** | **£13,544** |
| First Floor Joisting | 61 m² | | 6.30 | 8.75 | | 384 | 534 | | 918 |
| First Floor Cover | 61 m² | | 3.60 | 3.75 | | 220 | 229 | | 448 |
| Studwork Walls, Bridgings | 14 m² | | 3.15 | 8.75 | | 44 | 123 | | 167 |
| Window Cills | 16 m | | 3.50 | 5.00 | | 56 | 80 | | 136 |
| Attic trusses (Birds Eye Area) | 62 m² | | 28.00 | 15.00 | | 1,736 | 930 | | 2,666 |
| Additional Roof Carpentry | | | | | | 150 | 500 | | 650 |
| House Fascias | 19 m | | 1.80 | 3.75 | | 34 | 71 | | 105 |
| Bay Window | 1 no | | | | | 400 | 500 | | 900 |
| Porch Roof | 1 no | | | | | 150 | 150 | | 300 |
| Roof Insulation | 102 m² | | 5.80 | 2.00 | | 592 | 204 | | 796 |
| Garage Roof Area (Birds Eye) | 15 m² | | 10.00 | 15.00 | | 149 | 224 | | 373 |
| Garage Fascias | 6 m | | 1.80 | 3.75 | | 11 | 23 | | 33 |
| **FIRST FIX CARPENTRY** | | | | | | **3,926** | **3,566** | **0** | **£7,492** |

## 2a: Benchmark House Building Costs: Table 2 (of 3)

| Item | Quantity | Rates per m² or item | | | Totals | | | Costs |
|---|---|---|---|---|---|---|---|---|
| | | Mats | Labour | Plant | Material | Labour | Plant | |
| uPVC House Windows | 15 No. | | | | 2,055 | 400 | | 2,455 |
| Garage Window | 1 No. | | | | 91 | 20 | | 111 |
| Velux Rooflights | 6 No. | 128.00 | 60.00 | | 768 | 360 | | 1,128 |
| External Door Frames | 4 No. | | | | 164 | | | 164 |
| External Doors | 4 No. | | 62.50 | | 1,280 | 250 | | 1,530 |
| Door Furniture | 20 No | 20.00 | inc | | 400 | | | 400 |
| Garage Car Doors | 1 No. | 270.00 | | | 270 | 60 | | 330 |
| Garage Back Door | 1 No | 140.00 | 62.50 | | 140 | 60 | | 200 |
| Garage Back Door Frame | 1 No | 50.00 | | | 50 | | | 50 |
| Low-e Double Glazing | 12 m² | 35.00 | 15.00 | | inc with windows | | | |
| Staircase | 2 No. | 300.00 | 300.00 | | 600 | 600 | | 1,200 |
| Door Linings | 15 No. | 9.00 | 10.00 | | 135 | 150 | | 285 |
| Internal (Fire 30) Doors | 15 No. | 60.00 | 30.00 | | 900 | 450 | | 1,350 |
| Airing Cupboard Doors | 1 pr. | 30.00 | 30.00 | | 30 | 30 | | 60 |
| Airing Cupboard | 1 No. | 30.00 | 50.00 | | 30 | 50 | | 80 |
| Skirting | 160 m | 0.60 | 3.00 | | 96 | 480 | | 576 |
| Architrave | 160 m | 0.35 | 2.00 | | 56 | 320 | | 376 |
| Pipe Boxing/Cover Strips | | | | | 30 | 180 | | 210 |
| Vanity Units | | | | | 150 | 180 | | 330 |
| Snagging/Ironmongery | | | | | 250 | 500 | | 750 |
| **JOINERY, GLAZING & SECOND FIX CARPENTRY** | | | | | **7,495** | **4,090** | **0** | **£11,585** |
| Roof Tiling (House) | 110 m² | 10.50 | 6.00 | | 1,154 | 659 | | 1,813 |
| Roof Tiling (Garage) | 24 m² | 10.50 | 6.00 | | 252 | 144 | | 396 |
| Leadwork to Bay Window | | | | | 50 | 150 | | 200 |
| Leadwork to Porch | | | | | 20 | 80 | | 100 |
| Rainwater Goods (House) | 34 m | 4.00 | 4.00 | | 136 | 136 | | 272 |
| Rainwater Goods (Garage) | 10 m | 4.00 | 4.00 | | 40 | 40 | | 80 |
| Scaffolding (House) | | | | | | | 800 | 800 |
| Scaffolding (Garage) | | | | | | | 200 | 200 |
| **ROOFING & SCAFFOLDING** | | | | | **1,652** | **1,209** | **1,000** | **£3,861** |
| Plasterboard Dry Lined Walls | 378 m² | 2.70 | 6.00 | | 1,021 | 2,268 | | 3,289 |
| Plasterboard Ceilings | 162 m² | 2.70 | 6.60 | | 437 | 1,069 | | 1,507 |
| Plaster Covings | 130 lin.m | 0.80 | 2.00 | | 104 | 260 | | 364 |
| Power Floated Floor Slab | 86 m² | no screed: floor finish dealt with in Groundworks section | | | | | | 0 |
| **PLASTERING** | | | | | **1,562** | **3,597** | **0** | **£5,159** |
| Power Sockets | 27 No. | | | | 360 | 440 | | 800 |
| TV Outlets | 2 No. | | | | 16 | 24 | | 40 |
| Phone Sockets | 3 No. | | | | 15 | 36 | | 51 |
| Lighting | 22 No. | | | | 220 | 550 | | 770 |
| Fans | 4 No. | | | | 200 | 230 | | 430 |
| Smoke Detectors | 3 No. | | | | 90 | 45 | | 135 |
| **ELECTRICS & ALARM** | | | | | **901** | **1,325** | **0** | **£2,226** |
| Central Heating & DHW | | | | | 2,300 | 1,400 | | 3,700 |
| Bathrooms & WC | | | | | 1,600 | 875 | | 2,475 |
| **PLUMBING & HEATING** | | | | | **3,900** | **2,275** | **0** | **£6,175** |

## 2a: Benchmark House Building Costs: Table 3 (of 3)

| Item | Quantity | Rates per m² or item | | | Totals | | | Costs |
|---|---|---|---|---|---|---|---|---|
| | | Mats | Labour | Plant | Material | Labour | Plant | |
| Kitchen Units | | | | | 1,630 | 300 | | 1,930 |
| Worktops | | | | | 140 | 200 | | 340 |
| Sinks/Plumbing | | | | | 180 | 200 | | 380 |
| Appliances(inc VAT) | | | | | 340 | 150 | | 490 |
| **KITCHEN** | | | | | **2,290** | **850** | **0** | **£3,140** |
| Mastic Frames/Sanitaryware | | | | | 50 | 200 | | 250 |
| Emulsion Walls/Ceilings | 540 m² | 0.45 | 2.40 | | 243 | 1,296 | | 1,539 |
| Internal Glosswork | 320 m | 0.16 | 4.00 | | 50 | 1,280 | | 1,330 |
| Internal Doors | 30 m² | 1.25 | 36.00 | | 38 | 1,080 | | 1,118 |
| Cills/boxings/stairs | | | | | 25 | 150 | | 175 |
| External Staining | | | | | 70 | 300 | | 370 |
| Kitchen Floor Tiling | 20 m² | 7.00 | 12.00 | | 140 | 240 | | 380 |
| Wall Tiling | 25 m² | 12.00 | 15.00 | | 300 | 375 | | 675 |
| Cleaning | | | | | | 200 | | 200 |
| **DECORATING & TILING** | | | | | **916** | **5,121** | **0** | **£6,037** |
| Ground Preparation | 100 m² | 2.00 | 5.00 | | 200 | 500 | 150 | 850 |
| Gravel Driveway & Kerbs | 50 m² | 3.50 | 5.00 | | 175 | 250 | 75 | 500 |
| Contribution to Estate Road | one contract for entire estate | | | | 1,500 | | | 1,500 |
| Paving Slabs | 25 m² | 5.00 | 6.00 | | 125 | 150 | | 275 |
| Fencing | 40 m | 15.00 | 15.00 | | 600 | 600 | | 1,200 |
| Turfing | 150 m² | 3.00 | 6.00 | | 450 | 900 | | 1,350 |
| **EXTERNALS** | | | | | **3,050** | **2,400** | **225** | **£5,675** |

| | Material | Labour | Plant | Total Costs |
|---|---|---|---|---|
| **ALL BUILDING COSTS** | 36,950 | 35,968 | 3,014 | 75,932 |

| | | |
|---|---|---|
| Raw Build Cost/m² | 162 m² net floor area | £470 |
| Raw Build Cost/ft² | 1,738 ft² net floor area | £44 |

| Item | Material | Labour | Plant | Costs |
|---|---|---|---|---|
| Planning Drawings | 100 | 800 | | £900 |
| Planning Permission | 250 | | | £250 |
| Other Design Work | | 400 | | £400 |
| Building Regs | 325 | | | £325 |
| Structural Engineer | | 300 | | £300 |
| NHBC Warranty | 500 | | | £500 |
| CDM Planning Supervision | 250 | | | £250 |
| Water Connection | 600 | | | £600 |
| Water Company Infrastructure Charges | 480 | | | £480 |
| Electricity Connection | 350 | 110 | | £460 |
| Site Management | 170 | 3,500 | 700 | £4,370 |
| Office Overheads (principally salaries) | 500 | 6,000 | | £6,500 |
| **DESIGN & PROJECT MANAGEMENT COSTS** | **3,525** | **11,110** | **700** | **£15,335** |

| | | |
|---|---|---|
| **ALL DEVELOPMENT COSTS** | | **£91,267** |
| Development cost/m² | 162 m² net floor area | £565 |
| Development cost/ft² | 1,738 ft² net floor area | £52 |

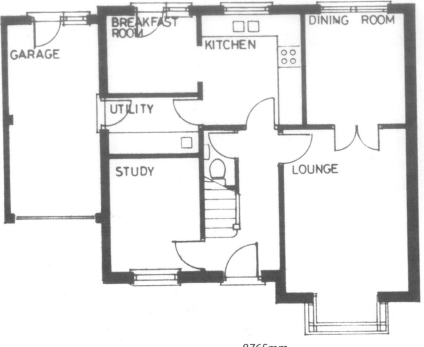

The benchmark house is brick and block construction built to the regulations applicable in 2000. This includes the Disabled Access arrangements (Part M) but not the 2002 thermal regulations (Part L). However the cost tables 2a have been adjusted to take account of the latest changes — more insulation, better windows and a more efficient boiler being the principal changes.

*GROUND FLOOR: Internal area is 61m², excluding the attached single garage which has an internal floor area of 14m². Note that internal floor area specifically excludes the external walls — this is the preferred way of measuring floor area in UK housing, but not everybody is this scrupulous.*

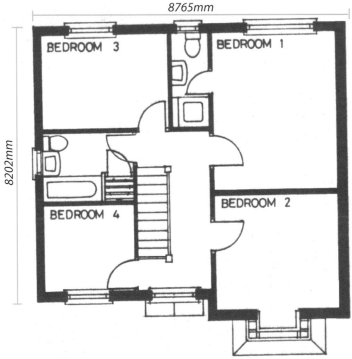

*FIRST FLOOR: Net floor area is the same as the floor below — i.e. 61m². Combined you get a total of 122m², about average for a four bedroomed developer built house. The arrangement of bedrooms and bathrooms (one en-suite, the other a family affair) is also absolutely typical.*

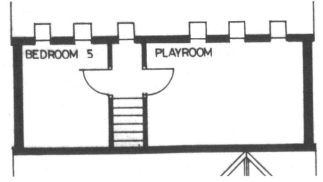

*SECOND FLOOR: here is where these homes stand out. An extra 40m² of loft space shown here as Bedroom 5 and Playroom. The undereaves cupboard space is not included in the measurements.*

The attic trusses, seen here being hoisted by crane, are used when you want to build a room-in-the-roof. AB Homes fit them to their Gidding house types where buyers express an interest in either having a full loft conversion or simply having a usable loft space which they can convert at their leisure.

Benchmark house builders Andrew (in the tie) and Roger Allen pictured outside their showhouse.

One significant change between the previous benchmark house and the current one has been the addition of level thesholds and access ramps for wheelchair users, required by the building regs since 1999. Neither Andy nor Roger was entirely happy about these ramps and felt they might well cause as many problems as they solve. Had they been redesigning from scratch they would probably have come up with a more elegant solution but this ramp was added to an existing house type.

Another area where the disabled access regs have made a difference is in the siting and size of the downstairs cloakroom. It was felt by many that the days of the understairs loo were over but Andy Allen came up with an ingenious design for fitting it all in. The door has been widened and the width of the cloakroom has been extended slightly. Note the angled cut off the door where it fits under the staircase.

## Benchmark Blues

The purpose of having a benchmark house is to use it to draw comparisons with other ways of building homes. The benchmark house chosen for this edition is not totally typical of what you might buy from a plc housebuilder such as Wimpey Homes or Barratt, but it is close enough to use as a cost model. What the table 2b on this page does is to compare this industry standard with an immensely expensive version of the same thing. So the first column, the Developer's House, illustrates the costs involved in building the benchmark house and the second column, the Expensive Alternative, shows just how much more it could cost.

What manner of things could cause you to spend twice as much money? Some may be beyond your control:

- A sloping site set 50 metres back from the road
- Difficult ground conditions needing special foundations
- No main drains or gas available
- Located in a conservation area requiring natural stone walls and roof coverings.

Add to this recipe some extras that you might select for your project in order to have a very high class home:

- Hardwood joinery throughout
- Expensive kitchen and bathroom fittings
- Inglenook fireplace
- Moulded covings, architraves and skirtings
- Professionally designed lighting system
- Super-efficient insulation levels throughout
- Underfloor heating combined with condensing boiler
- Mains pressure hot water delivery
- Intelligent alarm system.

### Outcome

Refer to table below. Much of the rest of the Housebuilder's Bible is concerned with exploring all these options and problems in much greater detail, frequently referring back to the benchmark house. But before I move on, it is good to take a brief look at just what damage all these accumulated changes could do to an ill-prepared budget.

## 2b: How To Double Your Building Costs

| | Developer's House | Expensive Alternative | Reasons |
|---|---|---|---|
| Design | £1,200 | £8,000 | One-off design work |
| Clearing Oversite | £413 | £5,000 | Sloping site |
| Foundations | 4,329 | 15,000 | Difficult ground |
| Foul Drains/Roadway | 2,000 | 6,000 | On-site treatment |
| Service Connections | 1,060 | 4,000 | Site > 50m from services |
| Road Access and Drive | 2,500 | 5,000 | Site> 50m from road |
| External Skin | 7,609 | 15,000 | Build in natural stone |
| Cavity Wall Insulation | 485 | 1,000 | Use 60mm Polyurethan |
| Chimney | 0 | 3,500 | Have two chimneys/fancy brickwork |
| External Windows/Doors | 4,260 | 7,200 | Hardwood joinery |
| Roof Tiling | 2,209 | 10,000 | Handmade tiles or Welsh slate |
| Rainwater Gear | 352 | 1,200 | Cast iron or seamless aluminium |
| Plasterboard/Dry Lining | 4,795 | 7,500 | Use Fermacell board |
| Staircases | 1,200 | 4,000 | Made to measure, curved |
| Skirting/Architrave | 952 | 1,400 | Specify hardwood |
| External/Internal Doors | 1,350 | 2,000 | Hardwood doors |
| Door Furniture | 400 | 800 | Specify higher quality |
| Lighting | 770 | 3,000 | Specify low voltage halogen lighting scheme |
| Ventilation | 430 | 2,000 | Whole-house ventilation and heat recovery |
| Heating system | 3,700 | 6,000 | Oil-fired condensing boiler/underfloor heating |
| Fireplace | 0 | 4,000 | Specify an inglenook fireplace |
| Range | 0 | 6,000 | Specify cast iron range or Aga |
| Alarm | 0 | 1,200 | Wired to police station |
| Kitchen | 3,140 | 12,000 | Specify Expensive style kitchen |
| Sanitaryware | 1,600 | 3,500 | Specify Continental bathrooms |
| Wall/Floor Tiling | 1,055 | 2,500 | Specify handmade tiles |
| Fencing | 1,200 | 6,000 | Brick walls |
| Unchanged Elements | 44,258 | 44,258 | |
| Total Build Cost | £91,000 | £187,000 | |
| Cost/m$^2$ on 161m$^2$ house | £563 | £1,127 | |

# Chapter 3
# Pitfalls

## Buying Land

"Where do I find the land?" is the most commonly asked question by wannabe builders. All the many selfbuild exhibitions have stands dedicated to selling building plots and often I am to be found just a few feet away, busy signing and selling this very book. And yet still the most frequent question I am asked is: "Where do I find a building plot?"

"Have you looked over there?" I reply.
"Oh yes, but they're all expensive."
"Well, land is expensive."

Shoulders shrugged. Conversation ends. Once or twice the conversation doesn't end there but develops along the lines of "How do I get building land for the price of farmland?" I say I wish I knew, if I did I wouldn't be here flogging my book. Then conversation ends with more shrugged shoulders.

People aren't dumb. They realise that the only way to make a killing at this property game is to get hold of the land for nothing or next to nothing. Once upon a time, back before they had such strict planning controls (I'm talking 50 years ago), land changed hands cheaply pretty much regardless of development potential. Houses were built with large gardens because people appreciated large gardens; farmland with road frontage changed hands because people wanted to grow things; barns were barns, not development opportunities. But these days anybody owning such a piece of land or an old outbuilding is well aware that these are considerable financial assets worth far more than their intrinsic value and they don't let them go for peanut prices. The planning policies adopted in England and Wales in 1947 – which have grown ever stricter since – have deliberately restricted the supply of building land in order to protect the landscape and one of the many side-effects of this policy has been to force up the price of building land to exorbitant levels. Every village, every street is subject to a local plan which involves drawing lines on maps around each and every settlement and deciding which infill spaces can be built on and which can't. Visit your district reference library and check out your Structure Plan (usually referred to as the Local Plan) and you'll understand how little land there is on which development will be permitted. Then you will understand just why building land is so expensive.

You may find odd advertisements in the press for outfits claiming to be able to locate untitled land, the implication being that you need only register it yourself to be able to lay claim to it. If only it were that easy. There is no unowned land in this country, certainly none you can build on. Other advertisements claim to be able to help you identify potential building plots: there are undoubtedly plenty of potential building plots about but just because you identify one doesn't mean that the owner will sell it to you for a song. After all, if someone offered you £500 for the back-end of your garden, wouldn't you be a bit suspicious? One thing this book is not going to tell you is how to get hold of cheap land this side of the Channel. France...now there's another book altogether.

### Mechanics
There are basically five methods by which property (inc. building plots) can changes hands in these islands.

1. Public auction: Pros: It's open. It gives the seller (or vendor in these circles) a legally binding agreement. Cons: The expensive pre-sale work has to be undertaken with no guarantee of success. Sometimes, in the excitement of an auction, it doesn't get done at all. A 10% deposit usually taken at the auction so buyer has to have funds to hand.

2. Formal tender: as practised in Scotland. Once a bid is accepted, the deal becomes legally binding. Otherwise similar to the auction in pros and cons.

3. Informal tender: buyers are asked to send in sealed bids for the property by a fixed date, together with details of their own financial position. All the bids are opened at the same time and the sale is agreed, usually with the party considered to be in the best position to buy. Cons: buyers are wary and object to the decision being made in private and with no opportunity to increase their bid. However it's probably less stressful than an auction and gives more flexibility to the vendor.

4. Informal telephone auction: the common method of property sales everywhere outside Scotland. It gives much more flexibility to both sides. This is both its strength and its weakness — you get flaky offers from purchasers and you get gazumping and other evils because the contracts are not binding until physically exchanged. And when there are more than three buyers competing for one property, it can gets very difficult to organise proceedings because someone is often away or can't make up their mind. In these situations agents often decide to switch to method 3, the informal tender, to close the deal.

5. Private sales: often referred to as 'Sale by Private Treaty.' If a buyer and a seller can agree on a price, then there is no obligation for them to go through the more public channels indicated above. A lot of land changes hands this way. You'd be surprised. Or may be you wouldn't.

The actual process of buying land (or derelict buildings) is similar to that involved in buying houses. And indeed the principles are exactly the same, though the detail is very different. You don't buy a house if you think it's too expensive or if you think it's going to fall down; you normally employ solicitors and surveyors to ensure that you are not buying a pig in a poke. Likewise with plots, you want to ensure that you can build what you want on it at a price you can afford. Having said that, the whole process of buying plots (and, especially, renovation opportunities) is more complex because there are more things that can go wrong. When buying an existing property at least you know that it is there, even if it might just fall down next week! With a building plot you are buying nothing more than a field which comes with a promise, a hope for the future. And unlike the conventional house market, the chances are that you will have to purchase your chosen plot without knowing exactly what you can build where.

## Professional Help

You don't have to hire any help but it's usual to do so because the stakes are high and you don't want to make a silly mistake. If you hire the services of a solicitor or a licensed conveyancer, look for a property specialist. If you are buying in an area new to you, you'd be well advised to look for a local rather than sticking with someone you've used before who might be 200 miles away from the action. Now is the time you need as much information, official and unofficial, as you can get. A good solicitor will uncover more than just that which is revealed by undertaking searches and checking for legal complications and boundaries. One common pitfall occurs when the planning permission only applies to one part of the building plot, a frequent occurrence when close to village framework boundaries and the like. Some solicitors spot this, others don't. But even the best solicitor is not going to be able to advise you as to whether the plot is an A1 purchase because there are a number of other areas that are outside the remit of even the most scrupulous legal beaver. To get an overview of these concerns, and it's no more than an overview, I have summarised them as human problems and physical problems on the following pages.

In truth, land buying is a complex subject and there is no one expert you can turn to to get it all worked out. Gen up: you could do worse than read *How to Find and Buy a Building Plot* by Roy Spear & Michael Dade. The biggest problem for many people is that the really nice plots and renovations tend to be sold in a matter of days and that very often you are in a hopeless position unless you have finance available and ready to go before you even hear about an impending sale. As I write, the property market in SE England is buoyant and most of the estate agents in my area had hardly any small development opportunities on their books at all during the year and, when they did, they usually sold them within a couple of weeks at or above the asking price. Narrow market, tough market, undoubtedly the main reason why selfbuild is not even more popular than it already is. If you are choosy about where you are going to live, then you have to be prepared to a) act fast and b) pay over the odds.

# Human Problems

The prospect of buying a duff plot is a nightmare that haunts professional builders as much as amateurs, and the consequences of doing so are likely to be with you for many a year to come. There is no absolute foolproof way of avoiding the lemons but a little bit of diligence (and a good lawyer) employed at the pre-contract stages of negotiations should uncover most of the problems. These problems broadly fall into two camps; the first to do with the technicalities of ownership and planning permission, the second with problems encountered on site.

## Legal

### Covenants

Building plots are often sold with legal constraints over what may and what may not be done to them. The most common form of constraint is the covenant whereby the vendor (i.e. the person selling the plot) requires that the purchaser should fulfil a number of conditions. Many of these might not cost a euro — i.e. no caravans to be stored in the back garden or no trees to be planted where they might block someone else's view — but others can involve substantial costs. The commonest type of covenant deals with boundary fencing and would read something like this:

*The purchaser covenants to erect 6' high fencing to the south and eastern boundaries of the plot before any building work takes place.*

Sometimes the covenant will be very much more specific and ask for a brick wall nine inches thick or something like that. A condition such as this is expensive to meet and should really be reflected in a lower plot price.

## Rights of Way

There are any number of complications that should, repeat should, be uncovered by your solicitor's search: rights of way crossing the plot, existing wayleaves for services and cables to cross the plot, complex shared ownership of access roads, to name but three. Even if you can live with these arrangements, they may well affect resale values and make finance much harder to get and insurance more expensive. Many of these problems can be sorted out by throwing money at them — but the canny buyer should ensure it's the vendor's money not theirs.

## Plot Access

Another likely cause of problems occurs when part of the land needed to successfully develop the plot is owned by someone else. Normally this would show up at an early stage of legal enquiry and would be down to the plot vendor to sort out, but one thorny problem that might get overlooked is the local highway authority's requirement for visibility splays at plot entrances. A visibility splay is a wedge of uninterrupted view either side of a driveway entrance which allows vehicles pulling out to see what is coming. Just how large this area needs to be is down to individual authorities and you would be well advised to check this matter personally with them before proceeding with a purchase. A typical snag here would be that planning permission has been granted for a house with access which is legally unbuildable; either you have to purchase a wayleave over a neighbour's land or you must alter planning consent.

The important principle to understand here is that the legal constraints on building a house (or access to that house) will not necessarily be the same as the planning constraints — and vice versa. A solicitor's or conveyancer's brief is to sort out the legal complexities surrounding purchase, not necessarily to advise on planning problems. Never assume that the development will be trouble-free just because it has detailed planning permission.

## Options

If it is any consolation, this is an area that causes big headaches to major professional developers as well as virgin housebuilders. If you are in any doubt about these issues, my advice is to use what muscle you have as a plot purchaser and, if possible, take out an option to buy your chosen plot rather than formally exchanging contracts.

What is an option to buy? The bare bones of a contract might look like this: you agree a price on a plot of land (though even this

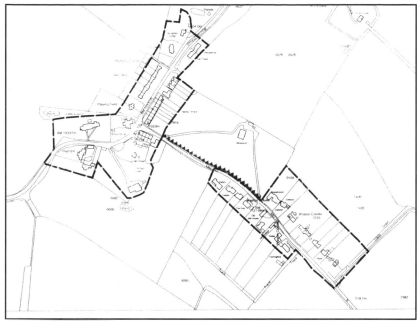

*Development is controlled around every settlement in the country. Here the thick dotted black lines are known as the village framework boundary. Land inside the boundary is worth around £1million/acre. Outside, around £2,000/acre.*

doesn't have to be fixed in stone). This remains in place for say 2-3 years (the length of the option is entirely up to you). During that time the vendor is prohibited from selling to anyone else. Some contracts involve interest payments to the vendor, this acts as a spur to the purchaser to get on with it and protects the vendor from time-wasters. The big plus from the purchaser's point of view is that an option protects you from gazumping and other forms of treachery.

How much would you be expected to pay for an option? Well, that depends. If the planning angle is difficult and you are taking on the costs of obtaining planning permission (which could be several thousand), then there may well be no payment made to the vendor at all. They would be very happy for someone else to do all this work for them. However if market conditions are buoyant, then you may have to part with up to 5 per cent of the plot price just to tempt the vendor into an option. Also the buyer may want to make the plot price conditional on what you manage to squeeze out of planning so that the price is £60k if you get one house but £100k if you get permission for two.

If there is a pitfall in all this, it is that you can spend a lot of money and get nowhere. But that's a pitfall that all property developers have to face.

## Planning

It is paradoxical that 18 years of Conservative government dedicated to "rolling back the frontiers of the state" presided over ever-

toughening planning laws. As I write, we've had nearly five years of New Labour during which time they've sat on their hands. If they do make changes to the planning system, it's odds on that the state frontiers will be rolling forward some more. The planners albeit accountable to elected local councillors — now have considerable and arbitrary powers over what you can and cannot do on a piece of land that you nominally own; in effect there is a level of "state ownership" over each and every building plot which supersedes individual ownership and you must fulfil the conditions placed on you before you can begin to put your own ideas in place.

## Time Lapses

One potential problem for the unwary is the fact that planning permission has a time limit on it. Normally this lasts for five years from the date the permission is granted, but there is one kind of planning permission, known as outline permission, which basically expires after just three years. As many small or self-builders will be buying a plot which has only outline permission to build, please note that you have to get detailed permission before the end of the three-year period or you have a very expensive field on your hands.

Once the work has begun, you no longer have to apply for planning permission. Exactly what the definition is of "work having been started" is a grey area, but it is universally accepted that if you have laid the footings then you have started. So if time is running short and you don't have the wherewithal to complete the building work, you can ensure your planning permission is permanent by undertaking just the foundation and footings work.

## Planning Concerns

The planners are concerned with far more than whether a particular plot can be zoned for building. Some of the major areas they will look at will be:

* size of the house: is it "too big for the plot?"
* site of the house: don't assume you can build anywhere on the plot
* neighbours' privacy and right to light
* style of the house: design and materials "must be in keeping"
* vehicular access and turning heads: a particular problem on narrow fronted plots, less than 12m wide. The highways department insists that not only will adequate visibility splays be provided, but that there must be adequate room on site for cars to turn around or, as they say in planning speak, "enter and leave in a forward gear."
* trees and hedges: often have to be retained or replanted. Sometimes this can become a real hot potato and Tree Preservation Orders (casually referred to in these circles as TPOs) can be slapped on inconvenient trees just to make life difficult for you. It doesn't have to be a big oak tree either — they can place TPOs on any tree with a trunk of 75mm or, failing that, little clusters of trees as well. TPOs are often slapped onto potential building plots that the planners, for some reason, don't want to become actual building plots. For builders, trees are a mixed blessing.

## Conservation Areas

These are areas defined by the planners as being especially sensitive and on which they maintain a whole raft of extra controls over what you can and can't do — for instance you need to fill out a three-page application in order to fell a tree. Conservation areas are typically the older parts of a town or the core area of a village, perhaps surrounding the village green, and the fact that you are buying in such an area should be apparent when you purchase — after all it is usually used as an additional sales bullet in the blurb and passes as an excuse to hoick the price. It affects new builders less than renovators because new build is already subject to stringent planning controls. But be aware that you will be unlikely to get permission for anything unusual in a conservation area.

Logically the issue of conservation areas ought to be dealt with by regular planning controls but logic and local government make uneasy bedfellows and conservation area issues are not dealt with by regular planners. There is of course a trap in here waiting to catch the unwary: if, for instance, you apply to build an extension to an existing house in a conservation area which involves the removal of some existing structure, you could find that your permission to build the extension gets approved by planning but your permission to demolish what already exists is turned down by the Conservation department. This is known, technically, as being kyboshed.

## Listing

The other great wedge of planning control concerns the listing of buildings thought to be of merit and which, therefore, need extra protection from unscrupulous owners and developers. The complexities of repairing and altering listed buildings really lie beyond the scope of this book. Yet it is important to realise that many of the current crop of potential barn conversions are already listed by virtue of the fact that the adjacent farmhouse has been listed. There are, amazingly, nearly half a million listed buildings in Britain so most villages have one or two and some places have whole rafts of them. In principle, you are allowed to develop listed sites but you need to obtain listed building consent as well as planning permission; this is almost always a very slow and painstaking process and the outcome is that you will almost always have to spend rather more on the building than you would if it wasn't listed. Listed building officers are attached to each planning department and this is the person to head for in order to glean more information.

## Unpleasant Surprises

When considering the problem from a perspective of hidden costs, it is the planners' interest in the design and materials of the house which is of most concern. Sometimes these concerns are easily predictable: if, for instance, you are building in one of the stone belts where there is a uniform vernacular style (as in the Cotswolds or the Yorkshire Dales), you will not be surprised to learn that you must build with similar materials. Expensive but not unexpected. However, most of Britain does not have a uniform building style and lowland England in particular is characterised by its great variety of building styles and materials. Despite this diversity, the planners can insist on any number of design details, examples of which now follow.

### Slate Roofs

Even in East Anglia, home of the (cheap) pantile, planners are frequently known to insist on slate roofs despite the fact that most roofing slate comes from North Wales and wouldn't have been known in England before the railway age. You may be able to argue that reconstituted slate will be adequate but it will still cost you about £6-£10/m$^2$ more.

### Dislike of Rooflights

They sometimes insist on dormer roof windows. A small dormer will add at least £400-£500 to construction costs; in comparison, a flat opening rooflight (a Velux) would cost no more than £250. Paradoxically, on barn conversions the reverse is true: planners hate dormers on barns.

### Altering Roof Pitches

A common planners' ruse. A steeper roof pitch is more expensive because it increases the roof area. A 45° pitched roof covers an area 16% bigger than one at 35° and will add around this much to roofing costs.

### Altering Windows

If they insist on a window radically different from a standard casement this could easily double joinery costs, possibly adding £1000 to construction costs on a four-bedroom house.

### Changing External Materials

Unless they insist on an expensive stone facing, the materials cost of differing wall constructions is not that large. And the brick market is such that insistence on a different kind of brick is unlikely to have a huge effect on price.

For more detail on the mechanics of planning permission, see Chapter 4 Design.

Only when a house has detailed planning consent without any reserve matters is it possible to accurately budget the above ground costs of construction. However, below ground, we come up against another set of unpredictable variable costs, determined to make a mockery of your budget.

The development costs of any new home can expand considerably because of problems encountered on site. These potential pitfalls fall into two main areas: problems encountered with the site itself, and difficulties encountered in getting access and supplying services to the site.

## Problem Sites

There are three basic causes of alarming cost expansion:
- slopes
- bad ground
- trees.

Straightforward excavation and foundation work can be relatively cheap. A detached house built on a problem-free site with good bearing ground, both flat and treeless, could have oversite and foundation trenches excavated, foundation concrete poured and footings built for as little as £4,000. However, any of the above problems could have increased foundation costs by up to another £6,000, and if you have more than one of these problems in combination, expect your costs to increase by more than £10,000. My benchmark house was built on clay soil and the foundation work cost around £6,000.

For more detail on these problems and how they are overcome, read Chapter 6 Groundworks.

### Visual Inspection

The first step in assessing any building plot is to take a walk over the site and the surrounding area. Be on the look out for clues as to what may have gone on in the past. Some points to watch out for are:
- Foundations of former buildings on site
- Evidence of drains, old water courses or wells
- Subsidence cracks in neighbouring buildings
- Overhead cables
- Springy ground — suggests high water table
- Slopes greater than 1:25
- Trees within 30m of your proposed foundations — species, size and girth should be noted
- Any evidence of ground having been disturbed or used as a dump.

### Background Detection

Investigations with local council, service companies, etc. should reveal more historical and geographical data on which to assess likely problems. Talk to neighbours, local builders or building inspectors who may well know the lie of the land.

### Trial Pits and Borings

To dig or not to dig, that is the question. Whether it is better to leave everything to chance and let the building inspector decide how deep your foundations must go when the time comes or investigate in detail beforehand and risk having to do more than you really need. Many cautious builders now tend to dig trial holes as a matter of course, whatever the history or geology of the ground. The normal practice is for the pits to be dug to a depth of 3m (close to but not under the foundations) in the presence of a structural engineer who takes a long gander at the ground conditions before the digger fills the holes back in. The engineer then decides whether the house foundations can proceed as normal or whether a more complicated foundation solution is needed. Expect to pay an engineer between £150 and £300 for this service, though their fees will be much higher if special foundation designs are needed, a JCB for an hour should cost an additional £50-£100 (depending on travel time). Augered boreholes are another alternative — likely to cost around £300 each (and you'll need two) but a good option where access to JCBs is not possible or you have other problems like high water tables. But there is also a natural tendency for the experts, having been called in, to suggest very expensive, fee swelling, solutions when they may not be necessary. Jeremy Bulbrook built three houses in the Cambridgeshire Fenland town of March during 2001 and he ended up feeling badly let down by his professional advice:

*I had a couple of bore holes drilled on my architect's suggestion. The soil report that came back from these recommended a piled foundation, on the basis that the first two metres or so could possibly be made ground, even though it was gravel/sand. My building inspector asked why I hadn't spoken to them first. He said that they would have been happy with strip footings, but as a recommendation for piles had been made, they had no choice but to force me down the piled route.*

*Now whilst I don't want the houses to fall down, I do wonder if some of the engineers that produce these reports are too scared to say that strip footings would be OK, because if it goes wrong in the future, then they have to bear some responsibility. After all, it doesn't cost an engineer a penny more to say he would recommend piled foundations. In fact he may earn more, if he gets to design the footings as well. If I was starting again, I would definitely talk to the building inspectors first. There's always the risk that when you dig you find something unexpected, but that could still happen even if you have bore holes drilled.*

In some extreme situations the professional fees can end up costing more than the foundations. I have reports of people having spent around £5,000 on site investigations in areas

*When digging a trial hole, the convention is to go down rather deeper than the proposed foundations. Normally you dig two or three holes just outside the proposed footprint.*

where mining activity may or may not have occurred; boreholes down to 30 metres are very expensive.

## Contaminated Land

Where the problems with the site are caused by the natural characteristics of the land, the solutions are usually fairly straightforward, if expensive. However, there is now a trend towards recycling building land and an increasing number of new homes are being built on sites which have had buildings on before — these sites are sometimes known as brownfield sites. If the previous building was a house or a barn, then a pollution problem is unlikely but if the site has been used as a tip or as an industrial plant then it is quite likely that the ground may contain a whole cocktail of nasties such as heavy metals, toxic chemicals or methane gas. Now local authorities up and down the land are currently preparing registers of contaminated land and they will be empowered to issue Remediation Notices which will require the landowner to make the site safe, which usually means either excavating and dumping the pollutants elsewhere (the Brent Spar option) or encasing them in concrete or clay (the Chernobyl option). Sometimes the solution may be relatively cheap — for instance specifying sulphur resistant cement — but it will be some time before housebuilders are able to accurately budget for contamination problems.

## Radon

Radon is a naturally occurring radioactive gas which is present in a few areas of the UK, most notably parts of Devon and Cornwall. It's a relatively low-risk hazard but there is increasing concern about the long-term effects of radon build-up in new homes which are built to much higher standards of air tightness and which, therefore, may act as potential radon traps. The good news for new housebuilders is that it is relatively easy and cheap to incorporate the recommended membrane beneath the ground floor which acts as a barrier through which radon cannot pass; however, renovators of existing properties should be aware that remedial work is much more difficult.

## Access Problems

When assessing a plot or a barn, you should take note of the distance you think you will have to take the services and the access you will have to build. Many backland developments come onto the market these days — typically the rear of someone's garden — and the prices asked for these sites are often little different to the prices asked for somewhere with a road frontage. Yet the budget cost of laying private driveways, drains, water and electricity combined with providing fencing

*Typical backland building plot, looking down past the existing bungalow towards the road nearly 100m away. Laying new drains and services plus building a driveway will add around £10,000 to development costs here.*

is upwards of £100/metre; that means that a plot set 50 metres back from a road is going to cost £5,000 more to develop than one with a road frontage. Whereas the layout of vehicle access arrangements are usually easy to work out, finding out about the services requires detective work.

## Driveways

The basic cost of laying a drive can be budgeted at around £50/lin.m., rather more if it is required to be fenced off as well. Often there is extra work involved in connecting to the public highway: typically you may have to construct a dropped kerb if you are crossing a raised pavement, at the very least you will have to provide a small apron of asphalt or tarmac so that there is no unsightly gap between your drive and the public highway. In some situations you may be required to create a visibility splay which may involve removing existing obstructions and rebuilding them further back from the road. On the other hand, you may have to construct a bridge over a ditch or even make an opening through an existing building. There are, in fact, so many potential access problems that it is almost pointless trying to summarise them — you will, in all probability, discover them when you first visit the site. Just be aware that whilst a straightforward highway junction will cost a couple of hundred quid, complicated access arrangements may well set you back several thousand.

## Drain Connections

Many isolated plots are too far from mains drainage to make connection feasible. To find out what the position is on any given plot you must contact your local council and/or your local water or sewage company. The detail and accuracy of records varies from area to area but they will have some idea of the location of your nearest drain.

If the mains sewer is reasonably adjacent and it's not obviously uphill from your plot, then the omens are fairly good. Excavation and drain connections are, however, fiddly and expensive on even short runs, and if your drain is, say, 50m away from your house it is worth talking to a groundwork/drainage contractor about the other possibilities.

Sewage disposal via a nonstandard route is going to add significantly to costs. A reasonable budget on a no-problem single site, draining straight into a main drain, would be £3,000. If you have to do something other than make a straightforward sewer connection, then you would be wise to budget these amounts in addition:

- Septic tank — add £1,000
- Mini-treatment works — add £3,000
- Cesspool — add £2,500
- Pumping station — add £2,000
- Foul drain runs longer than 50m — add £20/m
- Rainwater drain runs longer than 50m — add £15/m
- Rainwater that won't soakaway — add £300.

One frequently met problem is the development of a site that is located on backland or down a lane. Main drains are present under the main road but your site is maybe 150m or more away. How do you assess the situation? Probably the best solution is to get a groundwork contractor to have a look and give an estimate on how much a connection would be. If the figure goes up much over

£2,500 then you would do well to think of using some of the alternative solutions. This is something else that is touched on in greater depth in Chapter 6.

## Water Connections

Unlike drainage work, which is usually left to the housebuilder to organise, water connections have to be carried out by the powers that be. In England and Wales that means the private water companies and their fees are notoriously high, frequently higher than £500 for connections which need very little excavation, involving perhaps just three hours work; if your connection needs a road to be dug up, then the connection fee will be in thousands. All new houses in England and Wales are now fitted with water meters and these are conventionally placed at the boundary of the property so that at least you can control the costs of laying pipe from the boundary to your house; but all work carried out under or next to a public highway must be carried out by the water companies and it will cost.

Fortunately, the one ray of light in all this is that water companies will provide a free quotation for their work. They will need location and site plans, but there is no need for you to own the property, so it makes good sense to get this quotation before agreeing a plot price.

In Scotland and N. Ireland the situation couldn't be more different. Here it is beholden on the local authorities to provide water and, providing the property is only a "reasonable distance" from the mains supply, then work is carried out at the council's expense.

There is always the possibility of drawing water from under the ground via a borehole; this is almost invariably a costly option and can only be recommended if you have a very remote site (or you have a particular desire not to connect to your local water company's supply). Costs depend largely on depth of groundwater and can vary from as little as £1,500 to as much as £10,000; if you are interested, check out Wellborers in your Yellow Pages.

## Electricity

Like water, installation to new sites is charged on a time and materials basis. Even a simple connection (say less than 25m from mains supply) is likely to cost in excess of £300 and charges rise in line with distance. However, the electricity companies offer a similar quotation service to the water companies and you should avail yourself of this.

## Other Services

It is unlikely that other service connections will result in budget busting costs. Gas supply to a new dwelling is either going to be reasonably cheap or it isn't going to happen at all. It all depends on how near the mains gas supply is. Very often supply is free if the gas main is nearby. Phone lines are costed on a flat rate: there is a one off connection charge, currently £70 (+VAT) per line for new BT residential lines, whatever the distance. Cable charges are set by local companies but, like mains gas, will tend to be either low or not available.

# Random Perils

## Overhead Cables

Power cables running across your plot are bad news. They may intersect with your proposed building, in which case they will have to be moved; even if they don't they will detract from the resale value of the property. Burying them is the obvious solution but it can be horribly expensive; even a low voltage cable can cost over £20/m to bury, which can easily make a short diversion cost £2,500 or more. Again, the trick is to get quotations for this before entering into any contract to buy.

## Existing Drains

This is one real nightmare for rookies and professionals alike: existing drains running across your proposed building. Do what ever you can to find out if drains are present, but sometimes there are no records and no surface evidence. Drains vary in their importance; small runs connecting one or two households to a sewer may very easily be diverted — depending on the lie of the land — but sewers and pumped drains cannot readily be moved and discovering one of these in your footings is a Grade A disaster, though thankfully this doesn't happen too often. Again the key is to find out as much as

possible about the plot before you exchange contracts to purchase. If there is any doubt in your mind, then try and place a retention in the sale contract which is only payable should nothing untoward be found under the ground.

## Conversions

Don't assume that any building that has once been occupied by humans will automatically qualify for residential planning permission. Councils take widely differing attitudes to what constitutes abandonment and the most telling factor in whether or not an old building can be converted into a new home is usually the quality of the building, not its previous usage. Always check on the status of a derelict property in the local plan to see whether redevelopment is likely to be controversial. Often the planners will allow the conversion of a particularly fine old barn just to stop it from disintegrating and sometimes this permission is dependent on the structure being maintained, even when this is a costly and relatively dangerous course to take.

There have been cases of planning permission being withdrawn from barn conversions after the builder has undertaken demolition of a few select walls.

## Archaeological remains

Finding interesting remains might sound like a bonus but it can be expensive and time consuming as well. I know of one selfbuilder in Bedfordshire who had to pay an extra £3,000 because they uncovered Roman coffins in the foundations. If your site looks at all interesting, then it may be a condition of planning that a qualified archaeologist is present during excavations — all at your expense.

## Borrowing Money

I have already touched on the perils of property developing on borrowed money but it would be amiss not to touch on them once more because borrowing money, large dollops of the stuff, is perhaps the most dangerous peril of all. Against this, it must be said that the borrowing climate has changed since the boom of the 80s when developers were only having to put up 10% of the total costs and lenders were quite happy to see the loans repaid from the sale values. Nowadays you are very unlikely to be offered building money unless the lender believes you have the wherewithal to service the debt. If you already have a large mortgage and feel comfortable that you can meet the repayments, then the fact that you transfer this mortgage to an unbuilt or partially built property should not make very much difference to you. But never forget that there are many things that can come between you and the large paper profit which you start out with. Don't assume that this profit will flow effortlessly to you as you complete your building programme. Always be prepared for a situation where you cannot sell the finished house at the price you hoped for, or indeed at any price at all.

## Over-specifying

It is said that the three most important factors in property development are location, location and location. Like many other jokes, there is a pearl of wisdom here and one which rookie housebuilders would do well to heed. Building plots, just like existing houses, have to be assessed in relation to the neighbourhood they are located in and what goes on around them. If you are interested in maximising the return on your investment, then don't fall into the trap of specifying a luxury house on a plot which is surrounded by houses of a much lower quality. Rich people like to live in quiet secluded neighbourhoods, well away from the noise and grime of traffic and industry, and close by other rich people; poor people don't get the choice and have to make do.

If you have no intention of moving for many years to come and really don't give a hoot that your house is next to a council estate or a rubbish tip or a chicken farm, then go ahead and build your mansion on that nice cheap plot you found. However, if you are hoping to maximise your profit, it pays to take careful heed of the location you are building in and to specify a house in keeping with the neighbourhood. This is not hard to do, just look around and see who your would-be neighbours are and, more importantly, how much their houses are worth. A well-built new house will tend to attract a premium price, perhaps as much as 15-20% more than second-hand stock nearby but it is vital that you realise that however much money you pour into your house, you will not improve much on this premium.

This is a particular problem for selfbuilders in SE England who have to compete with each other and end up chasing up prices paid for quite humble plots of land. Naturally enough, they want to build the best house they can afford because they want to live in it but this often means ignoring the time honoured rules about the importance of location. The general inexperience of selfbuild purchasers also means that the lessons contained in this chapter are often ignored or, more likely, just not known about so that there is often precious little difference in price between an A plus plot and a C minus. Most estate agents have only the dimmest ideas about building costs and tend to value properties and plots almost entirely by amenity and location. It is up to the buyers to assess the development costs and the likely resale value. This is particularly so with barn conversions: these are usually considerably more expensive to build than equivalent new houses but the prices paid for derelict barns with planning permission doesn't reflect this at all.

## Bad Design

There is a dangerous tendency for selfbuilders to cut right back on the design costs in order to cram more features into the house. I've been into new homes which are about as attractive as a cardboard box but are stuffed to the gunnells with home theatres, central vacuum systems, sprinklers, heat recovery systems, Agas, closed-circuit TV, saunas, gyms, you name it. Turns out the plans for the house were knocked out by some bloke in his spare time for about £300 because they thought that six grand for a proper architect was a rip-off. Well, maybe it is, maybe it isn't but, in terms of payback, good design really does seem to pay for itself and good design rarely (never) comes cheap. Skimping on design comes about from concentrating on the cost of everything rather than the value.

## Pitfalls Checklist

Before buying a plot of land, you should check the following points. None of them is a reason for not buying, but all of them present potential extra costs which you need to be aware of and, perhaps, this knowledge may even enable you to negotiate a lower price.

- Are the described boundaries accurate?
- Are there any restrictive covenants on the plot?
- Are there rights of way crossing the plot?
- Would you own all the land necessary for access and services? If not, are wayleaves readily obtainable?
- Are there any tree preservation orders?
- Are there any other "legal encumbrances" which might hinder you in any way?
- Is access adequate for cars? Are there stipulations from Highways that could be difficult to meet?
- Is the plot wide enough? Plots narrower than 12m can present problems for turning vehicles.
- Are there any planning conditions in effect?
- Does planning permission apply to the whole of the plot?
- When does planning permission run out?
- Is there a slope steeper than 1:25?
- What are ground conditions like?
- Is there evidence of existing drains on site?
- Are there any large trees within 30m?
- Are there any overhead cables to be moved?
- Are there likely problems with service connections?

Many of these potential administrative snags should be unearthed by your solicitor. The more technical ones are normally dealt with by building professionals — i.e. architects and structural engineers. If the plot looks dodgy in any way, don't hesitate to get help. Consider commissioning a feasibility study from your designer before contracts are exchanged — because this should unearth most of the bugs. At the end of the day though, it's caveat emptor — buyer beware — because you are where the buck stops and it'll be down to you to sort out any do-dos.

# Chapter 4
# Design

## Overview

House design is undoubtedly the trickiest issue faced by every potential builder. The central point that shouldn't be forgotten is that you want to build the best possible house for a price you can afford. Easily written, but how the hell do you do it? What is the "best possible house"? And how do you go about designing it?

Questions abound. Is an architect necessarily an expensive option? What about using a designer who is not a qualified architect? Isn't it cheaper to use a package build design? Won't the planners force me to redesign the whole thing in any event?

Well steady on, I'll cover these issues in due course. But first let's take a look at the design process because...well, it's a good place to start. The design process can be subdivided into a number of parts, some fixed points with known costs and others elastic in the extreme. Below is a list of the stages that you need to go through. You don't have to do it in

this order (you could for instance apply for building regulations approval before you have planning permission) but it would be frankly very strange not to do it this way.
- Site Survey and Feasibility Study
- Design Process leading to Sketches of Options
- Commission Drawings for Planning Permission
- Submit Plans for Planning Permission (fee)
- Try and Negotiate Positive Outcome to Planning Application
- Do this Over and Over Again till Outcome is Positive
- Detailed Designs and Specifications
- Submit Detailed Designs for Building Regs Approval (fee)
- Negotiate Positive Outcome.

### Site Survey
Unless you are very confident of your surveying and drafting abilities, you should have a professional carry out an accurate site sur-

vey to measure and plot all the existing buildings, boundaries, levels, access arrangements, trees, drains, neighbouring buildings and any other information thought to be relevant. On simple sites this might cost £100-£200. If, by chance, you've read the previous chapter Pitfalls, then you'll realise that a smart plot buyer will have carried out much of this work before signing any contracts. Don't rely on professionals to sort these problems out for you after the event.

### Feasibility Study/Sketches
Assuming you have a plot and a budget, the most important questions are: what can you build on it and how much will it cost? It may seem very early in the whole mysterious design process but you have already reached crunch point. This is usually the key moment when you start to commission the whole building process and your decisions at this point will have costly implications on down the line. I have distinguished between a stage called Feasibility Study and another called

31

Sketches of Options; this is helpful in understanding how one grows out of the other but in reality there is no hard and fast dividing line between them, and how you and your designer get from an empty page to a full planning application will vary enormously from case to case.

Nevertheless, there tends to be a clear path which leads from the site survey stage into a feasibility stage (which, if you like, is about eliminating impractical options) and then into outlining practical solutions and, from there, plumping for your best choice, at which point the designer changes gear and starts to look at the nitty-gritty decisions which spring from the choice you have made. A professional at £20-£50/hr may seem a luxury, but they will (or at least should) understand the issues and concentrate your thinking on the relevant areas. There may or may not be any consultation with local planners at this stage, depending on how confident you or your agent feels. If doing it yourself, then a visit to the planners would be advisable. Use books of house plans for inspiration (despite the fact that they're mostly anything but), but do not expect to fit an existing plan on to your plot; the chances of it working without amendment are small and amending existing plans can be almost as expensive as starting from scratch.

The cost of this stage is naturally very open-ended: some short-of-work designers will undertake the early parts of this process for free on the understanding that more work will follow. For many independent designers and architects, the early part of the process is the most challenging and the most interesting and they would anticipate spending around a third of their time on this stage. The biggest variable is you, the client. The more sussed out you are, the better your brief, and the shorter and cheaper this process will be. Even if you are planning to build a kit house or use an off-the-shelf design, it is still worthwhile getting a professional designer to undertake some sort of study if only to sort out practicalities like drain runs (though note that many kit suppliers have their own designers who will undertake this work).

## Planning Drawings

A good designer with a thorough working knowledge of local practices and trends will be able to help you marry your ideas with the views of the planners, hopefully pre-empting any potential areas of conflict. Planning departments are surprisingly diverse in their ideas, often reflecting the individual tastes of the chief planning officer, and knowing the whys and wherefores of local planning decisions is one way in which local knowledge scores heavily over nationwide services.

Whoever you choose, they will have to produce a set (in fact several sets) of planning permission drawings to present to the local planning department. Budget anything from £200 for pre-drawn plans through to £3,000 for architect one-offs.

For a detailed look at the mechanics of applying for planning permission, and the likely fees, see the following section. There are a number of plans and drawings that the planners require and your chosen designer/agent should know this rigmarole backwards — indeed if they don't I would be tend to be rather suspicious.

## Working Details

If designing from scratch, it is conventional not to decide on all the construction details until planning constraints are established. This is simply to make sure that work does not have to be done twice in case of later amendments. However, construction details on conventional houses are remarkably similar and often the details can be lifted from previous jobs. On simple projects, the plans, construction details and specification (known as the spec with a soft 'c') can all be contained on two sheets of A1 (840x592mm) plans which would detail:

- Floor plans'
- Foundation plan
- Drainage plan
- First floor joist layout
- Roof truss/rafter layout
- N,E,S and W elevations (or views)
- Section or sections through the middle of the house, showing room heights, floor levels, wall constructions, joist depths, staircase dimensions.
- Window and door schedule (list of joinery manufacturers codes)
- Text explaining construction standards (lots of BS numbers here).

On more complicated jobs, there may be extra plans perhaps running to many pages, showing various complicated details like eaves or dormer windows. Upmarket jobs tend to have the specification written separately from the drawings and a serious architectural practice may write a specification running to fifty pages or more. How much of this is necessary depends on a) the complexity of the work and b) the attitude of the client. Rookie builders would be well advised not to attempt anything too unusual first time around, in which case the standard two-sheet plans are probably adequate. Many experienced subcontractors never look at plans in any event — quite a few can't read — and complex plans could be wasted on many.

I know of a number of small builders who basically dispense with the working drawings stage. They work from little more than the planning drawings, littered with notes like "To be confirmed onsite" or "To Building Inspector's Satisfaction"; they are on site everyday and they prefer to work out these details as they go along. Once you've done it a few times, it works fine provided you stick to fairly standard solutions (they do). But if you are new to this game and/or you can't be there on site a good deal, then you would do well not to skimp on working drawings as these form, in effect, your detailed instructions to your builder. Much of this detailed work and, in particular, the writing of the specification, forms the very heart of any forthcoming building contract. If you want an element of protection from the perils of badly executed building work, then a professionally written specification is worth far more than any off-the-peg contract that you might be tempted to sign.

In budget terms, these design details are the area with the most variance. If purchasing a set of predetermined house plans (typically for £300-£500), then all this detailed work will be included with the plans so the effective cost is zero. If using a package build, then again these details will come integrated with the package. But be wary of assuming that pre-drawn plans are necessarily the cheapest option, because 90% of the time they require significant amendments and sometimes it proves to be just as expensive as starting with a blank sheet of paper. However, even a one-off design may cost no more than a few hundred pounds if it sticks to tried and tested solutions; on the other hand, this part of the design work can also very easily cost £2000-£4000 for unusual houses, as unusual features take time to design — and build. Here you would expect workshop joinery, arched openings, fancy staircases, patterned brickwork — generally expensive features which are also expensive to design. If you are building to a tight budget and are happy with conventional solutions, then make it clear that you do not want unusual detailing and, as a result, a) your working details should not cost too much, b) your house isn't likely to be expensive to build and c) it is much less likely to run over budget.

The danger in trying to put a price to all this is that you may lose sight of the fact that, as with so many things in life, you get what you pay for; if someone knocks up a set of plans for you over a couple of weekends for a few hundred quid, the chances are that your finished house will reflect the fact. On the other hand, if you are interested in creating a wonderful home you'd be daft to skimp on the design stages. If you want to save money, you'd probably do better to build a smaller house. There is a real conundrum in here. People don't want to be ripped off by some fancy-dan architect charging the earth. Yet a good architect can often justify the fees because they actually add value to the finished product. If an architect or designer can do the business, then the thousands of pounds they want for employing them is money well spent.

## Structural Engineer

Having been called in during the digging of the trial hole, the structural engineer may have to make another appearance if the designs take on any non-standard features. All beams, lintels, roofs and foundations (the so-called structural elements) of a building require proof that they are sufficient to do the job asked of them. Standard solutions to standard problems are regarded as tried and tested, but anything out of the ordinary will require "proving" to the satisfaction of the building inspector. A structural engineer will calculate the forces applied to beams or foundations and come up with adequate solutions. If the ground you plan to build on is at all dodgy, then an engineer will be required to prove your foundation design; also many very ordinary situations like using steel beams or opening up a loft space require structural proving. If you want to build in timber frame

without going via a specialist supplier, you need to get the design proved by a specialist engineer qualified to issue an HB353 certificate — in Scotland it's called an HB210. This would normally cost between £300 and £500 per dwelling.

Detailed drawings and structural calculations (if needed) are presented to the local council's building control department for examination.

## Sub-designs

Design and specification of finishes is often left to the client or builder to sort out and this is more often than not passed down the line to the tradesmen involved on the job. Therefore, the plumber designs the central heating system, the electrician designs the lighting, a kitchen specialist will take over design of the kitchen. This sort of arrangement obviously works as it is what happens in 90% of homes built, but arguably it could be much better coordinated by a single designer.

On large, commercial contracts these areas are all dealt with separately by specialist professionals who draw up a specification and arrange quotes from it. One-off housing is really too small to justify the expense of all these extra professionals, and much of the work, designed and installed by the various tradesmen, is consequently very unimaginative. The degree of competence varies enormously: many act as much as salesmen as designers: most make no charge provided

you buy their product, which is all very well but it makes you very vulnerable to uncompetitive practices.

It's really a very difficult area to negotiate, even for hard bitten professionals. Many architects are not qualified to give advice on, say, lighting design or interior decorating. If you are happy with tried and tested solutions to problems then you will be well advised to keep it simple and deal directly with your chosen contractor; if, however, you want to explore the many and varied options open to you, then you could do worse than read the rest of this book which is peppered with contact names and numbers.

## In Conclusion

Design and professional expenses are the hardest areas to budget for because they are so variable. To a large extent, they are dependent on the brief that you, as a client, present to the designers. An off-the-peg house plan can be purchased for a few hundred pounds but will very probably require a great deal of alteration to fit both the site and your ideas. In contrast, an architect might charge over £5,000 for designing a detached four bed roomed house; however, it does not follow that the off-the-peg plans are necessarily better value. The resulting house might be £5000 less expensive to build and might also be worth £10,000 more when finished! Here you must use your own judgement and intuition.

# Planning Permission

Planning permission and building regulations are two big hurdles that every would-be housebuilder will have to jump. They are complex and not easily mastered, and many building professionals have bald patches on their heads where they have torn their hair out from negotiating paths through or around the maze of regulations and precedents that govern our construction activities. For a rookie builder this can seem all rather daunting, especially when you're not even clear what's the difference between planning permission and building regulations — or regs as they are known in the trade, as in "God, there's been another bloody change in the regs." The regs are dealt with later in this chapter — first planning permission.

## What Exactly Is It?

Various Acts of Parliament (notably the Town and Country Planning Acts), mostly introduced since 1945, require that local authorities should control what can be built where and how buildings (and land) should or should not be used. Planning permission is not concerned with how you build (that's the building regs), nor with who owns the land on which you wish to build. There are many small construction projects that do not require planning permission but something of the size of a new house invariably does.

The power-that-bees in this respect is your local council. Not your County or Metropolitan Council, but your District or City council. In Scotland and N.Ireland the system works slightly differently, as it does in National Parks, but then they wouldn't want to make it too straightforward, would they? It gets worse. Officially, the licence to build is granted by the elected councillors, but every council has a full-time planning department which consists of civil servants known as planning officers, and these are the people

who actually deal with planning applications. Indeed, the chief planning officer has powers to make certain decisions off his or her own bat. Even when they choose not to exercise these powers they make "Recommendations" to the committee of councillors as to whether an application should be accepted or refused. The planning committee rarely goes against the recommendations of its planning officers.

## Foreplay

You don't have to have any contact at all with the planners before submitting your application, but it is commonplace to do so. Tactics are involved here and there is no such thing as a correct way of going about it — every case stands on its own. On the one hand, you don't want to be faced with the expense of drawing up plans only for the planners to fall about laughing at the very thought that anyone could build on that piece of land; on the

## Guide to Planning Speak

### Outline
*Often used by landowners who are trying to find out whether development would be acceptable in principle without going through the hassle of having detailed plans drawn up. Outline permission to build is what turns a garden or a field into a building plot; getting it makes you seriously rich but it doesn't, on its own, allow you to build. Outline permission lasts for five years, but a detailed application must be agreed within three years or else the permission lapses.*

### Full Application
*As its name suggests, a full planning application seeks to approve both the principle and the details of development. It lasts for five years.*

### Approval of Reserved Matters
*This is used to convert outline permission to detailed.*

### Renewal
*Planning permission can be renewed, but only if consent has not expired so this route is used to get an extension to an existing permission. If the permission has lapsed, then a new application has to be made.*

### Relaxation
*Sometimes planning permission comes with a load of irksome conditions. You can apply to have these lifted at a later date but don't hold out too much hope.*

### Amendments
*If you purchase a plot with detailed permission for a house that you don't actually want to build, you may be able to amend the plans without submitting a whole new application. There is no charge for amendment but if your changes are substantial the planners may not accept them as amendments and you'll be back to square one.*

### Extensions/Conversions
*If your building project involves work to an existing structure, you may not need planning permission. Phone your local council's planning department and ask their advice. They issue a free 22 page booklet called Planning – A Guide for Householders which makes a fair stab at explaining the rudiments.*

other hand, if you wander into the planning department with questions like "What sort of house could I build on this spot?", then you are inviting the planners to design the house for you. This they won't do, but what will happen is that they will get in their minds all kinds of constraints that will severely limit your options: "You must do…" and "You can't have…" Like our legal system and our parliament, our planning system is adversarial; you may not get exactly what you want out of it — most planning decisions are the result of compromise — but you stand a far better chance of getting more of what you want if you choose the battleground on which to fight; i.e. submit plans with minimal reference to the planners. Getting the planners too closely involved before submitting your application can be seen as ceding this battleground.

Now it may be that your planning application is not terribly controversial and that the planners will be delighted with your ideas. In which case you may think I am a paranoid old nutter. But don't forget that it's your money and that they have the right to make you shell out for things which you think are completely unnecessary. Adopting a "lie down and think of England" pose may earn you brownie points at City Hall but may also fire off alarm bells around the corner at the bank or building society.

## Submitting an Application
The mechanics of submitting an application are straightforward, if time- and tree-consuming. There are, however, several different types of planning permission that can be granted and these are summarised in the adjacent box.

### Application Forms
The actual application consists of a number of forms which you have to fill out, together with your plans and your cheque. Exact requirements vary from council to council but are not likely to be less than six copies of each of the following:

- Location plan (taken off OS map at a scale of 1:1250)
- Existing site plan (boundaries outlined in red) at 1:500
- Proposed site plan — showing position of house, garage, driveway, access
- Layout plans and elevations of any existing structures on site
- Layout plans and elevations of proposed dwelling at 1:100 or 1:50
- Details of materials to be used
- Details of trees to be felled — even though your application arrives in a wheelbarrow, they won't see the irony.

In addition to these, it sometimes helps to have three-dimensional bird's-eye view drawings (isometric projections) which show how the house fits with its neighbours. Some people even go to the trouble of building models and circumstantial evidence suggests that this can be an effective way of communicating ideas on what might be seen as controversial applications.

### Ownership Certificate
You also have to fill out a form stating ownership of the land in question. You don't actually have to own land in order to apply for planning permission over it but you are required to notify the owner of your intentions.

### Fees
At time of writing, outline fees in England & Wales are £220 for each 0.1 hectare (=1000m$^2$ = small plot) of site area applied for. Detailed permission for one dwelling is also £220 and if you apply for outline and then move on to a detailed application it will cost you twice £220 (my calculator makes that £440 but it could be playing up). The only way to avoid this double fee is to go straight for detailed permission which involves more costly drawings: in some situations this is a risk worth taking but if the application is likely to be controversial, just go for the outline. There are no fees for consultation with planners or for making amendments to plans to satisfy planners' concerns.

## Chances of Success
After submitting your application, the planners then go to work on assessing it. These days they all seem to work in teams, and this makes it even harder to get any sense out of them as to how they think the application is progressing. They are meant to take eight weeks to reach a determination, but in practice it depends on how busy they are—it can all take much longer. Keep ringing them to find out what's happening to your application; sooner or later they will reach some sort of provisional verdict and this is the point at which negotiations start. If they are completely hostile, then you may do better to withdraw the application and start anew; if they express some reservations (they usually do), then you must be prepared to compromise hard. Eventually, the planning officials will either grant planning permission (unlikely on a new house) or refer it to the planning committee of the local council who, typically, meet once a month. This referral will come with a recommendation either way — which the committee usually accepts. Planning permission is often granted with conditions attached; if you are Sainsburys wanting to build a supermarket, these conditions may be something big, but for a one-

off housebuilder they are not likely to be terribly onerous.

## Reasons for Refusal

There can be any number of reasons why planners take a negative view of your proposals. In rural districts the land is zoned (via the "local plans" which you can inspect at your library), and if you are applying to build in a non-building zone then you've got your work cut out trying to get anywhere. Assuming they accept that the site is suitable for development, here are several reasons why they may still not play ball:

- Lack of adequate parking
- Can't turn a car around on the hard standing
- Overlooking neighbours
- Roof too high
- House too big for plot
- Not enough garden
- Development out of keeping with neighbourhood
- Wrong position on the plot
- Don't like your choice of materials or overall design.

I could go on. Suffice it to say that many of these reasons are perfectly justifiable and if you weren't so greedy and pig-headed you would be able to see the sense in them. But applicants are apt to feel aggrieved whenever the outcome goes against them.

## Lobbying

You don't have to take the views of the planning officials lying down. Many people have taken to lobbying their councillors to overrule the recommendation for refusal. This is real grass roots politics and in many parts of the world sums of money would change hands in order to get planning permissions through on the nod, but in Britain, of course, we don't do that. I don't wish to sound too sarcastic because by and large this is true — people tend not to go into local politics for money, but they do have a tendency to self-importance and many are not averse to a little bit of flattery. This is the network at work: it all depends on personalities and who you do or do not know. Even if you don't get very far with councillors, you should at least consider lobbying your neighbours. A couple of letters from neighbours saying positive things about your plans is worth a lot at a planning committee meeting. However, there is every chance that your neighbours may not feel as enthusiastic about your plans as you do and this tactic can backfire.

## Appeals v New Applications

If you shoot your bolt and, despite all your lobbying, your application is refused you are faced with three choices:
- Give up
- Submit a new application
- Appeal.

The first is the cheapest but it doesn't get you very far. If you want to persist, then there is no reason why you can't go to appeal on your first application whilst simultaneously submitting a new one. Surprisingly, there is no charge for making an appeal but it does take time, around six months, and many people can't wait that long, especially if there's borrowed money riding on it. Appeals are presided over by an independent inspector, often a QC, sometimes an architect, and on small projects like individual housebuilding the usual way of going about it is to produce written evidence. Basically, you must write your side of the story and explain to the inspector why you think you should have been granted planning permission in the first place. On the due date the inspector will visit the site and shortly afterwards they will make their ruling known. That's it. There are alternative methods of appeal, notably using the informal hearing method which gathers all the interested parties together to discuss the issue at hand, but the written representation is the simplest and least time consuming (and cheapest, if you are paying a professional to act for you).

Only one in three appeals succeed and from my limited experience it is difficult to predict the outcome in advance, so you are taking a big gamble in going to appeal. You can hire a professional to make the appeal for you, but this will be expensive and may not add to your chances. As there is no further drawing work to be undertaken — you can't amend your plans between first refusal and appeal — the appeal process can easily be undertaken by any lay person capable of using pen and paper, although a thorough understanding of planning issues will obviously stand you in good stead.

For many people, it will be cheaper and much quicker to submit a new planning application. When an application is refused, the planners have to state grounds for refusal. In an ideal world these issues could have been sorted out before the application ever came before the committee, but sometimes it takes a refusal to actually bring the problems out into the open. Armed with refusal reasons, you can make suitable amendments in your next application and, provided you can genuinely sort out the issues, you should have a much better chance of gaining planning permission, although the outcome is likely to be some way from your original ideas.

Changes to the planning system are always being mooted but all that ever seems to happen on the ground is that the whole process becomes ever more troublesome and time consuming. And I haven't even discussed Listed Buildings Consents — these can take over a year to obtain! Good luck.

# Building Regs, Warranties, Party Walls

As mentioned at the beginning of the previous section, the building regs are a different matter altogether from planning permission. As with planning permission, there are a number of small works that are excepted from having building regulations applied to them, but again a project as large as a house will invariably fall inside building control. Each local council has a building control department which employs building inspectors, who both assess plans submitted to them and visit sites to ensure that the plans are actually put into practice. The plans submitted to building control are more detailed than those used for gaining planning permission and so this work is usually commissioned as an additional service after a successful planning application. Note, however, that much of the detail needed to satisfy building regulations is to do with written specifications rather than drawings and that much of this is standard to all housing. Phrases peppered with BS numbers and sentences finishing with "to the satisfaction of the building inspector" are commonly placed in specifications precisely to meet the regs. Furthermore, what is often the most important part of an inspector's job, checking that the foundations are adequate, can really only be done on site.

Getting approval for building regulations is not a political matter and there are no committees to go before or councillors to lobby. You just have to reach agreement with your appointed building inspector — which, by and large, means doing as he (occasionally she) says. If you stick to conventional methods of construction this is generally not too difficult. However, expect problems if you are inclined to unusual techniques.

## What are they?

The building regulations actually consist of a number of separate booklets known as Approved Documents, generally referred to as Parts. Each part is given a letter and currently the English & Welsh versions of these run from Part A (which deals with Structure) to Part N (Glazing). You can buy the complete pack of 14 parts for £60.00 or for about £20 less you can buy an HMSO publication called Home Builder which attempts to make the whole thing digestible to the small housebuilder. You can also download the parts from the dtlr website.

These are technical publications and most builders have never clapped eyes on them; instead they rely on their designer to have satisfied the regs in the drawings and their building inspector to put them straight if the situation on site requires it.

From time to time, the regs are amended. The building regs are always getting tightened and recently we've seen changes to the fire regs and the energy efficiency regs and are about to get changes put through on the sound regs. In 1999, Part M (which deals with disabled access) was brought into effect in housing for the first time. Note that in Scotland and N.Ireland, they operate slightly different regulations — the Scottish ones have Parts as well but the letters are not equivalent to the English and Welsh versions.

## Building Control Fees

Local authority fees are no longer set nationally. However the fees for new houses tend to cluster around the £300 mark. My local authority charges £165 for plan approval and an additional £160 for site inspections on new houses up to 300m² internal floor area (both these figures include VAT). With smaller works like extensions, the fees are correspondingly less. VAT is charged on building control fees for new dwellings (unlike planning application fees) and is generally not reclaimable.

## NHBC

Whilst planning is exclusively the domain of the local councils, building control has been "privatised." For many years there was only one other option and that was the National House Builders Council (the NHBC), who run a building control scheme for their members side by side with their 10-year warranty. The NHBC is a force to be reckoned with in new housebuilding and it publishes its own standards which are, in general, slightly higher than the government's regulations. Professional housebuilders are mostly members because the 10-year warranty scheme is seen as essential to secure sales; besides this fact, the NHBC's fees for administering building control are a little lower than those charged by local councils. The NHBC is aimed at professional builders and charges a one-off joining fee of over £500 plus an annual membership of at least £250 (dependent on how many houses you build) which is meant to deter the casual builder.

## Warranties

I have already touched on the NHBC's 10-year warranty but it is important to realise that this is something quite distinct from the building regulations. Both are enforced by a series of onsite inspections; building control inspections occur at several pre-defined stages whilst warranty inspections occur unannounced so as to inspect other aspects of the work. Whereas it is mandatory to obtain building regulations for a major building project like a new house, the requirement for a warranty comes largely from mortgage providers who like it to be in place before advancing money on a finished property.

Now, if a house is built to satisfy the building regs, then it should be good for ten years so in many ways the whole warranty scheme is a bit of an expensive red herring. The NHBC's warranty scheme does provide some (arguably rather limited) protection for new housebuyers, particularly useful when your original builder goes bust, but it is nothing like a fully comprehensive guarantee and many new housebuyers are dismayed to find that after just two years the guarantee limits itself to "major damage caused by a defect in the structure" and just what that means is up to the NHBC alone to decide. Having said that, the NHBC accepts around 4,000 claims annually against its member firms (that's roughly one in every forty homes built) so it can hardly be accused of not facing up to its responsibilities. The NHBC warranty scheme has had a hammering in the press recently, mostly as a result of aggrieved new home owners learning too late just how little is covered by this warranty.

The question facing many selfbuilders is whether it is worth having this extra insurance offered by the NHBC warranty, which costs the builders between 0.3 and 0.8% of the selling price of the house, dependent on size of house and the builder's previous claims record. Well, there are alternatives. There is another warranty scheme from Zurich Municipal called Custom Build which is similar in many ways to the NHBC scheme but is tailored more to one-off builders who don't want to join the NHBC. There is a low registration fee of £50 but the policy itself is not cheap—expect to pay over £1000 for a one-off four or five bedroomed house. Zurich's Custom Build has been successful: it has caused the NHBC to launch its own version, a selfbuild warranty scheme called Solo. And others have also started venturing into this market, notably a scheme called Project Builder and another launched by the local authority building control departments.

There is also the possibility of having your work certified by an architect which is a realistic option only if you have employed an architect to design and oversee your build: it's not quite the same as a warranty, as any later claim you might have would be against your architect — i.e. you have to sue them — rather than an insurance company, but most mortgage lenders are happy to accept architect's certification. Your fee for this would be negotiated independently with your architect, but bear in mind that many architects don't like certifying work (understandably — it's quite a risk and it has to be backed by expensive professional indemnity insurance) and will try and steer you towards using Zurich or the NHBC. Also bear in mind that if you are financing your housebuilding by other means than a regular mortgage, then a warranty is not needed at all, although absence of one could make resale within ten years more difficult.

Finally a note for barn converters. Both the NHBC and Zurich offer a warranty scheme for conversions, though these are both costlier and of shorter duration than their new build equivalents. Also note that there is more on the ins and outs of warranties in the Insurance section of Chapter 5.

## The Party Wall Act

There is more to the red tape than just Planning Permission and Building Regs. If you are lucky these two will be the only bits you encounter but there are other things to consider as well. Close by a neighbour? Within six metres? You may have to treat with...

The Party Wall Act has been in effect since 1997 throughout England and Wales — prior to that it was restricted to London. The idea behind this piece of legislation is to protect the neighbouring properties from damage when your construction work is carried out. The Act is very specific about just where and when it comes into effect. If your foundations are to be deeper than your neighbour's buildings, you must observe the Party Wall Act provisions if you are within three metres of those buildings — note not boundary, but buildings. In addition to this, there is a provision which states that if you are building much deeper than the neighbouring house's foundations, then you may still be affected by the provisions of the Act at a distance of six metres. You draw a line at 45° down from the bottom of your neighbour's foundations and if it strikes your projected foundation works within six metres, then Ka Boom — you are in the net. It's likely to be pointed out to you when you put a full planning application in.

If the Party Wall Act does come into effect — and in many urban areas it is likely to if you want to build a basement or if you have to pile — you are obliged to notify your neighbour and to assuage their concerns that your building work may damage their property. Often this can be done with an informal exchange of letters but, if the neighbour is worried about what you are up to, then he or she is entitled to hire, at your expense, a qualified structural engineer or surveyor to verify your plans. You must state whether you propose to strengthen or safeguard the foundations of the building or structure belonging to the adjoining owner. Such aspects need to be considered at the design stage of the project to avoid unexpected costs arising. This can, naturally, become a long and involved process as the two surveyors have to reach agreement about just how the work should be undertaken. Your neighbour cannot prevent you undertaking this work but they can delay works. If the next door building is split into flats, then you have to entreat with each occupier individually. Doesn't that prospect fill you with joy? You can obtain a copy of the Party Wall Act for free off the web at www.hmso.gov.uk/acts1996/96040.

# Which Route?

There are two distinct approaches to house design. One is to hire a designer (be they architect or not) and to let them get on with the task of melding your ideas with their expertise; the other is to approach a package build company who specialise in selling standard houses which can be adapted to particular needs. In some ways the differences are not that great — after all both involve building houses — but conceptually it's the difference between painting from scratch and painting by numbers.

## Package Build

Whilst the creative types would probably be appalled at the idea that you could buy an off-the-peg kit house, package build does have one big advantage going for it and that is WYSIWYG. For those not up in computing circles, WYSIWYG (pronounced Whizz-Ee-Wig) stands for What You See Is What You Get, and it describes perfectly the attraction of the package build philosophy in that you know in advance what your home will look like. Furthermore, you know you'll have a conventional, resaleable property because it wouldn't be on offer if it wasn't. This is a very comforting and reassuring selling factor for self builders, who are terrified of losing their construction virginity to some way out weirdo architect with ideas.

Package builds will almost certainly not be the cheapest route to a finished house: in fact, as reference to the next section of this chapter will show, they are often considerably more expensive than the route taken by volume developers. However, they do offer the novice housebuilder something which few architects ever do and that is a price in advance — though I should add that in reality they only offer a price for the parts of the house they actually supply and erect, which is often no more than a quarter or a third of the total building costs.

Take a hill-trekking holiday in the Himalayas as a comparison. Many people would want to go on such a holiday first time with a package deal, but having done it once, would realise that it was not so difficult to organise and that, if they ever went again, they would go on their own, have more independence and save money. Housebuilding is not so dissimilar; the comfort of having a professional organisation behind you in your first venture and a feeling that you know what the final bill will be is worth a lot more than the vague hope that you just might be saving money.

What buyers of package building services should realise is that they are not getting free design. Rather, the design work is being paid for within the package price. The package build companies all employ architects or designers and these people get paid just like their freelance cousins, and who do you think pays their salaries? Now the logic of using predrawn house plans is that the whole design process is reduced to a matter of a bit of photocopying which should be much cheaper for all concerned. However, British planning restrictions being what they are today, there are virtually no uncomplicated building plots on which you can plonk an off-the-peg house: the houses all require "adaptation" which is tantamount to admitting that the brochure designs are just sales hooks to entice you, and that the actual house you have built will have had a fair amount of additional design work done to it in order to get it to fit both your ideas and the limitations of the plot. This extra work is invariably charged and you may well end up having a package build company designing your home from scratch.

Which begs the question "Why start with an off-the-peg design at all?" In theory, a freelance architect or architectural designer should be able to provide a similar service as a package build designer and really shouldn't cost any more. But, for many people, the prospect of hiring a freelance is off-putting and not just because they think it will be expensive.

If you happen to know somebody in the trade, then there is every chance that you'll appoint them (however inappropriate) just because it takes away the difficult task of finding a compatible stranger. Many people without any contacts will, however, be lured into the package build option just because it's there (coupled with the fear of the unknown). Eyeing up package build companies is like visiting Amsterdam's red light district: you can trawl up and down all night looking at the wares on offer but you don't have to consummate any deals if you don't like what's on offer. However, involving freelance architects and designers is much more personal: if you don't know them then it is akin to going on a blind date. You may or may not end up in bed together but you have to go through a courting stage just to find out where you want it to end up. It's a time-consuming and involved process and the outcome is just as likely to hinge on personal — not to say sexual — chemistry as it is on the designer's suitability and competence to carry off your briefs (shouldn't that read "carry out your brief"? Ed.).

Of course it doesn't have to be thus. If you're the professional, organised type, there is absolutely nothing to prevent you having a sort of beauty contest between three or four designers, in which you interview them and ask to see photographs of their previous work, ask for references and even ask them to prepare a quotation for design work, and possibly building work as well. The fact that architects hate this sort of thing is by-the-by: you'll be paying their bills and there is no reason at all why you shouldn't organise a parade of talents so that you can make an informed judgement.

Red light districts, blind dates, beauty contests — it's all getting a bit far away from building houses. So who are all these people?

## What's in a Name ?

### Architect

Use of the very word architect is a touchy subject. The general public thinks an architect is someone who designs houses but the title architect is, in Britain at least, protected in law just like the titles doctor and lawyer. To be qualified to call yourself an architect you must have completed seven years' training and passed all the relevant exams; an architect will regard him or herself as the natural choice for a commission such as designing an individual house and most architects love to take on such projects; trouble is, they may be rather high falutin' for your simple project and — worse fears — expensive. Just how expensive an architect is depends on how desperate they are for work but what can't be denied is that only a small fraction of new homes in this country are designed by architects. Traditionally, architects worked on a percentage fee basis, so that if they were just supplying plans and specifications they might charge around 5% over and above the value of the building contract, but if they were overseeing the work as well, this figure would rise to around 10%. However this particular tradition has more or less died out and now architects work for what they can get. Designers and architects have even been known to give quotations in advance for their work so they are showing every sign of rushing headlong into the 20th century. A newly qualified rookie might cost less than an a technician — say £150/day — whereas a top-notch, in-demand architect could go out at that much per hour. One of our internationally renowned architects quotes £70,000 for designing and administering a one off house, more than many more humble abodes cost to build. That's exceptional — though the house probably would be as well. But fees of £15,000 - £25,000 for upmarket projects costing a quarter of a million to build are now common-

place. But there are still loads of small architect's practices which work for much less.

Most (but not all) chartered architects are members of the Royal Institute of British Architecture (RIBA) and they run a nationwide Client's Advisory Service which will supply a list of suitable local practices who are actively looking for your sort of business. There is a collection of architects who got together to cater specifically for selfbuilders (known as the Association of SelfBuild Architects or ASBA) and although, as a group, it has a patchy reputation, it has done some innovative marketing including quoting for architectural services on a unit area cost basis. Incidentally, this rate was, until recently, around £30/m², about the same as the cost of wall to wall carpeting. Another useful lead is Design for Homes, a body set up to promote the use of architects in housing. The Design for Homes website has a searchable catalogue of architects where you can view their work. Incidentally, there is a body called the Architects' Registration Council, who you can call to check whether someone calling themselves an architect is fully qualified.

### Architectural Technologists

There is a second body, the British Institute of Architectural Technologists, which issues a quite separate qualification (architects would say it is a lesser one) which is relevant in the field of house design. Traditionally this group was thought of as mere draughtsmen, beavering away in offices on turning architect's sketches into working drawings but in fact many of them work in practice independently. And some of them are very good. BIAT oversees and publishes a Directory of Practices and a regional list of self-employed members interested in taking on new work.

### Building Surveyors

Lots of good design work is carried out by chartered building surveyors. The problem is finding them. As a professional body, they are administered by the Royal Institute of Chartered Surveyors (known as the RICS) but this amorphous group includes every flavour of surveyor including estate agents and building inspectors. They key is to find the right grouping — the Chartered Building Surveyors. If you ask for a list by post, you'll wait a long time but again you can search by region on the web at www.rics.org/ resources

### Many Others

There is in fact no requirement for anyone to have any qualifications to design houses. The country is stuffed full of unqualified but nevertheless competent designers. Some may have undertaken some architectural studies but never qualified, some may have qualifi-

cations in other related fields, notably structural engineers, quantity surveyors and building inspectors. And there are whole rafts of individuals who are "qualified by experience" — often designer builders — who do perfectly good work, some of it every bit as good as professional architects turn out. Obviously these designers are not regulated in the way that architects and surveyors are and you should be aware that if you hire an unqualified designer they are unlikely to carry professional indemnity insurance; on the other hand, unqualified designers are likely to steer you down a route where insurance is handled by third parties, such as the NHBC, so this is not actually as big a risk as you might imagine. You pays your money, you takes your choice.

### Design and Build

This is a method of building that straddles the traditional distinction between designers and builders. In some ways it is similar to package build in that you are faced with an all-in-one solution but, unlike package build, there are usually no predrawn plans on the table, so in other respects, design and build is more akin to hiring a freelance designer. In fact many design and build businesses are based around the skills of a designer who also happens to run a construction business. It is hard to generalise because individual businesses will go about things in markedly different ways and, indeed, may rarely have two similar contracts. I worked in a design and build business for ten years from 1986 to 1996 and if anything characterises this particular business it is the wide variety of projects taken on; some clients used us just as designers, some as just as builders, most as both. Some clients subjected us to beauty contests, some to competitive tendering, some to both of these and some to neither, preferring to work in an atmosphere of trust all the way from initial contact to completion of building work.

Unqualified designers will tend to be a little cheaper and will also tend to be a little less imaginative, which can be a good thing if you want to build cheaply. Engineers and surveyors in particular have a reputation for designing to a cost, something which has been known to elude more upmarket architects.

### CAD Packages

Computer-aided design (CAD) has been around for decades but only in the last few years has its presence begun to be felt in the housebuilding arena. In truth, architects still tend to look down their noses at it all: they continue to sketch stuff on paper in the time honoured fashion and then hire a "CAD operator" to turn their works of art into engineered drawings. Operating a full blown CAD package (the market leader is AutoCAD) is no mean feat but what has changed recently is that there are a number of really very cheap 3D software products around which anyone can pick up and play around with on their home PC. And some of it is very powerful indeed — a good example is Online Warehouse's ArCon which costs around £60. There is even passable good freeware that you can use — log onto www.povray.org if you want to check this out. If you like working with computers and you have plans for a home, you will probably love building virtual homes on screen and it may well help you work out some of your ideas.

## DIY Design

You can, of course, go the whole hog and design your own home. It's not as unusual as all that and it's not desperately difficult to undertake planning drawings — I have recently written an article for Homebuilding & Renovating magazine about a 77-year old grandmother who did just that, having sacked her architect because he kept trying to "improve" her plans. She knew what she wanted and successfully undertook all the negotiations with the planners. However, there is a large chasm of knowledge between doing outline sketches and filling in all the construction details, a chasm which can only realistically be filled by training and/or experience (preferably both). Most DIY designers get an experienced professional on board at some stage if only to satisfy all the building regulations — as indeed did my intrepid old lady.

The problem with DIY design is that it's difficult to get pleasing results if it's your first time. Design sense and spatial awareness are not skills that can be quickly or easily mastered and you have to be supremely confident in your own abilities to be entirely happy with your own work. Fine if what you were producing was just a set of drawings but, of course, it's not, it's a recipe for a real, live house. People are naturally afraid that they will be building an ugly or impractical structure and so the vast majority are keen to get some professional opinion on board. Most architects expect to feed in ideas and improvements to your initial ideas and most people reckon that they are very good at this and welcome the added input. But not everyone.

There is in fact a groundswell of opinion that rates building professionals in general and architects in particular as a nothing less than a cancer working to destroy an otherwise simple and healthy process called building. Colin Harding runs a medium sized building business in Bournemouth called George & Harding and also contributes an occasional column in Building magazine. In June 1999 he let rip on this topic:

*Very few architects have the construction management skills to justify their claims to be team leaders. Most of the contracts we work on suffer to a varying degree as a direct result of the designer's failure to do their job properly and professionally. Typical lapses are*

* *specifying inappropriate materials and systems, then being incapable of devising professional solutions to overcome the technical problems created*
* *lack of knowledge of basic construction techniques*
* *no understanding of buildability*
* *unwillingness to accept budget constraints*
* *inability to manage the design process so that information is often late or inaccurate.*

*What is so disappointing is that, in my opinion, the standard of professionalism among architects is still falling.*

Harding's is not a lone voice. Here's selfbuilder Rick Hughes's assessment of the service he received on his project in Swansea: *I would NEVER use an architect again, this practice has proved difficult, frustrating, incredibly slow, and, although very good on conceptual items, struggle greatly once things leave the drawing board and enter the real world.*

Hmm. Doesn't look good, does it? But in defence of architects I hear of rather more successful relationships than failures. Indeed I have heard many selfbuilders go as far to say that their project would have been hell without an architect on board and that using one had got them a far nicer house for much less money. Try this one for a counter blast from home extender Marc Arnall. *I decided to build an extension and, in order to save money, I wanted to use a person to draw the plans as opposed to using an architect. Meanwhile I talked to an architect that I knew, after explaining to him that, unfortunately, I couldn't afford to make use of his services. He was most understanding and offered to check over my ideas and costings, with no charge to me. The end result? Richard (the architect) has designed a far better extension, organised and put in my planning application, organised a good discount with suppliers and has reduced my costings by some £8,000. He is going to supervise the work, thereby ensuring that I comply with all regulations and that any labour I hire fulfils his/her part of the deal. Thank goodness for architects!*

Well this game of architectural ping pong could go on all night. It seems you either love 'em or hate 'em. What would be fair to say though is that there is a significant minority of architect/client relationships that are bedevilled with problems and that if you choose to work with an architect, choose very carefully. By and large, the design professionals who are not qualified architects don't arouse nearly so many hackles. It must be something they do to them in architecture school during those long seven years.

## Selecting a Designer

For many people there is no selection procedure, they just happen upon someone. Perhaps the chap plays golf with you or you went out with his sister when you were students or maybe she's an old friend of your mother-in-law — the network. Logically, this a daft way to pick on a designer, but it doesn't half take away the difficult decisions of how to choose, and it does provide some limited protection from hiring a real bozo. Building is one of the ultimate network businesses, there being very little formal long-term work around (no wonder the original Freemasons were builders), so it is not surprising that your designer should arrive on your (yet to be) doorstep by word of mouth. But bear in mind that all designers have tastes and quirks that are individual to them and even the simplest house commission is likely to receive radically different treatments. Make sure that you can at least live with your chosen designer's ideas by taking a look at their previous stuff. If you have very particular ideas yourself, then you would be well advised to seek out a like-minded soul.

The key to hiring an architect or designer and not paying through the nose is to be very upfront about money from the first meeting. Ask for an estimate to undertake design of your house and don't be afraid to specify that your project should cost no more than £XX,000 and that it has to be designed to a budget. Most architects/designers would actually appreciate such specific requests from their clients — a lot get very tired of the polite to-ing and fro-ing that goes on around issues like this. The more specific your brief, the better you will be pleased with the results.

If it's a safe, packaged product that you are looking for then the package build route may well be your best choice. Package build also wins out if speed of construction is paramount. There is much going for the package build route but it won't get you a unique home nor will it get you a cheap home. Whilst you would expect to turn to a freelance designer for a one-off house, surprising as it may seem, I think they are also the route to use if you want to build very cheaply, though I doubt very much if it would be the same designer.

# Timber Frame Homes

One of selfbuild's most frequently asked questions is "Which is better? Brick and block or timber frame?" and you'll not be surprised to learn that there is no easy answer to it. There are dozens of ways of constructing a house and they all have something going for them; there are at least five different techniques for building in timber frame, some of them ultra fast, one about as slow as you can get, and they each have their own advocates.

A key point to grasp is that the phrase timber frame usually applies only to the internal, structural parts of a house. It can be difficult to tell from the outside whether a house is built with a masonry blockwork or timber walls because the choice of your external walling material is largely unaffected by your choice of internal walls.

In England, Wales and Ireland (though not Scotland), the building trade traditionally builds houses using masonry blockwork for the structural walls. They are of course happy to use timber in the roof and usually for the floors above ground level so, in a sense, even these houses have some timber framing in them but masonry walls have been the preferred way of building homes since we ran out of forests around three hundred years ago. As the sources of timber dried up, we learned to build in brick and, later, using concrete blocks. It's a familiar story in other European countries, especially the Mediterranean ones, but also in Northern France, Belgium and Holland where our masonry techniques originated.

## Green Oak

In Tudor times, timber was readily available in most areas and houses tended to be built around large hardwood frames, the voids in between getting filled in with anything to hand. In the past twenty years there has been a revival of these old building methods and there is now a small but thriving green oak school of timber framing on offer from a number of suppliers, the best known of which is Border Oak. Green oak building is not quick and it's not cheap but it produced superb houses in the past and it continues to do so today: the green oak revivalists are much in demand today not only in Britain but all over the world.

## Modern Timber Frame

However modern-day timber framing is a very different animal. It is reputed to have been invented in Chicago in the 1830s: it was at the time a revolutionary method of construction. Instead of walls being built in situ as the house went up, there were hammered together in frames on the ground and then hoisted into place. It was called balloon framing because the houses went up so quickly. There was some scepticism at the time that they would come down just as fast, but the technique was used to transform Chicago within twenty years from a 100 inhabitant cattle station into one of the largest cities in America and many of the original homes are still standing. It became — and remains to this day — the standard way of building homes throughout North America. Speed of erection was of the essence and this is still one of timber frame's main attractions. There is a huge pool of North American construction workers who have grown up with this method of timber framing and the frames are still conventionally built on site, a technique which is also sometimes called stickbuilding. In Europe, the framing tends to be done in factories and then gets transported to site for erection.

*Two of our best known timber frame house suppliers. Above, Border Oak who build in traditional forms using green oak. Below, Potton Homes Heritage range use a mix of modern timber frame methods and softwood post and beams.*

Either way, the actual construction techniques are similar. Step One: relatively lightweight softwood timber studs are first cut to length and then nailed together in a rectangular frame. Step Two: a thin (usually around 8-10mm thick) board is then nailed to the outside of the frame — this both strengthens the frame and locks it into a rectangular shape. It's essentially that simple. Most designs call for the addition of extra layers, a breather paper on the outside, a vapour check barrier on the inside and, of course, insulation within the voids of the frame, but these are often added at a later stage on site. The skeleton of the house can be erected in a matter of days and then one can turn one's attention to finishing off the internal and external details; even here there is a speed saving because on a masonry built house you have to complete the external elements of the house before you can roof it and you have to cover the roof before you can start work on the internal finishes. With timber frame, the roof is conventionally left watertight by the erection crew which allows work to start on the inside immediately their work is done.

If it's that quick and simple why doesn't everyone use timber frame? Well, as already discussed, in many parts of the world they do, though admittedly these are usually the cold northerly latitudes, from which Scotland should not be excluded — current estimates suggest that between 60% and 70% of newly built homes in Scotland are timber frame, a figure on a steady upward trend. In the rest of Britain, timber frame housing accounts for less than 10% of new housing starts, though this figure is also on an upward trend. There are three discernible reasons for low uptake of timber frame overall.

## Cost

Timber frame is perceived to be more expensive than masonry construction. Straight cost analysis suggests this is true but the differ-ence is marginal, of the order of 1% or 2% on overall construction costs. Advocates claim that this added cost is easily clawed back through time savings, reducing finance costs. In Scotland, timber tends to be cheaper — though curiously only the external boarding, Stirlingboard OSB, tends to be sourced from Scotland — and this will tend to make timber frame a cheaper option overall

## Prejudice

There is a prejudice against timber frame, much of it dating from an infamous World in Action documentary screened in 1983 which exposed some sloppy housebuilding practices of the time and — erroneously — pointed the finger of suspicion at timber frame. You still hear all manner of things against timber frame houses such as "They are harder to sell", "They are difficult to insure", "They don't last as long." All complete rubbish. If there is one area where timber frame is inferior, it's in its sound proofing qualities between floors and rooms, but even here the difference is marginal and if you are particularly worried about sound transmission there are techniques available for uprating timber walls and floors.

## Tradition

It's harder for builders to "add value" by using timber frame. By taking much of the labour input off-site and putting it into a fac-tory, builders are in effect doing themselves out of a job and there is little incentive for them to change their ways. Architects are similarly disadvantaged in that timber frame construction requires an extra stage of panel drawing and extra structural calculation, both of which are highly technical in nature and best dealt with by specialists. There is thus an unwritten understanding between design professionals and builders to leave things as they are.

## Advantages

Selfbuilders, of course, don't have to run along with the crowd and selfbuilders throughout the UK have taken to timber frame in a big way for much the same reasons as Scotland as a whole has. Not only is a timber frame house potentially much quicker to build than a masonry one, but — because the frame itself is largely hollow — it is easy to insulate to a high standard and yet still maintain a clear cavity between the frame and the outside walling material. Timber frame houses are therefore inherently energy efficient and they are warm and comfortable to live in, even in the depths of the coldest winters.

At least as important as any technical differences between the building systems is the question of procurement. I've touched on the fact that most architects and most builders like to use traditional masonry construction

# Timber Frame Glossary

### Stickbuilding

The American school of timber frame house-building. Here the timber and boards are de-livered to site and the frame is constructed and erected by carpenters working directly for you. It has its advocates, many claim it to be substantially cheaper, but you need to have people around who know what they are doing and there is a shortage of them in Britain. You also need to allow for panel drawings and structural calculations, both of which are time consuming and expensive.

### Closed-panel systems

Usually timber frame houses are delivered to site with only one side of the walls boarded. The insulation and the inner linings are put in after the frame as a whole is erected. How-ever, it's a common practice in Scandinavia to deliver walls and floors to site with both sides boarded out and the pre-glazed join-ery already in place. Closed-panel systems (which are a sort of halfway stage on the route towards complete prefabrication) are being adopted by an increasing number of UK suppliers as well as being available from companies importing from Scandinavia.

Some businesses are now incorporating closed panel roofs as well as walls.

### SIPS

Structural Insulated Panels or SIPS are a fur-ther development of the idea of closed panel systems. Much of the timber element in the timber frame wall or roof panel is eliminated and instead the panels get their strength from bonding insulation (either expanded polysty-rene or one of the polyurethane types) to OSB boards, making a sort of sandwich panel. It's both very strong and very quick to erect. SIPS have been around in North America for some time but recently a number of British busi-nesses have got interested and we are start-ing to see a lot of interest from selfbuilders and the selfbuild press.

### Energy Efficiency

Good insulation has always been a feature of timber frame houses because they're essen-tially hollow skeletons. But as of 2002, the thermal regulations require U values better than those which standard timber frame walls used to provide. The standard wall thickness of timber frame houses is 90mm which has a U value of around 0.4 when stuffed with fibreglass or Rockwool. The re-quirement is now for a U value of just 0.35 (even lower in Scotland, 0.3) which means that the walls have to either be thickened or a better insulation has to be specified instead. It's not difficult to meet these new standards in either timber frame or masonry builds — but the standard designs will be changing a little.

### Breathing Walls

There are two conflicting theories of how best to build timber frame walls. The standard method is to exclude water vapour from the insulation layers inside the walls by covering the inside of the walls with a vapour barrier, usually a sheet of plastic. The alternative method, developed in Germany, is to allow a little of the water vapour from the house to seep through the walls and out into the air outside. This is called a breathing wall. Al-though there is still some debate about just which walls designs can and which can't breathe, the breathing wall design is becom-ing increasingly popular and is frequently specified with Warmcel 500 insulation, made in South Wales largely from recycled news-paper, and promising better thermal per-formance than conventional wool-type insu-lation.

because it suits their own purposes. Because of this there has grown up a quite distinct timber frame industry in the UK which has had to specialise in meeting all or most of the would-be housebuilder's needs. A timber frame company can't just build a factory, set up its jigs and wait for the orders to come rolling in — they won't. Instead they have to go out and grow the business by attracting the end users. As there are few independent architects prompting clients down the timber frame route, the companies themselves need to attract selfbuilders at the initial design stage and, by and large, they do this with attractive brochures of houses they have already built or a set of off-the-peg house types which you can choose or adapt to your own requirements. In effect, most timber frame companies design your house as well as provide and erect the superstructure.

It follows therefore that the timber frame is only one part of the service provided by these businesses. What they are really about is what is known as design and build or what the Americans call custom home building where you can pitch up with a few ideas, maybe a few sketches, and they will transform these into a workable home, delivered and erected on your site. The fact that your superstructure is made of timber is almost incidental to the procurement process — in order to sell you a timber frame kit, it is first necessary for them to capture your imagination and your confidence. Often they have a range of standard house types from which you can choose or adapt but most of them admit to rarely, if ever, building these standard houses. These days, selfbuild clients are choosing to have a much greater say in how their houses should look and function and consequently most timber frame houses start life as a sketch done by the selfbuilder or a more detailed drawing carried out by their architect. Even companies with an established reputation for standard house ranges such as Potton find they are doing more and more "one-offs". Potton's Mick Jewell commented to me: *Planning permissions are getting increasingly difficult to obtain and we find ourselves getting more and more involved with bespoke designs so although we are best known for our standard ranges we now undertake to work with almost any designs.*

## The Businesses

There are a surprising number of timber frame businesses throughout the country catering for the selfbuilder. By and large they tend to offer a similar range of services. Almost all the businesses offer a design service to turn your preliminary drawings into a fully engineered structure. In this respect a timber frame house is quite different to a masonry brick and block house: the design for a timber frame structure needs to be proved so that the building inspector is satisfied that it won't collapse in a heap or that it won't take off in the wind. This work is normally carried out in house, though you can commission a structural engineer to undertake it for you if you want. To do it on a one-off basis is a complex and time-consuming process and you also need to draw up technical drawings for the timber frame wall panels which, by hand, can take almost as long as it does to actually assemble them. This is all work which can be carried out easily on computer and this is another contributory factor helping to develop the timber frame industry into a unique entity, quite distinct from the mainstream building industry.

Beyond the design and assembly of the timber frame, the businesses offer various levels of service from frame erection right through to a complete build, often known as a turnkey service. Many of the businesses tend to offer different levels of service depending on distance — for instance, they will be happy to quote for an entire build or a waterproof shell within, say, a forty mile radius but beyond that feel that they are bound to be uncompetitive. Others have developed contacts all over the country and feel comfortable taking on entire builds far away from home — indeed some of the timber frame builders think nothing of going overseas. If anything characterises the industry it is the word flexibility. Having said that, it often pays dividends to work with a local business — the level of service is usually better.

Some of the businesses are known for specific styles or designs. Market leader Potton are best known for their Heritage range, half timbered Tudor cottages. They have spawned several imitators. There are a clutch of Scandinavian or Scandinavian-inspired companies, a couple of American ones and one German one — the selfbuild magazines are the best place to get information and contact details.

The majority of timber frame companies offer to work with any and every style. In all there are around sixty businesses active in the field, although around half are based in Scotland, reflecting the popularity of timber frame there. There are one or two offering to do very similar things with steel frames and Design & Materials is unique in working in a similar method to timber frame companies but actually supplying masonry materials to build houses in the traditional way. The concept homes are expensive; for instance, a Potton Heritage home of equivalent size to our benchmark house is going to cost over £10,000 more to build. A 162m$^2$ Caxton house kit from Potton costs over £27,000 — the kit really just covers the superstructure of the house. Foundations and finishes are additional costs. In contrast AB Homes spent just £16,000 on providing the equivalent work on our benchmark house. Typically the price of the kit is between a third and a quarter of the overall build costs though the amount of goods supplied with the kit varies quite considerably.

When making comparisons you have to become adept at looking at the small print to see what's provided and what isn't. The Scandinavian kit home suppliers tend to provide the bulk of what you need but at a considerable price; they also have a nasty habit of listing their floor areas gross — that is including the external walls — which makes the homes appear to be 15% larger than the competition which works with net floor areas. Watch out for this. In Scotland, the timber frame market is more mature than elsewhere and there tends to be a standard Scottish package (which includes the plasterboard), which makes cost comparisons more straightforward.

## Pre-payment issues

Because a large amount of work is being carried out off-site, most timber frame companies want some form of pre-payment. The timing and amounts of deposit required vary enormously from some businesses who want 100% of the frame costs before delivery to others who expect payment after work has been carried out. From a client's point of view, the nightmare lurking over the horizon is that the company they are dealing with may be about to go bust and that their cheque will be cashed before anything has arrived on site. Timber frame companies are no more secure than any other type of business and one piece of advice frequently given to selfbuilders is "Never pay for anything upfront." On the other hand, the suppliers have legitimate fears that the customer can't or won't pay and many have learned the hard way that a contract as large as a timber frame house, usually measured in tens of thousands of pounds, should not be undertaken without some form of deposit and some form of guarantee that the client is able to pay. Unlike other expensive items such as cars, timber frame kits are bespoke and can't just be sold on to another customer.

One way around this problem is to use a solicitor's stakeholder account where the majority of your payment is lodged, usually about a week before delivery of the main frame. This way the supplier can see that you have cleared funds in place, but they are not drawn down until the frame is on site. Another often acceptable solution, used widely for car purchases, is to get a bankers draft or a building society cheque — i.e. the sort of cheque that won't bounce — made out to the supplier a week or so before delivery. This is then shown but not handed over until goods are on site.

However, this raises another problem for self-builders borrowing to fund their build. Many lenders will not release funds against goods still being fabricated in a factory and consequently many selfbuilders get caught in a Catch 22 situation where they are unable to proceed. However, there are now mortgage products on the market, like Buildstore's Ac-

celerator Mortgage, which are designed to unlock funds before a critical stage is reached. Alternatively, many timber frame suppliers will accept undertakings from lenders to pay them directly on delivery. The important thing to bear in mind is that you must plan ahead and discuss the matter with your chosen supplier and your lender.

# Two Freelancers

Whilst it is relatively straightforward to analyse the ins and outs of using package build systems, it is very much harder to pin down what you get from using a freelance designer. The service varies, as you would expect, from the excellent to the incompetent. As with the rest of the building trade, freelancers usually find work by word of mouth — the old network again — but there are more formal routes through which you can contact designers which I've looked at in the last but one section.

Rather than list a load of old tripe about how much money an architect will save you or how you'd be crazy not to use one, I thought it would be more interesting to look at the work of a couple of designers who work in this area and to examine just what it is that you get for your money. Neither of these guys is cheap and you'd be most likely to end up with a building cost of £800/m² or even more these days. But then Mercedes cost more than Fords and this doesn't make Mercedes poor value. Both men are exceptional designers and provide a very specialised service some way removed from the average jobbing architect.

## A Traditionalist

Steve Mattick is a designer — not a qualified architect — who works from an office in the Essex village of Newport and who has a nationwide reputation for building houses in the old styles. And I'm talking old styles, not the Olde Worlde styles of the showhouses at the Ideal Home Exhibition with their timbered beams and leaded double-glazed sealed units. A new Mattick house will look almost indistinguishable from a 200-year-old one; the walls may not be perfectly perpendicular, the windows may not be exactly level and the roof will almost certainly sag (or "have movement"). The materials he uses are almost always natural and are often salvaged, and windows and doors are always made locally in a joiner's shop. Much attention is given to getting details right and many of these are worked out on site by Mattick and his crew for, above all, he is a designer builder.

Or he used to be. In recent years he has eschewed building and concentrated on design.

Now, going to the trouble of building roofs which gently undulate along the ridge is expensive. Carpenters are taught to erect roof trusses by hauling them up off the back of a lorry and arranging them all like a pack of

cards, stringing lines along the ridge to ensure perfect alignment. In contrast, Mattick's roofs will all be hand cut on site and will actually be packed out in certain spots to ensure that they do not align along a string line. Builders working for him tend to have to relearn the old craft skills, long since abandoned in the rush towards mass production

*The difference in the designs of these two can hardly be more extreme. Above, Mattick works in the Arts & Crafts or English vernacular style. Below, Ellis-Miller is a cool modernist although he has been known to undertake the occasional barn conversion. Maybe they are not so different.*

and streamlined products which are more and more made off-site. Coupled with his insistence on detailing workshop joinery, handmade tiles and cast iron guttering, Mattick's building costs are 50-80% higher than the standard fare of the big developers.

Mattick tends to have few problems from planners (who by and large drool over his work) and yet is often in conflict with building inspectors. Many of the techniques he employs are no longer considered adequate though, as he points out, they have stood the test of time. He particularly dislikes the current mania for double glazing, which makes it that much harder to build good-looking, traditional windows. One of his trademarks is the sideways sliding sash window, once common in eastern England but now all but abandoned. You can't really draughtproof such a window; you can't even stop water penetration when it is lashed by gales and so it has been relegated to the status of a vernacular has-been. Mattick is quite aware of the problems but reckons it's a price worth paying to achieve an authentic reproduction. As well as being well-heeled, Mattick's clients need to be enthusiasts capable of living with minor inconveniences like this.

Somehow, we assume that because a house is a new product it must perform to the same standards as a new camcorder or a new car; but if we bought an old wreck to do up we would expect to have a few wonky things going wrong with it from time to time, even after we'd shovelled a fortune into it. To some extent, an authentic new/old house is bound to perform in the same way. The current trick of aping old styles with modern materials and techniques comes at a price; it reduces art to artlessness, style becomes pastiche. As a nation we know this intuitively because we flock to National Trust properties and to villages like Castle Coombe and Lavenham to see beautiful buildings, but as a nation of house buyers we seem to be happy with imitations which are usually executed rather poorly.

## A Modernist

Which all rather begs the question why — if we want to live in smoothly functioning machines which never break down—don't we design houses that look like cars or computers? Well, why not? There are many architects working in the machine tradition but most of their work goes into commercial developments. Jonathan Ellis-Miller is one of the few who are interested in housing.

He designs in the modern style, has been much written up in the architectural press but was until recently ignored by all the self-build magazines (unlike Mattick). This is a shame because his approach has much to offer the selfbuilder who wants something out of the ordinary.

Ellis-Miller's most widely seen house is a timber frame built by Stewart Log Homes at the FutureWorld exhibition held in Milton Keynes in 1994, which attracted rave reviews from most visitors, but here I will describe the glass and steel home he selfbuilt on a plot at Prickwillow in the Fens near Ely. The plot was bought for £20,000 in 1987, the price being that low because the ground was poor and the foundation work was complex. He chose to build using a raft foundation rather than the more conventional pile. Either way it proves expensive and for a floor area of $110m^2$ (not all of which is built on) he had to pour $60m^3$ of concrete. In all, substructural works came to £10,000. In areas like the Cambridgeshire Fens where ground conditions are difficult, most plot buyers are aware of the problems involved and the plot prices tend to be cheaper to reflect the excess works needed.

The total building costs were £45,000 for a building which measures $70m^2$. Apart from the £10,000 substructural works, another £6000 went on made-to-order patio doors, £1000 on blinds by Hunter Douglas. Parquet flooring from the local salvage yard was cheap, granite worktops in the kitchen were not. The kitchen doors came from IKEA (cheap) though the handles and door furniture throughout is by Modric (expensive). Internally, the house is thus fitted with a mixture of cheap, off-the-shelf items intermingled with some pricey architectural fittings. The style is unashamedly modern (in the old-fashioned sense of the word) and Ellis-Miller is striving for that simple, uncluttered look which characterises the style. The quiet, slightly monastic feel to the house would suit anyone with a lifestyle to fit; children, I suspect, would not fit in so easily.

His building cost is around $£645/m^2$, though had he been building on good ground this figure would have fallen to $£540/m^2$. Had he not used expensive patio doors and spent money on fancy fittings, then he might have got the price down to near $£430/m^2$, but then he would have lost a lot of the style he was striving for. Other expensive detailing includes galvanised steel box guttering which drains to a soakaway via the centre of the house, bespoke aluminium windows at the back of the house, floor lighting and under-floor heating.

This style would be unlikely to appeal to more than a few aficionados of modern architecture, but it is by no means as avant-garde as you might think. If you have a site with a good view where single-storey development is preferable, this solution could provide a stunning house. In the case of his own house, the view out through the west-facing glazed wall looking over Ely Cathedral is a Fenman's delight, and despite the cool, semi-industrial look of the building it sits remarkably well in a side road in a fen village. Some people's immediate response to the thought of living in a glass-walled home is "What! No privacy?" but this problem is reasonably overcome with the use of external louvre blinds which are adjusted to suit conditions. Ellis-Miller's glass wall faces on to the road in order to get the view he wanted and there would probably be few people who would be happy with such a degree of overlooking. However, if the orientation had been more conventional (so that privacy could be maintained) then I think there would be few people who would not be bowled over by the effectiveness of the idea.

If you want to build in an unconventional style, you will likely have problems obtaining planning permission. Only estate agents are more conservative than planning officers and Ellis-Miller had a planning officer who was implacably opposed to such a dwelling. No way is Prickwillow a sensitive, conservation type area (quite the reverse) and no way does his plot impact on the casual visitor. Yet when he approached his local council planning department, he met with stares of disbelief and what can only be described as prejudice against his submitted plans. However, despite a recommendation of refusal from the planning officers (which 90% of the time carries the day), the councillors on the planning committee saw otherwise and let him build.

Without some support from more enlightened planning officers, plans to build in any but the tamest vernacular styles will be stillborn. If you're interested in building in an unusual style, then first check with your local authority to get their views about your favoured site. Obviously, if the area is a conservation area or next to a listed building or the church, then you will expect to have to stick to a prescribed style. On the other hand, most building plots are not in such sensitive positions and arguably it's really none of the planner's business what style of building goes up. Needless to say, planning officers do not see it thus. To them, everywhere is sensitive, which unfortunately translates as "If you want planning permission you'd better conform." Ellis-Miller's tale indicates that there is still room for innovation.

# Renovate or Rebuild?

As virgin, greenfield building sites become more and more difficult to obtain, increasing numbers of people are looking to purchase dilapidated dwellings which they then seek to demolish and to build afresh. These are basically recycled building sites, sometimes referred to as brownfield sites. Planning permission is usually much easier to obtain on a site with established residential usage and there are also usually considerable savings to be made because the service connections are already in place. A few sites will have problems with contaminated ground but mostly the requirements of today's foundations to go much deeper than was previously thought necessary means that any existing foundations will be excavated and disposed of, just as if it was regular subsoil. In addition to buying a serviced plot, you have an existing structure from which you may well be able to salvage some useful materials.

So far so good. The decision to demolish, however, is often not as clear cut as this. For a start, few people care to sell their existing properties at building plot prices. To do so is to admit that your home is worthless which can be a bitter pill to swallow, even if it's true In any event it's usually the case that the house is not worthless, it's just old and dilapidated and with a little bit of tender loving care and a whole lot of money it could continue to make a very serviceable home. So problem No 1 is the extra expense of buying such a site.

Then you are faced with a decision whether to knock down and start again or whether to work with what is already there. Now here things start to get complicated because the chances are that it is not a clear cut issue, most renovation opportunities fall somewhere between the two extremes. Added to which it is a fiendishly difficult exercise to compare costs between the two approaches because this major decision has to be made at a pre-plan stage and you will have to work with ballpark figures. Whether the building is worth saving at all is an issue that only you (and the planners) can decide — each case will be argued on its merits and there is no point trying to make any broad generalisations. However, I will now attempt to summarise the cost implications of the various routes.

## Demolish and Rebuild

Budgeting for this is comparatively simple. The new build aspect of the work will probably cost upwards of £500/m², if you build to

*The complete renovation and modernisation of this house cost around £400/m², not far different from the unit cost of building from scratch*

a fairly basic standard. The demolition side of the equation is less predictable but is not, as a rule, very costly. If there are valuable materials in the existing structure, then you can either reuse them yourself or you can sell them on. Some contractors will even pay you for the right to demolish and keep the materials. More typically, a demolition contractor will charge between £2,000 and £5,000 to remove a reasonable sized house. Watch out, however, for asbestos materials which are an expensive and dangerous pain to dispose of.

## Renovate and Extend

Obviously this all depends on the condition of the existing structure but, to give you an example, my business undertook the refit of a 120-year old detached brick house near Newmarket. All the old plaster was hacked of, all the floors lifted and the timbers were repaired or renewed and treated, the slate roof was replaced, the windows were all replaced with double glazed timber replicas of the originals. The house had a new staircase fitted, and bathrooms, plumbing and wiring were installed for the first time and a small 15m² extension was constructed to house a modern kitchen. The only underground work was the installation of drains to the street. In other words, the house was stripped to little more than its brick shell, which was actually in good condition and needed no repair work. It was a major piece of work for the family. They had to move into a caravan in the garden for six months as the house was basically gutted. But by the time the job was completed, there was a four-bedroom house with all the

amenities of a brand new one but with the charm and style of a Victorian cottage.

And the cost of all this in 1995? £40,000 for a 120m² house. Rises in labour costs would probably make that around £70,000 today. What hasn't changed is that VAT would be payable on these sums. Ouch. Unlike new builds and conversions of redundant buildings into homes, renovating existing dwellings does not qualify for zero-rating of VAT and this can itself sometimes tilt the balance towards new build. On the other hand, in this particular case, the family were able to obtain a £19,000 grant from the local council because the house was sited in a conservation area; it's not all stacked in favour of the zero-rated new builders.

## Comparison Costs

How does this major renovating compare in cost with building from scratch? Ignoring the grant and the VAT, the cost per square metre is very similar to building from scratch. Despite the fact that much of the shell of the original house remains in place, this saving is all but cancelled out by the requirements to use more expensive fittings such as bespoke joinery and real slate on the roof plus the clients' understandable desire to refashion some of the internal walls to make new rooms. Had there been considerable structural repairs to make as well (there often are), then the complete renovation of this building would have worked out to be as much as 25% more expensive than the demolish and rebuilding option.

# Shape & Size

Before you even approach a designer or a package company, you would do well to take on board a few home truths about the cost implications of your design decisions. If you are after cheap space, then you need to build your house in a simple shape, preferably a simple box with a simple roof. This doesn't have to look cheap — indeed it doesn't have to be cheap — but the point is that it is almost always going to be the simplest (and therefore cheapest) form of construction available to you. Many traditional houses take this form and they are not all peasants' cottages.

So why should a rectangular box shape be cheaper than say two rectangular box shapes stuck together? In a word, junctions. You are introducing junctions at every stage of the building process and junctions involve head scratching and sometimes even expensive detailing. Your brickwork will take just that little bit longer to build, your carpentry will become just that little bit more complicated, your roofing will become much more complicated. However, it is important not to exaggerate the cost implications of building complex shapes: I estimate that the cost ef-fect of these junctions is probably of the or-der of between 0.5 and 1% on your total building budget per junction. Therefore if you were to build in an L shape, for instance, you would scarcely notice the extra cost. How-ever, wherever you interrupt the basic shell shape of a house you are adding junction costs and if you choose a complex form with extensions, dormers, porches and the like then you can take it that the overall cost will increase by much more than the unit cost per square metre at which you build the main shell.

## Circulation Space

There is another hidden cost brought about by using non-standard shapes in house de-sign and this is to do with having adequate circulation space — i.e. hallways, stairwells and landings. This is virtually impossible to quantify because no two situations are the same, but the basic tenet holds that the more complex your form, the more difficult it be-comes to provide adequate circulation space or, put another way, the more space you end up using just to get around from A to B. For instance, in our lean, box-design benchmark house, circulation space occupies just over 20m$^2$, which is 12% of the internal floor area. That's a pretty tight ratio. Reconfigure the house in a 'T' shape and you'll probably be looking at circulation space taking up 25% or more of your internal floor area. Now you may not mind that, you might even want a minstrel's gallery set under a glass atrium in your entrance hallway, but do be aware of the constraints you put on your space by choos-ing more complex designs.

It's worth bearing in mind that the amount of space you need to actually live in is sur-prisingly small: a bed, a loo and a comfy arm-chair does for most people. Arguably every-thing else is either storage or circulation space. The past century has seen us becom-ing progressively richer and we own more and more possessions which, of course, re-quire more and more storage, which in turn requires more and more circulation space. And this I believe is the main motor behind our desire for more and bigger homes. Enough of this cod philosophy. How do you get a bigger home?

# Extra Space

The quest for extra space is on. Where is it going to go? Conventionally people have cho-sen to build larger houses but this is becom-ing an increasingly difficult option because of planning restrictions. Going up into the loft space is cheap but is not always an option. Could one of the solutions be underground? Maybe...

I have compared the cost of creating extra space using five different methods. There are some assumptions which need further com-mentary. Firstly I have assumed that we are faced with a situation where someone has plans to build a detached four or five bed-room house say of 150m$^2$: they are then hit by the desire to have more space, another 40m$^2$ in fact, equivalent to three good-sized bedrooms or a very generous double garage. I have looked at five different ways of achiev-ing this extra space which are:

- Build a 40m$^2$ basement
- Build a 40m$^2$ single storey extension
- Add 20m$^2$ to both the ground floor and upstairs
- Convert the loft space into usable space
- Build a large double garage

I looked at just the structural costs and ig-nored the fitting out costs as I figured these would be pretty much the same whichever option you chose. If the overall prices look low, this is why — the structure often costs under 50% of the total. Here they are briefly examined in order of increasing cost.

## Lofts

Just about the cheapest option for our space-hungry builders is to convert the loft space: it involves re-jigging the roof carpentry and building in studwork walls and a new stair-well but otherwise much less in the way of structural changes than all the other options. It comes in at around £10,000 (£250/m$^2$). Bear in mind that you need to double that figure to get arrive at a cost for a typical small loft conversion — remember here I am just on about structural alterations and am not including finishes.

Loft conversions are not an option on all houses; you need a headroom of at least 2m to make lofts usable for anything other than storage and many house designs start with the upper storey already built into the roof— in these situations you can't borrow any more space from the loft. And if your fancy is to open out the roof so that your headroom is not confined to the existing roof line, then you are adding significantly to your costs. Also note that most post-1965 houses have been built with trussed rafters which cannot be altered in any way, thus preventing any form of loft conversion. Our benchmark house which boasts converted loftspace has specially adapted attic trusses in order to be able to build in this space.

There are a number of niggly little problems that come with loft conversions. Chief amongst these is a requirement to have a fireproofed stairwell which exits close to the front door: in itself it's not that expensive to construct, but you may have to redesign your internal layouts to accommodate it. If designing a new house, this doesn't have to be a big problem but in existing houses it can be surprisingly disruptive. In fact the whole subject of building loft conversions in existing houses can be surprisingly complicated and it really lies beyond the scope of this book.

## Two Storey Extension

The other option which looks cheap is to expand both the ground floor and the upper floor of your house, the two storey extension option. Adding 3m to the length of a typical four bedroom house will probably be enough to create an extra 40m² of space and because this can be spread between two floors you are effectively halving the costs of extra foundations and roofing, though not, of course, external walls. I cost this option at just over £10,000 (£260/m²). In many ways it remains the most flexible option but, and it's a big but, it's not always feasible to just add 3m to the length of a house: plot boundaries and/or planning consents may very well prohibit this course of action. You will also end up with two extra decent sized rooms but if you want a really large space, a two storey extension will only get you halfway there.

## Single Storey Extension

Single-storey extensions are about 20% more expensive to build than two-storey ones. There are some savings, notably in having no staircase, but the extra foundations and roofing more than cancel these out. Incidentally the same cost penalty applies to single-storey house designs. Other costs being equal (they ought to be), this makes bungalows about 10% more expensive to build overall than the same floor area built on two floors. Yes, the price difference continues up into the loft space so that a three storey house should be a little bit cheaper to build than the equivalent size on two storeys.

The bungalow has rather gone out of fashion in recent years and tends now to be built to satisfy a particular requirement. This requirement, more likely than not, emanates from the planning department and relates to the fact that the plot overlooks other houses and that only single-storey development is felt to be appropriate. Alternatively, they are commissioned by clients who wish to avoid staircases. When starting from scratch with a two storey house, a single storey extension would seem to be a strange addition unless it is a solution to a specific problem such as a sloping site.

## 4: Options for Space-Hungry Builders (NB shell only prices)

| 5 options for increasing size of structure by 40m² | 40m² Basement | Single Storey Extension | Two Storey Extension | Add 40m² in Loft | 40m² Outhouse or Garage |
|---|---|---|---|---|---|
| Oversite Excavation | £ 2,500 | £ 500 | £ 300 | | £ 400 |
| Foundation Excavation | | £ 200 | £ 100 | | £ 200 |
| Concrete Foundations | | £ 700 | £ 400 | | £ 900 |
| Masonry Footings | | £ 400 | £ 200 | | £ 500 |
| Concrete Slab/Floor | £ 2,800 | £ 800 | £ 400 | | £ 800 |
| Screed Costs | £ 500 | £ 500 | £ 200 | | £ 500 |
| Extra Floor Costs | £ 0 | | £ 500 | £ 900 | |
| External Walls | £ 2,500 | £ 1,800 | £ 2,200 | | £ 2,200 |
| Reinforcement | £ 2,500 | | | | |
| Waterproof Tanking | £ 3,000 | | | | |
| Rainwater Drainage | £ 1,200 | £ 200 | £ 150 | | £ 200 |
| Joinery and Lintels | £ 1,000 | £ 1,800 | £ 2,200 | £ 2,200 | £ 2,200 |
| Insulation | £ 500 | £ 600 | £ 500 | £ 300 | £ 700 |
| Stairs | £ 1,000 | | | £ 1,000 | |
| Fire-Proofing Details | | | | £ 1,200 | |
| Roof Covers | | £ 3,000 | £ 1,500 | | £ 3,000 |
| Add Roof Carpentry | | £ 1,700 | £ 900 | £ 3,400 | £ 1,700 |
| Less Foundation Work | (£ 1,400) | | | | |
| Scaffolding, Making Good etc | £ 300 | £ 500 | £ 800 | £ 800 | £ 400 |
| ROUNDED TOTALS | £ 16,400 | £ 12,700 | £ 10,400 | £ 9,800 | £ 13,700 |
| Cost/m² | £ 410 | £ 320 | £ 260 | £ 250 | £ 340 |

Note that there is a saving on many basements because the existing foundations are being replaced

"THIS TABLE IS DANGEROUS." So says a builder in Letchworth, Herts who rang to tell me that the going rate for two storey extensions in his area is £800/m². I don't doubt it. Please bear in mind this table is referring to the added cost of building the structure only onto a new house, not coming in and adding an extension to an existing house. And also bear in mind that the finishes in a new structure tend to cost at least as much again as the shell. So HANDLE THIS TABLE WITH CARE. Its purpose is to compare the different methods , not to price your extension.

In London and the South East, land values are so high that basements are beginning to appear again. These Huf Haus basements were shipped in from Germany and will more than cover their costs on this tight site in South London.

## Garage/Outhouse

By and large, most new housing gets built with garage space whether it's needed or not. The radical thing is to axe the garage from the spec, not to build a second one. I take a closer look at garages in Chapter 11. Note that the garage attached to the benchmark house is a single garage and the price reflects the fact that it's one third of the size of the one quoted on Table 4 opposite.

## Basements

What price a basement? The basement is, by some way, the most expensive option. At first this might seem to be illogical: after all there are no roofing costs and much of the expense that goes to make up kerb appeal in a new house — fancy brickwork, nice joinery — is, of course, absent from a basement. The added costs come with the hole excavation, the extra strength required by the walls, the waterproofing details and the addition of another staircase. However, to get a fair comparison, you must subtract the cost of providing regular foundations which normally work out at around £50/m² and can cost two or even three times as much on difficult sites. If you have a problem site requiring such elaborate techniques as piles or rafts, then the addition of a basement makes even more sense since the increase in your foundation work will be proportionately much less.

Of the five options I've looked at, only the basement and the loft conversion satisfy the demand for extra space without increasing the footprint of the house. And the footprint of the house — that is the area of ground that

is actually built on — is crucial in determining the density of housing. A 60m² footprint will give you 120m² living space on two floors and up to 180m² on three floors. By utilising basements and/or lofts, you should be able to build 50% more houses on the same area. Although this line of argument ignores the requirements of vehicle access and the desire for decent-sized gardens, it cannot but help the situation we are facing where we apparently require space for four million new homes in the next 20 years and no one, but no one, has a clue where to build them.

## Approved Document

One of the chief reason for this lack of basements in the UK is that the skills and knowledge that went into basement construction have largely vanished. The building trade are generally a pretty conservative lot and if you were to ask a builder or an architect for a basement, the chances are you would be met by a wall of tut-tutting and head shaking as they explained that the problems would far outweigh the benefits. It is easy to mock but, to be fair, they have a good point as the ramifications if it all goes wrong are probably worse underground than anywhere else and most experienced architects and builders are wary of courting trouble. In an attempt to relaunch the basement in Britain, a group of interested parties including the British Cement Association and the NHBC have published an amendment to the Building Regulations entitled Basements for Dwellings. This draws together all the relevant building regulations with some best practice notes so that for the first time there is an easily accessible

reference source for design and construction professionals. There is much to understand that is beyond the ken of regular house designers: water tables, hydrostatic pressure, retaining walls, tanking details, reinforcement. Also it contains a complete reworking of the U value requirements to take into account the different thermal conductivity of materials below ground. The technical information is all in here so there is no excuse to be fobbed off by ignorance. The *Approved Document on Basements* is available from the British Cement Association (price £15.50 plus £1.00 P+P).

## Real-life experience

The following is the experience of Emyr George, a selfbuilder in North Wales who was building a basement in 1999.

*I've been busy over the last few weeks supervising the build of a basement. I found it very difficult at the start to find anybody to 'hold my hand on basements'. I read the British Cement Association's many publications on basements which half frightened me but, at least, led me in to the principles and jargon. I found it impossible to get a comprehensive design service which included the waterproofing so got the basic design from a structural engineer, some tanking information from a reputable supplier (RIW), and attempted to let a contract for the complete work. The results were frightening, about £28,000 for a 50m² basement. My ultimate solution was to let a contract for the slab (plus base steelwork plus base tanking) to a groundworks contractor and then used brickies and other labour to build the basement blockwork walls, insert the reinforcement and carry out the remaining tanking to the RIW specification. Whilst the tanking still remains to be completed, the final cost should be less than £20,000. If I subtract the foundation cost, the differential cost will of course be less. My plot has a considerable slope with rock about 2 metres down. This has dictated the size of the basement, and surprisingly the results of the ground tests were accurate so that I just touched the rock on one edge. I will be using the basement for a utility room, a workshop, a store room and somewhere to stick overexcited grand children (I'm 66). I will be installing a mechanical ventilation which gives adequate basement ventilation. The biggest problem has been to bring in the water services without penetrating the tanking. I have however persuaded the water company to allow me to bring the water first into the garage and then, via an insulated duct, into the house. I am by no means an expert on basements and can't guarantee that mine will be O.K.*

# Chapter 5
# Project Management

What exactly is project management? It's become a buzz word among builders who assume that it's the be-all and end-all of running a building site. There are now professional project managers who apparently keep building sites going armed only with a mobile phone and a fast car, the yuppies of the building trade. It's all about networking and contacts, being at the very centre of a huge web of information.

Well, yes, there is this aspect, but don't get carried away. Really, project management is nothing new; it's what contractors have always done, which is to organise building work. There is power here and, if you've never employed anyone other than a baby-sitter, that is an undoubted attraction to many of us frustrated prefects. But, as the old saw goes, with that power comes a responsibility and, in the case of the contractor, that responsibility is considerable, because whilst you are hopefully making a bit on everybody's labour you also have to pick up the tabs for everybody's cock-ups. You are where the buck stops.

So, project management goes on at every building site, even out-of-the-way ones where they've never even heard of it. It's really rather a holdall term that covers just about every non-manual aspect of running a building site. And there are no rules as to who can and who can't be a project manager; it could be the selfbuilding client, or their architect or quantity surveyor, or it could be the main contractor or their foreman. And of course it doesn't all have to be carried out by one individual — the various functions may be split between people, though when this happens you can expect even more cock-ups than usual.

# Raising Finance

The first step in the management of a project such as building a house is to have the finance organised to pay for it. For the majority of selfbuilders and small developers, that translates as how much you are able to borrow. Well how do you go about borrowing on a property that doesn't even exist? You will find it a lot easier to borrow money if you have a) substantial assets and b) substantial income, preferably both. If you don't fall into either of these categories then you are by no means ruled out of the game; you'll just have to work harder at impressing the mortgage lender. In fact, people of quite modest means are now regularly becoming DIY property developers.

There are currently around 30 institutions actively seeking selfbuild borrowers; most of these are prepared to lend up to 75% of the finished value of the property and several will lend rather more than this including such big names as Barclays, Lloyds TSB and the Woolwich — though most will expect you to come up with a hefty deposit for land purchase. The number of active lenders is now larger than ever but many of them just dip their toes in the selfbuild market only to withdraw a year or two later (often when they are taken over by a bank or some such). There aren't that many institutions who really understand this specialised market and the ones that do are generally pretty active with the advertising and exhibition appearances. Judged by these standards alone, the Norwich & Peterborough Building Society is currently the pick of the bunch, actively courting the selfbuild market by offering to lend up to 80% of a plot's value provided it has outline planning permission and up to 85% of the value of the completed house. The selfbuild magazines run with current data and contact details on who is doing what — Homebuilding & Renovating's guide is particularly good.

If your fortune is modest and your income small, you don't necessarily have to give up any idea of building your own home, especially if you are prepared to rough it for a while by living on site in a caravan. It means that a house such as our benchmark house, with a market value of £120,000, would be within the reach of a young couple with joint income of around £30,000/annum and equity or savings of no more than £20,000.

If you are self-employed or you are actively wanting to sell on the finished property for a profit, then the regular avenues may well be closed to you but there are still a number of specialist brokers who it is worth approaching, many of whom advertise in the selfbuild magazines. Another very useful contact is the Ecology Building Society who are particularly helpful in lending to those undertaking unusual constructions and renovations which mainstream lenders shy away from. Professional developers have traditionally borrowed from the major clearing banks but there are a number of finance boutiques catering for them as well such as Alban Marshall: again many advertise in trade journals such as the NHBC's Housebuilder.

## Your Presentation

Many lenders recommend that you contact them early, when you are still at the dreaming stage. If you have an existing mortgage, start by talking to this source and trying to gauge their attitude to your ideas. Talk in broad sweeps about what you are trying to achieve and try and winkle out of them how far they will be prepared to come along with you. Together you may be able to shape up a budget to work to. If you feel they are being unduly negative, then start looking at other lenders. The lenders themselves are tending towards centralised decision making which can make things more transparent but also rather less flexible: however they are not yet entirely monolithic—the Woolwich for instance still grants an unusual degree of leeway to the individual branch managers and a sympathetic Woolwich manager may be able to do rather more for you than a sympathetic Bradford & Bingley manager. It all rather depends on the individuals involved.

When the time comes to act, you will in all probability have to act quickly and you will need whatever ammunition you can get hold of — agent's details of the proposed purchase, copy of planning permission, your salary details, a building budget. If you've no plans, then show them a copy of this book and say you've read it from cover to cover — that'll impress them. You shouldn't have to show any plans at this stage because it is ludicrous to expect there to be any yet but this is one area where the timber frame package companies tend to win out because you can actually present a budget AND a plan, even if the house you end up building is nothing like this.

## Scheduling

Unlike conventional mortgage lending, development loans and selfbuild mortgages are released in stages as the work progresses. For someone new to this, it can be a daunting process, especially if they are having to borrow to complete the plot purchase for a house that's not even designed, let alone built. The key to doing this is to prepare a schedule of works, the sort of thing that is outlined in the diagram opposite. This shows how a typical British house is built, taking around eight months to complete. The costings are for something very similar to the benchmark house, which cost £75,000 to build. It's interesting to note that the rate of spending is surprisingly constant — it's actually very close to one pound per square foot per week. Eight months is generally a good time to set to build a simple house, especially if you've never built a house before. As you can see from the timeline, there are over twenty major tasks to accomplish, all needing coordinating and timetabling so that they occur in the right order at the right time. At this speed, you are actually paying the wages of three men to be on site continually and if that's how houses got built there really wouldn't be any problems trying to schedule a workforce. But in reality each house is built by upwards of 30 people, each with different skills and each with their own schedules to work to; you can't expect everyone to turn up at the drop of a hat so you have to program some slack into the schedule to allow for this.

## Speedy Builds

Some houses do get built in much less time than eight months. Refer back to the opening of the book and look at the quick-cheap-good triangle; even though we're now in Chapter 5, I'm afraid that this rule still holds good. If you want to build quick, then either be prepared to spend good money on professional supervision of the whole construction process or to have a half-finished house with lots of snags which will probably never get sorted out. It's quite feasible to build a house from scratch in just three months but in order to do so you have to concertina all the events and, realistically, this means planning the whole process months in advance so that everybody involved in the construction knows exactly what they are required to do and when they are required to do it, just the sort of intricate project planning for which British builders are famous! It also requires that the correct materials are delivered to site on the appropriate day (ditto British builder's merchants).

Speedy builds? It can be done, but...be prepared to spend the time you saved in the building process planning the whole thing instead.

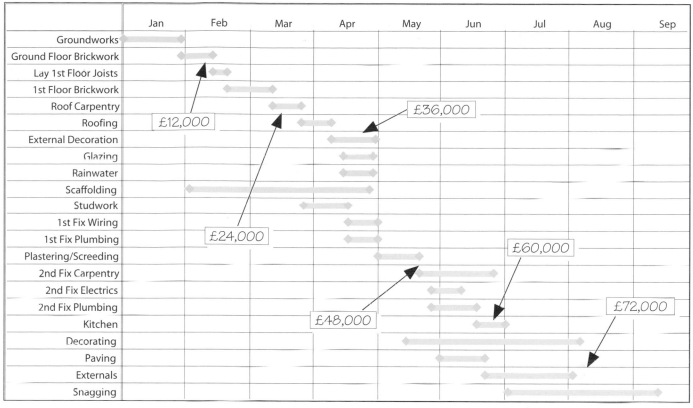

*A scheduler for the construction of an £80,000 brick and block house. The figures in the boxes are running totals for the amount spent. A timber frame house isn't so very different — the three month shell building stage (Feb - Apr) can be squeezed into one month, but only if you are very well organised.*

## Stage Payments

Almost all development loans and selfbuild mortgages are made in stages — they are sometimes referred to as progress mortgages. There are certain points in the construction process which, when completed, trigger the release of the next tranche of the loan. Each lender seems to use slightly different criteria to define when each stage is completed but a typical regime would involve three or four stage payments coinciding with
• Groundworks complete
• Structure watertight
• Plastered out
• Finished.
Normally the lender will insist on a surveyor making a site visit to check that the work has progressed as far as you claim, although some of the more intrepid bank managers will do this checking themselves.

## Managing Cashflow

One critical point to take note of is that the lenders only ever release payments after a stage is completed, so that you have to be able to float the works between the payments. This fact has undone many a small builder in the past and will doubtless continue to do so in future; typically, the builder runs out of cash towards the end of the job and gets stuck in a Catch-22 where they can't get the final (largest) instalment of the loan because they

haven't finished building and they can't finish building because they haven't got the final stage of the loan. A tricky little pitfall made all the worse because builders (and surveyors) habitually underestimate the cost of finishing building works off, and the time that the finishing soaks up. One of the major advantages of building reasonably quickly is that the strain on cashflow is minimised because the subcontractors may well be happy for you to withhold payment for a couple of weeks until the next stage payment is authorised; if that couple of weeks becomes a few months, then this option is effectively removed. However, there are now mortgage products on the market, like Buildstore's Accelerator Mortgage, which are designed to unlock funds before a critical stage is reached.

There is another little pitfall here awaiting the slower-than-average self builder: the VAT reclaim procedure. The what? Check out the VAT section of this chapter.

## Where Do We live?

Selfbuilders are faced with the problem of finding somewhere to live during the construction of their new home. The lucky ones can stay on in their existing homes and, if the market is rising, enjoy a two for one tax-free punt on the property market whilst their build takes place. However, the majority are faced

with having to sell up their existing home in order to raise enough money to buy the plot. In this situation you have to find somewhere short-term. The two main options are a short-term rental or a caravan on site. The first is expensive, often costing rather more than servicing a mortgage, and you can use this fact to try and persuade your mortgage lender not to have to make you sell up in the first place. The caravan is seen as the cheap and cheerful option but it's not without its hidden costs as well. Usually people buy static caravans. Purchase costs vary from around £2000 to £6000 depending on size and quality. Add to this the costs of getting it to site and installing it once there, usually between £500 £1000. Many firms supplying static caravans will buy them back off you though only expect to get between a half and two thirds what you paid. You need to have drainage, water and electricity supplies sorted before the installation which can make it hard to move into directly from selling an existing house. Also consider the cost of storing your possessions. Quotes to do this professionally usually come in at around £50/month plus the added cost (say £500) of moving everything twice. Amateur storage is feasible but often results in damaged furniture — fabrics, bedding, books, pictures, none of these should be stored in unheated sheds through a winter, if you value them at all.

# Working With Builders

The question everybody wants answered is "How do I find a good builder?" I suspect that people have been asking the same question all over the world for several thousand years now and I've yet to come across a convincing answer. I'm not going to even try. Instead I think it's a good idea to look at the question from a number of different angles, to try and grasp just what it is that goes wrong with construction work that causes people to tear their hair out with exasperation. In an effort to close in on the main question, I'll take a look at several supplementary questions

### Do I need a builder at all?

The building trade is a free market but, all in all, it's not a very good advert for the free market. It is widely perceived as being expensive, inadequate and inefficient, certainly when it comes to domestic work. Indeed one of the main drivers behind selfbuilder's willingness to take on the project management role themselves is a widespread lack of trust with general builders. When times are tough in the building trade, builders are falling over themselves to try and get work but an alarming number are simultaneously going bust. On the other hand, when times are good (as they have been, at least in SE England, since 1997) it can be extremely hard to even get builders to quote for work — some of the more reliable builders I know are now booked up with work for over a year. The problem becomes one of finding a builder at any price rather than one at the right price. There is an added danger that less scrupulous builders will take your job on knowing full well they are inadequately resourced, hoping their contact book will see them through. Mistakes multiply when main contractors get stretched beyond their capabilities.

So is a builder, a general builder, necessary? The essential ingredient that a general builder brings to the party is this magic phrase project management. Coordination of material deliveries, subcontractors, building inspectors, plant hire, office administration, you name it. Anyone who has ever managed a business of whatever size will know that it's a time consuming business and anyone who has ever managed a building business will know that it's almost impossible to get it just right. Rookie builders with experience in management can and frequently do take on the role of general builder and do the hiring and firing of tradesmen together with all the other activities. However what should not be underestimated is the amount of time and energy this all takes up. Realistically, you need some sort of professional management help if you can't be on site every day (although not necessarily all day). For many people, hiring a general builder makes a lot of sense.

### Why aren't builders any good?

However much sense it makes in theory, in practice many people end up feeling let down by their main contractor. More often than not, this is because contractors tend to be incredibly busy people and they are forever juggling timetables and deadlines. Whilst the typical general contractor would make a good project manager on one particular job, the wheels start to fall off when the number of sites being supervised gets above three. Yet in order to make a decent living and to keep a run of work going for various tradesmen, most general contractors simply have to keep going at several jobs simultaneously. I know from experience that it's incredibly demanding and stressful trying to coordinate building work going on across a wide area. As a builder you may start out with the best intentions in the world but you rapidly end up employing the same knee-jerk excuses used by everyone else in the trade (and despised by its clientele). Appointments start to get missed, calls start to go unanswered, promises start getting broken. Why can't builders deliver?

Well I'm not sure there is an easy answer to this. The glib answer is "You try doing it and see if you are any better." But that's not terribly helpful. In truth, most general contractors do deliver eventually but often at a standard well below their customers' expectations. So perhaps the advice should be by all means use a main contractor but don't set your standards too high. Or perhaps we are not prepared to pay enough for the level of service we want.

### What scares the builders?

Money for a start. It is an axiom often repeated that you should avoid paying a builder upfront for anything, wherever possible. However there is another side of this coin — it is the builder who is consequently extending you credit, which immediately puts him at a disadvantage. And despite the so-called power of the consumer these days, the levels of unsecured credit you are likely to get from a builder are way beyond anything else you are going to be offered on the high street. Try buying a new car by offering to pay in 30 days only if you are completely satisfied and then withholding 5% of the price for six months.

Little wonder that so many builders experience cashflow problems. Sure, they are buying their materials on credit but only lasts 30 - 60 days and the subcontract labour they employ will down tools if not paid much more quickly than that.

So one way you can smooth your relationship with your builder is to agree how payments will be met before the contract starts and then stick rigidly to those terms. If you are having to borrow large dollops of money to finance your building work and this money is only released in stages, then be open with your builder about this and make it clear just what he has to do to trigger the stage payments — at least he'll know that you are being realistic about money. One of the bugbears of today's builder is to be told at the end of the job that although the client is perfectly happy with the finished result, the final £20,000 is going to have to wait a bit because they've overspent and run out of money: yet it happens all the time, builders getting used as sources of interest-free finance.

Another frequent scam foisted on builders is the excuse that the money is locked into a 30 or 60 day savings account and that payment is being withheld until the full withdrawal period is up. The builder is quite likely to be struggling with an overdraft as big as a mortgage. Yet such behaviour by clients is all too common and is verging on being really abusive but, when the builder is the creditor, he can basically do very little about it.

As you can see, the builder is actually in a very vulnerable position. But clients play still worse tricks; some will withhold payment of many thousands of pounds on the flimsiest of excuses, such as resolving a few snags which might be worth just a few hundred pounds. Sometimes these machinations are born of frustration with the performance of the builder but sometimes the client uses these excuses to cover up for the fact that they never had enough money in the first place. Yes, these are the real cowboy clients. My business was "locked out" on a couple of occasions on the excuse that the standard of workmanship was not good enough when subsequently it emerged the real reason was that the client was in financial difficulties and simply had no way to settle the bill. Rather than admit to the humiliation of being unable to settle a debt, it is altogether easier and more convenient to tell everyone that the builder is an incompetent rogue from whom you have had to withhold money — or even more likely, an extortionate bill for extras. Whilst the client is telling everyone who will listen just how awful the builders are and receiving a sympathetic ear, able to point to work which is half finished in evidence, the builder is often forced to bear such indignities in silence. Often the amounts at dispute are too large for the small claims court but not large enough to warrant risking a full blown legal challenge and many thousands of pounds get written off this way. Clients withholding money for whatever reason is easily the commonest reason for builders going bust and it can happen to even the best builders.

### Does the builder choose the client?

Small wonder then that builders are just as wary of potential customers as the customers are of them. The vetting process that goes on between contractors and clients is very much a two-way thing and part of the skill of being a good builder is knowing which clients to work with and which to avoid. You are chosen by your builder as much as you choose your builder. It's back to that marriage thing again. People are often staggered by the huge range in quotations they receive from builders: commonly the cheapest quote will be no more than half as much as the most expensive. How can this be when the labour rates are little different from one builder to another and the materials are likely to come from the same sources at very similar prices? Often this discrepancy is explained by the fact that some builders are busier than others and therefore weight their pricing accordingly, but there is more to it than that because the builder also weights certain jobs with a risk premium because they suspect that they will not get paid in full or that the job will be more trouble than it's worth. Bear in mind that a small builder needs to make an average mark-up of at least 12-15% on his labour and materials costs just to survive in business and that, out of every ten jobs, the chances are that as many as two or three probably won't make any money at all. Unprofitable jobs are often referred to in the trade as lemons and the more experienced a contractor gets, the better he becomes at spotting lemons in advance. More often than not, a builder who suspects that such and such a job is a potential lemon will not even bother to quote for it or, if they do, they will add a very high percentage to the overall profit figure to cover their back should they win the contract.

### What's wrong with competitive tendering?

One practice which is now becoming prevalent is for busy builders to get together and divide up the work in a way (and for a price) that suits them — it's called covering. It works like this. A job is put out to tender — typically by an architect — to four or five local builders. Some of them are so busy that they simply don't want to take on any more work. Architects tend to regard refusals to quote rather badly and the builders feel that, rather than risking losing the possibility of quoting for future work, they would like to put in some price, any price. So the next step is to chat with the competition — it's not hard, it happens naturally anyway — and soon an informal cartel is in place.
Reg: "Have you been asked to quote for the old Rectory Job at Chipping Butty?"
Charlie: "Yes. I like the look of it."
Reg: "I really can't see any way we could do that one — could you do us a favour and cover us."
Charlie: "Sure — I've no doubt you'll be able to return the favour soon."

So Charlie puts in his price and tells Reg to put in a price maybe £10,000 higher. Reg knows he won't get the job but he hasn't spent any time or money quoting for it and he hasn't upset the architect so he'll stand a chance next time around when he does want the work. Occasionally the builders know all the other tenderers on any given job — in matters like this the grapevine works extremely efficiently — so that there are cases where every builder on the tendering list has been in on the scam. They all know who is providing the lowest quote and, consequently, the lowest quote is in reality quite a high one. Such a complete stitch-up is perhaps rare but frequently two or three of the quotes will be for show purposes only.

Partly this problem stems from the way building work is procured in the first place. And in particular the practice of builders quoting for free causes a lot of problems. It sounds too good to be true and of course it is. It takes a good deal of time to generate an accurate quotation and most builders simply send tender documents off to a quantity surveyor who carries out the work for them (for a scaled fee, depending on the size of the job). Now builders often end up quoting for five or six jobs in order to win one so the overheads of quoting for jobs they don't get becomes a significant business expense in itself. Anything that helps to ease the load of having to quote for jobs is manna from heaven for builders so you can see the attraction of any informal price fixing arrangements they might concoct.

### Are there any other options?

What's advantageous to the builder is obviously less welcome news for the consumer. What ways are there for clients to avoid being on the wrong end of one of these cartels? Well the obvious one is to avoid using general contractors at all, as previously discussed. You can elect to be your own main contractor and hire all the labour yourself but for many busy people this is an unrealistic option and in many parts of the country it is becoming harder and harder to track down good labour. Alternatively, you can hire a project manager who will do all this work for you for a fee. However, such people are thin on the ground and there are potential contractual problems when the job overruns or goes wrong in some way. There is also little guarantee that the project manager will succeed in hiring the best labour at the best price unless you hold him to a fixed price for the whole job — in which case — hey presto! — he's just become a general builder.

A third approach is to select a builder first, preferably even before the design stage, and to work in a sort of loose partnership with them throughout the project. Design and build — it's a buzz word in big commercial construction at the moment (where, incidentally, the problems are remarkably similar if only on a different scale). Rather than trying to tie builders down to the lowest possible price for a set of plans they have had no part in formulating, start by asking them what they think are the most cost effective ways of getting what you want and who is the best person to design such a house. This way you can work to the strengths of your builder and hopefully use these to drive down costs. Some builders will respond very positively to such an approach — others will run a mile, much preferring to work in the traditional ways. And whilst a more open, trusting approach to building can reap dividends, it's also not without its share of problems. Just because you start out talking partnering and understanding doesn't mean that you'll end up there — and untangling a messy design and build contract can be more work than sorting out the more traditional adversarial way of working. Informal ways of working end up in dispute as well.

### What makes a good builder?

Hugely successful contractors (or project managers if you prefer) are a rare breed. Though they almost invariably have their roots in one of the building trades, the skills that are required for managing building work are quite different. Good, clear communication is perhaps the most important and, if you are weighing up potential contractors, it is probably the aspect to which you should give the most careful consideration. After all if you can understand what they are on about then chances are that they will understand what you are on about and anyone working for them will understand their instructions. 90% of the things that go wrong on building sites go wrong because of misunderstandings or plain bad instructions.

In some ways this is good news, because if you meet someone face to face then you do at least get an immediate impression. If you can understand them it doesn't mean they will do a good job but there is a much higher chance that they'll do the job you want them to do rather than one they want to do. This calls into question your judgment of character: can you tell the difference between the hard-working, trustworthy, reliable characters and the shifty, slapdash and chaotic ones? It's terribly difficult, particularly as long exposure to the building game has a habit of turning the most upright people ever so slightly cynical and bitter. I suspect that the truth is it's always a bit of a gamble; there is no cast-iron way of making sure you are entering into a marriage made in heaven. This doesn't mean that it's not worth taking some elementary precautions.

### How to select a good builder

1. Try and start with a sensible shortlist. Get one or two of the bigger local builders on board who you suspect will do a good job even though you expect they might be expensive. Try and choose the smaller ones from recommendations rather than pins in the Yellow Pages.

2. Don't waste everybody's time by selecting fifteen or twenty contractors. It's much better to have three of four who you contact (even visit) personally beforehand to see if they have the time or the inclination to do your job. If the response is lukewarm, don't bother to send documents for quotation, look elsewhere.

3. If you want to check on financial standing and/or membership of trade organisations now is the time to do it. Don't get someone to quote for your work if you are going to reject them later because they don't meet your standards. Now is the time to check to see whether or not your builder is a member of any trade organisation.

4. The more detailed your plans, the more meaningful will be the quotations. Ideally, you should send drawings already approved by the building inspector. If you have a separate written specification, the process of quotation becomes much more straightforward (and therefore tends to increase accuracy).

5. Ask what the day-work rates are and what mark-ups will be applied to materials sup-

plied which were specifically excluded from the quotation — usually done to allow you to make up your mind nearer the time.

6. Be suspicious of very low quotations. Often you may find that most of the replies cluster around a figure (say £70,000) but one comes in way below (say £45,000). Without revealing your hand, try and elicit how this quotation was arrived at: what does this guy do that the others don't know about? Why is he so desperate for the work? It may just be the cheap one is the only one not in on the price fixing scam but, even so, be wary.

7. If there is no clear winner on price, then have a second informal round of interviews (probably by phone) to elicit more information. Are they busy? Are they very busy? If you haven't got a contract specifying completion dates, find out when could they start and how long would they take? Who would actually be running the job? Could you meet this person on their current site (good chance for a snoop)? Do they have a mobile number? Are they contactable out of hours?

8. If all still equal, then go for the best communicator. The one who you understand best, or just get on with best, will also be the one who will understand you best. It's that old chemistry at work again. If you've got to this stage and still haven't made up your mind, then trust your instinct.

Some of the very best of our small builders are extremely unambitious and don't go out chasing work. They keep a gang of three, four or five guys going and will turn work away rather than take on twice their normal workload. They don't advertise and you won't find them in the Yellow Pages. Often they don't even do quotations. Clients willingly wait months, even years, to get hold of these builders and work is almost always carried out in a spirit of trust and cooperation, usually with very few subcontractors involved at all. If you value quality above price and informality above deadlines then this may be the route for you. If there are any of these mediaeval craft gangs in your neck of the woods, chances are your architect or building inspector will know of them.

### What makes a good client?

- Be straight about money. If money is tight then sit down at the beginning of the job and discuss how and when payments will be made. Don't leave it until the end.
- Communicate well. Choose a builder you can talk to easily and one who you in turn understand. If you choose to use a main contractor, then work with him all the time.

- Don't issue instructions to the subcontractors over the head of the main contractor. There is a chain of command and you should stick to it. It's sometimes very tempting to short-circuit it but it very quickly gets messy. This dictum gets terribly hard to stick to when the main contractor has gone AWOL.
- If you enter into a written contract, then understand what the basic terms are. This applies even if the arrangement is less formal.
- Don't be afraid to ask questions. If the job starts taking off on a course you hadn't envisaged, then find out why at once.
- Realise that part of the key to getting good building work done is to be a good client which translates as being a good manager. Don't be a passive consumer. And avoid letting things decline into a "Them and Us" situation.
- Don't keep changing your mind. And don't abuse the "free quotation" ethos that general contractors operate on. It's one thing to get a free quotation at the outset of the job, its quite another to demand costed alternative quotes for every finish item in your house. Main contractors spend an inordinate amount of time generating quotations and the more they are asked to provide them, the less time they have to spend on managing their business.
- If you want to withhold money because you feel something has not been done satisfactorily then be specific about exactly how much you are withholding and why. Explain what you want the builder to do in order for you to release the payment.

This still doesn't guarantee that you and your builder will be a match made in heaven. No, unfortunately there is no guarantee of that any more than there is of starting a happy marriage. But if you as a client play your part to the full and don't mess your builder around, then you won't be doing your chances of success any harm. In my experience, a good client is the single most important element of a successful building project — indeed, good clients tend to get good building work done for them. And if there is a key to being a good client, it is understanding just what your role is and playing it to the full.

If you've chosen to dispense with the main contractor then you'll almost certainly be in the business of hiring subcontractors. Project management — piece of piss, mate. Subcontractors — no problem — there are simple ground rules, aren't there! I mean.

Well there are. They go something like this.

## What Should Happen
- Never hire anybody who hasn't been personally recommended to you
- Always check on their previous work
- Always get three quotations in writing
- Never hire anybody on an hourly rate; get all work priced before hand
- Check to see if they are members of a reputable trade organisation
- Check to see what guarantee they offer
- Never pay up front
- Always get "extras" priced and put in writing before they are carried out
- Impose a time schedule with penalties for late completion.

All sounds good, sensible stuff.

## What Actually Happens
• *Never hire anyone who hasn't been personally recommended to you*

You might have to wait a long time.

• *Always check on their previous work*

Has anyone seriously got time to do this? Chasing up old working contacts for subcontractors who may only be on site for a day or two doesn't feature highly on most "To Do" lists.

• *Always get three quotations in writing*

You must be joking. You may have to approach about ten to get three to respond in writing and even then you may have to wait (and chase) for two months.

• *Never hire anybody on an hourly rate; get all work priced before hand*

Fine for most trades, but sometimes this is totally impractical. You have to have a detailed specification ready and chances are, if you are trying to save money, that you won't have.

• *Check to see if they are members of a reputable trade organisation*

They'll probably be more expensive if they are.

• *Check to see what guarantee they offer*

Worth checking on for kitchens and plumbing but a bit meaningless for most subbies. They've either done it right or they haven't and it'll be down to you to check.

• *Never pay up front*

Good advice for anybody anytime.

Sometimes it's very hard to keep.

• *Always get "extras" put in writing before they are carried out*

Alright in principle but, again, sometimes totally impractical if you are in a hurry (you will be). Get a site diary instead. If you want it to go down in writing be prepared to do the writing yourself.

• *Impose a time schedule with penalties for late completion*

Risk losing your subbies.

## What is a Subcontractor?
Legally a subcontractor (or subbie) is a worker who gets hired and paid by a main contractor. If a subcontractor works directly for you then they are, strictly speaking, not subcontractors at all but ordinary (or main) contractors. The difference is crucial because if you become a main contractor you also become responsible for policing your subcontractors' tax affairs (lots of unpaid admin.). However, if you are the client, this all flows over your head — i.e. you don't have to know anything about it. Even though your subbies won't be subbies at all when they are working for you, everybody still refers to them as subbies.

Generally speaking, when we say "subbies" we are referring to tradesmen providing a specific skill, like a plumber or a brickie. Sometimes subbies will be one-man bands. Sometimes they will be small firms employing several people. The one-man bands will tend to work for a cheaper hourly rate but may well be just as expensive when it comes to quoted works.

## Essential Subbies
Generally, you will be able to build a house by hiring the following characters:
- Groundworkers. Someone with a JCB and access to a lorry.
- Brickwork (brickies). Often overlaps with groundworkers — one of the two (or you) will have to lay the drains. Often work in gangs of three (two brickies/one labourer). Don't usually supply materials.
- Carpenters (chippies, or joiners up north and in Scotland). Often work in twos (no labourer). Don't usually supply materials.
- Roofers. Most often hired in small gangs who supply and fix, sometimes doing the scaffolding as well.
- Plasterers/dry liners. Mixture of one-man bands and small firms.
- Plumbers. Same mixture of one-man bands and small firms.
- Electricians. Same mixture.

- Decorators. Most selfbuilders do this themselves but there are plenty of "professionals" around.

There are a number of other specialist subbies who you may want to use: glaziers, garage door fitters, kitchen specialists, pavers and drive layers, landscapers, scaffolders. Refer to Chapter 11 Shopping for more details.

## Choosing a Good Subbie
I'd like to come up with an easy rule for picking good subbies but I don't know what it is. If you've found one perhaps you would let me know. Obviously, you can go to great lengths to see that you appoint a master, but this can be very time-consuming and if the guy is only going to be on site for a few days it seems like a big case of overkill. Generally, contractors and subbies know the going rates for various trades and they can usually work out an amicable agreement over a cup of tea and a ten minute chat and this is how 99% of subbies get hired. It's easy come, easy go and if someone is useless they usually get asked to move on. However, if you want to ensure high standards from the start then you have to do a great deal more work, taking up references and talking to other contacts.

NB Don't forget the builder's dilemma. High standards don't tend to go with cheap prices. You gets one or you gets the other.

## Labour Only v Supply & Fix
Subbies tend to come in two distinct flavours. The labour-only subbies are usually hired singly (or in small informal gangs) and often on an hourly or day rate. They tend to be concentrated in the heavy building side (brickworkers, carpenters, plasterers). Many of the later trades — i.e. those concerned with finishes — are more often organised by small businesses, which prefer to sell a package whereby they supply the materials and the labour to fix the materials: typically, roofers, plumbers, electricians, glaziers and kitchen fitters. These supply and fix subbies will tend to be more organised — you'll be able to get quotes out of them — and possibly a little more expensive, particularly as they are in the business of marking-up materials they buy on your behalf. In effect, you are introducing an extra layer of management which has to be paid for. From a small builder's point of view, the big advantage of hiring small firms rather than singletons, is that cost control becomes much clearer. If someone is quoting to supply and fit a kitchen into your

*A common sight on British building sites — the vanishing subbie!*

new house for £5,000 then you know in advance what the damage is. However, if you rely on your own buying power plus Jim's joinery skills (paid for on an hourly rate) then you will just have to hope that it'll be less than £5,000; logic says it should be, but such finishing jobs have a habit of running over budget. You could ask Jim to quote to install your kitchen but Jim might well be reluctant to do so, especially if you are supplying the kitchen fittings. And what about coordinating with the plumber, the electrician and the tiler? Who will do this? If it's to be you and they end up keeping Jim waiting (they will) then it's you who is taking advantage of Jim's fixed price and he'd have every right to cry foul. This sort of finishing work involves so much intricate planning that it is unrealistic to expect every part of it to be quoted separately, so it tends to be either subbed out in its entirety or done on a time and materials basis.

## Daywork v Price Work

Daywork is the term commonly used to describe payments by the hour (or day) and it contrasts with price work, where payments are related to specific works having been completed. For example, a brickie on daywork might hope to get paid, say, £100 per day: if he was on a price he would hope to get paid something like £200 for every 1000 bricks laid. All things being equal, you would hope that he would lay about 500 bricks per day whichever system was being used to pay him, but human nature being what it is, it is widely assumed that the person paying the brickie will get better value from priced work. Many advisors say you should only ever hire builders on a price work basis but there are many situations where a daywork arrangement is both easier and more flexible.

If you are building to a tight budget, price work is almost certainly the route to take. For a rookie builder this is perhaps doubly important because you don't know what's in a day's work. Ask yourself how many doors a chippie should be able to hang in a day; if you haven't got a clue then you qualify as a rookie builder.

The main problem with always insisting on price work stems from the fact that it is, contractually, a much tighter type of agreement and that, for it to work, you need to be able to describe the work accurately before you can readily ask for it to be quoted. So really you need to have a professionally written specification for it all to make sense to subcontractors. It's not enough to say "Here is a set of plans. How much will you charge to put the brickwork and blockwork up?", because there are any number of little incidentals that increase the size of this work and make a mockery of your attempts to limit the damage.

## Measured Rates

Another problem is that many subbies find plans about as easy to read as you do. This is less of a problem with the finishing trades where they can come and give the house a once over and don't have to resort to plans, but often the hardest parts of a job to quote are the first parts when no house shell yet exists. Here a common ruse is to agree a rate for each section of work (say £300/1000 bricks laid) and then to total up when the work is completed. This is a perfectly sensible way of going about it and protects the subbie from any dispute about differences between what's on the plan and what actually got built: however, there is a great scope here for disagreements over the quantities actually built. Even qualified quantity survey-

ors will disagree by 2 or 3% and they work to an agreed set of measuring rules: a contractor and a subcontractor may end up 10% apart.

## PAYE v Subcontract

Until 1997 almost every subbie you would meet on a small building project would have been technically a subcontractor as opposed to an employee. Many of them worked for the same gaffer week in, week out, year in, year out and yet were still subcontractors for tax purposes. The Inland Revenue and the Contributions Agency have seen fit to reclassify these workers as employees which is a very different kettle of fish for everyone concerned. From a client's point of view, the major change will be that many small building operations have put their prices up to cover the extra tax burden placed on them. In theory. In practice the market decides, as it always has done, and the true effect of these tax changes is very hard to analyse, especially against a background of skills shortages and rising labour rates.

Not all workers have been reclassified. There are still many genuine self-employed building workers who negotiate their own contracts on a job by job basis. However they will have to work as individuals (or small partnerships) to remain self-employed, and it may be that, in time, they start to gain market share because of the tax changes.

## Cash Payments

One of the big advantages of organising your own building work is the ability to negotiate discounts with tradesmen in return for paying them in cash. This is, of course, illegal and any serious publication such as this cannot, naturally, condone such behaviour. But cash payments for casual work are not going to stop because I start being self-righteous. The normal builder's scam is to take off VAT in exchange for payments in cash, but this does not make much sense in new housebuilding because almost all the work is zero-rated so you can reclaim this tax in any case. Unlike the professional contractor, a selfbuilder is not required to police subcontractors' tax arrangements and if you choose to pay them in cash then that is a matter between you and them — it is not illegal simply to pay cash. Should the subcontractor then fail to declare this income it is they who are committing an offence, though subsequent inquiries might get back to you to uncover these payments. Cash payments actually do very little to benefit the new housebuilder unless they are used to negotiate lower prices from subcontractors, something most subbies are reluctant to do.

### "Do I need one?"

You've already got one. It's a principle of contract law that every time you buy something or hire someone (or something) you enter into a contract. Any item you purchase should perform adequately, any person you hire should carry out the work described competently and you, in turn, should pay them the agreed amount. In essence, it's that simple and this basic principle holds whether you are hiring a baby-sitter or building the Channel Tunnel.

All building work is covered by these principles — after all it's why builders are referred to as contractors — and don't think that just because you haven't got a written contract then you have no redress should things go wrong. However, it is also true to say that if things do go wrong, the more written evidence you can produce to show how and why, the stronger your case will be. If you can produce a written contract, signed by the builder, to say that he should have been finished by the end of August, and it's now November and you still haven't got any glazing in, then you've got a pretty good case for withholding payment. Without something written down it's your word against his and — well there might just be two sides to the story: you're not in a completely hopeless position, but your case is much weaker.

### "So a written contract is essential?"

Not at all. It's actually one of the most over-rated of safety features devised by professionals largely to justify their fat fees. Take the aforementioned Channel Tunnel, the largest construction project undertaken in these parts in recent times. Teams of lawyers will have been drafted in by both sides to negotiate contracts as watertight as they hope the tunnel will be. Did it get the tunnel built on time and to budget? Of course not. Re-enter those same teams of lawyers to argue about compensation, etc. Who benefits out of all this? The contractors, Eurotunnel and its shareholders — or the lawyers?

### "It's all down to a handshake?"

Not at all. That's throwing the baby out with the bath water. The basis of a building contract is that the client contracts to pay a specified sum in return for completion of a list of specified tasks. The more detailed this list, the stronger the contract becomes. If you have a professionally drawn up specification of works, then you already have about as good a contract as you can get. Signing a formal written contract for work that is only specified in the loosest terms is, in comparison, a complete waste of time and money.

### "So you think that acceptance of a quotation is enough?"

Yes. If a builder has seen whatever plans and specifications you have, by quoting for them he is committing himself to carry out the work competently. If there are further conditions you wish to set (such as time limits), then you should add these to your specifications. Should it later prove that your specifications are inadequate then so be it; the situation would be no better had you signed a written contract.

### "Is the spec. that came with my off-the-peg plans OK?"

You've missed the point. No contract is ever completely watertight. The more detail you put into a contract, the tighter it gets. There isn't a point at which it suddenly becomes OK; rather you get what you pay for. It's like asking how much life insurance is enough when you know that there's a 99% chance that you won't need any and a 1% chance that £2million would be very useful. Very detailed specifications are time-consuming to produce and are, therefore, expensive; only you can decide whether you need one.

### "But I'm planning to organise the building work myself."

It's unusual to sign contracts with labour-only subcontractors or indeed to put anything down in writing. Normally, the work is described verbally or with reference to any plans and specifications to hand. However, the contractual principles involved in hiring subcontractors are no different and neither are your chances of redress, should things go wrong. One of the penalties of building on the cheap is that you are more exposed to bad practice, but hopefully you can compensate to some extent by your frequent site presence. In the absence of any written undertakings, keep a site diary to record the comings and goings and at least you'll have some written evidence in case of trouble. Even to be able to say "Gary and Pete were there just two days in that week and no-one else turned up till the 27th" puts you in a much stronger position than saying "They were hardly ever there."

### "I say, I say, I say."

The above section appeared verbatim in the original edition of the Housebuilder's Bible and its assertion that you don't need a contract has caused one or two people to hop up and down with indignation. Perhaps they have a point. The fact that I've never built with contracts doesn't necessarily prove that they are a waste of time. Julian Owen, a well known selfbuild architect, pointed out that he was required professionally to work with a contract and that they didn't have to be expensive or difficult to understand. He particularly favours the simple 16 page JCT Minor Works Contract which is written in clear English and helps all sides to understand their responsibilities. I won't argue against this but I stand by my original line that a contract is no substitute for a detailed written specification of work.

### "Anything else to sort out?"

There are some things which you need to be clear about which are not to do with the technical specifics of building. The formal way of dealing with them would be to enclose the terms along with the plans and specs you send for quotation; by putting in a quotation, the contractor implicitly accepts your terms. However, you could choose to sort these terms out more informally after acceptance of quotation; if you are confident that the terms are not too onerous on the builder, he should be happy to accept and, if he isn't, then you've just been given the clearest indication you'll ever get that this marriage was not made in heaven. Reconsider. Sorting out these matters is in the interest of both parties and very often the first move will come from the builder.

## Insurance

For terms and rates, see Insurance section later in this chapter. Whoever is organising the building work should have cover. Make sure it's in place.

## Payments

Agree payment terms. If your money is being advanced by a lender in stages, be open with the builder about when and what these stages are. Generally it's the builder who is advancing you credit and this makes him even more vulnerable than you are.

## Retention

It is quite common to withhold a little money (between 2 and 5%) until snags are adequately sorted out. However, don't try and spring this on a builder halfway through a job as if it was a matter of course. It's not. Furthermore, it's always a delicate issue — it reeks of a lack of trust — and some perfectly good builders find it all rather insulting and often choose to steer clear of such contracts. After all, how would you feel to be told you were having 5% of your pay withheld until such time as your employers saw fit. If you want a retention clause included, it's one to get into the open very early on.

## Time Penalties

Usually, these take the form of damages which are to be deducted from the overall contract value if the work is not completed to an agreed schedule. For some reason I've not been able to fathom, these are conventionally referred to as liquidated damages. Again, it's one to sort out right at the outset and it's a very adversarial condition to place on a builder.

Time penalties make sense when you will suffer financial hardship (such as paying extra rent). However, when a job overruns it is more often than not very hard to decide who is to blame. You have to be prepared to keep your side of the bargain, which means no delays in agreed payments along the route and no changes to the specification of works. This still leaves the messy grey area of unavoidable delays (weather, strikes, illness, disputes with architects) which could keep an impartial referee busy for weeks. You need a very tight specification to be able to argue your side effectively.

These added conditions are really nothing more than specialised forms of insurance and, if you load a contract with retention clauses and time penalties, you can expect to pay more overall for the works described.

## Extras

The biggest single contractual nightmare any builder faces is how to adequately negotiate what the trade calls variations but what everyone else refers to as extras. People call them extras because, like Topsy, they seem to grow and grow. Some do shrink (hence variations being a more accurate term) but for every one that shrinks or even disappears there must be a dozen that expand. It's a particularly critical problem with renovations and smaller works (where often 40% of the final bill is made up of items not originally quoted for), but the new housebuilder is not immune from catching these particular bugs. If you've got plenty of time and money and like a nice loose specification where you can make up your mind as you go along then you'll be wondering what all the fuss is about, but if you belong to the 95% of builders who break out into a sweat every time a bank statement arrives you will want to know how to avoid these nightmares.

The good news is that you can inoculate yourself against most of them. The bad news is that immunisation is itself expensive and time-consuming. Many extras can be avoided by having a professionally written specification, but people wanting to save money will probably have avoided paying for one in the first place and these are usually the same people who can least afford extras.

As if the fact that extras occur at all isn't bad enough, when they do occur, you, the client, are negotiating with a gun to your head; you can hardly hire another builder just to do the extras. If you've gone in a bit hard at the beginning — including onerous time penalties and retentions, you can be sure that the builders will have their revenge here. Not only can they potentially stitch you up pricewise, but they have a cast-iron excuse for blowing your time penalty clauses out of the water. Even if things haven't descended to this sabre rattling, adversarial level there is still ample scope to misunderstand and to misconstrue — "Oh I didn't realise that meant the glass had to be toughened as well." "Well that's an extra £80." If you are the kind of client who expects your builder to give you fully costed options for free throughout the job, as in "How much extra would it be if we had a bidet in the kitchen?", you probably deserve to pay over the odds in any event.

Each little decision forms a mini-contract in itself and accounting them can take up over half the total admin. time spent on a job. The golden rules are:
- make it clear that extras need to be authorised by you before work starts on them
- always negotiate extras direct with the main contractor — that is the person with whom you placed the initial contract, not with anyone working for them
- write down what you've agreed — even if it's just in a site diary.

The reasons for extras are many and various. Sometimes it is down to unquantifiable works discovered after the building work has begun — in new building this type of problem usually occurs underground. Most often it is down to the client adding to the original specification of works as the job progresses or, as it's known in the trade, "changing their bloody minds again." There are two specialised forms of extras, or variables, which deserve closer attention.

## PC Sums

PC Sums are not a new form of anti-sexist arithmetic but a good old builder's routine for dealing with loose specifications. Prime Cost Sums are put into contracts to allow you,

the client, the freedom to select a particular product at a later date. For instance, you might put a PC Sum of £300 for a bathroom suite into a specification. The contractor will have included this amount in the quotation but the actual figure you pay will be down to which bathroom suite you choose.

There is a nasty little problem here because things like bathroom suites have list prices and they have trade prices — indeed the trade price is a matter for negotiation. Don't bulldoze in and buy the kit yourself, because the builder (or perhaps plumber in this case) is expecting to make a profit on this deal and they would have every right to expect you to reimburse them for their lost profit. The normal arrangement is that the builder buys what you specify and that you get to pay list price and the builder pockets the difference between list price and his trade price, but this can work out very expensive, particularly if you up the spec. There is no reason why you shouldn't negotiate a radically different deal whereby you pay trade prices, but make damn sure that you negotiate it beforehand — preferably right at the beginning. Again, the sure way to avoid these sorts of problems is to have a tight specification and that mean ones without PC Sums. This means deciding on things like kitchen and bathroom finishes before the job starts.

## Provisional Sums

Like their cousins, the PC sums, the provisional sums are placed in contracts where there is an element of doubt about the amount of work to be carried out. They are much more common in renovations than in new building but there are nevertheless areas — notably underground works — which most builders will only estimate rather than enter into a fixed price quotation. Understandably so. It's a buck-passing device, a way of saying that if there's more work to do than can reasonably be anticipated, then you, dear client, will be the one who has to pay. Well, you knew it was a risky game. Provisional sums are just one of the things that makes building work such a gamble. You can try to force contractors to take on the risk themselves but their understandable response is to hoick prices through the roof; more realistically you can establish guidelines for how provisional works will be charged: a labour rate, a mark-up applied to materials, that sort of thing.

Plan your site as if you were Wellington planning the downfall of Napoleon, or Montgomery about to attack Rommel. Think of it as a military campaign. Montgomery defeated Rommel because he realised that a battlefield was like a building site and that the best building sites were well organised with things happening when and where you wanted them to happen.

Don't just order 14,000 bricks and think how clever you are to have got them so cheaply. Think about how much space 14,000 bricks will take up, where that space is to be found, who or what will put them there, whether they will stay there when you dig a trench in front of them and whether your hod carriers will be able to get to them if there are 200m² of concrete blocks stacked in front. Build the house in your head before you pick up a shovel in anger and you will be some way towards having a strategy for negotiating the obstacles that you will encounter along the way.

Always assume the worst. Plan for rain, lots of it; plan for sub-zero temperatures in which your tap freezes and your bricklaying sand sets hard like rock; plan for delays as your subbies slip off to finish another job. Don't be gobsmacked if materials turn up damaged or if the wrong materials get delivered or if nothing gets delivered at all. Keep calm when your mortgage advance fails to come through on time and four large roofers move threateningly towards you demanding payment.

It'll be alright. It won't be that bad.

## Who? When? With What?
I cannot stress how much it is worth sitting down with a blank sheet of paper before you start building. In my experience, builders actually find this incredibly hard; they are, by nature it would seem, always wanting to "push on" or "get ahead" and they think admin is for accountants and blank sheets of paper are for poets. It's almost as if the child in us can't resist the lure of the sandcastle whereby you start digging and piling and gradually the structure appears as if by magic, because everyone is digging and piling. Perhaps it is the natural way to build— after all how many children do you see designing sandcastles before going onto the beach. Natural or not, building this way is a luxury which only the rich and frivolous can afford. Your preparation doesn't have to look incredibly professional — it may indeed look like nothing so much as a glorified shopping

list — but it does need to identify who is going to do what, when and with what. As a rule of thumb, every hour spent planning the job beforehand saves between three and four hours tying up the loose ends at the end of the job.

Some of these whos? and with whats? will be blank at the beginning of the job — for instance, you may not know your plumber or your plasterers at that stage — but the key point to take on here is that you need to identify a time by which you should make a decision, otherwise you will lose the so-called critical path and the whole building programme will slide gently off the rails.

## How to Finish
Following on from this thread, there is another identifiable problem which you need to address from the word go and that is to do with the finishing details, the key ones listed below:

- Kitchen
- Bathroom furniture
- Light fittings
- Socket placement
- Decorating schemes
- Wall tiles
- Floor finishes
- Shelving, cupboards
- Pavings, driveway finishes.

Very often, and quite understandably, people don't want to make decisions about these features until the structure is finished and they can walk around it and visualise everything. Architect's drawings (and 3D computer walkthroughs) are no substitute for being there anymore than watching the Travel Show is a substitute for going on holiday. The ability to successfully visualise completed building projects when they are still on plan is something that is generally only picked up after years of experience. If you feel unhappy about making these crucial buying decisions before you have a building you can walk around, then be realistic about the scheduling of these delayed purchases.

Refer back to the eight month building schedule which appears at the beginning of this chapter. Notice that your first fix wiring and plumbing are taking place whilst the roofing is being completed, in Month 4. Well first fix wiring and plumbing can't actually take place until there has been some decision making about what is being wired and plumbed in and this effectively means that you will have had to plan both the kitchen and the bath-

room layouts, even if you have yet to decide on what the fittings are to be. Usually these layout options will have been drawn in on the initial plans but note also that the socket outlet and lighting positions will also have to be inked in at this stage and this will affect your positioning of beds and desks and TVs, which is normally left off the plans.

## Plan for a Pause
If you refer back to the timeline diagram at the beginning of this chapter, you will note that the finishes are booked in to Month 6. Note also that the plastering stage isn't booked to be completed before the middle of Month 5 and realistically this is the point at which the visually challenged can at last see what their schemings have produced. Most people are surprised to find that some rooms seem larger than they had imagined, some seem smaller, some lighter, some darker. If you are of the sandcastle persuasion of builder, you've reached the natural point at which decision making about finishes should take place — you know, a dark oak kitchen would look just so, or perhaps you feel like stretching to those sensational Provencal tiles you saw in the Fired Earth catalogue which would look a wow behind the bath. Now phone up your chosen supplier, be they MFI or Smallbone kitchens.

"Yes, madam, we'd be pleased to supply you with these items. They will be shipped to you in six weeks time."

"Six weeks! But I've only got ten days!"

"Well perhaps madam would like to choose from our Salmon Slash range which can be delivered to you in three working days."

"But I don't like any of those."

I could go on but my point is made. If you want the time to step back and think and then seek out obscure items, and you don't want to do it before your house is plastered out, then plan a quiet period in the building program so that you can engage on a second stage of the planning. If you are working to stage payments, then try and arrange for a stage payment to coincide with the completion of the plastering stage so that the financial pressure is taken off.

## Site Tidy
A clean site is a happy site. It is also a more productive site and a safer site. However, keeping a site tidy takes time and some people regard this as wasted time. It's not. Take time out each day to clear away the crap and

*Isolated barns provide rich pickings for ne'er-do-wells. With slates fetching £1 each, it's a bit like leaving your car unlocked with the keys in the ignition.*

to return tools to the spot where they should be kept and it will repay dividends in time saved later on.

Subcontractors tend to be very messy; if someone is working for you on a price then they will tend to think that clearing up after them is your business. Typically, the issue doesn't even get discussed when the subbies are being hired but as a general rule if the subbies are supplying materials then they should be responsible for seeing that they clean their waste away after they've finished — after all, in this instance they own the waste materials. On the other hand if you are supplying materials then they are yours and it's down to you to decide what to do with them. If you demand that your subbies spend half an hour at the end of each day clearing up their own mess they may well turn around and demand extra money for work which would normally be done by an apprentice (whatever happened to them?). Clean subbies are a blessing, but if yours aren't don't just stand there and moan, get on with it yourself.

### Rubbish Disposal

Often the reason a site degenerates into something resembling the aftermath of a small bomb is that there is no coherent way of disposing of all the rubbish. Indeed, many builders are a) loath to spend money on keeping a site clean and b) loath to throw anything away because it might come in handy later on the job, or on another job. There is a balance to be struck here between a sensible amount of recycling of waste materials and a stubborn refusal to admit that 98% of what is not used the first time will never get used anywhere else. What this invariably hides is the refusal to admit to an earlier buying mistake.

The easiest option for most small sites is to have a skip on site all the time. It costs around £5/week to keep a skip in an off-the-road location which I reckon is very good value. The expense comes when skips are exchanged —

expect an exchange to cost £100 or more, depending on your location, but don't forget that you can have sand and aggregates delivered economically in the new skip, which can make a considerable saving. Many builders are tempted to economise on the rubbish and let the pile grow bigger and bigger, thinking that they'll sort it out later on. Just piling rubbish up in one corner can cause more problems than it solves — a windy day may send it all out over the site again, and into your neighbours' gardens as well. Another solution is to dig a pit on site which you will cover on completion — this sounds attractive but it is usually rather a dodgy way of going about things because you'll find that covering it over is easier said than done and you'll be unlikely to use the resulting land for anything useful because it will keep subsiding. Bonfires are OK for disposing of timber offcuts but most building waste is either inert (which won't burn) or is plastic (which shouldn't be burnt). Whatever you do, do plan to do something. Building work produces copious quantities of all kinds of waste and it won't just go away.

### Security

Theft is a problem on building sites the world over. It's usually on a small scale and it's typically tools that get nicked, often by casual ne'er-do-wells rather than organised gangs. Fortunately, the way most sites work, the early stages of the work involve a large amount of largely low value commodities like concrete and blocks which are not easily stolen. Only after the shell is watertight (and hopefully lockable) do the expensive fittings arrive on site. If you want to beat the threat of any potential theft, then don't provide any tempting morsels for light fingers:

- Have valuable materials (joinery, sanitaryware, kitchen goods) on site for as short a time as possible before fixing.
- If you have nowhere to lock up kit like cement mixers, barrows and handtools then at least hide them so that the casual visitor does not see them from the road.
- Take small tools (especially power tools)

home with you.
- Get the windows glazed and the external doors hung as soon as is practically possible.
- If your site is particularly vulnerable, consider building the detached garage first (if you have one) to use as a strong room. Alternatively, do what many of the professionals do and hire a container for the duration.
- Temporary fencing-off is expensive and usually unjustified on small sites. However it may be worth considering if you are in a particularly high crime area or if your site is particularly hazardous and it is likely that people may be wandering around after hours. You can hire 2m high steel fencing such as SGB's Heras Readifence for around 50p/m/week—less for longer periods. If you need security fencing for more than five months it will probably repay you to buy it and resell when you have finished.

## Safety

Building sites are by their very nature dangerous places. We demand finished buildings which are themselves structurally sound, weatherproof and safe to live-in but in order to create them we have to go through a series of steps which are inherently unsafe. Anyone managing small building sites is legally required to be aware of these risks and to take measures to minimise their impact. New housebuilding is actually one of the safer sectors of the construction industry — a fact borne out by lower insurance premiums — but there are still a large number of potential hazards to be negotiated.

### Excavations

Trench work is usually fairly safe at levels down to about 1m (waist height), but thereafter the dangers of trench collapse become very much greater. There are well proven techniques for shoring up trenches and if you are not sure what you are doing then for God's sake get hold of someone who is. Deep foundations are potentially very dangerous and you need to guard against not just trench collapse but also materials and people falling down into them. If you are working close to or underpinning an existing structure there is the additional problem that you could undermine it and cause a potentially catastrophic collapse.

Another problem to always be aware of is encountering buried cables and pipes, something that is common when you are opening roads to make service connections. You can reduce this risk by doing your homework and trying to establish just where cables are likely to be buried.

## Plant

Control machinery. Heavy plant can kill or maim if not properly controlled. If you get behind the wheel of a dumper truck don't play silly buggers, be very wary. They are not difficult to drive but they can be difficult to control, particularly if it's wet and muddy. They can easily end up crushing someone. Dumpers are often used to pour concrete into foundations and this frequently leads to accidents. Also, ensure cement mixers are properly seated before you start loading.

## Ladders

Don't be tempted to be macho — anchor the top end on to something secure. Don't make do with funky old ladders with broken rungs. And wonky step ladders are a nightmare you can live without.

## Scaffolding

Don't be afraid to spend money on extra scaffolding. If you are uneasy about doing some task off a ladder (or a scaffold tower) then get proper scaffolding erected. It's surprisingly cheap and you'll get the job done in half the time. Also be very wary about "rearranging" scaffolding. Usually, this means nicking boards off the scaffolding to use elsewhere. Think who might be going to use the scaffolding in the near future and make sure they know what's been going on.

## Power Tools

If you don't already have a kit of power tools but are planning to buy some, then buy 110v ones rather than 240v. You'll need a transformer to get them to work but they are far safer. When you hire power tools you should be offered a choice of 110 or 240v. If you are committed to using 240v power tools then ensure that your temporary electricity supply is protected with RCDs (Residual Current Devices).

## Electric Cables

Long extension leads are a menace (though sometimes unavoidable). Try and avoid trailing them across site where vehicles may drive over them. Get a cordless screwdriver — they are brilliant and you won't need all those extension leads. Cables on building sites tend to get gashed and generally bashed about and it's not unusual for bare wires to get exposed. Keep your eyes open for this sort of thing and if you come across badly frayed cable then replace it, don't bodge it with insulating tape.

## Steel Toe-Caps

Bruised and broken toes are still one of the commonest of accidents. Yet you still see subbies wearing trainers on site. If you are buying purpose made shoes, get some with steel toe caps (from most builder's merchants from around £30). If you manage to acquire a pair with Doctor Martens written on them you'll have a valuable fashion accessory to boot. Most builder's merchants also do a line of steel toe-capped wellies.

## Head Injuries

Most "serious" sites insist on hard hats being worn at all times, yet you won't even find a hard hat on most small sites — which is a shame because small sites are no less dangerous and, when people are working above you, a hard hat makes good sense. Yet, because they have an image of being "for the big boys only," the small builders and their subbies tend to shun them at all times. At least make an effort. Have at least a couple of hard hats on site and wear them when people are working on scaffolding above you.

## Sharps

Remove nails from loose timber lying around site. Common sense really but it usually gets overlooked. If you keep a clean and tidy site, this will be no extra work. If you don't then chances are the only way you'll even know that nails are lying in wait for you is when you tread on them. Ouch.

## Lifting

Back injuries are by far the commonest cause of lost time for builders. They can usually be easily avoided by asking for some help when lifting heavy objects like bags of cement. Again, don't feel you have to be macho just because you're on a building site. Ask for help.

## Minor Accidents

Have a small first aid kit on site. Most injuries are minor and can readily be treated with TCP and a bandage.

## CDM Regs

In 1995, there was a significant upgrade to the health and safety regulations in respect to building sites when the Construction (Design and Management) Regulations came into effect. The key point in the new regulations is that building work should be organised in accordance with a Health and Safety Plan which should be written by the designer and administered by the main contractor. If you are deemed to be a Domestic Client — definition = a client for whom a project is carried out, not being a project carried out in connection with the carrying on by the client of a trade, business or other undertaking (whether for profit or not) — your job does not come under the CDM umbrella. However, professional developers will have to begin by appointing a Planning Supervisor who will be responsible for seeing that the design is safe to build and then later a Principal Contractor, responsible for seeing that the health and safety plan is put into effect on site.

The CDM regs are statute law and failure to comply with them can result in criminal prosecution. The risks encountered on a building site haven't changed: the management of those risks has. It's a fair amount of extra work and red tape for builders and unfortunately there is no evidence as yet that it has done anything to improve safety on building sites. It's a technical subject and there's not room to cover it all here; the Health & Safety Executive (HSE) publish several booklets and I recommend one called Health and Safety in Construction, price £7.95 inc P+P, available from HSE Books. Local authority building regs departments and the NHBC now offer a Planning Supervision service for professional developers: on my last benchmark house, the NHBC charged £225 for acting as Planning Supervisors.

Now, selfbuilders and other domestic clients may not have to comply with the letter of the CDM regs, but you should be aware that all other construction jobs lasting longer than 30 days are required to be notified to the HSE, though technically this is the responsibility of the contractor not the client. Note that if you are managing your own build then you are regarded as the contractor.

## Notes for Converters

As if it wasn't complicated enough already, there are a number of grey areas connected with the application of the CDM regs. One of these is the issue of demolition: demolition is the bête noire of the construction industry with alarmingly high accident rates and such is the concern of the HSE that the preamble to the regulations suggests that any building work involving demolition should automatically come under CDM legislation. Alright in theory, but the policing of the new regulations is already so thin as to be verging on the non existent and it would now appear that the HSE have softened their line to exclude demolition of anything less than whole structures: it would be impractical to go through the CDM rigmarole every time you wanted to knock a wall down.

However, it is as well to be aware of the increased dangers of conversion work. In addition to all the regular safety hazards encountered in new build, conversion work introduces another tier of problems to be sorted through. Falling masonry and roofing timbers, support of temporary openings, removal of materials such as asbestos, application of noxious chemicals for timber treatment, to name just four that readily spring to mind. The principles of assessing and managing these risks are identical whatever the work, but the potential for accidents in conversion work will always be much higher than on new build.

# Insurance

There is a great deal of risk involved in building. One of the keys to successful building is to be able to manage this risk so that it doesn't overwhelm you and one of the most useful tools, in this respect, is insurance. Risk comes in two flavours. Physical and financial. The physical risk on building sites is largely a health and safety matter and managing that risk is looked at in the previous section Running a Site. But there is an overlap between the two types of risk because an injured subbie or passer-by may well choose to sue you for negligence and so the first (and arguably most important) layer of insurance rears up at you. In fact, you need two separate policies in place to cover this risk because the risk to the general public is dealt with quite differently to the risk to people working for you.

## Employer's Liability

If you employ any subcontractors — and if you undertake your own project management you are deemed to be an employer, at least from an insurance angle — and any of these subcontractors then has an accident which might be your fault, then they can sue you. If this is a serious accident the sums of money at stake will be large. Most policies now cover you for £10 million. A general builder is required by law to have an Employer's Liability policy in place and if you, as a client, are using a general contractor then you don't need your own policy in place as well. But you should check to see if your chosen contractors' policy is in place.

## Public Liability

This covers people (or objects) who you are not employing but might, nevertheless, still have cause to regret your building site ever existed. Maybe the mud from your site led to an accident, maybe your scaffolding fell down on someone's car, maybe some kids were playing in your foundation trenches when... This is "what if" insurance with a vengeance, but though the chances of a claim are small, any such claim could be extraordinarily large. Most standard policies cover you for £2 million worth of damage.

## Contract Works Insurance

Financial risk can never be entirely covered — for instance no one is going to insure you against your finished house being worth less than it cost to build. But there are various catastrophes that you can, to a certain extent, guard yourself from. The basic level of insurance here is covered by the Contract Works or All Risks policy, used to cover theft of plant and materials from site (usually with a hefty excess) together with fire or structural damage to any structures that you may be working on. Your lender will probably insist that you have all risks cover just as a conventional mortgage lender will insist that buildings insurance is in place on any property they mortgage. If you are employing a builder to erect your house, again you shouldn't need to take out your own policy as well but again you must check to see that they have current all risks insurance in place and that it's large enough to cover the value of your completed house — very often the policies stipulate a maximum contract value above which they won't pay out.

One important point to note is that contract works insurance does not cover any existing structure you may be altering, converting or extending. You would be expected to have this covered by a regular buildings insurance policy. There is another particular problem which occurs with unconverted barns with valuable planning permission riding on the back of them. The nominal value of the structure may be very low indeed — in fact it may well be a liability rather than an asset — but the planning permission depends on the building continuing to exist. Were it to burn down before conversion work is started, you could theoretically have the planning permission revoked which would be far more expensive than replacing the original fabric. So the risk you are insuring in these cases is not the value of the building but the value of the planning permission. Make sure that your insurance company understands the difference.

Contracts Works or All Risks policies are not mandatory and they usually come with dozens of options for you to pick and choose just which risks you want to cover. These go from the catastrophic (such as the building being destroyed) down to the inconvenient (such as some kid nicking your power tools). Just where you draw the line and just what excess you choose to bear yourself has an enormous impact on the cost of the policy.

There are only a handful of insurance companies active in the construction market and most of them are now very open to the needs of selfbuilders as well as the professionals. Quotation for construction projects is a complex area and you would do well to seek out the advice of an insurance broker before parting with cash, but expect to pay around 0.66% of the total project value to get all the cover you really need to build with a safety net. That translates at around £500-700 for a house such as our benchmark, four-bedroom detached house. Small builders pay much the same rate on their overall turnover. This would cover you for all the main areas that professional builders are supposed to cover, being employer's liability, public liability and all risks insurance, all summarised above. If you are selfbuilding, then these policies cease to have any validity once you have completed and so then you need to transfer to regular building and contents policies.

There are a number of specialist brokers selling policies to selfbuilders, most of them advertising in the selfbuild press. I have found DMS particularly helpful: they offer both a fast track, short term policy and a slow and steady build policy.

## Warranties

Most people have heard of the NHBC (the National Housebuilding Council) — usually because it's being attacked in yet another TV programme about bad housebuilding practices. But most people are only dimly aware that the NHBC is actually an insurance company and that the so-called NHBC guarantee is really nothing more than a latent defects policy. A what? If you buy a car or a computer, it is usual for it to come with a one year or two year guarantee, provided free of charge by the manufacturer. The new homes market once operated in exactly the same way but back in the 1930s depression, there was such a huge number of housebuilders going bust that the housebuying public lost all confidence in the guarantees being offered by individual builders. The housebuilders who remained in business decided to pool together the risk and the NHBC was born. It's really rather a peculiar organisation because it's part policeman, part arbitrator, part insurer and partly a club for housebuilders. The builders themselves pay the premiums (based on their turnover and their claims record) and sell it to the purchasers as a ten year guarantee. But it's not the same thing as buildings or contents insurance and many housebuyers have had cause to feel very poorly done by the NHBC policies when they finally get around to reading the small print and find out just how little is covered.

But over the past fifteen years there have been a lot of changes in this area. For a start there is some competition, principally from Zurich Municipal and latterly from the local authority building inspectors. And partly driven by this competition and also partly by wave after wave of bad publicity, the NHBC has substantially improved its terms of cover to include things like roof tiles and double glazing. And in 1998 the NHBC introduced a policy called Solo aimed specifically at selfbuilders. Zurich CustomBuild has been around for a lot longer and remains the market leader but we also have latent defects insurance from other sources as well now, including FE Wright and Trenwick Willis Corroon.

How do they work? Well any substantial piece of building work has to be inspected to insure it's been carried out correctly. This work is traditionally undertaken by your local authority's building inspectors. Initially you submit your plans which they scrutinise and often call for one or two amendments on. Then they carry out on site inspections to see if you are building what your plans suggest you should be building. Having satisfied themselves that you have carried out the building work correctly, you then get a completion certificate. If you are just building an extension, that is basically the end of the story. The NHBC warranty worked under a rather different system which used building inspectors to carry out random checks before issuing a completion certificate but now the two systems have overlapped and the distinction is becoming confused. The crucial difference between ordinary building control and a warranty scheme is that the latter is turned into an insurance policy which allows you to make a claim against the builder (or its insurance company) in the event of defects arising in the future. But of course you have to pay for this policy and, for selfbuilders, it's an expensive exercise — usually costing a little over £1000 per dwelling. You don't have to have it in place but you may well find your mortgage lenders insist on some form of warranty.

## Architect's Certificates

There is an alternative. If your job is being supervised by an architect (or in some cases a surveyor or a chartered builder), you can elect to have them issue progress (and completion) certificates throughout the job which say, in effect, that the work has been done to their satisfaction. Most lenders are more than happy to take the word of a suitably qualified (and insured) professional instead of a latent defects warranty such as NHBC or Zurich. However, your professional is unlikely to provide such a service for free and the overall cost may well end up being very similar to third party insurance.

There is a pitfall here too for the unwary. Your architect is not an insurance company and making a claim against an architect is no easy matter. If your double glazing (say) was to fail after five years you would have difficulty establishing whether this failure was down to poor design or to manufacturing defect. If you think the blame lies with your architect's design or supervision, you would then have to pursue the architect for compensation. Now it is part of a properly qualified architect's job to have Professional Indemnity (PI) insurance in place for just such eventualities so they can't just roll over and play dead the moment you get heavy, but what isn't often understood is that their insurance policy will cover their costs but not yours. And unless you have all costs awarded to you (which is extremely rare) then you are likely to end up with huge legal bills.

Another financial risk looming and, lo and behold, there is yet another policy available to cover this particular risk, although I only know of one such policy, the Selfbuild Legal Protection scheme. It will pay reasonable legal expenses for actions you might wish to take against a whole raft of characters over and beyond your architect: your main contractor, your subbies, your materials suppliers, even your solicitor. It costs about £125 and is valid for up to two years after you move in.

What if you are using a designer who doesn't carry PI insurance? Many very good house designers are not formally qualified and would find it very difficult to get PI cover. In these instances, your protection would lie in using one of the third party warranty providers instead. Once your plans are accepted by the likes of the NHBC or Zurich, then they are taking on responsibility for their outcome.

# Book-keeping

### Site Diary
Even if you loathe the thought of record keeping, do try and keep a site diary and write down a summary of every day's action:

- Weather
- What work was done
- Who was on site and how many hours they worked
- Quotations, orders, deliveries, shopping trips
- Payments made
- Contacts made, phone numbers
- Site visits by building inspectors, surveyors, etc.
- Comments, feedback from casual visitors, neighbours
- Accidents (however small), breakages, theft.

Not only does this provide a fascinating historical record, but a site diary has a more immediate benefit if a dispute arises; you have a written record of transactions as they occur. Whether you choose to work with or without a formal contract, a site diary will provide you with loads of unexpected ammunition should things ever turn nasty.

### Basic Accounts
What level of accounts you keep on a project like a selfbuilt house is very much up to you. Because you are able to reclaim VAT on most purchases going into a newly built house, it is a must to keep every VAT receipt that comes your way (I recommend a lever-arch file and a hole puncher for filing). When the time comes to make your claim, you will have to total all the figures, but whether it's worth keeping a running total of costs going whilst the job is in progress is doubtful. Running trading accounts with builder's merchants and plant hire shops can be a big help; not only is buying more convenient (and often cheaper) but just the fact that tax invoices get sent by post to your home address makes it much easier to keep tabs on paperwork. Trading accounts is a subject dealt with in greater length in Chapter 11 Shopping.

### Management Accounts
If money is tight then you should consider putting a lot more effort into job accounting. You need an early warning system in place to warn you when costs start to overshoot. The key to doing this is to split your whole project down into a number of little joblets such as Groundworks, External Masonry, Roofing, etc. Prepare a detailed budget for your house showing how much you expect to spend on each joblet and prepare a job schedule sheet showing how long each stage of the job should take. Analyse costs as they occur and use your site diary to estimate how much of each stage is completed each week.

You don't go into a project like building a new home without some sort of a budget. Sticking to the budget is obviously crucial to the success of the project, but in my experience you are more likely to come adrift through making an unrealistic budget in the first place rather than overspending on budgeted items. The other great budget breaker is the unavoidable extras (often to do with extra foundations or drains). There is only one safe way around this and that is to make a largish — say 5% — contingency sum available for such eventualities. If your budget doesn't stretch to this, then how about building a smaller house? The more loosely organised your management of the job is, the higher the chance there is of encountering unavoidable extras. No amount of clever management accounting will make up for an incomplete specification.

### Correspondence
Keep handy copies of all correspondence to do with your house from plot purchase to suppliers' terms. A lever-arch file with about ten subdividers should be sufficient. Don't forget that correspondence means keeping copies of your letters as well as ones received, so work out some system of making and keeping copies of your side.

### Literature
When you express any kind of an interest in building, you soon find yourself getting snowed under with mailshots for this, that or the other. Some of this is junk, some of it is incredibly useful, but you will need to be on the ball about organising it or you'll never be able to retrieve the useful bits when you need them. Again a subdivided lever-arch file is a real winner here, though you may need to invest in a heavy duty hole puncher (round about £25) to pierce the thicker tomes. In addition, get a pack of cardboard magazine files which you can use to hold really thick literature like you get from kit home suppliers and certain kitchen manufacturers.

# VAT

IMPORTANT NOTICE: VAT rates can change. Indeed they may well do during the lifespan of this edition. It only takes a single announcement in the House of Commons. This edition is based on the situation that applied in 2002: all prices mentioned in this book are VAT-free (unless otherwise stated). If there are major changes, they are likely to receive wide publicity but if you are not sure what has happened, you are advised to contact the VAT query line — 0845 0109000.

New housebuilding (and conversions of non-domestic property into homes) enjoy a privileged position in the UK VAT world. They are zero-rated. This means, in layman's terms, that you can reclaim almost all the VAT charged to you in the course of creating your new house. This is something of an anomaly. Since the introduction of VAT in 1983, almost all other building work has been standard-rated, which means that you cannot reclaim the VAT. The reason new housebuilding survives VAT-free is that VAT cannot be levied on second-hand house sales since such sales are private, and so it would be regarded as inequitable for new housebuilders to have to charge VAT on their product when 85% of all house sales escape it. Nevertheless, the imposition of VAT on new housebuilding is a possibility that all new housebuilders must face and it's recently come to the fore in the political debate about the future of housing. Change may well be on the way during the lifetime of this edition so that VAT reclaims may become a thing of the past. Having warned you of that, the changes in VAT rules for homebuilders recently have actually been pretty helpful. The definition of a non-domestic property was widened in 2001 to include anything that hadn't been lived in for ten years so conversions of all kinds of buildings into homes was brought into the zero-VAT net — prior to that they had to have been unoccupied since 1973. Gordon Brown also introduced a new 5% VAT band which applies to work on properties empty for more than three years and also to changing the number of living units in a building. This latter was presumably brought in to encourage builders to convert large houses into flats but it seems to equally well apply to people that want to turn a block of flats into a large house.

## Reclaiming VAT

So much for politics. Here follows an explanation of the VAT position in Great Britain as of 2002. The position varies depending on how you organise your construction. If you are a professional builder undertaking a spec build for the first time, it could hardly be simpler; you just reclaim the VAT inputs each quarter when you do your VAT returns. The only complexities come with certain costs where VAT is not reclaimable. More on these in a minute. For selfbuilders, Customs & Excise runs a special scheme called VAT refunds for DIY builders and converters. Really, this Claim Pack is a must have item unless of course you think the government deserves the money more than you do.

How you run a job has a bearing on the VAT situation. Design fees and professional services are not normally eligible for VAT refunds but if you start by appointing a builder who then subs out design and other fees, then it's all considered one design and build contract and you can reclaim all fees (provided the invoicing doesn't separate out the fees from the construction). It's called creative invoicing.

If you are taking on the project management yourself, there are quite a few groundrules you need to be aware of.

• You can't reclaim VAT from subcontractors for their labour. Make sure they don't charge VAT in the first place. Just to make things complicated, if the project you are undertaking is classed as a conversion not a new build, then you are able to reclaim VAT on labour, even though VAT on the labour is probably being charged at the reduced rate of 5%.

• You can only make one claim and this must be within 3 months of completion. Completion is not the same thing as occupation: they expect you may well occupy before technical completion but if the delay between the two is longer than six months then they become suspicious and will demand explanation. Tread cautiously here.

• All purchases you wish to reclaim the VAT on must be supported by valid VAT receipts, made out to you. A VAT receipt is one that includes the supplier's VAT No. (but doesn't necessarily separate out the VAT). Credit card slips, cheque stubs, delivery notes are not VAT receipts. Also Customs & Excise want to see the originals; they don't accept photocopies. Note also that if some of your material supplies are purchased through a subcontractor who is not VAT registered, you will not be able to reclaim VAT — the original invoice must be made out to you.

## What is Zero-rated?

As discussed already, recent changes in VAT rules have somewhat simplified the rules and made definitions of what can and cannot be zero-rated much easier to grasp. There are two areas to consider. Firstly how does the job as a whole stack up in the VAT reclaim stakes And secondly, which costs incurred can you reclaim? The first area has always been looked on as a minefield. If you are in doubt, you can get hold of the rules on the web at www.hmce.gov.uk where you want to get hold of two documents, VAT notice 708 (Buildings and Construction) and VAT information sheet 0501 (which explains the 2001 changes in a mere 11 pages). There are of course still grey areas — for instance what happens when you convert a pub which has a self-contained flat — but it's still simpler than it was. A bit.

Provided you can establish that your project is a new build, almost all the construction costs are eligible for zero-rating of VAT. That is to say, that suppliers who are knowingly supplying a zero-rated project should not add VAT to their invoices and if VAT is applied (currently at 17.5%) you should be able to reclaim it. The situation with conversions is subtly different. Here you are expected to pay VAT on all supplies, including labour albeit at a the new reduced rate of 5%. You can still reclaim using the DIY builders VAT refund system (snappily referred to in these circles as VAT notice 719)

As your house nears completion, you will find a number of items which Customs & Excise, in their wisdom, regard as fittings which lie outside the zero-rating net. If there is any ground rule at all it is that if the items are fixed into the building then they are zero-rated but if they are removable then you must pay the VAT. However, there are so many exceptions to this rule that it is necessary to run through the list. Again this whole area was reviewed in 1994 and many fixtures and fittings previously excluded from zero-rating are now allowed. I present the following list for general guidance only; your VAT office may view things differently to mine and please don't jump down my throat if you find you are unable to reclaim VAT on something I've said you can. It's your VAT office you should be arguing with and, if you're canny, you will do this before you start construction. VAT Notice 719 includes a similar list which you should refer to for the latest views from the VAT office.

Having tried to get myself off this particular hook, let's look at the current state of play. Personally, I find this catalogue of what's in and what's out ridiculous, and I'd be tempted to laugh at it if there wasn't so much damn money riding on it. Don't keep telling your VAT official that "This is crazy!"; they know it and they've heard it a thousand times before.

• KITCHENS: Fitted kitchens are zero-rated but white goods (cookers, washing machines, dishwashers, etc.) are not. There is no distinction made between integrated and freestanding equipment — you must pay VAT on them — so things like waste disposal units and water softeners are standard-rated. However there are some zero-rated appliances, most notably cooker hoods and built-in vacuum cleaners.

• AGAs: standard-rated except when they have an integral boiler; then they are regarded as part of the heating system and you can reclaim the VAT.

• FITTED CUPBOARDS: At present the ruling seems to be this — if you build the cupboards (i.e. fitting doors across alcoves formed in the walls) then it seems that you can reclaim the VAT on all the materials, but if you buy in fitted cupboards then you can't. If that's not clear then ask your VAT office.

• FLOORING: All forms of carpeting are standard rated. Everything else is zero-rated.

• HEATING / PLUMBING / SANITARY WARE: All zero-rated except water treatment units. Fireplaces are also zero-rated. Solar panels, heat recovery systems and air conditioning also qualify for zero-rating.

• ELECTRICS: All zero-rated. Light fittings should be OK provided they are fitted, but a zealous inspector may disagree.

• ALARMS: Both smoke alarms and burglar alarms are zero-rated. Also fire safety equipment is now zero-rated.

• FURNISHINGS: Movable furniture is invariably standard-rated. The status of fitted shelves is unclear. Curtains and blinds are standard-rated but you can reclaim VAT on curtain rails.

• DECORATING: Paint is zero-rated and you shouldn't have any problem with wallpaper. Also, if you want to have decorative finishes (like pine matchboarding) you should be able to reclaim the VAT.

• GARAGES and DRIVEWAYS: Zero-rated.

• LANDSCAPING: They will generally accept a limited amount of turfing and paving as zero-rated. However, trees, shrubs and plants will all be VATable.

• SWIMMING POOLS: Standard-rated unless it's inside a building which is at least

attached to the main house.
- OUTBUILDINGS/CONSERVATORIES: Detached outbuildings (except garages) are standard-rated. However, attached extensions like conservatories are zero-rated.
- PLANT HIRE, SCAFFOLDING: These are standard-rated items which you cannot reclaim, although note that scaffolding erection and dismantling is technically zero-rated whilst the hire is not. Therefore you can save money by getting your scaffolder to invoice separately for the two services.
- PROFESSIONAL FEES: standard-rated.

## End of the Party

A selfbuilder can only make one reclaim from the VAT office and so when it's done, it's done. This presents a major cashflow problem to many as there is usually several thousand pounds waiting to be reclaimed, several thousand pounds which most selfbuilders could well use to finish off their project; many end up forgoing further VAT reclaims in order to get their hands on this money before the house is complete. If you employ a VAT registered builder to construct your house this reclaim problem does not occur as the builder's invoices are zero-rated for all but the exempt items though note that you can still use the DIY reclaim scheme if you buy just the odd can of paint and a few curtain rails on your own account.

## Listed Buildings

If you think the list of what you can and can't reclaim VAT on has just a touch of the Alice in Wonderland about it, then Lewis Carroll must have gone into overdrive when dreaming up just how the tax should be applied to listed building work. The purpose of listing buildings is to preserve them so you might think that the Treasury might just help out a bit with repairs. But no, what actually happens is that alterations to listed buildings are zero-rated whilst repairs to them have VAT charged on them at the standard-rate. So there is a tax incentive to alter a listed building but none to keep one in good repair. Yes, I agree, it's an extraordinary state of affairs. Enter the creative specifier who can save 17.5% of the building costs with a nice turn of phrase!

Most major works on listed buildings involve a mix of repairs and alterations and the usual route taken is to agree a proportion of the two with Customs & Excise before work commences. If it's 60:40 alteration:repair, then they should allow you to charge (or be charged) VAT at 40% of the standard-rate. So if the total bill was, say, £100,000 net of VAT then you would be expected to pay just 40% of the standard VAT amount of £17,500.

## VAT in the EC

The VAT regimes for new housebuilding vary substantially around the EC. There is no such thing as zero-rating anywhere else (as far as I can establish). In the Republic of Ireland, VAT is collected at over 20% on all building materials though there is a tax break if you employ a registered builder on a new house — you pay VAT at 12.5% instead. But one piece of good news is that if you are undertaking zero-rated building in the UK you can reclaim VAT on materials purchased anywhere in the EC. This is particularly useful for selfbuilders in Northern Ireland who want to buy stuff from the Republic. Also note that there is an increasing cross-Channel trade in light goods which currently seem to be significantly cheaper in France and Belgium than in the UK. French DIY sheds Castorama and Leroy Merlin are now getting almost as many UK visitors as the wine warehouses (I'm exaggerating) and there is an IKEA in Lille which seems to be much cheaper than its UK counterparts. This arbitraging of building materials is something which may grind to a halt if (or is it when?) the UK joins the euro. But of course by that time we may no longer have zero-rated building supplies.

# Other Taxes

Whereas professionals and selfbuilders are on a level playing field when it comes to VAT, selfbuild really comes into its own when you start to look at other taxes. If you are building your one and only house, then you really don't have to pay any taxes at all on the profits you make. The two taxes which you might expect to get clobbered by are income tax and capital gains tax (CGT). If you are a professional, you will get caught by one of these two. Typically, income tax is levied on you if your livelihood involves building homes for sale and CGT cuts in if you buy and sell second homes or houses to let out. Here you would be expected to pay income tax on any rental income and CGT on any gains you make when you come to sell the house. However neither income tax nor CGT have ever been levied on 'your principal private residence' so any profits you make on your private homebuilding are consequently tax-free. Even if you sell off part of your garden for someone else to build a house, you don't pay any tax on the proceeds, although you can trip into the tax net if the garden area exceeds 0.5 hectares.

Now the selfbuilders' tax exempt status raises a few interesting possibilities. What if you

move into a house you have built, make it your 'principal private residence' and then sell it shortly afterwards? What if you step from one selfbuild house to another to another? Welcome to the world of the serial selfbuilder. It's actually a long established practice in the UK. I remember a builder doing exactly this in the Cambridgeshire village I grew up in. My parents bought a house off him in 1950. By the time we left the village when I was 13, he'd moved house about five times and was at work on yet another, all in the same village. Many small builders live a semi-nomadic, selfbuild lifestyle like this, interspersing regular work with the odd homebuilding or renovating project. As long as you establish each house as your 'principal private residence' you should be in the clear tax-wise, although there are signs that the Revenue is beginning to take an interest in this area. There is no published guidance on how long you have to stay in a house before it is accepted as your 'principal private residence' which would distinguish you from a commercial developer but 12 months is often quoted as a broadly acceptable period. The key point to establish isn't how long you live in a house but that the project wasn't undertaken with profit in

mind. "Private residence relief is not intended to relieve speculative gains," reads the Inland Revenue Help Sheet 283. "Relief is not therefore available where you acquire or spend money on your dwelling-house wholly or partly to realise a gain on its disposal." Ominous wording, if ever, especially as it could be applied to just about anyone who ever bought a house in Britain. It's worth bearing in mind. Although the number of people pursued for tax on their "speculative" profits on selfbuild is tiny, it would be as well not to make too much of a song and dance about how much money you may have made.

In reality, not that many people will keep on moving house and building and moving and building indefinitely. Whilst it's a great way to build up equity and reduce mortgages, it doesn't actually bring in any extra cash (unless you start trading down) and it's also pretty exhausting and doesn't fit easily into the requirements of family life. But it probably beats babysitting as a way of eeking out a little bit extra. Until such time as the property market decides to take another tumble…

# Chapter 6
# Groundworks

Groundworks is the term most often used to describe all the things that builders do beneath ground level. It's actually a hotch potch of different activities — excavation, drainage, service connections, concreting, some brickwork. It also conventionally includes the laying of the ground floor but I deal with that in the next chapter where ground floors can be more easily compared with upper floors. The advent of JCBs, readymix concrete and plastic drainware has taken a lot of the graft out of this part of building, but it still remains an exacting and potentially hazardous task. It is also incredibly messy, especially when there's rain about. Whilst neighbours will look on in horror as you recreate the battlefield of the Somme, you must shrug your shoulders and utter asinine comments like "You can't make an omelette without breaking eggs." Groundworks is really a question of getting from A to B as cheaply and easily as possible. There are many reasons for using something other than the standard solutions for your underground work, but all of them involve sorting out or avoiding problems, not increasing amenity value. This is not to say that the housebuilder does not face choices of how best to get the groundworks completed, but these choices are for the most part to do with ease, speed

and cost of installation. This chapter concentrates on these issues as well as taking a closer look at how some of the problems, outlined in Chapter 3 Pitfalls, are solved.

Given a straightforward site and a straightforward house design, the groundworks can progress with remarkable speed at a comparatively low cost. However, a problem site can easily double or even treble the base costs, so I cannot emphasise enough how important it is to thoroughly analyse the costs involved in just getting your house out of the ground. Groundworks is also one of the areas of housebuilding most prone to mistakes being made. The setting out of foundations and levels and the correct siting of drain terminals is not a job to be undertaken lightly; add a slope into the equation and you have a job to tax the most skilled surveyor. Yet the supervision of groundworking is often left to harassed digger drivers who "want to get on with it" and often barely refer to any plans that may have been drawn up. The horror stories that you occasionally hear of completed houses having to be taken down because they were put up in the wrong place are a testament to the consequences of rushed excavations. If you've never been involved in setting out foundations, you can sit back and laugh at the incompetence; not until

it's just you and a stroppy JCB driver do you begin to realise just how difficult it is and how easy it is to go badly wrong. Of all the areas of housebuilding, groundworks is the one that needs the most management and the best management. If you are a DIY project manager, this is the big one. Crack this and you will have no problems on down the line.

Most builders choose to subcontract all the groundworks but, whilst this makes it very much easier to navigate this stage, it is still vital to check that you are getting exactly what you asked for. You must check that the foundations are in the right place, that they are square, that they are at the right height (this last can be very difficult to measure). You must check that the access arrangements have been properly constructed, with falls going the right way. You must check that the drains and the services have been installed correctly. Your building inspector will provide some guidance and will be able to pinpoint errors and bad practice but building inspectors are not paid to be surveyors and they will have no idea if your trenches are off-square or in the wrong position. It is much harder to ferret out mistakes on groundworking than on later parts of the build but it is also usually much more expensive to rectify at a later date.

# Excavations

A flat site is a cheap site; clearing debris off the oversite will not take long and digging normal depth foundations for a four-bedroom house will take a JCB no more than a day. Note, however, that the crucial task of setting out the foundations on the ground has to be carried out after the undergrowth is stripped away. It's not a job to rush, especially if you are new to the game, and so you ideally want to leave a couple of days between site clearance and the start of excavation. The consequences of setting out in completely the wrong place are often disastrous.

Unless you are working in a confined area where mechanical plant cannot reach, then you will want to get hold of a JCB or some similar digger. Some builders have diggers and digger drivers in their armoury, but most just have contacts with guys who are self-employed and own their own machine. They tend to charge for travelling time so it's worth getting someone local and — depending on how busy they are — they often charge for a minimum of half a day even when they're only around for a couple of hours. But at around £150-£200/day for driver plus JCB, they can do the work of around ten to twenty men and therefore represent a bargain not to be sniffed at. They can also do a lot of damage. The one-man band digger drivers tend to be the most helpful, but they do like to get on with it. If you're not 100% on top of what's to be done then chances are that you'll get rushed into mistakes. Trench excavations happen remarkably quickly (at around 50m/day, enough for a 120m$^2$ house) and inexperienced groundwork managers will have their work cut out to keep up.

## Demolition Man?

If you've an existing structure to demolish, then you'll have a choice of taking it down slowly and salvaging materials or getting a machine to demolish it (which is not very green but it's far more exciting — one for the camcorder). I'd suggest that it is almost entirely dependent on the value of the salvaged materials. There are also health considerations whichever method you employ — watch out for asbestos, which was very common in much of the 20th century housing now being demolished.

## Muck Away

Charming expression for getting rid of the spoil. The topsoil is stripped off and stored on site for later use, but the subsoil is usually dumped somewhere else. Many digger drivers operate in tandem with a 15- or 20-tonne lorry and will have local dumping contacts. Alternatively, it is worth chasing up local landowners to see if they have any holes to fill. Subsoil taken out of the ground "bulks-up" at least 30% when piled in a heap (or on a lorry). This means that just under 12m$^3$ dug out of the ground will fill the 15m$^3$ space on a 20-tonne lorry. Some ground conditions, notably clay, bulk-up at much more than 30%: a 50% or even 60% bulk-up rate can be expected. Make sure if you get a quote per cubic metre whether you are dealing with muck in the ground or bulked-up on the lorry.

## Landfill Tax

Since 1996, a tax has been applied to muck away at a rate of £2/tonne if the spoil is classed as inert and up to a whopping £15/tonne if it has man-made detritus in it. The tax is paid when spoil is tipped at a licensed pit and it has had the effect of increasing the cost of a 20-tonne muck-away lorry from around £60/load to £100/load. Our benchmark house had around 45m$^3$ of muck taken away during the excavation stage and this will have resulted in a Landfill Tax bill of about £150, adding 25% to excavation costs.

Ouch. A stealth tax if ever there was.

All the more reason to find a friendly farmer with a hole to fill. Many builders are choosing to put all excavated spoil in the back garden, then compacting it with heavy machinery and placing topsoil back on top. It's an option to consider but it's just not possible on all sites.

On many sites you will be unable to get heavy plant like JCBs to the back of the house once you have completed the trench excavations. If you have plans for landscaping or drainage or even plan to build a swimming pool or a summer house at a later date, this may be your only opportunity to get the groundwork done quickly and cheaply and a change of plan or an oversight can have costly ramifications on down the line. Another area to sort out on day one is the site access; it pays to get your drive levelled and hardcored as early as possible.

## Summary

For more information about muck removal see the Hiring in Plant section in Chapter 12. In summary, look to pay between £10 and £15/m$^3$ bulked up — equivalent to £12-£20/m$^3$ in the ground — for excavation and removal of subsoil to a licensed tip.

# Pull down your home, couple told

**Doomed: The £250,000 house**

A COUPLE have been told their £250,000 retirement home must be pulled down because it was built in the wrong place.

Ken and Doreen Walker, both 65, were looking forward to years of peace in the four-bedroom brick and timber mansion with views over the Downs.

However, neighbours at Lindfield, near Haywards Heath, West Sussex, complained when they discovered that it had been put up 20ft away from the spot which had been proposed and cast a shadow over their homes.

When the case went to a public inquiry the inspector found against former businessman Mr Walker, who served on Haywards Heath planning committee and in 1992 was deputy major.

Fighting back tears, his wife, a retired primary school teacher, said: 'We made a terrible mistake and it's going to cost thousands.

'We had planned this as our little project for when we retired. We put our savings into building a dream home that our four daughters and their children would want to visit. We put the house up but set it further back from the road than was shown on the plans.

'It was only after the roof had been put on and tiled that neighbours complained. It's almost complete and everything has to be taken apart piece by piece.'

Mr Walker said: 'We cannot believe people can be so miserable-spirited to exaggerate out of all proportion what the loss of amenity was.'

But neighbours in Lyoth Lane were celebrating.

Fireman Dave Harding, 39, said: 'The house casts a large shadow over our property and stops the sun for everyone.'

Richard Walker, deputy director of planning at Mid-Sussex District Council said: 'If anybody fails to build in accordance with the approved plans they will always run the risk of incurring abortive expenditure.'

*Daily Mail August 1995. This story is getting a bit long in the tooth now but in never fails to put the wind up. Especially the types that want to "get on with it." Take care over your setting out.*

There are two competing techniques for laying house foundations on problem-free sites. One is to pour the minimum amount of concrete possible into the foundation trenches and then build upwards in brick or blockwork — known as traditional footings. The other system reverses this logic altogether and pours as much concrete as possible into the trench before starting on the bricklaying — this is usually called trenchfill. Note that when you are pouring concrete into clay soils, you will probably have to use the trenchfill method.

## Which is Best?

Both methods have pros and cons. The traditional method, laying footings below ground level, is cheap on materials but heavy on labour; it is also slower.

Our benchmark house uses trenchfill. Most professional developers do. They value the speed and comparative ease with which trenchfilling is done. What really tends to swing it for the trenchfillers is that a high proportion of the labour element goes into setting levels for the concrete to be poured to and that this work is the same whatever the concrete level. Add to this the fact that much of the graft of foundation pouring has been taken away by the increasing use of concrete pumps which do away with the need for barrowing, and you can see why trenchfill is tending to win out. A new development is the arrival of self placing concrete which finds its own level around a set of foundation trenches. This reduces the labour input still further and may do away with the use of pumps. The most widely available self placing concrete is RMC's Foundation Flow.

The depth and length of the trenches are not in your control, but the trench width is largely down to which bucket the JCB uses to dig with (the general choices being 450mm and 600mm wide). Using a 450mm wide bucket is going to reduce the amount of readymix used by a quarter (as well as reducing excavation costs) but it is not to be recommended to rookie builders. Cavity walls—generally now 300mm wide—sit uncomfortably on such a narrow trench; single skin masonry (as used in the garage) is obviously less of a problem, but the key factor in all this is accurate setting out of trenches. Unless you are an experienced surveyor, you really want to play safe and set trenches at 600mm wide, because not to do so is to risk not having square footings. This will end up costing you far more money than the few hundred quid (maximum) you may save through having narrow foundation trenches.

So is there still a case for traditional footings? Well, yes there is, particularly for selfbuilders. It is still marginally cheaper to build this

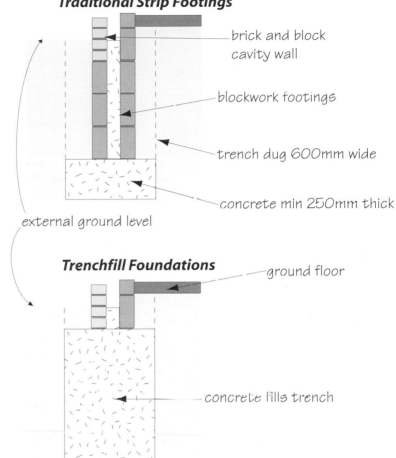

# Foundations

### Traditional Strip Footings

- brick and block cavity wall
- blockwork footings
- trench dug 600mm wide
- concrete min 250mm thick

external ground level

### Trenchfill Foundations

- ground floor
- concrete fills trench

way, even when compared to a house being done with all its trenches at 450mm width.

You can — and some people do — design a house so that it sits on a series of concrete pads rather than a continuous trench. It helps to have a relatively lightweight structure — timber frame is ideal— and you need an external skin that doesn't have to sit on the ground. It's much more of a fiddle setting it all up but it is possible to reduce the amount of foundation concrete used by around 70% when using pad foundations, though any cost saving here is likely to be clawed back in structure above. The post and beam Walter Segal houses tend to use pad foundations.

*The width of the foundation trenches follows the size of the digger buckets*

# Slopes, Bad Ground & Trees

If you have worked through the book to this point from Pitfalls you will have twigged that, though groundworks can work out to be very cheap, they can also turn into a budget crippling nightmare. Whether you have or haven't, the crucial groundworky bits went as follows:

There are three basic causes of alarming cost expansion:
- slopes
- bad ground
- trees.

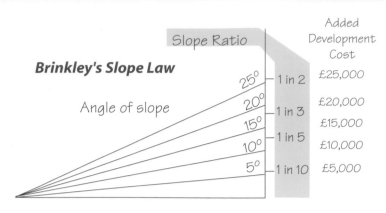

**Brinkley's Slope Law**

Angle of slope

Slope Ratio

Added Development Cost

| 25° | 1 in 2 | £25,000 |
| 20° | 1 in 3 | £20,000 |
| 15° | 1 in 5 | £15,000 |
| 10° | 1 in 5 | £10,000 |
| 5° | 1 in 10 | £5,000 |

## Slopes

Obviously, it all depends on how much it slopes, but even quite gentle slopes can create havoc with a tight budget. Brinkley's Slope Law, pictured right, states that, no matter how you deal with it, each 1° of slope will add £1000 to your development costs. Obviously this represents an enormous over-simplification of different situations but you will be disappointed to discover that it rarely works out less than this and sometimes it can be a whole lot more, especially if you are constructing a mansion larger than 200m². You just can't get away with building a sloping house and so adjustments have to be made between the lie of the land and the lie of your house and these adjustments are expensive. It's not just excavating out the ground so you can build on the level; if the slope is greater than 5°, there are complications with access roads and pavings, drains, and landscaping. Steeper still and you are likely to require retaining walls and possibly even safety railing. Faced with a sloping site, there are basically three options for the new housebuilder.

### Excavate and Cart Away

Here you dig large house-sized hole out of your slope, dispose of all the excavations and fit the house into the hole. This is perhaps the simplest and the one that the planners are likely to prefer, as it will keep your roofline low. There will be the cost of excavation and carting away which, depending on the lie of the ground, could easily cost £1000-£4000. Add to this the cost of any retaining walls that might have to be built: budget £100/lin.m for a 1m high retaining wall.

### Build Out From High Point

Here you substitute the cost of excavating with the cost of building supporting walls. There may not be much to choose between the two in cost terms, but this method is likely to leave you with expensive steps to build up to the back/front of the house. The overall

structure is also likely to be far more imposing and, consequently, much less likely to pass muster with the planners.

### Fit House To Slope.

Arrange the house as a series of steps, running up the slope. Building basements and/or mezzanine split levels may well be architecturally the most pleasing but it is also the most expensive. Split levels have cost implications at almost every stage of the building works: stepped foundations, shuttering for floor slabs, special stair joinery, complex service routes, complex roof details. Split level building adds 10—20% to your overall building costs.

Whichever method you choose to overcome the problems set by a sloping site, you will be faced with extra landscaping expenses — steps, turfed banks, rockeries. Although these costs can generally be deferred over a number of years, they will add significantly (£1000+) to the overall development costs. The extra thousands might well be better spent on building a semi-submerged basement.

## Bad Ground

A variety of problems are dealt with under the category of bad ground. The commonest are clay soils and the presence of tree roots, but also you must be prepared for bog conditions, mining subsidence, wells, water courses, old factory workings, disused refuse tips, even problems when ancient remains are discovered. It's worth carrying out any amount of detective work to ascertain exactly what has happened on your site because the ramifications can be expensive. A fairly recent new menace (or, rather, newly described menace) is radon, a naturally occurring radioactive gas, which is being found in more and more parts of the country.

A site appraisal is likely (but not definitely) going to uncover the problems you will meet below ground and your foundation design is almost definitely going to be in the hands of an engineer. There are three likely solutions to bad ground:
- Deeper foundations (sometimes reinforced with steel)
- Raft foundations
- Piling.

### Deeper Foundations

You will have to excavate to good bearing ground (if it's there). If it's just a question of going down to 2.5m, you may get away with the regular trenchfill foundation. But this will be expensive; on a four-bedroom house it will add around £300-£500 for every extra 100mm depth you have to dig down. If the ground is soft or wet (which is likely), then extra will have to be spent on shuttering and shoring. Deeper than 2m, it usually becomes cheaper (and/or easier) to specify one of the alternative foundation systems — i.e. rafts or piles. Trouble is if you are discovering how bad it all is as you dig, then it's realistically too late to switch to one of the alternative foundations systems.

### Clayboards

One technique commonly used in clay areas is to fit a collapsible board against the side of the trench, rather like lining paper on the side of a cake tin. The idea is that clayboard is flexible enough to allow the clay to heave without moving the enclosed concrete foundations. There are a number of dedicated products available for this application; the two best known are Claymaster which is made of polystyrene and Clayboard which uses a honeycomb filler very similar to that used in moulded doors.

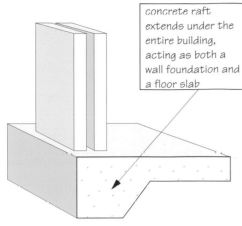

concrete raft extends under the entire building, acting as both a wall foundation and a floor slab

## Rafts

On a problem free site, the floor slab is laid a couple of stages further on than the foundations. However, with rafts, you pour the foundation concrete together with the floor slab concrete in one operation. With various cambered design profiles and a whole mass of steel reinforcement, you create a concrete raft which will move as one. If subsidence occurs, the raft will absorb the changes without imposing extra strains on the superstructure above.

A raft foundation uses vast amounts of concrete and, if one had been specified for the benchmark house and garage, it would have cost as much as £10,000 but, unlike the alternatives, it would provide you with a floor slab to build off. In effect, it's similar in price to piling or digging foundations greater than 2.5m, that is to say around £6,000 more than the bog standard solution.

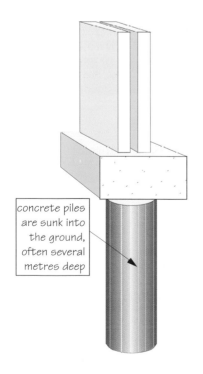

concrete piles are sunk into the ground, often several metres deep

## Piling

Reckoned to be cost effective in situations where foundations would otherwise have to be deeper than 2m. The number of piles and the depth of each pile can only be determined by a test pile being dug (budget £300), but a typical installation would place piles 2.5m apart under every load-bearing wall (including detached garages) and each pile would go down till solid ground was reached. All the piles are then filled with concrete and tied together with a concrete ground beam, which would be all that you would eventually see of the operation, and would look much like a regular trenchfill concrete foundation. Budget prices are £30/metre depth for individual piles (depth anywhere from 3-10m) and £60/lin.m for ground beams. A 5m depth piled foundation for the benchmark house and garage would cost around £8000, around £5,000 more than standard footings or trench fill on a non-problem site. There are various other techniques which can be used as an alternative to concrete piling or reinforced rafts but these are really the province of the specialist engineer. One interesting option is Abbey Pynford's Housedeck which is designed to be cost effective for single house developments; it's actually a floating or suspended raft which gives you a well insulated slab. Housedeck will typically cost between £10,000 and £15,000 for a 100m² footprint. Abbey Pynford's Phil Jones commented to me: "Our unit area rate gets lower as the footprint increases, up to about 250m². We are never going to be competitive with simple strip foundations but we find that Housedeck starts to make sense if you have to dig down more than 1.5 metres."

## Trees

There are two different ways in which trees may affect your development costs. One is visual; planners and neighbours may view the importance of your trees quite differently from you. The other is to do with the effect of tree roots on your foundations. A site with mature trees will tend to look immediately attractive but you should pay close attention to just where these trees are located in relation to your proposed foundations.

## Tree Roots

Tree root systems can spread a very long way from the trunks and they can suck water from even greater distances causing movement and shrinkage in soils, which is bad news for house foundations. The solution to this problem is not to cut down the offending trees — this can actually make the situation worse for up to ten years afterwards — but to have deeper foundations, or specialist ones. Both the NHBC and Zurich publish tables showing the foundation depth needed for differ-

ent tree species at varying distances but this is too technical in scope for this humble work: the summary table is designed to let you roughly gauge the affect on construction costs. There are four variables which determine the foundation depth when tree roots are present; these are:

* Shrinkability of the soil — clay soils are bad news
* Water demand from tree species: some species such as poplar, willow and elm, are very thirsty whereas others, such as beech and birch, have much less impact on your foundations.
* Mature height of tree species
* Distance of tree from foundations

The worst case scenario would be to have a tall and thirsty tree, located 7m (or less) from your foundations which are in clay. God help you! The NHBC would want you to dig foundations over 3m deep or use piles or rafts. And of course it would cost.

## Action

If your plot has any of these problems it will pay dividends to seek advice at survey stage. The person who would normally deal with such matters is a structural engineer, but if you are employing a designer to solve your problems, it would be as well not to engage another professional off your own bat; let the designer choose how (and who) best to overcome the difficulties. A possible source of free and impartial advice is your local building inspector. See Chapter 3 Pitfalls.

If there is good news in here it is that there is now effectively some sort of cap on the amount your foundation costs may grow. The new techniques coming on stream — especially piling and ground beams — are slowly but surely getting cheaper. If you have bad ground, your total groundworks costs (including laying of the ground floor) may well double from a base of around £70/m² footprint but they are unlikely to treble.

## Underpinning

If you are involved in restoring an existing structure, you may well have to strengthen the foundations, particularly if you are adding loads like extra floors. This conventionally involves digging out short sections under the existing foundations and infilling or underpinning with concrete. It's slow, laborious and expensive work. It's usually carried out under the supervision of an engineer and you should make sure that you have assessed the situation before embarking on the work. Allow £500/linear metre for underpinning.

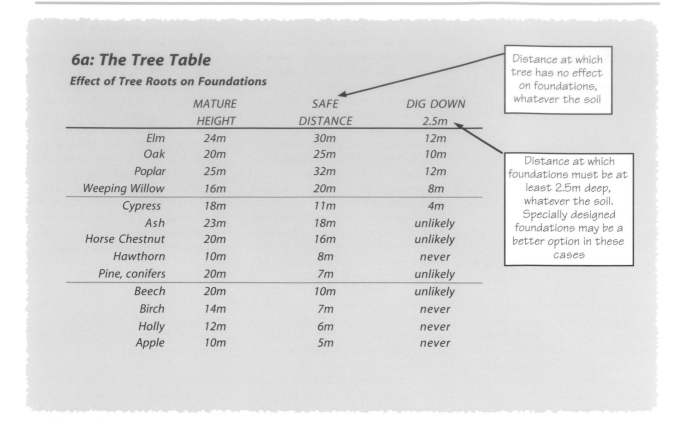

## 6a: The Tree Table

**Effect of Tree Roots on Foundations**

| | MATURE HEIGHT | SAFE DISTANCE | DIG DOWN 2.5m |
|---|---|---|---|
| Elm | 24m | 30m | 12m |
| Oak | 20m | 25m | 10m |
| Poplar | 25m | 32m | 12m |
| Weeping Willow | 16m | 20m | 8m |
| Cypress | 18m | 11m | 4m |
| Ash | 23m | 18m | unlikely |
| Horse Chestnut | 20m | 16m | unlikely |
| Hawthorn | 10m | 8m | never |
| Pine, conifers | 20m | 7m | unlikely |
| Beech | 20m | 10m | unlikely |
| Birch | 14m | 7m | never |
| Holly | 12m | 6m | never |
| Apple | 10m | 5m | never |

Distance at which tree has no effect on foundations, whatever the soil

Distance at which foundations must be at least 2.5m deep, whatever the soil. Specially designed foundations may be a better option in these cases

# Services

The service connections are an administrative heavyweight. The actual amount of work is often relatively small but it will usually take many hours sorting out just what goes where. Most of the utility companies have something like a New Homes Division which is what you need to get hold of; this will arrange site surveys and quotations for installation and also offer advice about the do's and don'ts. It is quite possible to lay drains and services in the same trench and this is usually the cheapest option – providing of course that your connections are all in the same direction.

## Water

New homes (and conversions of existing buildings) in England and Wales are almost always fitted with water meters which are themselves almost always fitted as near to the highway as possible – though there is a move afoot to start fitting internal water meters. The water company will usually put a temporary standpipe next to the meter which will enable you to have a water supply on site immediately and it is worth considering just where the meter is best located so as to avoid traffic.

You need to lay your water pipe at least 750mm below ground so as to avoid frost – and your water company will want to inspect this before you close the trench. If your main drain run goes more or less in the direction you want to go you can often lay it in the same trench. You don't have to duct it except where it comes through the foundations of the house; if you bring it up into the house against an outside wall or through a suspended floor, you need to lag the pipe with insulation as it comes up out of the ground (again to avoid frost damage). These days people tend to use alkathene (aka MDPE) for water mains and it will pay you to use a wide bore 25mm pipe (costs around £20/25m roll) if you are considering a mains pressure hot water system. Avoid underground joints at all cost — you are responsible for leaks on your side of the meter.

## Electricity

Included in your quotation for electricity supply will be (hopefully) enough plastic ducting for you to get from the local supply to your meter. The route you take between these two points is up to you but the ducting should be buried 450mm below ground level. These days the local electricity companies prefer you to locate your meter in a white plastic box, recessed into your wall; whilst convenient (allowing for meter reading when you are not at home), they are pretty ugly and if you haven't got anywhere you can hide them you can insist on an indoor meter.

It is very useful to have a temporary supply to site whilst construction is underway but you have to do a bit of construction work first to create a suitable housing for it. For more details, see section on Standard Electrics in Chapter 8.

## Gas

If you have a mains gas supply to lay, then you are usually best advised to install ducting (available free from British Gas) at the groundworks stage. You are conventionally aiming to get from the gas main to an external meter box which you can place pretty much where you please. British Gas supply a Semi-concealed meter box which is mostly buried in the ground and is much less obtrusive than the wall boxes. The incoming gas service pipe, which connects the gas main with your meter, should be buried at least 375mm below ground level.

## Telecoms, Cable

Both BT and the cable companies will supply plastic ducting for free. BT supply may be overhead in which case don't trouble yourself. My local cable company will supply ducting for their service even in areas which may not receive a supply for many years to come. The routes and the depths of these runs are up to you though note that they prefer their lines to come out of the ground on the outside wall of the house, rather than inside. Mains water, electricity, gas and telecoms are often laid in ducting which is laid across the site during the drain-laying excavations. The water company will want to inspect the ducting but the other services will let you fend for yourself, so you need to know exactly where you want them to run. Industry standards are to set electricity and gas mains at least 450mm below ground level.

## Infrastructure Charge

First introduced in England and Wales in 1990 to help pay for environmental improvements, these charges are raised by the local water companies and are additional to their already high connection fees. The infrastructure charge is nothing more or less than a tax on new building. It's applied to every new dwelling created — including flats converted from existing houses — and it is applied at the same level regardless of the size of the dwelling. Until 1994, water companies were free to set their own charges and — surprise, surprise — they tended to charge the earth (often over £1500) but then OFWAT, the water regulator, stepped in and set a ceiling for the infrastructure charges (£236 for water and an additional £236 for main drainage connections in 1999). In Scotland and N Ireland the situation is very different; there the water industry is still publicly owned and infrastructure charges are unheard of. The infrastructure charge is made up of two parts, a charge for water provision and a charge for sewage disposal. Each water company sets its own rate; if you dispose of your sewage by other means than connecting to the main drains, then you will be exempted from the sewage charge. Normally the infrastructure charge is not levied until the house is finished, but some water companies get around this by forcing you to pay an equivalent sum as a deposit before they will connect you up to the mains.

Despite OFWAT's success in limiting the scale of these charges, this sort of back-door tax (which loses few votes) is probably the coming thing and expect other similar charges to appear over the next few years. In America they are called impact fees and they get levied not just by utility companies but by the local councils as well to pay for roads, schools, etc. which the new development is deemed to need.

# Drains

First things first; it is important to understand the difference between foulwater and rainwater.

- FOULWATER is the waste generated by normal household usage — flushing loos, emptying baths and sinks, washing machines, dishwashers, etc. Foulwater is sometimes subdivided as black water (toilets) and grey water (most other outlets).
- RAINWATER, as its name suggests, is what falls out of the sky and flows down the gutters and downpipes from off the roof.

Generally our sewage systems are working at near capacity levels and therefore it is a standard requirement that rainwater is not added to the load. Hence it is normal to lay two separate drain systems to dispose of their respective wastes in different ways. In certain locations it may be possible to run rainwater into the main sewerage system (refer to your water company) but it would be unwise to assume that this is the case. You will need to prove that there is no alternative.

Our benchmark house has its foul drains running into the estate's main drains and thence out to the drains under the main road; its rainwater drains collect in a couple of soakaways either side of the house. This is the usual arrangement for UK housing.

Rainwater drains typically cost more to install than foulwater drains. Bear in mind that not only are there downpipes at every corner of the house, but there is a garage which also has to have its rainwater disposed of and this contributes to some very long drain runs. When planning rainwater drains it is sometimes possible to replace a relatively expensive underground drain run with a relatively cheap gutter run overhead. Alternatively, you can sometimes use a larger size of guttering, which will enable you to cut down on the number of downpipes and therefore the length of rainwater drains. But I digress; this stuff really belongs in the section on Rainwater — see Chapter 7 Superstructure.

## Where To?

In assessing the likely costs of any individual scheme there is one overriding question that must be answered at the outset. That is, "Where the hell am I going to dump all this crap?" There are other questions as well, notably: "How do I get it there?"; but "Where to?" is the BIG ONE. So, though it may seem illogical to start at the end, we'll look at the drainage options this way around.

All these dumping options are extremely variable from case to case. Table 6b indicates ballpark figures for many options but — I can't emphasise enough — you would be wise not to set too much store by these figures as they can often prove to be higher.

## Running into the Main Drains

Even a relatively simple mains drainage connection can be an expensive business. In England and Wales, you'll have to pay a sewage infrastructure charge — currently £236 — from which off-mains disposal is exempt. Locating main drains can be a problem; what records exist are held by the water companies and, whilst access is open to all, accuracy is not guaranteed. The amount of work in excavating and connecting to the main drain (usually referred to as "doing a road opening") can vary enormously depending on the depth of the drain, whether there are vacant junctions (known as laterals) already present to connect onto, the presence/absence of other utilities, and the attitudes and charges of local authorities and water companies. To open a public highway, you must contact the council highways department in order to purchase a road-opening permit (prices start from £300). Inspections of the opening and connection need to be carried out by a) your water company, b) your own building inspector and c) the council highways department, who inspect no less than five times to ensure the surface reinstatement is in order. A busy road may require traffic lights and if your main drain runs under the other side of the road, the whole process becomes very much more complicated. The water company is going to insist that you employ a competent groundworker to make

## 6b: Dumping Options

These figures do not include the costs of drain runs between house and dumping ground, only the costs of final dumping

### Foulwater

| | |
|---|---|
| Road Opening to Main Drains | Budget min. £2000 |
| add for Deep Drains/Complications | extra £2000 |
| add for Situation Needing Pump | extra £3000 |
| Septic Tank + Land Drains | Budget £3000+ |
| Mini Treatment Works | Budget £5000 + |
| Cesspool | Budget £4000 + |

### Rainwater

| | |
|---|---|
| Soakaway | Budget £100 per soakaway |
| Storm Drain Connection | Budget £300 |
| To Main Foul Drains | Budget £250 for interceptor |

the connection and therefore it is a sensible idea to get some quotes for this work before proceeding with the work.

### Backdrop Manholes

It is much cheaper, easier and safer to lay house drains at depths of between 600 and 1200mm below ground level. Normally, drains are best laid at gentle falls (around 1:80) and sharp inclines are discouraged. If your main drain level is way beneath your optimum house drain level, you will probably find it easiest to construct a backdrop manhole near your boundary line (cost £200-£400). A backdrop manhole works a bit like a waterfall: it's a sudden drop from one level to another and it requires special construction methods and access arrangements. Our benchmark house used a plastic version called a marscar bowl (£80 to buy).

### Pumps

If your main road drain is higher than your house drains you have the option of pumping the waste up hill. This is often done by building in a tank of some description, similar to a small septic tank (say, 2m deep and 1m in diameter) into which the house drains run, and fitting either a solid handling pump or a macerator or grinder pump. The macerator pump is the more expensive but allows the waste to be expelled in a 32 or 50mm pipe, which makes it a better bet for long distances. A control panel is placed somewhere indoors or in a weatherproof casing. Expensive though a pump is, it can be cost effective to install one when the main drain connection is further than 300m away even if it is downhill. This is because it can pump out into a 40mm pipe which can be laid in a flat trench, much reducing excavation costs. On the other hand, any system that works by gravity alone is ultimately preferable because it isn't going to break down.

Budget between £2000 and £4000 for making a road opening and maybe a further £3000 if you need a pumping station. Occasionally road openings can be done for less but don't count on it. However if your costs look like being any higher than this you should start to look at an off-mains drainage solution.

### Off-Mains Drainage

The simplest and the cheapest off-mains solution is usually to install a septic tank. It's a tried and tested method and there are millions of them in operation, dotted around the countryside. A septic tank is one of the simpler concepts to understand in the field of sewage treatment: it is an underground chamber (traditionally constructed of brick, more recently from concrete or GRP), into which your foul waste system empties. The septic tank first separates the solids from the liquids before carrying out a limited amount of bacterial treatment on the liquids which form by far the greater part of the waste. The solids collect at the bottom of the tank and need to be pumped out, usually annually, but the liquid (or liquor as it gets called in these circles) passes out of the septic tank to end up, conventionally, in a series of linear soakaways — called a leaching field — located downstream from the tank, probably underneath your lawn. Here the liquor soaks away into the subsoil. As waste water enters on one side of the tank, the semi-treated liquor overflows on the other side. There is no power needed, there are no moving parts and, as long as the solids at the bottom of the tank are regularly pumped out (or desludged), then the septic tank should give decades of trouble-free service. The cost of the tanks varies depending on the volumes they are designed to deal with but single household units are often priced between £400 and £600. Added to this is the cost of the groundworkers installing the tanks (often around £1500)

and the cost of excavating and installing a herringbone soakaway system — again depending on the volumes to be dealt with and also ground porosity. It would be wise to budget £3,000 to £5,000 for a new septic tank system.

However, in order to be able to install a septic tank, you need to convince your building inspector that the ground on which you are building is capable of actually absorbing the liquor and this you attempt to do by undertaking a porosity test, sometimes known as a percolation test. Carrying out such a test couldn't be simpler. You dig a hole in the ground, you fill it with water once and let it soak away: you fill it with water again and this second time you stand there with a stopwatch and note how long the water takes to drain away. The quicker it drains away, the more porous your subsoil. The length and complexity of your leaching field is determined by the time the water in the hole takes to soak away. If the water level takes longer than 15 minutes to fall 25mm, then you have a problem: your building inspector will tell you your subsoil is officially non-porous and you have to find some other method of disposing of the liquor.

This is where the Environment Agencies step in. For in most circumstances, especially if the ground is non-porous, there will be a ditch, a stream or a burn within striking dis-

*The Klargester Septic Tank*

tance of your property and if you clean your liquor to a higher standard than that achieved by a septic tank — which means using one of the systems described below — then you will be allowed to discharge it into this water course. But in order to do this, you need to apply for a Consent to Discharge.

## Consent to Discharge

In England and Wales, sewage disposal into water courses comes under the aegis of the Environment Agency (National number 08459 333111 — should be the only contact number you need but paperwork is done via local offices, listed in phone books under Environment Agency). A Consent to Discharge currently costs £94 (no VAT) if the plant is outputting less than 5m³/day — a typical single household discharges between 0.5 and 1 m³ per day so virtually all single households will discharge less than this amount. It can take up to four months to get an approval. You can start to install the plant but you can't discharge from it until you have the consent. It is often a condition for obtaining a consent that a service contract is taken out with the plant installers.

In Scotland, you need to contact the Scottish Environmental Protection Agency (SEPA) and in N Ireland it's the Environment Heritage Service. If you can't get away with a septic tank or don't have a water course to discharge into then your options are limited to having a cesspool.

## Cesspools

Sometimes confused with septic tanks, a cesspool is different because there is no outflow at all. Everything that empties into your cesspool has to be pumped out and removed from site. Whereas a septic tank or a treatment plant need be desludged perhaps once a year, a cesspool is likely to fill up every few weeks: tank desludging usually costs between £50 and £80 a time, so you can see that a cesspool is very expensive to keep on top of. They are also traditionally rather larger than septic tanks or treatment plants so that their installation cost is also pretty high. A cesspool is the option of last resort, only to be specified if every other avenue is closed. And the cesspool is not acceptable at all in Scotland.

## Package Treatment Plants

If you can obtain a consent, then the normal course of action is to install a small sewage treatment plant. There are around twenty businesses in the UK producing such plants suitable for single dwellings and they employ a wide variety of different technologies to achieve their aims. What they all have in common is that they are all designed to treat your foulwaste to such an extent that you will be

able to obtain a Consent to Discharge, so that the outflow can be run off into a nearby watercourse — in contrast, the outflow from a simple septic tank is unlikely to meet the required standards. In effect, a package treatment plant works rather like a super-charged septic tank and the outflow is measurably cleaner. The simpler plants use little more than an air pump whilst the unique Klargester Biodisc is designed around a series of rotating metal discs. And there is one, the Bio Bubble, which acts like a super-super-charged septic tank and eats the solids as well as the liquor and therefore doesn't need any desludging. What they all have in common is that they consume a certain amount of electrical power in order to work. This means that they also need looking after, to a much greater extent than a simple septic tank. Consequently, all the package treatment plant suppliers offer annual service contracts — indeed in order to obtain a Consent to Discharge into a watercourse, you have to sign a declaration confirming that you will pay annual charges. The cost of these service contracts vary between suppliers and also vary by region so it is important to be aware of these charges when comparing systems. Typical service contracts are currently costing between £80 and £150/annum — though note that these do not include desludging costs which are paid to the local council to remove solid wastes.

Not everyone will be installing an entirely new drainage system. Repairing or upgrading an existing septic tank is a commonly met problem. Many of the existing septic tank systems have been around for a long time and have been either poorly maintained or just become saturated — often the ground soakaway drains become blocked and the effluent going into the tank just backs up as if it was a cesspool. In situations like this it may be possible to reuse part of the old system — typically the original tank — and to bolt-on a smaller treatment plant downstream. If you have an existing septic tank that's not functioning as well as it should, then don't automatically assume that the whole system has to be replaced.

## Alternative options

There is a growing interest in alternative forms of sewage disposal. Some of these are seen as being greener than the conventional methods but it's a tag which many of the alternative practitioners themselves are reluctant to emphasise: most readily admit that there is a time and place for almost all the sewage systems on the market and it is often stretching things a bit far to make out a case that any one system is greener than another.

The best known of the alternative disposal systems is the use of reed beds (aka Constructed Wetland Sewage Systems). A reed bed system can be used to upgrade the effluent coming out of a tank so that it meets the same discharge standards as a package treatment plant and can, therefore, be discharged into a water course. Although it sounds very organic and natural, successful reed bed drainage involves a surprising amount of construction and no way is this a cheap option — installation costs are similar to a package treatment plant and you require an area the size of half a tennis court. And like a septic tank or package treatment plant, you still have to pump out the solids which are collected in a primary settlement tank. Reed beds also require some weekly maintenance so they tend to attract enthusiasts rather than the fit-and-forget brigade.

Reed bed treatment is now well accepted as a sewage treatment method and is now being specified on a large scale by some of our water companies. There are however other options, including the use of dry composting toilets. Increasingly, selfbuilders are turning their attention to the whole picture of water and waste management and seeking to combine aspects such as rainwater harvesting and grey water recycling with efficient treatment of sewage waste. Normally it is a principle of all foulwater drainage systems that rainwater should be disposed of separately: the problem being that whereas most sewage digestion systems need a steady supply of blackwater to keep working smoothly, rainfall has a habit of arriving in large quantities which can disrupt the workings of the sewage systems. However, if rainwater is being collected separately, it is usually used to flush toilets and this way the two systems can be effectively combined at one stage removed.

## Siting of Tanks

Any off-mains drainage system that uses a tank which needs desludging (and that includes most of the options) has to consider tanker access — 30 metres is reckoned to be the limit that a tanker's hose can extend to. In Scotland, tanks must be a minimum of 15m from the house. No minimum exists in England and Wales but if you have a sensitive nose you would do well to stick to the Scottish standards.

## Rainwater Disposal

### Soakaways

The normal destination of rainwater is a simple soakaway which is nothing more than a 1m deep hole in the ground, usually filled with free draining hardcore or brick rubble. Soakaways are conventionally sited 5m away from buildings, but the building inspector must be convinced that the water will percolate away. In heavy clay soils, for instance, a soakaway may not be appropriate and you may have to look at other ways of disposing of rainwater. Budget £50 if machine dug, £75 if hand dug.

### Storm Drains

Common in urban areas, rare in the country, they are actually designed to stop the roads flooding, but can sometimes be used for house rainwater. Budget £300 to make a connection to a storm drain. Storm drains are often over 100 years old and in a poor state of repair, and locating them can be a hit and miss affair. Typically, they are managed by the highways department of the local council (rather than the local water company) and they often flatly refuse to accept any additional rainwater discharge, even when it is obviously the best option. If you have well-honed negotiating skills, here is a good place to put them into practice

### Rainwater Into Main Drains

Attitudes to this vary from area to area, but nowhere is it encouraged. But when soakaways and storm drains are impracticable, this course will often be accepted as a last resort. There must be an interceptor between the two drain systems to prevent pongs coming back up the rainwater gullies.

### Rainwater Harvesting

The sensible Germans have for two decades now practised the art of saving rainwater for household use (rather than just spraying on the garden via a water butt). There are now a handful of businesses in the UK selling (mostly German) gear with which you can filter, collect and pump rainwater around the house for flushing loos. More information can be found on this in Chapter 10 Green Issues.

## Routes

This is the other major decision to be made when looking at drain runs. The idea is to get from the house to the final dumping point with as few bends as possible. Drains have a tendency to get blocked, so access is important at all but the gentlest bends, and access is expensive.

### Ballpark Drain Run Costs

Straight 110mm plastic drain runs can be machine excavated (to average depths), laid and buried for around £12/lin.m. The building inspector may allow you to have a few gentle radius bends on your drain runs, provided they don't prevent rodding — that is clearing future blockages with drain rods — but generally the accepted practice is to have access to the drains every time there is a bend. The addition of inspection chambers, gullies, rodding access, etc. ("fittings") more than doubles the basic metre rate for drain laying to between £20 and £25/lin.m — the cost of one manhole is equivalent to 10lin.m of straight drains. So the general idea is to plan your drain runs with as few bends as possible.

## Eight Drain Tips

### The Plans Need...

Drawings and specifications should include drain layout, invert levels (depths), junctions, inspection chambers and access (rodding) points.

### Plastic or Clay?

Although the trade is still split between using clay and plastic (uPVC) drainage, someone new to the game would do well to use plastic. There is little to choose between the systems on price but the plastic systems are more user friendly. There are six major players in this field and, underground at least, there is little to choose between them on quality or price. Osma are the market leaders and their installation guide tells you much of what you need to know about laying drains. They do a free (but slow) design service but you must know your main drain invert (drain depth) levels for it to be worthwhile.

### Buying Plastic Pipe

Plastic pipe is sold with heavy discounts off list price. A new house project should be able to get discounts of 30-40%. All the manufacturers produce guttering and internal waste fittings as well and, if you combine your order, you will have more muscle to negotiate better discounts.

### Excavation of Trenches

Drain trenches are normally 450mm wide (the width of a digger's narrow bucket). If drains are to run parallel and close to wall foundation trenches, then you will be doing yourself a favour if you can set the drains higher than the concrete in the adjacent trench — NB this won't work with trenchfilled foundations. Where this is not possible, drains will have to be concreted-in, whereas they are normally just bedded in pea shingle.

### Drain Sizes and Depths

100mm drain (the standard) is going to be adequate for all situations where there are less than five loos. There is no set depth, but less than 600mm and you may have to cover the pipe with paving slabs, deeper than 1200mm and you will have problems working. The optimum fall is 1:80 which is equivalent to 250mm on a 20m run. If you have to cope with gradients much steeper than this then take specialist advice, don't assume that drains will work just because they are going downhill.

### Pea Shingle

Plastic pipe should be bedded on pea shingle, which is a particularly fine grade of gravel. Allow one ton of pea shingle (cost £6 - £15/ton) for every 8lin.m of drain. When calculating excavation quantities, allow for 80% of excavated material to go back into the trenches once the pipes are laid.

### Rodding Access

It is good practice not to have to rod from inside the house, so try to give every waste point a direct run to a manhole rather than joining drain runs together under the house in the assumption that they can be rodded from above.

### Drains Under Driveways

Plastic drains less than 900mm deep under a driveway need a reinforced concrete capping. Note that clay drains only require capping when the depth is less than 450mm. Allow £5/lin.m extra for this, but note that it is a very useful place for excess Readymix to be dumped, which can effectively reduce price to near zero.

# Chapter 7
# Superstructure

*Superstructure is a long and pretentious word and I would like to use some funky Anglo-Saxon alternative, altogether more down-to-earth. Trouble is, I don't know one. Some use the term shell — as in "Putting up the Shell" — and perhaps this isn't bad, especially if you think of it in terms of sea shells, not egg shells. But, to confuse matters, the outer walls that make up the shell get referred to as skins or, sometimes, leaves; one suggests bodies, the other trees, neither eggs nor sea creatures. It all seems a bit of a mess; hence I'll stick with the term Superstructure. Definition? Well you have hopefully figured it out by now — it's all the above ground bits of a house up to but excluding the finishes and the wiring*

*and piping. Literally, the super (i.e.above) structure as opposed to the sub (i.e.below or under) structure. So in Superstructure we'll look at walls (as in inner and outer skins), doors and windows, roofs and all the fiddly bits that hold them together. Floors? As mentioned earlier, ground floors are normally considered as part of the substructural works whilst upper floors are regarded as superstructural. I'm abandoning tradition here in favour of ease of comparison and you'll find the entire floors section buried in this*

*chapter. If you buy a timber frame house kit, it's the superstructure that you are getting. Or at least part of the superstructure. The roof covers and the external wall finishes are left to you to sort out along with the substructural works and the finishes.*

# The Inner Skin

The inner skin refers to the structural, load-bearing part of the external walls. For many years that was just about all there was to it, but these days the requirements for insulation have made the decision of just how best to build the inner skin a complex and involved subject. Our benchmark house is built in brick and blockwork, the traditional and commonest form of house construction in England, Wales and Ireland; it is well understood and relatively cheap to construct and its only serious challenge, at least on single house sites, comes from timber frame.

## Cavities

The practice of building two separate walls separated by a cavity became widespread in the 1930s. It was introduced to combat the problem of damp internal walls. The original point of having a cavity was to keep it empty so that water could not cross between the outer and inner skin but since the 1970s we have become more concerned by heat loss and the cavity has started to be used as a convenient spot to stuff wads of insulation. Now you might think that these two alternative uses for a cavity are completely at odds with one another and essentially you'd be dead right. Yet bit by bit builders are learning that insulation and cavities are not an impossible marriage and many builders are now enthusiastically stuffing their cavities with all manner of insulants without suffering horrendous damp penetration problems. But an even greater number of housebuilders have continued to build homes with empty cavities; up till 2002, over half of all new homes in Britain were built this way — i.e. with no insulation in the cavity.

That all changed with the introduction of the new thermal standards in April 2002. Just how builders choose to achieve the new U value standards will appear in due course but if they stick to blockwork as the preferred material for inner skins, they are confronted with three basic options: fill the cavity with insulation, put insulation in the cavity but leave a gap (known as partial fill) or insulate on the inside of the wall.

### Cavity Fill Insulation

This is both cheap and easy to do — but you do lose your empty cavity. Cavity batts designed to completely fill the void between the walls — known as Full Fill — are invariably made out of one of the woolly insulators such as glass fibre or mineral wool; these are "wicked" (rhymes with licked) to stay rigid and are cut to fit in around cavity ties. An alternative would be to blow the insulation (either polystyrene beads or glass fibre) into the cavity after construction. The benchmark house was insulated this way with blown polystyrene; it is marginally more expensive but is a simpler operation. Cavity fill is becoming increasingly popular but the NHBC does not accept it anywhere in Scotland and also in a few other exposed locations outside Scotland.

### Partial Fill

Most of the regular insulation materials are available in formats designed to partially fill the cavity. The empty part of the cavity should be as wide as 50mm and here is the problem with this method: despite special "retaining" wall ties being available (which, at 25p each, actually cost more than the insulation), the wet Tuesday in February syndrome means that it is often extremely difficult for brickies to maintain a partially clear cavity. If you want a decent amount of insulation plus a 50mm cavity, your overall wall thickness is starting to blow up to 300mm plus, and this starts to eat a significant chunk out of your internal floor area. There may also be knock-on costs on foundations and lintels.

### Insulated Dry Lining

This method involves using plasterboard laminated to expanded polystyrene and sticking the whole thing on the room side (i.e. inside) of the inner skin wall. British Gypsum's version is called Thermal Board. In theory this is a good solution, but in practice it is rarely used because of a reluctance to "dot and dab" polystyrene to walls (some form of mechanical fixing system is needed, usually Nailable Plugs). It is also more expensive than setting insulation inside the cavity. Although it gets around the problem of having to partially fill the cavity wall (rarely successfully

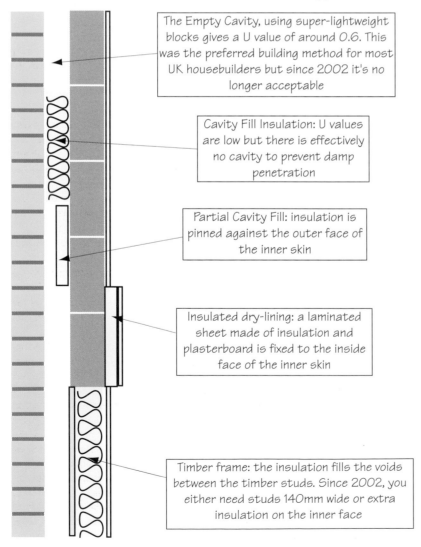

The Empty Cavity, using super-lightweight blocks gives a U value of around 0.6. This was the preferred building method for most UK housebuilders but since 2002 it's no longer acceptable

Cavity Fill Insulation: U values are low but there is effectively no cavity to prevent damp penetration

Partial Cavity Fill: insulation is pinned against the outer face of the inner skin

Insulated dry-lining: a laminated sheet made of insulation and plasterboard is fixed to the inside face of the inner skin

Timber frame: the insulation fills the voids between the timber studs. Since 2002, you either need studs 140mm wide or extra insulation on the inner face

## 7a: Cost Comparison of the 5 Main Walling Systems (all costs per m²)

| WALL SYSTEM | BRICKWORK | CAVITY TIES | INSULATION | INNER SKIN | INSULATION | PLASTER | TOTAL | COST ON 162m² BENCHMARK HOUSE |
|---|---|---|---|---|---|---|---|---|
| Cavity Fill | £38.00 | £0.50 | £3.00 | £14.00 | | £9.00 | **£ 65** | £10,500 |
| Partial Fill | £38.00 | 1.10 | 5.80 | 14.00 | | 9.00 | **£ 68** | £11,000 |
| Insulated Dry Lining | £38.00 | 0.50 | | 14.00 | 10.70 | 6.80 | **£ 70** | £11,300 |
| Super-lightweight Blocks | £38.00 | 0.50 | 4.50 | 17.40 | | 9.00 | **£ 69** | £11,100 |
| 140mm Timber Frame | £38.00 | 0.80 | | 23.50 | 6.30 | 9.00 | **£ 78** | £12,600 |

achieved), it leaves a number of cold bridges between floors and where internal walls meet external walls and this makes it hard to meet the 0.35 U value rating required for walls (let alone the 0.3 in Scotland). To get better insulation levels, you'd have to use a product like British Gypsum's Thermal Board Super, which uses a polyurethane substitute called phenolic foam: this however is very expensive at around £10.00/m².

### Super-Lightweight Blocks

For the past 20 years, super lightweight or aircrete blocks have been the No 1 choice for our professional housebuilders. Each manufacturer has different names for them — Thermalite's Turbo, Durox's Superblock, Celcon's Solar — but the idea remains to do for concrete what Aero did for chocolate. By introducing more and more air into the manufacturing process, the insulation capacity of the blocks increases until, hopefully, it's light enough to satisfy the U value requirements. However the new improved 2002 U values are just a bit too tight for these blocks, at least at widths that we are familiar with. In fact, Celcon's technical literature shows to get a U value down to 0.35, you have to add insulation somewhere; the only wall design they show that doesn't require any added insulation is the 350mm solid block which is a rather different animal to the usual ways we have of building cavity walls. Despite their popularity, these blocks are not without their critics; they do appear to settle more than conventional blocks which leads to surface cracking problems. But perhaps their main drawback is that they cost around 50-80% more than ordinary run-of-the-mill concrete blocks. Whilst most housebuilders felt this was a reasonable trade-off for not having to bother with dedicated wall insulation, now that this is no longer true aircrete may rapidly lose its allure.

However, the aircrete block makers have a reputation for innovation and they have recently been hitting us with a number of new products designed to address the thermal shortfall. Step forward thin-joint blockwork and solid masonry houses. Read about these in the next section, Alternative Skins.

### Timber Frame

Timber frame housebuilding is currently in a period of sustained growth. Over 60% of houses built in Scotland are timber frame and over the UK as a whole it has breached the 10% mark, many of these being selfbuilds. However, switching to timber frame requires a much greater leap of the imagination than just juggling figures. It doesn't have to be built off-site — but it usually is — and it involves different skills and expertise which tend to mark timber framers out as a race apart. Even the follow-on trades (plumbers, electricians, kitchen fitters, second-fix carpenters) have to rethink the way they go about things when the walls are made of studwork and the first floor is a structural element holding the whole building together. Lintel and wall ties change, and allowances for differential movement between brickwork outer skins and timber frames have to be built-in.

Whilst timber frame internal walls are cheaper to build than blockwork ones (£10/m² v £14/m²), when these walls become external and structural, as required for timber framing, they become more expensive because they usually have structural sheathing, breather paper and vapour barriers added; these combined more than double the cost of the basic studwork. The benchmark house has an external wall area of 172m² and an internal wall area of around 90m². Had AB Homes switched to timber frame, they would have saved around £500 on their internal walls but lost around three times as much on the externals.

Such sums are almost entirely hypothetical because what would actually happen is that they would get someone to quote to supply (and probably erect) the basic structure in a timber frame. There are a number of companies that perform this service, converting plans for brick and block houses into plans for timber frame houses and then quoting for manufacture and erection. Factory prefabrication is, however, relatively expensive and you would expect to pay between £2,000 and £5,000 more for such a service. The best known name in England and Wales doing this service is Taylor Lane. In Scotland, there are dozens of companies who supply whole house packages either working to their own designs or adapting others. In fact almost any timber frame company (there are currently around 70) will offer to convert a masonry designed house into a timber one. Check the selfbuild press for more contacts.

### Other Differences

• Wall ties: Timber frame requires a different shape of wall tie (Catnic's are called BT-2) and slightly more of them. They are more expensive to buy than blockwork wall ties (£25 for 100 instead of £10 for 100).
• Brick/timber frame lintels are about 35% cheaper than brick/block lintels, saving around £150 on the benchmark house.
• Perhaps the most significant extra cost comes from having to have the design proved by a structural engineer. Your building regs officer will require an HB353 certificate (HB210 in Scotland) which may well set you back £500/house, unless you are buying an off-the-peg design.
• Timber frame has always sold itself on being 'energy efficient,' largely because it's so easy to fill the voids with insulation. However the 2002 U value requirements mean that standard timber frame detail, as practised in the UK since the 70s, is no longer acceptable as it only gives a U value of around 0.4. Expect to see slight changes to the detailing, either wider walls or, more likely, more efficient insulation boards being used, typically the foam boards made by Kingspan and Celotex. Table 7a is priced on the wider, 140mm, wall option as opposed to the old 90mm standard.

# Alternative Skins

The previous section Inner Skin covers the two main building systems for UK housing. Needless to say, there are dozens of others and each year there is a steady trickle of pioneers doing something rather different. Some of these are definitely minority interests, others are gunning very much at the mainstream of housebuilding. I can't possibly hope to do any of them justice in such a short space so let's hope I manage to avoid any injustice.

## Green oak/post and beam

The traditional way, that is to say Tudor way, of building large timber houses was to erect a large post and beam skeleton (usually using oak) and then to hang the house off it. Post and beam housing has undergone a revival in recent years and it's used for both retro designs (Border Oak, Potton Heritage) and modern (Carpenter Woodland Oak, Huf Haus). It's also essentially the form you get when you take on a timber barn conversion. It's very good for creating large open plan spaces as you don't require structural walls. However, you do require an external weatherproof cladding. Here you have basically two options, infill between the posts or clad the entire structure. The infill technique used to be carried out with wattle and daub but today's insulation requirements rely on rather more hi-tech solutions. Attention has to be paid to the fact that green oak shrinks so that what starts out as a nice tightly fitting infill panel can work itself loose by year three. This is addressed by using flexible foam gaskets which expand to take up the slack.

## SIPS

SIPS stands for Structural Insulated Panels and they are the hottest thing in town at time of going to press. It's an American way of homebuilding that can best be described as timber frame without the timber. By laminating sheets of plywood or OSB around a core of insulation board, you get an incredibly strong building board which combines many of the qualities of plywood with great insulation values. Ideal for our new exacting U values? Many people think so, hence the excitement. SIPS are very flexible. You can turn up on site with a load of blank panels and simply cut window holes and door holes into them wherever you choose — only the widest openings require stiffening. You can also build roofs with them. Where they are not so clever is when it comes to jointing the panels together — lots of foam gets sprayed about on site — and they are still trying to figure out neat ways of running the services around SIPS walls.

Like many overnight sensations, SIPS have actually been around a while, in this case since the 1950s, but never really developed beyond the prototype level because they were too expensive to build compared to traditional methods. But in the early 90s, American post and beamers (known confusingly over there as timber framers) started to use SIPS to clad their newly built homes and this seems to have kick started the market. In North America there are a hundred or more producers and some developers have started using SIPS to build estates. In all, around 12,000 SIPS homes are being built each year across the Atlantic. To date developments in Britain are in their infancy but several small manufacturers have started to produce SIPS and, in 2001, Kingspan, one of our big insulation producers, acquired a small German system (Tek Haus). Perhaps even more significantly, one of our major housebuilders, Westbury Homes, who build around 4,000 new homes every year, opened a factory (Space 4) producing a SIPS style product for their walls and roofs which, in due course, they plan to roll out across much of their own homebuilding programme as well as offering it for sale to selfbuilders. Watch this space.

Actually before we leave SIPS, an honourable mention for Marshall's Panablok which is a panelised building system which is a sort of cross between SIPS and steel frame. It's been around for around ten years without ever having really taken off though it's currently found a little niche with people building blocks of flats.

## I beams

Timber I beams have become a common sight on British housebuilding sites. Being an engineered product (basically like a steel RSJ, only made of wood products), I beams are lightweight and stable and they don't shrink. Like SIPS, they are also comparatively strong. Where they have been getting used mostly is to replace conventional timber floor joists. But some people have been building whole houses out of them. A Hull-based company called Fillcrete has come up with an interesting design called Tradis which makes heavily insulated panels where the strength comes from Masonite I beams and the insulation from blown cellulose (aka recycled newspapers). It's not really as flexible as SIPS (you can't cut it up on site very easily) and it shares the same jointing problems but because of the strength of the I beams it can span huge distances which makes it suitable for applications like floors.

## Steel

In some parts of the world — notably Australia — steel-framed housing is big bananas. In Britain, its heyday came and went in the 1940s in the post war prefab boomlet. Since then, it's remained something of a curio.. There are two approaches, mirroring timber frame. You can have a post and beam structure (which is what most office buildings are) or you can build lightweight wall panels (which is where most of the house-

*SIPS panels can be easily adapted on site though a number of modified tools are required*

builder's interest is). Advocates reckon it's superior to timber frame in many ways — it's lightweight, it's fast, it's accurate — but it's mostly been aimed at the mass housing end of the spectrum. For several years, British Steel's (now known as Corus) Surebuild was the only game in town and they regularly produced about 1,000 homes a year from an antiquated plant in South Wales. For a couple of years, their supply simply couldn't keep up with demand as one or two of the plc housebuilders began to get interested. The situation is changing thanks to some new kit developed in Australia and New Zealand that allows you to cold press steel without having a huge plant — indeed one of the systems works from the back of a lorry with just three people needed to press the steel into channels and assemble it into frames. And Irish housebuilder, Fusion Homes, is planning to offer a bespoke steel housebuilding and erection service across the UK. Their design fuses insulation around a steel frame so that you end up with something not a hundred miles from a SIPS panel. Steel has traditionally only made much sense when you have an order for many identical units but the new CAD CAM techniques potentially change all that. Another space to watch.

## Pods and Prefabs

The past five years have seen renewed interest in prefabrication as a solution to our housing needs. Bathroom pods in particular are migrating from commercial office space into housing. They are assembled and finished in a factory and then craned into place on site, bolted into place and the plumbing is connected from the outside. Completely prefabricated dwellings are also back — steel-framed containers have been used to build hotels and MacDonalds for years and now innovative housing groups such as the Peabody Trust have started using them as well. However, neither pods nor prefabs are likely to be of the remotest interest to self builders or small developers because, to make economic sense, you have to replicate the work many times — opinions vary as to how much many consists of but it's not less than 30 and it may be as much as 100.

Timber and steel frame homes are conventionally supplied in what kitchen suppliers would call a flat pack state, wall and floor units ready to be assembled on site. In contrast, pods and prefab units are supplied as ready assembled units — indeed they tend to have as much work done in the factory as possible. Transportation thus becomes the limiting factor — you can't realistically transport anything which won't fit onto the back of a lorry.

Above: steel frame housing accounts for less than 1% of new homes in Britain but many predict a big future if production bottlenecks can be sorted. Below: Britain's No 1 PIF supplier is Beco Wallform. Here it is being used on a house near Banbury.

## PIFS

Another technique. Another acronym. Just to prove not all innovation is happening in the lightweight framing, this one uses polystyrene moulds and lots of concrete. PIFS stands for Permanent Insulated Forms. It's the approved British acronym but in North America they are known by a different one, ICF (Insulated Concrete Forms). Rather like SIPS, PIFS have taken off in North America where again they are reckoned to be building more than 10,000 homes each year using this technique. Unlike SIPS, it's originally a German idea — it's still widely used there as well though not in equivalent numbers to the USA and Canada. In the UK, by far the best known name is Beco Wallform, started in the early 90s by Robin Millar, who has built around 150 homes using this technique.

The idea behind PIFS is that you start with a delivery of hollow polystyrene blocks which you then stack up into a house shape. You stop at each floor and get lorry loads of readymix which you pour into the hollow walls. It's a variation on how concrete building work is usually carried out where you take down the formwork after the concrete has set. With PIFS the polystyrene acts as formwork for the concrete and then as insulation for the finished house - hence permanent formwork.

The polystyrene can be covered on the outside with polymer (flexible) renders; inside, however, there are many unusual techniques for fixing internal walls, frames and floor joists which would probably completely flummox the average British builder. And whilst the idea is engagingly simple, it's not without its problems as I've seen on site when the wet concrete sometimes bursts through the side of the polystyrene blocks.

## More concrete

PIFS are but one form of concrete housing. There are others. The Dutch are masters at building in concrete and they have developed a number of ways of industrialising the produced some stunning homes amazingly quickly and relatively cheaply. Good, quick and cheap? Heard that before somewhere? Well to date no one has even built an Airform house over here so how could we tell!

## Celcon's Jamera

Aircrete blocks have been briefly touched on in the last section about conventional inner skins. I expressed some doubts as to whether they would weather the new U value requirements. They insulate much better than conventional concrete or concrete blocks but they are frankly not a patch on the dedicated insulation materials like polystyrene and polyurethane. And because they cost more than ordinary blocks, there must be many people thinking "Oh we'll switch back to ordinary blocks and use insulation for the first time." Well, Celcon have an intriguing answer to this which, if it succeeds, will end up with us using about 15 times more aircrete than we have done. Jamera is a Finnish method of housebuilding — that's kinda warming in itself — that is based on building whole houses out of great planks and slabs of aircrete, often 350mm thick. You don't use any 'dedicated insulation', you just allow the thermal properties of solid blocks of aircrete to do their work. Jamera homes have walls, floors and roofs all constructed from nothing but aircrete. This may sound strange but it does have a lot going for it. For a start, it's made to very high tolerances so you don't (or shouldn't) end up with any awkward bits protruding or any gaps that need filling with foam. The wall blocks glue together with a thin-joint mortar not unlike tiling adhesive. The floor and roofing planks are tongue and grooved.

Celcon are deadly serious about Jamera and are about to go into production in a big way in Yorkshire. And several of the major housebuilders are chaffing at the bit here as well. Whereas they all profess immense interest in all the new techniques, deep down most of the English housebuilders love brick and block and Jamera is still blocks as they know them, albeit bloody big ones. I've seen a few thin-joint block sites and I've always been impressed by how clean they seem compared to conventional mortar based brickwork. The problems with Jamera come from the fact that you've lumbered yourself with a wall 350mm wide and you've still got to face it with something. Anyone for a 50mm cavity and some nice facing bricks? Not if it means a 450mm wide wall. But just when you think this idea is a non starter, the brick companies all appear to be developing brick slip veneers which give you a conventional brick facing just 33mm deep. In Finland, of course, they don't bother with bricks but just plaster or render everything.

## Others

Having been very traditional in our approach to homebuilding for decades, suddenly there has been an explosion of interest in how differently we might do it in future. All I've tried to do here is summarise some of the methods which are putting themselves across as mainstream alternatives. There are several more ethnic methods about which I know very little and can't really do much more than point you in the right direction.

Here are some useful contacts.

- Earth-sheltered or underground homes. These take the concept of a basement to its logical conclusion and build the entire house underground. Actually, more typically, earth is banked up on three sides so that you still end up with one wall of glass. However don't assume this is a natty way of avoiding the planners. Current contact via website www.besa-uk.org
- Centre for Earthen Architecture, University of Plymouth, Nottle Street, Plymouth (01752 233630). All things to do with building in cob and earth, increasingly of interest in restorations. Linda Watson runs courses and acts as an informal contact for other regional groups.
- Straw bale homes. A small phenomenon in North America, they have started to sprout in Britain and Ireland as well. Our best known straw bale builder is Barbara Jones who runs Amazon Nails. 01706 814696.
- Hemp? Architect Ralph Carpenter of Modece Architects is the man 01284 761141.
- Centre for Alternative Technology, Machynlleth, Powys (01654 702400). Mine of information, especially on timber and also straw bales. Wide number of residential courses on offer and good bookshop with details of all these and more.
- Construction Resources — a green builder's merchant specialising in unprocessed building materials (as well as many other things). 16 Great Guildford Street, London SE1 0HS (Tel. 0207 450 2211)

The one thing you will have noticed about this section is that I haven't mentioned any prices — not once. Most unlike Brinkley. There is a reason this. Most of these non-traditional techniques are expensive. Several of them are still in their infancy and haven't really sold enough for meaningful prices to develop. For instance at time of writing Kingspan are still importing their Tek Haus panels from Germany and Celcon their Jamera floor planks from Finland. Where prices have emerged, they tend to look high. For instance, the standard Beco Wall costs around £30/m$^2$ just for the insulation blocks. And SIPS panels are certainly no cheaper than conventional timber frame.

*At first glance this appears to be a normal house. Look closely and you can see the walls are made of straw. Straw bale homes are a fascinating if tiny niche.*

Reference to Table 7b: External Walling Costs shows that there isn't a great difference between the various options. It's hard to build an outer skin for less than £35/m$^2$ though it's not difficult to vastly increase this figure if you specify expensive materials and finishes. Before embarking on a look at what the regular options are, a word about mixing up walling materials, something that's become very popular with developers (though not with AB Homes, builders of our benchmark house, who stick with brick). Mixing materials invariably creates an extra layer of complexity and therefore adds to costs. Not only are different materials and trades being brought in for relatively smaller amounts of work, but junction details need to be built in as well. It's difficult to be too precise about this because every situation is different but bear in mind that simplicity helps if your primary aim is to hold down costs.

*Wimpey Homes, one of the UK's biggest housebuilders. Their product is typical in that it employs different exterior claddings, in this case brick and render.*

## Brick

In England it remains most people's first choice because it looks good — or at least it can look good — and it is the most durable of facings. There is an enormous choice and prices vary from as low as £150/1000 (for semi-industrial looking bricks) up to £800/1000 for hand crafted gems. Most developers stick to the ranges costing less than £250/1000 where there is a good choice of simulated handmade ones (like Ibstock's Bradgate range) which housebuyers appreciate.

Much of the trick with bricks is in getting the detailing right. A very ordinary brick can look stunning with the right windows and the right cill and coping details; equally, a beautiful brick can be rendered dull and flat in an uninspired elevation. Much of this depends on the skill of the designer but brick manufacturers are increasingly aware of this problem and now proffer advice on how to get the detailing looking good. The Victorians were masters at brick detailing and you only have to look closely at some of their buildings to realise what I am on about. It's an art which has been largely lost to us in this century but it is showing tentative signs of making a comeback.

A basic facing brick can be purchased and delivered direct to site for around £200/1000. Laying costs are around £300/1000 (it varies depending on where you are); allowing for cuts, wastage, ties and mortar makes a minimum price of around £40/m$^2$. By using a better quality brick — say at £500/1000, this price ups to £60/m$^2$.

### Buying Tips

If brick is your chosen facing material, then you may already have ideas about which brick you want. Indeed, the planners are quite likely to have tried to make the choice for you. However far you have got down this road, you would do well not to get fixed on a specific brick before you start chasing best prices because, given the range of bricks available, there is more than likely a very similar brick to the one you like at a much better price. Don't try to describe a brick to someone on the phone, take photos of the brickwork you like and send copies to your potential suppliers. In my experience, there is usually one supplier who tries significantly harder than the others and they usually come up with the best price too. But I should also point out there are one or two scams at work here as well — to find out more check the Bricks section in the Shopping chapter.

Note that the brick manufacturers are beginning to offer brick veneer systems for use with some of the wide wall designs which are appearing. Although you might think a thin brick slip would be cheaper than a full width brick, you'd be wrong.

### Render

Rendering is the expression most commonly used for an external plastered finish, a treatment which has been enjoying something of a return to fashion in contemporary house designs. In Scotland it's known as harling, and in Ireland it's never gone out of fashion. Two alternative techniques are used to get a rendered finish — rendering directly on to

blockwork or rendering on to metal lathing which is nailed on to battens. The first would normally be used on masonry-built houses, the second on timber frame. Pricewise there is little difference between the two systems.

### Decorative Render

A nearly lost art which is undergoing a small revival. The finish is rather like an upmarket artex applied to the face to enliven the outlook. In East Anglia it is known as pargetting and there are so few exponents that ballpark figures are meaningless.

### Pebble Dash

Uncommon on new build nowadays, pebble dashing involves throwing (or sometimes spraying) small stones into wet render to make a rough cast finish. Now perceived as downmarket, it costs little more than conventional smooth finished render. Rough Casting and Tyrolean finishes are two other variations on this theme.

## Timber

Plain timber boarding (sometimes known as clapboarding) is coming back into fashion with the increasing popularity of barn conversions. There are several different styles which you can use. Roughsawn timber (featheredge) looks more rustic; planed timber (shiplap) can look a shade more sophisticated. The most upmarket is cedar, widely used in N. America and with a potential lifespan of 60 years, but three times the price of regular shiplap. Shiplap itself is about £3/m$^2$ more expensive to buy than roughsawn featheredge but saves a large amount on

Shiplap

Half-timbering

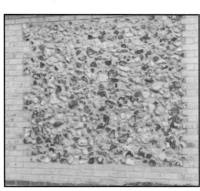

Brick noggins

Flint

Pargetting

decorating costs — sawn timber drinks wood stains by the gallon. Coupled with the waste which is bound to occur, stained external timber panelling usually costs less than brick, though the final outcome is heavily dependent on what you are attaching it to. Timber on timber frame is very cheap. It's much more expensive when you have to attach it to a second skin of blockwork in order to get enough insulation into the wall.

Incidentally, with all external timber, it is good practice to put at least one coat of paint or stain on the boards on the ground before fixing. Timber shrinks, and if the whole board is not covered with a uniform colour you will end up with 1-2mm flesh-coloured strips wherever boards overlap.

### Half-Timbered Tudor Look

This is usually achieved by planting 50x100mm or 50x125mm timber on to either a block work or timber frame backing. A typical gable would have between six and twelve verticals and two or three horizontals, plus framing around any windows. A simple arrangement such as this with planed timber would add around £8/m$^2$ (Mats £3 Lab £5). Complex patterns with distressed timber or oak could easily treble this figure. Further expense could be added by doing the infill panels in brick rather than cement render. This is a beautiful old technique (called brick noggins) and it can be carried out in several different ways. It is very time-consuming and it would only look good with interesting bricks and timber, so allow £60/m$^2$.

### Vertical Tiling

Using vertical tiling is another Victorian building feature that is coming back into fashion, particularly in SE England. Costs are very similar to plain tiles laid on roofs, although vertical hanging tends to be a little more expensive because there is more work involved in cutting corners, angles and around openings. Generally it looks best with small format plain tiles or slate and it is more important to select a good looking (i.e. expensive) tile for a wall than it is for a roof. Cedar, in the form of small tiles called shingles, also features as a wall cladding.

### Rubble Walls

If you know the right quarries this kind of walling material can be extremely cheap to buy, but it tends to be very time-consuming to lay. Traditionally rubble walling was independent of any backing materials, but now it is much cheaper to lay if it is set against a background of blockwork — which makes it a bit like very rough pebbledash. Each area

of the country has its own local "rubble" stones and seaside locations often tend to find theirs on the nearby beaches.

In East Anglia, flint is the usual material and prices vary enormously depending on how it is finished. Flint can be laid as wholestones — which gives a rough "agricultural" look — or it can be knapped, which involves breaking the stones open to reveal a shiny black inside which is then set as the facework. Wholestone is available for under £10/tonne, but knapped flint is three or four times this amount. Expect to pay around £6-10/m$^2$ for rough walling materials (inc. sand and cement) and around £80/m$^2$ for laying. As you can see from these prices, laying is slow. It is, however, not particularly difficult and it could well suit a DIY builder who has more time than money. You can now buy pre-finished flint blocks which take all the hard work out of it — you just lay them like a conventional block.

### Artificial Boards

There are many artificial materials which can be used to clad buildings although they tend to look a bit too industrial for most people's tastes. None of them cost under £20/m$^2$ and you'll be unlikely to gravitate towards them without the promptings of a keen designer. There are too many products to give anything like a comprehensive overview; here are details of three to give you a taste:

- uPVC is used as a substitute for timber cladding as well as fascias and soffits. It is sold in timber width strips but is usually available only in white. It has very little going for it except the promise of no maintenance.
- Eternit makes a glass fibre panelling called Glasell which is popular with some architects. It costs £25/m$^2$ to buy, including fixings, and is used as an alternative to cement rendering, often combined with the half-timbered look.
- Eternit also produce a fibre cement shiplap board called Weatherboard 50 which can be used as an alternative to timber.

### Stone

If you live in one of the so-called stone belts you may well have to build in stone to satisfy the local planners. You may actually want to build in stone — it's usually very attractive — but it's likely to be very much more expensive than the developer's standbys, brick and render.

There are basically three approaches: you can use real stone quarried out of some hillside, you can use reconstituted stone which is stone dust glued together with cement, or you can use stone cladding which gets stuck on the outside of cheaply erected blockwork.

## Natural Stone

Building stone tends to be a very local affair. It was, after all, hewn from quarries and, in the days before cheap transportation, could only be carried the shortest of distances. Many of these old stone quarries survive and supply the demands of the local construction trade. In some areas there are thriving second-hand markets in stone walling materials, yet nowhere is natural stone a cheap material. You may be given brownie points for using natural stone in your house — more likely the local planners will insist on it — but you'll probably be adding £10,000 to the overall cost. Civil Engineering Developments are a major stone factor and have depots and contacts all over the country.

## Reconstituted Stone

A cheaper alternative is to use a reconstituted stone. Marshalls and RMC Peakstone are two of the largest producers. Although, to the practised eye, reconstituted stone will never look as good as the real thing, it will cost about half as much and, if done well, looks as good as many of the cheaper bricks.

## Cladding

Stone cladding has got a reputation for being naff as hell, but this is because it's often associated with people who fix it to their brick terrace houses to "make a statement" (such as "I'm naff as hell"). Out of context like that it does look more than a touch ridiculous, but on a new house in a stone village chances are most casual passers-by would not even know it was stone cladding. However, artificial stone claddings are now virtually unobtainable and natural stone cladding is very expensive — it is unlikely to cost less than £50/m² — so if you are starting from scratch you might just as well use real stone.

## Glass

Certain designs call for lots of glass, so much that you have to start thinking in terms of glazed walls rather than large windows. In the accompanying table, I've costed up for a screen wall of sliding patio doors and fanlights, the sort of thing you might use around a swimming pool or a conservatory. The glass has to be suitably energy efficient to meet the new building regs and on the surface it appears to be an amazingly expensive walling option even when you take into account the low fixing costs and the reduction in costs from not having to build an inner skin. There is a basic costing law at work here. Windows cost twice as much as the walls they sit in.

## Porches and Bays

Thus far I've been looking at exterior finishes but there is, of course, much more to the external design of a house than just the mate-

## Table 7b: External walling Costs

| | BASIC MATERIALS | ACCESSORIES | LABOUR | PAINTS or STAINS | LABOUR on TIMBER FRAME | LABOUR on 2nd BLOCKWORK SKIN | EXTERNAL INSULATION | TOTAL COST/M² | COST ON TEST HOUSE |
|---|---|---|---|---|---|---|---|---|---|
| Cheap Brick @ £250/k | £17.00 | £2.00 | £20.00 | n/a | n/a | n/a | n/a | £39 | £5,900 |
| ExpensiveBrick @ £500/k | 34.00 | 2.00 | 20.00 | n/a | n/a | n/a | n/a | £56 | £8,400 |
| Render on 2nd Blockwork Skin | 4.00 | n/a | 12.00 | 1.00 | n/a | 4.00 | n/a | £35 | £5,300 |
| Render on Timber Frame lathing | 4.00 | n/a | 12.00 | 1.00 | 4.00 | n/a | n/a | £39 | £5,900 |
| Render on External Insulation | 4.00 | n/a | 12.00 | 1.00 | n/a | n/a | 15.00 | £36 | £5,400 |
| extra for Half Timber effect | 3.00 | n/a | 6.00 | n/a | n/a | n/a | n/a | £9 | £1,400 |
| Sawn board on 2nd Blockwork skin | 7.00 | 3.00 | 12.00 | 4.00 | n/a | 8.00 | n/a | £48 | £7,200 |
| Sawr board on Timber Frame | 7.00 | 3.00 | 12.00 | 4.00 | 8.00 | 0.00 | n/a | £34 | £5,100 |
| extra for Planed Shiplap | 3.00 | n/a | n/a | n/a | n/a | n/a | n/a | £3 | £500 |
| extra for Artificial panelling | 18.00 | n/a | -5.00 | -4.00 | -8.00 | n/a | n/a | £1 | £200 |
| Tiles hung on 2nd Skin Blockwork | 17.00 | 7.00 | 18.00 | n/a | n/a | 14.00 | n/a | £56 | £8,400 |
| Tiles hung on Timber Frame | 17.00 | 7.00 | 18.00 | n/a | 14.00 | 0.00 | n/a | £42 | £6,300 |
| extra for Handmade Tiles @ £700/k | 25.00 | n/a | 18.00 | n/a | n/a | n/a | n/a | £25 | £3,800 |
| Rubble Walling/Flint on 2nd Skin Blockwork | 10.00 | 4.00 | 80.00 | n/a | n/a | n/a | n/a | £110 | £16,500 |
| Reconstituted Stone | 15.00 | 2.00 | 40.00 | n/a | n/a | n/a | n/a | £57 | £8,550 |
| Natural LimeStone | 35.00 | 2.00 | 60.00 | n/a | n/a | n/a | 14.00 | £97 | £14,600 |
| extra for quoins, stone cills and lintels | 13.00 | n/a | n/a | n/a | n/a | n/a | n/a | £13 | £2,000 |
| Glazed Patio Door Walls | 170.00 | 5.00 | 10.00 | n/a | n/a | n/a | -14.00 | £170 | £25,500 |

*This costings table is complicated. The reason being that you can't just look at the cost of the facing material, you have to also look at the cost of what it gets fixed onto. In the case of brick this is ignored because a brick skin is self supporting. But render, timber and tile hung facings need either an extra block wall or a timber frame background. This makes timber frame a much cheaper option as the support wall is built-in. Except in the example of render where additional costs are incurred (Renderlath) and/or the alternative option of external insulation is also an option. As I said, it's complicated.*

*A stone facade never fails to attract and confident developers sometimes build with natural stone. This one was built by Prowting Homes, one of just two major housebuilders to experience a dramatic profits decline in 2002. And subsequently, they were taken over by Westbury, the SIPS builders.*

## Cills, Arches

One of the classiest effects you can get on external facades is to use feature lintels above and cills below your openings. There are a number of options for doing this. The cills and lintels can be formed from special bricks or made on site with a granite and cement mixture, which is fine if they get painted afterwards. Another variation is to have reconstituted stone ones made up in a workshop: this is the most expensive option (see Table 7b) but also probably the most attractive.

Insetting joinery into the facade is not a merely decorative process. By its very nature it helps to protect windows and doors from the worst of the weather, and the building regulations acknowledge this by making recessed joinery compulsory in Scotland and in many exposed parts of the rest of the country.

## Don't Ruin It

Having gone to all that trouble to get good-looking materials correctly proportioned, it is worth taking on board a cautionary word about the effect of those little elements which can ruin the overall effect — like a wart on the face of a much loved friend (shouldn't that have been a carbuncle? Ed.). Whether you go for period charm or ultra-modernism really makes no difference, just think about the details — remember the devil is in the details. Here are a few style tips:

- Rainwater downpipes — the fewer the better
- Plastic meter boxes — hide them round the side
- Security floodlighting — don't point it straight at people walking towards it
- Alarm bells — potential burglars will still see them on a side wall
- Satellite dishes — they can sometimes go out in the garden.

rials used. Features like bay windows and porches have been coming right back into fashion despite the fact that they are expensive to build. It's quite hard to separate out how much extra these features cost because they tend to get lost in the whole job costings. A bay window, for instance, involves minor additions to almost every aspect of the construction — excavations, foundations, flooring, brickwork, joinery, roofing, guttering, carpentry and decorating (to name just nine). Individually these changes are not great but added together I estimate that a two-storey bay may add as much as 3% to the costs of erecting the house superstructure. For an area less than 3m² that's expensive — getting on for double the amount spent on ordinary living space.

Porches are easier to quantify, although bear in mind that the standard of construction varies enormously from something little more than a rain shelter to what amounts to a mini-extension. Being (usually) rectangular in shape, porches are not appreciably more expensive to construct than the main structure, but bear in mind that any complications that might ensue will end up taking a disproportionate amount of supervision time. One recent development is companies producing GRP bolt-on porches and bay window canopies; it's proved to be a big hit with developers. One company, Storm King, produce a whole range of architectural conceits such as pseudo-lead infill panels and clock towers. Their bolt-on porches start at just over £100.

*A glass walled house (designed by Jonathan Ellis-Miller) built at Milton Keynes FutureWorld in 1995*

All materials insulate to a greater or lesser extent — see section on U values in Chapter 13 — but only since the 1970s have we seen the widespread adoption of materials that do very little else except insulate. By and large, these materials are not prohibitively expensive and most will pay for themselves — in terms of reduced heating costs — within a few years. So whilst you could design your home to avoid using insulation wherever possible, there would be very little point in doing so.

## Material Choices

There are several materials available to insulate housing. All have pros and cons and not all are suitable in every application; mostly they are available in a number of different formats — often in combination with other materials like chipboard and plasterboard — which makes describing them all extremely complicated. The basics are as follows:

### Fibreglass

Cheap, reasonably good insulator. Excellent when laid flat in lofts but when placed in walls it will sag. But help is at hand: it can be "wicked" which stiffens it up and allows it to be placed into wall cavities without risk of sagging or, as they say in insulation speak, to "perform well in the vertical." Here they tend to get referred to as batts as in cavity batts or timber frame batts. Although nearly double the price of unwicked quilts, they are still good value compared to other materials.

### Mineral Wool

Production is dominated by Rockwool. In most ways it performs very similarly to fibreglass and can also be wicked to perform well in the vertical. However, Rockwool is noticeably superior to fibreglass (and almost all other insulation materials) in terms of fire resistance. It is usually priced to compete with fibreglass though sometimes it is 5-10% more. The current U value requirements for flat ceiling areas is 0.16 which requires at least 250mm of fibreglass or mineral wool. For many people that seems excessive but it still pays for itself within a few years.

### Expanded Polystyrene

It gets used in buildings in two formats. The first is as a vast amorphous mass of little white beads which get blown into cavity walls from lorries. The second is in rigid boards; here two brands dominate, Jablite and Kaycell — it is often referred to by builders as Jablite. It performs very similarly to fibreglass and mineral wool in terms of insulation capabili-

ties (but not fire protection) and is similarly cheaply priced. Used widely in cavity wall construction (in both formats) and underfloor insulation (where the regs now require around 100mm of EPS). It is much the cheapest material when you are having to build with a partial cavity fill.

### Extruded Polystyrene

This is a different version of polystyrene which is much denser and much stronger — expanded polystyrene sheets are notoriously brittle. In terms of insulation capabilities it lies midway between polyurethane and the much cheaper alternatives, but its big selling point is that it is resistant to water penetration. Again, production is dominated by two businesses, both American, Dow Chemicals (who make Styrofoam) and Owens Corning (Polyfoam). Drawback? Price. It's even more expensive than the polyurethanes (see below).

### Polyurethane

The most efficient of the main insulators on the market, it is usually sold in rigid sheet format, usually foil backed. However, it is pricey even if you buy second hand, where a company called Seconds & Co. is busy. The domestic market is dominated by two manufacturers, Celotex and Kingspan. A big problem with polyurethane has been that its production involved the use of CFCs, now implicated in the demise of the ozone layer and therefore environmentally incorrect. This has led the manufacturers on a frantic search to find ways of making their boards with a different blowing agent and it has produced a range of similar insulation boards made with either polyisocyanurate foam or phenolic foam. In terms of performance they are both very similar to the older polyurethanes. Despite their cost, polyurethane (and substitutes) are being increasingly specified because their superior performance as insulators means that they are space efficient — in that you can get the desired insulation levels from a thinner sheet — and that means there are sometimes reductions in other construction costs. Basically these boards are twice as good but three times the cost.

Another application for the polyurethanes is to get blown into cavities and increasingly under old roofs to keep them going a bit longer. It's expensive and traditionalists howl with indignation when they see this being done. But it works.

### Cellulose Fibre

This is sometimes promoted as a green alternative to the other materials. For a start, it's made from recycled newspapers (so that's where they go) and it can also be used in timber frame walls without a vapour barrier which is reckoned — by some — to be an advantage. It has one major disadvantage in that it is not available in a sheet form so it has to be blown in by specialists. There is one main manufacturer in the UK, Exel Industries, who market their product as Warmcel.

### Radiant Heat Barriers

There is a relatively new group of insulation materials which work on the Bacofoil-behind the Radiator principle. That is to say they have shiny reflective barriers which bounce the heat back into the room. There are three, Actis (from France), Alreflex 2L2 (from Holland) and Airtec (British) which have some body to them and therefore tend to act like conventional insulation; there is a fourth, Thermo-Brite (from the USA) which is no more than a thin reflective sheet and which claims to reflect 95% of radiant heat, in a similar manner to Low-e glass. Whilst they have all passed tests to demonstrate that they work, industry sceptics cast doubt on what will happen to them if (or is it when) their coats lose their shiny surfaces. In any event, they mostly cost around £8-10/m² so they can hardly be seen as cheap substitutes for conventional insulation. They are particularly useful where you haven't much space. Although I really don't understand exactly how they work, feedback from users has been pretty positive. So perhaps we should put skepticism to one side and enjoy.

### Buying Tips

Generally the best place to buy insulation materials is from the insulation specialists. Sheffield Insulation (SIG) and Encon are the best known national distributors but there are numerous local ones listed in Yellow Pages under Insulation Materials. Some of the Insulation Installers are worth checking out for supply only. The supply and fix services offered are often a good deal; it is hard to beat them on price (or speed) except where you are not paying for site labour.

## Vapour Barriers

Insulation works by trapping air within its body. To continue to work well, the insulation needs to remain dry and, because of this, it has become a common practice in timber frame housing to fit a vapour barrier on the warm (room) side of the insulation layers.

## 7c: Insulation Guide Prices

> Thermal conductivity = the effectivness of each material as an insulator. The lower the number, the better it insulates

> Bangs per Buck simply divides the Thermal Conductivity by the Price to give an indication of how much insulation you get for your money. The higher the figure here, the more cost effective the insulation is.

All prices/m²

supplied and fixed

| MATERIAL | Thermal Conductivity | 25mm | 38mm | 50mm | 75mm | 90mm | 100mm | 140mm | 200mm | BANGS PER BUCK |
|---|---|---|---|---|---|---|---|---|---|---|
| Mineral Wool/Fibreglass Quilt | 0.042 | | | | | | £1.40 | | £2.80 | 1.70 |
| Full Fill Cavity Batts (Glass/Wool) | 0.038 | | | £1.50 | £2.25 | | £3.00 | | | 0.88 |
| Expanded Polystyrene (Jablite) | 0.040 | | | £2.40 | £3.50 | | £4.60 | | | 0.52 |
| Blown Fibre | 0.037 | | | | | | £6.00 | | | 0.45 |
| Timber Frame Batts | 0.038 | | | | | £2.50 | | £4.30 | | 0.95 |
| Styrofoam/Polyfoam | 0.030 | | £6.00 | £7.80 | | | £15.00 | | | 0.21 |
| Kingspan/Celotex | 0.025 | | £4.50 | £5.80 | | | £11.00 | | | 0.34 |
| Vermiculite | 0.075 | | | | | | £7.00 | | | 0.19 |
| Sound Deadening Quilt | n/a | | | £7.00 | | | | | | n/a |

*STANDARD THICKNESSES*

This vapour barrier (fancy title for polythene sheeting) stops condensation occurring within the insulation which would cause the insulation to hold water and thereby cease to be effective as an insulator. Vapour barriers were a technical hot potato back in 1983 when an infamous World In Action programme did for timber frame construction what BSE has done for beef sales; the programme claimed that badly installed vapour barriers were leading to "Big Problems" with timber frame building which was, at the time, catching on in a big way in England. Most leading developers immediately dropped timber frame construction methods because — even though at the time the veracity of the accusations was doubted — they couldn't afford to be selling a product which had a question mark over it. Twenty years on, timber frame has still not recovered its position in the English market and yet the debate about vapour barriers has long since died down. The fact that they are not always installed with the thoroughness they deserve is now seen as a bit of a red herring; indeed research coming out of North America is beginning to suggest that the important thing to build in is an air barrier, subtly different to a vapour barrier. It's a highly technical issue which lies beyond the scope of this book

### Cold Bridging

Cold bridging is what happens when parts of your insulated shell is interrupted by things that don't insulate very well. What on earth am I talking about? The returns where cavity walls join around window and door openings are the best known example but there are many others. The timber studs in a timber frame wall or the rafters in a roof, the edge of a floor where it meets the foundation walls. All effectively leak heat rather faster than their better insulated surroundings. Even things like steel wall ties used to tie cavities together act as heat sinks. Now the more insulation you stuff into your fabric, the greater the relative importance of cold bridging becomes. As insulation levels rise, there are more and more products appearing which address cold bridging effects, most notably the group of products known as cavity closers which you use in the gap around window and door openings. The best known is the original one, RMC's Thermabate but there are lots of others.

The benchmark house has uPVC windows made by Spectus, one of the largest national manufacturers. It's the first of my benchmark houses to use uPVC joinery and in doing so it reflects a widespread change going on in the housebuilding industry generally. uPVC first started to be used for joinery in the 1960s and it has slowly but surely spread throughout the housing market to establish itself as the No 1 material. In fact, new housebuilding was really the last citadel of timber windows but the relentlessly rising tide of uPVC has finally broken through and in the space of three or four years it has established itself as the material of choice for developers.

Andy Allen, designer and builder of the benchmark house, has misgivings about using uPVC. The demand to switch to uPVC is coming from the customers who associate it with the magic phrase "maintenance-free." If AB Homes don't fit uPVC windows, their customers will go down the road and buy a house that does and with this sort of clamour going on, you have to run with the crowd.

The success of uPVC has brought about significant changes to the ways windows are bought. For a start, the old timber joinery majors have been taken apart by the onslaught. The two big names in this business, Boulton & Paul and John Carr, first merged into one company — Rugby Joinery — and then were taken over by an American joinery business, Jeld Wen. For years, these businesses, Boulton & Paul in particular, had set the agenda for how windows were made and how they were sold. They had decided that the future lay in turning out thousands and thousands of standard timber windows in modular sizes and selling them at deep discounts via the builder's merchants. It was a vision that worked, up to a point. They could produce windows far more cheaply than local joinery shops and they took the lion's share of the window business.

In contrast, the uPVC suppliers were singing to a different hymn sheet. They started out in the replacement market and they learned to manufacture to all kinds of odd sizes and styles. And to do it quickly and cheaply. Their production techniques were influenced by Japanese ideas of lean production and quick turnaround and they weren't carrying huge stocks of unsold material. Also they quoted for every job on an as seen basis so didn't mess around with complex catalogues that needed the skills of a librarian to understand. They also supplied a finished product which was ready double glazed and furnished. Plug it in and play. The writing was on the wall. The Boulton & Pauls and John Carrs of this world responded to the challenge by selling uPVC windows but even so they pumped them out in modular sizes, the way they always had done. They couldn't get the hang of the big picture. When they offered to supply ready glazed timber windows, they made them so expensive that no one in their right mind would buy them. They were losing money and losing heart.

What's important to grasp here is that what has sparked the demise of the traditional timber window business is not the fact that the windows are made of timber but rather the way they were made and sold. There are other manufacturers, notably the Velux Rooflight company, who make excellent timber windows and they continue to flourish. But they are specialists and never tried to be all things to all people. There is nothing wrong per se with timber windows — in fact many people continue to rate them rather higher than uPVC on all sorts of grounds — but the traditional joinery manufacturers had become a dinosaur simply waiting for the extinction event to occur. They will continue to sell windows in great numbers but, increasingly, they will be made of uPVC rather than timber.

## Standard Options

Such was the hold of Boulton & Paul on the housebuilding market that designers had learned to work around the modular sizes which were presented to them. To be easily buildable, a house had to work bricks and the bricks had to work window openings. Everything was measured out so that cutting was kept to a minimum. To introduce odd-sized windows was to add unnecessarily to costs so everyone got in the swing of producing houses with the same sized holes in. Of course, now that the uPVC suppliers can handle bespoke sizes with the same speed and at less cost, this hangover from the past has to all intents and purposes gone. In theory. In practice, the habit has become so ingrained that it will continue for some while yet and it's as well to have an understanding of just how the frame sizes work. There is a second generation of uPVC manufacturers growing up, like Speedframe, who choose to work mostly with the standard sizes, simply because the housebuilders know them so well.

## Understanding Frame Sizes

The unit heights are easy to fathom: they are in 150mm steps, which represents two bricks courses — the height options are 450, 600, 750, 900, 1050, 1200, 1350, 1500. The width options — 488, 630, 915, 1200, 1770mm — would at first glance seem to be selected by a random number machine. It appears that the widths were changed in the early 80s after a directive from Brussels indicated that the 300mm brick was about to take over Europe and that they'd better have joinery to suit. The joinery manufacturers all obliged but bricks remain 225mm long! To add to the confusion, the sliding sash window styles are made with a different selection of widths. These are based on the rules of classical architecture and to find out more ask Prince Charles next time you see him.

It is by producing windows in this modular fashion that the likes of Boulton & Paul made their economies of scale which, in turn, made their product cheap. The penalty for choosing a different size from them is around 50% costwise and often a six week delay whilst they make it. Compare that with a typical uPVC window fabricator who will turn out any size to order usually within two weeks. Not much of a contest.

But in terms of headline prices, the timber joinery businesses still look cheaper. There are several volume joinery manufacturers besides Jeld Wen who are turning out enormous quantities of standard-sized timber joinery — Crosby Sarek, Dale, Magnet, Abbott. Of these manufacturers, Magnet are alone in maintaining a substantial branch network of depots through which they sell exclusively. All the others sell through the established builder's merchants. There are numerous others in this business (like Howarth and Hill Leigh) who sell directly to housebuilders and the trade.

Many so-called quality window producers complain of the low standards of the volume producers. They may have a point, but it is worth bearing in mind that these standards have improved substantially in recent years. All timber is now vacuum treated with preservatives, opening casements are draught stripped and window locks and ventilation are now fitted as standard. The depth of the glazing rebates — the ledge where the sealed units sit — has yet to come to terms with universal double-glazed units (i.e. they are still too narrow), but even this is beginning to change; Jeld Wen now offer a Stormsure

## 7d: Guide Prices for Jeld Wen Windows

| | SMALL 630x1050 | MEDIUM 1200x1200 | LARGE 1770x1200 |
|---|---|---|---|
| **SOFTWOOD WINDOW FRAMES (to take 24mm Glazing)** | | | |
| Plain Casement | £60 | £80 | £120 |
| Cottage Plain | £80 | £110 | £170 |
| Swept Head Casement | £70 | £110 | £160 |
| Cottage (Swept Head) | £90 | £140 | £210 |
| Top Hung | £70 | £100 | £120 |
| Regency (with vertical bar) | £130 | £150 | £260 |
| **FACTORY GLAZED WINDOWS** | | | |
| Softwood Plain Casement | £100 | £160 | £240 |
| Hardwood Plain Casement | £150 | £240 | £360 |
| Softwood Georgian Style | £120 | £250 | £360 |
| Security Windows (softwood) | £140 | £230 | £370 |
| PVCu Plain casement | £90 | £150 | £220 |

range with wider rebates capable of handling the glazed units now standard in uPVC windows. Much of what people used to demand from a so-called High Performance window is now available right throughout the ranges.

## The Catalogue

In days of yore, you couldn't design a cost effective house without a joinery catalogue to hand. Even though this connection has been broken, the joinery catalogue remains a thoroughly useful tool. And the grand-daddy of them all was Boulton & Paul's catalogue, now of course Jeld Wen's. Even if you don't plan to use anything from their range, it's still a useful reference because it gives you a feel for what is possible or at least what is commonly available.

## The Styles

The Jeld Wen catalogue has 100 pages of standard windows. At first glance the choice can seem mind-boggling, but growing familiarity shows that the choice is rather like the menu at an Indian restaurant, where every dish is available in every sauce and the length of the menu actually disguises a paucity of actual choices — i.e. it's really just a question of which sauce you want with your chicken, lamb or vegetables.

The backbone of their window production is the casement window, by which is meant any window that opens on hinges (as opposed to a sliding action). A window that cannot be opened is known as a fixed light, but most casement windows incorporate a fixed light or two and still get called casements. The hinging can be arranged either on the side of the casement (side-hung), from the top (top-hung) or pivoted in the middle (well-hung?), and many windows have a combination of these arrangements. Add in a varying number of glazing bars (supposedly to give a window more character) plus a swept top rail (oozes charm) and you can almost taste the poppadums.

To compare the products I have produced a simplified summary table so you can see how small (630 wide), medium (1200) and large (1770) windows compare in price through some of the major styles. I have assumed a discount off list price of 40% which should be within your negotiating powers if you are buying in whole house lots.

## Sliding Sash Windows

There is a wide choice to be had. At the tacky end are the top hung windows that merely look like Sliding Sash windows (until they are opened): Jeld Wen call them Regency or Colonial. There are also a range of contemporary sashes. The modern version of the Victorian sliding sash, which worked with concealed weights, has adjustable spiral balances that are a bugger to adjust and, even when well adjusted, can be very stiff to open and shut, but are in other ways superior to the original. Typically these windows offer a tilt facility so that you can clean them from the inside. At the top end, there are restoration specialists like Mumford & Wood who are producing a product very similar to what the Georgians built. And the sash window is not restricted to timber: there are a number of uPVC fabricators, some, such as Masterframe, producing a surprisingly convincing product.

## Other Features

There is a range of other options you can specify. You might want Easy Clean or Projecting Hinges (extra £10) which enable you to reach the outside of the glass from the inside; maybe coloured fittings (£7 extra) tickle your fancy. Most timber windows are available in either a stain basecoat or a white primed finish. The default is the stained basecoat because you can paint or stain on top of that but you will be saving yourself time and money to get the primed finish if you are going to paint over the top. Just remember that all these options will delay your delivery schedules by weeks so they are only an option if you are planning well ahead.

Oh, and there's trickle vents. If you want to know about trickle vents, delve into the Ventilation section in Chapter 8.

There really isn't a lot to choose between the quality of the joinery turned out by the volume timber manufacturers, though the finer detailing does vary a little. Occasionally, you will find that one is offering much better terms than the others and you may have cause to switch horses. This is usually possible because, despite the different naming systems they use, the sizes are standard and therefore interchangeable.

## Other Options

### Bespoke Timber

Although there are many types of timber suitable for manufacturing external joinery, if you choose to have your windows supplied cheaply from a volume manufacturer then

## The Seven Styles of Window in the Jeld Wen Catalogue 1200 x 1200 size

Plain Casement
£80 unglazed or
£160 factory
glazed

Swept Head style
£115 unglazed
£190 factory
glazed

Top Hung
£100 unglazed
£170 factory
glazed

Horizontal Bar
£95 unglazed
£190 factory glazed

Cottage style
£110 unglazed
£280 factory
glazed

Georgian or All Bar
only available factory
glazed
£250

Regency
Vertical Bar
£150 unglazed
£250 factory glazed

they will almost certainly be made from European Redwood, probably from Scandinavia. Although it is not particularly durable, it can be readily treated with wood preservatives; more importantly it is the cheapest type of suitable timber. It machines well and generally looks good, which makes it suitable for translucent finishes like wood staining.

There are better woods to use for external joinery but they are all very much more expensive and won't necessarily result in better (or longer-lasting) windows. Most hardwoods are inherently more durable than softwoods — oak, teak and Brazilian mahogany are particularly suitable — and there are some N. American softwoods such as Douglas Fir which are nearly as durable as the better hardwoods — certainly durable enough not to require treatment with wood preservative. However, it must be realised that the design, installation and maintenance of the joinery is at least as important in determining how well the items perform over the long term. Specifying more durable timber will probably double your joinery costs at a stroke. Most joinery manufacturers offer "hardwood" alternatives in most of their ranges but you don't get any choice as to which hardwood. If you particularly wanted something like Douglas Fir for your windows then you would have to search out a small joinery shop to make them for you; this route would probably treble the cost of using a bog standard casement from a volume producer.

### uPVC

Almost every window style is available in a uPVC finish. And much that I have written about the style choices for the timber windows applies equally to uPVC. If you are happy with a white uPVC finish it will generally be no more expensive than fitting a timber window — in fact refer to table 7f and you'll see that uPVC is now substantially cheaper once you take into account the cost of finishing the windows. Timber can only be the cheaper option if you want to put a lot of your own unpaid labour into glazing and decorating. Note however that the woodgrain effect PVC windows are at least 50% more than the plain white ones.

The question is, is uPVC any good? Well, uPVC windows have a stranglehold on the replacement market. What sells them is the fact that they are usually replacing clapped-out timber or steel windows which may have been in place for fifty years or more, and they are offering comfort and warmth together with the promise of being maintenance free. It's actually too early to say if uPVC windows will be trouble-free (uPVC guttering certainly isn't), but the indications are that they are performing well. uPVC as a material may last for 30 or 40 years but it's hard to repair: in contrast, timber windows can last much longer — if they are regularly painted or stained.

Note also that Greenpeace are leading a vociferous campaign against the use of uPVC in buildings. They argue that both the production and the eventual disposal of uPVC is a toxic process involving the releases of a number of unpleasant chemicals, dioxins being the most prominent. Their claims are naturally denied by the British Plastics Federation.

### Composites

There are a number of suppliers who offer timber on the inside and uPVC or aluminium on the outside, thus combining the good looks of timber with a more durable exterior. Best known of these is Andersen Windows, an American Joinery giant, who produce a huge range of timber doors and windows with an external uPVC coating. Aluminium-clad windows are available from the likes of Velfac and Sampson and recently Jeld Wen have begun importing an American range called Norco. Composite windows are approximately double the price of basic timber or uPVC, but note that if you want sliding sash style windows, the American designs are good value. Also note that American window dimensions are completely different to ours — they don't "work" bricks.

### Finishes

Whilst non-timber materials invariably come pre-finished, with timber windows you have a number of choices. The current standard is to coat the joinery before it leaves the works with a honey-coloured woodstain which leaves you with the largest number of options. You can apply darker woodstains or you can apply paint. Left to itself, the woodstain provides limited (6-month) protection for the joinery. Some period windows, notably the sliding sash styles, are only available primed (unless by special request) as it is assumed that they are always painted on site.

Now the volume producers are offering prefinished (either painted white or stained dark) timber windows which just require glazing and touching up on site — look for a high build finish. These tend to be around 40% more expensive than the standard. And there is a move to also supply a totally finished and glazed product as well — though here look to pay around three times the price of the raw timber joinery as described in the catalogues.

## Barn Conversions

 Conversions usually pose problems quite different from new builds. There may be existing windows to match but more often than not you will be punching new holes in an existing wall and hoping to fit something that looks in keeping with the period of the original building. Incidentally, the expression "punching holes" is very hip in barn converting circles at the moment, used widely by both planners and architects, so much so that you might be forgiven for thinking that the decision on where exactly to punch those holes is the be-all and end-all of barn design. As you may have noted, made-to-order joinery tends to cost an arm and a leg and specifying it is one of the factors which makes converting barns more expensive than building new. However, if you want to keep costs down there are a number of options that may be of interest to you (or your planners) which can be bought off the shelf. First, the oh-so-modern looking Top Hung window can actually look just so in a barn elevation; certainly less obtrusive than the cottage or swept head styles. Also note that the Narrow Module casement windows tend to look better than standard width windows in barn-type buildings.

## Detailing

The Victorians set their windows and doors back into the brickwork. Not only does this decrease the effects of weathering on joinery but it tends to look better as well. However, it is an expensive way of going about things, primarily because it requires a masonry projecting cill underneath and some form of arched lintel overhead, adding perhaps £100 per opening.

Today's volume joinery is made with integral cill sections and is designed to fit just 25mm back from the outside face of the brickwork. This is easy and cheap but it also looks cheap, especially in brick facades. Rendered and timbered exteriors normally feature cottagey windows perched on the external face, but traditionally brickwork was associated with recessed joinery. Consider recessing your joinery if you are building in brick or stone:

- It will be cheaper than specifying hardwood windows
- It will almost certainly look better
- A softwood window, set back, will probably perform better than an exposed hardwood one.

Look at the relative performance of Victorian sash windows and timber or steel casements on 20th century housing. By and large the old sash windows last about 100 years, or three-times as long as exposed casements.

If you live in an area rated severe weather exposure (and this includes all Scotland and N. Ireland), you will have no choice but to recess your windows into the walls.

## "Good Fenestration"

Architects and planners talk loftily of something called "good fenestration." By this they mean that there are some ways of placing windows (and entrances) in walls that look good and others that look ugly. You'd think that what looks good and what doesn't would be a matter of individual taste, but in fact there is a surprising amount of consensus about it.

Until this century, virtually all buildings that we constructed had "good fenestration." Whether we are looking at the great country houses now presided over by the National Trust or at the humble peasant's cottage or indeed at spec. built Victorian terraces, there is a general consensus that they look right. Throughout the course of the 20th century we've gradually lost the art of fenestration, so that by the 60s we were mostly building in ways that look all wrong to us now. Quite why this should be so is still a subject of some controversy (i.e. is it just fashion or is there something more basic?), but most designers and customers are now aware of the mistakes that have been made and in the 80s there was a movement to build back in, what developers call, kerb appeal, which refers to the visual impact a house makes on passers-by — what advertisers would refer to as sexiness.

The movement to build in kerb appeal has not been an unqualified success. Visit any modern housing development and you can't fail to notice what the current fashions are. Half-timbering, ornamental leadwork, rustic pantiles and cottage style windows all suggest that developers are trying to recreate ye olde village look and yet, and yet it still all seems so unconvincing. You can get a house to look convincingly old fashioned, but you have to avoid things like standard joinery which tends to be made out of comparatively heavy sections which rarely looks authentic. The art of fenestration is partly to do with getting the openings in the right place but also partly to do with making sure that these correctly placed openings are filled with good-looking joinery. Much as it pains the purists, good design doesn't always equate with timber windows.

## 7f: External Joinery Schedule for Benchmark House

| Softwood Windows | | Width | | Ht | Jeld Wen Joinery Codes | Net Price | Glass | Painting | Total | uPVC Alternative |
|---|---|---|---|---|---|---|---|---|---|---|
| W1 | Downstairs Bay (Front) | 1770 | x | 1350 | LEWH313CC | £ 325 | inc | £ 143 | £ 468 | £ 257 |
| W1 | Downstairs Bay (Side) | 630 | x | 1350 | LEWH113C | £ 134 | inc | £ 51 | £ 185 | £ 106 |
| W1 | Downstairs Bay (Side) | 630 | x | 1350 | LEWH113C | £ 134 | inc | £ 51 | £ 185 | £ 106 |
| W2 | Study | 1200 | x | 1200 | LEWH212C | £ 199 | inc | £ 86 | £ 285 | £ 157 |
| W3 | Garage | 630 | x | 1050 | LEWH110C | £ 120 | inc | £ 40 | £ 160 | £ 91 |
| W4 | Breakfast Room | 630 | x | 1050 | LEWH110C | £ 120 | inc | £ 40 | £ 160 | £ 91 |
| W5 | Kitchen | 1200 | x | 1050 | LEWH210C | £ 186 | inc | £ 76 | £ 262 | £ 142 |
| W6 | Upstairs Bay (Front) | 1200 | x | 1350 | LEWH213C | £ 220 | inc | £ 97 | £ 317 | £ 169 |
| W6 | Upstairs Bay (Side) | 630 | x | 1350 | LEWH113C | £ 134 | inc | £ 51 | £ 185 | £ 106 |
| W6 | Upstairs Bay (Side) | 630 | x | 1350 | LEWH113C | £ 134 | inc | £ 51 | £ 185 | £ 106 |
| W7 | Landing | 1200 | x | 1050 | LEWH210C | £ 186 | inc | £ 76 | £ 262 | £ 142 |
| W8 | Bedroom 4 | 1200 | x | 1050 | LEWH210C | £ 186 | inc | £ 76 | £ 262 | £ 142 |
| W9 | Main Bathrrom | 488 | x | 600 | Special | £ 102 | inc | £ 18 | £ 120 | £ 78 |
| W10 | Bedroom 3 | 1200 | x | 1050 | LEWH210C | £ 186 | inc | £ 76 | £ 262 | £ 142 |
| W11 | En suite bathroom | 630 | x | 1050 | LEWH110C | £ 120 | inc | £ 40 | £ 160 | £ 91 |
| W12 | Bedroom 1 | 1770 | x | 1050 | LEWH310CC | £ 284 | inc | £ 112 | £ 396 | £ 218 |
| | | | | | **Total** | **£ 2,769** | **£ 0** | **£ 1,082** | **£ 3,850** | **£ 2,146** |

| Rooflights | | Width | | Ht | Velux Codes | Net Price | | | | |
|---|---|---|---|---|---|---|---|---|---|---|
| Loft | Velux Rooflights | 550 | x | 980 | GGL 3000 | £ 104 | | 6 units | £ 624 | |
| Loft | Flashing for Rooflights | 550 | x | 980 | EDZ 104 | £ 24 | | 6 units | £ 144 | |
| | | | | | **Total** | | | | **£ 768** | |

| External Doors and Frames | | Width | | Ht | Door Codes | Net Price | Frame Codes | Net Price |
|---|---|---|---|---|---|---|---|---|
| D1 | Timber Front Door | 932 | x | 2100 | Special | £ 300 | FN29M-MOB | £ 63 |
| D8 | Timber Back Door | 856 | x | 2100 | E2XGG (inc glass) | £ 137 | FN26M | £ 50 |
| D12 | uPVC Patio Doors | 1800 | x | 2100 | CLAY18 | £ 779 | n/a | £ 0 |
| D9 | Utility/Garage Door | 850 | x | 2100 | Fire Door F3XBF | £ 63 | FN26M | £ 50 |
| D10 | Garage Back Door | 858 | x | 2100 | E2XGG (inc glass) | £ 137 | FN26M | £ 50 |
| D11 | Garage Car Door | 2275 | x | 2100 | Steel Panelled | £ 223 | UF7066NS | £ 48 |
| | | | | | **Total** | **£ 1,640** | | **£ 262** |

> Apologies if this table seems confusing. The left hand side (up to and including the joinery codes) is what is called The Joinery Schedule, an essential part of the specification for any building work. The prices on the right hand side merely try to show the cost of that joinery schedule, including the add-ons such as glazing and decorating. In fact, our benchmark house has uPVC windows so these add-on costs should be ignored in this case.

# External Doors

Many of the things that I've written about windows apply equally to external doors. Furthermore, there is a polite convention that your choice of door should not clash with your choice of window — a convention that's well worth following whatever your chosen style. As with windows, the door manufacturers tend to stick to pretty conventional ideas and all produce variations on some remarkably similar themes. One of the more daring ideas is to put a little bit of stained glass in the pocket window on some of the designs. By and large, the best that can be said about the design of these doors is that "it blends in quite well" or "isn't that unobtrusive?" If you want a door that makes a statement about you — and, after all, the front door is the first thing visitors come into contact with — then you'll have to look to a bespoke joiner's shop or a salvage yard. And expect to pay.

## Materials

Timber is still the most widely used material for external doors (just) but whereas it once enjoyed a near monopoly it now has to share the field with other materials. As with windows, timber doors are the cheapest to buy off the shelf but they are not universally loved by developers because they are prone to twisting and warping, entailing unwelcome call backs. Switching to hardwood doors is one option but, by all accounts, hardwood doors are almost as likely to move as softwood ones A reasonable compromise for those who want something better than a softwood door but are not keen on specifying tropical hardwood is to go for hemlock, a durable N. American softwood particularly well suited to doors.

As Table 7e indicates, there are now several other materials in regular use for making doors. All are more expensive than softwood and all share the plus point that they are dimensionally stable — which no timber door will ever be. Steel is the cheapest alternative; widely used in N. America, it has an aura of security about it which is perhaps unjustified, since a door is no stronger than its frame (which is usually softwood) or its locks (which are no different whatever the door). Steel paints well but is susceptible to bodywork damage like a car. The market leader for steel doors is the IG Weatherbeater. uPVC is widely used in the replacement market but suffers visually in comparison with its competitors. The most interesting of the alternative materials is GRP — that's glass reinforced fibre or good ol' fibreglass. It's well established in the garage door market but is now beginning to make inroads into house doors. The wood grained effect is far more realistic than anything uPVC can achieve and the material can be stained to match other joinery. Look out for Lindman's Fiber-Classics.

## Patio Doors

The idea of opening up a largish hole in the house facing the garden is attractive to most of us; it's a sort of poor man's conservatory. You have a basic choice here between sliding doors and hinged ones which we conventionally refer to as French doors (though the French more accurately call them porte fenetre or window doors). There is not an awful lot to choose between them pricewise, but the overall visual effect can be very different. You see, the patio door is that rarity in new housebuilding, an essentially modern design feature, a sort of junior relative of the glass walled office block. If you are spending money (lots of it) on creating an Olde Worlde look, then a set of patio doors — even with leaded lights — is going to look out of place. In contrast, a pair of French terrace doors tends to add a little bit of Brideshead to the elevation; they're nothing if not old-fashioned. French doors may look the part but

## 7e: External Door Options

| FRONT DOORS COMPARED | FRAME | DOOR | FURNITURE | HANGING | DECORATING | TOTAL |
|---|---|---|---|---|---|---|
| Softwood | £60 | £120 | £90 | £63 | £70 | **£400** |
| Hardwood | £100 | £220 | £90 | £63 | £70 | **£540** |
| Steel | inc | £300 | £90 | £25 | 0 | **£410** |
| uPVC | £50 | £270 | 0 | £25 | £10 | **£360** |
| Fibreglass | inc | £310 | £90 | £25 | £20 | **£440** |
| Secured by Design | inc | £560 | £15 | £25 | £70 | **£670** |

*Comparisons are for a single, solid panelled door, all taken at 40% discount from Jeld Wen*

| FRENCH DOORS and PATIO DOORS COMPARED (c. 1800w) | | | | | | |
|---|---|---|---|---|---|---|
| Softwood French Doors | £110 | £390 | £50 | £100 | £120 | **£770** |
| Softwood Patio | inc | £900 | inc | £25 | £60 | **£985** |
| Aluminium Patio | £120 | £260 | inc | £25 | £10 | **£415** |
| uPVC Patio | inc | £780 | inc | £25 | £10 | **£815** |

Comparisons are for 1800wide frames. French Doors are smaller but these have been quoted with sidelights to make up the opening to 1800. Patio doors are sold preglazed and furnished, hence additional costs of near zero.

they are notoriously fickle in their behaviour and are a bugger to hang well. Too tight and you'll forever be planing bits off every time it rains; too loose and the wind will whistle through them as if they were wide open.

Patio doors, whether sliding or hung, present security problems. French doors are relatively easy to force open; this can to some extent be countered by fitting sliding and locking bolts to both doors, not just the first leaf to open. They are also unusual for external doors in that they open outwards which leaves their hinge knuckles exposed and vulnerable to being cut off, though there is a little gizmo called a hinge bolt which can counteract this. Patio doors present a different problem in that they have frequently been prised, frame and all, from their moorings; very often they are secured only by three screws at either end.

### Handles

Whilst in theory there are innumerable materials that you could use to make door handles from, in practice the range is surprisingly limited: aluminium, wrought iron or brass (or rather brass effect). Aluminium has the reputation for being cheap (though there are some very expensive aluminium fittings available) and brass is the preferred material for most developers, both inside and out. Its styling is usually either Victorian (plain) or Georgian (fancy scrolled edges). Black wrought iron is favoured for the country cottage look, but is out of place on anything else. If you want something a bit different you can look out modern stainless steel designs (check out Modric) or plastic (Normbau).

### Heat Loss

As regards overall heating costs, the role of the door is pretty negligible, largely because their overall area is small compared to other elements in the house. However since the new thermal regs came into effect in 2002, you have to consider the U value of your external doors as well as your windows. The JeldWen catalogue is a treasure trove of information on this front — the 2002 catalogue included U value figures for the first time. Timber doors don't score well, averaging well over the 2.0 figure that is anticipated in the regs. In contrast, the steel and GRP doors achieve U values between 1.2 and 1.5 because they have hollow cores which can be filled with insulation. uPVC doors also tend to perform reasonably well; expect U values down below 2.0. Solid timber is the poorest insulator, then glazing, then insulated panels, be they steel, GRP or PVC. The requirement is for an overall joinery U value of 2.0 so if you want a solid timber door with a U value much higher than this, you can still fit it if you fit windows with a lower U value -- there is a trade-off allowed.

# Glazing

Glass and glazing is one aspect of housebuilding where the changes are ringing out. Until the 1990s, most new homes were routinely fitted with single glazing. A decade later, standard double glazed units no longer meet the building regulations and we are having to familiarise ourselves with all kinds of new energy saving techniques, from low e coatings to argon filling and warm edgings. We have also had to cope with new glazing techniques and new safety features.

### Double glazing

The idea of double glazing is to reduce heat loss and, to a lesser extent, increase sound insulation. The work is done not so much by the extra pane of glass but by the air between the two panes, known as the air gap. The early forms of double glazing were a significant improvement on single glazing. U values for single glazing tend to be around 5.0; in contrast a basic double glazed sealed unit is around 3.0. But the technology has kept on developing and the most advanced glazing systems available today have U values as low as 1.0. The most recent changes in our thermal building regs reflect this state of affairs and now require windows to have a U value of no more than 2.0. What was a state of the art window ten years ago now won't even pass muster. It's not exactly Pentium Processor type change but it's still a lot for the dear old building industry to cope with.

In fact the building trade took a long while to come to grips with basic double glazing. There was a horribly high failure rate, usually manifesting itself in the form of misting between the panes. The air in the air gap was sealed, and meant to stay sealed, but when the edge seals broke down, the air would mix with moist external air and condensation would take place. Hundreds of thousands of double glazed units have failed this way over the years and only recently has the industry worked out how to combat the problem. Builders were using the wrong kind of sealants and squeezing glazing units into rebates that weren't designed to take them. The results were that the units got wet around the edges and the seals disintegrated. Double glazing failures was one of the bete noirs of the warranty providers because they didn't include them in their ten year guarantees something which the new housebuyers never seemed to twig until they came to make a claim. But such is the confidence in the new installation techniques that both the NHBC and Zurich have, since 2000, added sealed unit failure to the list of items covered by their latent defects policies. The key change has been the uptake of drained and vented bottom rails that allow any accumulated moisture to either drain away or evaporate before it starts doing damage to the seals. Deeper glazing rebates in the joinery help matters as well and these are becoming mandatory thanks to changes in the thermal regs. Misting in units was a problem for both timber and pvc windows but the problems were worse with timber because these were often site glazed, rather badly.

## Energy efficiency

Various measures improve the efficiency of double glazing. The simplest is to increase the distance between the panes. A 6mm gap was the old standard. By upping this to 16mm or 20mm you reduce heat loss by nearly 25%. It's easy for the glazing manufactures to alter the gap and there is no cost penalty here. The difficulty comes in building joinery that will take deep units like this. The PVC manufacturers didn't have any problems but the timber window makers proved very reluctant to switch to wider glazing rebates though the new legislation effectively insists on it — the old high performance windows are now the basic standard.

The next trick is to fill the air gap between panes with something other than air. The inert gas argon is the common choice (though some use krypton). Argon filling tends to add about £5/m$^2$ to the costs of the units and it results in only a marginal improvement in efficiency, typically between 5% and 10%.

Then switch to coated, low emissivity (or Low E) glass. Low e glass works by absorbing short wave solar heat, just like other glass, but then acting as a reflective shield to the long wave heat emanating from inside the house. In effect it introduces a layer of one way insulation into the sealed unit. Low E is applied as a micron-thin coating to the inside of the inner pane and, although some people claim to be able to tell the difference between low e coated and uncoated glass — apparently it has a blue tint — I can't. Low E coating is a developing technology and there are now hard coatings and soft coatings with varying emissivity levels. Soft coatings are better and, needless to say, more expensive. A hard coat will reduce the overall U value by 25%; a soft coat by as much as 35%.

Another emerging technique is to use warm edge spacers around the sealed units. Traditionally, the spacers have been made of aluminium which is, of course, a very good heat conductor. A classic case of cold bridging. By replacing the aluminium with something less conductive (typically plastic) you get a much more even U value across the entire sealed unit. The smaller the units, the bigger difference warm edgings make.

Beyond this, there are adjustments you can make to the frames which can have a major impact on heat loss. And ultimately, you can add an extra sheet of glass and move to triple glazing which also improves efficiency by around 25%. Triple glazing is also much better for sound proofing. Add all these 25%s here and 35%s there plus the odd 10% and you can see how a state of the art double or triple glazed unit can get a very low U value, far in excess of what is required by the new UK regs. In fact if you want state of the art triple glazing you will almost certainly have to import it because there isn't anyone in the UK producing triple glazed units.

## Rating

Comparing glazed units and windows is a complex business. For instance glass is unique amongst building components in that it can absorb heat as well as lose it. A highly efficient window on a south facing wall is probably a net contributor of heat over a year as a whole (though of course it is never easy to measure such things). In order to try and bring some simplicity to it all, a new body called the British Fenestration Rating Council (www.bfrc.org) has plans to introduce an energy rating system for windows. It's something similar to that used by the white goods manufacturers where it is now mandatory to show the energy consumption of every machine on sale, but unlike it, the system will not be mandatory. However some of our large joinery firms are on board and will be using the rating system from 2003 so watch out for it.

## Renovations

The 2002 reg changes brought about another significant change in that, for the first time, replacement windows were required to meet the new standards as well. Exactly how this is going to be policed remains something of a mystery at time of writing. But expect the glazing firms to stop selling units that don't match the 2.0 U value figure. And expect the joinery firms to stop making windows that

---

### 7g: Glazing Guide Prices

*All prices are £/m$^2$*

| | MATERIALS | LABOUR | SUPPLY + FIX |
|---|---|---|---|
| **DOUBLE GLAZING PRICES** | | | |
| *Minimum charge per sealed unit* | | 25% of m$^2$ price | |
| *Fixing charges for sealed units* | | £15 | |
| | | | |
| *Standard clear 4-16-4 sealed units* | £25 | £15 | **£40** |
| *Obscure 4-16-4 sealed units* | £28 | £15 | **£43** |
| *Toughened 4-16-4 sealed units* | £33 | £15 | **£48** |
| *Laminated 6.4-16-4 sealed units* | £60 | £15 | **£75** |
| *Low E glass with argon filled cavity* | £35 | £15 | **£50** |
| *Low E glass available in all options* | | add £12/m$^2$ | |
| *Imitation leaded lights* | | add £25/m$^2$ | |
| *Swept head glazing* | | add 20% | |
| **SINGLE GLAZING PRICES** | | | |
| *Fixing charge for single glazing* | | £2/pane | |
| *Minimum charge* | | £ 25 | |
| *4mm Float* | £12 | | **£15** |
| *6mm Float* | £18 | | **£20** |
| *6mm Toughened* | £20 | | **£24** |

can't take at least 24mm wide double glazed units. One area that will remain exempt from the new requirements is listed buildings. English Heritage are one body that doesn't approve of the new regs — they see it as a pvc window salesmen's licence to rip out all that is wooden and lovely with our national treasures. The exemption may also apply to properties situated in Conservation Areas though this isn't abundantly clear. The conservators' point is that thick windows (whether pvc or timber) don't look as good as thin ones.

## Safety Glazing

Another important factor to consider is the regs requirement for safety glazing on
- Any window less than 800mm off floor level
- Any window less than 300mm from a door
- All doors and sidelights where pane width is greater than 250mm
- Internal glazed doors with pane sizes more than 250mm x 250mm

There are two common forms of clear, strengthened glass:
- Toughened: Baked hard to about five times the strength of float glass and, when broken, shatters into (hopefully) harmless lumps. Toughened glass costs about 50% more than standard float glass.
- Laminated: Consists of two sheets of ordinary glass sandwiched around a plastic film: when hit it breaks but doesn't collapse. This is now how most car windscreens are made. Laminated glass is conventionally 6.4mm thick and it costs around double standard float glass, considerably more than toughened glass. Consequently for these applications, toughened glass is now almost universally specified, but laminated glass is preferable if you are worried about security; it's harder to break through.

## Cleaning Windows

Fed up with cleaning windows? Another innovation is self cleaning glass. All the big producers seem to have something on the market, new in 2002. St Gobain's is called Aquaclean. Like low e glass, it uses a transparent coating but this one is hydrophilic (literally 'water-loving') mineral material, so that water spreads out over the surface of the coating and causes a washing effect when it comes into contact with the window. The water then quickly evaporates, leaving no marks from dried drops of water. They don't actually claim that you'll never need to clean windows again, rather that you won't need to clean them so often.

## Decorative Effects

The addition of imitation leaded lights is popular in many Tudor style developments. It can be added either as squares or diamonds. It is a relatively expensive operation (costing around £25/m$^2$ — that's an extra £300 on the benchmark house) and it can look awful. In fact it often does; it's another effect that rarely looks good with thick double glazed units. However, when the design is carefully handled (which usually means using it sparingly), the effect can be to simulate a much older style of window.

## Georgian Look

Fitting sealed units into Georgian style windows and doors can be a very expensive business, because most glaziers have a minimum charge for each unit made and small units therefore get heavily penalised. For instance, Solaglas, one of the largest of the national glazing firms, set a minimum charge per unit of 25% of the square metre rate; this means that double-glazed units do not get any cheaper when the size falls below 500x500mm (or its equivalent area). Now, a typical Georgian style bedroom window has 16 small panes measuring 250x275mm; you don't have to be a financial genius to work out that that's going to be one hell of a lot more expensive to kit out with double glazed units. In fact it's likely to cost 16 x £9 or £144 as opposed to just £35 for a more conventional arrangement with just two units.

Small wonder that a number of manufacturers like Andersen Windows are offering imitation Georgian glazing bars, rather like imitation leaded lights. If your heart (or your planner) is set on Georgian style joinery then look out early on for glass suppliers who won't exact such a savage cost penalty.

## 7h: Heat Loss Through Glazed Joinery

| SEALED UNIT MAKE UP | GAP BETWEEN PANES | | | | |
|---|---|---|---|---|---|
| | | 6mm | 12mm | 16mm+ | |
| Single Glazing | 5.0 | | | | |
| Solid timber door | 3.0 | | | | |
| Insulated door | 1.2 | | | | |
| Air filled DG unit | | 3.1 | 2.8 | 2.7 | |
| Argon filled DG unit | | 2.9 | 2.7 | 2.6 | |
| Argon filled low-e DG unit | | 2.3 | 1.9 | 1.8 | |
| Air filled Triple glazing | | 2.4 | 2.1 | 2.0 | |
| Argon low-e triple glazing | | 1.8 | 1.4 | 1.3 | |

*Figures above are U values: the lower the more efficient*

| | HEAT LOSS THROUGH GLASS | | | | |
|---|---|---|---|---|---|
| U Value of glazing | 5.0 | 2.0 | 1.7 | 1.3 | 1.0 |
| Extra Installation costs | | regs | £250 | £750 | £1250 |
| kWh heat lost/annum | 146 | 59 | 50 | 38 | 29 |
| Annual cost of heat lost | £ 67 | £27 | £23 | £17 | £13 |

*Figures are for 22m$^2$ glazing as per benchmark house*

### Swept Heads

The Georgian look has been drifting out of fashion in the last decade — possibly because of the high glazing costs — but it has been replaced by the Country Cottage look and, from the developer's point of view, the quintessential part of the Cottage look is the curved head to the window. Again, there are knock-on effects to the glazing costs, but there is an important proviso here that the cost conscious should know. Whilst the real swept-head windows involve manufacturing curved glass units — adding around 20% to the cost — there is an alternative, which is to stick timber swept-head inserts over the top of rectangular glass units after they have been fitted. Almost every major joinery manufacturer offers this option and it makes both the glazing and the joinery cheaper. However it is an imitation swept head at best, and though you might not be able to tell the difference from the outside, from the inside you can actually see that the insert has been stuck on top of the glass.

### Obscure

People generally only fit obscure glass in bathroom windows, the reason being that they are often N-N-N-Naked in the bathroom and they don't want the neighbours to have a gander. This arrangement may well suit 90% of UK households, but think about you and your bathroom before blithely specifying obscure glass. You may not need privacy in every bathroom or you may not need privacy all the time, in which case venetian blinds or curtains might serve you better. You might even enjoy lying in the bath looking out of your window, perhaps having a gander at your neighbour.

Obscure glass doesn't add much to a room from the inside and doesn't look that good from the outside. The plainer patterns tend to look least obtrusive but none of them look as good as a real window. So think whether you really need obscure before you specify it.

### Daylight Quality

The primary function of glazing is to let light in. Keeping heat in and not breaking when hit (either intentionally or accidentally) are lesser but more frequently discussed properties, but before passing on let's consider this primary function for a moment. Generally, the thicker the glass, the less light gets through. Low E glass (which saves heat) actually cuts out quite a lot of light: it acts rather like Polaroid sunglasses do in reducing glare. In rooms with lots of glazing this can be a positive benefit in itself. On the other hand, if your design keeps glazing to a minimum, remember that daylight quality is improved by having windows in two walls of a room so that daylight arrives from more than one direction: this may be worth considering in kitchen design.

*Two examples of the effect of adding leaded lights to modern double glazed windows. For me, the top one look fine and the less said about the bottom one the better.*

The "industry standard" is to build a concrete or masonry ground floor and a timber first floor. This is how the benchmark house was built, and my costings confirm that this is indeed a sensible course and you should have good reason to vary from it. However, note that I used the phrase "concrete or masonry" for the ground floor; there is a choice here between solid concrete slabs and precast concrete floors that are delivered to site.

Before we move on, a word about table 7j on Subfloor costs, because even I find it a bit confusing. Why sub-floor costs? To distinguish the costs from floor finishes (dealt with in Chapter 10). By and large, builders do not supply floor finishes and here we are looking at the floor costs strictly from a builder's point of view. But note that I have labelled the last few rows Covers; this is to try to distinguish between the floor base and the base supports if you like between the sub-floor and the sub-sub-floor. The problem is that you can lay either cement screeds or timber deckings over the floor supports and this makes direct comparison costings a minor nightmare. The two top sections Ground Floors and First Floors will give you a basic price for the floor support but neither group will give you a completed sub-floor until some form of cover has been laid over it.

## Solid Slabs

A solid concrete slab is usually laid 100mm thick over a layer of compacted hardcore. This is the most labour intensive system and, conversely, the cheapest on materials, which makes it suitable for DIY builders with access to cheap or free labour. It also remains the best way of doing garage floors. Industrial buildings have power-floated floor slabs which do away with the need for expensive slab coverings and this technique is creeping into housebuilding vis a vis our benchmark housebuilders, AB Homes.

## Pre-Cast Flooring

Pre-cast concrete floors are not economical below areas of 50m² but become increasingly cost-effective on larger areas. Beam and block is gaining in popularity with developers, largely because it's fast and dry. It is an option on upstairs flooring as well, but here it gets expensive because a crane is usually required on site. It has better soundproofing qualities than timber and so is an excellent choice for multi-occupancy dwellings like flats. Another reason for specifying suspended beam floors upstairs is that it can make it easier to fit a whole house underfloor

heating system. The downside is that a masonry first floor can make it a nightmare to run services. You need to plan carefully to avoid such hassles, though all the floor suppliers have systems in place for hanging false ceilings which helps a bit.

Beam and block floors are provided by specialists who work from drawings supplied. A number of businesses cater for this market and many have links with builder's merchants who act as middlemen; if you want to go direct, try Tarmac Topfloor or Rackhams. Note that the infill blocks that are laid be tween the concrete beams are the same in size and specification as the standard 100x225x450mm blocks used in wall construction, and you will usually be able to effect savings if you supply the blocks. These floors, in common with all suspended ground floors, need ventilation, which is usually done by providing airbricks in the external walls; indeed the presence or absence of airbricks around the damp-proof course is very often the only clue as to what sort of ground floor a new house has.

Understand also that precast flooring is an engineered solution for each situation. There is very often more than one way to run the beams and you may be able to take advantage of a system like Rackhams 225 beams which can span up to 8m and can sometimes enable you to do away with sleeper walls within the main floor area.

### Marshalls Jet Floor

This is a unique variation on the standard beam and block floor that uses polystyrene

infill blocks to fill the voids between the beams. It is, therefore, thermally very efficient. Only an insulated timber ground floor could come close to this. However the insulation blocks are rather expensive and are unlikely to be as cost-effective as laying your own polystyrene sheeting on top of a more conventional sub-floor.

### Hollow Core

Hollow core planks are another form of craned-in precast floor. Instead of concrete beams being laid and infilled with blocks, the whole floor is laid in a series of wide concrete planks — hollowed out to reduce the weight, hence the name. Hollow core is the most expensive of the options but leaves you maximum flexibility: you don't have to align your walls on beams, you can build anything anywhere. However, the internal walls where the planks meet end to end have to be double thickness in order to bear the weight.

### Timber

Timber ground floors are discriminated against by the NHBC, which insists on there being a concrete capping and damp-proof membrane laid over the oversite underneath the suspended floor, which effectively adds around £4/m² to the costs. Upstairs, of course, no such extra work applies and here timber joisting is still the cheapest option. However, it can also be a viable option when considering a timber-finished ground floor. Around £10/m² — 50% of the cost of a timber ground floor — goes into the sheeting (usually chipboard or plywood) that is laid over the joists and where a plank floor finish is desired this sheeting can be dispensed with. The prob-

*Concrete beams laid ready for block infill*

lem with doing this is that either the planking will be exposed for the duration of the construction, which will almost certainly lead to damage, or some form of temporary sheeting will have to be installed, which will cancel out most of the perceived cost advantages. However, the technique works well with reclaimed boards which need to be sanded and sealed in any event and can serve as both temporary and finished floor covering.

Note that AB Homes chose to build a first floor with timber joists but they also wanted to build blockwork walls upstairs. They got around this problem by building in three steel beams which act as bearers for the block walls above.

### I-beam Floors

An interesting new system is now available in the UK from Trus Joist MacMillan. It is called SilentFloor (because it claims to be squeak free) and it involves building floors out of timber I-beams instead of masonry beams. On upper floors it is quick and lightweight to install and doesn't need any bridging: the board covering can be nailed directly into it. Using an I-beam system would cost around £600 for the upstairs in the benchmark house, around 40% more than sawn carcassing, but should enjoy similar speed advantages as beam and block floors do. It's a particularly useful system if you want to have floor spans wider than 4m but don't want to have to mess around with supporting beams. It also makes running services a doddle. I beams have experienced a rapid take up and there are now several alternative suppliers.

### Chipboard

The lowest grade of timber floor covering in widespread use, chipboard is made out of tiny wood particles suspended in a sea of glue. At around £4/m$^2$, chipboard is nearly half the price of the much stronger plywood but is not nearly as durable. The NHBC now requires that all chipboard used in new housing should be moisture resistant, but this is far from being weatherproof and it is not recommended that chipboard be built into a house before the structure is watertight — nevertheless it regularly is. One mid-priced alternative is to use Sterling Floor, a waferboard now manufactured in 2400x600 tongued and grooved sheets like chipboard. Chipboard is now frequently laid as a floating floor: that is to say that it is laid — or rather wedged-in without any fixings at all — on top of polystyrene floor insulation sheets. This technique — sometimes known as a polychip floor (as in polystyrene and chipboard) — is bound to become more common as floor insulation is now laid as standard. Whereas chipboard has for a long time been the standard material for covering upstairs timber floors, where it is nailed — using ring shank nails — to the timber joists, its use without any nails or screws at all is still in its infancy. Problems have been encountered with chipboard sheeting curling at the edges and with sheets getting wet and consequently expanding and cracking walls above. In theory, there is much to recommend floating chipboard floors, especially where a carpeted finish is required, and costs are no higher than the traditional cement screed topping given to ground floors. In practice it pays to use the technique with caution; lay timber battens underneath where

extra support is needed such as underneath stud walls, at external doorways and at the foot of staircases.

### Insulation

Underfloor insulation on the ground floor is not quite mandatory but the 2002 changes to the building regs make it expensive to avoid. There are several methods of insulation available, the cheapest and most readily understood being to lay flooring grade expanded polystyrene at 75mm or 100mm thickness over the sub-floor and under the screed or chipboard. Alternatively, you could opt for the nu-Trenchfloor system being championed by the Readymixed Concrete Bureau — this places the insulation under the concrete slab itself. Or a thinner layer of more efficient insulation board. These techniques of underfloor insulation are relatively new and there are possibly problems building up in the future should the insulation not prove to be as rigid as expected: more cautious builders will use some form of reinforcement in their screeds (such as Fibrin) to counteract any such failures. The really cautious can specify Celcon's Jamera Flooring planks which are 250mm deep and don't require any additional insulation to meet the U value standard of 0.25.

Aficionados of underfloor heating will wonder what all the fuss is about. Such systems only work well with very high levels of underfloor insulation — otherwise much of the heat would be lost — and, whatever problems there may have been with underfloor heating systems, laying insulation under heavy cement screeds does not appear to be one of them.

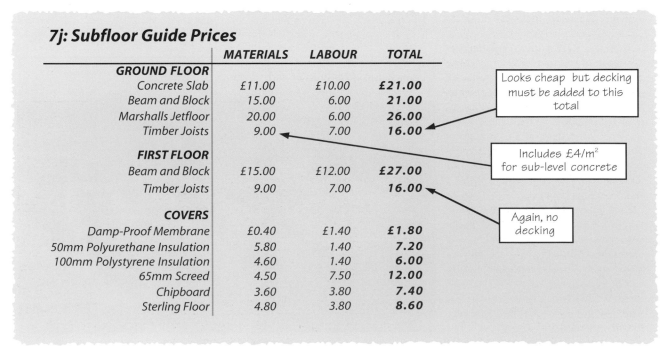

## 7j: Subfloor Guide Prices

| | MATERIALS | LABOUR | TOTAL |
|---|---|---|---|
| **GROUND FLOOR** | | | |
| Concrete Slab | £11.00 | £10.00 | **£21.00** |
| Beam and Block | 15.00 | 6.00 | **21.00** |
| Marshalls Jetfloor | 20.00 | 6.00 | **26.00** |
| Timber Joists | 9.00 | 7.00 | **16.00** |
| | | | |
| **FIRST FLOOR** | | | |
| Beam and Block | £15.00 | £12.00 | **£27.00** |
| Timber Joists | 9.00 | 7.00 | **16.00** |
| | | | |
| **COVERS** | | | |
| Damp-Proof Membrane | £0.40 | £1.40 | **£1.80** |
| 50mm Polyurethane Insulation | 5.80 | 1.40 | **7.20** |
| 100mm Polystyrene Insulation | 4.60 | 1.40 | **6.00** |
| 65mm Screed | 4.50 | 7.50 | **12.00** |
| Chipboard | 3.60 | 3.80 | **7.40** |
| Sterling Floor | 4.80 | 3.80 | **8.60** |

Looks cheap but decking must be added to this total

Includes £4/m$^2$ for sub-level concrete

Again, no decking

The traditional routine for internal partition walls is to build blockwork walls downstairs and timber studwork upstairs. Internal studwork (at around £8/m²) is cheaper and quicker to build than blockwork (at £14/m²) but it is felt by many developers to be a bit tacky. Timber framers will, of course, hotly dispute this, but it would be churlish to deny that a certain amount of prejudice still exists against timber stud partition walls. By the way, don't assume from this that timber frame houses are cheaper to build than block built ones: the costs of timber stud walls more than doubles when specified as the load bearing skin of your external wall, largely because of the essential addition of a layer of plywood bracing. And most houses have a larger area of external walling than internal.

There is another reason for favouring the block wall downstairs, and that is to do with the fact that many of the downstairs walls are load-bearing, whereas upstairs, with the widespread use of roof trusses which transfer all their loadings to the external walls, the walls serve no other purpose than room division. Now, timber stud walls are quite capable of bearing normal floor loadings but their construction needs to be more carefully designed, and this is a hassle that most builders could do without. Also, there is the problem that people automatically assume that any studwork wall is not load-bearing and that this may cause problems in years to come if alterations are undertaken.

## Alternatives

Every year or so someone comes along with another system which will "completely revolutionise building techniques" and make "blockwork and studwork redundant." We've had Stramit straw partitions, Paramount plasterboard wall units, Premaco gypsum wall blocks, Streamline system walls. All promise great savings and yet none ever really catch on. Part of the problem is that you need to have a very large site going to start enjoying real savings since the amount of initial head scratching is large; I may be doing these manufacturers a great disservice, but I don't think the one-off house builder will be particularly interested. However, the steel partition systems like British Gypsum's Gypwall Rapid and Knauf's Diamond Dry Wall system, have begun to make significant impact on the volume housebuilders and may well trickle down to smaller sites in time.

## Steel Beams

Every designer will tell you that you can build rooms to any size that you want — "Your imagination is the limit" or some such nonsense. But they may not explain that once a room gets wider than the normal span for a floor joist you will run into extra costs because you have to fit a beam across the middle to split the loading. This width varies with the size and frequency of the floor joists, but once you get over 4m, your costs start to rise substantially. Well they do if you are working with timber joists: some of the alternative materials mentioned in the flooring section (i.e. concrete precast floors and timber I beams) are capable of much longer spans.

Steel beams themselves are not wildly expensive — a 102x178mm steel channel would cost less than £12/lin.m — but fixing them is a lot of work, no matter which method you use. If they are set inside the floor void, the floor joists will all have to be hung off the steel; if the steel is put below the ceiling then it will have to be boxed in with plasterboard. Steel also needs looking after; it needs a coat of paint and it needs protecting from the threat of fire — usually this is achieved by fixing two thicknesses of plasterboard around it. Despite its inherent strength, steel is actually one of the first things to give in a serious fire so steel beams normally get extra fire protection.

Inserting a steel beam of around 5m length is likely to add around £200 (Mats £70, Lab £130) to construction costs. If you decide to make a feature of it and add an arch below, this will add another £100 to the total, depending on the complexity and size.

## Other Beams

Timber framers tend to use specialised beams when they want to create wider than average rooms. If you are using a post and beam system of construction such as employed by some timber frame companies like Potton Timber or Border Oak, the solution comes complete with the house as they use the massive post and beam timbers to hang the rest of the house off. A more usual situation is to use a flitch beam which is a piece of steel sandwiched between timbers. Flitch beams can be made up on site and are subject to the same sort of cost provisos as regular steel beams. There are various other types and styles of timber beam available; one worthy of mention is the glulam (pronounced glue-lam) beam which is made up of hundreds of small timber sections glued and laminated together. Glulam beams are rather more expensive than steel on a strength for price basis but they have the big advantage that they look good, good enough to leave exposed even though they look a little too modern for some traditional tastes. Most specialist timber merchants will stock several sizes from around £15-£40/lin.m depending on girth.

## Sound Insulation

Poor sound insulation through hollow timber or steel walls is seen as a distinct disadvantage by many individual house builders. Indeed it is stated as one of the major reasons selfbuilders choose blockwork construction. But timber or steel walls can perform excellently in this respect, given the right wall coverings. In particular a heavyweight building board called Fermacell used in place of regular plasterboard makes an enormous difference, easily replicating the sound deadening qualities of blockwork.

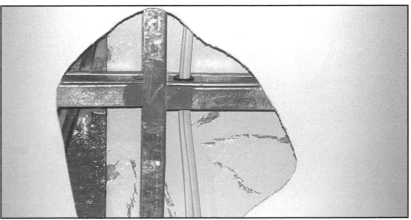

*Steel partitioning is gaining wide acceptance with housebuilders. It's quick, lightweight and cheap.*

# Roof Carcassing

There are two major competing techniques for building roofs. Traditionally, roof timbers were measured, cut and assembled on site — a skilled job involving complex setting-out procedures and cutting lots of obscure angles and notches. Traditional roof carpentry is an art form in itself and it has its own rich jargon involving the likes of rafters, purlins, collars and birdsmouths. However, the rise of the prefabricated roof truss is slowly but surely putting an end to all this. With trussed roofs, the brainwork is done by computer, the cutting by machine and the jargon is reduced to fink and fan, the two commonest truss designs. Erecting a series of roof trusses is generally a straightforward matter — hoist them into place, straighten them up, nail them on and add diagonal bracing. On a simple rectangular box-shaped structure, roof trusses are about three times quicker to erect than traditional roofs and, because of the inherent strength of each individual truss, they use considerably less timber — usually about 30% less by volume. On a detached house with a simple roof shape, the roof carpentry using trusses would cost around £1800 (Mats £800 Lab £1000) compared to £2800 (M £1000, L £1800) for a traditionally cut roof with purlins.

Whereas traditional cut roofs are built from sawn carcassing, readily purchased from any builder's merchant, trussed roofing tends to get fabricated by specialists. Not that this should present a problem to builders: provided you can present a set of dimensioned plans, you will get a quote back usually within a few days. You can contact specialists or you can take your plans to any builder's merchant who will do the donkey work for you.

If you choose to build using trusses, bear in mind that prefabricated roof trusses are sensitive things and they perform well only if they are treated well:
- Care should be taken not to put any twist or undue load on to them, both whilst being handled and when being stored before erection.
- They should be stored upright on bearers (not standing on their feet).
- They should never be altered on site. They can't be cut around chimneys and openings, so you must get the plan accurately built.

Another tip is to set the truss spacings as accurately as possible using a 600mm spacing. This will pay dividends when it comes to tacking the metric length plasterboard sheets to the ceilings formed by the trusses.

So why doesn't everybody use roof trusses? Well, mostly they do but there are some situations where the traditional cut roof holds sway:
- Roof truss manufacturers sometimes get very busy and cannot deliver for several weeks.
- Complicated roof shapes take longer to build whichever system you use and the difference in erection speeds — which is the trusses' big selling point — is much less marked.

Consequently, many builders specify trusses for their main roofs, but prefer to stick with the traditional methods when it comes to odd jobs like building dormer windows, porches or garages.

### Attic Trusses

There is another reason why many builders dislike the trussed roof; it effectively eliminates use of the loft space for anything other than storage. The cross members which make up each truss cannot be removed or altered in any way and this prevents the roof space being opened up at a later date. There is, however, the possibility of using specialised attic trusses which are designed to leave the main loft space open so that any future loft conversion can be arranged with a minimum of fuss and expense. However, whilst the speed of installation is maintained, attic trusses are between two and three times the price of regular ones and this means that they effectively lose their cost advantage over traditionally cut roofs.

### Room in the Roof Designs

Where overall roof heights are restricted, it is common to build the upper storey of a house projecting partly into the roofspace. When added to an existing dwelling this is usually referred to as a loft conversion but in a new build the convention is to give the upper floor at least a metre of vertical wall before the sloping (or raked) ceiling cuts in. This type of design is sometimes known as a one-and-a-half storey house.

If you are going for a room in the roof design — and many timber frame companies specialise in this style of home — there are a number of knock-on effects which you

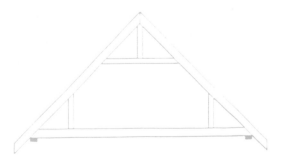

*Contrast the ubiquitous fink truss (top) with the attic truss (below). The fink truss is the cheap option but it prevents you using the loft space because of its support posts. The attic truss is a beefier affair and the pitch is usually steeper (45°) so that you can get reasonable headroom.*

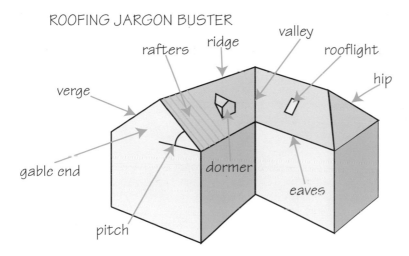

ROOFING JARGON BUSTER

verge · rafters · ridge · valley · rooflight · hip · gable end · dormer · eaves · pitch

should be aware of. The internal sloping ceilings on these houses greatly limit what goes on underneath them; beds are usually OK, cupboards are difficult and planning a bathroom in such a space is something you should consider very carefully. You can end up with a lot of expensive dead space; you may like the idea of under-eaves cupboards or a basin in a sloping alcove, but you'll probably live to regret it and end up wishing for convenience rather than character. When comparing floor space costs, consider space under raked ceilings to be worth just that little bit less than space with full-height ceilings.

The prefabricated roof truss works most effectively when you are designing roofs that sit entirely above the upstairs room space. Then the horizontal section of the trusses can sit directly onto the wallplates at the top of the surrounding walls and form the ceiling joists for the upstairs rooms. When you introduce a raked ceiling you change the truss loadings and start having to use much wider rafter sections and if you have long sloping ceilings you will have to introduce a midway support beam known as a purlin: in effect you are back to constructing a traditional roof so again the supposed economies of prefabricated trusses largely disappear.

However there are roofing systems appearing now which address these problems, replacing rafters altogether with a series of insulated panels stretching from the ridge down to the eaves. It's a variation on the theme of using attic trusses to create an open space in the roof but its selling point is that it is lightweight and quick to install. I've actually already dealt with these panels in a section called SIPS in Alternative Skins. There they were being used for walls, here the same principle applies to roofs. Look out for Jablite's Roof Element and Millbank Roofing as well as the usual SIPS suspects.

## Vaulted ceilings

Some designs call for the room in the roof idea to be extended all the way up to the ridge beam at the apex of the roof. Here you have no flat ceiling area at all. This is a visually dramatic effect, often employed in barn conversions and new oak buildings where you have attractive timber rafters which are worth displaying in their own right. This is a world away from prefabricated roofing trusses, employing techniques of roof design similar to those used in mediaeval times.

## Roof Windows

Once you have opted for a room in the roof design, you have to sort out how you will treat the windows for these rooms. When your natural window height coincides with a sloping ceiling you have two choices. You can "go with the roofline" and fit a sloping rooflight window or you can "break through the roofline" and build a dormer. A dormer window is a fiddly construction. However it is formed, it involves building a sort of miniature house with walls, roof and a window and then joining it seamlessly on to the main roof structure. Whilst this may appeal to the model makers amongst you, harassed builders in a hurry will not appreciate all this intricate detailing. People buying kit homes with dormers placed on the roof might think that they are avoiding all this hassle, but they will find that finishing dormer details is still a time-consuming business. The roofers have to form valleys and often stepped lead flashings, plasterers or bricklayers have to come back to fill in tiny wall spaces on the outside, and even tacking plasterboard on the inside calls for an ability to think three dimensionally. Another pitfall associated with some dormer designs occurs when they break the eaves gutter line of the main house, which results in extra rainwater downpipes; I have seen various ways people have tried to disguise this detail but none of them look particularly convincing.

Planners permitting, you can of course forget about dormers and fit opening roof lights. Velux is the big name in this field (though there are several others) and Velux rooflights are very quick and easy to install; on a new building an opening rooflight will cost between £100 and £250 depending on size and will add virtually nothing to labour cost—it taking no longer to install than it does to fit the roof covering over the same space. In comparison, a simple dormer is likely to cost over £800. It may well be that your overall desired effect demands dormer windows in your roof and, if so, so be it. Just be aware that these types of windows (like bay windows) are not only expensive in themselves but are also heavy on management time. Unless very well planned out, they are more than likely to cause snags further on down the line.

If you are converting a barn you are likely to find that the planners will not allow dormer windows and will force you to use a rooflight. In response to this now well established pattern, Velux have produced a range of conservation rooflights which are designed to blend in with centuries-old buildings whilst still providing ease of opening and double glazing expected of modern roof windows. These conservation rooflights are however priced at a 30% premium to standard rooflights.

## Sunpipes

For those of you still in the dark, a sunpipe or light pipe is a highly reflective tube that allows you to pipe daylight from a roof down into the house. What you actually see is a transparent dome sitting on your roof and a translucent light diffuser — looking for all the world like an electric lampshade — fitted onto the ceiling of the room below. What you get is a credible amount of natural daylight into the darkest recesses of your home. A medium sized 350mm light pipe will produce much more light than a 100w bulb even on a dull winter's day and will be adequate to light a room up to 15m$^2$. At around £300, they are similar in cost to rooflights but they can have advantages in certain situations — you can bend the pipes round corners if necessary.

## Edge Details

One important detail to consider when thinking about roof designs is how to treat the roof edges. The ridges, hips and valleys will be sorted out by the roofing contractors, but the eaves and verge details are largely a matter of roof carpentry. Here, it makes no difference whether you've built a traditional cut roof or a trussed rafter one; you still have to sort out some sort of effective junction between the roof cover and the underlying structure.

*Roof verge here sits straight on top of the gable wall*

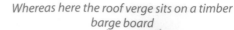

*Whereas here the roof verge sits on a timber barge board*

## Eaves

There are numerous variations on this theme, none of which is likely to cost less than about £15/lin.m (Mats £6, Lab £9) to fix (excluding decorating costs). If there is an industry standard detail it is the closed or boxed eaves. It would cost around £500 to surround a four bedroomed house and garage with this detail.

An alternative is to have open eaves. These are reckoned to look less modern and often more attractive. Some designs dispense with fascia boards altogether and allow guttering to be strapped on to the rafter feet — this is a particularly useful technique to employ with timber barn conversions where a fascia

would look out of place — but the more usual method dispenses with just the soffit boards and leaves the rafter feet exposed. An open eaves detail is a little more expensive than boxed or soffitted eaves as you still have to provide a plywood plate (albeit above the rafter feet to catch the felt) and you are left with fiddly finishing details on the exposed underside.

More expensive still is to use the Georgian-style parapet. Here you build your external walls up above the eaves line and collect the rainwater draining off the roof in a hidden lead gutter behind the parapet. This technique was once common in inner-city housing terraces and large country houses, but

nowadays tends to look a little bit pretentious — unless you happen to be building a large Georgian-style house.

## Verges

Verges are only found over gable ends, so many houses without gables will have only eaves details. There are, again, two classic treatments of verge junction details. One is to lay the tiles or slates straight on to a bead of cement at the top of the supporting gable wall, the other is to oversail the wall and to finish the roof cover over a (usually timber) bargeboard. Each technique has its merits: the direct method can look horribly cheap but, equally well, is capable of being enhanced by using some fancy dog's-tooth

*Open eaves (left) contrasts with the more common closed or boxed eaves*

brickwork: the bargeboard method is rather easier to install (it too can be enlivened by adding decorative effects).

## Ventilation

It is surprising to many people that roof timbers do not need to be treated with preservatives (unless you live in a long-horn beetle area, mostly south of London) but you do need to consider moisture penetration very carefully. For a conventional trussed roof where the upstairs living space does not project into the roofspace, the ventilation requirements are satisfied by the provision of a 10mm continuous air gap all the way around the eaves. You might think that this is a very straightforward matter, but there is also concern that a ventilation gap shouldn't become an open doorway to birds and insects, and therefore there has grown up a whole industry making plastic roof vents which let air in and keep bugs out. There are several different types; some are cut into the soffit boards, some are nailed on top of the fascia and some get fixed between the rafters. They range in price from £1-£3/lin.m. The roofing giants, Redland and Marley, both make proprietary ventilation systems but you will find better value from specialist producers like Glidevale and Rytons. Rytons, in particular, are geared to mail-order sales and

*Plastic roof ventilation keeps bugs out but keeps the air flowing through the roof timbers*

produce a most helpful catalogue explaining the ins and outs of roof (and sub-floor) ventilation.

### Ridge Ventilation

When you have a room in the roof design, roof ventilation becomes a more complex problem and care has to be taken to leave a airflow gap between the roofing felt and the insulation surrounding the living space. There is also a requirement for ventilation at the top of the roof, the ridge, and this can be expensive to achieve.

One way of achieving this is to fit a ventilated ridge, a plastic extrusion which fits under the ridge tiles: this has the advantage of being visually unobtrusive but it comes at a cost of around £18/lin.m, much more than the cost of the ridge tiles themselves. Alternatively there are several formats of ridge ventilation tiles now available: they are invariably expensive — expect to pay between £30 and £50 each — and unlike the dry ridge systems they are all too obvious from the ground.

Roof or ridge vented tiles are also useful with an internal soil pipe or an extract fan that are most conveniently ducted up through the roof space. Glidevale produce the most complete catalogue of roof ventilation and also some of the best solutions for these types of problems.

If you are working with a handmade tile, Tudor Roof Tiles produce an Invisible Venting System which uses the natural camber present on most handmade tiles to provide adequate ventilation space to take the foul air away from extractor fans and soil pipes.

RedBank produce a vented ridge tile suitable for taking the exhaust from gas fired appliances: it's called a low resistance terminal and it costs around £60. Smoke from solid fuel fires has to be expelled via the more traditional chimney arrangements.

### Unvented Roofs

If all this ventilation seems to be more trouble than its worth, then you'll want to know about other options. In fact, if you are building a room-in-the-roof design then you would also be well advised to use an alternative because they are likely to be cheaper and easier. The 2002 changes to the thermal building regs demand a sloping roof U value of just 0.2 which in turn requires an awful lot of insulation (approx 200mm of mineral wool or polystyrene or 120mm of Pu board). There simply isn't the depth of rafter to stuff this much insulation in and still have room for a 50mm vent gap under the roof. But just when all seems lost, Tyvek and the breath-

able membranes ride in to the rescue. These materials are at once waterproof but vapour permeable and their manufacturers have convinced the authorities that if you specify one of these so-called breathable membranes instead of traditional roofing felt, then you don't need to have the 50mm vent gap within the rafter space and you don't need to worry about eaves and ridge ventilation. Although they are expensive compared to roofing felt, you claw this money back by saving on other materials. It's not quite true to say you don't need a vent gap at all because most designs call for counter battening under the tiles or slates — this effectively gives you a vent gap on the outside of the roof, above the rafter line.

There are many variations on the unvented roof design, sometimes known as a warm roof design. It's complicated in Scotland by the requirement for roof sarking which is a layer of solid timber boarding traditionally nailed over the rafters but the insulation manufactures and the breathable membrane suppliers all have details showing ways of satisfying both the U value requirements and moisture management — every roof design has to pass what is called a Condensation Risk Analysis. The 2002 changes will have a significant impact on how we design and build room-in-the-roof but it may be some time before a clear winner emerges.

# Roof Covers

There are many different materials you can use to cover your roof but before we go on to examine them consider first that virtually every housing estate in the country has a concrete tiled roof. Why? Simply a question of cost — concrete tiles are an amazingly cheap way to provide a roof cover and, designed well, they can look very effective. Sometimes but not, unfortunately, always.

Another plus point for concrete interlocking tiles is that they can be laid at very shallow pitches, some at as little as 14°, whereas the more traditional tiles often demand roof pitches of 35°. Low-pitched roofs have two advantages over steep-pitched roofs: their surface area is less — this makes for savings on roofing materials — and they are less visible, therefore the visual impact of any roof covering is diminished. Note, however, that

if you are trying to recreate an older style of building, a low pitched roof will probably look out of place.

## Concrete v Clay

In contrast to concrete, a clay tile is seen as an upmarket product and people often enthuse about how much better they look but, as ever, it's a question of personal taste. Concrete and clay can look virtually identical when laid — the difference becomes apparent as they weather. After ten years a concrete tile looks washed out, the colour flat, the roof lifeless. In contrast, the look of clay actually improves with age as it develops an interesting patina. Clay tiles hold their value too — see if you can find a concrete tile in a salvage yard. The price differential between concrete and clay used to be wide but it has been steadily falling in recent years — currently there

is a 20% premium for clay. At the really cheap end, concrete has the market more or less to itself with what are known as large format or interlocking tiles — often measuring 330x270mm, the size of six plain tiles; you don't need very many and this fact alone makes them much quicker to lay. Large format tiles start losing their cost advantage on complex roof shapes with lots of cuts, so you tend to see them on very simple roof designs.

Small format tiles, known as plain tiles, are available from a wide range of suppliers in both concrete and clay. At the top end of the plain tile market come the handmade clay tiles: these are something else and, like handmade bricks, they tend to lend a strong vernacular flavour to any building they are put on. However, handmade clay tiles are also amazingly expensive, costing around five times as much to supply and fix as the basic concrete interlocking tile.

The roof tile market in the UK is dominated by two giants, Redland and Marley (both recently taken over, by Lafarge and Eternit respectively). Redland set the standards to which others aspire and if you want to get a better understanding of the possibilities with tile coverings, you should get hold of their Guide to Roofing Systems; it's free and it's an incredibly useful 46-page booklet which will tell you more than you will ever want to know about roof tiling. It's also available in Pocket Guide format — you should see it, it's a work of art. Redland tend to be more expensive than the competition (at least on single site developments) and you may find better prices if you chase Marley roofing or one of the smaller manufacturers such as Sandtoft, Russell or Weatherwell. Most roofing contractors have cosy relationships with one particular manufacturer and you may well find that it pays you not to be too picky as to whose tile goes on your roof. Handmade tiles tend to be the province of smaller producers: if you

*Above: Large format concrete tiles are the cheapest roof covering and are consequently used extensively by commercial developers. Handmade clay tiles (below left) will cost around five times as much whilst natural slate (below right) two to three times more.*

# 7k: Roof Coverings Guide Prices

ACCESSORIES includes underfelt and battens together with an allowance for standard roofing fittings like ridge tiles, eaves tiles, valleys and hips, verge undercloaks, lead flashings around chimneys and at roof abutments. The benchmark house is a good example because it has all of these features: if you had an extremely complicated shaped roof your accessories figure could easily double up costs.

| | COST per 1000 | NO. NEEDED per m² | COST per m² | ACCESS-ORIES per m² | TIME in MINS/m² | LABOUR £18/hr | SUPPLY + FIX RATE per m² | OVERALL COST ON TEST HOUSE 134 m² |
|---|---|---|---|---|---|---|---|---|
| **TILES** | | | | | | | | |
| Concrete Interlocking | £500 | 10 | £5.00 | £5.50 | 20 | £6.00 | £ 17 | £ 2,200 |
| Clay Pantile | 430 | 16 | 7.00 | 7.00 | 30 | 9.00 | £ 23 | £ 3,100 |
| Concrete Plain | 220 | 60 | 13.00 | 7.00 | 45 | 13.50 | £ 34 | £ 4,500 |
| Clay Plain | 280 | 60 | 17.00 | 7.00 | 45 | 13.50 | £ 38 | £ 5,000 |
| Handmade Tile | 700 | 60 | 42.00 | 15.00 | 60 | 18.00 | £ 75 | £ 10,000 |
| **ARTIFICIAL SLATES** | | | | | | | | |
| FibreCement | 600 | 13.3 | 8.00 | 5.00 | 25 | 7.50 | £ 21 | £ 2,700 |
| Simulated Natural | 1400 | 13.3 | 19.00 | 5.00 | 25 | 7.50 | £ 32 | £ 4,200 |
| Redland Richmond | 600 | 11.1 | 7.00 | 5.00 | 25 | 7.50 | £ 20 | £ 2,600 |
| Redland Cambrian | 1300 | 13.3 | 17.00 | 5.00 | 30 | 9.00 | £ 31 | £ 4,200 |
| **NATURAL SLATE** | | | | | | | | |
| Spanish | 950 | 20 | 19.00 | 5.00 | 45 | 13.50 | £ 38 | £ 5,000 |
| Reclaimed Welsh | 1000 | 20 | 20.00 | 5.00 | 60 | 18.00 | £ 43 | £ 5,800 |
| Welsh | 1700 | 20 | 34.00 | 5.00 | 45 | 13.50 | £ 53 | £ 7,000 |
| Westmoreland | varies | | 50.00 | 7.00 | 75 | 22.50 | £ 80 | £ 10,700 |
| **SLATE/TILES** | | | | | | | | |
| Mini Stonewold | 550 | 9.9 | 5.40 | 6.00 | 25 | 7.50 | £ 19 | £ 2,500 |
| **OTHERS** | | | | | | | | |
| Lead | | | 20.00 | 5.00 | 150 | 45.00 | £ 70 | £ 9,400 |
| Reed Thatch | | | | | | | £ 80 | £ 10,700 |
| Cedar Shingles | | | 24.00 | 6.00 | 50 | 15.00 | £ 45 | £ 6,000 |

have a deep wallet, look at Acme, Keymer and Tudor, who produce visually stunning roof tiles that are brand new yet manage to look at least 200 years old.

If you crave the look of a traditionally tiled roof but your budget doesn't stretch that far, Forticrete produce a large format concrete tile called the Gemini which simulates the plain tile look by planting a groove down the middle of a large format tile. Slightly more expensive but rather better looking comes Sandtoft's 20/20 and HF's Beauvoise, imported from France: both are middle format clay tiles available at around the £20/m² laid. .

## Slate

Slate became the preferred roofing choice of the Victorians when the railways provided access to the cheap Welsh slate quarries. The slate is still there but it is no longer cheap; indeed it is up there with handmade tiles and thatch as one of the most expensive options for the pitched roof. In rural areas, slate is unlikely to be most people's first choice. How-

ever, planners often insist on slate roofs for the flimsiest of reasons and it is as well to be aware of that possibility.

If you want slate but are reluctant to pay the going rate for new Welsh slate there are a number of other options. You can look to source your slate from Spain: prices are much cheaper than Welsh slate but quality has been patchy and it's worth looking out for slate carrying a 30 year guarantee. Alternatively you can track down a supplier of second hand slate. Prices are similar to imported slate and quality is similarly variable but, if you know what to look for, it's relatively easy to assess the quality of a recycled slate and it can make a very good buy. There are also a number of slate substitutes on the market. The cheapest are the fibre cement slates but these are liable to warp and discolour over time.

There are also a number of interesting slate products, usually made out of reconstituted slate dust. Redland produce the best known reconstituted slate called the Cambrian and Eternit have one called the Melbourn: they are, in fact, not traditional slates at all but

interlocking tiles. It is a mid-priced alternative to the natural slates and the unimpressive artificials. However, many planning officers will insist on you using natural slates, even though they couldn't tell the difference when laid on a roof.

## Stone Belt Roofing

Don't think that you can get away with just a stone facade if you live in an area where stone is the predominant building material. For sure, you will be required to lay a stone tile roof to match your neighbours. Local material prices vary from quarry to quarry but are invariably high. I was quoted "a penny a square inch" (£16/m²) by one salvage yard for Westmoreland slate which puts it on a par with the other very expensive roof covers you could possibly choose. There are numerous cheaper, artificial alternatives around (e.g. Redland's Stonewold range) which will not look in the least bit convincing but using them may save you several thousand pounds. Again you face a tricky task reconciling your budget with the demands of your local planners.

### Shingles

Another old vernacular standby is the cedar shingle. A shingle is a tile fashioned out of cedar wood and is usually supplied in random widths to give a broken up effect. It is a reasonably hard wearing material — though not as good as clay, slate or concrete — and it is used just as often to do vertical wall panels as it is pitched roofing. Cedar is a naturally durable timber which doesn't require any treatment or staining, and if you covet a genuine timber house then shingles will be your chosen roofing material.

### Thatch

This is really one for enthusiasts. People do build new thatched houses — about one every year. Not only is it very expensive, but there are numerous regulations about where thatch can go on new building — for a start it has to be 12m from any neighbouring dwellings. Thatch is not something that can be added as an afterthought; if you are really serious about it you must design the roof around the thatch. You are more likely to come across thatch if you are involved in renovating or converting.

### Turf

Turf roofing is vernacular in places like Iceland but in the UK it's distinctly organic. There have been a number of new turf roof houses in the last few years, most famously the Integer BBC Dreamhouse built in 1998, and they always make for very interesting features. No, you don't have to mow them, not if you get your planting right. Their success depends to a large extent on having a top notch underlay and here Erisco Bauder seem to be the company of choice.

### Sheet Roofing

Sheet roofing is often associated with flat roofing and there is very little flat roofing being built today. There is nothing intrinsically wrong with flat roofing, but too much cheap felt got stuck on too many cheap houses in the 60s and the bitter taste of continual roof repairs has yet to fade away.

You might, however, be considering flat roofing for, say, a roof garden or a balcony. Be aware that the durability of a flat roof is almost entirely dependent on how much you spend on it. Mineral felts are the cheapest covering (at around £10/m², supplied and fixed, but don't expect much more than about fifteen years lifespan); areas which are to get walked over really require something a bit stronger like asphalt (about £25/m²) or lead (around £50/m²).

Sheet metals such as lead and copper actually make very stylish coverings for pitched roofs but their expense means that they are rarely seen on new housing.

### Tile Weight

Roofing materials vary enormously in weight. For example:

- Lightweight slate     20kg/m²
- Concrete interlocking tile     45kg/m²
- Plain tile     90kg/m²

Does this matter? Well it matters to the roof designer that the timbers holding up the roof should be strong enough to bear the imposed load but the effect on cost is surprisingly small, particularly if roof trusses are being used. The cost of using a roof truss system for a heavy roof covering will add about 10% to the truss cost — probably less than £100 for a detached house.

### Felt and Battens

Building regulations require that whatever (pitched) roof covering you decide on there should be a layer of roofing felt underneath. At a cost of less than 50p/m² this is no great cost and it has the added advantage for quick builders of providing a temporary waterproof cover for work going on below. Felting takes place simultaneously with battening, which is necessary to provide fixings for the tiles or slates. On all but the largest houses, the whole process of felting and battening usually takes roofers no more than a day and costs around £2.00/m² (Mats £1.00, Lab £1.00). Don't make the mistake of felting and battening before choosing a roof covering: the spacing of the battens is set by the gauge of slate or tile and the gauges are very variable. Note that the Scottish practice is to build a solid timber sarking layer on top of the rafters before laying felts: this adds significantly to the roofing costs.

Felts are now tending to get replaced by breathable membranes — Tyvek remains the best known but there are many others such as Klober, Monarperm 450 and Daltex Roofshield. Although expensive — two to three times the price of ordinary roofing felt — these membranes enable water vapour inside the roof space to permeate through them thus eliminating the need for other expensive ventilation gear.

### Additional Fittings

As most roofing is carried out by specialist contractors, usually on a supply and fix basis, there is perhaps not the need to know so much about the intricacies of roofing. However, there is a lot more to a roof than slates or tiles and on a typical detached house the actual roof tile may make up no more than 50% of the overall roofing material costs. The most visible additional element is the ridge and/or hip tiles (usually around 20% of cost); the underfelt and battens (12%) are the other significant costs. Ventilation gear, which is often fitted by roofers, is another expensive item. Table 7l illustrates the extent of additional items on the roof of the benchmark house.

### Hip Treatments

The hip is the name given to an external angle in a roof — an internal angle is called a valley — and the standard way of finishing a hip is to use something very similar to a conventional ridge tile, although the hipped version is sometimes slightly differently shaped. This is a cheap and quick specifica-

*Coursed stone tiling: the courses shrink in size as you get closer to the ridge. An attractive vernacular detail but time consuming and expensive to achieve*

tion, costing no more than about £10/lin.m (M £4, L £6) and it is really the only practical way of finishing a concrete interlocking tiled roof. However, if you are planning on a plain tiled roof there is an alternative which is to fix bonnets which look very rural and vernacular. However, bonneted hips are way more expensive both in labour and materials (you'll need something like 10 bonnets/lin.m as opposed to 2 hip tiles) and the rate per linear meter works out at over £40 (M £25, L £15). An even more expensive option, which is most often seen on slate roofs, is to cut the tiles or slates to meet exactly over the hip. This is known as a close-mitred hip and it tends to be preferred by those going for neat, unfussy solutions. It is heavy on the old labour and it relies on underlying lead soakers to be effective which makes it cost in excess of £50/lin.m.

Bonnets and close-mitred hips may sound like unnecessary extravagances, but although they are way more expensive than hip tiles, the total length of hips to cover is often not that much and specifying something different here has a marked effect on kerb appeal.

## Valleys

Another cost-sensitive area of roofing is the valley which is formed when two roof lines meet on an internal corner. The valley is not as visually prominent as the hip and this makes it a candidate for treating as cheaply as possible. The commonest way of doing this is by fitting a purpose-made valley gutter and cutting the tiles or slates around it. Here, fibreglass is tending to replace lead; it's quite a bit cheaper and much quicker to lay but labour costs are still significant. Valley gutters cost around £20/lin.m. when done in fibreglass, rising to £30/lin.m when finished in lead.

On plain tile roofs there is the alternative of using purpose-made valley tiles which are very similar to inverted bonnet hip tiles. Again, this is an expensive option — £45/lin.m (M £25, L £15) — but it is worth considering around features like dormer windows where the valleys are visible from the ground.

## Verges

If you are roofing up to a gable wall, you will need to form some effective junction at the verge. The simplest method is to lay a mini-soffit board (known as an undercloak) on top of the brickwork (or timber bargeboard if one is specified), run the roof cover up to the edge of the undercloak and then fill the void between with cement. Such an arrangement costs no more than £3/lin.m to execute and is no different whether the roof cover is slate,

tile or stone. There are alternatives — Redland make a concrete wrap-over tile that can be used with certain tile covers and there is even a plastic verge system. However, these other methods all cost around double the cement undercloak technique and they add nothing to the look of your roof edge.

An interesting innovation in this field is a product called Roofblock, marketed by Forticrete. This is a masonry alternative to fixing fascias, soffits and bargeboards — i.e. all the roof edge details which drive builders mad. With Roofblock you simply lay a special shaped block on top of the wall and the detail is sorted. It does equally well for eaves and verges.

### Decorative Accessories

Whilst most fittings are purely functional, occasionally a decorative touch can make a very plain roof exciting. Caught by the general trend for all things vernacular, roofing manufacturers have been busy reproducing Victorian embellishments like cockscomb ridge tiles and fleur-de-lys finials. Handle with care; in the right place these can look fantastic but on most roofs they look plain silly. Similarly, two-tone effect roofing (either with contrasting tile colours or accentuated ridge tiles) is invariably very striking — but that doesn't always mean it works. If you see a roof you like, photograph it and show it to your roofer for quotation. Chances are it will be out of your price bracket!

### Dry Tech Systems

The parts of the roof most vulnerable to weather damage are the perimeter areas like ridges, hips and verges. The traditional way of fixing ridge, hip and verge tiles is to bed them in cement. For some time now the tile manufacturers have been trying to persuade us to use dry systems, which clip together with a series of mechanical fixings, but there is a general reluctance to take up their offers partly because of the higher prices charged

for these fittings and partly because the look is even more modern and nondescript than the conventional roof. Note that in Scotland, dry verges are the norm and that housebuilders seeking a low maintenance finish are also specifying them — cement fillets on roof edges are notoriously brittle.

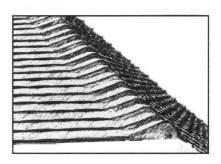

Three ways of detailing hips. Top: Hip Tiles, cheap and cheerful at £10/lin.m. Middle: Bonnets, at £40/lin.m. Bottom: Close Mitred Hips, at £50/lin.m

## 7I: Roofer's Shopping List for Benchmark House

| WHAT WAS NEEDED | HOW MANY | HOW MUCH |
| --- | --- | --- |
| Redland Grovebury | 1380 | £ 690 |
| RidgeTiles | 34 | £ 80 |
| Valley Gutters | 6m | £ 100 |
| Marley's Ventilated Ridge | 6 packs | £ 200 |
| Nails and Ironmongery | | £ 50 |
| 15x1m Felt Rolls @ £7.00ea | 12 | £ 84 |
| 25x38 Battens @ 22p/m | 400m | £ 88 |
| Verge Undercloak | 40m | £ 45 |
| Mortar to Verge | 40m | £ 15 |
| Lead Step-flashings | 9m | £ 50 |
| **TOTAL** | | **£ 1,400** |

# Rainwater

Getting rainwater off roofs and down into the drainage systems is one of the small but very important details that can make or break the appearance of a house. Done well, with appropriate materials, it can add a little to the overall visual appeal of a house. However done badly, it can ruin a fancy facade. The key to getting the look right is the placing of the downpipes and, as a general rule, the fewer the better.

## Plastic

The low maintenance, low budget option is plastic (PVCu). There are around half a dozen manufacturers in the UK and they all sell through the builder's merchants. Note that there is a compatibility problem here: even though the designs are very similar, the rival manufacturers products rarely fit each other so don't mix and match your guttering. Generally PVC guttering is available in four colours, black, brown, grey and white though Hunter Plastics have a range with additional colours. There are also a range of sizes and styles: both half-round and square-box are common plus there are a few more ornate sections such as ogee.

When designing rainwater systems, you have to bear in mind the likely flow rates which naturally tend to vary with the area of roof being drained: if your roof areas are large you may find yourself having to fit more downpipes than you wish and one way around this is to use a larger guttering and downpipe. The manufacturers all hold data to help you specify appropriate sizes. For instance, Osma produce an Amazon gutter section which will drain over 100m$^2$ of roof area, as opposed to the 57m$^2$ maximum specified for their standard RoundLine section. Now, the Amazon is over twice the price of the RoundLine, but specifying it can sometimes actually save money by cutting down on both the number of downpipes and the length of underground drainage work.

Fixing PVC guttering off scaffolding is at best a semi-skilled job easily mastered by a competent DIYer — the manufacturers all have concise installation guides. But note that whilst it is a relatively easy task to do from scaffolding, it can be a very dangerous and difficult thing to undertake using just a ladder. Also you need to pay attention to the brackets used to hold the gutters and downpipes in place. There is quite a choice available, designed to cope with the whole range of materials that you may have to fix into or around. Note that there are adjustable brackets available which can accommodate situations where you are unable to fix into your preferred location — very useful when working with uneven surfaces that you might expect to find on barn conversions or stone buildings.

There are two drawbacks to using plastic guttering. One is that, as discussed, it all looks rather naff; the other is that it isn't actually any good. uPVC guttering generally, and the rubber jointing gaskets in particular, seem to break down under the effects of bright sunlight and the effective lifespan of a uPVC rainwater system is probably only about 10 years. Expect to start replacing bits after this time.

Manufacturing standards have increased somewhat over recent years and you can improve the overall performance of your guttering by choosing a plastic system with a high-gloss finish (Osma, Terrain) which is better at reflecting sunlight, but if you want a much better performance, then you should consider using different materials.

## Other Options

All the other options are more expensive but all promise greater durability. The traditional British material used for guttering before the advent of plastic was cast-iron and this is still widely available in a range of period details. It is now mostly used on conservation work and listed buildings. With proper maintenance (which means repainting every five years or so), cast-iron guttering does last a long time — there are many examples of Victorian rainwater systems still in good working order.

Copper is another material, widely used on the Continent. It's very resistant to the elements and doesn't need any painting. Copper of course changes colour over time to eventually achieve a lime-green patina which will suit some properties better than others. Copper is also used with chain pipes, an interesting technique which does away with the conventional enclosed downpipe and allows the rainwater to run down a chain to the ground — only to be recommended when you have a good overhang on your eaves.

Aluminium and plastic-coated steel are also used. Aluminium now tends to be the province of specialist suppliers who provide seamless welding. Both these systems are available in a wide range of colours and promise many years' maintenance free service.

## Rainwater Harvesting

There is no reason to stop you putting some of this mildly acidic rainwater to good use before pouring it all away. Many people will be interested in building in rainwater butts and these can be made much more useful and more productive if they are designed in from the beginning. For around £10, you can add a rain diverter to your downpipes which will not only redirect your rain into a tank but is also intelligent enough to know when the tank is full and then redirect the rain back down the downpipe. If you want to use the rainwater for domestic purposes — and there's good money to be saved here — you are talking more serious underground storage tanks and pumps. May I refer you to the section called Saving Water in Chapter 13.

*Downpipes, inspired by the Richard Rogers school of architecture*

# Chapter 8
# Plumbing & Heating

# On Heat

Deciding on a heating system is one of the biggest bugbears facing a builder. It's such a complex field and there are so many options available that it is terribly easy to get swamped by the sheer volume of information. It's all very well saying something smarmy like "You should choose the system that suits you best" but that doesn't actually make it any easier to know what that system might be. There's nothing for it but to start at the beginning. A little background on the physics of heat will improve your understanding of all the areas discussed. Here answered for you are seven questions that you'd never even think to ask.

## What is Heat?

Heat is a by-product of "work" going on or, if you like, energy being spent: this usually involves one substance turning into another. Our bodies (like our houses) leak heat and this leaked heat must be replaced, which we do by eating (calories are a measurement of energy, there are 13 calories in a kilowatt hour). The colder it is outside our bodies and our houses, the more heat we leak and the more energy we have to take on board to stay warm.

## What is "Feeling Warm?"

The rate at which we lose heat determines how hot or cold we feel. "Feeling cold" is a signal that we are losing high and potentially dangerous amounts of heat; "feeling warm" signals that all is OK.

## What Determines How Warm We Feel?

- The insulating effect (U value) of our clothes (or duvets)
- The temperature of the surrounding air
- Wind speed (wind chill factor)
- Level of water vapour around
- Whether our skin is wet or dry
- How much heat is being "given off" (radiated) by surrounding objects (including the sun).

When assessing heating systems, we use air temperature as a shorthand indicator of background comfort but it is important to be aware that air temperature is just one of several factors at play. Anyone who has ever had a thermostatic control dial in their home will be well aware that what's warm on a dry day can be 2-3°C too cold on a wet or a windy day.

## Is There an Optimum Comfort Level?

Not as such, but the general consensus is that you need to be dry and free from draughts, and that, of the two forms of heat, radiant heat is more pleasurable than convected heat.

## Radiant v Convected Heat

Radiant heat is the glow you feel on your face when you are standing near a bonfire; the air temperature may be minus 10°C but you feel as warm as toast. Convected heat is warmed air: car heating is the ultimate form of convected air heating: when combined with the forced draught of the fan heater, it dries your throat, makes your eyes water and induces drowsiness.

## Does it Have to be One or the Other?

No. In fact all heat sources are a cocktail of convected and radiant heat. Bonfires (and sunshine) will tend to heat the air and warm air will tend to heat the objects it comes into contact with. Convected (or warm air) heat is characterised by being very responsive — i.e. you feel warm very quickly: radiant heat can take a long time to get going (and a long time to cool down).

Having said that, a couple of readers have been at pains to point out that radiant heat is much less significant at low temperatures (say below 80°C) and that what is often referred to in manufacturer's blurb as radiant heat is no such thing. Rather it would seem that what is happening is that warm, draught-free air is being mistaken for radiant heat or, to put it another way, the pleasant effect of warm, draught-free air is being wrongly attributed to heat radiation when it may be nothing of the sort. I never said it was easy.

## So What's the Perfect Heating System?

Hopefully you have just twigged that there is no such thing. Like most design decisions, you must make a series of compromises and your aim should be to make the least bad compromise overall.

## Watts it All About?

Finally a word about how we measure power output, because I know everyone finds it confusing, not least because there are different systems of measurement in operation. Here I try to plump for one, the watt (W), and it's big brother the kilowatt (kW) which is, as you might hope, 1000 watts. British Thermal Units (BTU) get a look in on the boiler section because generally boilers are still rated in BTUs:

- 1W = 3.41 BTU
- 1kW = 3410 BTU.

These are all measurements of heat output. However, you will also be frequently coming across the kilowatt-hour (kWh) which is a measurement of heat actually consumed.

The simplest way to understand the difference is to think of an old-fashioned two-bar electric fire: each bar puts out 1kW of heat. If you leave one bar on for one hour, it will have used 1kWh of energy: if you put both bars on it, its output will obviously double and the kWh will be used up in half the time. So its output is measured in kilowatts but the power actually used is measured in kilowatt-hours — output through time. Thus when I am rabbitting on about boilers I'm mostly referring to kilowatts and BTUs, but in the sections on fuel costs it's all kilowatt-hours.

All this theory is fine but how well does a standard central heating system stack up? The "wet" central heating system described below was pretty much standard in most detached British housing for the last three decades of the 20th century, both for new builds and refurbishments. Although many aspects are beginning to change as new, more efficient technologies come along, it's still a good place to start.

## Heat Loss Calculation

This is carried out, usually by the plumber, on a room by room basis, and the results are used to assess the size of the radiators needed in each room. The boiler itself is sized up by adding all the outputs of the various radiators and adding "a bit."

## Boiler

The boiler is fitted against an outside wall and the exhaust gases are ducted horizontally outside by way of a balanced flue. The boiler heats water to 80°C and this water is then pumped through the primaries (large copper pipes) and thence to the cylinder and the radiators.

## Cylinder

Placed in the airing cupboard, this acts like a giant (bath-sized) kettle for heating domestic hot water (DHW). It starts to empty every time a hot tap is turned on; it is simultaneously filled from a tank of cold water in the loft space which, in turn, is filled from the water main. The cylinder is indirect which means that the water inside never passes directly through the boiler but is heated at one stage removed by the boiler water passing through copper loops inside the cylinder.

## Radiators

These are fitted and connected by two copper pipe circuits: one — the flow — takes the hot water from the boiler around the circuit, the other — the return — takes the cooler water coming out of the radiators back to the boiler. A small plastic tank (feed and expansion tank) is placed in the loft which gives the hot water in the circuit space to expand — which it does as it gets hotter. Note that the current benchmark house eschews all tanks in the loft and uses a mains pressure hot water system instead. Mains pressure systems are beginning to replace gravity as a means of delivering hot water around the house.

## Controls

The system is electrically pumped to supply even heat around the house. There is a programmer and a couple of thermostats which turn the system on/off and also switch motorised valves so that the hot water pumped from the boiler can be switched between heating the water in the cylinder or circulating around the radiators.

## Labour Content

In a new four-bedroom house, the pipework and control cabling will be "first fixed" in 3-4 days; first fixing needs to take place after the structure is up but before the plastering starts. The "second fix" (including hanging radiators) will take 5-6 days. Conventionally, the heating engineer also fits the sanitaryware, kitchen plumbing and the above ground waste runs, and all this work tends to get lumped into one quotation and carried out together.

## Cost Summary

The table on this page shows the costs for a 20kW, 15-radiator installation of the type that was fitted into our benchmark house. Materials are at prices which non-plumbers should be able to obtain at specialist merchants like Plumb Center. The grand total figure is derived from quotations and so includes an element of profit which a small plumbing firm would charge.

## Open Fires

Most large family homes are still built with an open fire in the living room. Despite modern central heating being quite adequate to provide warmth in the most extreme winter conditions, housebuilders are still apparently happy to pay £1000 plus for an open fireplace with accompanying chimney. Whereas central heating is regarded in entirely functional terms (fuel efficiency, programmed control, water pressures, etc.), the open fire is altogether much more of a romantic dream — and a very potent one. So what if 70% of the heat goes up the chimney, so what if it has to be cleaned out daily? To the average British household, fire in the living room is as fundamental as sex in the bedroom.

Because fires are both expensive to install and largely unnecessary, the current trend is to only see them specified on upmarket homes. Open fires are dealt with in their own section in this chapter and any heat given off by open fires will be treated as free background heating in the same way that we treat winter sunshine, heat from electrical appliances and, of course, body heat. Solid fuel stoves and kitchen ranges, together with other nonstandard forms of heating are looked at in another section of this chapter, Alternative Heating.

## 8a: Benchmark House: Central Heating Costs

|  | MATERIALS | LABOUR | TOTAL |
|---|---|---|---|
| 20kW Gas Boiler + Flue | 550 | 200 | £750 |
| 150lt Mains Pressure Cylinder | 500 | 100 | £600 |
| Primaries/Valves/Pumps | 250 | 200 | £450 |
| 15 Radiators + Pipework | 650 | 550 | £1,200 |
| Heating Controls (inc TRVs) | 250 | 150 | £400 |
| Wiring and Commissioning | 100 | 200 | £300 |
| TOTALS | £2,300 | £1,400 | £3,700 |

# Which Fuel?

When considering which fuel to use to provide space heating and domestic hot water (DHW) there are a number of considerations:
- Availability
- Installation and storage costs
- Capabilities of each fuel
- Fuel costs
- Environmental impact.

## Availability

Piped gas from the North Sea reserves is currently available to over 70% of UK households, which includes almost all urban areas. However, large tracts of rural Britain and Ireland are deemed too remote to justify laying gas mains and most of these areas will never have the option of a piped gas supply. If in doubt, a phone call to the local office of British Gas will illuminate the situation in your area. Sometimes an initial enquiry will trigger the offer to extend a gas main along a side road.

All the other fuels touched on here are available everywhere except the remotest corners.

## Installation

### Electricity

Installation to a new site is charged on a time and materials basis. Even when it's straightforward it is unlikely to be less than £300. However, as its use in modern housing is universal, when considering electricity as a heat source it is effectively there for nothing. An Economy 10 (two-rate) meter can be installed at no extra cost and is generally well worth doing even if you don't plan to use electric heating — more information on two rate meters can be found in Chapter 10, Kitchen and Laundry.

### Gas

British Gas subsidises the installation costs because they want new customers. If gas supply is adjacent then connection is usually free. Longer distances are possible, subject to negotiation with British Gas new supplies. Beyond a distance of a couple of hundred metres or so, it becomes prohibitively expensive unless the costs can be borne with neighbours.

### Oil

The costs are solely to do with onsite storage. Storage tanks are available in steel or plastic. The usual sizes are 300 gallons (1365lt) and 600 gallons (2730lts). Steel is much cheaper (£220 for a 2730lt tank compared to £400 for an equivalent in plastic) but plastic is guar-

## 8b: Fuel: Raw Costs Compared

| | STREET COST | CONVERSION | COST /kWh | ANNUAL TARIFFS |
|---|---|---|---|---|
| **ELECTRICITY** | | | | |
| Standard Rate | 6.5p/unit | none | 6.5 p | £ 25 |
| Economy 7 - daytime | 6.5p/unit | none | 6.5 p | £ 38 |
| Economy 7 - night time | 3p/unit | none | 2.5 p | |
| Economy 10 - daytime | 8p/unit | none | 6.5 p | £ 38 |
| Economy 10 - night time | 3.3p/unit | none | 3.2 p | |
| **MAINS GAS** | 1.5p/unit | none | 1.5 p | £ 35 |
| **LPG (Calor Gas)** | 17.7p/lt | Divide by 7.1 | 2.5 p | £ 55 |
| **OIL (28-second)** | 16.5p/lt | Divide by 10.2 | 1.6 p | £ 0 |
| **House Coal** | £150/tonne | Divide by 8300 | 1.8 p | £ 0 |
| **Anthracite** | £220/tonne | Divide by 9370 | 2.3 p | £ 0 |

**ALL FIGURES INCLUDE VAT at 5%**

## 8c: Fuel: Effective Costs Compared

| | Fuel Cost/kWh | Appliance or Boiler efficiency | Effective Cost |
|---|---|---|---|
| **ELECTRICITY** | | | |
| Daytime Peak Rate | 6.5 p | 100% | 6.5 p |
| Off-peak Rates | 3.2 p | 100% | 3.2 p |
| **BRITISH GAS** | | | |
| Elderly Cast Iron Boiler | 1.5 p | 60% | 2.5 p |
| New Boiler | 1.5 p | 78% | 1.9 p |
| Condensing Boiler | 1.5 p | 90% | 1.7 p |
| **LPG** | | | |
| Elderly Cast Iron Boiler | 2.5 p | 60% | 4.2 p |
| New Boiler | 2.5 p | 80% | 3.1 p |
| Condensing Boiler | 2.5 p | 90% | 2.8 p |
| **OIL** | | | |
| Elderly Cast Iron Boiler | 1.6 p | 70% | 2.3 p |
| New Boiler | 1.6 p | 85% | 1.9 p |
| Condensing Boiler | 1.6 p | 95% | 1.7 p |
| **COAL** | | | |
| Open Fire | 1.8 p | 35% | 5.0 p |
| Stove | 1.8 p | 65% | 2.7 p |
| **ANTHRACITE** | | | |
| Open Fire | 2.3 p | 35% | 6.6 p |
| Stove | 2.3 p | 65% | 3.5 p |

**ALL FIGURES INCLUDE VAT at 5%**

anteed for ten years. If you are building for a largish detached house you would do well to get the large tank size which should be enough to last a year at a time — buy in the summer when oil prices are low. Steel tanks have been known to start leaking after five years and are meant to be painted every year (nobody ever does). Add to this figure building up supporting piers (Mats £25, Lab £50), initial placement (L £50), measuring gauge (M £40), filter (M £40), fire check valve (M £30) and microbore connection to boiler (M £10, L £30), and budget around £450 for a steel tank, £600 for a plastic one. The tank can be placed up to 2m below the boiler, but then a tiger loop will be needed as well (extra £40). Attention must be paid to placing oil tanks; they must be outside and they must be 1.8m from any openings. Recent upgrading of the regulations means that ideally an oil tank should be placed 1.8m from the house and 760mm from a boundary, though if you build a reasonably fireproof structure these distances can be relaxed. If there is a danger of leaking into watercourses, then a catch pit or bund must be constructed. Oil tanks are also ugly and their careless siting can spoil an otherwise attractive elevation. They can be buried underground (like a petrol station) but the cost here soars to more than £2000. Camouflaging with trellis and climbers is a cheaper option but allows access for tank replacement.

## Liquid Petroleum Gas (LPG)

Storage tank needs to be 3m from any buildings or boundaries so there are comparatively few sites that it is suited to. Calor Gas are the biggest supplier and they take on full responsibility for installation and maintenance of tanks. They usually charge around £300 to install a tank: this includes pipe laying to boiler. Occasionally they are prone to doing special offers at around £100. Note that alternative suppliers such as Shell supply tanks for free — but you are then bound to use them as suppliers. Bulk gas tanks are even more of an eyesore than oil tanks and their placing is a matter that the planners will want to consider — don't plump for an LPG supply as an afterthought, you may be letting yourself in for big problems. Note that, like oil tanks, LPG tanks can be buried underground but this is likely to cost £400 extra plus excavation costs.

## Solid Fuel

This all-embracing term includes just about everything you can burn which isn't a liquid (oil) or a gas: housecoal, anthracite and the processed coals (coalite, fernicite, coke) wood, peat, you name it. Solid fuel can be stored anywhere under cover (the bath?) but purpose-built coal bunkers would cost a minimum of £200 (M £80, L £120). Plastic ones are available from £90. If you use wood, it is important to have somewhere dry to store it; this takes space but can be an attractive feature in its own right.

## Capabilities

### Gas

Gas is the preferred fuel for most people and gas is at the leading edge of heating technology. Nearly 80% of central heating systems run on mains gas and, where it is available, it is the overwhelming choice in new developments. The market responds to this by making far more gas-burning products available — and at keener prices. Another plus for gas is that it is, arguably, the best fuel for cooking.

### LPG

Despite having a tiny fraction of the market (around 2%), LPG versions of many gas boilers are available, though usually around 10-15% more expensive — LPG boilers can be converted to mains gas. Note that LPG can also be used for cooking.

### Oil

Oil-fired systems account for around 10% of the market overall, and are much the most popular choice in rural areas where mains gas is not an option. There is a much smaller range of boilers available and prices are 20-50% more than gas equivalents, though this is partly because they use the more efficient pressure jet burner which reduces running costs. Oil cannot be used to cook with (unless using an oil-fired range).

### Solid Fuel

Solid fuel heating systems are available as kitchen ranges, living room stoves or utility room boilers. Anything that the other fuels can do, solid fuel can do; compared to the other fuels, though, solid fuel heating is unresponsive, inefficient and plain hard work. Wood-burning stoves do not generate enough heat for DHW and wet heating systems combined.

### Electricity

Using electricity as a main heat source invariably means latching on to one of the off-peak tariffs. This, in turn, means restricted hours of use which is the biggest limitation. In other respects electricity is the most capable of all fuels because it can be used for just about every household function requiring power.

### Green Power Sources

There is always a healthy interest in non-fossil fuel sources and there are some interesting — if experimental — houses being built which hardly use any fossil fuels at all. The problem with all of the green alternatives is that they don't provide an all round energy solution: they'll give you some of your hot water, some of your electricity but you will still need some form of fossil fuel backup. For instance, warm water solar panels are, at best, a top-up energy source which can provide most of the hot water needs for a UK house in summer and less than 15% in winter. Using solar power is unlikely to save more than 10% of overall fuel bills, whichever system you use for your main heat source. There are also green heating systems around such as heat pumps which take energy from the ground. But these require electricity to run.

## Fuel Costs

Prices in the Fuel Costs Table are for the Cambridgeshire area, where the benchmark house is located, during 2002. There is inevitably some regional variation in prices but these tend not to be greater than 10% up or down, and so these figures give a reasonable guideline to likely charges. Table 8b shows the apparent cost of each fuel and gives a method for converting these costs into kWh for easier comparison. I have only covered the main fuel choices and if the fuel you are planning to use is not listed get in touch with Sutherland Associates who publish a very comprehensive guide to comparative fuel costs. The Effective Costs table shows the cost of the heat after it has been converted from the raw fuel by your boiler; this effective cost is dependent on the efficiency of your appliance.

### Electricity

Electricity is charged by the kWh and so price comparisons are straightforward. Also, electric heating is virtually 100% efficient so what you pay for is what you get. Electricity suppliers (RECs) are free to set their own tariffs and there is some variation between them. And since 1999, domestic customers in England, Wales and Scotland have been free to buy their electricity from a range of suppliers — currently over 20 and rising (a current list can be found on OFFER's web page at www.open.gov.uk/offer). Not only are there more suppliers but each has its own tariffs and its own payment options. Your electricity bills can be reduced by careful shopping about, by using as much cheap-rate nighttime electricity as possible (look to use Economy 10 tariffs or similar) and by paying your bills by direct debit — usually worth a 5% reduction on its own. You can increase your bills by between 5% and 7% by opting for an Eco Tariff which promises to match your demand with a similar amount of electricity generated by renewable sources such as solar panels and wind power. To get prices contact Bill Enquiries at your local electricity supply company who are — much as it perplexes them — obliged to give you a list of alternative suppliers as well.

Note that one of the alternative suppliers is British Gas who promise great savings simply by combining the two utility bills. It seems almost fatuous, but apparently something like one hour in four spent working for a utility company is spent collecting the monies it is owed, so there is certainly logic in offering to combine the billing. Where are you Tesco?

## Gas

Gas is also billed in kWhs which makes comparison with electricity easy — again, phone your Bill Enquiries for local rates. How much of the gas you consume actually ends up heating your house depends on the efficiency of your boiler, hence the variable efficiency ratios suggested in the accompanying table 8c. As with electricity supply companies, British Gas also offers a favourable tariff to customers offering to pay monthly by direct debit; doing this should save you more than 5% on your gas bill. The comments about combining utility bills apply just as much to the gas industry as the electricity industry and you can now purchase your gas from a number of suppliers, including electricity companies.

## LPG

Although there is no tariff as such, Calor Gas — the main supplier — make a charge of around £50/annum for tank maintenance. For local prices, check Yellow Pages under Gas Suppliers or Bottled Gas.

## Oil

The most common fuel of this type is known as 28-second burning oil. The modern generation of pressure-jet oil boilers are more efficient than non- condensing gas boilers by up to 5% but only if regularly maintained (which means replacing the burner every year or so). Otherwise, the same general principles of boiler efficiency still operate — although note that oil-fired condensing boilers are very expensive.

For best local prices, check Yellow Pages under Oil fuel distributors & suppliers. Oil prices have been fluctuating wildly for the past three years but over the past twenty years oil has been the cheapest fuel on average. There is also usually a significant seasonal fluctuation, and having a tank large enough to allow buying once a year — in summer — will lower your fuel bills.

## Solid Fuel

More complex to price because of the variety of different types of fuel and the enormous variation in boiler/stove efficiencies. I have priced two of the most common solid fuels, household coal and anthracite, but there are numerous other processed, smokeless coals around. Their effective cost is unlikely to be less than anthracite. For local prices, see Yellow Pages under Coal & Solid Fuel Merchants.

Wood is altogether too variable to present any comparative costings; although it burns well and results in a garden-friendly ash waste, it is unlikely to be cost effective when compared to coal, which burns very much hotter.

## Environmental Impact

To get a better understanding of the environmental issues involved with home energy use, refer to Chapter 13, Green Issues. There are two particular areas where concern focuses: firstly how clean (or dirty) any particular fuel is and secondly how much carbon dioxide ($CO_2$) each fuel releases into the atmosphere. $CO_2$ is the gas readily associated with the greenhouse effect, which is reckoned to be causing long term global warming.

- Solar power is generally a very green power source. As yet its impact on the environment is limited because it's too expensive to install.
- Gas is the cleanest of the fossil fuels in that it produces very little sulphur dioxide or nitrous oxide (the acid rain gases). It's also efficient in that little is lost in transmission from source to end user and so its combustion produces comparatively little $CO_2$.
- Oil is a slightly dirtier fuel than gas (acid rain wise) but tends to produce even less $CO_2$ than gas. Transporting oil around the world is cheap but occasionally hazardous when tankers run aground.
- Electricity is a form of converted energy so it is much processed before it enters the home. It is generated in a number of ways — by burning coal, oil, gas and other fossil fuels, by hydroelectricity, by wind and solar power and, most controversially, by nuclear fission. Some of these are clean, some are not, whilst nuclear power is, paradoxically, both the cleanest major energy source available and potentially the most dangerous. Whatever the merits or demerits of electricity generation, much of its energy is lost in transmission along the national grid, which adds to its expense and reinforces its poor environmental rating.
- Coal, British Coal in particular, is a dirty fuel which contributes loads of sulphur to the atmosphere. Despite cutbacks in coal-mining, it remains the one British fossil fuel with long-term reserves. Anthracite and the smokeless fuels are much cleaner than housecoal, but do still not compare well with gas or oil.

## And the winner is..

There is actually remarkably little in it.

The table 8d summarises the comparative costs of using different fuels on the benchmark house. The three main fuel choices, gas, oil and LPG are each assessed in two different ways, firstly with a new but conventionally-fired boiler and next with condensing boilers — more on these anon. Electricity and solid fuel are assessed in the last two columns (or the top two rows, seeing as how the table has been turned sideways in order to fit on the page). The table looks at space heating and hot water costs in a house built to the new thermal standards which came into effect in 2002. In addition cooking costs are added to the blend. It is assumed that where gas is available it will be used for both oven and hob. Actually the fuel used for cooking has quite a significant impact on the whole equation, enough to make mains gas look about £50 a year cheaper than oil. If you chose to have electric cooking instead, the running costs would be almost identical. The condensing boilers are more expensive to install but do pay for themselves by lowering running costs.

The option that does surprisingly well is electric heating. It's so cheap to install that even though its annual running costs are nearly double that of mains gas, it takes around ten years before the aggregate cost of installation and total running costs overtakes mains gas. This is looking at a fairly conventional electric heating system, either storage heaters or underfloor elements. Switch to an electrically powered ground source heat pump and you'd have a heat source that is a) the most expensive to install and b) by far the cheapest to run.

There are of course many other factors at play. The more insulation you build into the structure, the less heat you require. There is more on this in the Green Issues chapter. And of course I have ignored things like solar panels which give you some free heat.

# 8d: Benchmark House: Fuel Cost Comparison

| | GAS Conventional Boiler | GAS Condensing Boiler | LPG Conventional Boiler | LPG Condensing Boiler | OIL Conventional Boiler | OIL Condensing Boiler | ELECTRIC HEATING | SOLID FUEL |
|---|---|---|---|---|---|---|---|---|
| **SPACE HEATING** | | | | | | | | |
| Fuel Connection Fee | £150 | £150 | £0 | £0 | £0 | £0 | £0 | £0 |
| Storage Costs | £0 | £0 | £300 | £300 | £400 | £400 | £0 | £100 |
| System Installation | £3,700 | £3,900 | £3,800 | £4,100 | £3,900 | £4,700 | £2,000 | £3,700 |
| Annual Tariff | £35 | £35 | £55 | £55 | £0 | £0 | £13 | £0 |
| Annual Service | £30 | £30 | £30 | £30 | £50 | £50 | £0 | £20 |
| Basic Fuel Cost (pence/kWh) | 1.5 p | 1.5 p | 2.5 p | 2.5 p | 1.6 p | 1.6 p | 3.2 p | 2.3 p |
| **SPACE HEATING REQUIREMENTS (HOUSE BUILT TO 2002 STANDARDS)** | | | | | | | | |
| Heat Required (kWh/annum) | 7,100 | 7,100 | 7,100 | 7,100 | 7,100 | 7,100 | 7,100 | 7,100 |
| System Efficiency | 78% | 90% | 80% | 90% | 85% | 95% | 100% | 65% |
| Fuel Used (kWh/annum) | 9,103 | 7,889 | 8,875 | 7,889 | 8,353 | 7,474 | 7,100 | 10,923 |
| Annual Space Heating Bill | £136 | £118 | £222 | £197 | £134 | £120 | £227 | £251 |
| **DOMESTIC HOT WATER** | | | | | | | | |
| Heat Required (kWh/annum) | 4000 | 4000 | 4000 | 4000 | 4000 | 4000 | 4000 | 4000 |
| System Efficiency | 78% | 90% | 80% | 90% | 85% | 95% | 100% | 65% |
| Fuel Used (kWh/annum) | 5128 | 4444 | 5000 | 4444 | 4706 | 4211 | 4000 | 6154 |
| Annual Bill for Heating Water | £76 | £66 | £125 | £111 | £75 | £67 | £128 | £142 |
| **COOKING** | | | | | | | | |
| Cheapest Fuel | BY GAS | BY GAS | BY LPG | BY LPG | BY ELECTRICITY | BY ELECTRICITY | BY ELECTRICITY | BY ELECTRICITY |
| Fuel Used (kWh/annum) | 1000 | 1000 | 1000 | 1000 | 1000 | 1000 | 1000 | 1000 |
| Annual Cooking Fuel Bill | £15 | £15 | £25 | £25 | £65 | £65 | £65 | £65 |
| **SUMMARY** | | | | | | | | |
| INSTALLATION COSTS | £3,850 | £4,050 | £4,100 | £4,400 | £4,300 | £5,100 | £2,000 | £3,800 |
| ANNUAL RUNNING COSTS | £227 | £199 | £372 | £333 | £274 | £252 | £420 | £458 |
| COMBINED COSTS after 10 YRS | £6,119 | £6,037 | £7,919 | £7,733 | £7,039 | £7,619 | £6,202 | £8,378 |

FUEL COSTS INCLUDE VAT at 5%

# Boilers

Boilers are rated according to the power they can produce. Manufacturers still work in BTU (British Thermal Units); I'm trying to be metric, but in the section, for clarity's sake, I'll use both. Just remember:

• 1kW = 3410 BTU.

A small application — like a one bedroom flat — might use a 20,000 BTU boiler (6kW); a large Victorian vicarage would require something in excess of 100,000 BTU (30kW). A new four-bedroom house built to the latest thermal regulations will need — well read on, it's a bit controversial.

Conventionally, boilers are sized by totalling the radiator output (worked out from the heat calculation) and adding a bit for heating domestic hot water (DHW), and then going to the nearest size above. This is a bit hit and miss, to say the least. For a more detailed explanation of heat calculations, see Chapter 13, Green Issues.

The industry standard is to design heating systems capable of keeping the house around 21°C warmer than the temperature outside. Now in a new house, built to 1995 building regs, the amount of heat needed to keep the structure 21°C warmer than outside is surprisingly small. As a rule of thumb, you need no more than 25 watts per m³ of living space. The benchmark house, with a floor area of 161m², has 355m³ of living space and this means that the heating requirement is (25 x 355) 8875 watts or 8.9kW (30,000 BTU). However, the Vokera gas boiler fitted into the house is rated at 20kW. How come the discrepancy? Are U values (the basis of heat calculations) meaningless or is there some conspiracy to sell us bigger boilers and radiators than we really need?

One little known reason for apparent oversizing is that radiators are usually only 70% efficient: outputs claimed in manufacturers' brochures apply to radiators connected at the top corner on one side and at the bottom on the other: these days radiators are usually connected bottom to bottom and this dramatically lowers their output. Mears calculators and various rules of thumb, used by plumbers to carry out heat calculations, take account of this discrepancy without ever explaining it. However, whilst radiators should arguably be oversized by as much as 50%, boilers themselves do not have to be 50% larger to deliver the anticipated heat from each radiator.

Another factor to take into account is that a central heating system has to be felt to be working and that means that it must be able not only to keep a house warm, but to heat it up from cold within a reasonable (say one hour) time-scale. This obviously requires extra heat but not that much extra — the benchmark house requires just 1.4kW extra heat to raise the temperature 10°C in one hour — and a 12kW (40,000 BTU) boiler really ought to handle background heating, boost heating and hot water needs. Such a boiler will be £100 cheaper to buy and cheaper to run. However, if you insisted on a 12kW boiler, your plumber would probably want you to sign a disclaimer in event of it being underpowered! I know of plumbers who have been sued by clients — albeit ones living in uninsulated old houses — because the system they installed didn't make the house warm enough, so perhaps it's not surprising that plumbers tend to view these things conservatively and to err on the side of caution.

Note I have lifted this section verbatim from the last edition. The building regs have of course been amended since then and since 2002 the minimum levels of insulation in the standard home are around 50% better than alluded to here. This in turn will reduce the heating rule of thumb figure right down to around 12 watts per m³ of living space or just 4.5kW output — you check this out on Table 13d on page 205. Trouble is that no one makes a boiler that small. The Plumb Center catalogue routinely refers to 30,000BTU boilers as five radiator ones and 40,000BTU boilers as seven radiator ones. In the replacement market, ideal but the post-2002 version of our 15 radiator benchmark house doesn't even need a 30,000BTU boiler to keep the place warm. In fact, 6kW output, just 20,000BTU would be adequate. The reason boilers don't get much smaller is that they have another job to do, which is heating up the hot water for the taps. The really low output boiler couldn't do that job in an acceptable timescale.

## How Size Affects Price

Typically, each model will be produced in six or seven sizes ranging from mini 15-30,000 BTU (4-8kW) up to 80-100,000 BTU (23-30kW). Plumber's merchants will regularly knock 30% off list for trade customers — more for regular clients. The price difference between sizes is not great; however that difference increases with the boiler sizes. The difference between the smallest and the next smallest is just £40, whereas the difference between the largest shown and the next size down is £100.

## PLUMBING SYSTEMS COMPARED

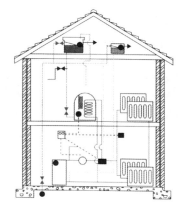

**TRADITIONAL BRITISH METHOD**
*Tanks in the loft and a hot water cylinder*

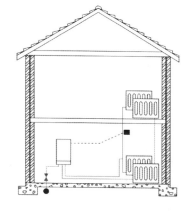

**COMBIS**
*No water storage involved at all. The cold feeds all come off the mains. The hot water is heated instantly as it passes through the combi boiler*

## Boiler Heat Exchangers

The older type of gas- and oil-fired boilers use cast iron heat exchangers and work by heating this cast-iron, which holds heat well and, in turn, transfers the heat through to the hot water. They are characterised by being easy to install, reliable and inefficient. The cast iron takes a comparatively long time to heat up and a correspondingly long time to cool down — hence the inefficiency of heat transfer.

The more modern style of boilers — which includes the combi and condensing boilers — are made with copper or other lightweight metal heat exchangers and operate with a much lower water content. They are more efficient but have to be much more carefully commissioned, and it is vital that the correct corrosive inhibitors are present. They also need more servicing.

## Combination Boilers

A combi has a second heat exchanger in the boiler which works as an instantaneous water heater, in the manner of the once popular Ascot water heaters, used to heat water bound directly for the hot tap. This second heat exchanger adds 50-80% to the price of the boiler but this cost penalty is clawed back by the elimination of hot water storage (in cylinders), and tanks and associated pipework in the loft. All in all, it is cheaper to install than a conventional system. Combi boilers are now well established in the UK — they account for around 50% of all new boiler sales — and the market is dominated by continental manufacturers like Vaillant and Vokera. Low flow rates mean they are not that wonderful for applications such as showers but they are good choices for households with erratic lifestyles, coming and going at all hours. The relatively low water content heat exchangers also mean they need rather more careful commissioning by the plumber and, even so, the heat exchangers scale up in hard water areas. Hard water scaling isn't a terminal problem — you can get the boilers descaled — but it won't do any harm to fit some sort of scale inhibiting device as well.

## Condensing Boilers

Condensing boilers, also known as energy efficient boilers, work by having extra large heat exchangers which extract a much greater proportion of the usable energy from the fuel; consequently, the exhaust fumes are much cooler and this causes condensation inside the boiler (hence the name), which in all other boilers would spell disaster. The exhaust gas comes out at a surprisingly low temperature, usually around 50°C to 60°C as opposed to 250°C on a conventional boiler and as a result the flue from a condenser can be plastic. They also give off a mildly acid condensate which should be piped into the soil stack or to an outside gully. To cope with the condensation, the heat exchangers are made of aluminium or stainless steel — one of the main reasons for their extra expense.

The overall market share for condensers remains tiny (less than 3% of boilers sold) and the plumbing trade in general remains very reluctant to embrace this new technology, despite early indications that they work pretty well. But this is expected to change rapidly as the 2002 changes to the building regs look at boiler efficiencies for the first time. There are now hundreds of models of gas condensers available and an increasing number of oil-fired ones as well. A gas-fired condenser is usually around £300 more than its conventional cousin whereas an oil-fired condenser is about £1000 more. Note that Baxi, our largest gas boiler manufacturer, introduced their first condenser, the Barcelona, at the tail end of 1998 and it is priced very competitively against conventional boilers. In common with several more advanced boilers, it modulates its own output so that one size is big enough for any application up to 30kW.

## The Plume

One problem that is present with condensing boilers is the plume of water vapour that issues from the waste flue. Its chemical composition is no different to waste gas coming out of conventional boilers but because the gas has been allowed to cool below 54°C, the large amount of water vapour present condenses and appears as a white cloud known as a plume. For each kilogramme of natural gas burnt, approximately two kilograms of water vapour is produced and a condensing boiler, when working in full condensing mode, can produce about a pint of liquid per hour. There are certain situations such as flats where the plume has caused problems for neighbours, but in a detached house this should be of minor importance, though it may well be worth locating the flue well away from windows — many condensing boilers allow you to duct the waste gas quite a distance.

## Boiler Efficiency

The changes to Part L of the building regs have had many profound effects on the way we build homes but one of the most surprising is the inclusion for the first time of boiler efficiency measures. Minimum standards were set for newly installed boilers in both new build and in the replacement market., these being a 78% efficiency for gas, 80% for LPG and 85% for oil boilers. At a stroke many old tried and trusted boilers were rendered obsolete. And whilst these efficiencies don't require condensing technology in order to comply, the U value trade-offs allowed in the regs, the so-called Target Method of compliance, meant that housebuilders could get away with less insulation in the fabric of the structure in exchange for fitting a condensing boiler. The key to understanding all this is to be found on the web at www.sedbuk.com where the efficiencies of over 500 different boilers is listed — the list is updated monthly and is growing all the time. SEDBUK stands for the Seasonal Efficiency of Domestic Boilers in the UK. Remember that. You'll be tested on it at the end of the chapter. What it is measuring is the percentage of fuel burned by a boiler that ends up as usable heat. So a 78% SEDBUK percentage means that 78% of the fuel turns into heat in the home and the other 22% gets wasted. Like GCSEs, boilers are now banded from A (excellent) down to G (terrible - suitable for the Albanian export market only). D is the pass mark for gas boilers — i.e. over 78% in gas, 80% in LPG or 85% for oil-fired. The best, most efficient boiler in the SEDBUK charts at time of writing was the oil fired Grant Vortex with a 95% efficiency rating. The best gas boiler was the brand new Potterton Promax in its small, 15kW version — it was rated at 91.3%. Most commercially available boilers are now SEDBUK rated but a few smaller boiler manufacturers don't

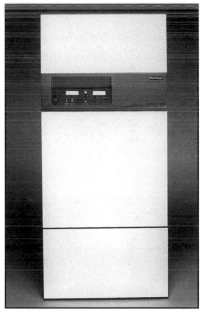

*1460 high x 550 wide x 600 deep, the Potterton Powermax HE is an all-in-one gas-fired condensing boiler and unvented hot water system. Its SEDBUK rating is right up there in Band A (90.5% efficiency); its hot water output is very fast, and my local plumber's merchant had "never heard of it." The only drawback I can see is the price — I was quoted £1875*

seem to have got around to it at time of writing. Note that the boiler efficiency rules do not apply in Scotland — a cynical sales ploy to get rid of old boilers that no longer cut the mustard south of the border?

### Flue Choices

Where you have a boiler, you must also have some form of exhaust pipe to get rid of the fumes. The flue, as it is known, is actually quite an expensive part of the kit and selecting the right flue is an important step. There are currently three options.

### Conventional Flues

This is the old-fashioned, low-tech solution and involves releasing the exhaust fumes into some sort of vertical chimney. However, conventional flues require an intake of air from the house. This presents no problem in an old draughty pile, but in a draught-proofed new house provision must be made for an air feed from outside or under the floor — which will add to the heat load of the boiler. Also, the possibility of these air vents becoming blocked at a later date presents a potential safety hazard.

### Balanced Flue

This draws fresh, combustible air in from the same opening through which the exhaust fumes are expelled. Nowadays, the preferable option with gas and oil-fired boilers; some balanced flue versions (Glow Worm's Fuelsaver) are the same price as conventional flues but most manufacturers add a 15-20% premium. In a new dwelling however, this is almost always going to be much cheaper than building in a conventional flue.

### Fan Flue

Popular in flats where boiler positioning is sometimes difficult. Specifying a fanned flue adds 20-30% to the cost of a conventionally flued boiler, but allows a far greater number of positioning possibilities because the fumes can be expelled a much greater distance.

### Flue Positioning

There are tightly enforced regulations about where you can and can't place boiler flue terminals in outside walls. For instance, they shouldn't be less than 300mm below an opening window or under the roof eaves and they shouldn't be less than 600mm from an internal or external corner. Your designer should be aware of these hurdles, but every now and then someone gets caught out and has to reposition the boiler away from its preferred spot. Generally, the regulations are not as stringent for fan flue terminals, and fitting a fanned flue boiler can sometimes be a useful (if expensive) way around an otherwise intractable siting problem.

### Kitchen Ranges

This is an option that appeals to many because of the intrinsic style and feel. The Aga is the best known, but it is basically just a huge cast iron cooker not a whole house-heating boiler. There are a number of products (e.g. Rayburn, Stanley, Esse, Eastwood) which will fit the bill and provide all three required functions — that is cooking, space heating and DHW — from one heat source. The Rayburn GD80 (costs around £3500) is a gas-fired cooker which can provide 23kW (80,000 BTU) of space heating, but is also capable of running on a summer setting which reduces output to around 1kW. There are limitations in using ranges for all your heating requirements — no mains pressure tanks, relatively unresponsive — but the top models now have electronic time and thermostatic control and Esse even make a condensing model. No way is this a cheap option but if you have your heart set on a cast-iron cooker (which is unlikely to cost less than £2500 in any event) it is worth considering upgrading to one that does space heating and DHW as well. Having said that, the space/DHW heating capabilities come at a price (£600-£800) for which you could purchase many more efficient gas- or oil-fired boilers as well as more sophisticated controls. It is also little understood that ranges are very expensive to run, whatever the fuel. The gas-fired GD80 uses around 30,000kWh/annum (cost £400) for just normal cooking usage; this is rather more than the anticipated space heating costs for the benchmark house and nearly twenty times the cost of conventional gas cooking. The water boiler on the other hand has a bench efficiency of 80% which compares well with other gas boilers.

### Overheating

I have come across one or two examples of people fitting all singing and dancing cast iron ranges into new houses only to be overwhelmed by the amount of heat they pump out. It's a problem in summer especially when it had been hoped to use the range as a cooker only and yet the cooker won't work without heating up copious amounts of hot water which has nowhere to go except around parts of the radiator system. The better insulated the house, the bigger the problem.

# Emitters

"Emitters" is a convenient tag to use for the bits of space heating systems that deliver the heat. Go into Plumb Center and ask for an emitter and they'd most likely direct you to the local psychiatrist, but if I just call them radiators (rads in plumber-speak) then I am ignoring all the other weird and wonderful heat emitters that exist. More on those later. Conventional wet central heating systems use rads, so we'll start here.

## Pressed Steel Radiators

These are what goes into most central heating systems today and most readers will be all too familiar with them. Functional rather than elegant, there are several well-known makes which tend to compete on price: e.g. Stelrad, Myson, Barlo, Brugman. Rather like windows they come in standard shapes and sizes, typically from 300mm to 700mm high and from 500mm to 3000mm long. Most manufacturers produce three or four height options, each available in lengths which increase in 100mm steps. There are also double-panelled and finned versions which give off more heat. The Plumb Center catalogues give charts for two manufacturers' products, which enables you to plan with some degree of accuracy. Roughly speaking, they produce heat in proportion to their size: the smallest (300H x 400L) will give out 0.25kW, the largest, double-panelled type (700H x 2000L) will give out around 4kW. Having carried out a heat calculation for each room, you will be faced with a choice of shapes and sizes as to how that heat load can be met and here thought can be given to radiator placing.

### Pricing

List prices are, as ever, indicative of where the haggling starts. Discounts off radiators can be huge (60-70% is not uncommon with some manufacturers); look to pay around £30 for each kW of output — discount outlets like Harrison McCarthy can go as low as £25/kW. Merchants tend to have special offers going and so it pays not to be too fussy as to make. On the benchmark house, 15 rads with a total output of 15kW were priced between £400 and £450. Piping up the rads with 100m x 15mm copper tube, fittings, valves would cost an additional £250 in materials. Using the "greener" heat loss calculations (see previous section on boilers), which estimate heat loss at less than 8kW for the whole house, would save around £150 solely on the cost of the radiators. Condensing boilers, which work at lower temperatures, would need rads about 15% larger to get the same effect.

## Alternatives

### High Efficiency Radiators

Faral are the market leaders with their aluminium rads. Their Italian styling is a wow — but perhaps too modern for many tastes — and they are designed to work at low temperatures which makes them very suitable for condensing boilers. Cost about £75/kW. Using Faral rads would add £600 to the standard radiator costs in our test house.

### Low Water-Content Rads

Designed to work with tiny amounts of water (less than 1lt sometimes), they are very quick response and efficient, but tend to give out little radiant heat which is a bad thing, but there should be fuel savings because less water is being heated overall (a good thing). Thermalpanel are a noted producer. Cost around £60/kW output, which would add £300 to the overall price in the benchmark house.

### Period Radiators

Traditional cast-iron radiators are still around and available from an increasing range of suppliers. In period bathrooms and the like they are just the ticket but they do not come cheap. Expect to pay around £180-£200/kW output — and that's just for rads supplied in grey primer that need painting.

### Skirting Radiators

Sometimes preferred because of their low visual impact. Leading name here is Myson's Wallstrip. It goes where you would normally fit skirting board — now there's a saving. Like skirting, it can go around bends and it tends to get priced by the metre and so it's a little difficult to compare with conventional rads. Look to pay around £30-£35/metre run (depending on the number of bends, ends, etc.). Heat output depends very much on water temperature. A conventional 75°C would give off about 0.5kW/m; a condensing boiler, working at 55°C, about half that amount. However you look at it they are not going to be less than £70/kW, about twice the effective cost of bog standard rads.

### Heated Towel Rails

These specialist radiators, usually hung in the vertical, are now becoming an item in the contemporary bathroom. Zehnder are the most elegant, complete with dinky little collapsible towel rails, but they cost between £140 and £250 (about £170/kW). Myson and Worcester are around half that price. All can be coloured to match your bathroom suite (add £40) and all are available with an electric immersion heater option for summer use (add £100 plus).

## Underfloor Heating

Available as either water-based (wet) or electric, underfloor heating (or UFH) is very popular in Germany and Switzerland and is now widely specified in the UK selfbuild market. It's just beginning to take off with developers as well. Overall, its market share in the UK is still minute (of the order of 2% of central heating installations) but this is expected to grow dramatically during the next ten years. With an underfloor heating system, the floor itself becomes the emitter and, so as you don't burn your tootsies, the wet systems need to work at lower temperatures than ordinary wall rads and they are often used in conjunction with condensing boilers (which are designed to work at lower temperatures), otherwise temperature reducing equipment is needed. They are mostly laid under a cement screed which is used as a heat reservoir (like an electric storage heater); this means that the heat is released slowly throughout the day — it is pleasantly draught free and the heat stays close to the floor. Electric underfloor heating is touched on in a following section in this chapter (Alternative Heating). There are now many businesses offering varying levels of service and most can be found at the selfbuild exhibitions.

Underfloor heating is not a homogeneous product: every system is different and the quotations need to be deconstructed carefully to see whether you are comparing like with like. Watch out to see if significant extras are included — insulation, heating controls, mesh to attach the pipe to. Note that whilst UFH does away with radiators, you still need to find somewhere to fit the manifold — these are large and ugly and are best concealed in a cupboard or a utility area. In cost terms UFH tends to work out about £1500-£2500 more than a standard radiator system in a largish house, pretty similar to using skirting heating or unusual radiators.

### UFH under Timber Floors

Whilst there is some debate about the suitability of UFH under timber floors — wood is regarded as an insulating material — virtually every supplier offers it as an option.

There are several methods of installing UFH under timber floors. Some use aluminium plates to spread the heat across the floor: some require a mortar "pug" to be built as an extra layer in the floor, some use nothing at all, the pipes being clipped to the underside of the floor after it is laid. Generally the aluminium plate system is rather more expensive than the other systems in terms of materials supplied but the mortar pug system requires a fair amount of extra building work. Some suppliers quote for installation using alternative designs: the mortar pug system usually appears to be significantly cheaper but bear in mind that it will involve other significant construction costs.

### Pipe Issues

People naturally fear pipe failure with UFH. Suppliers go to great lengths to ensure that the pipe is up to the job, but as it is still a relatively new technique there is some justification for at least being worried about it. Most warm water UFH is run in PEX pipe, now widely used all over Europe and reckoned to be the safe choice. An alternative is to use one of the polybutylene pipes like OsmaGold or Hep2O. It's best to specify one with an oxygen barrier as this reduces the risk of rust getting into the system.

### Energy Saving

Many suppliers claim that UFH is inherently energy efficient and will save you money in the long term. I have my doubts. Just because it works at low temperatures compared to radiator-based system doesn't necessarily mean it will cost less to run — you are after all heating up a much larger area, using much more water. When placed in a cement screed, UFH is a very slow response system: it takes a long time to heat up and a long time to cool down. It is therefore best suited to lifestyles where people are around all day, otherwise you end up heating an empty house. Under timber floors the response times are quicker but the efficiency is reduced because of the insulating qualities of timber. Ditto when placed under thick carpets.

One common route taken by selfbuilders is to run UFH downstairs and radiators upstairs. It makes a lot of sense because a) it's a bit cheaper and b) radiators are not quite such a problem in bedrooms.

# Domestic Hot Water

The standard system, used in Britain for most of this century, uses a copper cylinder, fed by a tank overhead or in the loft, and is heated by copper tubes inside. These tubes transfer heat from the boiler primary circuit to the water in the cylinder: the domestic hot water (DHW) never passes through the boiler at all and thus it is known as an indirect system. All cylinders these days come ready insulated (lagged).

## Cost

Fitting a regular cylinder (inc. backup electric immersion heater) costs around £200 (Mats £100, Lab £100). Quick recovery cylinders (which heat cold water to 60°C within half an hour) cost around £50 extra.

### Plus

Cheap, easy to install and well understood by the average plumber. Replacement is straightforward; facility for electric immersion heating if the boiler is out of action.

### Minus

Having water tanks and pipework in the loft. Poor flow rates achieved from hot water taps due to inadequate head (or pressure) of water — this poor flow rate only really matters where a powerful shower is valued.

## Loft Plumbing

In conventional systems, there are two tanks in the loft: one (usually 227lts) feeds the cylinder, the other (usually 18lts) supplies the central heating system. Having to put a tank in the loft — avoiding this is sold as a big plus for other systems — actually costs around £220 (M 100, L £120) for the water storage tank and around £80 (M £40, L £40) for the feed and expansion tank (aka the Jockey Tank). Therefore, any system that does away with all loft plumbing is going to save you around £300.

## Instantaneous Hot Water

Small instantaneous hot water heaters are still sold but in a new house the normal way of achieving this is by fitting a Combination Boiler (or combi). Although combi boilers are 30-50% more expensive than conventional boilers, the savings in avoiding cylinders as well as loft plumbing combine to make this system as cheap and possibly cheaper to install than the standard DHW system.

### Plus

No cylinder: no loft pipework or tanks: hot water on demand, 24hrs a day: simplified controls: no switching valves needed.

### Minus

Poor flow rate remains the big problem — anything below 15lts/minute is not adequate for a family home and many combis produce as little as 10lts/minute. Also problems with scaling (in hard water areas) in the hot water heat exchanger which reduces flow rates still further.

## Mains Pressure Hot Water

These systems use unvented (i.e. no loft pipework for expansion) hot water cylinders which are strong enough to withstand storing hot water under mains pressure. They answer the problem of low flow rates to showers but at a cost of around £500. To operate to full effect they need at least 2.5 bar of mains pressure and a mains flow rate of 35lts/minute. Unfortunately, UK water companies are only obliged to provide mains water at 1 bar pressure so many situations will not benefit at all. Phone your water company to determine your local pressure. Despite being a British invention which went on to be the most popular hot water delivery method in the rest of Europe and North America, mains pressure hot water cylinders were actually prohibited by our water bylaws until 1987. On grounds of safety. Not that they are particularly dangerous. They are now available with a whole raft of safety features attached (which is partly responsible for their comparative expense) and a requirement that they be installed by a qualified person. Despite all this, they have been rapidly taken up and account for around one in six all new cylinder sales and as much as 50% of cylinders going into new homes.

### Plus

No loft pipework: mains pressure hot water delivered to all parts of the house, particularly valued by shower users: a small saving on being able to use smaller bore pipework throughout.

### Minus

Expensive (extra £200 on standard): need certified installers (also likely to be expensive). Don't use with cheap taps: leaks, when they do occur, are much worse when under mains pressure. No back up storage if supply is cut off. It's worth paying extra for a stainless steel or enamel version if you live in a hard water area.

## Variations

I have outlined three approaches to delivery of DHW. Needless to say there are a number of other options that sort of mix and match these three approaches.

## Thermal Stores

A variation of the unvented hot water cylinder is the thermal store. These systems work by reversing the logic of the standard setup and use a cylinder of hot water to heat cold water channelled through it at mains pressure. Result? Hot water at up to 30lts/minute comes straight out of the hot taps. As hot water is not actually stored under mains pressure, it doesn't have to be installed by a qualified plumber. Thermal stores also usually work without the need for tanks in the loft; instead they come with integral feed and expansion tanks. For a four-bedroom house, expect installation costs of around £300 (including mixing valves), about midway between using the standard route and using mains pressure unvented systems.

Thermal stores were first developed by British Gas in the early 80s and are produced by a number of small British manufacturers. They are particularly good when you want to combine different inputs; e.g. if you have a solar panel or a heat pump supplying hot water as well as a boiler. You can get thermal stores made to order to fit your particular application from a couple of thermal store boutiques, Chelmer Heating and DPS Heatsave.

## All in One Units

Another approach is to combine both boiler and cylinder in one box, a systems approach if you like. A piece of kit such as Potterton's Powermax HE has a mains pressure condensing boiler and a stainless steel mains pressure cylinder plus a pump and a programmer all in a box just 550 wide by 600 deep — the height varies with the size of the water tank but the biggest, the 150lt tank version, is still only 1460mm high. All the installer has to do is fit six copper connections and the flue. All you have to do is fork out £1800 for the kit.

## Shower Pumps

When all is said and done, the main reason for having mains pressure hot water is to enjoy decent showers — that's the place you really notice the difference. If you want to stick with a gravity system but value a good shower, then you will need to fit a shower pump. There are single impeller pumps which boost the water after the mixing valve, and double impellers which boost both hot and cold before they enter the valve. There is also an increasing number of all-in-one pump and valve shower units like the Triton Aquasensation (£170). Which you choose is partly dependent on the layout you have. Prices are largely dependent on the power of the pump. They can be purchased for just over £100, but a pump delivering 30lts/minute (equivalent to a good mains pressure system) will cost £180 plus. Most work on a timed switch. Add the costs for extra wiring and fitting and you can see that a shower pump is not a very clever option in a new building, where you would be quids in by starting off with a better DHW system. Leading manufacturers: Mira, Aqualisa.

# Background

- A bath takes about 70-80lts of hot water and so water storage needs to be above this level (or instantaneous) to be adequate. Hot water cylinders usually hold around twice this amount.
- A typical household of four uses between 200 and 250lts of hot water a day, conventionally heated to 60°C.
- It takes 12kWh to heat 200lts of water through 50°C (the difference between the temperature of the cold water and the hot water) and the average cost of water heating (by gas or oil-fired boiler) is £100/annum.
- Just under half of all water consumed in the home is heated.

## Showers and Flow Rates

- A good power shower needs a flow rate of 25lts/minute. This will not be achieved by the conventional system where the flow of hot water is determined by the height of the loft tank above the outlet. A pump will be required (or else feeble showers endured).
- In an unvented mains pressure system (or a thermal store), the flow rate is dependent on the mains pressure supplied by the local water company.
- With a combi boiler, which produces instantaneous hot water, the flow rate depends on the design of the boiler. It is unlikely to be much better than 10lts/minute.

## Recovery Rates

The time taken for cold water from the mains to get to 60°C inside the cylinder is referred to as the recovery rate. This rate is dependent on the size of the boiler or the cylinder heat exchanger, whichever is smaller. For instance, a typical cylinder for a four-bedroom house needs 8kWh of energy to heat its 140lts of water from 10°C to 60°C; an 8kW heater will accomplish this feat in one hour, whereas a 16kW heater will take just half as long. In theory a 32kW heater would achieve the same

feat in 15 minutes, but in practice this would not happen unless the boiler was also rated at 32kW, which is unlikely. Here the boiler size becomes the limiting factor in the recovery rate. Unlike boilers, cylinders are not advertised by the size of their heat exchangers; however, most manufacturers sell a "standard" version (Cost £80) which takes about one hour to heat up and a "quick recovery" version which takes 20 minutes (Cost £130). The latter simply have larger heat exchangers.

## Efficiency/Heat Loss

All new cylinders are insulated to reduce heat loss to less than 3kW of heat during a 24-hour period. Effectively, this heat loss can be ignored for six months of the year as it is simply transferring heat from water to space heat; during the summer you might leak something like 500kWh of heat — value £10-£15. Many new cylinders (like the Megaflo) are encapsulated by 50mm of polyurethane which reduces heat lost over a 24hr period to under 1kW — nothing to all intents and purposes. Annual DHW costs using an average 225lts/day should be about 5,000kWh or £100 for a gas or oil system. A super-lagged cylinder will save around £10/annum.

## Dead Legs

The hot water piping running between the cylinder and the hot water taps is effectively an extension to the cylinder; water sitting there loses its heat very quickly. An efficiently

designed installation would have around 5lts of water sitting in the hot pipes. This may sound insignificant, but bear in mind that every time a hot tap is opened some of this water is replaced and so if every hot tap is turned on just 3 times a day, then 15lts of extra hot water has to be heated (cost per annum 300kWh or £6-£10). An inefficient design with much longer dead legs — i.e. bathrooms and kitchen all at opposite ends of the house — might use four or five times the length of hot water pipe. Not only does the cost of supplying hot water to the dead legs then become significant (£30 plus/annum) but you start getting 20-30 second lags between opening the hot tap and getting hot water. Avoid long dead legs if possible.

There is a way around this problem which is to create a pumped hot water loop around the house so that there is always hot water at each hot tap. However you have the added cost of installing and running a circulation pump and, to be effective, you have to insulate the hot water pipes to a high standard otherwise you will gain very little.

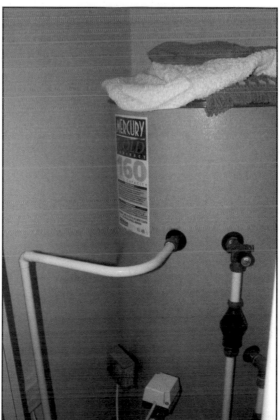

*AB Homes, our benchmark housebuilders, fitted these mains pressure hot water tanks throughout their development. The UK didn't allow them to be fitted until 1987 because of safety fears but they have since taken off in a big way in the new homes market and are now fitted in over half of all new homes.*

# Heating Controls

Before the days of central heating (c.1950), heating controls consisted of putting (or not putting) coal on the fire or, at best, an on/off switch on an electric heater. Here is an industry that has grown at a prodigious rate and there is now a bewildering range of options open to the householder. Yet the purpose of controls is quite simple:

* to increase comfort
* to decrease fuel consumption
* safety.

This section concentrates on wet heating systems; other heating systems (warm air, electric, solid fuel) tend to have different control systems which will be touched on in the following section, Alternative Heating.

## Programmers

Timers to the layman. These are basically the on/off switch for the whole heating system and, as such, override all the other controls (except safety features like frost thermostats). Digital display has brought big improvements to programmers and now for little more than £30 you can get separate control for hot water heating and space heating which you can switch on and off 21 times a week. Changing the setting is about as easy as recording a film on the video — i.e. it helps to be young. Also, plumbers just love being called back to find out why the heating isn't coming on, only to find that you've been messing around with the programmer.

Look for ones with a boost (or "Extra Hour") facility which allows you to turn the system on at odd times — mostly a standard feature now. A basic electronic programmer is now considered an absolutely essential component of a central heating system. Digital displays are now almost universal — although it hasn't made them easier to use or understand than the older ones with plastic knobs.

## Thermostats

Known by plumbers as just stats, these provide a secondary level of on/off switching, controlled by temperature. So if the air or water temperature is higher than the thermostat setting, these controls will switch the heating system off, even though the programmer says "run."

* ROOM STATS: cost £12. Will cut off hot water to radiators when the set temperature is reached. Placing them requires care. To some extent being replaced by TRVs and programmable thermostats — see below.
* CYLINDER STAT: cost £9. Does much the same for hot water cylinder. Some are integral with the cylinder, some are strapped onto the copper walls.
* BOILER STATS: Usually integral with the boiler, these set the temperature of water passing through the boiler, which is the hottest part of the system.
* FROST STAT: cost £20. A safety device which turns on heating if there is a danger of any components freezing — e.g. boilers in garages or other unheated spaces. It can of course take precedence over a timer which says the system should be off. Malfunctioning frost stats can be expensive to run and difficult to pinpoint.
* HIGH LIMIT STAT: cost £30. A safety device to stop sealed system boilers overheating (or boiling). Ask if your preferred boiler needs one.

## Motorised Zone Valves

These are what the programmer operates; they are used to switch the flow of hot water around different parts (or zones) of the system. The cheapest systems use a 3-port valve (£40) but it is better to use two 2-port valves (2 x £30). The simplest valves switch all water either this way or that and therefore give rise to something called hot water priority, which means that the hot water stops being pumped around the radiators when the domestic hot water is being heated in the cylinder. There are more costly valves that are capable of opening in a middle position which allows a flow of hot water both ways.

A standard set of heating controls (excluding TRVs) for a four-bedroom house would cost around £200 (Mats £100, Lab £100). These controls are often sold in packages which usually include a pump, motorised valve, a programmer, a room stat and a cylinder stat. Note that wiring must be provided between all these components.

## TRVs

Thermostatic radiator valves (TRVs) are apparently simple little gizmos fitted on to the bottom of the radiators that can sense the air temperature and switch off supply to the radiator when satisfied. They are cheap (£7); they increase comfort levels by stopping overheating and they reduce fuel bills. They are becoming almost standard — they are fitted throughout the benchmark house.

### Minus

There have been problems with the operation of TRVs. Many people do not understand the principle of thermostatic control and, when feeling cold and seeing a dial, turn the TRVs on fully, thinking this will make the radiators hotter. It won't. Furthermore, because they require manual operation, there is no way of knowing (other than learning from experience) how high to set them to achieve comfortable space heating in any given room — though note that the latest versions (Danfoss) allow you to adjust the highest/lowest settings.

### Another Minus

TRVs have been prone to sticking (usually in the off position) and many people have reported radiators not working at all at the beginning of the heating season. Drayton TRVs had a particularly poor record; I know of someone who took all their TRVs off because they appeared to stop the radiators working at all. Manufacturing controls now appear to

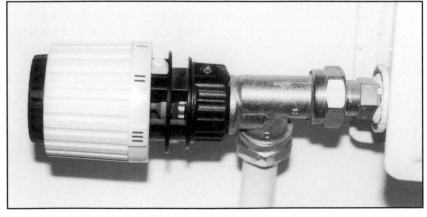

*The near ubiquitous TRV — but is it any good?*

be better and this problem should be eliminated, but only time will tell. Honeywell TRVs are said to be among the more reliable.

### Yet Another Minus

TRVs don't reduce fuel bills by as much as you might think — or that their manufacturers might claim. Although they can stop supply of hot water to the radiator to which they are fitted, they have no way of letting the boiler know this fact. In some systems which replace the room stat with TRVs, all radiators can be satisfied yet the boiler will continue to push hot water around the flow and return runs controlled only by the timer and the boiler thermostat. Don't be talked into doing away with the room stat just because you've fitted TRVs. They really only offer fine adjustments to the heating in each room.

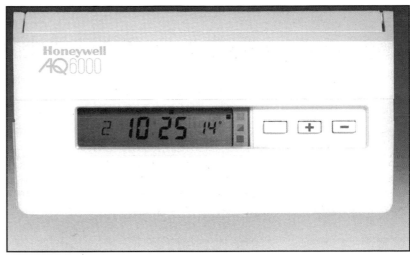

*The Honeywell AQ6000 was the first boiler manager to be aimed at the home market*

## Underfloor Systems

If you want underfloor heating controlled on a room-by-room basis, you have to use wall mounted room stats, which is an expensive option when compared with TRVs.

## Programmable Thermostats

These combine the functions of the ordinary programmer (time switching) with that of the room stat (temperature switching). They also allow you to pre select different temperature maxima for different times of day: very clever but even less user-friendly than the ordinary electronic programmers. A potential energy saver; a potential comfort increaser and no more expensive than a programmer and room stat separately. Whereas ordinary programmers can be placed anywhere that's convenient, once you introduce a thermostat you have to think very carefully about its location and which temperatures it will be measuring.

## Boiler Managers

(aka optimisers or weather compensators). Currently the most upmarket controls option available, the use of these is slowly filtering down from large industrial buildings to housing. The price reflects the variety and complexity of controls from relatively simple systems like the Honeywell AQ 6000 (costs around £170 — around double the basic controls) to multi-zoned systems like Landis & Staefer's's RVP 75 or the DCD Heating Controller which cost around £300.

They aim to stabilise room temperatures whilst reducing the fuel consumption of boilers. You programme the manager to have your home heated to the temperatures you choose at the times you select and the manager decides the most efficient ways of achieving this. A microprocessor is fed data monitoring outside air temperature and heating water tem-

perature and it is able to independently switch the boiler and the pump on or off to maximise efficiency. Their use is particularly recommended with condensing boilers where they are able to maximise the length of time that the boilers can work in condensing mode (which increases fuel efficiency).

### Minus

There have been problems to do with rusting heat exchangers when boiler managers have been coupled with a cast-iron boiler. Check with your boiler manufacturer to see if it is compatible with a boiler manager running a low temperature heating system.

### Another Minus

The controls are even more difficult to understand than programmable thermostats; many people are likely to be flummoxed by them, which partly accounts for their slow uptake in domestic situations. This is particularly true of the more upmarket systems like the Landis & Staefer's. If you lead an erratic lifestyle, in and out at all hours, the supposed efficiencies of a boiler manager will be wasted on you: but for homes with regular occupation patterns, a boiler manager should produce tangible savings

## Two-Zone Heating Systems

An energy saving idea which splits the space heating into two heating zones — typically upstairs/downstairs — in addition to heating the hot water. It involves using a 3-zone programmer such as the Horstman Channel Plus. Again, the benefits very much depend on lifestyle — i.e. whether you really use your house in a predictable way. If, for instance, you hardly ever went upstairs before 9.00pm then you could have upstairs heating off all day which could conceivably save 10-15% of space heating bills. You could achieve similar

results with TRVs but these would need daily manual adjustment. Zoning more complex than upstairs/downstairs is possible, but would probably involve longer and less efficient pipe runs which would tend to cancel out any advantage. The 2002 energy efficiency regs suggest that a building larger than 150m$^2$ should be split into heating zones: it is not quite a requirement, the wording in the Approved Document is a bit woolly.

## Are They Worth It?

The savings achieved by superior heating controls are extremely difficult to estimate because they depend to a large extent on how the house is lived in. Often manufacturers will claim 15% or 20% savings on running costs but these are usually comparisons with systems with no automatic controls, which are most unlikely to be fitted today.

A more reasonable assumption would be that any one of these extra levels of heating control might save 5% on fuel costs for heating. At the present time you cannot run a boiler manager covering more than one heating zone unless you pay around £370, so it's either/or but not both.

On a detached four-bedroom house, fitting a cocktail of sophisticated heating controls might save around £50/annum. However, had you already decided to spend extra money on super insulation and condensing boilers your prospective fuel bills would be halved, so your 15% saving would also be halved, down to something like £25/annum. Even so, the cost of more effective heating controls should not be more than £300 and so they are what you might call a moderately attractive investment.

# Alternative Heating

## Electric Heating

The electricity supply companies would be horrified to learn that they are an alternative heating supplier, but a scan of comparative fuel costs (see Which Fuel? earlier in this chapter) will show you why I have placed them in this category. The popularity of electric heating with developers is due almost entirely to its low installation costs. At peak rate it is a prohibitively expensive fuel to run (7p/kWh); off-peak is less than half this price, but still twice the price of gas. Off-peak night-storage heating is also about the most uncontrollable, unresponsive heating system ever designed, delivering the bulk of its heat when it's hardly needed.

To counteract these failings, the supply companies have tariffs with off-peak rates in the afternoon and evenings (ask for Economy 10). Also, they recognise that night-storage heaters are not everyone's idea of beauty and so they currently recommend underfloor heating topped up with ceiling heaters, which are designed to run on the new Economy 10 tariffs. These developments represent a big improvement in the outlook for electric heating — the pluses that apply to wet underfloor systems apply just as strongly to electric heating — yet as long as oil and gas remain half the price, electricity is unlikely to be many people's first choice. It will also remain a relatively uncontrollable heat source as long as the effective hours of use are limited to 10 per day.

A night-storage heating system for a four-bedroom house would cost just under £2000. This would involve fitting 7 or 8 night-storage heaters and providing convector radiators for the rest of the house. An electric underfloor/ceiling system would cost around £1500 for underfloor heating downstairs and ceiling heating to both downstairs and upstairs; adding an underfloor system upstairs (which would necessitate a beam and block first floor) adds £250 to the whole system. Electric underfloor heating is now controlled automatically as standard in ways not dissimilar to how boiler managers work; both outside temperatures and screed temperatures are monitored to adjust the levels of heat input needed.

This under and over system, as it is known, is by some margin the cheapest form of central heating to install. Electric heating systems have come on leaps and bounds in the last few years and it is certainly worth considering as an option, particularly if you're interested in underfloor heating.

Your local electricity supply company will have a New Homes Dept. which will design and cost (and arrange installation of) a suitable system for your house. Other underfloor/overhead specialists are ESWA and Devi. One of the areas where electric heating systems fall down is that they don't give you any hot water and for that you need to either fit a cylinder with an immersion heater or use a wet boiler such as the Amptec Boiler.

### Plus

No additional connection charges: available everywhere; cheap installation costs; low maintenance costs as the "boiler" is located at a distant power station; doesn't leak; no radiators with underfloor heating; underfloor heating coupled with convector booster heaters are actually a very good team, the first giving comfortable heat, the second giving quick response.

### Minus

Expensive to run; generally unresponsive; underfloor heating concept does not work so well upstairs; not very green; when comparing quotations don't overlook the fact that electric heating makes no allowance for domestic hot water; Economy 7 cylinders are expensive and limited.

## Warm Air

Warm air or forced air heating systems work by blowing heated air around the house in a series of ducts. All you see of it are inlet and outlet grills, usually a pair per room. It's the most common form of heating in American homes but in Britain it's fallen right out of favour after many systems fitted in the 60s and 70s proved to be noisy and ineffective. I don't think any private developers have fitted warm air heating systems into new homes since about 1985. Johnson and Starley are the only firm left producing warm air units in this country, mostly satisfying the retrofit market. They work with a conventional flued, floor-standing gas-fired boilers. The system must be installed by a CORGI registered installer and would cost around £3300 for a four-bedroom house. This would include a gas-fired boiler and all the ducting to push the hot air around the house, but domestic hot water (DHW) would have to be supplied by other means. It's not a completely bleak outlook. A recent entrant into the market is Schrag, a warm-air system from Germany, which comes with the very upmarket Huf Haus. I am told it's marvellous.

### Plus

Very responsive — heat house quickly; no radiators; air can be filtered; possibilities of being combined with heat recovery systems and air conditioning.

### Minus

Warm air is arguably the least comfortable form of heating; lacks any radiant heat and, despite air filtering, tends to throw up dust particles. Not well understood in UK; poorly designed and installed they have been known to be noisy. However, recent users have reported high satisfaction rates.

## Heat Recovery

see next section on Ventilation.

## Underfloor Heating

see previous section on Emitters.

## Solar Power

Solar power now splits between two options: panels for heating water and panels (or cells) for creating electricity. Neither option comes cheap. For a water heating system, a standard installation on a 160m$^2$ family house would cost over £2000 for the flat plate collector and about £3500 for a vacuum tube collector. The vacuum tubes are a considerable improvement; they are sensitive to light rather than sunshine and they are not as affected by wind chill. However, even when working at full whack the output is only going to be around 3kW: this would easily be enough to provide DHW in the summer and provide some DHW in the winter. The problem is that the cost of DHW heating with a well insulated cylinder and a gas-or oil-fired boiler is remarkably small — just £100/annum in the benchmark house. Getting £40 or £50 of "free" hot water each year is paltry when compared to installation costs; the payback period is as much as 70 years. The electricity-producing panels, known as photovoltaic cells, are even more expensive to install though you can connect these to the grid which enables you to sell electricity back to your regular supplier (albeit at a miserly rate).

Having said that, there are signs that solar panels will become cheaper as they become much more widely installed in places with warmer, sunnier climes than ours. If you are interested in alternative energy production generally (and I've overlooked a number of other options), you should point yourself towards the Centre for Alternative Technology in North Wales. They have carried out much excellent pioneering work in this field and they also have a good bookshop. Also consider joining the Association of Environment Conscious Builders (AECB) who will put you in touch with dozens of very useful contacts.

The most significant recent change in this field has come via the deregulation of the electricity supply industry. Now several of the major suppliers are offering EcoPower options which allow you to buy your renewable electricity over the grid. For a small premium (usually between 5% and 10%), the supplier will match any power you use with power created by some distant wind farm or photovoltaic solar panel. Green energy for £30 or £40 a year sounds like an inviting option and a lot less hassle than installing and maintaining your own power plants on site — maybe this will prove to be the catalyst which will really get renewable power sources off the ground.

## Solid Fuel

Solid fuel stoves exist which can handle heating for the largest houses. This means that they can be harnessed to provide hot water to be pumped around radiators and through the hot water cylinder as well as giving off more than a pleasing glow in the room where they sit. They come in three basic styles, the decorative cast-iron finish to go in the living room, the kitchen range which adds cooking capabilities, or the utilitarian box to be hidden out of view.

They are never going to win on the convenience stakes as in order to perform the task equivalent to a gas/oil boiler they will have to be kept going all through the winter, which means frequent stoking, riddling and emptying. Attempts by manufacturers like Charnwood to market automatically loading and emptying stoves have been abandoned because of high cost. And in the semi-cold seasons (September-November and March-May) you'll never be quite sure if or when to fire up and so you'll need some sort of backup system (probably electric), which rather defeats the purpose of spending all the money in the first place. There is still a place for them as whole house heat sources, but realistically only in homes permanently occupied. Many remote locations still suffer regular power cuts and the ability to heat the home without recourse to electrically controlled components remains important yet, like other wet central heating systems, solid fuel systems are nowadays designed with electric pumps and valves to distribute the hot water so even this potential advantage is largely lost.

### Living Room Stoves

The Coalbrookdale range (made by Aga Rayburn) are well known and readily available. There are four sizes and each size is available with or without a boiler. Without a boiler, the stoves are really just efficient room fires; the boiler (which absorbs around 60-70% of the stove's heat output) is essential if a wet whole house heating and DHW system is wanted. The benchmark house would require at least the second largest Coalbrookdale, the Severn, which belts out 10kW of hot water as well as 3kW of room heat. It weighs a quarter of a ton and costs around £900. There are a number of other manufactures, both British and European, who produce variations on the same theme some with highly individualist styling (Euroheat, Waterford's Erin, Morso) but prices are remarkably similar.

### Kitchen Ranges

Another approach is to use a cast-iron cooker as a centre piece in a kitchen. The Aga is the best known and, at around £3300 to buy, the most expensive. However the Aga only has a small boiler, capable of supplying DHW but not further space heating. There are a range of good-looking stoves which can cook, heat and do DHW — e.g. Rayburn, Stanley, Wamsler, Hergom. Strictly speaking, we're moving away from solid fuel because these cooker/heaters can be (and most frequently are) fired by gas or oil. In its solid fuel version the top of the range Rayburn would be big enough (16kW) to provide for the benchmark house — but it would require refuelling every 2 hours! Overnight its output would drop to just 2kW, which would make those January mornings a bit too nippy and would necessitate electric backup heating. At around £2400 plus installation costs it's an expensive but stylish option. Wamsler produce a solid fuel central heating cooker that looks more basic (as you might see in a restaurant kitchen) which is about 25% less than Rayburns and Stanleys. All these ranges can be run in summer, thus doing away with the need for separate cookers, but then they belt out more heat than you'd really want.

To find out more, check out dealers in the Yellow Pages under Heating Eqpt - solid fuel.

### Plus

Style; reliability; doesn't pack up during power cuts (although central heating at least is usually electrically pumped); many stoves are "multi-fuel" which means they can burn virtually anything, which may be an attraction if you own a wood or a peat bog.

### Minus

Initial price is high; need backup heating; extra housework; fuel not especially cheap; inefficient (unlike gas or oil the boiler can't be turned off at the flick of a switch); unresponsive: fuel needs storage; need open flue (and probably chimney); room stoves get hot and are not child friendly.

## Cooling

Air conditioning and cooling had always been thought of as unnecessary in UK homes because our summer climate never got that hot. But in recent years we have experienced one or two summers which were nothing short of sweltering. Plus we are seeing the widespread adopting of air conditioning in our cars — it's now almost standard on new models, having only recently been considered a luxury. There are home air conditioning systems available in the UK but whilst new housebuilders show increasing interest in more and more sophisticated ways of staying warm during the 20-odd week annual heating season, there remains approximately nil interest in staying cool during the 10-week high summer period.

Why? Well for a starter, it is expensive to install. A whole house air condition system for a detached house would set you back in the region of £5000, rather more than the most elaborate heating systems on the market. A one room system would cost around £1500. The existing models are all electrically powered and a whole house model would consume around 3-5kW of power when going at full blast — typically it would run for only 50% of the time, even on the hottest of days, providing you remember to keep the doors and windows shut. The units also tend to be noisy, though this problem can be reduced if the design of the installation is good. Like boilers, air conditioning needs to have exhaust ducting and this means that the system has to be built in permanently and is connected to an outdoor unit. To my knowledge, there are no portable air conditioners that you could move around the house with you. There is a new system on the market called Idrosplit that piggy backs on to a radiator central heating system, available from Plumb Center, clever but pricey. Alternatively, some of the heat recovery units offer an air cooling facility; the Villavent 4 unit provides something called comfort cooling — it will not turn the house into a fridge like the ones in American homes, but will be able to drop incoming air temperature by several degrees.

# Ventilation

Buildings need to be ventilated. Trapped water vapour in particular can be very damaging, causing condensation and encouraging mould growth and wet rot. It's a potential problem in both the external structure of a house — especially under ground floors and in roofs — and the enclosed living space.

The building regulations deal with the need for ventilation in both areas. Underfloor ventilation (only applicable with suspended ground floors) is by way of air bricks; roof ventilation is by eaves or soffit vents and occasionally air bricks too.

The building regs dealing with internal ventilation specify that habitable rooms must have opening windows fitted with trickle vents (more on these later) and that kitchens and bathrooms must have extractor fans (or "adequate means of extraction"). A cooker hood ducted to the outside is acceptable in a kitchen or else there must be an extractor fan capable of shifting 60 lts/s (litres/second); the bathroom fan must be capable of shifting 15 lts/s, equivalent to a small bathroom full of air in about ten or fifteen minutes. A separate toilet can make do with an opening window or a small fan.

## Standard Solutions

Fit trickle vents in the windows. Extractor fans in kitchens and bathrooms.

### Trickle Vents

These slimline plastic inserts have now become nearly universal on standard joinery — indeed it is now an a problem to find windows without them. Trickle vents, which can be open or closed from inside, are slotted into a hole drilled out of the head of the window. Some manufacturers still charge £6 extra for fitting them, some supply windows with just the slots cut out and supply the vents separately at around £6 each.

### Cooker Hoods

Normally fitted as standard in kitchens, although they don't have to be ducted outside — they are said to "recirculate" if they don't. It makes very good sense to make sure your cooker does duct directly outside as it works much better and saves the cost of a second, more powerful extractor fan. Cooker hoods are usually sold as part of a package with hobs and ovens. They start at around £50-60: automatic versions with humidity controlled switching are available at around £90-£100.,

but the current fashion if for rather grand stainless steel ones which typically cost £300 or more.

### Bathroom Fans

A basic, 15 lts/s, fan can be controlled by a pull switch, or linked to a room light switch. Bathrooms without windows have to have models fitted with automatic overrun timers, and where ducting is required a centrifugal fan is recommended. Higher up the range, the fans have humidistats which can automatically switch fans between off, low and high settings dependent on humidity in the bathroom. And at the top of the range are a small number of heat recovery fans which do all these things as well as recycling some of the heat normally pumped out by the fan.

Not included in the above prices for fans are exterior wall grilles (£5) or any ducting (£12/3lin.m). Fans can be ducted horizontally through external walls or vertically into the roof space and then out through the ridge via a ridge vent tile (£50) or through a roof vent tile (£35). Fitting is normally done by the electrician and budget charges will be around £20 for the switch (Mats £5, Lab £15) and around £25 labour for fitting the fan, more if there are complex ducting routes involved.

The total cost of these measures on the benchmark house was around £500, made up as follows:

- Trickle Vents  18@ £6          £108
- Cooker Hood and Ducting     £100
- Bathroom Fans  3 @ £100     £300

## Whole House Systems

### Mechanical Ventilation

The building regs allow for radically different approaches to ventilation. One is to do away with trickle vents and to provide both extract and inlet ventilation via a series of ducts controlled by electric fans. A number of manufacturers produce units which will recapture some of the heat being sucked out of the house, mixing it with fresh air being brought in through the loft. A new house has such high insulation levels that the fabric (i.e. walls, roof, floor) lose comparatively little heat. If careful attention isn't paid to airtightness and ventilation, then much of this saved heat will just trickle away. It is estimated that 25% or even 33% of the heating bill goes on replacing unwarranted ventilation — in the

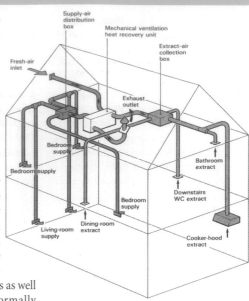

*Typical installation layout for mechanical ventilation with heat recovery. Note the large amount of ducting involved.*

benchmark house, that would amount to £50-£70/annum. Worth saving. Unfortunately, a heat recovery system will cost at least £1500 to install and as much as £70/annum to run because it is powered by two electric fans on continuously; in addition there will be occasional servicing costs. In terms of power saved v power used (known as the efficiency ratio), heat recovery systems perform reasonably well, but when costed it turns out that the power saved usually costs about 2p/kWh, whereas the electricity to run the unit is costing around 7p/kWh. The evidence suggests that, in our temperate climate, airborne heat recovery systems are not good value. In response to these criticisms, manufacturers have been introducing systems powered by low wattage fans (such as VentAxias HR200V) which improve the overall returns.

When pressed, most manufacturers will admit that the economic return is negligible but will still insist that there are benefits in increased comfort levels. This may well be true but it will have to be taken as an act of faith because it is notoriously difficult to predict how an as yet unbuilt house will behave: most people find warm, well insulated housing remarkably comfortable and free of condensation without recourse to mechanical heat recovery systems.

## Passive Stack Ventilation

This is another option that can be used if you are interested in whole house ventilation. Passive stack ventilation also uses ducts to extract stale air from the house but there the similarity ends. Trickle vents are fitted in all the dry rooms (i.e. living rooms, bedrooms) whilst ducts run from the wet areas (bathrooms, kitchens) up to a vented ridge tile; air pressure does the rest, drawing air in through the house and away through the roof. A simple concept, essentially no different to a chimney stack (hence the name). Each extract duct has to be connected to its own vented ridge tile via an insulated flexible pipe and will cost £120-£150; in certain situations (bathrooms with no external walls) this will be cheaper than using a centrifugal fan with ducting. A whole house system (with four passive stacks) would cost around £800 (Mats £400, Lab £400). Add a cooker hood (which is recommended) and the overall cost will be around 60% more than the standard route.

There are currently two passive stack suppliers, Passivent and Johnson & Starley (Aereco). Passivent have a couple of variations on the basic module including a system which introduces humidistats on both the inlets (trickle vents) and the extract grilles. This effectively cuts down excessive air-changes as the vents close below a certain level of humidity. Strictly speaking, this would seem to be contrary to the building regs standard that half an air-change per hour should take place throughout the house, but humidity levels are a good indicator of the level of use a room is getting (people produce water vapour) and no one seems to be complaining. The "intelligent system" with humidistats costs around £250 more than the ordinary stack system, by now nearly double the standard route — though still half the price of mechanical heat recovery. For around £400 above the standard solution, you get a system that works without anything mechanical to go wrong and introduces an element of heat saving. Passive stack systems are still relatively new and many architects and designers are unaware of their existence. However passive stack ventilation took a huge step forward in 1998 when Wimpey Homes, the UK's biggest housebuilder, started using it throughout their range, though for first floor bathrooms only. Their kitchens and downstairs WCs are vented with conventional fans; this arrangement is now known as the Wimpey option.

### Plus

Quiet; no running cost; nothing to break down; no filters to change; the "intelligent" systems reduce overall heat loss in well sealed housing.

### Minus

Doesn't suit every situation - the taller the building the better they will work; because there is so little to them, many people simply don't believe they work; they want fans! It's also difficult (verging on the impossible actually) to configure when you are building into the loftspace — it doesn't work so well when you start angling ducts into the rafter space.

## Comment

The subject of ventilation is intriguing because it is as yet very poorly understood. There is a general consensus that ventilation needs to be planned into modern buildings but there is no agreement on how much ventilation is really needed. If it were a question of just replacing oxygen used by the inhabitants, the ventilation rate would have to be no more than 1lt/s/person: some authorities think a minimum figure should be about 2.5 times this level, others think it should be no less than 40 times this level. Our current building regulations suggest that 0.5 air-changes/hr is sufficient — this equates to around 50lts/s in our 350m³ benchmark house which puts it bang in the middle of the range of assumptions.

Both mechanical and passive stack ventilation systems work on the assumption that, without their intervention, houses would be inadequately ventilated and would suffer from:

- excess water vapour
- condensation
- smells
- stuffiness
- general lack of oxygen
- build-up of toxic gases like radon, formaldehyde or volatile organic compounds given off by synthetic carpet and the like.

However, it is worth emphasising that before spending good money on fancy ventilation systems, you should ensure that you have a reasonably airtight structure. The "air-leakiness" of your house may make the installation of such fancy ventilation schemes quite redundant. Even with trickle vents all sealed, it would appear that many UK homes will "self-ventilate" at a level of around two air-changes per hour just through leaks in the structure — for instance, where there is imperfect draught sealing around doors, windows, skirting boards, pipe holes and loft hatches; an unsealed chimney alone extracts 20lts of air/s.

A cursory glance at heat-loss calculations for the benchmark house (see Chapter 13) will show what a large part heating air-changes plays in the overall heating costs. At half an air-change/hr (50lts/s), the benchmark house will lose about a third of it's heat through ventilation. However, if the house is built "leaky" — at say two air-changes/hr — then this heat-loss figure will multiply fourfold to around £200 per year. In comparison, the so-called building fabric (walls, roof, ground floor, windows) ships no more than £100 of heat during the course of a year, so you can see what an important place ventilation has in the scheme of things.

So if you are interested in installing something more advanced than the standard ventilation requirements, you should pay careful attention to draught proofing beforehand. To this effect, you should fit a damper on your chimney to shut it off when not in use, you should seal all cracks, holes and joints with a flexible silicone sealer — dry-lined plasterboard walls have a particularly bad reputation in this respect — and you should consider fitting a proprietary sealed loft hatch (like Marley's, cost £50). Pay attention to door furniture so that you do not have open keyholes, and note that french doors and stable doors are particularly difficult to draught proof.

### Pressure Tests

If you want to take this process to it's logical conclusion, then you can have a pressure test carried out on your house for around £200. They attach a giant vacuum cleaning type device which puts the house under pressure (up to 50 Pascals, which sounds like a lot but it's not noticeable if you are inside) and then measures the rate the device draws air in through it to replace the air being displaced through all the cracks in the structure. At 50 Pascals, the leakage rates are five or ten times more than you would get under typical atmospheric conditions. This may seem an expensive and unnecessary test to put your house through, but if you are about to pay out a great deal more than this for a whole house ventilation system, not to mention an elaborate heating system, it's possibly worth ensuring that it's at least going to work as planned. Contact Retrotec.

# Fires and Chimneys

Functionally, central heating has made the fireplace redundant yet the fireplace lives on in most new family homes. If you want to save money building your home and you want a "green", low-running cost style of house, then you will be doing yourself a great favour by cutting out all plans for room fires of whatever type. Trouble is — what do you put in the middle of the living room wall? Without a fireplace something is missing. It's like a church without an altar — it just doesn't look right. A living-room fire on a cold winter's night feels so good because it strikes a chord with the caveman or woman inside us all, whose control of fire was the very thing that separated us from the wild beasts roaming outside. In other words, we are in the land of the adman's "aspirational purchases."

Feeding this aspiration is now seen as a bit of a luxury and the majority of smaller homes being built do without the open fire altogether. Some plump for a gas fire, some for nothing at all. AB Homes, our benchmark house builders, are in the latter camp. They don't do fires; their homes don't have chimneys. Actually, chimney spotting is an interesting exercise — take a look around and see who is building them and who isn't; the results can be quite surprising.

## Fire Options

### Open Fires

If you want an open fire, the simplest option available is to form an opening using a fireback unit. Ventilation is provided by an airbrick somewhere in the vicinity of the fireplace, and you decorate the opening with some sort of simple mantelpiece. For just over £100 more you can fit a purpose-made fire

basket complete with ventilation and removable ash can — the Baxi Burnall is the best known — and if you want a regular fire this is a worthwhile addition.

### Stoves

Another approach is to take the fire out into the room space and contain it in a metal surround — the stove. This is a much more efficient way of heating a room (though even the most efficient cast-iron stoves are no match for a new oil- or gas-fired boiler) and is much favoured by hippies living in isolated cottages. However, in a new house it probably represents the worst of both worlds in that a) you don't actually need a stove for room heating and b) you lose the sexiness of having open fire in your living room. Most solid-fuel stoves are very traditional in appearance and they are not cheap. For more modern designs, you need to look to the Continent and a price tag of £3,000 plus.

A more detailed discussion of the merits of stoves appears in the section Alternative Heating a few pages back.

### Gas Fires

For those who cannot be doing with the hassle of solid fuel but still want a focal point, then gas fires may be the answer. You can buy a student digs style gas fire such as Valor's Firelite for around £80, or you can get gas fires which can be inset into a fireplace (£200 upwards). Of more interest to new housebuilders will be the balanced-flue gas fires like the Canon Coalridge and the Valor Flamenco (£280 plus) which can be set on any outside wall and don't need a chimney at all, which makes for a very cheap way of getting a focal point fire into a living space. There is also a range of decorative effect gas fires — what I

have learned to call Loggy-Glows — which heat up ceramic coal and logs. By the time you've fitted them with decorative fire baskets and decorative fire surrounds you won't have much change from £250 and you still have to fit a chimney to take away the exhaust gases.

### Electric Fires

Ever keen to compete with gas, there are a number of electric Living Flame effect fires. As these are a poor imitation of a gas fire making a poor imitation of a coal fire I can't see them being hugely fancied by new housebuilders but, in this business, choice is king and it would be ungracious of me not to mention them in passing. Prices range from £70 for a free standing 2kW (bar) fire with plastic logs stuck on top to £300 for ones which have a flame effect glow going on in the background. Naff as you like.

## Chimneys

### Masonry

The standard way of evacuating smoke from fires is via a brick- or block-built chimney, the higher the better. The standard way to do this is to use concrete or clay flue liners set into an insulated cement screed, built up with the masonry work. It makes little difference to cost whether this chimney is built against an internal or an external wall — though there is a small cost penalty when building a masonry chimney in a timber frame house. In many traditionally styled homes, a large fireplace and chimney are designed to be the very heart of the house; for instance, Potton Homes, who specialise in creating Tudor style interiors, indicate that the construction costs of an inglenook fireplace and chimney suit-

## 8e: Fire and Chimney Costs

| | QUANTITY | | RATE | TOTAL |
|---|---|---|---|---|
| Brickwork | 10 | m² | £ 39.00 | £390 |
| Extra Blockwork | 10 | m² | 14.00 | £140 |
| Extra for High Work | 8 | Lin.m | 40.00 | £320 |
| Form Lead Roof Flashings | 1 | | 50.00 | £50 |
| Redbank Fyrerite Chimney Units | 1 | No. | 75.00 | £75 |
| Flue Liners 300hx225mm | 25 | No. | 7.00 | £180 |
| Chimney Pot | 1 | No. | 12.00 | £12 |
| Firebacks | 1 | | 45.00 | £45 |
| Extra for Fireplace Construction | 1 | | 200.00 | £200 |
| Fire Surround | 1 | No | 25.00 | £25 |
| Tiled Hearth | 1 | m² | 30.00 | £30 |
| Damper/Airbrick | 1 | | 40.00 | £40 |
| **TOTAL** | | | | **£1,500** |

This is a 'what if?' table. The benchmark house has no fires and no chimney. The costs are based on a previous benchmark house with a simple fire surround with a masonry chimney

able for one of their Heritage homes would cost around £4000; this figure could be quartered if you specified a simpler style of chimney but you would of course lose the splendour of the timber-beamed, brick-faced fireplace.

Feature chimneys, as opposed to feature fireplaces, are another money soaker. The old English (or Jacobean) chimney is enjoying something of a revival. On a steeply pitched roof with a handmade roof tile it can look fantastic, but it is likely to take a week or two to build and will add a minimum £500 to the chimney costs. If your budget doesn't stretch to ornamental brickwork, you might be interested in just an ornamental chimney pot. Salvage yards usually have stacks of them and Redbank produce a wide range at costs between £10 and £700.

### Stainless Steel

There are a number of outfits producing stainless steel flues which can be used instead of a conventional chimney. Check out Selkirk and Brefco. A stainless steel insulated flue is not cheap: it would cost more than £500 to purchase an 8m-long system for the bench mark house, which is about twice as much as the materials for a conventional chimney — but there are a number of plus points worth examining:
- They allow total flexibility as regards siting
- They are quick and easy to install
- They work rather better than regular chimneys.
- They need very little cleaning
- They are particularly well suited to timber frame construction.

*Stainless steel flue terminals can ruin a traditional roofline. Despite this, planners are implacably opposed to allowing masonry chimneys in barn conversions. "Out of character" they claim.*

The biggest downside to using these systems is the look of the flue terminals. Instead of a traditional brick chimney you get an industrial looking stainless steel flue terminal; this can look fine in modern designs of housing but if you aspire to the trad then it looks pretty awful. Having said that, many barn conversions sport these aluminium flue terminals because planners are dead set against building masonry chimneys into a barn because it is not seen as being in keeping.

### Prefabricated Chimneys

Very popular in Scandinavia, the best known names in the UK are Isokern and Anki. They produce a pumice stone chimney lining system which fits together like Lego and has the advantage of being pre-insulated. One of the problems with conventional, flue-lined chimneys is that the temperature of the escaping smoke drops substantially as it rises up the chimney, causing both condensation and tar deposition; this is a noted problem when relatively high temperature stoves are being used. Ideally, the chimney linings should be insulated as constructed but this is frequently not done and specifying a pre-insulated lining such as Anki or Isokern (or one of the stainless steel ones) should alleviate the problem. These prefab chimneys are typically around £300 more expensive in materials than traditional flue liners and blocks, but they save something in construction time.

# Plumbing

Plumbing and heating, together with roofing and electrical work, is conventionally undertaken by specialist subcontractors who usually supply materials as well as labour. In analysing the labour costs, I've subtracted from quotations the amount a general contractor would hope to spend on materials: this leaves a labour rate of nearly £25/hr which is rather more than a plumber would charge. The difference is explained by the mark-up a plumber would normally put on materials, so that though he would expect to be buying somewhat cheaper than a rookie builder, he would price the job as if the materials were list price. The difference is perhaps academic

but it explains why the rate/hr looks so high You should be able to hire a one-man-band type plumber for nearer half this rate but he might not be happy for you to buy materials. However, if you are working on a zero-rated job (new build and barn conversions) and you hire a non-VAT registered plumber (or for that matter any other tradesman), you should insist on buying the materials yourself otherwise you will not be able to reclaim the VAT. Conventionally, plumbers are hired to fit heating and sanitaryware; this includes all aboveground waste fittings, but rarely underground drainage or rainwater goods. Traditionally, plumbers also undertook sheet-

metal work on roofing, but now this is tending to be carried out by roofers. There are a couple of grey areas that it is good to be aware of. The first concerns the wiring of heating controls (which is sometimes carried out by the electrician) and the second concerns the installation of kitchen sinks and dishwashers, which is sometimes undertaken by specialist kitchen installers. Be clear, when you are hiring, who is to do what. The table runs through these tasks on an hour and cost basis; one of the plumbers who've checked over this, commented simply "I wish it was always that quick!"

## 8f: Plumber's Labour Charges

| FITTING A WET CENTRAL HEATING SYSTEM TO A 4-BEDROOM HOUSE | HOURS | CHARGED at £25/hr |
|---|---|---|
| Fit Boiler + Balanced Flue | 8 | £200 |
| Fit Cylinder | 4 | £100 |
| Fit Tanks in Loft | 6 | £150 |
| Run Cold to Loft | 2 | £50 |
| Connect Primary Pipework | 8 | £200 |
| Fix 14 Radiators | 8 | £200 |
| Flow and Return to 14 Radiators | 14 | £350 |
| Fit Heating Controls | 6 | £150 |
| Commission System | 8 | £200 |
| **TOTAL FOR WET CENTRAL HEATING** | **64** | **£1600** |
| **FITTING A BATHROOM** | | |
| Fix Bathroom Suite (Bath/Basin/WC) | 6 | £150 |
| H+C Plumbing to Same | 4 | £100 |
| Waste from Suite to Stack | 2 | £50 |
| Fit Waste Stack (Ground to Roof) | 4 | £100 |
| **TOTAL FOR ONE BATHROOM** | **16** | **£400** |
| **ODDS N SODS** | | |
| Shower Fitting (inc H+C, Waste) | 8 | £200 |
| Bidet Fitting (inc H+C, Waste) | 4 | £100 |
| Fix Cloakroom Suite | 4 | £100 |
| H+C Plumbing to Same | 2 | £50 |
| Waste from Cloakroom to Stack | 2 | £50 |
| Fit Kitchen Sink (inc H+C, Waste) | 5 | £125 |
| Fit W/M or D/W (inc H+C, Waste) | 2 | £50 |
| Fit Outside Tap | 2 | £50 |
| Place and Plumb-in Oil Tank | 6 | £150 |

*Prices are labour only and do not include any material costs*

### Check the Spec

Many contractors have only the vaguest understanding of the ins and out of heating and plumbing systems and are more than happy to let their plumber design, price and install whatever system they like, and plumbers have become quite used to acting almost autonomously, as long as the kit works and the price is about right. Comparing quotations between plumbers is consequently a very difficult business because the specifications of the competing heating systems are almost bound to be different unless a professional has been employed to design the system beforehand, something which hardly anyone bothers with on smaller residential construction jobs.

Points to watch out for when comparing quotations are:
- Are the design considerations identical? What temperature is each room to be heated to? How many air changes an hour have been assumed in the calculations?
- What fuel is being specified to run the system? Have the costs of connecting to or storing the fuel been fully taken into account?
- What controls are being provided? How efficient will the system be? How easy will it be to service the system? Will pumps and cables be concealed? What insulation is being provided to the hot water pipes?
- What sort of emitters are being specified? If standard panel radiators, where will they be sited and who is responsible for painting them? Will they have TRVs fitted as standard? If so, will these be in addition to or instead of a whole-house thermostat?
- What provision has been made for towel radiators? Heating airing cupboards?
- What arrangements will be made for hot water storage? What will hot water flow rates be like?
- What sort of pipework will be used? Where will the overflows run to?
- What sort of guarantee is offered? Does the business offer any form of regular servicing contract?

### Plastic Plumbing

Indoor plastic plumbing has been kicking around since the late 70s and in its time it's come in for a fair amount of stick from the professionals who were content to look at it as just a DIY product. It's also resulted in numerous floodings resulting from duff joints or, more often, lazy installers. However, it's very easy and quick to install; it's mostly push-fit and it comes on a roll so you don't have to bother with soldering joints as you do with copper. So quick and easy that, at long last, it's really taking off in professional plumbing circles as well. Partly it's because it's used exclusively for underfloor heating (where it seems to perform fine) and partly because new building techniques such as I beam floors are becoming widespread and it's difficult to get copper tube through an I beam floor. The product itself has matured. Hepworth, the originators, have redesigned their joints to make them hopefully idiot proof and there is now competition from other big names in the field like Osma and Marley. It's hard not to come to the conclusion that copper plumbing is on the way out, although it will continue to be used extensively for many years to come. Gas plumbing, for instance, has to be done in copper.

# Chapter 9
# Wiring

1 House wiring

2 Lighting

3 Built-in vacuums

4 TV, phones and cables

The housebuilding industry's standard for electrical provision is some way in advance of the minimum requirements. This will surprise many who automatically assume that professional developers always try and get away with the bare minimum, but in fact the NHBC standards for power supply to any new house are absolutely basic and most house buyers and selfbuilders will want around double that number of outlets. Certainly, the power and lighting specifications for the benchmark house are way above these standards you could hardly have less than one light per room. The benchmark house has a rather superior lighting specification and, without going over the top, the builders have spent rather more than many developers would. It's worth bearing in mind that even if you chose the NHBC minimum standard for lighting, you would probably spend a lot more money on lampshades, table lamps and fittings, all of which would attract VAT at 17.5%, whereas built-in light fittings are zero-rated in a new house. It's probably a fair estimate

to assume that you won't be leaving naked bulbs hanging for more than about five years and that in the long run you'll spend an additional £500 on shades and separate table lamps. You may feel that the NHBC minimum requirements are a red herring but, be warned, costs derived from these standards are widely used by businesses selling the bits of houses that don't include the wiring, to illustrate how much (or how little) it will cost to finish off the house. So it is as well to be aware that by current market standards the minimum requirements are unrealistically low. The accompanying table 9a shows just how each element of an electrician's quotation would be made up and how this translates into a whole house quotation — in this case the one used on our benchmark house.
More than most aspects of

construction, electrical fittings vary enormously in quality. For many years, the market has been dominated by two British businesses, MK and Crabtree: indeed many specifiers indicate that fittings should be by either of these two firms. But there is a huge gulf between MK/Crabtree prices and some very cheap imported gear that you can get hold of. The current TLC catalogue has MK Logic Plus 13amp double sockets at £4.37 each; however, they also have their own brand version (Telco) at £1.90 each. If you want a mid-priced alternative, I can recommend MEM who produce a comprehensive catalogue.

## 9a: Guide Prices for Wiring and Lighting

**WHAT WENT INTO THE BENCHMARK HOUSE**

| ITEM | MATS | LABOUR | TOTAL | NO. | COST |
|---|---|---|---|---|---|
| **POWER CIRCUITS/CONSUMER UNIT** | | | | | |
| Double Socket | £8.00 | £12.00 | £20.00 | 20 | £400 |
| Single Socket | 7.00 | 12.00 | 19.00 | 7 | £130 |
| Fused Spur | 7.50 | 12.00 | 19.50 | 2 | £40 |
| 5-amp Socket | 7.50 | 12.00 | 19.50 | | |
| Cooker Switch | 12.50 | 15.00 | 27.50 | 1 | £30 |
| Cooker Outlet | 5.00 | 10.00 | 15.00 | 2 | £30 |
| Shaver Point | 25.00 | 20.00 | 45.00 | | |
| Immersion Point | 8.00 | 20.00 | 28.00 | 1 | £30 |
| External Sockets | 15.00 | 30.00 | 45.00 | | |
| Consumer Unit | 30.00 | 10.00 | 40.00 | 1 | £40 |
| Residual Circuit Devices | 40.00 | 4.00 | 44.00 | 1 | £40 |
| Each Fuse | 4.00 | 2.00 | 6.00 | 10 | £60 |
| **TV/TELECOM WIRING** | | | | | |
| Coaxial Point | 8.00 | 12.00 | 20.00 | 2 | £40 |
| Telephone Point | 5.00 | 12.00 | 16.00 | 3 | £50 |
| Loft Aerial | 20.00 | 20.00 | 40.00 | | £0 |
| Door Bell | 5.00 | 20.00 | 25.00 | 1 | £30 |
| **SAFETY** | | | | | |
| Smoke Detectors | 30.00 | 15.00 | 45.00 | 3 | £140 |
| **LIGHTING** | | | | | |
| 1-gang Switch | 4.00 | 10.00 | 14.00 | 15 | £210 |
| 2-gang Switch | 6.00 | 15.00 | 21.00 | 5 | £110 |
| 3-gang Switch | 8.00 | 20.00 | 28.00 | | £0 |
| Pull switch | 6.00 | 10.00 | 16.00 | 3 | £50 |
| 2-way Switching | 2.00 | 5.00 | 7.00 | 2 | £10 |
| 3-way Switching | 4.00 | 8.00 | 12.00 | 2 | £20 |
| Central Pendant | 4.00 | 10.00 | 14.00 | 20 | £280 |
| Fixed Ceiling Light | 3.00 | 10.00 | 13.00 | 3 | £40 |
| Down Light | 2.00 | 10.00 | 12.00 | 2 | £20 |
| Wall Light | 2.00 | 15.00 | 17.00 | | |
| Extra for Light Fittings | 25.00 | 20.00 | 45.00 | | |
| External Light Points | 5.00 | 20.00 | 25.00 | 1 | £30 |
| **FANS** | | | | | |
| Bathroom Fans | 50.00 | 50.00 | 100.00 | 4 | £400 |
| Kitchen Fan | | 30.00 | 30.00 | 1 | £30 |
| | | | **TOTALS** | | **£2260** |

### Connection Fees

Regional electricity companies (RECs) are free to set their own connection fees and, being monopoly suppliers of an indispensable power source, they tend to charge a lot. Even a straightforward connection is likely to cost in the region of £300; if you are considering electric heating in your house, you may find that the REC offers to halve or even waive the entire connection fee as a sweetener. Long cable runs (say in excess of 50m) can be prohibitively expensive, costing thousands, and should be carefully costed when assessing the plot. Each REC has a New Supplies Department, which is where you should look for quotations; you don't need to own the plot before getting a quotation.

### Temporary Supplies

Some builders manage without temporary electricity supplies, relying on generators and diesel-powered mixers; indeed most of the house superstructure can be easily erected without power tools. However, plumbers, electricians and second-fix carpenters are big users of power tools and you can't have your permanent supply turned on until they're finished so, for most builders, a temporary supply makes good sense. Current regs insist that the temporary supply board is adequately housed; on most sites this means building a blockwork box with at least a paving slab roof and a lockable door. Budget a day's work and £100 materials to build an adequate shed with consumer unit and sockets on a backing board inside. Care should be given to locating the temporary supply so that long cables are not left trailing over the site where they could be run over by diggers, dumpers or lorries. Discuss your requirements with the REC's new supplies estimator; there will be an extra charge for temporary supply but it's usually not large, provided there are no major cable detours.

### Meter Boxes

The industry standard is to install white plastic boxes built into the external wall. The RECs like them because they can access the meter without entering the house; builders like them because the RECs supply them free (as they do lengths of underground ducting) and they can be built into the outer skin brick wall without a lintel. Only problem is that they are ugly, ugly enough to ruin a fancy period facade. If this bothers you then either look to locate the plastic meter box where it won't detract from your kerb appeal or insist that the company supply comes into the house where it can be concealed in a cupboard. Gas

supplies have the same problem but they offer an alternative meter box concealed in the ground; however, this is felt to be unsafe for an electrical supply. Water meters are always concealed in the ground.

### Consumer Units and RCDs

The consumer unit — what used to be known as the fuse box — is the place where the REC's supply is split into a number of separate circuits for distribution around the house. There are conventions on how these circuits should be arranged, although the exact design will depend on each particular layout. A 10-gang unit will suffice for all but the largest houses and it is recommended not to economise too much on this item. Miniature circuit breakers (MCBs) have now all but replaced the traditional fuses; instead of

fusewire blowing, a little button pops out and reconnection is never more complicated than pressing the button in again.

Another recent development is the advent of residual circuit-breaking devices (RCDs) — now mandatory — which provide increased protection against electrocution in event of contact with live wires. One drawback of RCDs is that they are very sensitive and can be triggered by thunderstorms or faulty equipment. This in turn may cause problems with things that must not have their power supply cut off — chiefly freezers and smoke detectors. An RCD-inspired power cut-out could have very messy consequences if it occurred during your two weeks in the Algarve, and for this reason it is recommended that freezers are run off separate circuits not pro-

*A temporary supply box — waterproof and secure*

*Plastic meter boxes — convenient but ugly, even when painted*

tected by an RCD. The net result of all this is that you'll be spending around £100 on your consumer unit whereas in the bad old days it might have cost only £20.

## Sockets

If you've got deep pockets, fit lots of sockets — but at £20-£25/outlet this can rapidly become a prohibitively expensive option. If you know how you are going to arrange beds and furniture in each room you can minimise the number of sockets needed; if you want to retain flexibility for each room then you'll probably need a minimum of three sockets per bedroom and four sockets in living rooms. Don't think that you are saving money by fitting single sockets instead of doubles. The work involved in installing them is identical; the materials price is only pennies different. You can step-up to brass-fronted sockets for an extra £3/outlet.

## Safety Issues

Britain is one of the few countries that allows unqualified people to install wiring. A new installation is routinely checked over by the REC before final connection is made, but the inspections are often rather cursory and often they only check that the earth bonding is in place. There are a number of areas where DIY housewirers — and professional electricians come to that — are prone to make untraceable errors and you would be well advised to steer clear of house wiring unless you have a thorough knowledge of the tasks in hand. Even if you are just supervising a subcontractor, you should be on your guard for the following pitfalls.

### Cables in Walls

Cables buried in walls must be set either vertically or horizontally from the outlets they supply. The idea is that the follow-on trades have some idea where not to drill holes. However, this requirement is frequently ignored in the rush to get jobs done and sometimes even to try and save money by using less cable. Even if you know where the cable is buried and, therefore, think it doesn't matter, don't forget that the cable will still be there long after you've moved on and some poor sucker thirty years hence could be in for a nasty surprise. Technically, you are allowed to run cables within 150mm of internal corners and wall/ceiling junctions, but this habit cannot be recommended.

### Earth Bonding

It is a requirement that exposed metalwork should be earthed to prevent it becoming "live." This is normally done with 10mm earthing cable (it's green and yellow). What exactly needs to be bonded?

- Water and gas mains as they enter the house. Also oil tanks
- Any exposed structural steelwork and oil tanks
- All services must be bonded together
- All metal in bathrooms must be bonded together

Note that if you are plumbing with plastic pipe (such as Hep20 or Speedfit), the requirement to earth bathroom radiators and steel baths is dropped.

### Circuit Lengths

Many electricians do not realise that there are prescribed maximum circuit lengths for any given cable size. For instance, a normal ring main run in 2.5mm$^2$ cable should not be longer than 66m. There are several guides available explaining the regulations; one of the best is EPA's The Electrician's Guide, price £16 inc P+P.

### Electric Heating

If you are interested in electric heating — and it's a much improved product — then your best bet is to contact your REC's New Homes Department. They are rather more entrepreneurial than British Gas — their product is harder to sell — and they are keen to suggest and quote for different types of electric heating (cf. underfloor, night storage, electric boilers). These can be installed by specialists or by your own electrician. The power supply to your house is likely to be uprated — in some cases to three-phase — but you are unlikely to have to pay excess for this. Off-peak electricity is what it's all about and your off-peak usage will be metered separately and controlled by a separate consumer unit. For a more detailed assessment of electric heating, refer to the section, Alternative Heating, earlier in this chapter.

## Off-peak Electricity

Even if you don't choose to install electric heating, you can still have an Economy 10 meter fitted at no extra cost and enjoy the savings of using half-price, off-peak power at night. For a more detailed discussion see Chapter 10, Kitchen and Laundry.

## Frequently Overlooked

When designing electricity supplies to a house there are a number of points to watch out for — and easily forgotten at the first-fix, cable-burying stage. Many electricians are used to doing what they are told and no more and will be of little help in designing a better system. Here is a bulletted list of commonly forgotten wiring details:

- Loft lights, cupboard lights — do you want them?
- Separate freezer circuit — preferably not protected by RCD
- Separate garage supply if garage is external
- Outside power points, security lights, welcome lights
- Kitchen unit lighting — usually fixed below wall units
- Check the rating of your electric cooking gear — 30 amps may not be enough
- Wiring for electric showers and power shower pumps
- Wiring and installation of fans in bathrooms and kitchen
- Separate circuit for immersion heater
- Outlets left for smoke detectors (now mandatory)
- Doorbell wiring
- Heating controls wiring: boiler, programmer, thermostats, pump and valves all need to be connected. This work is often undertaken by the plumber but the electrician must leave at least a fused spur to power the controls. If the plumber does this wiring, then a separate test certificate will be needed from him
- Fused spurs for waste disposal units and/or water softeners
- Wiring to sewage treatment plants or for any external water pumps (water features, swimming pools)
- Wiring for electric garage door operators: needs an accurately placed single socket, not really a problem if power is in the garage
- Burglar alarm first-fix.

The best light is natural sunlight. Lux is a measurement of light density and whereas 500 lux is the generally accepted level of electric light needed for reading, bright sunshine delivers 100,000 lux and even a cloudy overcast day will produce 5000 lux of light.

The older you get the more light you need. A 60-year-old requires ten times more light than a 10-year-old.

Apart from brightness, there are two qualities of light that are important.

## Colour Rendering

Some light sources show colours close to their natural daylight colours and are said to have good colour render. Other sources — notably orange street lamps — are incapable of showing any colour variations at all. Fluorescent lighting (including low-energy light bulbs) tends to give a washed-out, faded look to colours. This bothers some people more than others, but before you install energy-saving lightbulbs everywhere in your house, make sure you can live with the light quality.

## Colour Appearance

Or How White is Your Lamp? The bog standard tungsten lamp which we all know and love is said to be orange white — others say warm; halogen is, like Daz, a whiter white — or crisp white; fluorescents give off a milky, cool white, though there are now some warm-coloured fluorescents available.

This may seem all very technical and uninteresting but the quality of the light source is an important feature of how a room looks. Some lighting designers will actually recommend that a multipurpose room (say an office by day and a living room by night) has two different lighting schemes — fluorescent for business, tungsten or tungsten-halogen for pleasure. The feel of the room is then transformed at the flick of a switch.

## Central Pendant Lighting

This is the basic standard lighting scheme much loved by penny-pinching developers. It provides adequate ambient (background) lighting and it will always be the most efficient way of distributing light into a room but it is, generally, a very poor source for reading by or carrying out intricate manual operations because you will tend to be in the shade. It is really only a very good light source when the light is wanted directly beneath it — e.g. dining tables — but most other light sources require multiple outlets in each room to work well and so pendant lighting will remain a cheap and cheerless option.

## Spotlights

Back in the 60s the appearance of spotlights on the scene was a breath of fresh air and they became the first popular form of directional lighting. They are still immensely popular but there are often better ways of achieving the required results. Because the entire fitting is fixed and visible, spotlights have the ability to completely ruin the look of a room, especially when mounted on tracks in the middle of ceilings.

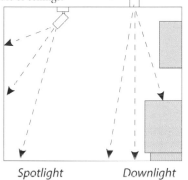

*Spotlight*      *Downlight*

## Downlighters

Light sources concealed in the ceiling have the big advantage of being stylistically neutral — i.e. they can blend in with any type of decor. They have the disadvantage of only being able to light a rather limited area and a large room lit entirely with downlighters might need as many as ten — which is expensive. Despite their name, downlighters do not have to point straight down: there are "eyeball" versions which beam the light off at an angle — in effect sidelighters.

Low-voltage halogen downlighters, which supply a very bright, good quality light, are now the height of fashion and some lighting specialists specify them almost exclusively. The low-voltage is achieved by the use of transformers and, whilst installation is not particularly difficult, incorrect wiring can be dangerous — there are still a few electricians who know nothing of low-voltage work. If you are fitting low-voltage, then make sure that yours does.

## Uplighters

These work by reflecting light off another surface (usually the ceiling) and many people assume that the light quality will therefore be low. However — provided the room has white or near-white ceilings — they are actually a very efficient way of providing ambient light and the light cast down from the ceiling is usually very good for reading under. Uplighters are normally fixed slightly above eye level to conceal the light source and they come in many shapes and forms; one particularly popular one is to fit unglazed ceramic bowls (cost £15-£25) and then to paint them with the same emulsion used on the surrounding walls. This provides a stylistically neutral form of lighting that blends well with natural wood finishes and off-white walls.

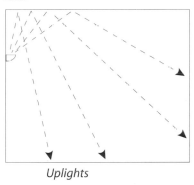

*Uplights*

## Sidelights and Table Lamps

People habitually refer to their sidelights as "reading lights" which suggests that the central light is good for vacuum cleaning and not much else. There is an enormous variety of shapes and styles to suit every taste; table lamps from £5 upwards, floor (or standard) lamps from £30. The one big advantage of independent lights is that you retain the flexibility to arrange your room in any fashion you choose, as long as you've got a socket nearby.

## 5-amp Plugs

A handy idea for living rooms where you want to have a number of sidelights is to fit a series of 5-amp lighting sockets (usually with small round-pin holes to distinguish them from 13-amp mains sockets). These can be linked together and all switched from one point. It's convenient not only because it gives you a master switch to control all the sidelights plugged into the 5-amp sockets, but it also gives you the ability to dim. By arranging the switching next to the door, it gives you the option of doing away with the central pendant lighting altogether. Budget £20-£30 per outlet plus a similar amount for the switch.

If you know nothing about the art of good lighting and you are in a hurry and don't want to waste a small fortune, you won't go wrong by specifying a handful of 5-amp sockets. You can create quite sophisticated lighting effects

## Light Bulbs

### Tungsten
*Ordinary lightbulbs (or GLS bulbs): cheap (30p), average life 1000hrs, power-hungry, good colour rendering, slightly orange light, easily dimmable; available in a huge choice of shapes and sizes (reflectors, tubes, pygmies, candles) which all cost a good deal more than 30p.*

### Mains-Voltage Halogen
*Also known as Halogen A: cost £2.50, average life 2000hrs, power-hungry, good colour rendering, pure white light, dimmable, fully interchangeable with tungsten bulb fittings.*

### Low-Voltage Halogen
*Come in specialist fittings (spotlights, downlighters) which vary enormously in cost from under £5 to £40 plus. Replacement bulbs costs around £3.50. Average life of bulb, 2000hrs; consumes around half the power of tungsten bulbs, good colour rendering, pure white light, dimmable with a appropriate electronic switch, now widely available. Best LV halogen lights are dichroic with reflectors and they require transformers.*

### Fluorescent
*Usually fitted as tubes; miniatures (as used in shaver lights or as kitchen surface lights) costing around £2.50; available in tubes up to 2.4m long (cost around £7). Average life 8000hrs; consumes around 25% of power of tungsten, cold flat light with poor colour rendering. Tends to be used in utility, garage spaces.*

### Compact Fluorescent
*Better known as energy-saving lightbulbs: cost £5-£15, performance similar in every way to long fluorescent tubes but compact shape makes them much more versatile when it comes to positioning. Interchangeable with GLS lightbulbs, but do not fit easily inside average lightshade and can look cumbersome. Note that they cannot be dimmed by regular methods and so don't try and replace dimmed GLS lights with compact fluorescents. There are a number of other light sources readily available — metal halide, sodium, neon — but their use is rare in the home and is unlikely to be specified by anyone other than a specialist lighting consultant.*

by using side lighting and, without spending a fortune on fittings, you can get pools of light wherever you want them whilst retaining a flexibility to change it all if you get bored and want something different.

### Dimmers
Dimmer switches give you the ability to control the amount of light given off by a bulb and thus set the mood for a room. They are particularly useful in living rooms where you may want to relax in front of the tele, watching the fire, and don't want to do it under the glare of 100 watt bulbs. Furthermore, dimmed lights save energy, and if you use dimmers which don't have a push on/off capability, you increase the length of your bulb life by having a "soft start" — most bulbs blow when you turn them on. As regular dimmers can be bought for around £5 (compared with £3 for an on/off switch), there is an argument for fitting them just about everywhere. You can dim just about any kind of light but the very basic dimming switches will only work on the standard GLS tungsten lightbulbs. There are now electronic dimmers widely available from around £10 which will handle either mains or low voltage halogen. Other kinds of bulbs require special dimmers which cost upwards of £30 for one-gang switching. Contact Home Automation.

### Alternative Lighting
If you wanted to improve on the basic developer's specification at the design stage, there are two other routes which you may be interested in.

### The Green Approach
An energy-efficient lighting scheme is looked at in some detail in Chapter 13, Green Issues. I estimate this would add around £300-£400 to building costs (but would cut furnishing costs by perhaps £150-£200) and could easily save £50/annum on electricity bills. Note that as from 2002, the building regs now require that you fit at least some energy-efficient lighting..

The 2002 energy efficiency building regs address lighting for the first time. They want you to fit some energy efficient lightbulbs. But where? And how many? They are a bit vague about where, merely suggesting "where lighting can be expected to have most use." And the number required is dependent on the number of rooms built. More than seven rooms, it's three. More than ten rooms, it's four.

### The High-tech Approach
In this low-voltage light scheme, the emphasis is on quality using ultra-bright, tungsten-halogen downlighters. Because of the comparatively narrow light fields of low-voltage downlighters, a bedroom would require a minimum of four and a living room probably eight or more. Costs of lighting the benchmark house would be in the £3000-£4000 range.

One stage on from this comes the concept of scene lighting. Here you programme banks of lights to come on together to create moods or scenes. It's something which is commonly seen in places like conference suites and lecture theatres but is beginning to migrate towards the home (via the USA). Products such as Lutron's Homeworks works with most types of bulbs and allows you to create and recall lighting arrangements, including dimming. Not only can you switch banks of lights on and off with one button but you can also do vacation settings for security. But I'm straying off here. This stuff really belongs in the Home Automation section coming shortly.

## Room by Room

### Kitchens
Central pendant lighting is particularly inept at providing light for kitchen worksurfaces, and this is one area where task lighting is now considered essential. The conventional place for this is under the wall cupboard units, hidden from view by the decorative downstand known as the pelmet. There is a choice of tungsten or fluorescent fittings; tungsten gives better light rendering but gets hot and tends to "cook" the contents of the overhead cupboard; fluorescent stays cool and is generally preferable, particularly if you choose a warm, white type like Sylvania Homelight de Luxe. An alternative is to fit downlighters in the ceiling over the kitchen surfaces, but placement has to be extremely accurate and you risk getting unlit areas under the wall units. If you have an extractor hood, make sure it has a light as well. Lumiance have introduced a range of low-voltage halogen downlighters which are only 20mm deep and are specifically designed to fit into a cupboard shelf. If your kitchen design doesn't want or need pelmets under your wall cupboards and you don't want exposed lights, then this is the answer for you.

### Dining Tables
A pendant light hanging over a dining table works very well, but make sure that the bulb is well concealed by the shade or fitting. Lighting from the side is much more difficult because of the shadows cast by the diners. As an alternative to a hanging light, go for a cluster of low-voltage downlighters — the way they do it in fancy restaurants. Avoid

fluorescent lighting if you are of the gourmet tendency and like to see what it is you're eating. And if you are the type who goes for candlelit dinner parties, it's very useful to be able to dim the ambient lighting.

## Living Rooms

There are no set rules for lighting living areas. Chandeliers, spotlights, uplighters, wall lights, downlighters, table lamps, sidelights — all have a role to play and it's very much a question of taste. Most developers and self-builders will be planning fairly conservative interiors, particularly in their living rooms, and an awful lot of the high-tech lighting schemes would be completely inappropriate here. However, the use of concealed fittings, such as downlighters, is compatible with virtually all settings. Lighting a room with downlighters is generally pleasing to the eye but it is expensive because of the numbers needed. Pendant fittings and wall lights may be preferred but considerable time and expense may go in selecting the right fittings for the room; downlighters actually require less thought. Another option is to go for three or four uplighters or wall lights, which will generally be enough to provide all the lighting needs (including reading) for a largish room; this presents a stylish mid-priced alternative between the expense of downlighters and the poor light quality offered by a central light.

Feature mirrors need to be set where they do not directly reflect lights. A traditional effect like a mirror above an Adam style fireplace will be ruined by a chandelier directly in front of it. Picture lighting is another problem area which you can ruin if you don't get it right.

## Bedrooms

For most people, bedroom lighting will be a mixture of an ambient central pendant and table lamps for reading. Although a central pendant light source will be cheaper to install, when the cost of task lighting is included, the alternative options of uplighters or downlighters look more pocket-friendly, though you must pay attention to switching from the bed as well as by the door.

## Bathrooms

The regulations require that bathroom light fittings should be concealed to prevent direct contact with water. Conventionally, this is done by placing a central light inside some sort of glazed casing. There are some extremely naff bathroom light fittings around and finding a good one can be difficult. An alternative approach is to use sealed downlighters.

Task lighting is also very useful around bathroom mirrors. The standard method is to fit a tungsten strip light (combined with electric shaver socket) which is adequate but rarely beautiful. Mirrors with integral lights are a stylish solution but they are very expensive.

## Hallways/Stairwells

- Don't be tempted to hang lights where you can't change the bulb without a ladder.
- Don't fit uplighters at the foot of stairwells where you can see the bulbs from above.
- Bear in mind that the building regs now require some energy efficient bulbs in new homes. Fitting them in to the halls and stairwells is probably the easiest way of complying, if you don't particularly want them throughout the house.

## External Lighting

The bane of external lighting is the 500 watt halogen floodlight. In the last few years these have become very cheap (under £20) and very common, yet their effect is blindingly unpleasant, unless well concealed. Security lighting need not be unattractive. It is worth giving a bit of thought to external lighting; unless you are building next to a well-lit road, you will find that some form of external light is essential just to negotiate the front path. By all means arrange to switch it on a timed Passive Infra Red (PIR) detector, but that doesn't mean you have to blast people in the face with 500w bulbs. PIR switches can be purchased on their own for around £25 and can be adjusted to trip on at different light levels and for different lengths of time — from a few seconds to several minutes. As alternatives to tungsten halogen floodlights, consider wall-mounted lanterns (c. £30), outdoor spotlights spiked into the ground (c. £10), free standing bollards (c. £60) or even brick lights (which replace a standard brick in your external wall) (c. £30).

The 2002 energy efficiency regs bring external lighting into their ambit for the first time. They demand that external lights should either be fitted with daylight detectors and timed switches or not use more than a 40w bulb — ideally a compact fluorescent lamp.

*The bane of external lighting is the 500w halogen floodlight*

# Built In Vacuums

Why bother to fit a built-in vacuum cleaning system? The big plus with central vacuums is that what gets sucked up stays sucked up. With a portable vacuum, efficiency depends on how well the filter works. Small particles of dust go through the filter and get recirculated which is why a house often smells a little bit different after vacuuming. By removing the motor to somewhere like a utility room or better still a garage, you are shifting all this dust out there, though it may not do much for the look of your shiny new car. And, by locating the motor out of the way, you also get another plus which is near silent vacuuming.

The biggest minus seems to be finding somewhere to stash the pipe. The fewer inlets you have the cheaper and easier to install but the longer the external pipe needs to be. Many people fit one inlet downstairs and one upstairs which means you need up to 10m of pipe to be able to get to the far corners of the house. Coiled up this makes a considerable heap - much bigger than a portable vacuum. The solution is to build in a rack, like a hosepipe rack, somewhere handy to get to but easy to conceal. A pipe cupboard no less. Canada is the spiritual home of central vacuuming; it gets fitted into the majority of new housing there. The Candians build homes which are nearly airtight and one of the side effects of living in near airtight housing is that people become very concerned with indoor air quality. They take planned ventilation very seriously, they avoid possibly toxic materials in construction and they pay close attention to things like vacuuming to ensure it does the job it's meant to..

There are a number of small manufacturers moving into this market in the UK, though note that the two most significant players Beam and Smart are both owned by Electrolux, the household appliance giant. Most advertise heavily in the selfbuild press and can be regularly found making pitches at the selfbuild exhibitions. If you are interested, most will quote from floor plans you send them. They aim particularly at the new build market because the system is most conveniently fitted at the first-fix stage so that the ducting is easily concealed. Put another way, it's more trouble than it's worth to fit the pipes into an old house but building into a new home is relatively straightforward. Prices for a built-in vacuum cleaner installed on a four-bedroom detached house are around £500 (excluding labour). Some businesses actually give away the wall ducting with timber frame kit homes, hoping this will create a sale later.

# TVs, Phones and Cables

Of all the sections in the Housebuilder's Bible that have required rewriting over its eight-year history, this one stands out because it has changed the most. As recently as 1995, this was a fairly short section: you stuck a phone line in, you put a couple of TV points in, an aerial in the loft, maybe a satellite dish and you were away. For many people this will still be a fine solution, but the past five years have seen the arrival of home office working, the internet, ISDN lines and digital TV, and suddenly the basic house wiring doesn't look quite up to the mark anymore. Now you have to make an educated guess as to what to put in and what to leave out, not only for your own requirements but for any possible future buyers as well. Time to knuckle down and take a hard look at what's in and what's out in home cabling.

### What are the essential changes in home wiring?
The twentieth century saw the widespread introduction of three different wiring systems into the home, electricity, telephones and television, with a few homes opting for a fourth system, wiring for burglar alarms. Of these, only the first, electricity, has conventionally been cabled all over the house. Telephones initially came into the house at just one socket, more recently two or three and likewise TV outlets have been restricted to one, two or three outlets. Whilst the electric cabling routes around the house remain largely unchanged, the demand for more complex phone wiring and TV cabling is causing these other systems to grow and converge. Phone wiring is changing because we want more outlets and because we are using phone lines for more than just conversations. TV wiring is changing because the methods of delivering TV signals are changing. Over and beyond this, the actual cables used for phones and TVs are changing and people are starting to cable for additional reasons, typically things like security and lighting control. I'll start with TV.

### What do I need to watch digital TV?
The government has let it be known that it wants to stop analogue TV broadcasts (i.e. terrestrial Channels One to Five) in order to auction off the airwaves but there is much doubt as to whether this will ever happen, at least for another generation, especially as these frequencies no longer seem to be quite as valuable as once imagined. So first point is that you needn't feel hustled into turning digital. There is however more to digital TV than Sky's £35/month subscription services; there are an increasing number of free-to-air channels which are available only via digital means. At present (and this is unlikely to change), TV signals are delivered to the home by three different methods, rooftop aerial (known as terrestrial), satellite dish and fibre optic cable. If you live in or near to a big city, you will have a choice of all three but this is not the case in many rural districts so you need to find out what is available and what works well in your area.

Analogue TV signals (the ones we have all grown up with since the 1950s) have conventionally been fed around the house in brown coaxial cable from the rooftop or loft aerial. The standard signal is usually adequate to service three or four TV sets — if you want more you need to add a small amplifier to the system.

Digital TV works rather differently to analogue. The signal needs to be decoded in the house, something usually achieved in a box of tricks called a digibox, although it can also be done inside a digital TV (that is a TV that has a built-in decoder). So you need to consider where your decoder should sit. Digiboxes are about the size of a video recorder and, like VCRs, are usually fitted around the main TV. Whether you receive your digital signal by aerial, satellite dish or cable, there must be a direct cable connection to the decoder and this then sends the signal to the TV or TVs. Digital decoders struggle to handle more than one channel at a time (though they can now record one whilst simultaneously showing another via the SkyPlus system) and if you link TVs in series they will all have to watch the same thing unless you purchase additional decoders and pay additional subscriptions.

So at present, if you want, say, three TV outlets in your home and you want to receive both analogue and digital at each outlet, you need two different cabling systems in place — unless you go for a structured cabling system. More on this later.

*Mains electricity, FM radio, digital TV, phone, computer network, CD jukebox. It's all here. The numbers on the RJ45 sockets on the right relate back to positions on the patch panel.*

### What are the options for phones?
Phone cabling around the house has traditionally been a simple affair. Your service provider (traditionally BT) install a master socket and you can run a small number of extensions out from there. If you started running a business from home, you would install a second line with a fax cum phone on it. It rarely got more complicated than that. And then came the internet.

### Ah, the internet. I guess that's made it all more complicated.
It rather depends on how you use the internet. If you are just an occasional surfer who likes to perhaps do a bit of home shopping and send the odd e-mail, then the typical phone arrangements we already have works just fine. But if you are a heavy user — and increasingly people working at home are heavy users — then a second line becomes almost essential because once online, the phone line is engaged and this becomes inconvenient to the rest of the household. Now that flat rate internet charging structures are becoming the norm, many people will stay online during the entire working day so a separate line for this becomes essential. If you work from home you have the prospect of a household with three phone lines — and it's beginning to get a bit silly. There are better ways of managing the situation.

One way around this problem is to opt for a single ISDN line — BT's offering is called Home Highway. This is a type of digital phone service that allows you to send more data down a phone line than normal - it's about twice the speed of standard modems. It also, crucially, allows you to do two things at once on the same line so that you could be online whilst receiving a phone call. ISDN has a complex charging structure but the net cost is roughly equivalent to installing two phone lines and it does promise faster internet access. However it does require ISDN compatible hardware — the computers need ISDN cards and you need a terminal adaptor, provided as part of the signing on fee.

However, an even faster phone technology than ISDN awaits in the wings. Broadband is already being rolled out in some parts of the country. Broadband connections cost slightly more than ISDN lines (usually around £40 per month) but promises permanent and unlimited internet access at speeds eight to ten times faster than the current crop of modems.

Broadband itself is subdivided into two different technologies, ADSL and cable modems. ADSL uses spare capacity on the BT phone line that comes into your house. Your phone service is unaffected and you can use the phone at the same time as surfing the net. Installation costs around £150 which includes an ADSL modem for use on either PC or Mac. Like ISDN, ADSL is only available where BT has enabled the local exchange to provide it and the signal is surprisingly vulnerable and it deteriorates very rapidly so that even if you are in an ADSL area, you may

not be able to subscribe if you are more than two miles from the local exchange. To find out if you can get ADSL, visit www.btopenworld.com and do a search by postcode. Cable modems are available to customers of the two cable networks, NTL and Telewest, who between them cover 50% of the UK population. The deals are broadly similar to BT's ADSL offerings though cable modems do require an additional cable to be run into the home. If you can't get ADSL or cable, broadband is shortly going to be available over satellite.

### ISDN, ADSL, this alphabet soup is getting confusing.
It's not just you that is confused. The whole telecoms and internet industry is watching anxiously to see how things pan out. But perhaps the most important thing to bear in mind, if you are planning to wire up a new house, is just what facilities you might want where. If your needs are predictable and fairly conservative, you don't need to put dozens of outlets around the house. If, for instance, you know which room you plan to use as a home office, and you suspect that you may need an extra phone line there, then it is a simple matter to wire it up conventionally at the outset. But if you want to retain maximum flexibility so that any room could be used as an office or a TV lounge, then it's time to consider a structured cabling system.

### A structured cabling system? What's that?
It's a way of wiring houses with high speed data cable, known as Category 5 or Cat 5 cable. It has migrated from offices where it is now as common as electric wiring. Instead

of haphazardly running cables from the various input points to the various output points around the house, you designate a place in the house as a central hub (known as the wiring closet) and you bring all the incoming cables to this point and then distribute them around the house to wall mounted data sockets which look very much like electric sockets.

A wiring closet doesn't have to reside in its own purpose built room — unlike the other kind of WC. The essential element in a wiring closet is a patch panel, a wall hung box the size of a small suitcase. The patch panel plays a similar role to an electrical fusebox in household electrical wiring where the power coming into the house is split up and sorted into different circuits. It is in here that the phone lines and TV cables are all connected. Rather than being connected up in series (or daisy chained) as many TV and phone outlets are in conventional set-ups, each outlet throughout the house is connected directly back to the patch panel. That means a double data socket will have two cables running next to each other back to the patch panel where each will terminate with its own unique number which corresponds to a number etched on the data socket.

### What's the advantage of installing a structured cabling system?

It really comes into its own if you want to gain a degree of flexibility in your home. A well designed system will allow you to plug TVs and phones in wherever you want to, not at the limited number of outlets you otherwise specify. You will also be able to set up small phone and computer networks which would allow you, for instance, to share printers or modems between computers or to back up your essential data without using disc drives or other media. Useful stuff in an office but arguably not quite so compelling in a typical home. But you only have to see how the numbers of electrical sockets have proliferated around the home over the past few decades to see that our attitudes to sending and receiving data will probably change substantially in years to come. Structured cabling gives you the built-in flexibility to do that.

### What else can you do with structured cabling?

The Cat 5 cable is capable of carrying all kinds of data. It's become the industry standard cable for computer networks — known as Ethernet — and yet it can be used for sending all manner of other signals besides voice calls and computer data, giving you remote control capabilities which only recently people would have thought were pure science fiction. You can pipe high quality sound signals along Cat 5 thus giving you the ability to have multi-room sound systems. You can use it to control lighting scenes around the house. You can use it to control motors which could open or close gates or windows. And you can use it for close circuit TV, security features and panic buttons. Provided you have built-in enough outlets, you have the capabilities of building an intelligent home and enough flexibility to add to the intelligence levels as and when you see fit.

Just about the one major weak point with Cat 5 cabling was that it didn't deliver a very compelling TV signal. Because of this it has been conventional to run CT-100 coaxial cable as well as Cat 5 around the house and back to the patch panel. But recently, two companies, IP Homenetworks and OMC, have developed a technique for sending TV and video signals along Cat 5 cable without any loss of quality. This is a considerable breakthrough because it greatly reduces the amount (and type) of cable needed.

### What does a structured cabling system cost?

The Cat 5 cable itself is not expensive, typically no more than electric cable. Similarly the patch panel and the RJ45 outlets are commodity items. The materials to fit out a four bedroomed house would typically cost around £800 - £1200 pounds, depending on the number of outlets that you require. This compares very similarly with the cost of electrical wiring. For many selfbuilders, the cabling is seen as just another DIY task to be completed along with the underfloor heating and the central vacuums system. There are now many companies offering to supply and fit structured cabling systems and prices start from about £2000 for a basic fit out, though

many of the more esoteric uses of structured cabling such as lighting control and multi-room sound systems are expensive extras costing many additional thousands.

### Are there any alternatives?

There are two main competing technologies for intelligent homes. The original one is mains-borne — that is using the existing electricity cables to move data around the house as well as electricity. There is a well established system called X10 which does just this. It's nothing new — in fact it's been around since the 1970s — and you can get a simple starter pack for no more than £50. X10 is the province of the dedicated home automation enthusiast who wants to be able to do things like closing the blinds remotely. It's never really developed into a whole house data system because it doesn't handle phones and data.

The other technology is wireless. We have become used to using mobile and cordless phones and the latest generation of digital cordless phones (known as DECT phones) enable you to do clever things like transferring calls between handsets. What is newly emerging is the capabilities for computers to send data between each other and to their peripherals using radio frequencies. Apple has a system up and running called Airport which does just this and great hopes exist for another similar technology called Bluetooth which works with all manner of appliances. There are now a number of heating controls that work without cables — usually referred to as RF — so it may be that all the switching signals which lie at the heart of the intelligent home may end up being done using radio waves and not cables.

That still leaves TV, video and audio signals which can't (as yet) be beamed around the house without loss of quality but in five, ten or twenty year's time this technical problem may have been overcome. So you could just do nothing and hope that technology will catch up with your future needs, but there is a risk that without a structured cabling system your house will begin to look very dated very quickly.

# Chapter 10
# Finishes

# Internal Wall Finishes

Plastering is the cheapest way of providing good internal wall and ceiling coverings. There are different systems of "plastering" but they all come within spitting distance of £7-£10/m² in price. There are alternatives which can be used when you know exactly what you want — exposed brickwork, tongued and grooved matchboarding — but they are considerably more expensive than a plastered finish and are normally only built as features.

The big question facing housebuilders is whether to go for a wet or dry system of wall coverings. The wet techniques use wet-mixed cement renders and gypsum plasters: the dry systems use dry-lined plasterboards. The wet techniques are traditional British building — the dry techniques are imported from countries where timber frame is prevalent. Ceilings are almost invariably fixed with plasterboard, but here there remains a choice about whether to cover them with a wet Thistle Finish plaster, to dry-line or to comb on Artex. Pricewise, there is very little to choose between the systems — though I estimate that dry-lining is a little bit cheaper.

## Wet Plastering

### Plus
It is well understood by builders and favoured by most plasterers; a well-skimmed plaster finish looks fantastic — at least initially.

### Minus
It's wet. Something like 1m³ of water (=12 bathfulls) is being built into the fabric of the house if it is wet plastered and this must in time dry out, which will take a summer at least. This drying out results in movement which causes cracking in the top coat plaster which looks naff and gets builders called back on site to carry out cosmetic repairs. This problem is particularly bad when plasterboard ceilings are skimmed with a plaster finish; here the movement in timber behind the boards causes hairline cracks around all the plasterboard joints. None of this cracking is in the least bit dangerous — it doesn't mean subsidence is occurring — and many people live happily with it knowing that these bedding in problems can be filled in at the first redecoration. However, for many unsuspecting souls it is a source of genuine grievance and complaint.

## Dry-lining

### Plus
It's dry — avoiding problems outlined above. It is relatively easy to correct out-of-plumb blockwork — you just adjust the thickness of the adhesive dabs. It also gives a comparatively soft wall with enough give for small children to bounce off unharmed, whereas a hard, plastered wall would bring forth tears.

### Minus
Dry-lining is not particularly difficult to learn — the plasterboard manufacturers all run cheap two- or three-day training courses — but it can be badly applied, leaving a ridged effect on walls and ceilings. Plasterboard has to be fixed more carefully than is normal trade practice so as to keep the number of cuts to a minimum. The wall finish is similar to what you would get if painting on to lining paper (which is basically what you are doing) and this may not be glossy enough for

some tastes. Plasterboard walls are not as damage-resistant as traditional plasters, though repairs can be easily effected.

Another problem with dry-lining is that it can be draughty. In theory the backing walls should be airtight — why do you have to put in all those expensive trickle vents in the windows? — but in practice air sneaks through the most unlikely joints. The solution to this problem is to seal all the joints between sheets and around openings prior to taping and jointing. However this is both expensive (Gyproc's sealer costs around £10/lt.) and time consuming. This air leakiness problem occurs with all forms of construction that use dry-lining, but its significance is greatly reduced when you build in timber-frame, incorporating a vapour barrier in the external walls.

## Blockwork v Studwork

You can only apply wet render on to a masonry background and it is, therefore, not an option for timber framers. Those using studwork walls will have to fit a wallboard, usually plasterboard — though, as already noted, plasterboard will take a 3mm wet plaster finish. On the other hand, if a dry method is desired in a brick and block house, then the favoured method is to stick plasterboard on to the blockwork using the dot and dab technique which uses specialised gypsum plasters as adhesives. This is the method currently in favour with over 70% of professional house builders — just goes to show how much they value not being called back because "there's cracks in me walls."

## Plasterboard

What is it? Gypsum plaster sandwiched between two layers of paper. It is characterised by being easy to cut, fairly easy to handle and it provides a good backing for paint and plaster. Note that wastage can be high when using plasterboard — up to 30% on small rooms and ceilings, between 10% and 15% on walls. It is available in several different formats: square edged (for wet plaster skimming) or tapered edge (for dry-lining); 12.5mm thick for 600mm spaced studwork and 9.5mm thick for 400mm spacings; foil-backed for providing an integral vapour barrier (it's cheaper to use a separate polythene sheet); small boards measuring 1800x900mm as well as the more normal, room-height, boards which are 1200x2400mm. There are also now a number of plasterboards which are laminated to insulation. Make sure you get the right format for the job and make sure that you've used metric spacings on your wall studs and ceiling joists as imperial-sized plasterboard is no longer made.

Plasterboard is a very competitive business with three companies (BPB aka British Gypsum, Knauf and Lafarge) slugging it out for the European market. Consequently, the price hasn't really changed much in 20 years — amazing value if you think about it. There is little to choose between the rivals either on price or quality.

## Alternatives

### Fermacell

Widely used in Germany, Fermacell is, in some ways, very similar to plasterboard and, in others, rather superior. It has a much higher racking strength than plasterboard and is therefore particularly useful when you want to hang radiators and bathroom furniture off timber stud walls and you don't know where the studs are. Fermacell also makes for better soundproofing. However, it is pricey in comparison with plasterboard, costing over £3/m², nearly three times the price. Consequently, it is mostly being used in the UK as a backing board for kitchens and bathrooms. It is usual to glue the boards together and simply paint over them for a finished surface. Another board worth seeking out is Knauf's Aquapanel, a cement particle board which is completely waterproof and can therefore be specified in shower enclosures.

## Exposed Brickwork

Costing between £20 and £30/m² — depending largely on your choice of brick — using exposed brickwork internally can be surprisingly cheap. With block and stud walls costing between £6 and £10/m², plaster finishes costing around £7/m² and painting costs of around £1/m², exposed brickwork from £20/m² doesn't look an expensive option. On internal walls, with both sides exposed, the arithmetic looks even more favourable. However, please note that £20/m² buys a pretty basic "developers" brick and that a "character" brick (i.e. second hand or handmade) will cost 50% more to lay. Also note that a masonry sealer (at around £4/lt) should be applied — and this is more expensive than emulsion work. More significant problems are encountered with fixtures like door and window lintels and electric cables which would normally be concealed behind the plaster. These problems mean that feature brickwork is most often seen in small areas such as fireplaces. Used adroitly, exposed

## 10a: Plastering: Guide Prices

|  | MATS | TIME in MINS | LABOUR £18/hr | TOTAL |
|---|---|---|---|---|
| Render and Skim | £2.50 | 20 | £6.00 | £8.50 |
| Carlite Browning and Finish | 2.50 | 25 | 7.50 | 10.00 |
| Tacking (Nailing) Plasterboard | 1.90 | 12 | 3.60 | 5.50 |
| Dot and Dab (Sticking) Plasterboard | 1.90 | 10 | 3.00 | 4.90 |
| Skim Finish on Plasterboard | 1.00 | 15 | 4.50 | 5.50 |
| Dry Lined Finish to Plasterboard | 0.80 | 10 | 3.00 | 3.80 |
| Artex Finish on Plasterboard | 0.80 | 10 | 3.00 | 3.80 |
| Fixing External Renderlath | 10.00 | 12 | 3.60 | 13.60 |
| Two-coat External Render | 4.00 | 40 | 12.00 | 16.00 |
| Floor Screed, 65mm Thick | 4.50 | 25 | 7.50 | 12.00 |
| Floor Screed, 50mm Thick | 3.50 | 20 | 6.00 | 9.50 |

*All figures are £/m²*

brickwork can be an effective feature at a cost little more than conventional plastering.

## Pine Matchboarding

Finishing walls and ceilings with timber matchboarded panels would cost around £20/m² (Mats £10, Lab £10). This price is made up of timber at £6/m², fixing at £6/m², sanding and filling at £2/m² and varnishing at £6/m². Pine panelling used to be very popular but is now rarely seen over whole walls, though its use as a stained boarding, fixed vertically between skirting and dado rail, is a currently fashionable effect. It is also an effective way of creating decorative service panels behind which can be run pipework and cabling, though this is a complex matter which ideally needs designing into the building from the beginning.

## Glass Blocks

One of the most intriguing trends in home interiors recently has been the re-emergence of glass block walls. They were widely used in the 1930s, mostly on public buildings, but then fell completely out of fashion. You simply didn't see them until about five years ago when the TV interior shows rediscovered them and suddenly glass blocks are everywhere. You can't get through B&Q without tripping over them. Many firms like Luxcrete, Shakerley and Vitra offer glass blocks together with everything you need to lay them — it seems to be a popular DIY job. Ballpark materials costs are around £60/m².

## Plastered Fancies

Coving is used to mask the joint between walls and ceilings. It used to be almost ubiquitous in new housing but it's beginning to fall out of fashion. It's not particularly expensive — rather cheaper than skirting board at around 80p/lin.m and is fixed for around £1.50/lin.m. Providing coving throughout the benchmark house cost around £300. For this price you just get a simple rounded profile but if you want something more ornate, it's available.

Artex produce a range of four classical styles which cost around £3/lin.m and are harder to fix than standard coving but do add a certain grandeur to a room that you might like. They can be combined with fancy ceiling roses (at around £10). There are a number of other specialist companies producing all kinds of plaster mouldings — arches, dado rails, corner details, wall plaques. Check Yellow Pages under Plaster Ware.

## Decorative Panelling

British Gypsum produce a number of decorative fielded panels out of a material called Glasroc which, as its name suggests, is gypsum plaster reinforced with glass fibre. They can be combined to provide a very smart looking interior wall detailing that would, in truth, look better in a shop or a restaurant than a home. They would be normally fixed on top of a wall finish (instead of replacing it) so the cost, at around £10/m² to buy, makes it similar to pine matchboarding.

## Ceramic Tiling

Tiling is not strictly speaking an alternative to plastering because it is usually applied on top, so "addition" might be a better word. Its use is often entirely functional when applied as a splashback behind sinks, basins and baths, but visit Italy or Portugal and you'll be amazed to see ceramic tiling in living rooms and bedrooms as well. In the UK wall tiling is seen in more functional terms; our benchmark house is unusual in this respect in that there is 25m² of ceramic tiling, far more wall tiling than you would normally expect in a house of this quality.

Whether you pay under £5/m² for some unadorned and unnamed import or £80/m² for some top of the range, handpainted tile out of the Fired Earth catalogue, the fixing costs remain remarkably similar. The adhesives which you use to stick the tiles down with and the grouts which you spread between the tiles tend to work out together at between £3

and £4/m² depending on the thickness and specification. The laying costs depend on the intricacies of the task in hand, but on fairly straightforward work, it takes a tiler around one hour to fix a m² of tiles and about 15 minutes to grout them up later. Big straight runs will be faster than this but most tiling work in new housing involves a fair amount of cutting and this takes the time.

## Buying Tips

Ceramic tiles vary enormously in style and quality from the cheap, mass-produced output of large factories to the exotic and individual handmade styles, often produced in the third world. The UK market is dominated by two big names, Pilkington (the glass makers) and Cristal. Their ranges are widely available at all kinds of outlets — DIY sheds, builder's merchants and tiling specialists — and their ranges are also largely complementary; at their simplest they have several earthy and pastelly coloured floor and wall tiles priced below the £10/m² mark. They both have acres of largely nondescript kitchen and bathroom motif tiles either with inoffensive patterns or odd adornments like wheatsheaves or dolphins. Very homely but not going to win any design awards. However, both Pilks and Cristal have some much more interesting designs that you might have to visit a tiling centre to gen up on. And, of course, there are any number of lesser known producers — check out Marlborough, Sphinx or any of the Italian imports.

The revived interest in all things handmade has produced a rash of simulated handmade tiles like Cristal's Linda Beard collection. Though nothing like the authentic ones, these tiles do represent a reasonable compromise between looks and price. For the real thing, you can do no better than phone Fired Earth for a catalogue.

# Floor Finishes

Nowhere else in building is there such a great variety of materials at such a huge variation in price. You could carpet a four-bedroom house for less than £1000 (inc. VAT); equally you could spend over £5000 and not risk being accused of extravagance. Normally, floor finishes are not included in building budgets unless they are an integral part of the construction; developers rarely fit floor finishes although they occasionally offer to carpet houses as a sweetener to encourage a sale.

## Carpet

Even when glued down, carpet is regarded by Customs & Excise as a movable item and therefore subject to VAT as a furnishing — all other types of floor finish are zero-rated and therefore effectively exempt from VAT when built into a new house. Even so, carpeting still provides potentially the cheapest form of floor covering available — especially the bonded cords which also happen to be reasonably hard wearing. Beware offers of free underlay and free laying; obviously these services are not free and the charge for them is included in the price. Usually priced by the yard, carpet laying can be subject to enormous wastage because of the limited roll sizes. The DIY builder might be happier to lay carpet tiles, but if price is the only consideration, then it will still probably be cheaper to look out for the absolute basic ranges supplied and fitted by one of the carpet warehouses. Some of these carpets sell for a good deal less than a decent underlay (which can cost £3/m²) so you can imagine what the quality is like.

For the novice, buying carpets is a bit of a minefield with enormous price variations for apparently similar products. The British Carpet Manufacturers' Association runs a grading scheme as follows:
- Grade 1: suitable for areas getting low use (bedrooms)
- Grade 2: average use areas (dining rooms, studies)
- Grades 3/4: heavily used areas (halls, staircases).

This grading scheme would be more useful if every retailer abided by it but they don't — some use their own grading systems and others blithely ignore the whole procedure. It can all be a particularly taxing affair for the selfbuilder who is often under great pressure to move in quickly. There often isn't time to make an informed decision and rash choices here can be expensive and hard to live with.

A Which? report (March 1994) into buying carpets provides good background reading. Key buying points to watch out for are:
- Don't be misled by incredibly low area prices quoted in newspapers and magazines. Get written quotations with details of underlay, fitting charges, and any extra that might get charged for gripper, door bars, delivery, etc. There are plenty of hidden costs for the unwary.
- Material. Wool is the traditional and natural material for carpets; it also tends to be the most expensive. Synthetics like nylon and acrylics are now commonplace and much carpet sold these days is a cocktail of wool and synthetics — and people walking on them would not know the difference. The very cheapest material is polypropylene which looks synthetic but may be fine for your needs, especially in bedrooms.
- Comparing prices over the phone is difficult because a lot of carpet is not branded and there are so many varieties on the market that very often no two outlets sell the same thing. Sticking to an established name like John Lewis will ensure that you are not ripped-off, but they are unlikely to be selling carpet below £10/m² which is higher than many people's budget will allow.
- Bear in mind this rule of thumb when estimating cost: you should double the advertised price of a fitted carpet to get an idea of what it will all cost when laid on your floors. This will allow for offcuts, underlay and laying costs.

### Bathroom Carpeting

Avoid woollen carpet in bathrooms as they will tend to go mouldy, especially if they have a hessian backing. Polypropylene carpets with foam backings are cheap and durable and will survive many years of bath time frolicking.

### Tiles

There are many different materials used to tile or sheet floors and there is not space to cover them all here. In particular, there are any number of synthetic rubbery plastic type floor coverings which are generally more at home in an industrial or commercial setting than a house. If you want to know more, check out your Yellow Pages > Flooring Services. Here I look at just the three most popular tiled finishes.

## Vinyl

The very word vinyl sounds cheap but don't be misled, it's not. Either in sheet or tile form, this can vary between the very cheap marble effects (like Polyflex) costing less than £5/m² — these tiles usually have only a small percentage of vinyl in them — to Amtico floor tiles costing over £50/m². The best results are to be had when the immediate sub-floor is covered either with a 5mm latex screed or hardboard sheeting. Adhesive adds around £1.50/m², laying costs between £2.50 and £5.00/m².

## Cork

Cheap cork tiles can be purchased in the DIY sheds, but they do not last very long. In any area receiving reasonably heavy wear, use vinyl covered and backed tiles. Wicanders is the main producer: their top of the range Cork Master costs around £25/m². Best laid on board; if laid on a cement screed ensure that it's completely dry — this takes around eight summer weeks. Adhesive adds £2.50/m², laying costs around £5/m².

## Ceramic/Quarry Tiles

Laying costs are higher when specifying ceramic tiles because it is a more involved process, requiring time-consuming cutting and a second pass to grout up the results. Adhesives and grouts add around £1.50 to £2/m² to prices. The very cheapest floor tiles are usually imported from Italy or Portugal and are displayed under little known brand names in the DIY sheds and discount tile shops at less than £5/m². The cheapest British quarry tiles — which are made from reconstituted stone rather than baked clay — are available in red at around £10/m², whilst Cristal, Pilkington and Wooliscroft produce popular floor tiles from around £9/m² upwards. At the other end of the scale, Fired Earth and numerous imitators sell a dazzling array of terracotta floor tiles, many of them reclaimed, from around £35/m² upwards.

Another popular option is to fit a stone floor. I have seen a lot of Indian slate laid recently — it looks good and it's very cheap but it seems to suffer from varying thicknesses which makes a pig of laying. Paving stones or flagstones are conventionally laid outside but they can also make stunning interiors as well; Classical Flagstones produce convincing replica York stone from £25/m² which is often used indoors.

## Timber Flooring

The rise and rise of hardwood flooring is notable trend in contemporary home design. It was always thought of as an aspirational feature but people used to get put off by the price. It's not got any cheaper but all of a sudden people seem to be quite happily paying £40 £80/m² for hardwood floor planking and are being increasingly daring as to the choice of wood — current top of the pops seems to be bamboo which sounds like it might be cheap but ain't. The best known brand names in this market are Junckers, Tarkett and Kahrs, all widely available, material prices starting at around £40/m². Cheaper options are to use a veneered floor which has a 4-5mm layer of hardwood stuck onto a composite backing. If anything, a veneer floor is going to be more stable because of the backing. However, every time you sand a hardwood floor you strip at least 1mm off the top surface so in the long term maintenance stakes, a solid floor wins out. But how many times are you actually going to sand a hardwood floor? Cheaper still is to use a wood-look alike floor cover but this is really cheating now.

How about a softwood floor? You can lay a new tongued and grooved pine floor; materials can be bought from as little as £7.50/m² but these need sanding and sealing after laying — allow around £5/m² for this — and will almost certainly shrink dramatically, opening up unsightly cracks between the boards. This shrinkage problem is a feature of all wood floors — though it is insignificant when using well-seasoned hardwoods — and the only way to ensure it doesn't happen is to let the timber dry out in your centrally heated environment before laying — rather impractical for most builders. But if you are prepared to source better quality pine planking from slow growth timbers in north Scandinavian latitudes, then you can match the performance of many hardwood floors at around half the price. You do, however, have to know what you are buying — don't just pitch up in a timber yard and buy tongue and grooved flooring.

Another approach is to use a reclaimed board which has been stored undercover and is, hopefully, dimensionally stable. These vary in price from around £6/m² up to £30/m² and will almost certainly involve you in a lot of extra work (de-nailing, sanding, hole filling, more sanding, sealing). The huge variation in prices for reclaimed boards is of course an indication that there is a huge variation in quality as well. If you go to one of the better salvage yards, such as Machell's, near Leeds, you'll find good quality board but prices to match new planks. Another option is to use wood blocks — reclaimed oak can still be picked up from salvage yards for less than £15/m² — but again be prepared to have to carry out a lot of extra preparation work. However, a wood block floor (sometimes known as parquet) has to be laid on a solid backing, which will generally involve laying some form of extra screed or decking beneath, especially as floor insulation is now mandatory.

## Matwells

It's always a nice touch to see people thinking ahead and building in a sunken matwell is usually a sign that someone has been. Now that the disabled access regs require level access, usually at the main entrance door, a sunken matwell becomes even more important, as the door now opens just a few millimetres above the floor cover. There is an industry standard matwell (which may surprise some) which is 760 x 460 x 40mm. If you stick to this you can buy galvanised steel surrounds for around £40 and these will take industry standard sized coconut matting (costs around £8 per mat). If you are putting down a timber floor, you can create your can of course create your own surrounds.

## 10b: Floor Finishes Guide Prices

| All costs are £/m² | MATERIALS | | | LABOUR at £18/hr | | | BENCHMARK |
| | PRICE | WASTE | EXTRAS | in MINS | LAYING | TOTAL | HOUSE COSTS |
|---|---|---|---|---|---|---|---|
| Cheap Carpet | £5.00 | £1.00 | £2.00 | 15 | £4.50 | **£13** | £2,100 |
| Decent Carpet | 18.00 | 3.60 | 2.00 | 15 | 4.50 | **£28** | £4,500 |
| Axminster Wool | 36.00 | 7.20 | 2.00 | 15 | 4.50 | **£50** | £8,100 |
| Cheap Vinyl Tile | 5.00 | 0.50 | 1.50 | 40 | 12.00 | **£19** | £3,100 |
| Expensive Amtico-like Vinyl | 50.00 | 4.00 | 1.50 | 50 | 15.00 | **£71** | £11,500 |
| Cork | 14.00 | 1.40 | 2.50 | 40 | 12.00 | **£30** | £4,800 |
| Red Quarry Tile | 12.00 | 1.80 | 4.00 | 60 | 18.00 | **£36** | £5,800 |
| Cheap Ceramic Floor Tiles | 7.00 | 1.05 | 4.00 | 60 | 18.00 | **£30** | £4,800 |
| Expensive Ceramic Tiling | 40.00 | 6.00 | 4.00 | 80 | 24.00 | **£74** | £12,000 |
| Softwood T&G boards | 8.50 | 0.85 | 7.00 | 80 | 24.00 | **£40** | £6,500 |
| Junckers-style Beech Floor | 40.00 | 4.00 | 2.50 | 60 | 18.00 | **£65** | £10,500 |
| Reclaimed Boards | 25.00 | 5.00 | 8.00 | 80 | 24.00 | **£62** | £10,000 |
| Wood Block | 16.00 | 1.60 | 8.00 | 80 | 24.00 | **£50** | £8,100 |

Timber floors have a hidden cost advantage in that they can be laid straight onto timber joists without the need for any decking; a potential saving of £5/m², but not without its problems. See text.

# Second Fix Carpentry

Second-fix carpentry is a bit of a rag-bag of different activities that covers just about everything that carpenters get up to after the plasterers are finished. It usually includes door hanging and staircase fixing, as well as fixing skirtings and architraves and pipe boxings; often it also includes fitting kitchens and vanity units in bathrooms and putting up shelves. Prices in this section are mostly just material prices; for an inkling of the current fixing costs refer to the table Chippies Rates in Chapter 12.

## Internal Doors

The world of the internal door is split between the hollow and the solid. The hollow doors are like sandwiches; the casings are layers of board and the filling consists of a material very similar to egg boxes. Where you would normally place the handle and latch, they put a solid hunk of wood called the lock block and foolish would-be chippies (like me) have been known to hang these doors in a hurry, only to find that the lock block is on the hinge side of the door. If you are observant, you will hang the door on the correct side — there is only ever one lock block in a hollow door.

This all sounds very cheap and tacky and, generally speaking, eggbox-style doors are, but they can also be purchased with expensive hardwood veneers, usually from some environmentally incorrect species like sapele (pronounced sa-pee-lee), and this pushes the price up to levels at which you can buy solid softwood doors, around the £25 mark.

The very cheapest doors you can get are eggbox-filled doors which are encased in, wait for it, hardboard. Expect to pay around £12 for one of these but don't ever kick it. A popular variation on this theme is the embossed or moulded door; they are no stronger but they imitate the fielded panels found on timber doors and some of them imitate wood grain texture. The simpler ones cost between £30 and £40 each and they look quite acceptable when painted, which is what they are designed for. Some superior ones use a type of fibreboard for the casing and they are strong enough to take glazing, although doors with glazing panels are much more expensive — around £70. All the major joinery manufacturers have a selection of these doors and, if you want to select a door, get hold of one of their catalogues. Premdor Crosby and Magnet both have good ranges. Most designs are also available in bi-fold format for use as sliding cupboard doors.

## Solid Wood Doors

For people who like their doors to go clunk rather than thwack when they shut. Not that these doors are that much heavier than their eggbox counterparts; indeed there are a number of incredibly cheap (i.e. less than £30) imported timber doors available in the DIY sheds which look as though they might actually disintegrate if you shut them too hard. They are usually stored about ten feet above ground level and when you get to see them close up you realise why.

Generally, internal timber doors fall into two categories; stainable and paint-only grade. The paint-only ones are made from inferior timbers that may well have dead knots — which are given to working loose — and are frequently made up of short sections of timber which are finger-jointed together. If you are planning to paint the doors you might just as well settle for a paint-only grade door costing around £40; the better quality, stainable doors are more than twice as much.

Hardwood is an option as well. Oak and meranti are widely available but expensive at around £150/door. The hardwood veneered hollow doors are about half this price and are solid enough for most people's demands.

## Cottage Style Doors

An increasingly popular option is to fit ledged-and-braced doors to all internal openings. This style of door used to be exclusively associated with back doors and outbuildings, but with the fashion for all things cottagey, they are beginning to move indoors. External doors are manufactured with a moisture content of around 18% whereas the ideal moisture content for internal doors is around half this amount. Hanging an external door inside tends to result in them twisting out of shape.

The joinery majors such as JeldWen now carry internal cottage doors (in their case known as an FL&B for Framed Ledged & Braced) but they cost twice as much as the ones designed for exterior use. Alternatively, seek out one of the small specialist suppliers such The Real Door Company; they will tend to charge between £140 and £200 for softwood doors.

## MDF Doors

Another approach which is gaining in popularity, especially as regards fitted cupboard doors, is to make them on site using MDF (medium density fibreboard). MDF is a manufactured timber board which can be worked like natural timber; the finish can be sanded to accept paint or even, at a pinch, stain. Mouldings can be either routed into the board or stuck on to the surface. This is obviously rather labour intensive and the doors tend to be a bit on the heavy side but it is cheap. If you have nonstandard sized doorways, which often occurs with alcove cupboards and the like, then MDF is often a good solution. You need a board that's at least 25mm thick or else you won't be able to hinge it; alternatively, you can stick two thinner boards together and cut bits out of the top one to make decorative panelling effects. A good timber merchant will be able to dimension MDF for you, a facility not to be sniffed at.

## Door Furniture

Door furniture is the phrase used to describe just about everything to do with doors excluding the door itself. That usually means all the bits made of metal and door ironmongery would be a much easier to understand expression, but the building trade likes the word furniture to be used here. I really don't know why. Perhaps it adds to the mystique of the whole thing or maybe they are just being pig-ignorant. Anyway, I digress.

The point to cotton on to here is that some door furniture is purely functional in that you don't see it or, if you do, you don't notice it; however other bits are very visual and — wait for it — tactile. Yes folks, door handles are sexy. Developers know this and consequently are prepared to spend above the bare minimum to create an impression on the would-be house purchaser. Door handles may indeed be the only part of the house that the viewer actually touches during an inspection and female purchasers are thought to be impressed by something strong and solid which responds readily to their grasp.

There is a wide range of quality available. The accompanying table shows the kind of money spent on the door furniture for the four external and 16 internal doors of the benchmark house. Without looking for more than ten minutes, I was able to re-specify at less than half price. And of course it would be just as easy to more than double the price to over £800. Quality here is a complex field; there are numerous manufacturers and several different materials to choose from. Each material is available in a wide range of grades — there are no generalisations to be had in this game. The very cheapest handles may well

## 10c: Benchmark House: Brass Door Furniture

| | NUMBER | UNIT COST | TOTAL |
|---|---|---|---|
| **EXTERNAL ITEMS** | | | |
| Hinges | 6 prs | £5.00 | £ 30 |
| 5-lever Mortice Locks | 3 No | 22.00 | £ 66 |
| Night Latch | 1 No | 25.00 | £ 25 |
| Rebate Sets | 1 No | 2.00 | £ 2 |
| Handles | 4 prs | 10.00 | £ 40 |
| Letter Plate | 1 No | 15.00 | £ 15 |
| Door Knocker | 1 No | 5.00 | £ 5 |
| Slide Bolts | 6 No | 5.00 | £ 30 |
| Security Chain | No | 5.00 | £ 0 |
| 2-point Locking System | 1 No | 50.00 | £ 50 |
| Door Bell | 1 No | 3.00 | £ 3 |
| **EXTERNAL TOTAL** | | | **£ 270** |
| excluding garage side door | | Allow £30 | |
| **INTERNAL ITEMS** | | | |
| Hinges | 24 prs | 2.00 | £ 48 |
| Latches | 16 No | 2.00 | £ 32 |
| Rebate Sets | No | 2.00 | £ 0 |
| Handles | 16 prs | 9.00 | £ 144 |
| Privacy Locks | 3 No | 2.00 | £ 6 |
| Slide Bolts | 2 No | 2.00 | £ 4 |
| **INTERNAL TOTAL** | | | **£230** |
| **GRAND TOTAL** | | | **£500** |
| Cheapest alternatives | | | £250 |

be aluminium or plastic or brass plated: equally well, these three materials may feature in some of the most expensive furniture available. If there is a discernible rule it is this: the British manufacturers are expensive. They will claim that this is because they are producing a quality product and that's bound to cost more, but isn't that exactly what the British motorbike manufacturers claimed in the 60s? Unlike most building materials, door furniture is small enough and expensive enough to be readily tradable along the world's shipping lanes and the signs are that overseas competition is putting the drops on us again. Most of the domestic grade stuff you can buy in the UK is imported.

### Style

Most developers fit brass-plated furniture to their doors. There are two basic styles: Victorian (or plain) and Georgian (frilly bits added). Both styles are catered for by builder's merchants and DIY sheds who sell shrink-wrapped pre-packs at fairly reasonable prices. These pre-packs have one big advantage going for them in that they've got all the bits you need in the pack; you may be able to buy at keener prices but you risk a) forgetting vital bits, b) having to overbuy on items like screws and c) buying the wrong bits — classic one here is to get the wrong-

sized hinges. If your tastes veer away from these mainstream choices you'll have to brave it and go and order your very own door furniture.

Our benchmark house is fitted out with brass furniture on both external and internal doors.

### Door Security

Door security features are dealt with in the Security section in this chapter. To summarise — if you can't be bothered to find this section — current NHBC guidelines recommend fitting 5-lever locks to all external doors but also recommend that the main exit door should be protected by a Yale-type night latch which can be readily opened from inside without a key; this is to make escape easier in case of fire.

### Espagnolettes

These are fancy multi-point locking systems that are fitted, as standard, on uPVC doors, but only because the basic material is so flexible that it would not be secure without bolts top, middle and bottom. The use of espagnolettes is creeping into the world of timber joinery and you can fit your own to any timber door simply by routing a slot down the closing edge. The espagnolettes cost

around £55; they have an integral handle but they don't replace the 5-lever lock necessary on any external door.

### Buying Tips

As already mentioned, the door furniture pre-packs are a moderately good deal if you are happy to stay within a limited range. If you want more unusual fittings then the DIY sheds have a surprising variety; if you want wood or ceramic knobs this is a good place to look. More specialised still are the Architectural Ironmongers: check the Yellow Pages in your area. Clayton Monroe make one-off wrought iron door furniture which is both traditional and very different.

Another tip well worth pursuing is to order all your external door locks "to pass." This means that all your 5-lever locks are adjusted so that they can be opened with the same key. It's not exactly the automated house but it's a big improvement on lugging around identical looking keys, each of which will only open one of your doors. A good merchant will be able to sell you locks to pass at no extra cost though they will take an extra day or two to sort it out.

### Knobs

Sorry to bring up this sordid subject again but the observant amongst you may have noticed that there are two distinct styles of door opening levers, otherwise known as handles and knobs. Whatever the merits and demerits of the two, there is one painful little trap to watch out for if you go for a knob — you need to fit a longer latch otherwise you will scrape your knuckles every time you open the door. For the technically challenged, the latch, in this instance, is the metal tube that fits inside the door and the hole in the latch determines exactly how far the handle or the knob sits from the edge of the door. The standard tubular latch is 63mm long and it's designed for handles; when fitting a knob on an internal door, fit a 75mm latch and an external door knob will require an even longer latch — say 95mm. The pre-packed knobsets normally include 75mm latches, but if you are buying independently then watch out.

### Stairs

By far the cheapest staircase you can specify is the straight-flight with 13 steps and a total rise of 2600mm, which is the industry standard distance between floors. Timber staircases like this can be picked up off the shelf for as little as £180; they are also much quicker to install and, generally, have far less in the way of newel posts and balusters. A straight flight staircase with all the trimmings is going to take a good chippie no more

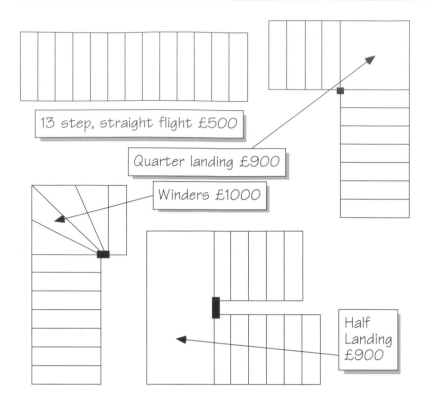

13 step, straight flight £500

Quarter landing £900

Winders £1000

Half Landing £900

lin.m whereas the fancy turned timber balusters start from around £45/lin.m. Even on a relatively straightforward staircase, the fittings will often cost as much as the stairs.

### Galleries

A surprising number of otherwise very conventional new homes incorporate an open-plan gallery area which links the two floors with a grand staircase arrangement. Typically there will be an area of hallway around the front door which is open right up to the upstairs ceiling or even the underside of the roof, lit by a Velux rooflight. It makes for a very impressive entrance with dramatic overtones of minstrel's galleries and the like. In a way it's pure theatre; it is an extremely impractical arrangement and it doesn't owe much to traditional housing styles which we British seem so keen to ape in other respects. Done out using acres of glass, white walls and chrome staircase, we would say "It's far too open plan for us"; however, dress up the same idea with pile carpeting and traditional looking balustrading and we react quite differently — "Gosh! Isn't that just like Gone With The Wind."

However you finish it, the gallery/open-plan stairwell arrangement is space hungry and is, therefore, a luxury. In itself it's not a particularly expensive detail (unless you start curving the staircase and the balustrading) but before you embark on a maximum impact entrance, first consider whether you wouldn't rather have an extra room or two instead. Chances are that if you want that kind of entrance then, frankly, you don't give a damn.

## Skirting/ Architrave

The amazing thing about skirtings and architraves is that we don't really need them at all. Indeed, many countries have already done away with them. Yet a glance at the building costs Table 2a generated by the benchmark house will reveal that AB Homes, in common with every other major UK builder and just about every selfbuilder, spent good money (around 1% of the total building costs) on fixing largely superfluous bits of timber to the base of all the walls and around all the internal door openings.

There is (or rather was) a logic behind fitting skirting boards. It used to be standard building practice to leave a 50mm gap between the floor and the bottom of the plaster on the wall so as not to breach the damp-proof course placed in the wall; however, damp-proofing techniques have changed and now floor membranes are lapped into wall membranes and the rising damp never (in theory) penetrates the room space at all. It

---

than two days to put in, and so anticipate a cost (without decoration or carpeting) of just £450 (Mats £300, Lab £150). The cheapest source of straight stairs is the Magnets of the joinery world; for more complex arrangements, a local joiner may well be very competitive, though note that Jeld Wen's bespoke staircase production is often excellent.

### Half-Landings

The commonest alternative is to split the staircase into two halves connected by a half-landing. This arrangement is better when you want a more open stairwell design and often makes it much easier to design the internal layout of the house. Half-landings (and the related quarter-landings) tend to double the overall staircase costs.

### Winders

Winders (pronounced wine-ders, not winders) is the name given to steps that turn corners whilst still climbing; a spiral staircase consists of nothing but winders but a more conventional arrangement uses three winder steps (usually at the top or the bottom of the flight) to navigate a 90° turn. They are space efficient and so are normally used in situations where space is tight. These days they are most commonly used with loft conversions, precisely because of this reason. They are not cheap — the staircase alone will cost

£600 plus — and in many ways they are best avoided, especially when you want to move furniture up or downstairs.

### Spirals

The ultimate in winding-staircases is the fully fledged spiral staircase. Usually done in steel, they are expensive and enormously impractical. The logic behind spiral staircases is that they save space but in reality the amount of spaced saved is minimal. They do certainly impose a style and in certain, modern looking interiors, they are just so. Realistically, the average UK housebuilder is going to find them far too ostentatious. Expect to pay over £1000 for a very simple steel spiral staircase.

### Fittings

At least as significant visually as the shape of the staircase is the specification of all the little bits that go with the stairs; the banisters, the handrails, the newel posts. These days banisters tend to get called balusters which is, perhaps, something to do with European integration, but the details remain wedded to the turn of the century (last time around). As with so much else in UK housebuilding, the standard options all hark back to our dearly beloved bygones: Georgian, Victorian, Colonial, Fluting, Rope Twist, etc. Easily the least fussy — and the cheapest — are the peasant variety known as Plain Balusters. The plain arrangements cost around £30/

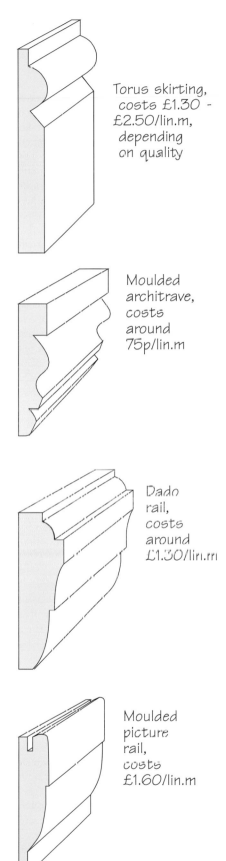

Torus skirting, costs £1.30 - £2.50/lin.m, depending on quality

Moulded architrave, costs around 75p/lin.m

Dado rail, costs around £1.30/lin.m

Moulded picture rail, costs £1.60/lin.m

still leaves the problem of filling the unsightly crack between wall and floor but the widespread incorporation of fitted carpets has made even this problem a thing of the past.

Not that I've anything against skirting boards; I love 'em — the wider the better. They look great and any room without them will look cold and, worse still, European. Both skirtings and architrave are available in a range of styles varying from the very plain to the thick moulded sections beloved by the Victorians. Fixing times don't vary much (prices usually hover around £1/m) but as regards material costs, the fancy sections are two to three times more than the utilitarian versions which are around 40p/m. To some extent this can be offset by specifying moulded sections from timber "fifths" (see section on buying timber in Chapter 11, Shopping), which are perfectly adequate for most people's needs. On the other hand, you can go for hardwood skirtings which — in my book — is pure unadulterated ostentation.

If you are in a hurry you can use prepainted MDF sections, which are now becoming widely available at builder's merchants. These are best nailed into the walls but, alternatively, can be stuck on with an adhesive like Gripfill, a "mastic glue" which can be used to bond all kinds of materials. Not only could you use it for all your skirtings and architraves, but it's fantastically useful for sorting out little problems like squeaky stairs. A true friend to the bodge merchant.

### Dados and Picture Rails

You may find it hard to believe that skirtings and architraves are purely cosmetic, but even the most sceptical amongst you will have to agree that dados and picture rails are not essential. However, they were regarded as essential in polite Victorian parlours. The dado rail was placed at waist height, the picture rail just a few inches below the ceiling. Their chief function was to provide a visual break in the eye feast that was the Victorian living room, whose walls consisted of two different kinds of wallpaper as well as (starting at the bottom) skirtings, dados, picture rails and plaster covings. Despite the fashions for all things Olde Worlde, this level of detail in new housing is now extremely uncommon. Nevertheless, good timber yards still keep these sections, mostly for restoration work, and you may choose to fit them in a new house if you are looking for a bit of style.

### Loft Hatch

Every house has one (unless you have a room in the loft) and they are not the most demanding of features. But take a little care in fitting a loft hatch as it is frequently a weak point in your home's battle against draughts. Furthermore, being an outlet for draughts rather than an inlet, you are never likely to be aware of just how much warm air you may lose through the loft hatch. Many an otherwise fastidious greenie (myself included) has insulated the top of the loft trap door — Gripfill is brilliant for this job as well — but neglected to effectively draught proof the strips of wood on which the hatch door sits. In terms of heat loss through loft hatches, effective draught proofing is ten times more important than the insulation. You don't have to do anything dramatic; just make sure it sits tight. If you are particularly fussy, you can buy proprietary loft hatches made from uPVC which clamp shut: they cost around £50.

### Loft Ladders

Not essential but nevertheless incredibly useful, even if you only go up there once a year. A decent aluminium sliding loft ladder will cost around £50 and take a competent DIY boffin around 2hrs to fit. However, if you are interested in making your loft hatch draught proof, it is really worth carrying out the installation of a loft ladder first because it usually leads to you having to make significant adjustments to the trap door housing.

Whilst we're on the subject, it's worth installing a permanent light in the loft just to make life easy when fixing a loft ladder. You won't regret it.

### Airing Cupboard

Airing cupboards are not actually required in houses with central heating but they are still very commonly fitted. There is one major drawback to the contemporary airing cupboard and that is that with the new generation of super-lagged hot-water cylinders, you no longer have a creditable heat source in the airing cupboard; hence, perpetually soggy towels. Well that's not quite true; any new house will enjoy a much higher ambient temperature than an old wreck and this will tend to dry damp clothes, albeit rather slowly. You can, of course, just put fully dried clothes in the airing cupboard, but this rather defeats the purpose of having an airing cupboard in the first place. Alternatively, you can fit a mini-heater or a 150w light bulb inside. It all seems a bit futile when the cause of your problem is the fact that you've wrapped up the hot water cylinder so well that it no longer gives off any heat.

What's really needed is an effective way of lagging and unlagging your hot water tank, controlled automatically by the relative humidity of air inside the cupboard. But this sounds very expensive and surely the world is full of more pressing problems. Still it's one to ponder on during those long sleepless nights.

## Boxing

Boxing in the pipes is a new facet of house-building that now forms a significant bit of a second-fixer's work. In the good-bad-indifferent-Olde days the pipes were left naked for all to see. The stench pipe in particular was usually run down the outside of the house. Current fashions are for internal stench pipes — concealed internal stench pipes — and this means boxing is de rigeur. Now, depending on your disposition, this type of job can seem like an incredible almighty drag or a marvellous opportunity to show the world just how creative you can be with a bit of dead space. Whichever camp you fall into, it helps to plan your pipe runs and attendant boxings well ahead so that the boxing can be incorporated into the overall scheme of things rather than sticking out into rooms like an ugly carbuncle ("monstrous," I hear you saying). Bathroom boxings are often best tiled over, but you must allow at least some of the panelling to be removable — a trick that's accomplished with mirror screws and flexible mastic joints. If you are painting the finish, then MDF is probably the best material to use, but if you plan to stick ceramic tiles on, then a waterproof 18mm plywood would be a better choice.

Boxing is also widely used in bathrooms to create a fitted vanity unit effect. There are a range of basins (known as semi-countertop) that are designed to sit over a boxed unit and there are also concealed cisterns which will be proud to flush behind your mini-wall. The usual choice of wall finish will be ceramic tiles but pine matchboarding is becoming fashionable once again, albeit painted not varnished.

## Shelving

The only quotation that The Duchess of Windsor is remembered for is "You can't be too rich and you can't be too thin." Had she been a keen builder, she might have added "You can't have enough shelves" because it is an axiom that, however many shelves you put up, you will still need more. I can discern three approaches to shelving:

- Buy some: go out and buy some ready made up units. DIY sheds have some pretty basic ones; IKEA has some basic ones which are a little better designed. Department stores like Habitat and John Lewis have some very nice expensive shelving systems. Free standing shelving units are not especially cheap but they are removable.
- Bash them up: utility shelving can be extremely cheap to fit. If you use one of the proprietary steel bracket systems like Spur or Element 32 you pay a lot more but you get a system that's very quick to install and easy to alter. It is also readily removable. Materials for a steel bracket shelving system work out at around £30/lin.m which is cheaper than almost any ready made system.
- Labour of love: design your shelving to fit a particular alcove or sit at a certain height. Think a little of the finished look; perhaps add some sort of pelmet and possibly some lighting as well. This sort of detail does not have to be expensive but it does require a certain amount of forethought. If you know what MDF is and know how to wield a router, you should be able to erect bespoke shelving (with no metal brackets showing!) for less than £20/lin.m (materials only).

# Painting & Decorating

## Exterior Work

You can avoid exterior decorating altogether by specifying pre-finished materials like uPVC. Indeed, many are doing just that: Wimpey Homes, one of our largest volume housebuilders, have recently switched to no timber exteriors. The windows, fascias and bargeboards are uPVC; the doors are steel; the garage doors are GRP. But although the move away from timber exteriors has been accelerating through the 90s, there is still a considerable number of housebuilders who chose timber — largely because it looks better — and timber needs some form of protective coating.

The main choice is now between traditional paint (usually white) and woodstains. Even though woodstains are more expensive to buy, the cost difference between the two systems is negligible because there is such a high labour content in decorating and, if anything, stains are slightly quicker to apply. What really causes decorating costs to tumble is reducing the number of coats needed to get a decent finish. Many builders do this with stains by dispensing with the third coat, which would be difficult with conventional paint, but there are now a number of one-coat paints (e.g. Crown Solo) which enable you to dispense with the undercoat — at a price.

## Wood Paints

The traditional way of finishing external timber is with oil-based gloss paint. This is applied in a three-coat system; primer, undercoat, gloss. If you want to use a traditional paint finish you can save money and time by specifying that your joinery arrives on site primed with paint instead of the current industry standard of a basecoat of honey-coloured stain.

Which paint to use? There is now a bewildering array of paints available: traditional oil-based gloss, non-drip gloss, one-coat gloss, microporous paints, acrylic paints to name but a few. Coupled with the fact that every manufacturer seems to use a different naming system to describe their product and it's no wonder the poor consumer gets confused. Which? magazine carries out an annual review of exterior paints (and stains) but it only scratches the surface of the paint market; their survey is just not comprehensive enough to provide a complete picture and, in any event, the canny manufacturers are forever reformulating their products and giving them new brand names so that the chances are, even if you went around B&Q armed with the latest Which? survey in your hand, you'd still not find their recommendations. Or if you did, how would you know it was the same as it was five years ago when Which?'s test started.

## Water-based Acrylics

Two factors have combined to increase the sales of these paints and they are both to do with user friendliness. Firstly, they are very easy to apply — afterwards the brushes can be washed out under a cold tap; secondly, there are increasing concerns over the health risks of using the traditional oil-based gloss paints. The people most likely to benefit from both these factors are the professional painters and decorators yet, paradoxically, they are the ones who are most resistant to using water-based paints, reckoning them to be useless. Expensive more like. Though they are still a comparatively new system (first introduced in the 70s) the indications are that water-based paints perform rather better than many oil-based alternatives. What they won't give you is a high-gloss sheen finish, but then the matt look is preferred by most people these days.

## Masonry Paints

As if to emphasise the last point about the durability of water-based paints, standard masonry paints, which are used to cover external render and masonry, are all water-based and many will claim to last for 15 years before needing recoating. They are easy to apply but their application should not be rushed; the underlying cement render must be allowed to dry out thoroughly. This is a drag because many builders are itching to strike the scaffolding by the time the external rendering is done and waiting for render to dry can take forever. Take the scaffolding down and it'll take you three times as long to paint the house. The moral? Only build houses with external painted panels when the sun shines.

## Stains

Woodstaining is one of the very few continental ideas to have really caught on in British housebuilding. The habit of applying woodstains has been a hit with the wood

stripping Habitat generation despite the fact that it's anything but a traditional British practice. This popularity is largely because the stains enable you to see the natural grain of the timber which they are covering. Generically, stains are divided into two subgroups, low-build and medium-build, but you are unlikely to hear these terms bandied about on a building site where they are known by their brand names. The build rating refers to the thickness of the stain and the higher the build the better the protection but the less you see of the underlying wood. The biggest names in this business are Sadolin and Sikkens, now both part of Akzo Nobel, though the British manufacturers are at last getting their act together (Ronseal, Dulux, Hicksons, Cuprinol). Sadolin's low-build stain is called Classic and is most widely used on sawn timber which drinks it like a Dublin bar on St. Patrick's night; their medium build stain is called Extra and this is much more oily — treacly almost — and you use this for covering timber joinery. All these stains are available in a range of woody colours but the really jazzy colours are usually restricted to the low-build ranges.

Conventionally, stains have been spirit-based but, as with paints, you can now buy water-based acrylic stains. Sikkens' Cetol BL range is reckoned to be one of the best.

## Creosote?

There are a number of wood preservatives which are way cheaper than the commercial woodstains. And of these, creosote stands out as being much the cheapest — you can pick up 25lts of the stuff for £15, which makes it six times cheaper than a Sadolin wood stain. The trouble is that creosote stinks and it goes on stinking for years. Use it out in the garden and even on the garden shed but don't ever put in on your house.

## Interior Work

## Walls and Ceilings

Most interior walls are finished with emulsion paints which are very cheap and very easy to apply, being water-based. The standard choice you need to make is between a matt finish and a silk finish. Matt finishes are characterised as being thicker (more opaque) and softer; silk finishes produce a harder, glossier look that has the added advantage

## 10d: Painting and Staining Guide Prices

| | UNIT | COATS | MATERIALS | TIME in mins | LABOUR @ £12.00/hr | TOTAL/m² |
|---|---|---|---|---|---|---|
| 1 COAT EMULSION | m² | 1 | £0.15 | 4 | £0.80 | £1.00 |
| 3 COAT EMULSION | m² | 3 | 0.45 | 12 | 2.40 | 2.90 |
| 3 COAT GLOSS (inc. preparation) | m² | 3 | 0.63 | 40 | 8.00 | 8.60 |
| Strips (in linear metres) | lin.m | 3 | 0.16 | 20 | 4.00 | 4.20 /lin.m |
| Windows (both sides) | m² | 3 | 0.31 | 300 | 60.00 | 60.00 |
| Doors (both sides) | m² | 3 | 1.25 | 180 | 36.00 | 37.00 |
| Balusters | m² | 3 | 0.63 | 180 | 36.00 | 37.00 |
| 3 COAT VARNISH/STAIN (+ prep) | m² | 3 | 1.50 | 40 | 8.00 | 9.50 |
| Strips (in linear meters) | lin.m | 3 | 0.38 | 20 | 4.00 | 4.40 /lin.m |
| Windows (both sides) | m² | 3 | 0.75 | 300 | 60.00 | 61.00 |
| Doors (both sides) | m² | 3 | 3.00 | 180 | 36.00 | 39.00 |
| Balusters | m² | 3 | 1.50 | 180 | 36.00 | 38.00 |
| 2 COAT MASONRY PAINT | m² | 2 | 1.80 | 40 | 8.00 | 9.80 |
| EXTERNAL STAINING (3 Coat) | m² | 3 | 4.00 | 40 | 8.00 | 12.00 |
| Strips | lin.m | 3 | 1.00 | 20 | 4.00 | 5.00 /lin.m |
| WALLPAPERING (1 layer) | m² | 1 | 1.00 | 15 | 3.00 | 4.00 |

STRIPS refers to narrow sections such as skirtings and fascia boards. Here prices are worked out in linear metres rather than square metres. For windows, doors and balusters prices are given for painting/staining both faces-i.e inside and outside.

## 10e: Paints and Stains: Guide Prices and Coverage

*All prices exc VAT: coverage and m² rates for one coat only.*
*All prices are for whites and magnolias*

> Some outlets supply colours for the same price. Usually standard colours are 15% more expensive. Paint off a colourising machine is 40% more than white.

| | REGULAR SIZE | PRICE | COVERAGE | COST/m² |
|---|---|---|---|---|
| Contract Emulsion (non-vinyl) | 10 lt | £ 10.00 | 12 m²/lt | £0.08 |
| Vinyl Matt Emulsion | 5 lt | £ 9.00 | 12 m²/lt | £0.15 |
| Vinyl Silk Emulsion | 5 lt | £ 10.00 | 12 m²/lt | £0.17 |
| Masonry Paint | 5 lt | £ 13.00 | 3 m²/lt | £0.90 |
| Regular Gloss/Undercoat | 5 lt | £ 12.50 | 16 m²/lt | £0.16 |
| Eggshell | 5 lt | £ 14.00 | 16 m²/lt | £0.18 |
| Acrylic Gloss or Eggshells | 5 lt | £ 18.00 | 12 m²/lt | £0.30 |
| Wood Primers | 5 lt | £ 13.00 | 10 m²/lt | £0.30 |
| | | | | |
| SADOLIN CLASSIC on sawn timber | 5 lt | £ 32.00 | 5 m²/lt | £1.30 |
| SADOLIN CLASSIC on planed timber | 5 lt | £ 32.00 | 10 m²/lt | £0.60 |
| SADOLIN EXTRA on joinery | 2.5 lt | £ 18.00 | 15 m²/lt | £0.50 |
| Polyurethane | 2.5 lt | £ 15.00 | 12 m²/lt | £0.50 |
| Floor Lacquers | 1 lt | £ 10.00 | 10 m²/lt | £1.00 |

> All prices in this column are for single coats only

*SADOLIN (together with SIKKENS) are the market leaders for wood stains.*
*Much cheaper alternatives exist (i.e. Kalon own brand)*

## 10f: Benchmark House: Painting Costs

| | QUANTITY | TRADE RATES | TOTAL |
|---|---|---|---|
| **WOOD STAINS** | | | |
| Fascia 25x200 | 25 lin.m | £ 4.40 | £110 |
| Ventilated Soffit | 19 lin.m | £ 4.40 | £80 |
| Porch | 3 m² | £ 61.00 | £180 |
| External Doors and Frames | 2 m² | £ 21.50 | £40 |
| Cedar cladding (bay window) | 2 m² | £ 12.00 | £20 |
| **PAINTS** | | | |
| Emulsion Walls/Ceilings | 540 m² | £ 2.90 | £1,570 |
| Internal Doors and Linings | 30 m² | £ 37.00 | £1,110 |
| Balusters | 4 m² | £ 37.00 | £150 |
| Skirting | 160 lin.m | £ 4.20 | £670 |
| Architrave (25 sets) | 160 lin.m | £ 4.20 | £670 |
| Window Cills | 16 lin.m | £ 4.20 | £70 |
| Vanity Units/Boxings | 12 m² | £ 2.90 | £30 |
| | | | |
| Mastic | 10-15 tubes, various applications | | £ 200 |
| **TOTAL** | | | **£4,900** |

> Trade rates are all-in labour and materials rates

> Various items in this table need decorating on two faces — doors, windows, balusters. The areas in the quantity column are measurements for one face only

> Still not clear? Well if you laid all the internal doors together on the ground they would cover an area of 30m²; but the rate of £26.00/m² is a trade rate for staining both faces of the door. Estimating can be a real hassle sometimes.

of being more readily washable. There is no difference in price. Satin finishes are a halfway house between matt and silk. One tip for new housebuilders is to apply your emulsions immediately after plastering or dry-lining is finished. You can get in and have a relatively free run at bare walls without having to fiddle around with skirtings, architraves, socket boxes, switch plates and radiators.

Another tip, this one for the stylistically challenged housebuilder, is to slap magnolia on everything. White is a bit too clinical for most people's taste; in contrast magnolia has enough cream in it to soften the overall effect without making any loud statements that will clash with furnishing choices made later on. If you are in a hurry and don't want to be bothered planning colour schemes, then magnolia is the answer. Dull but true.

### Woodwork
Interior woodwork gets very similar treatment to exterior woodwork. Traditionally, that meant a three-coat gloss paint system. Increasingly it means that woodstains are used instead.

### Varnish
I'm tempted to say that varnishing is vanishing but I wouldn't be so daft; its use is, however, much more limited than it used to be. Externally — where it is prone to blistering and flaking — it has been replaced almost entirely by the woodstains. However there is still a place for varnishes indoors on any exposed timbers. The fashion these days is to use matt lacquer varnishes (like Sadolin's excellent Holdex) which give a subtler, understated sheen. And there are also now acrylic varnishes (like Cuprinol's Enhance) which are so subtle you'd hardly know they were there. Wood floor finishes are another area where clear seals get used, usually with rather poor results. It looks fantastic when first applied but after a depressingly small number of weeks it comes to look worn and tired. If you are looking for an alternative to wax, check out Dulux's Diamond Glaze, a water based lacquer said to be ten times harder than conventional floor varnish.

## Specialist Finishes

### Artex Textured Ceilings
Don't think that Artex is a replacement for painting as well as plastering. It has to be painted to stop the smell, and emulsioning Artex is a good deal more time consuming than going over a flat surface. Many of the big housebuilders still specify Artex on their ceilings throughout, presumably because of problems they have experienced with cracking in plastered ceilings. Dry-lining, which is now prevalent on internal walls, can of course be applied to ceilings as well but the taping and jointing work needed to finish it is more complicated because there is always a much higher number of cuts and joints on ceilings than on walls.

### Wallpaper
Summary Table 10d just about says it all. Or at least it covers the basics. The price of £4/m² is for a very basic covering and obviously the sky is the limit when it comes to buying wallpaper. It is worth noting that a basic wallpaper is not so very expensive; you could wallpaper the benchmark house throughout for around £500 over and above the cost of slapping on a basic emulsion.

### Paint Effects
There has been a considerable revival of interest in near-forgotten painting techniques like stippling and rag rolling. If you are at all interested you will probably already have a book by Jocasta Innes and there's really nothing more to add. However, if you want to dip your toes in it but are afraid that you might get stoned on scumble glazes then you can cheat and use one of the new proprietary two tone paints like Dulux's Duet. However, I don't think Jocasta would approve somehow.

### Mastics
Mastics are something of a new feature in building, or at least the ways we use them today are new. They now tend to get applied to just about every conceivable join between materials; so wherever joinery meets brickwork or a tiled surface meets a worktop or a bathtub, there's a bead of mastic. There are mastics for sealing between plasterboard sheets and decorator's mastics for filling cracks (Painter's Mate); just about the only thing that is common to them is that they are packaged in tubes. Where water penetration is a problem — and that includes most external applications — it is worth paying more for the silicone based ones which, whilst remaining flexible, are less likely to break down.

It is said by some that mastics are the bodger's friend and that if you build to very high standards your joints will all be tight and you shouldn't need mastics at all. While there is some truth that good building standards are usually reflected in tight joints, mastics, particularly the silicone based ones, are now so widely used that it is inconceivable you will not have any need of them at some point. It is, however, very difficult to estimate just how much mastic you will need — that, at least, often depends on how wide your gaps are. And it is also true that mastic is a whole lot easier to apply against tightly fitting backgrounds. Note that if you are subcontracting decorating, you should make it absolutely clear where you want mastic to be applied and which type of mastic you want to be used.

*Junctions* **like this often prove to be excellent spots to fill with mastic: note the mastic bead between brick and render gets wider as it travels right, sure sign that something isn't level**

# Curtains & Blinds

It hardly seems like building but it's still a cost to be considered: a development cost for sure. Normally you buy curtain material by the yard (or metre) and this is the price that tends to stick in the mind. Yet on all but the most expensive materials, this is only about a third of the final cost if you include making-up costs and curtain rails. Now for many DIY enthusiasts, these costs are absorbed in their own time. You put up all the curtain rails while your husband runs-up all the material on the machine. But to pretend these costs are not there would not be in the spirit of the rest of the book, which assumes that your time is worth something (albeit not very much).

## Curtain Rails

Unlike the materials which hang from them, curtain rails are zero-rated for VAT purposes and so, if you are a selfbuilder, it is worth buying these before any reclaim is made. The rails look best when they are at least 400mm longer than the opening they cross and they don't look out of place if they are much longer. The usual materials are plastic (£3/m), wood (£9/m) and brass (£10/m) — though watch out for whether things like rings are included: the raw price of a wooden pole can double by the time fittings and rings have been added.

## Curtains

As a rule of thumb, to establish the overall widths of curtain material needed, double the length of the track from which you are going to hang it. Most curtain material comes in 54" or 136cm (1360mm) widths and to work out how many widths of material you need, you divide your doubled track length by the width of your chosen material. The table shows a worked example of costings for a standard bedroom window.

Making-up costs are also usually worked out on a width basis; Star Curtains of Newmarket charge around £10/width — the length of the curtains is immaterial. Some sort of lining material is recommended (though not essential) and also a taped heading is standard for a pencil-pleated finish. Thus the costs for a reasonably good but not extravagant material, like Jonelle's Bergereac which retails at £13.00/metre run, on a 1200 x 1200mm window work out at just over £120 and, if you transpose these prices on to our benchmark house, you would expect to pay around £1500 to curtain the whole house.

You can, of course, buy ready-made curtains and these can be much cheaper. But will they actually fit your windows? Good luck when you go looking. Alternatively, many selfbuilders will have curtain material available from their old house and, using their own labours, will be able to drape all their windows for much less than this figure. On the other hand, I'm not being in the least bit extravagant in my choice of materials (less than £15/m) or fittings. Fancy designer-label fabrics, Austrian blinds, cast iron hanging rails — this sort of detail could easily double or even treble the cost.

## Blinds

The cheapest type of blind available is the roller blind. It's also the cheapest way of providing a window cover as it comes with its own integral hanging brackets. A blind in a 1200mm-wide bathroom window will set you back no more than £40 and possibly a lot less — some manufacturers produce roller blinds in standard widths which you can then cut to size. Venetian blinds are a shade more sophisticated; in aluminium they are two to three times the price of a roller, in wood they are around five times the roller blind price.

## 10g: Estimating for Curtains

### TRACK LENGTHS and MATERIAL QUANTITIES for a BEDROOM WINDOW

| | | |
|---|---|---|
| Window Width | | 1200mm |
| Curtain Track Length | add 400mm | 1600mm |
| Standard Curtain Width | | 1360mm |
| Total Width of Curtains | Twice the curtain track length | 3200mm |
| No. of Standard Widths Needed | Total width divided by standard width | 2.35 |
| | Rounded up to nearest half width | 2.5 |
| Window Height | | 1200mm |
| Curtain Drop | add 300mm | 1500mm |
| Extra Material for Repeat Pattern | add 200mm | 1700mm |
| Curtain Material Needed | 2.5 widths x 1700mm drop | 4250mm or 4.25m |

| COSTS | | |
|---|---|---|
| Wooden Curtain Pole | 1.6m @ £10/lin.m | £16 |
| Wooden Fittings, Rings | | £10 |
| Curtain Material | 4.25m @ £15.00/m | £65 |
| Lining Material | 4m @ £2.00/m | £8 |
| Taped Headings | 3.2m @ 70p/m | £2 |
| **Materials** | | **£101** |
| Costs for Making-up Curtains | 3 widths @ £10/width | £30 |
| Fitting Curtain Rails | 0.5hr @ £14/hr | £7 |
| Fitting Curtains | 0.5hr @ £14/hr | £7 |
| **Labour** | | **£44** |
| **ALL-IN TOTAL** | | **£145** |

# Driveways & Pavings

Driveways are included on the list of external works which are exempt from VAT on new buildings, so there is every reason to finish the drive before occupation. Almost invariably these days, planning permission for new homes requires provision for off-road car parking and this means that some attention has to be paid to both where and how this is to be accommodated. So whilst a garage is arguably a luxury you could dispense with (or postpone), driveways and hardstandings must be accommodated within the initial design and costings.

## Foundations

Whatever drive finish you decide on, the base you lay should essentially be the same: ideally 100-150mm of hardcore (which can consist of a number of different materials, none of which should cost much more than £10/tonne). A 1m$^3$ void needs 2 tonnes of hardcore to fill it, so:
- To lay hardcore 100mm thick, 1 tonne will cover 5m$^2$ — budget £2.00/m$^2$
- To lay hardcore 150mm thick, 1 tonne will cover 3.3m$^2$ — budget £3.50/m$^2$.

A superior method, particularly recommended on clay sites, is to use a Terram or Geotextile sheet underlay beneath the hardcore layer. These cost around £1/m$^2$ but they allow water to pass through whilst stopping mud mixing in with the hardcore overlay. Laying hardcore can be done by hand but this is backbreaking and time-consuming. The most efficient method is to use machines to spread and tamp hardcore — digger buckets are particularly effective tampers. It is very useful to have hardcore laid as early as possible on a building job as it aids access and stops the site becoming a quagmire, but drain-laying timetables do not always allow this use of machinery and whether it is worth getting machinery in later just to lay hardcore depends on the size of the driveway.
- Budget £1/m$^2$ for spreading hardcore with excavating machinery
- Budget £100 for getting a JCB to come in especially
- Budget £3/m$^2$ for barrowing, spreading and hand tamping.

Overall, laying hardcore on already dugout ground should not cost more than £7/m$^2$. If you dispense with or skimp on this hardcore sub-base, you will end up with a drive which will initially look good but will rapidly disintegrate. The other problem to be aware of here is rainwater drainage; on flat sites, water will tend to pool if it is not adequately planned for. To this end, it is normal to lay the drive so that rainwater collects in certain points then drain the water away off to a soakaway. Whilst the falls can usually be constructed when the actual driveway is being laid, the drainage obviously has to be installed before the sub-base. A minor detail? You won't think so if you overlook it.

## Concrete Block Paving

This is becoming an increasingly popular way of finishing the front access (and also for doing paths and patios). There are large price breaks available for bulk orders and full loads (144m$^2$) should be available at less than £6/m$^2$ in greys or buffs (which makes them as cheap as plain concrete paving slabs and almost as cheap as wet concrete laid 100mm deep). They are usually laid dry (i.e. without any cement) on a 50mm bed of sharp sand, and finished with jointing sand brushed over them and whacked with a compactor plate: dry laying is cheaper than wet and this makes them a cheap and attractive option for patios and paths as well as drives.

Supply and fix prices tend to come in around £15/m$^2$ (excluding hardcore foundation preparations). Kerb work obviously has a big impact on the overall costs and the value of this varies from site to site but averages about 20% of the overall costs. More elaborate pavers than what is typically found on garage forecourts will bump the overall price up by 50-100%. As with bricks and roof tiles, there is a choice between clay and concrete; clay invariably costs more but is said to look better or, more accurately, to wear better.

Builders can usually make significant savings by negotiating paver prices off the back of brick and block orders placed at the beginning of the job and thereby taking advantage of full load deliveries. Money can also be saved by using machines (JCBs, etc.) to place pallet loads at convenient places; later on this work can often only be done by hand.

## Tarmac

The preparation is much the same as for pavers; kerbs need to be set in concrete round the perimeter, though these are usually cheaper than the special kerbings used with block paving. A pukka job should consist of a 80mm base course laid below a 35mm top course, known as the wearing course. A 50m$^2$ driveway with 20m kerbings should cost around £15/m$^2$ (Mats £6, Lab £9, hardcore works excluded). This would fall to around £10/m$^2$ for areas over 100m$^2$. Some tarmac prices appear to be far lower than this     this is the Wild West of the building trade remem-

## 10h: Guide Prices for Driveway Finishes

| | MATS | LAB | COMBINED | BENCHMARK HOUSE COSTS | |
| --- | --- | --- | --- | --- | --- |
| | | | | PER ITEM | OVERALL |
| Hardcore foundations/m$^2$ | £3.00 | £3.50 | £6.50 | £490 | £490 |
| Concrete Block Paving/m$^2$ | 8.00 | 6.00 | 14.00 | £700 | |
| Kerb Work/lin.m | 6.00 | 6.00 | 12.00 | £430 | £1,620 |
| Tarmac/m$^2$ | 5.00 | 6.00 | 11.00 | £550 | |
| Kerb Work/lin.m | 2.00 | 3.00 | 5.00 | £180 | £1,220 |
| Concrete/m$^2$ | 5.00 | 5.00 | 10.00 | £500 | |
| Kerb Work/lin.m | 1.00 | 3.00 | 4.00 | £140 | £1,130 |
| Shingle/m$^2$ | 1.00 | 5.00 | 6.00 | £300 | |
| Kerb Work/lin.m | 0.50 | 3.00 | 3.50 | £130 | £920 |

Hardcore foundation costs are common to all applied toppings and additional to other costs

Assumes 30m$^2$ driveway with 18m kerbs

*Top: block paving is traditionally laid in this herringbone pattern. Not only does it improve the look but it is also reckoned to produce a stronger bond. Above: granite setts are here being used to create a mosaic-like pattern*

## Key Drive Prices

### Concrete Block Paving
*Pavers: £8.00-£10.00/m² (down to £6/m² in full loads)*
*Matching kerbs: £8.00/lin.m (down to £5.00/lin.m. in full loads)*
*Labour rates for laying pavers: £6.00/m²*
*Labour rates for setting kerbs: £6.00/lin.m*
*Allow a contingency for levelling hardcore, setting falls and moving blocks around the site.*
*Incidentals include 50mm sharp sand bed (12m²/tonne @ £10/tonne) and jointing sand (15m²/50kg bag @ £3.60/bag). Recessed manhole covers which can be filled with blocks are available at £75 .*

### Tarmac
*Tarmac (base or wearing): £25/tonne*
*1 tonne of base coat will cover 7m² at standard 50mm depth: 1 tonne of wearing coat will cover 14m² at standard 25mm depth.*
*Materials cost of base and wearing course: £5/m²*
*Labour rates for laying: £5/m² (more on small areas).*

### Wet Concrete
*PAV 1 Readymix : £50-£60/m³ or £5-£6/m² at standard 100mm depth*
*Labour rates for laying: c. £5/m² (rising to £8/m² on small areas)*
*Edging formers: c.£2.00/lin.m.*

*For quotations and for other finishes, check your Yellow Pages under Paving Services.*

ber — but the specification is unlikely to be the business and the finished drive may not last very long.

## Concrete
Base preparations are similar to pavers and tarmac; kerbs can be ignored in favour of shuttering (or road forms) for which steel formers are available to hire. The designated readymix for driveways is PAV 1 — strong and relatively expensive — and it is normally laid at 100mm depth. Reinforcement should not be necessary. A 50m² driveway with 20m edgings should cost around £10/m² (Mats £5, Lab £5, hardcore works excluded). This would fall to around £8/m² for areas over 100m².

## Patterned Concrete
A number of specialist operators now offer patterned concrete paving where imprints of pavers are set into wet concrete to give a pave effect drive. This technique is widely used elsewhere around the world but is having difficulty catching on in the UK because of the low prices for standard concrete block paving. Patterned concrete drives start at around £20/m² (excluding foundation work) which, if anything, is rather more expensive than concrete block paving.

## Shingle and Gravel
This is the cheapest option and, in many rural situations, the most attractive. It's particularly suitable for long drives. However, note that the better gravel driveways are actually labour intensive as they involve laying three or four layers of stones, each rolled and then left for a day or two between coats. Edgings need to be placed — treated timber strips are adequate — and the success of the drive overall depends on good hardcore beneath. Top coat materials shouldn't cost much more

than £1.00/m$^2$ but laying costs are likely to be high, especially if there's no mechanised plant available.

Quotes to supply and lay a gravel drive often specify a simpler two layer application as this keeps the price down to around the £7/m$^2$ mark (excluding foundation works).

## Resin-Bonded Driveways

Available from specialist firms, these work by sticking small stones into a rigid sheet to give a shingle-look driveway which is as hard and durable as concrete or tarmac. Fantastic product if it's done properly but can be a disaster if not. Prices tend to start around the £30/m$^2$ mark (excluding hardcore foundation work).

## Fancy Paving Options

There are many other materials available to lay paths and, in particular, patios. Labour costs for laying vary widely (£5-£15/m$^2$) depending on whether they can be laid wet or dry and whether they need pointing-up afterwards. Wet laying involves using cement (albeit usually a dryish mix) and tends to be very much more labour intensive. Some hardcore backfill is usually advisable though when it is designed for foot traffic only it does not need to be laid as deep as it is under driveways. Materials choices include:

- Plain paving slabs — £4.00-£5.00/m$^2$
- Riven paving slabs (textured surface) — £6.00-£7.00/m$^2$
- Heritage paving (simulated natural stone) — £15/m$^2$
- Natural York stone flags (the real McCoy) — £50/m$^2$
- Granite setts — £40/m$^2$
- 75mm Beach Cobbles — £15/m$^2$
- Reconstituted stone — £25/m$^2$.

Marshalls of Halifax are the largest supplier of manufactured pavings (and garden walling effects). Their brochures, which are widely available at builder's merchants, are a good starting point in assimilating some possibilities. They also have a wide choice of block pavers (both concrete and clay) and paving slabs.

Natural stone slabs, setts and cobbles are widely available though you have to search them out from smaller suppliers and quarries: try Harris & Bailey. Blanc de Bierge produce an attractive honey-coloured range of reconstituted stone slabs and setts which cost around £20/m$^2$. Be aware that prices are usually quoted ex-works and that transport costs are likely to add between £100 and £250 to the total depending on amount and distance.

## Specialists

Laying a drive should not be beyond the competence of a good builder yet many people prefer to subcontract the whole process to a specialist, typically found in the Yellow Pages > Asphalt and Macadam or Paving Services. Before you do this, I would like to draw your attention to a 1995 Which? report which revealed a staggering range of prices as well as some uncompromising high pressure selling tactics associated with national companies advertising through magazines and usually (but not always) selling patterned concrete or resin-bonded driveways. In this Which? report, prices for one 60m$^2$ driveway varied from £329 to £6210! Table 10h gives a flavour of the middle range of driveway prices. I would tend to steer clear of both the very cheap quotes and the very expensive ones.

Finally a plug for www.pavingexpert.com, a website maintained by paving guru Tony McCormack where you can find out more than you ever wanted to know about the black art.

# Fencing & Turfing

## Fencing

If you just want to mark a boundary and are not too bothered about privacy or security, then the cheapest permanent option is the timber post-and-rail fence. This arrangement shouldn't cost more than £10/lin.m (Mats £4, Lab £6); it looks fine and is easily maintained. If you have longish (30m plus) lengths to erect, then the cheapest suppliers are to be found in the pages of Horse & Hound (down below £8/lin.m). Alternatively, a chain link fence will cost a similar amount and, though less attractive, is more secure and should stop dogs and children straying to boot.

1.2m-high chestnut palings are another cheapish option (costing around £5/lin.m) which, being vertical, are much harder to get

over. They are easily fixed — just whack posts in every 2m or so — but have a temporary air about them which may not appeal to all. The picket fence is similar in design but altogether more permanent in appearance but it costs around £15/lin.m (M £9, L £6).

If you require privacy and security then you will have to go for a solid or near solid fence with a height of 1.8m (above head height). The traditional way of doing this is to erect something similar to a post-and-rail fence and then to cover it with vertically fixed, featheredge boarding. This is known as a close-boarded fence. Expect it to cost around £25/lin.m (M £15, L £10). It is a little cheaper to use ready-made panels of the type you see in garden centres but the result is very flimsy in comparison. There are many variations on

the theme of boarded fences, you can set the boards horizontally or diagonally, or alternate the boards between the inside and the outside of the fence posts (called hit and miss fencing). You can achieve quite stunning effects very simply and they don't have to be stained dark afterwards. If you want to investigate further, I recommend you get Jackson's Good Fencing Guide — it's free from Jacksons. They also deal with wire fencing which, I am assuming, is of lesser interest to would be housebuilders.

## Brick Walls

Whilst timber fencing is getting expensive at around £30/lin.m, you are not going to get even a whiff of a brick boundary wall under £100/lin.m and, if you use a nice brick and build up to head-height, the cost will be around £200/lin.m. This is a different animal altogether and ideally should be erected along with the main house so as to combine economies of scale — not to mention getting JCBs into the back garden. A 1.8m-high brick wall is actually a rather vulnerable construction, prone to blowing over in howling gales, and best practice advice now recommends that all unsupported walls over a mere 650mm high should be built two brick skins thick (225mm). In exposed locations, a 1.8m-high brick wall should be built 330mm thick. Whether your wall is freestanding or is being built as a retaining wall against some high ground, your building inspector will advise you as to the exact requirements needed. Dry stone walls are, needless to say, even more expensive, costing around £300/lin.m for a waist-high one.

## Turfing

A detailed look at landscaping lays beyond the scope of this book, but I feel I must cover turfing at least because most developers consider it part of their remit to make a garden look acceptable, if not exactly inspired. Indeed, as with fencing, the VAT office allows you to reclaim VAT on purchases of turf when erecting a new house: unfortunately for keen gardeners, the VAT line is drawn at turf.

Of course there's more to it than just laying the turf. After the builders have done their bit, the average plot resembles a World War One battle ground (hopefully without the bodies) and the site has first to be cleaned of debris. Usually, it is then rotavated, levelled and rolled, and normally a selective weed killer is applied to prevent thistles taking over. Turf itself usually costs around £1.30/m² to purchase; the preparation work and the laying will cost around £2.00/m², more if the work is particularly arduous or if there are slopes involved. If extra topsoil is needed, this costs around £10-£20/m³. You can halve the cost of turfing if you seed the area instead but this can be a bit hit and miss: seeding is best carried out in September, though you can often get away with it in springtime as well. You need to be lucky with the rain or else you will have to water for about eight weeks.

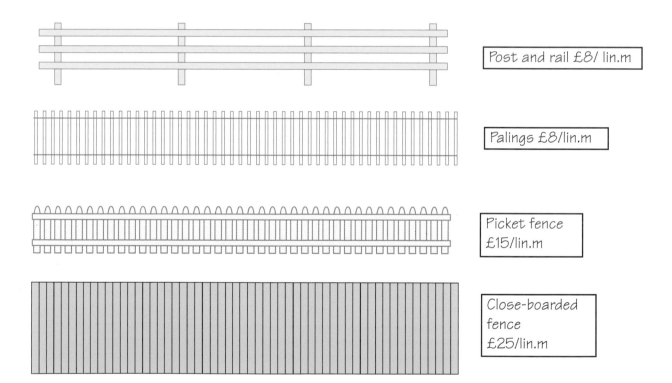

Post and rail £8/ lin.m

Palings £8/lin.m

Picket fence £15/lin.m

Close-boarded fence £25/lin.m

# Chapter 11
# Room by Room

# Kitchen Design

The kitchen is the most expensive part of the house to build. Whereas unfurnished spaces (such as bedrooms and living rooms) clock in at around £400/m$^2$ and bathrooms at around £700/m$^2$, the spend on the kitchen area is likely to be in excess of £800/m$^2$.

This is perhaps a slightly misleading statistic because only the kitchen and bathrooms are finished at the building stage; everywhere else has to be furnished by the homeowner. But even so, if insurance company figures are anything to go by, the average home has just £20,000 of stealable fittings and, looked at on a £/m$^2$ basis, that only adds £250/m$^2$ to floor area costings. So, whichever way you look at it, kitchens remain far and away the most expensive item in the contemporary house.

### Benchmark Kitchen

AB Homes kitchen for the larger Gidding is a modest affair by today's standards. It's split into three zones — a kitchen preparation area, a utility room and what is called a breakfast room. All three bits together account for 20m$^2$ of the ground floorplan or 12% of the overall internal floor area. The kitchen working area is an L-shape, the units themselves and the worktops were supplied by a local joiner Paul Donnelly. Donnelly acts as a sort of semi-fabricator, buying in the basic carcasses and dressing them with drawers and doors to suit. His price to AB Homes is very keen: for all the units, worktops and white goods including the utility area, they pay less than £2000.

The Gidding benchmark house comes in two different versions. The smaller version includes the single garage in the main footprint of the house: in the larger version, the garage moves outside and the space gained is split between a study and a breakfast room. The breakfast room has the effect of doubling the size of the kitchen space — even so it's hardly what you would call open-plan but realise that without the breakfast room you still have a very workable galley kitchen. What prominence you decide to give to the kitchen is the most difficult internal design decision that you will be faced with. The two extremes to opt for are:

- the kitchen as utility area (hidden from view and servicing a separate dining room)
- the kitchen to be the main living area of the home, typically called an open-plan arrangement.

The trend is towards the open-plan kitchen; this suits the kitchen suppliers as it means a) bigger kitchens and b) consumers are more conscious of the way their kitchens are going to look. If you accept the notion that you want your kitchen to be the most important room in the house, then you are probably prepared to spend a much larger sum on making it beautiful. On the other hand, if you want to keep costs down, design your kitchen more as a utility area and have a separate dining room where you eat.

### Mud Rooms and Larders

Many designs relegate the utility area to little more than a laundry room, but for many people, particularly country dwellers, a proper mud room would be far more useful; somewhere warm and light to take off wellies and wet coats, to air clothes, for dogs to sleep in. It's the natural place for a back door, but to do it properly requires a surprising amount of space. They are not called mud rooms for nothing; for as much as six months every year, just going out into the garden is a seriously mucky business and the interface between inside and outside needs thought.

The separate larder is an old idea coming back into fashion. This can be small room and doesn't need any daylight but to work well it needs to be easily accessed from the kitchen preparation area. Ideally you locate it against an outside wall that doesn't face south and you exclude it from the insulated shell of the house — that way it stays cool. You may want to give some attention to airflow (strategically placed airbricks) and to draught proofing around the door. If your design can't handle all this, then even an internal, heated larder is useful if only to store dried food and crockery: it's much cheaper than fitting it all into expensive kitchen units.

### Grasping the Kettle

When you've come to some conclusion about how you want your kitchen to work with the rest of the house, you can then get down to the nut and bolt design matters of what goes where. It is usual to start with a list of household appliances. If you have opted for a separate utility area, this will be the natural home of washing machines and tumble dryers and, possibly, freezers. The kitchen proper must have a sink, some sort of cooker and a fridge. Dishwashers are increasingly sought after and are conventionally placed close to the sink. The positioning of your appliances around the kitchen becomes the skeleton on which the kitchen furniture is hung. There are some conventional dos and don'ts to consider:

- DO locate sinks and plumbed-in appliances where waste pipes can get to the drains. Usually this means placing them against an outside wall.
- DO locate cooker hoods against an outside wall where exhaust fumes can be evacuated. You can run ducting to get around this problem but it is a fiddle best avoided.
- DO leave worktop space either side of both the sink and the hob (or cooker top).
- DO keep the sink, the hob and the fridge reasonably close to each other. Simply for the sake of convenience. Some kitchen planners will go on at length about the importance of the work triangle in the kitchen. Politely ignore them.
- DON'T place a hob or a sink in a corner unless you consider an angled corner arrangement (expensive); corners tend to make poor working/storage space.
- DON'T place a fridge or freezer next to or under a heat source (hob, cooker, radiator).
- DON'T forget to consider the boiler if it needs to be in the kitchen. Not only will it be hot but there are rules concerning just where you can and can't place boiler flue terminals (see Chapter 8, Services, section on boilers).
- DON'T put wall cupboards over the sink; conventionally, sinks go under windows and for most small- or medium-sized kitchens this will always be the most practical location.

If you're a neat, logical kind of person, having got this far you should be able to draw a layout plan on some graph paper and begin to get an idea of the number of units you will need. Congratulate yourself because you're the kind of client any kitchen supplier would be pleased to have — you actually know what you want!

## 11a: Benchmark House: Kitchen Costs

| | NO. | NOTES | VALUE |
|---|---|---|---|
| **APPLIANCES** | | | |
| Kitchen Sink | 1 | 1.5 Bowl/Single Drainer in St. Steel | £60 |
| Utility Sink | 1 | 1 Bowl/Single Drainer in St. Steel | £40 |
| Taps | 2 | | £80 |
| Hob | 1 | | £80 |
| Hood | 1 | | £60 |
| Oven | 1 | | £200 |
| | | | |
| **KITCHEN UNITS** | | by local supplier PD Kitchens | |
| FLOOR STANDING | | | |
| U/worktop Housing | 2 | 600mm wide | £180 |
| Corner Unit | 1 | 900x900mm | £120 |
| Drawer Unit | 1 | 600mm wide | £160 |
| Base Units | 2 | 600mm wide | £200 |
| Base Units | 1 | 500mm wide | £90 |
| Base Units | 1 | 300mm wide | £80 |
| Utility Base Unit | 1 | 600mm wide u/sink | £90 |
| WALL UNITS | | | |
| Cooker Hood Unit | 1 | 600mm | £50 |
| Glazed units | 2 | 600mm | £250 |
| Corner Unit | 1 | 600x600mm | £200 |
| Wall Units | 1 | 600mm | £80 |
| Wall Units | 1 | 300mm | £70 |
| **WORKTOPS** | | 38mm thick laminate | |
| Kitchen and Utility | 3 | 3m long | £140 |
| FLOOR PLINTHS | 4 | | £60 |
| **KITCHEN FITTING** | | including appliances | £850 |
| **TOTAL COST OF KITCHEN WORKS** | | | **£3,140** |
| plus | | | |
| Wall Tiling | | 8m² ceramic tiling | £ 80 |
| Vinyl Flooring | | 15m² | £ 150 |
| Over sink downlighters | | 2No | £ 70 |

> Floor plinths run along the foot of floor units similar to skirting board. Often sold separately and fitted to unit legs with spring clips. They have to be returned back to the wall at open ends

> Pelmets do much the same as plinths but run around the top of the wall units instead of along the floor

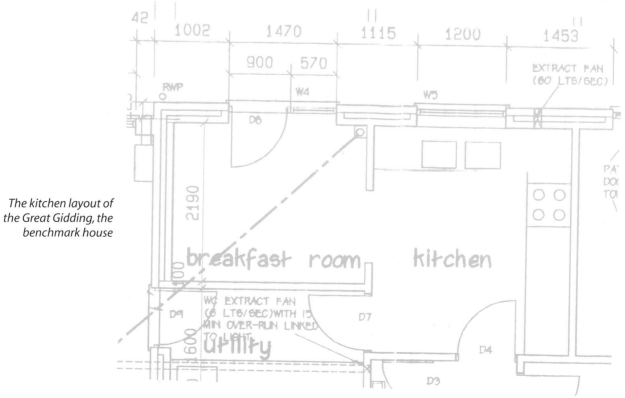

*The kitchen layout of the Great Gidding, the benchmark house*

# Kitchen Units

The fitted kitchen is an invention of the late 20th century. In the 1960s, a kitchen cabinet was thought of as something to do with Harold Wilson's unique government style. But shortly thereafter, the fitted kitchen arrived in the home in a big way. And, bit by bit, we have learned to spend more and more money on our kitchens. There are several procurement routes, each with its own pitfalls. Whilst the bulk of the new kitchen market now goes into replacing existing kitchens, a significant chunk gets accounted for by the 150,000 new homes built each year. And whilst a penny pinching spec housebuilder may spend as little as £2,000 on fitting a kitchen on a starter home you only have to open a Sunday newspaper to realise that some people are happy to spend over £100,000 on a fitted (or perhaps an unfitted) kitchen. Bigger of course, better undoubtedly, but not fifty times bigger or better.

## *Just Shelves with Fancy Doors*

When we think of fitted kitchens, we think of how the door fronts look. The kitchen dream sellers are well aware of this and, although the actual units may make up only 25% of the final bill, these are how kitchens are sold to us. New fashions have come but they've never really gone so kitchen design continually expands to incorporate new ideas whilst simultaneously recycling the old ones. The basic manufacturing process is relatively simple and cheap so that no new idea can ever be free from imitators for more than a few months.

The kitchen business is fully metricated and works in modular units which increase in 100mm intervals. Thus any given range of floor units or wall cupboards will be available in widths of typically 300mm, 400mm, 500mm and 600mm; 600mm is the key one, this is the building block of the fitted kitchen — appliances are conventionally made to fit into 600mm gaps. The other sizes tend to get used to fill awkward gaps between the 600mm units. By twiddling the plan about a bit, you can fill any space on any wall to the nearest 100mm — and they sell blanking-off pieces to cover any little gaps left over. So give a kitchen designer a space that's 3600x2400mm and they will tend to think of it as 6 units long and 4 across.

All but the most expensive kitchen unit carcasses are made from a wood pulp board like chipboard or MDF, usually covered with a melamine veneer which serves both to make them stronger and moisture resistant. The cheaper doors, which are hung over these carcasses, are made of similar materials, though here the melamine covering is usually decorated with some trim. Solid timber is a more upmarket door option and there are more adventurous designs using such materials as stainless steel and plastic.

There are several ways of getting fixed up with a kitchen. About the cheapest is to go to one of the giant DIY retailers such as B&Q, MFI or IKEA and buy yourself a flat pack. The cheaper kitchens tend to be supplied flat packed and need assembling on site, a feat which in theory is straightforward but in practice can be damned difficult, especially when it takes you two days to realise you haven't got all the bits. Which? magazine surveyed six major flat pack outlets in Jan 2002 (namely, B&Q, Focus Do It All, IKEA, Jewson, MFI and Wickes (owned by Focus Do It All but continuing to trade independently). On price there wasn't much to choose from (as you might expect). They concluded that the two key things to look for were adjustable legs (to take account of uneven floors) and drawer quality. Only the most basic units didn't have adjustable legs but the drawer quality varied considerably from inadequate wooden runners (MFI) to poorly designed metal runners (most) to three rollers (IKEA). Pretty much on this count and this count alone IKEA came out tops in their survey. "The best quality units we tested," they wrote, adding the barb "provided you can follow the instructions."

They might have added a few more barbs because as any experienced IKEA shopper knows buying things from IKEA is often a fraught experience. My old mucker, Robin Gomm, fits a lot of IKEA kitchens these days and he reckons his main problem is in getting hold of all the right parts. "Always allow for at least two visits to the store, sometimes three," he says. Apparently, IKEA's service is nothing short of excellent in the most of the many other countries they operate in but not so in the UK where pre-ordering is a no-no but items are routinely out of stock. Per head of population, the British are the world's largest consumers of IKEA products so the Swedes who run the operation have obviously worked us out to a tee. Some suspect it's a deliberate ruse to get us to go back time and time again because we can't stop spending money in the stores.

If you have seriously set your heart on an IKEA kitchen, get hold of their kitchen catalogue which is distinct from the main IKEA catalogue. There are items in the former which don't appear in the latter.

## *The Continentals*

The more innovative and interesting designs are the preserve of the upmarket kitchen. The Germans were the first into this pond in the 70s when names like Wellman, Allmilmo and, most notably, Poggenpohl came to the UK. Like all things German, they have built up a reputation for superbly crafted kitchens. In terms of style however they've been left in the slow lane. The high-tech, Continental look is now led by the French and, especially, the Italians — look out for Boffi's futuristic designs from Alternative Plans.

## *Smallbone, etc.*

Despite exporting barely any kitchens at all (we import about 20%), the British have responded to the threat of mainly upmarket invasion by inventing a whole new romantic theme — sometimes known as the English Revival style or, more often, doing a Smallbone. Smallbone — which started as an antiques business in Wiltshire — led the way in creating a new vernacular kitchen, which managed to strike some chord in the English middle-class psyche and led people to pay vast sums to recreate a past that never existed. Using many revived techniques and idioms (rag rolling, marbling, Welsh dressers), they created a magnificent, seductive illusion. To purchase the actual Smallbone marque is now outrageously expensive — though not necessarily poor value — but the style has spawned hundreds of imitators. This school of kitchen design has grown away from providing modular boxes towards what has become known as the unfitted kitchen — an Aga here, a beech block table there, terracotta tiles on the floor, wicker baskets hanging on rails, you can almost smell the garlic and olive oil.

Some of these upmarket companies must be approached directly, many have just one UK outlet. The nearest thing to a directory exists in the back of Kitchens, Bedrooms and Bathrooms magazine which will give you an overview of the market's top end.

## *Kitchen Boutiques*

Another approach is to ignore the plethora of manufacturers and concentrate on your local kitchen specialists. Most small towns have at least one, and a regional shopping centre will have several — check Yellow Pages. Most will stock only three or four manufacturers' products but as manufacturers offer sometimes hundreds of options (especially in door colours) this can still be quite bewildering. Typically, they will stock a mass-produced British flat-pack product (like Ram Kitchens or Symphony) which they will use to try and compete with MFI and co, but the bulk of their showrooms is given over to displaying a middle market Continental range. They make more money on the more expensive kitchens so it is understandable that it is these that they promote, even though they may sell only one or two a month.

Many people are rather reluctant to set foot inside a kitchen specialist as they think it would be a) too expensive and b) involve high-pressure selling. By and large, this is not the case; though they probably cannot compete with MFI on kitchen unit price alone, they are usually owner-managed and tend to give a high level of personal service without resorting to any pressure tactics. Unlike the major retail outlets, prices are usually negotiable and this makes it hard to compare on a like for like basis.

Almost all kitchen specialists are tied to certain manufacturer's products; there are very few independent fee-based advisers and one of the best known is Roma Jay Designs who offer a very competitive postal design service for £90 — but note that a full design resulting from a site visit with working drawings would be very much more expensive.

## The Builder

If you are fitting a kitchen as part of a much larger project (i.e. building a house) then it may make sense to keep the work in house and ask your builder to fit it. That's if you are still on speaking terms by the time you have reached the kitchen fitting. There are several outlets (principally builder's merchants and joinery centres) which aim to sell mainly to builders and they will have kitchen catalogues available to browse through and sometimes showrooms to visit. The major joinery firms — Jeld Wen, Premdor, Magnet — all produce fitted kitchens though, stylistically, they tend to be the most conservative of all. Their catalogues are easy to get hold of and clearly priced. The builder can buy these units (and the accessories) at discounts of between 20 to 40% off list price and many will be happy to negotiate to share at least some of the discount with you — see section on Contracts in Chapter 5, Project Management, in particular find out what a PC Sum is. Even so, the prices from the volume joinery majors, even with full discount, will be slightly more than the cheapest available from the likes of MFI; but there is one big advantage if your builder fits the units and that is that he will remain responsible for sorting out any snags. If, on the other hand, you supply your own units to your builder and, say, the hinges work loose or there are unsightly gaps here and there, then you'll have your work cut out trying to convince him it's his fault: indeed you'll have fallen into one of the contractual traps placed along the route.

## Bespoke Kitchens

Before the advent of Smallbone, getting a joiner to make up a kitchen for you was always thought of as the most expensive option. If you choose to have doors made up out of gale-blown timbers, etc., this can still prove to be expensive enough but, with the advent of MDF, simple handmade and handpainted kitchens can be surprisingly cheap. Almost all kitchen carcassing (i.e. the bits you don't see) is made up of chipboard or MDF. You can buy 18mm thick MDF board in 2.4x1.2m sheets for as little as £15/sheet and get it machine cut for under 50p/cut. A sheet will make up an averaged-sized kitchen carcass and door; add a little for ironmongery and knobs, paint or varnish, design a simple trim and plinth detail and — lo and behold — you've got all the materials for our standard kitchen at less than half the price of MFI's cheapest. Get hold of the Hafele catalogue and you suddenly have access to all the same ironmongery as the kitchen manufacturers do (because they use the same catalogue). Carousels, fancy pedal bins, you name it, they are all in there.

Even though a competent joiner would take little longer to assemble this kitchen than he would a flat-pack, there are still remarkably few takers for such a design. This is probably a result of marketing failure as much as anything else. There are many economies in fabricating on site but most people are simply unaware what they might be. There are substantial design limitations — glass doors, friezes, fielded panelling and other complicated motifs are best carried out in factories — but there is, however, undoubtedly a niche for kitchen designers to create simple made-on-site kitchens which will accommodate the limited budget. This would be much closer to the ideal of the Shaker kitchen than those maddeningly expensive ones that carry that currently fashionable title.

*In 1999, IKEA joined the unfitted kitchen set with a range called VARDE. All the units are completely free standing making it easy to alter, renew or add on to. The birch worktops are built on top of the units. There are matching wall units from a range called FAKTUM.*

# Sinks & Worktops

## Sinks

### Stainless Steel

Stainless steel sinks now represent the cheap and cheerful option, which is perhaps surprising because in many other contexts stainless steel is regarded as an expensive material. Steel is actually a very good choice of material for a sink; it's strong, lightweight and easily cleaned. However, it is something of a victim of its own success because stainless steel sinks became so ubiquitous in the 60s and 70s that people started to choose other materials just to be different. It also suffered from the fact that it was a one-colour product at a time when kitchens were becoming colour coordinated.

The very cheapest kitchen sinks now tend to be stainless steel; single bowl/single drainers can be picked up for less than £30, a set of taps for less than £20. However, the products from the big names in kitchen sinks (Fordham, Leisure, Carron, Franke, Blanco) can be every bit as expensive as coloured ones. Expect to pay £120plus for something as good as a Franke one-and-a-half bowl sink.

### Asterite

Asterite (which is made by ICI) is just the best known of many resinous silicone-based materials, all of them revolutionary and all with names that sound like bit players from Star Trek: Resan, Sylaca, Silquartz, Silacron, Novean, Astracast. Every sink manufacturer seems to have developed their own material (mostly made in conjunction with ICI). Whilst steel became stigmatised as being downmarket, these synthetics, typically coloured white, brown or something in between (usually christened Mocca or Cappuccino to add sophistication), took off in a big way. In terms of performance they offer no advantages over steel — in fact they are a damn sight harder to clean — but they do look good in kitchen showrooms, particularly with colour coordinated taps.

Asterite sinks are most commonly sold in packs. What this means is that you'll get a bundle of extras like sink racks, drainers and (maybe) a hardwood chopping board thrown in along with taps and waste fittings. If you don't mind obscure brands, then expect to pay around £135 for a one-and-a-half bowl sink pack. Generally it's worth paying an extra £15 to get taps with ceramic discs which, it is claimed, never drip.

### Butler's Sinks

The old fashioned butler's sink also tends to look a wow in the kitchen showroom, particularly when it is inset in a hardwood surround with drainage grooves. It's not changed from the original Victorian design (i.e. a large white rectangular box) and this adds an air of authenticity to it which nothing else in a modern kitchen can touch, not even an Aga (which hails from the 30s). Consequently, it's become an item in all Smallbone-inspired kitchens and its very size and weight stand as statements of contempt for the standard mass produced fitted kitchen. Butler's sinks, such as the Armitage Shanks Belfast, cost between £110 and £150 depending on size. Taps and waste are extra: these sinks are most definitely not sold in packs.

## Kitchen Worktops

The worktop is the name given to the main shelf in a kitchen where all the action happens — the food preparation, the cooking and the cleaning. Everything else is just storage. Getting the worktop right is a crucial part of kitchen design and, though it may not be the first thing you think about when selecting a kitchen, it will be the single most important element in your kitchen. The standard width for worktops is 600mm which is sufficient for most kitchen configurations. Peninsulas, islands and breakfast bars may all require wider surfaces; there are a few extra-wide sizes available with two good edges, designed for these types of applications. The cheapest option is 28mm thick white or near-white laminate which costs around £20 for a 3m length, available at DIY sheds or trade outlets like Magnet. However, if you want irregular shapes or fancy trims then you will need to go via a kitchen specialist and probably have to buy a more expensive laminate.

### Expensive Laminates

The patterned varieties are what the kitchen showrooms push. There are a few well known names like Formica, Polyrey, Resopal, Duropal and Beaumel; the showrooms often try to sell their own versions. They are usu-

---

## 11b: Guide Prices for Kitchen Worktops

| | COST/lin.m |
|---|---|
| **LAMINATES** | |
| D-I-Y Cut-on-site Post Formed Laminate | £10 |
| Superior Post Formed Laminate | £30 |
| Same with Wood Trim | £50 |
| Same with Acrylic Trim | £80 |
| **HARDWOOD** | |
| 40mm Beech | £60 |
| **STONE** | |
| Granite/Marble | £200 |
| **TILED** | |
| Cheapish Tile with Wood Trim | £70 |
| Cheapish Tile with Acrylic Trim | £100 |
| **SYNTHETIC STONE** | |
| Silkstone | £200 |
| Corian/Surrell | £300 |

Prices are for a linear metre of 600mm wide worktop. A little something has been added to cover mitred corners except the DIY option, where it is assumed that metal trim is used.

Price could easily double if expensive stone is chosen

Fancy £50/m² tiles would add another 30%

Inset sinks - add £200. These prices include installation

ally sold in 40mm thicknesses which gives them a beefy feel — though provided the front is supported every 600mm the extra thickness is unnecessary. There is a far wider choice of colours and patterns but prices will be around three times the cheapest options — i.e. they start at around £60 for a 3m length or, if you prefer, £20/lin.m.

### Hardwood

These usually appear as thick strips of woods such as beech or oak which are glued and laminated into a solid board. Both Junckers and Texwood produce a range of worktops, available in a 27mm and a 40mm thickness in beech, maple, ash and oak. They look fantastic but cost around £70-£80/lin. m. It's not particularly difficult to build your own hardwood worktops but you will probably need the skills of a good joiner's shop to enable you to work the wood into a usable 600mm wide strip.

### Marble/Granite

Costs for marble or granite range from £150-£300/m² (£90-£180/metre run of worktop). Normally this supplies a 20mm thick slab which is usually fitted on to a timber sub-base for extra support. Holes can be cut for sinks and hobs (at around £50/hole) and intricate moulded edges can be applied at £10/lin.m; drainage grooves can be cut at around £20 each. Marble is not a particularly good choice for worktops as it stains and reacts to acids like lemon juice and vinegar (though some would regard this as "patina"). Granites are the preferred option for those wanting stone work tops. Whilst marbles tend towards whites and pinks, granites naturally tend to blacks and greys, which makes a granite worktop too dark for many people's tastes. Nevertheless, granite has emerged as the worktop of choice in the majority of upmarket (i.e. over £20k) kitchens.

### Tiled Worktops

A base is built of ply or blockboard (cost £4.50/lin.m) on to which tiles are stuck. The cost largely depends on the type of tiles chosen: budget perhaps £20/m² to lay, more if it's a complex pattern, and for tiles anything from £10/m² for mass produced plain tiles up to £40-£80/m² for something which would look good in a Fired Earth showroom. They can look spectacular and can be run in or set off against tiled splashbacks, but the irregularity of the surface (particularly on the more expensive tiles) can become an annoying feature and tiled worksurfaces are much harder to clean. In fact, largely because of their impracticality, tiles worktops have gone right out of fashion.

### Corian

Corian is a product which is used to make both worktops and sinks. It is best known for making it possible to "weld" sinks seamlessly into the worktop so they appear to be one and the same item. It remains a bit high-tech for many people's tastes and a bit high priced for many people's pockets. What is it? Well, it's an inert mineral filler fixed in a matrix of methyl methacrylate polymer. Nuff said? It's a synthetic panel product but unlike the regular melamine laminates (which are actually just thin coverings stuck on chipboard) these boys are solid, heavy and smooth. Every kitchen specialist showroom boasts a Corian (or Corian look-alike such as Surrell) sink-cum-worktop but they don't actually shift very many. There are an increasing number of alternative makes and some are beginning to get very much cheaper than original Corian. Look out for Silkstone which looks very similar but costs something akin to a mere £100/m run, about half the price of Corian.

### Trim Options

The standard edge detail for laminate worktops is what is called Postform, which gives a curved finish to the front edge. You can get square-edged finishes but they are not recommended unless you are going to add some sort of trim to it. An otherwise cheap and cheerless laminate top can be made to look very much more attractive with the addition of an edge trim. These can be applied by hand but it is difficult to do a professional job on site; if factory applied, it will approximately double the cost of a laminate worktop (budget £50/lin.m). Even more expensive trims are available — like Corian — which would push the price up by over £70/lin.m.

### Jointing Options

One of the problems in specifying laminate worktops, particularly ones with curved, postformed edges, is how to get around corners. The cheap option is to use metal jointing strips which stand up proud of the worktops and cover the gap where the two worktops meet. They are cheap, at around £3 each, but seamless they are not. Worktop fabricators offer various options for jointing worktops so that they appear to be one piece; straight runs are butt jointed from about £10; angles get a mason's mitre for around £15. If you are not going through a kitchen specialist then a useful contact is Allied Manufacturing who supply a wide range of kitchen fittings besides worktops.

*If you are wondering why I have placed Sinks and Worktops in the same section, here is the answer. If you can afford to have a Corian worktop, you can simply mould the sink into it.*

# Kitchen Appliances

All prices quoted in this section will include VAT. Trade prices invariably exclude it whilst retail outlets invariably include it. Whichever way, new housebuilders in the UK cannot reclaim VAT on kitchen cookers or appliances with the sole exception of cooker hoods which are regarded as a ventilation item.

## Cooking

The standard practice today is to buy a built-in oven with a separate hob and a hood, often sold together in a package. Every supplier offers a choice of gas or electricity for your hob without any effect on price, but a gas oven is more expensive than an electric one. The budget developers' packages (Ariston, Whirlpool) are priced at around £300: you can buy similar packages from MFI or Comet for even less. Note that IKEA, such good value on kitchen units, is actually quite a rip-off on appliances, their best deal for a Whirlpool cooker/hob/fan package being £565. You can pick up a better regarded brand name like Neff from one of the suppliers like Arrow for less than £400.

Appliances are mostly made to modular sizes so that they slip easily into any kitchen unit assembly so there is no compulsion to source your appliances from the same place as your units. Neither of course is there any compulsion to stick to the same brand of appliances throughout the kitchen though for convenience many people do.

## Stand Alone/Slot-in Cookers

Go into Currys or Comet and you will still find a range of very 1950s style gas and electric stoves. I don't think very many go into new homes (unless you are specifically going for that 50s retro-look) but they are very cheap. However, 21st century housebuilders all go for fitted ovens and hobs. The question is which oven, hob and hood? In recent years the choice has multiplied alarmingly making this once simple task extremely taxing.

## Ovens

At the basic end you get a single electric oven with a timer clock and two or three functions. In fact that is enough for 90% of us. It'll cook a Christmas dinner, what more can you ask? Well a lot. What's happened with oven rather mimics what's happened with computers. They have grown more functions and controls. Take a top of the range Miele single oven. It comes with ten functions; true fan heat, top heat, conventional heat, bottom heat, intensive bake, fan grill, automatic roast, defrost, full grill, economy grill. It also has

ThermoClean plus pyrolytic cleaning with Air Clean catalyser. Don't yer luv this stuff? You need to go on a course just to see how it works and, not surprisingly, Miele, along with a handful of other manufacturers, run cookery demonstration courses.

You can opt for a double oven which gives you a second cooking chamber, useful if you want to cook things at different temperatures but for many people, the top oven gets used as an eye-level grill — you don't really need any other functions.

## Gas Ovens

Built-in gas ovens are widely available but much less common than electric ones (though note that MFI stocks them); they tend to be more expensive and don't have many of the features of an electric oven. They also produce much more moist waste than an electric oven, especially on grill settings. Their big selling point is low running costs — around 25% of conventional electric cooking. The extra cost of a gas oven will pay for itself within 5 years if burning mains gas and 10 years if burning LPG. Only Stoves make a true gas double oven: more usually you get a grill compartment set over a separate oven but the grill chamber cannot be used to cook conventionally.

## Specialist Ovens

The relentless rise of the microwave has seen it elevated from being a countertop accessory to being a built-in second oven in its own right. Most people find it far more useful and flexible than having a double oven. Despite being limited in their uses, microwaves are excellent in a number of areas (cf. cooking casseroles and fish, boiling vegetables, reheating, defrosting) where conventional cooking is cumbersome. They are quick, clean and energy efficient. As an alternative to fitting a separate microwave unit, most manufacturers now make multi-function or combi ovens that include a microwave function. You can use these as either conventional only, microwave only or both functions at once which allows you to halve the cooking time for something like a joint or a chicken or roast potatoes but still get an element of crispy browning. However operating them in combined mode is quite complicated — it requires a whole new set of cooking skills.

Steam ovens sell themselves as healthy alternatives to microwaves. They tend to be quite small, not much bigger than a microwave, and they work by boiling water and blasting

steam into the cooking chamber (some of them do this under pressure). Like microwaves, they are surprisingly versatile and can do much of the cooking undertaken on a hob as well as useful little jobs like defrosting and sterilising bottles. Again, it's a whole different approach to cooking which has to be learned afresh. Steam ovens are still quite a specialised item and they are not cheap, prices starting from about £600 from de Dietrich or Miele.

## Hobs

Most people instinctively go for a gas hob, where they have the choice. Gas is fast, responsive and cheap to use: its drawbacks are harder cleaning and a dislike of pans boiling over. If mains gas is unobtainable, then consider having bottled gas just for the hob. A 19kg gas tank costs around £12 and should last about six months if it's only being used for a hob. If you use it for oven and grilling as well, you can switch to 47kg tanks with lower unit costs. Gas cooking has another big, often unspoken plus going for it in that it continues to work in power cuts, something many rural areas still suffer from frequently.

Whilst electric hobs have been seen as the poor relation, there are a number of developments that make them more interesting. First the ceramic hob came along which was easier to clean if nothing else but they perform only slightly better than conventional electric plates. They do, however, make a pleasing orange glow. More recently we have seen induction hobs which work via a magnetic field rather than an element. When magnetic pans are placed on the surface, a field is generated to produce heat. The field is only generated where the pan touches so induction cooking is efficient and extremely quick — faster even than gas. Induction hobs are also horribly expensive — expect to pay around £750 for one of these beauties. And buy new cookware — it has to be magnetic.

The more upmarket suppliers can also fit you out with specialist hoblets where you can mix and match your cooking surfaces and include griddles and fryers as well as the more usual plates. Most manufacturers also give you the option of having extended hobs if you find the standard 600mm width a bit limiting.

Be aware that the standard electrical supply for electric cooking in the kitchen is a 30 amp cable. This is only capable of supplying 7.5kW of power (you need 4 amps for each kW). Double ovens will use as much as 6kW with everything on and an induction hob or a five or six plate ceramic hob can take as much as 8kW with every ring in action. You can elect to either uprate your supply to 45amp or run separate circuits for the oven and the hob.

## Cooker Hoods

In a new, draught-free house, condensation and cooking smells will not easily disperse without opening windows, so a cooker hood is nigh-on essential, especially as you have to have some form of extract fan in a kitchen in order to satisfy building regs. You can have cooker hoods that merely 'recirculate' the air back into the kitchen but these are really nothing more than glorified grease filters. It's accepted as far better practice to enable your cooker hood to extract to the outside which obviously involves knocking a hole in the wall and connecting ducting to it. However, if you have a whole house ventilation system, you may want to hang onto some of the usable heat you are extracting and here a recirculator may make sense.

Cooker hoods now seem to come in four flavours. The standard version is a rectangular box which sits between 650 and 750mm above the hob: you get a three speed fan and a light (actually v. useful) but they are cheap and usually noisy. There is an "integrated" variety which gets concealed in an overhead wall cupboard and is activated by pulling the top hung cupboard door open. Next a slimline or telescopic version which is typically no more than 25mm deep and these are turned on just by a gentle tug towards you; the fan itself sits in a dummy cupboard above. The most upmarket option is to go for a canopy cooker hood which acts more like a conventional chimney: usually finished in stainless steel, look to pay north of £350 for this type. If you want to study how basic functional items have morphed into high fashion items, then the cooker hood would be a good subject. You can get one for £30 if you look carefully. You also pay more than £1500 if you want, as much as a basic chimney costs.

## Which Make?

There is an awful lot of snobbery about kitchen appliances. Classy kitchens need white goods with German (or at least German sounding) names like AEG, Bosch, Neff or Miele (it's pronounced like Sheila). Very classy kitchens need classy German makes like Gaggenau. British manufacturers like Hotpoint, Tricity Bendix, Creda have reputations based on price rather than quality, as have Philips Whirlpool and most of the Italian manufacturers with the exception of Smeg (yes, they are Italian) who have levered themselves up to Premiership status. The

very cheapest appliances often come with little-known brand names and obscure East European origins.

Getting confused? It gets worse. White goods branding is an extremely complicated area. There is much cross-manufacturing of parts and "country of origin" labelling should more correctly read "country of final assembly." As an example, most European cooker hoods are made in Italy and perform to much the same (rather noisy) standard whether they are branded Candy, Neff or Creda. Much of the upmarket German kit is actually assembled in Turkey or Portugal.

No wonder purchasers often subcontract the decision making as well as the installation. Broadly speaking, if you want to create an impression then the brand names have to be German. The very best cookers tend to be German, but don't assume that a German brand name is necessarily a sign of quality. Also, if you want anything unusual like a built-in griddle you will need to seek out the high quality brand names. However, if low price is your main concern, then you should check out Curry and Comet own brands or alternatively, if you want integrated appliances, look at MFI or specialists selling to developers — phone Arrow, Allied, BDC or Crangrove.

## Agas

The Aga remains the item for the complete country kitchen. Despite their exorbitant cost (nothing less than £5000 to purchase new plus the need for adequate foundations, suitable chimney arrangements and £300 fitting costs) and their exorbitant running costs (nothing less than £7/week in fuel and annual servicing costs of £200), otherwise rational people still salivate at the thought of having an Aga in the kitchen. They can't do chips, they can't grill and boiling a kettle takes forever but, to quote the sales blurb: "An Aga transforms even the most functional kitchen into a warm and welcoming gathering place for all the family. It becomes the heart and hub of your home." The fact that this description is often spot on usually says more about the state of the rest of the house than any unique attributes of the Aga. Any large radiant heat source will be immensely attractive on a bitingly cold day and it's this aspect of the Aga — over half a tonne of hot cast-iron — which fuels its seemingly unending popularity. A large storage heater would fulfil the same function at a fraction of the cost but, I'm afraid, it would completely lack the necessary style.

If you are contemplating an Aga for your home, you must plan for it from the ground upwards. Though not designed as water boil-

ers, for an extra £200 you can go for an Aga with a boiler capable of heating not less than 400lts of water/day (i.e. enough for about eight people) and — provided yours is a new house qualifying for VAT zero-rating — you can reclaim VAT on the purchase which instantly saves around £500. Customs & Excise are usually happy to accept this distinction and they cannot insist that the boiler is ever connected to your hot water cylinder. Agas come in gas-fired, oil-fired, solid fuel and electric (Economy 7) versions. There are a number of cast iron stove makers besides Aga and they are usually quite a bit cheaper. Many of them incorporate boilers so that you can use them as both cookers and house heaters but although this sounds economical, it can be a mixed blessing when it's your only heat source — it's not so much a case of being warm in winter as boiling in the summer.

## Ranges

There are alternatives between the splendour of the Aga and the industry standard "tin boxes" which are sold as part of a fitted kitchen. When the first edition of this book came out in 1995, hobby cookers were unheard of. Now every kitchen showroom has them on display at prices starting at around £800, even less at Currys. They are now referred to as range cookers and they are about half as wide again as the industry standard 600mm so you get six rings instead of four. You can get them dual fuel so that you get an electric oven and a gas hob: indeed this is the most popular option. Which? road tested 12 ranges in Feb 2002 and was rather sniffy about them all. It's best by was the dual fuel Flavel Cookmaster, costing around £850. But there are quite a few that cost over £2500.

## Dishwashers

If you want a dishwasher, the big decision facing you is whether to go free standing or integrated. If you are buying a fitted kitchen you will come under a little pressure to go for an integrated one which will slip behind a kitchen door so that you wouldn't know there was a dishwasher there at all. Now despite the integrated ones having less in the way of metal casing, they invariably cost more though sometimes it can be hard to compare because the models are not directly equivalent. But take a good, solid German make like Miele whose basic 638 model is available as both a free standing and an integrated unit. Free standing costs around £350, integrated — you'll do well to get one for less than £450. The divergence in costs is even more clearly illustrated at MFI where they sell a freestanding dishwasher (under their own Hygena label) at £199 but their cheapest integrated one (also badged as Hygena) is £399. Incidentally, if you want white goods with recognisable brand names like Bosch or Smeg, MFI is not the place to get them. Buy direct from a trade outlet or over the internet.

If you succumb to the allure of an integrated dishwasher, you have a further choice to make. Whether to hide the entire machine behind your chosen kitchen unit door — that's known as fully integrated — or to let the control panel peep out at you in a way referred to as semi-integrated by some and as drawer line by others. Just as girls wearing tight Lycra cycle shorts are prone to exhibit an elastic knicker line, so kitchen units are said to have a drawer line, conventionally located at 200mm below the worksurface. The semi-integrated or drawer line units have the control panels located above the drawer line (same as the free standing dishwashers) and leave an infill space below designed to take a matching door panel. In contrast, the fully integrated dishwashers engineer the control panels so that they are actually located on the top edge of the door. You can only get to them by opening the dishwasher.

If you find the distinction between fully and semi integrated dishwashers all a bit too precious, then save yourself a couple of hundred quid and bung a free standing one in. And avoid stainless steel and save yourself another couple of hundred quid. Stainless steel looks good, photographs well but as anyone who has lived with one will tell you, they don't half show the fingermarks. If you want the stainless steel look to stay looking clean, then you need aluminium which is even more expensive.

## Laundry

You can get integrated washing machines and tumble dryers but generally these items get placed in a separate utility room and they are therefore normally purchased as free standing items. Hotpoint remain the biggest name in washing machines, accounting for 50% of the UK market. Their basic stand alone models start at around £280; their Aquarius range starts at £400 and incorporates a number of green features (less water, less power, less powder). Hoover are one of the very few to offer a machine with a delay timer. The last time Which? surveyed washing machine reliability in May 2002, Hotpoint and Hoover scored down near the bottom of 16 brands. The most reliable? Miele (pronounced like Sheila).

## Tumble Dryers

You don't have to get a tumble dryer to vent outside but it makes good sense. Full-size, air-vented dryers cost around £180 whereas the alternative option is to have a condensing dryer which are getting on for double the price. Tumble dryers are notorious energy guzzlers and one way you can save on running costs is to fit a gas tumble dryer. They are made by Crosslee under the White Knight brand name (though note that White Knight also do electric tumble dryers) and though they cost around £300 they will dry a drum of wet clothes for 10p, as opposed to 40p or so on an electric dryer. Whilst they may cost an extra £50 to plumb in, they will save that in running costs within two years.

## Washer-dryers

The trend towards separate utility areas in larger houses has meant that there are few built-in washing machines and no built-in tumble dryers. Instead there are a large number of extremely expensive washer dryers costing from £500 upwards. They do save space but they are not as convenient as you might hope — they are only capable of tumble drying half a wash load at a time so they need unpacking between programs. They are also the most unreliable of all kitchen appliances.

## Cold Storage

There are numerous options of above- and below-freezing point storage and there are also numerous arrangements for their housing. You have the same decisions you get with cookers — whether to integrate or go free standing. Free standing is invariably cheaper. Or was until the arrival on our shores of the giant American fridges which you haven't a hope of integrating into any MDF kitchen unit. Now a whole raft of new names (to us) like Admiral, Amana and Maytag are selling enormous fridge freezers with ice dispensers and are getting over £2000 for some models. Quite a change from a Whirlpool under the counter-job for £155. And Smeg have appeared with some curved edge 50s style fridges in a range of pastel colours, looking fabulous and definitely not for concealing, especially with an £800 price tag. Ice dispensers: don't forget they need a water supply. All attempts to add value to what are essentially nothing more than cold cupboards. Again, if you are trying to save a little money, consider building an old fashioned larder, located off the kitchen, where you can store even more than you would get in a 26.7 cubic foot Maytag Sovereign. I figure even a small larder will be five times the volume — but where would you put the ice dispenser?

## 11c: Reliability of Kitchen Appliances

| | Washing Machines | Tumble Dryers | Washer Dryers | Dishwashers |
|---|---|---|---|---|
| **MOST RELIABLE** | Miele (1 in 12) Candy Bosch AEG Tricity Bendix Siemens Zanussi | Crusader (1 in 100) Creda Hotpoint Servis Electra White Knight | Bosch (1 in 6) Indeit Zanussi | Neff (1 in 10) Bosch Miele Siemens Tricity Bendix Zanussi |
| **AVERAGE** | 1 in 5 | 1 in 10 | 1 in 4 | 1 in 6 |
| _Chances of a breakdown in any 12 month period_ | Indesit Whirlpool Creda Electrolux Servis Hotpoint | AEG Bosch Zanussi Miele | Zanussi | Hoover AEG Hotpoint Whilpool Ariston Candy Indesit |
| **LEAST RELIABLE** | Ariston Hoover (1 in 3) | Whilpool Hoover (1 in 6) | Hoover Hotpoint (1 in 3)) | Hygena Indesit (1 in 4) |

Source: Which? Magazine May 02

# Kitchen Waste

The average kitchen design pays far too little attention to the dirty business of waste disposal. The standard solution is to fit a 20lt plastic bin behind the door of the sink unit and to leave it at that. This is hardly ideal even for one person flats. Large kitchens produce large amounts of waste and processing this waste efficiently should be part of a good kitchen plan. Growing interest in waste recycling means that more people are paying attention to separating waste and this means separate storage areas being made accessible. There is often no need for anything more complicated than a cardboard box, but boxes tend to take up space and become untidy.

## Organic Waste

There are two reasons for wanting to separate organic waste from the rest:

- you can't stand the smell or the mess
- your garden or your chickens love it being thrown over them.

The two approaches call for radically different solutions. The Clean Jeans will be fitting a waste disposal unit under their kitchen sink. This is a gizmo which macerates all animal and vegetable remains fed to it and then pumps it out into the foul drains. Cost from £100 to £300 depending on power and capabilities. Leading makes: Tweeny, Maxmatic, Waste King.

The Smellie Nellies will be going for a compost bin, which will also probably be located under the sink, conventionally in a 20lt plastic bin. Leading make: Addis, cost £3.50. More elaborate bins are available which clip on to the back of the door and have a cunning lid which lifts up only when you open the door. It pays to keep it pretty simple and have a bin which you can wash frequently.

There are some very fancy "green" sinks which have extra holes down which you can put organic waste which falls seamlessly into plastic-lined bin below — look for a Blanco Box Sink, prices start at £300. This is a composting option for the clean and green Jeans but they will have to pay dearly for this ability to keep the surfaces spotless.

## Other Recycling Options

Visit your local recycling centre and decide what it is that you can or want to recycle. Glass, aluminium, newspapers (but not cardboard), cork, batteries, clothes are the most frequently observed bins in my part of the woods, but your local council may have different priorities. It is worth giving some

thought as to how you will store these items until you next visit a bottle bank. It seems absurd to use up expensive kitchen space which has no doubt been ergonomically planned so that not even the spice rack is out of place. The utility room may be the place but note that if you've got dogs or children they may appreciate boxes filled with all kinds of interesting things stored at ground level. Garages or external covered bin spaces may be better solutions but bear in mind that the further away from the kitchen you get, the more likely it is that everything will get chucked in the bin marked "General." A little thought at the design stage can make all the difference. Note that the most frequently recycled materials — glass and paper — are also two of the least cost-effective to recycle. There is a good market for clear glass but green and brown glass is almost valueless and many bottle banks don't differentiate;

and newspaper recycling is itself a difficult and polluting process of doubtful economic value. In contrast, plastics and metals — especially aluminium — are well worth somebody recycling. If you are serious about recycling, find a centre that takes many different kinds of waste — and don't drive twenty miles out of your way to get there!

Don't be fobbed off with a mini-swing bin of 20lt or less. Even the greenest households need a waste bin that will hold a dustbin liner. If storing this quantity of waste is a problem, you can get over things with a rubbish compactor which reduces the volume four or five times. They are an expensive option, costing around £700 and taking up as much space as a large bin! Contact In-Sink-Erator.

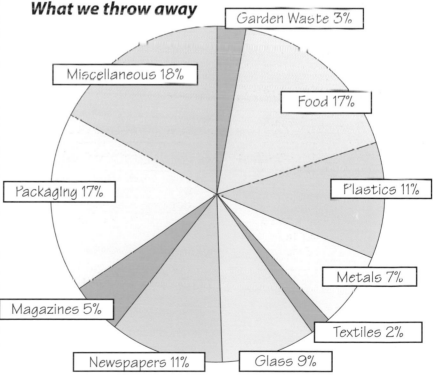

**What we throw away**

- Garden Waste 3%
- Food 17%
- Plastics 11%
- Metals 7%
- Textiles 2%
- Glass 9%
- Newspapers 11%
- Magazines 5%
- Packaging 17%
- Miscellaneous 18%

# Bathrooms

Bathroom fixtures and fittings are areas where standards have risen dramatically in the last century; the provision of a bathroom only became obligatory in the 1985 Building Regs and there is still no minimum size for bathrooms nor any obligation to build in more than a bath (or shower) and a loo. (This standard rises to a bath and two loos in houses where five or more people might be expected to live).

The basic minimum standard adopted by new housebuilders is way in excess of this. All contemporary bathrooms include wash-basins and virtually all houses with four bedrooms or more have a second bathroom, usually known as the en-suite and accessed directly from the master bedroom. A downstairs cloakroom is also now an extremely common feature in family homes. Professional housebuilders are not known for their largesse and they would claim that the effective standards are those imposed by the housebuying public, which seems to be about thirty years ahead of the building regulations in this instance.

## Costs

The bathroom is a multi-trade zone. Do not be fooled into thinking that bathrooms are all about plumbing-in sanitaryware: that's just the beginning. Ventilation, wall tiling,

mirrors, accessories, obscured glazing, enclosed light fittings, pull switches, towel rails (heated or otherwise) and specialised floor coverings all combine to make bathroom fitting a complex and elaborate process — and one that is easy to neglect in the hurry to finish a house. Bathroom planning is even more important in timber frame buildings because timber bearers should be present in the walls to secure all the fittings.

Bathrooms are expensive. The accompanying table shows costings for the two bathrooms plus downstairs cloakroom in the benchmark house. This is a typical installation with a bath in the family bathroom and an enclosed shower in the en-suite bathroom. Bear in mind that it's not the size of the bathroom that is expensive but the fittings in it. Big bathrooms are becoming very popular; many people want to fit cupboards and furniture in them and the en-suite bathroom, in particular, seems to be getting bigger and bigger, eating chunks out of its attached bedroom.

6% (10m$^2$) of the overall floor area of our benchmark house comprises bathrooms and it's an expensive 6%; the combined bathrooms cost way in excess of ordinary bedroom space. If you want to save money, don't build more than one bathroom. A bedroom

costs about £400/m$^2$ to build; a fairly basic bathroom will nearly double that figure and specifying fancy period fittings or modern continental styling, together with matching towel rail and tiling, could easily double that cost again.

Shower cubicles are three times the price of a basic bath. Don't think you are saving water (and therefore money) by showering; an enclosed shower space is a luxury, and the extra £250-£300 over and above the cost of a cheap bath will not be paid for out of water saved, especially if you fit a power or mains pressure shower which uses a bath load of water in three minutes.

## Bathroom Suites

Budget bathrooms are most usually sold as three-piece suites. Normally a bathroom suite includes:

- Bath, bath taps, plug
- Bath panels (to conceal the fact that the bath is plastic)
- Basin and supporting pedestal
- Basin taps and plug
- WC, cistern, seat, handle.

If you don't buy a suite, you'll have to remember to get all these items separately — items like cistern levers are easily overlooked. If you want to opt for a separate shower instead of a bath you may be able to find a two-piece "cloakroom suite" (be warned: cloakroom basins are often minute). A very basic bathroom suite will cost £200-£250. You won't get high style at this price but you will get a choice of six or seven pastel colours which can be coordinated with tiles to, at least, suggest that you've tried. Most bathroom outlets have a range of four or five suites going up in price to around £400; after that you get into more upmarket designs where all items come priced individually. Prices tend to get softer as they get higher and trade discounts of "no more than 10%" on budget lines suddenly rise to 30% or more when your spend rises above £1000.

## Accessories

Most suites offer a wide range of matching accessories (shelves, soap holders, loo roll holders, toothbrush holders, toilet brush holders, towel rails) at prices well over the odds for what you would pay in a DIY shed. Even on a fairly basic suite, you could easily spend over £100 on buying matching fittings, adding another 20% to your suite price. If you want a bidet, expect this to add around 30% to the basic three-piece suite price.

## 11d: Benchmark House: Bathroom Costs

| ITEM | FAMILY | EN SUITE | CLOAK ROOM |
|---|---|---|---|
| Loo (inc Seats) | £150 | £150 | £150 |
| Basin (inc. Taps) | 60 | 60 | 40 |
| Bath (inc. Taps) | 200 | | |
| Shower Tray 760x1000 | | 150 | |
| Shower Door | | 100 | |
| Shower | | 150 | |
| Copper Pipe/Plastic Waste | 90 | 80 | 40 |
| Labour To Fit | 250 | 250 | 125 |
| Waste and Soil + Vent Pipe | 80 | 50 | 50 |
| Labour To Fit | 150 | 50 | 50 |
| **ACCESSORIES (inc. Fitting)** | | | |
| Pipe Boxing | 60 | 60 | 60 |
| Vanity Units | 150 | 150 | |
| Fans | 100 | 100 | 100 |
| Wall Tiling (5m$^2$) | 100 | 250 | 50 |
| Enclosed Light Fittings | 60 | 60 | |
| Shaver Sockets | 40 | 40 | |
| **TOTALS** | **£1490** | **£1700** | **£665** |

## Styles

There are currently two discernible streams of bathroom styling, mirroring the fashion in contemporary kitchens. One is towards modern looking, built-in fixtures; the other is harking back to Victorian and Edwardian times. The more money you spend, the greater the divergence of styles become. The major UK producers (Armitage Shanks, Ideal Standard, Shires, Twyfords) all plough this well worn furrow. If you want something that transcends these styles, you'll have to look at continental brands names like Sottini or Roca or, if you want to get thoroughly minimalist, check out Vola UK who import all manner of weird and wonderful sanitary sculptures like glass sinks. Sales literature is available at most plumber's merchants and many builder's merchants; also check out the growing number of bathroom boutiques — try looking in the Yellow Pages under Bathroom Eqpt. If you want something out of the ordinary, be aware that it may take many weeks for it to be delivered.

## Period Styling

Up till fifteen years ago, people were still stripping out period porcelain and nothing new had been produced since the 50s. The return to fashion of these styles (always white or off-white) has been the one big success story for sanitaryware producers in the last few years and now every manufacturer produces sanitaryware to fit the period. The cheaper suites are priced at £350-£400 but they don't look very authentic (Plumb Center's Bramham Suite is as good as any) Ideal Standard have produced suites in four period styles (Victorian, Edwardian, Art Deco, Country Cottage)

*Visit any bathroom showroom or trade fair and it immediately becomes apparent that there is a style war in progress. Top: the Continental look, all sleek lines and curves. Bottom: Ancient British look, profoundly Eurosceptic*

Authenticity comes at a price; the Victorians never had mahogany bath panels nor glazed shower screens. To get the full period effect, attention must be paid to the detailing throughout the bathroom. A roll-top, cast-iron bath that can stand on its own will cost £500 plus; a Dorchester heated towel rail £400. There are small craft producers, like Sanitan and Vernon Tutbury, producing authentic designs but such a bathroom can cost £3000 just for the sanitaryware.

## The Modern Look

This is the other dominant style in contemporary bathrooms. The porcelain styling is all curves and pastel colours, the taps look like mushrooms and lavatory cisterns are concealed. Basin vanity units can be purchased from the merchants (from £70) but a more pleasing alternative is to build tiled work surfaces on to which you place a semi-countertop basin (like Ideal Standard's Tulip, £70 plus taps). The essence of this style of

bathroom is, not surprisingly, to match colours. If you want to do this, check that the British Standard colour numbers are the same — don't assume that "Ivory" or "Misty Peach" is the same colour for tile producers as it is for bathroom suppliers. You can also have your heated towel rails spray-painted to match bathroom suites (costs about £40 extra).

Whirlpool baths like the Jacuzzi will cost £2000+ though the plumbing-in is relatively straightforward. Other ideas that you may come across are building in saunas or gyms; all of which will cost a great deal of money and good luck to you.

## Showers

A rapidly growing market, showers are popular both as attachments to bath taps (known as shower mixers) and in their own right in stand alone shower cubicles. Apart from style

— and there are showers to fit every style — there are two things to look out for; thermostatic control and adequate flow rate.

## Thermostatic Control

Thermostatic control automatically adjusts the balance of hot and cold water flowing through the shower head as other taps in the house turn on and off. It is expensive, usually adding around £70 to the cost of a shower. A cheaper alternative is to have a shower with a high-temperature limiter which will avoid scalding but may still leave you drenched in cold water when a hot tap opens somewhere else.

## Shower Power

There are many routes to getting a good pressure through your shower head. The most effective are to install a mains pressure hot water system or a thermal store (see section on Domestic Hot Water in Chapter 8, Services). The least effective are to install an electric shower or a combination boiler, both of which heat water instantaneously and therefore suffer from low flow rates. In between these extremes come a whole gamut of power showers which aim to add whoosh to feeble pressure from tanks in the loft. There are single impeller pumps which boost the water after the mixing valve and double impellers which boost both hot and cold before they enter the valve. Which you choose is partly dependent on the layout you have and prices are largely dependent on the power of the pump. They can be purchased for just over £100, but a pump delivering 30lts/minute (equivalent to a good mains pressure system) will cost £180plus. Leading manufacturers: Mira, Aqualisa.

There are a also number of integral pumped shower valves like the Triton AS 1000 . These tend to be a cheaper option (the styling is naff) and you end up with an unsightly box of tricks in the shower cubicle. There are also electric showers which work entirely off the cold main and don't need a hot water supply, and electric showers like the Triton T90 (£300) which heat, pump and make thermostatic adjustments. The most ingenious (and probably the cheapest option) is the Croydex $H_2O$ shower (around £80) which uses the pressure from the cold main to force the hot water flow rate up. Alone of the power showers it doesn't need a power supply, but there's no thermostatic control and you can't use it with a combi boiler.

If you want a power shower in a new house, you would be well advised to avoid all these products and go for a mains pressure or near mains pressure hot water system.

## Shower Trays

Acrylic trays can be had for under £50 but they are not recommended because of problems with leaking caused by the trays flexing. The most popular option is the ceramic stone trays: Matki's is good (cost £75). For another £15 you can buy them with an undertile upstand which will eliminate any possibility of leakage. The standard size is 760mm square (which suits the standard pivot doors). There is a significant (100%) cost penalty if you want a larger tray.

## Shower Doors

You have a choice of building the shower into an alcove (with three side walls tiled), into a corner or free-standing against one wall. Pricewise there is little to choose — the cost of a tiled wall being similar to the cost of a glazed side panel. The alcove option usually looks the most professional; you finish the opening with either a pivot or a bi-fold door which will cost anything from £80 (Elbee, Laconite, Ram Niagra) to £200 or more (Matki, Daryl, Showerlux, Nordic). Matching side panels tend to be 60-80% of the door price. If your shower is incorporated with your bath, then you have a choice of a simple shower curtain hung from a rail (from £30) to a glazed shower screen (£50 upwards).

## Open Showers

What price open showers running into a floor drain? It's a detail regularly seen on the Continent and has been widely specified in this country in special needs bathrooms. You dispense with the tray and your enclosure need only be a shower curtain. The key component is the floor drain which has to be able to sit inside a floor void, to be able to cope with the 30 litres per minute which a power shower will throw, to include a trap and yet be readily cleanable which means that the grate and the assembly must be removable. In consequence, shower drains are relatively sophisticated and good ones cost over £100. Manufactures include Harmer (part of the Alumasc group) and Caroflow and designs allow incorporation with either regular floor tile sizes or sheet materials such as Altro Safety Flooring. Altro's main shower product is Marine 20 which is a 2mm covering laid over floors and can be continued up walls as well. At just under £15/m$^2$ (material only), it is no more expensive than ceramic tiling.

The key to getting a floor shower drain to work well is to build in a fall of 1:40 for a metre around the floor drain. In masonry floors, this can be achieved relatively easily with a 25mm depression in the screed — the Harmer floor drain requires only a 25mm deep screed. However, you can rarely shave 25mm off the top of a timber joist without seriously weakening the floor so the usual solution is to build a fall up with firrings laid across the tops of the joists; this leaves you with a 25mm threshold at the bathroom door which needs to be addressed.

## Avoiding Leaky Showers

In theory, this is no problem; in practice, tiled shower cubicles often ship water where they shouldn't and tiled floors will tend to fare even worse. It really is worth paying a lot of attention to the construction of shower enclosures generally because their failure is one of the commonest faults in new buildings. Don't skimp on the linings — use a water proof plywood or a waterproof board like Knauf's Aquapanel rather than regular plasterboard — and use the best adhesive you can afford to fix ceramic tiles with. The key failure point, however, is the joint between the walls and the floor (or more likely tray) and with most designs you are dependent on a bead of silicone mastic to stop water finding a route through the defence. Your silicone sealant will stand a much better chance of success if the joint is tight and even, something which usually depends on how good your carpentry is.

One ingenious way around the problem of leaking showers is to install an all-in-one moulded cubicle. Advanced Showers produce a range of elegant, stand alone enclosures which, whilst not cheap (costing upwards of £600), are very quick and easy to install and will be valued by all those who have experienced the frustrations of shower leaks. Another option is to avoid timber joists in your first floor: it's the shrinkage in these joists (often as much as 8mm) when the house is drying out that causes all these shower leaks. Specify either a beam and block first floor or something like a Trus Joist floor (see Chapter 7, section on Floors).

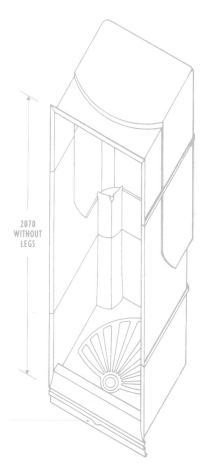

2070
WITHOUT
LEGS

*Advanced Showers produce this all-in-one moulded shower enclosure. They are not cheap — they start at around £450 — but they are absolutely leak free*

For developers, bedroom space is cheap space. All that really has to be provided is enough room to fit a bed and an item of furniture plus enough space to manoeuvre about between them — the technical term for this is swinging a cat.

## Design Considerations

You can of course give far more consideration to the whole issue. It's worth visualising the layout of the bedroom furniture so as to work out where to place radiators and power sockets. Also it's a nice touch to arrange light switching so that it can be reached easily from the bed. On the other hand, if you want to maintain maximum flexibility, then fit power sockets on every wall so you can accommodate various layouts. In reality there may only be one sensible place where a bed can go, but there may be other considerations. What is appropriate as a nursery for a toddler is unlikely to suit a teenager and you should consider how the uses a bedroom gets put to will change over the years. Don't always assume that a bedroom will remain a bedroom.

## Size

It is conventional to rank bedrooms by size. Now, you might think that in a four-bedroom house you would provide a double bedroom for mum and dad (or whoever tickles your fancy) plus three smaller but similar sized rooms for the children. But no; the British way of doing it is to build bedrooms in ever decreasing sizes. It's also the British way of doing things to rank houses according to the number of bedrooms they have. Almost all developers switch to four bedrooms when the overall floor size creeps over 110m². Our benchmark Gidding house with its loft converted sounds enormous with its six bedrooms but it really doesn't appear so when you visit and it still only has 161m² of internal living space — many so-called four bedroom houses are larger than this. Judging the size and amenity of a house by the number of bedrooms can be very misleading but that is the way we do it. Ask a man how many cc in his car engine and he'll be able to answer off the top of his head: ask him how many m² internal living space he has in his house, he won't have a clue. My previous benchmark house had only three bedrooms but was actually 5m² larger than the six-bedroom Gidding.

The Gidding benchmark house bedroom sizes are as follows:

### First Floor
- BEDROOM 1   14.8m²
- BEDROOM 2   11.6m²
- BEDROOM 3   10.0m²
- BEDROOM 4   6.2m²

### In Loft
- BEDROOM 5   12.5m²
- BEDROOM 6   21.4m²

The arrangement on the first floor is pretty standard for a tight four-bed arrangement. The bedrooms are ranked by size (often 15-12-10-8 are the floor area ratios). Whether Bedroom 4 at just 6.2m² is contravening the trade descriptions act in calling itself a bedroom at all is a moot point, but it's the way it's done so I really shouldn't be churlish. However the size of the loft rooms is such that it puts the tightness of the first floor arrangement into perspective. At 21.4m², Bedroom 6 is easily the largest room in the house.

If you are not designing a house for immediate resale you can afford to ignore these bedroom conventions and to work out the number of rooms that you really need. Personally, I have never understood why the minor bedrooms come in varying sizes — rather than 12m², 10m² and 6m², why not three at 9m²? Or do you in fact need lots of small rooms at all? Another alternative is to build larger rooms which can be partitioned at a later date if needs arise.

## Wardrobes

Not usually included by developers and not usually included in any summary of building costs, the wardrobe is, nevertheless, a near essential item in any bedroom. As with shelving, outlined in the previous section, there are basically three approaches to creating bedroom storage space:

- Use free standing furniture: it costs but you can take it with you
- Use specialist bedroom fittings
- Make your own.

The last method has one major advantage, recently agreed by Customs & Excise, in that it is regarded as zero-rated for VAT purposes. Typically you would design your bedroom wall partitions with various strategically placed kinks into which you slip a hanging rail and a few open shelves and then hang a door or two in front. It's probably the cheapest option for new housebuilders as the cup-

boards can be created as you go rather than being added on afterwards. Budget between £100 and £250 per fitted wardrobe, depending on the size, finish and complexity of the design; this would include shelving, hanging rails and a door or two. Magnet and the DIY sheds sell melamine wardrobe fitting kits, complete with hanging rails, at around £35 each.

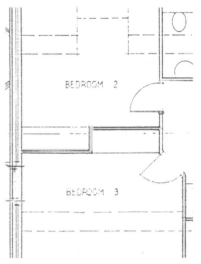

*The kinked bedroom wall creates wardrobe space — and avoids VAT.*

# The Home Office

Pick up any paper or magazine and you're likely to find articles about working from home, as if it had just been discovered as the panacea of all modern ills. This is completely daft. Working from home is what most of us always did, long before they invented factories and offices and there are still loads of trades and businesses which have always worked from home. What is new is that there is a whole host of office workers who would previously have commuted some distance to work now padding a few feet down the passageway. Journalists in particular are able to work from home which is, just possibly, why you read so much about it in the newspapers and magazines. But my farming friends just scratch their heads and wonder what everyone is talking about.

What's the upshot of all this? Well, what most people think when they think of working from home is that they need an office, or at least some office space. The physical requirements for all this are remarkably small, usually satisfied by a few shelves and a working space serviced by a couple of power outlets and a telephone socket (two if you are greedy). There really isn't much designing to be done, you just take over the box bedroom and have done with it. Even if you are inclined towards the hi-tech office with PCs, faxes, printers, scanners, copiers, modems and the like, you still don't really need anything more in the way of infrastructure — though extra power points and phone sockets would certainly come in handy.

## Planning Issues

However, for many others, working from home will need considerably more thought. You may require meeting space or consultation rooms which are best kept quite separate from the rest of the household in order to maintain a professional atmosphere: sometimes this can be quite neatly achieved with an additional ground floor room which has its own external entrance. On the other hand, you may need workshop space which will create dust or noise or smell and which is ideally situated in a separate building. These are specialised concerns and really no one is going to understand them better than yourself, so it is pointless me whittering on. What I should point out though is that the more specialised and separate your workspace becomes, the more problems you are likely to encounter at the planning stage.

These problems are likely to hinge on whether you can extend the terms of the planning permission to include non-residential uses. Solo home office working is frankly not going to be an issue but anything that a) makes a lot of noise or smell or b) attracts a lot of visitors is not going to be passed through on the nod; in fact, it's probably unlikely to get passed at all if the area is zoned purely residential. However the buzz word of contemporary planning, sustainability, is on your side here. For decades the planning system has worked to separate the residential zones from the industrial zones on the premise that the two don't mix well, but as much of our working activities have become cleaner and quieter, the wisdom of this zoning has been called into question. Now the boot seems to be on the other foot because the car — more particularly the car journey — has become the bete noir of planning departments. Anything which can be done to reduce the number of car journeys is said to be sustainable, which is planning speak for a good thing.

## Dedicated Office?

Spec. housing is still being built without dedicated office space though this is changing quite rapidly. Our benchmark house (at least in its larger version) has a room designated as a study and there are now many examples of developers building in a far more sophisticated level of home working. Just a few miles from our benchmark house in Peterborough, Stamford Homes are currently fitting out every home on a large estate with state of the art digital TV and data cabling, giving the flexibility to have an office in any room you choose or, indeed, to network computers together so that you can have more than one office. Within 10 or 20 years, I expect this level of sophistication will be as standard as electrical power cabling has been, though there are difficulties in knowing just which standards will end up being adopted. More elaborate specifications are touched on at the end of Chapter 9.

If you are designing a one-off house and have no need for an office-level data infrastructure, should you be concerned? Probably not. Any future developments in home cabling systems will have to be capable of being retrofitted into existing houses so you can afford to sit and wait and see what the future may bring.

It would be as well to bear in mind that, though you may not want a dedicated home office, future purchasers are likely to have such space high on their wish list. If there is a lesson to be learned here, it is to plan a little flexibility into the scheme you are designing. If you definitely want a home workspace then you should fit it out accordingly, but many people are not altogether sure that they do: instead of fitting one out from the word go, identify which room you think would be best for this purpose and at least specify a couple of extra power sockets and maybe first fix an extra phone line in.

# Conservatories

Adding a conservatory is big business in the home refurbishment market (200,000 new ones built each year) but comparatively small beer in the world of new building — only about 1% of new homes are built with conservatories. Why should that be? Well, for one thing, a conservatory is usually more expensive to build than an ordinary extension. The substructural works are no different but both glass walls and glass roofing are more expensive than traditional building methods, and these combine to make the costs of conservatories range from around £500/m² to over £1000/m². In comparison, the basic cost of an extension would be less than £500/m² (before fitting out). The reasons for this are not hard to fathom; whereas a developer might spend around £50/m² on external walling and £60/m² on roof carpentry and coverings combined, the cost of toughened double-glazed units alone is £50/m² and normally a conservatory's glazing costs are much less than the cost of the surrounding frames.

Conservatories also cost a lot to keep warm in winter and require specialised (i.e. expensive) blinds and fans if they are to be kept cool in summer. You can, of course, choose to not use your conservatory when it's either too hot or too cold or too dark, but that's an awful lot of times for a room that's so expensive to build and it makes little sense when you consider the size of the initial investment. Furthermore, conservatories add little if anything to house values — not everyone loves them.

## Alternatives

Adding a conservatory onto a new house is often a sign that the original design work is not what it might have been. Conservatories are expensive and problematical, and whereas they may make stunning and effective extensions to existing houses, their role in a new house is not at all clear. If you feel you need a conservatory to add that certain panache to your dream home, then you may just have under-designed the house in the first place. A rethink on the basic layout would probably save you money and give you a better house to boot.

If you want more living space, think of incorporating a south-side summer room (with lots of windows and a french/patio door) and a north-facing winter room designed for cosy dark nights around the fireside. If you really want glazed roofing, consider fitting two or more large Velux rooflights in a lean-to section. Veluxes are much easier to clean and are easily openable, making ventilation a doddle; this way you can achieve some of the benefits of a conservatory without the drawbacks.

## Aspirations

Despite my reservations I must admit that there are certain situations where a conservatory comes into its own. Sunday lunch in April, reading the newspaper on a sunny winter's morn, sundowners on long summer evenings among the potted plants. Rather like an Aga, the conservatory forms part of many peoples dreams of stylish living and, however inappropriate in a new house, some people cannot be without them. In advertising jargon, conservatories are another "aspirational purchase" for romantics and who am I to decry their pleasures? Shame on my puritanical self.

Though not fundamentally different to any other types of building, conservatory construction has evolved into a specialist trade. Many glazing firms have branched out into designing and building conservatories, and many of them offer an all in one design and build service. Styles range from utilitarian greenhouse to ornate Victorian complete with fancy ridge pieces; structures are commonly built from timber, aluminium or uPVC. Budget conservatories can be picked up from the DIY sheds and Wickes, whilst the more upmarket structures are dominated by the likes of Amdega and Portland who advertise heavily in the national press.

If you are interested in designing and building your own conservatory there are a number of specialists who produce the structural aluminium channel sections to order. Check BACO (British Aluminium) or Pilkington.

## Polycarbonate sheets

One of the extra expenses incurred with a conservatory is the glazed roofing panels. If double-glazed, the spec on these is usually one skin laminated and the other skin toughened glass = mucho expensivo. One way of greatly reducing costs is to use polycarbonate sheeting at around £25/m². However it's a somewhat threadbare alternative to the real thing and it does get incredibly noisy when there's a hailstorm about.

## Building Regs

Conservatories are problematic when it comes to energy efficiency. At times they can contribute just enough solar gain to heat the entire house; at other times they can be a huge heat sink, sucking heat out of the house; and at still other times they can provide so much heat that you need air conditioning to stay comfortable. How do our energy efficiency regs get to grips with them? They make a crucial distinction between conservatories which are separated from the rest of the building and open plan ones. Separation is defined as being built outside the heated envelope so the division must be done with either external walls or doors, built with the appropriate U values and draught stripping. If you choose to build your conservatory as an open extension to the rest of the house, then it has to comply with the 2002 Part L regulations, one of which is that glazed areas should not exceed 25% of the total floor area. That could be tricky.

*New homes tend to work better with integral sunrooms rather than conservatory extensions, with which we are all familiar.*

# Garages

In common with almost all new house developments in the UK, the benchmark house has a garage. The way AB Homes have designed the Gidding is so that it is available in a couple of different versions. I have written elsewhere about the ingenious loft options offered; something similar occurs with the garage. The cheapest version includes a single garage integral with the basic rectangular floorplan. In 2002, this was being sold for £133,000. For £18,000 more, the garage is shifted off to one side to become an attached garage, accessed via the utility room. What the buyer gets for this extra £18,000 is not a larger garage (they are exactly the same size) but a study and a breakfast room where the integral garage once sat. And the extra £18,000 reflects not just the cost of building the garage (which is actually around a third of this amount) but the fact that the larger house occupies a larger plot.

## Is a Garage Necessary?

Before you commit yourself to spending good money on garage space consider for a moment whether it is really necessary. Although current fashions in house styles tend towards the traditional, there is absolutely nothing traditional about a garage. Its nearest equivalent in pre-20th century housing is the stable or, perhaps, the cowshed; but the housing of cars is an altogether different affair. Furthermore, whilst thirty or forty years ago it was a good idea to keep vehicles undercover to facilitate winter starts and to stop rust, cars these days are made to very much higher standards and it is really not necessary to keep them undercover. Nowadays, security is often cited as a reason for building garages — but does this really justify spending as much on a garage as it costs to buy a small car? And for many practised car thieves, a locked garage doesn't really represent much of an obstacle in any event, especially as people tend to be much less security conscious on outbuildings.

## Other Functions

Of course, garages have many other uses besides providing undercover car parking, as is shown by the numbers of people who have them but never park their cars inside them. Solid fuel, tools, lawnmowers, gardening equipment, bicycles, golf clubs, baby buggies, deep freezes, paddling pools, paint, you name it, it gets stored out there, and very useful it is too. But if you are designing a house from scratch, you may come to the conclusion that what you need is a larger utility room or a basement, not a garage. Garages are obviously valued by a great number of people otherwise speculative developments wouldn't include them as a matter of course, but don't just fall into the trap of assuming that a house must have a garage because it's not a proper house without one.

## When To Build It?

You can, of course, decide to leave the construction of a garage until an unspecified later date. If it is included in on your planning permission drawings, then the right to build it cannot be taken away once you have started the main house. NB This ruling goes for conservatories, swimming pools and any other fancy accoutrements that you aspire to but can't afford. Therefore just drawing the plans in might represent a good compromise solution for those who don't really need a garage but worry that the house might be difficult to sell without one. Against this, you should be aware that any building work that takes place after you move into a house will not be exempt from VAT, so it will cost you 17.5% more to construct. Also, it is worth pointing out that many people find it very useful to build the garage before the rest of the house as it provides a useful and secure store-cum-site hut whilst the main construction work forges ahead. Indeed, with a little bit of adaptation, you could just about live in a garage for a few months — certainly not much worse than the average caravan.

## Siting

By and large, house designers do not like garages. They are difficult. On most sites, access demands that they are located somewhere prominent near the frontage and yet, by their very nature, they are more akin to outbuildings and sheds. Now, polite architectural convention dictates that you don't put a humble shed in the front garden and so you are left with the problem of having to make the garage look good without costing too much.

## Integral

One way around this conundrum is to have an integral garage, that is, one that is built into or at least attached to the main house.

### For

- It makes for a more effective utility room type garage if that's what you have in mind
- You can use it to house boilers and freezers
- The arrangement fits better on narrow fronted sites (under 15m wide).

### Against

It doesn't usually do much for the look of a house. Most garage doors are better suited to largely unseen parts of your estate — i.e. they are naff — and placing one prominently in your front elevation can be very ugly. The problem of the garage door is particularly acute when you are building in a traditional style. One way of alleviating it is to have an "L" shaped house and to tuck the garage into the bit of the L that projects forward towards the road. This softens the impact of the integral garage on the all important kerb appeal.

## Detached

Given a site without space constraints, most builders will plump for a detached garage. The main attraction of this arrangement is that it maintains the integrity of the house design but, even so, this can still be overwhelmed by the siting of the garage. Ideally, this will be well away to one side but most plots these days are not large enough to make this a viable option and so very often the house is half-hidden by the detached garage in front of it. Effectively, this means that the garage plays a crucial role in people's initial views of a house, and developers have responded to this by spending more and more money on external appearance, commonly including fancy roofing effects not seen on the main house.

## Building Costs

Many of the costs of building a garage — whether integral or detached — are no different from the costs of building the main house. Garages do not have to meet the standard building regulations as regards insulation and damp penetration and this allows them to be constructed with thinner, single-skin walls. However, groundwork costs and roofing costs are basically identical, and despite the fact that garages are rarely fitted out with all the paraphernalia of a finished house, the construction costs of a garage are still as much as 60% of those of a finished house when compared on a floor area basis.

## Alternatives

### Car Ports

One alternative approach is to build just a lean-to car port or undercover car parking bay. You need some form of hard standing for the car and then the rest is up to you. The finished result could be anything from a flimsy timber construction which might look better as a garden pergola to a fully fledged garage without a door.

### Prefabricated

There are several small manufacturers who produce prefabricated garages at prices way below standard construction costs. But what you are buying is probably little different in quality to a garden shed. That may be exactly what you are looking for of course. They are very utilitarian and would probably be best sited away from the main house.

### Underground

Budget costs for a fully submerged basement (shell only) are £430-600/m², around double the cost of an above ground structure. Consequently, an underground garage is unlikely to be a cost-effective option unless space is at a premium. Access ramps (budget £8000) and potential drainage problems make the totally underground garage an expensive luxury. However, the economics look far friendlier when sorting out sloping ground. There are instances where burying car parking below ground can actually free up ground elsewhere for more cost-effective uses (like building extra houses), but this is unlikely to be relevant to many single housebuilders.

### Garage Doors

For many designers, the problem with garages begins and ends with the garage door. Until the 1970s garage doors were strictly functional and utilitarian, often made of steel with no attempts at embellishment. Since then, a large number of imitation traditional door styles have sprung up, aping the move back to other traditional forms. The trouble is, that whilst a window or a front door can be made in styles copied from old doors, there are no old garage doors to copy from. Hence a mock Georgian or mock Tudor garage door looks more than faintly ridiculous. Double doors, over 4m wide, look particularly strange and attempts to mould classical patterns on to them merely serve to emphasise how strange and out of place they look.

If there is a traditional British garage door it is the side opening style that you see on houses built in the 20s and 30s, made from solid timbers and lit by small square frosted glass panels. Magnet still produce such a door and it is remarkably good value at around £150 for a pair large enough for a single garage (though these need glazing and painting). The current trend is to go for doors which open vertically and there are a number of manufacturers producing especially for this market, e.g. Cardale, Henderson, Garador and Hormann. As with front entrance doors, there is a choice of different materials, the main ones being timber, steel and glass fibre (or GRP as it gets called in this business). Garage doors are large and therefore tend to get pricey. It's a specialist business and your best bet is to trawl through Yellow Pages to "Garage Doors" and seek quotations from there. Steel is much the cheapest material but also the least attractive. Timber and GRP are around twice the price. GRP doors are usually produced to look like timber — in fact they can look incredibly realistic. They can also be stained; their main advantage over timber is that they are (hopefully) maintenance-free, yet many people will prefer to stick with timber.

If you don't like any of the commercially available doors yet still crave the convenience of an up-and-over door, then check out Hormann's sub-frames which you can fill in with your own designs at your leisure. They are called Open-for-Infill doors

### Opening Mechanisms

As already stated, most garage doors these days open vertically. But it's not quite that simple. There is vertical and vertical.
• The simplest type of opening is the canopy or up-and-over door; when open about a

## 11e: Benchmark House: Attached Single Garage Costs

| | |
|---|---|
| *Clearing Oversite* | 80 |
| *Excavating Foundations* | 90 |
| *Concrete Foundations* | 300 |
| *Garage Floor* | 310 |
| *Rainwater Drains* | 220 |
| **GROUNDWORKS** | **£1000** |
| | |
| *Footings* | 210 |
| *Garage Blockwork* | 160 |
| *Garage Brickwork* | 1140 |
| *Steel/Lintels* | 140 |
| **MASONRY** | **£1650** |
| | |
| *Trussed rafters* | 373 |
| *Extra Garage Roof Carpentry* | 130 |
| *Garage Fascias* | 30 |
| **FIRST FIX CARPENTRY** | **£533** |
| | |
| *Garage Door* | 330 |
| *Back Door + Window* | 480 |
| **JOINERY/GLAZING** | **£810** |
| | |
| *Roofing* | 400 |
| *Rainwater Goods* | 80 |
| *Scaffolding* | 200 |
| **ROOFING/SCAFFOLD** | **£680** |
| | |
| **PLASTERING** | **£ 0** |
| | |
| **PLUMBING/HEATING** | **£ 0** |
| | |
| *Lighting* | 50 |
| **ELECTRICS** | **£50** |
| | |
| *Mastic* | 30 |
| **DECORATING** | **£30** |
| | |
| *Gravel Driveway + Kerbs* | 475 |
| **EXTERNALS** | **£475** |
| | |
| **GARAGE BUILDING COSTS** | **£5228** |
| **INTERNAL FLOOR AREA in m²** | **14** |
| | |
| **COSTS/M² of FLOOR AREA** | **£373** |
| **COSTS/FT² of FLOOR AREA** | **£35** |

*Double garages can be difficult. Two single garage doors tend to look better but are a lot less practical when it comes to getting cars in and out.*

*A traditional stable door approach suitable for a barn conversion*

*The Hormann Open-for-infill doors allow you to improvise a little with the finish. A double door like this is best opened with an electric door operator.*

locating the supporting frame behind the walls rather than between them. Height is also an issue. Some big cars won't fit under a 7' doorway.

If you are planning a double garage, you have the choice of a double door or two singles. Two single doors usually work out cheaper; although you have to build a dividing pillar, the cost of this is offset by the extra cost of a 4.5m lintel to cross the gap above a double door opening. Opening double doors by hand can also be quite a hassle, particularly if the spring mechanism works out of adjustment. On the other hand, if you plan to use an electric door operator you save yourself the cost of installing a second one.

## Remote Control Operators

An increasingly popular item which allows you to open and close your garage door automatically from both a switch inside the garage and a remote control unit which you can keep inside the car. They are not cheap — coming in at around £250 which includes just one operator (extra ones cost £45ea) — but they do make a lot of sense when you consider the hassle involved in opening garage doors manually. All the garage door suppliers sell these and they come in varying levels of sophistication. Hormann and Bosch market multi-function ones which can switch on welcome lights and open entrance gates as well. However, even the most basic ones come with timed welcome lights which come on whenever the door is opened: this is very useful.

Electric operators also come in different flavours. Most work with a geared chain but there are some (Hormann's Supramatic) which work on a Kevlar belt which promise virtually silent opening. They tend not to work on the basic canopy up-and-over doors although Cardale's Autoglide is an exception: in fact it can be retrofitted onto existing doors.

If you are going to spend £6000 plus on a garage, then it's probably worthwhile spending the extra £350 on an operator so that you actually get to use the garage for its intended purpose.

third of the door protrudes outside the frame, forming a canopy. They are usually hand operated and canopy double doors are something you could live without as they can get very heavy and awkward to lift.

- As its name suggests, the fully retractable door glides all the way back into the garage on a set of tracks. These are much more suitable for double doors and for remote operators.
- The North Americans like to fit sectional garage doors. These split into, typically, four horizontal sections which slide up a set of vertical tracks and then, one section at a time, turn through 90° and end up under the garage roof. The advantage of this is that the door doesn't protrude when opening so that you can park hard up to

both the inside and outside face and still open the door.

- Finally, there are various makes of Roller Doors around which perform in much the same way as sectional doors. However instead of turning through 90°, these doors roll up like a carpet. They look like steel shutters, which is what they are, and so the kerb appeal aspect is limited.

## How Wide?

The traditional width for a single garage door in the UK has been 7ft (2134mm). It's mean. There are an awful lot of cars around that will struggle to get through such a gap, particularly so if the entry angle isn't dead straight. If you have the room, go for doors which are 7'6" wide (2286mm). If space is very tight, you can usually gain a crucial few inches by

# Chapter 12
# Shopping

*If you love shopping, it's a given that you'll love housebuilding. One of the secret joys of building homes is that you can indulge yourself on the greatest shopping trip of your life. But successful housebuilders are always canny shoppers, not spendthrifts, and there are a few basic lessons to be learned before you launch into it all. Firstly, do not get carried away with the thrill of it all and choose items way beyond your budget. Secondly, know where to look. And thirdly, know how to shop, how to strike a bargain. It's well worth studying the whole buying process. This is the logic of this chapter. It doesn't cover everything but it does cover many of the important areas that have been otherwise ignored up to this point.*

# Taking Off Quantities

A bill of quantities is a fancy, construction professional's term for a shopping list. Making a comprehensive one is fundamental to controlling costs and is one of the major benefits to derive from having a properly designed, properly specified job. Many times in the past I have measured off plan to estimate a cost and then gone and measured again on site to order materials. I must also admit to having measured three or even four times when the bit of wood I write the measurements on gets nailed into some studwork or gets painted over. If I had taken the advice that I'm offering now I'd be a little bit richer and a little bit fatter. It may just be that you have built so inaccurately that your house does not resemble the plans that were drawn up, but if this is the case then you're playing in a different orchestra to me and there's no help to be proffered; go ahead and skip the rest of this section.

Now, serious construction professionals will engage the services of a quantity surveyor (known on site as "the QS") to work out what is needed. However, QSs don't come cheap and many small builders work on their own rules of thumb for estimating the right quantities. These are not usually as accurate as a QS would get them but they are much better than nothing.

## Free Take-offs

If you've no experience of this sort of quantification work, then I would tend to steer well clear unless you have loads of time and patience, particularly as many builder's merchants now offer a free take-off service ideally suited to the needs of rookie builders. Much of the repetitive grind of measuring and recording is carried out by computer and, provided the job is relatively straightforward, they are pretty accurate. The closer you stick to industry standard solutions, the better the outcome and they are quite capable of generating accurate results from a basic set of plans and elevations. The materials-buying sheets generated for the benchmark house included amount for foundations, masonry work, joinery, lintels, roof covers, carpentry, rainwater gear and sanitaryware; not exhaustive but a good start.

## Traditional Route

Let's compare it with the traditional way of doing a take-off. Traditional here means that your source document is a written schedule of works (often known as the spec), not the plans. You use the plans to calculate the areas and volumes but you work methodically down the written list so as not to miss anything out. To give you a flavour of what I'm on about, here is a clause taken from the spec of a previous benchmark house.

• 7.1 External (house) walls of 275 - 280mm 3.5N clinker blockwork cavity work incorporating 75mm Rockwool or similar full fill cavity insulation and 200mm s/s butterfly brick ties at max 900mm horizontal and 450mm vertically and at every block course adjacent to openings. Additional 105mm skin of face brickwork (bricks to clients choice) forming plinth wall and tied to blockwork with s/s butterfly ties as described above. Plinth wall extends 10 courses above DPC.

Hardly a riveting read, but it's clear enough. The job of the QS is, if you like, to rewrite this specification with the quantities added in so that it might read:

• 7.1 158m$^2$ double skin external (house) walls of 275 - 280mm 3.5N clinker blockwork cavity work incorporating 145m$^2$ x 75mm Rockwool or similar full fill cavity insulation and 580No. 200mm s/s butterfly brick ties at max 900mm horizontal and 450mm vertically and at every block course adjacent to openings. Additional 55m$^2$ x105mm skin of face brickwork (bricks to clients choice) forming plinth wall and tied to blockwork with 130No. x s/s butterfly ties as described above. Plinth wall extends 10 courses above DPC.

You don't need any specialised equipment. All you need are your finished plans, a decent ruler, a calculator and a pen and pencil (rubber would be handy). And bags of common sense. If you've got a computer and you know your way around a spreadsheet you'll save yourself a bit of work, but not that much.

## Measurements to Take

Take your measurements from your detailed plans (which are now conventionally drawn in metric scale which makes scaling up a damn sight easier). If the distance you want is referred to on the drawings then use it, otherwise you must measure off plan in millimetres and scale up to get actual sizes; thus, if drawings are 1:50, then you multiply your measurement by 50 to get the actual measurement.

Many of the dimensions you need will be written in on the plan so you won't need to measure. Where an area is needed you multiply the two sides together, but when this area is not a simple rectangle you must split the overall area into a number of smaller rectangular boxes and add these together. Remember that the area of a triangle = Half Base x Height.

For all but the very largest houses all this measuring should take about four to six hours. Complicated building details like split levels, curved work, dormer windows or raked ceilings make the measuring much more complex too and it is well worth double-checking as a mistake here will have costly ramifications on down the line. Oh, and don't forget to write the answers down where you won't lose them.

I also find it incredibly handy to make little notes next to the calculations which remind me what assumptions I have made when doing the calculations. Typically these read as "have assumed no skirtings in conservatory" or "have allowed for three courses of face brickwork below DPC." It's a good idea to decide whether your derived quantities are "as measured" or whether you have added an allowance for waste. It really doesn't matter which method you employ but you must be consistent otherwise you will end up adding 15% to the quantities several times over and you will over-order by miles.

The further your house gets away from the good old box shape, the more complicated it gets to measure out and, if a feature like a bay window or a fancy chimney is difficult to quantify, then you can bet that it will also be difficult to build.

## Working Through the Spec

You work methodically through the spec quantifying everything that is quantifiable. You then have to sweep through the whole thing a second time to generate a shopping list; some of the things you have quantified will have to be amalgamated with other sections, others will have to be broken down still further.

Blockwork is a good example. The bulk of this house's blockwork appears in this section 7.1 that I've already highlighted, but there is more blockwork in the garage, in the internal walls downstairs and around the chimney. All these have to be totalled to get an overall total for blockwork. And then consider that blockwork includes not just the blocks themselves, but the sand and cement making up the mortar not to mention the labour to lay them with. These totals have to be extracted from the blockwork total and added to the brickwork total which, to add to the confusion, will have different square metre labour rates and uses different volumes of mortar.

### Written Specifications

Well that's the traditional route. It's time consuming but it works. If you plan to do your own project management it may even be worth going through this exercise to familiarise yourself with the job in hand. However, many housebuilders never bother with anything so elaborate as a written specification of works but just make do with plans on a couple of A1 sheets. This is fine if you know what you are doing, but using a set of plans without a written spec can be a bit like trying to cook a new dish for which you have a list of the ingredients but no instructions on how they go together. Arguably it doesn't matter which order you measure quantities in but the danger is that if you don't work methodically through a list, you will miss whole chunks out. If you have skimped on this stage of the design process, then this is where your chickens come home to roost.

### Applying Measurements

From all these measurements plus various details drawn in on the plans you should be able to construct a reasonably accurate bill of quantities. You may not actually want to make up a shopping list for paint at the planning stage, but the point is that by having taken all these measurements you shouldn't have to keep taking them throughout the job. You have the figures. From these figures plus a little close scrutiny of your house planned you can work out quantities for:

- Excavation
- Concrete (approximate)
- Flooring materials
- Walling materials
- Roofing materials

- Insulation
- Plasterboarding and plastering
- Decorating materials
- Skirting and architrave
- Covings
- Scaffolding
- Guttering and downpipes
- Whole house heat-loss calculations.

Joinery is treated rather differently. If you've got a pukka written spec, there will be a joinery schedule attached which will list all the opening sizes and the window and door styles which will fit in the openings — see Table 7f on page 93 to see what I'm on about. I find it helpful to start with the joinery: I work out the overall areas and use this sum to subtract from wall areas. The joinery schedule can also be used to calculate approximate quantities for glazing, lengths for lintels and cavity breaks and a subsidiary schedule for door furniture.

### Average Prices

The rates I quote later in this chapter are all rates current for building work in southern England in 2002, especially around my home town of Cambridge. Your area may (almost certainly will) have different prices in operation by the time you start building, but bear in mind that Cambridgeshire is close to the national average on building costs. Early editions of this book (it first appeared in 1994) were able to neatly summarise both material and labour costs right across mainland Britain — only Ireland diverged significantly. But the few years has seen that change. Labour rates in boom areas seem to be up by 50% 100% whilst slack areas are little changed from the mid-90s. London in particular is very hot but there are other parts of the country where labour can be just as difficult to get hold of, let alone wring sensible prices out of. It's certainly not an exclusively a South East

of England problem — Edinburgh appears to be almost as expensive as London — but the result is that many of the labour rates will have to be adjusted up or down by 30% or more — I have tried to pitch them somewhere in the middle. In any event, my prices are intended only as a guideline by which you can compare your own quotations.

The current benchmark house was built in a relatively cheap area (near Peterborough). In 2002, the day rate for carpenters in this area was around £80: less than 100 miles away, in London, the day rate was around £150. One of the side-effects of this was an awful lot of commuting chippies, struggling to get to London building sites by 8a.m.

### Wastage

If you manage to work out the theoretical quantities of just about everything you need, you are still faced with the problem of knowing how much extra to order to cover wastage. Wastage is a wonderfully vague term that covers just about any and every mishap that can occur on a building site from defective materials being delivered to perfectly adequate materials apparently walking off site. There's really no way of knowing in advance what your wastage rate will be, but experience suggests that you'd be wise to over-order by between 8 and 10% on heavyside materials like bricks, blocks, sand and cement and also plastering materials. You should be able to work out timber quantities exactly, but here you will probably be blighted by timber quality not being what you require and again you would do well to add extra lengths to your totals. Buying more than you actually need is, of course, expensive but so are the frequent shopping trips which happen when you buy too little.

# Entering the Bazaar

The British consumer is used to being able to see what something costs. Visit any high street or supermarket and the price you pay will be clearly labelled on the goods or, at least, on the shelf underneath. Haggling over the price is something that you might do on holiday in Morocco or Turkey but it's thought not to be part of the British way of life.

This is far from the truth. Step off the high street and into the world of commerce (or house buying or even car purchase) and we Brits are out there haggling with the best of them. Generally speaking, when there are three or more zeros on the end of the price

tag, the gloves come off and any pretence at civilised shopping goes out of the window. Anyone responsible for purchasing building materials would do well to bear this in mind because a well organised buyer can achieve savings of 20% or more over the unprepared novice.

It helps to be an established builder. To have a proven trading record stretching back over some years and, better still, to have had a record as a prompt payer will stand anyone in good stead with their suppliers. But these days merchants are keen to attract any custom (except the doubtful payers) and if you

can establish your credit worthiness and the fact that you might be a substantial customer, if only temporarily, then you will have a strong bargaining chip.

### Inside a Builder's Merchant

Like any business, builder's merchants and all the related building trade suppliers are buying in goods and selling them on at a mark-up. The services that a merchant provides for this mark-up are:

- accessibility
- delivery (usually free)
- advice.

After a round of take-overs and mergers, there are only three national chains left, Jewsons (which took over Harcros in 1997 and Grahams in 1999) is now the largest, Travis Perkins (which swallowed Keyline in 1999), and Builder Center (part of the giant Wolseley group). In addition there are around thirty regional operations (typically with 5-10 outlets) and still a fair number of small independents, one- or two-branch outfits which may well turn over less than £1million/annum. In addition, there are specialist trade outlets dealing with plumbing (cf. Wolseley's Plumb Center), electrics, roofing, joinery, ironmongery and glass. Whether they are any good or not depends an awful lot on the quality of the staff working in any particular branch and, especially, the branch manager. Needless to say, the smaller operations tend to give a more personalised service but can't always match the prices offered by the large chains.

A general merchant will hope — indeed need — to make an average mark-up in excess of 50% to stay in business. Thus, if they purchase some paint for, say, £100 then they will need to sell it for £150. An awful lot of their business is conducted with preferred clients at mark-ups much lower than this 50% and so to balance this out they must sell a great deal at mark-ups of 70, 80 or even 100%. So, one of the keys to getting good prices from a builder's merchant is to become known as a preferred client. Step one is to open an account.

## Trading accounts

To set up an account with a builder's merchant, you would normally be asked for a bank reference and two trade references. The bank reference shouldn't be a problem (de-pending on your relationship with your bank of course) but trade references could prove difficult if you've never had a trading account. Instead, write a letter of introduction saying who you are and what your project is. This will carry far more clout if you include a copy of the plans, which they may well offer to quote on.

If you've never had a trading account (and if you are not in business on your own account there is no particular reason to have had one), they operate under a very simple code. When you pick goods up or have them delivered you get a dispatch or delivery note. The tax invoice arrives a few days later by post (this is the one you must keep for VAT records) and every month you are sent a statement of account which summarises all the invoices you have run up on your account in the previous calendar month. Normal terms are that you must pay off the outstanding balance on your account at the end of each subsequent month; i.e. if you spent £500 on account with Jewsons during April, you would be required to give them a cheque for £500 at the end of May. In effect you get between 30 and 60 days credit depending on whether your purchase happened at the beginning of the month or the end of the month. Sometimes postponing a purchase by a day or two — so as to avoid the month end — can get you an extra 30 days credit. Builders merchants know all about these tricks and they consistently get more sales in the first week of a month than they do in the last week.

Don't just open an account and start purchasing materials as and when you need them — you'll pay top whack this way. If you've get the whole job priced up you know that you will have some serious prices back because they suspect you will have got prices from the competition. You may well be able to improve on these quoted prices. A question you occasionally get asked over the phone by a builder's merchant is "Is this a job you are actually doing?" Probably sounds rather silly but they are sounding you out: if you're just estimating you get one price, if you are buying you get a better price. They quite expect you to go the rounds of local suppliers and they want to have a bit of fat they can lose on the next call.

This practice of haggling over prices is common to almost all areas of building supplies except the DIY sheds (Homebase, B&Q, etc.). It's partly volume driven (that is, if you buy 150 sheets of plasterboard you'll get a better rate than if you buy just one), but it also has much to do with the cosy understanding that exists between builders and their suppliers, which goes to make builder's rates look cheaper than they actually are — or to put it another way, to discourage the DIY enthusiast from getting out of bed. The levels of discount vary from product to product and just to make it complicated some merchants operate two, three or even four levels of discount off the retail price. Some products are sold with a list price from which you have to negotiate the biggest discount you can get; other products have no list prices and the prices paid for them just come down to negotiation. Purchasing well is of course an art. Get too pushy and the merchants will get annoyed and shut up shop. Too relaxed and they'll squeeze whatever extra they can get out of you.

Now, as recently as the 80s what I have just written would have practically barred me from ever setting foot in a builder's merchant again. But slowly the worm is turning and the trade merchants are far more aware of a) the competition from the DIY sheds and b) the growth of the selfbuild market. Most merchants I talk to are only too willing to supply one-off builders at somewhere near their best prices. They have had too many cosy relationships with "trusted trade customers" turn horribly sour and now the order of the day is to do any business which pays. So even if you are a coven of Bangladeshi single-parent lesbians, don't feel you'd not be welcome — although you'll probably still get funny looks in the cement shed.

A new development is the arrival of selfbuild buying clubs which promise to cut right through all the delicate negotiations of trying to nail down best prices. Clubs isn't strictly speaking what they are; they are businesses juts like any other but in exchange for you offering to put almost all your business

*Despite the tales of financial irregularities, Wickes remains a reliable source of cheap building materials, used widely by both the trade and DIY enthusiasts*

their way, they promise unbeatable prices. You trade flexibility for price. There are currently two competing businesses in this market, Buildplan (part of the Buildstore group which also does land and finance) and HousebuilderXL. Both will undertake take-offs as well as quotes for materials.

## Buying Direct

This whole question of who supplies whom is still a pretty murky area. Most manufacturers take the view that they should support the established distribution channels (i.e. the general merchants) and consequently you will have to shop there for the product. For instance, you can't buy plastic drain ware direct even if you are Barratt Homes. On the other hand, there are manufacturers like Rytons (who produce roof ventilation) who readily sell via mail order to all comers but who, consequently, tend to get blackballed by builder's merchants so that their product is little known. As a general rule, manufacturers do not deal direct with end users except where they set up their own distribution channels, such as Magnet. To make the whole picture thoroughly confusing, you will find that some distributors (notably Jewsons) will have own brand items on sale which suggests that they are manufacturers. Just like Sainsburys are farmers. But this doesn't mean you are buying direct. What really matters is not which brand or where you bought it from but was it cheap and was it any good?

## B&Q and Homebase

One of the reasons for the success of the edge of town DIY sheds is the perceived unfriendliness of the builder's merchant to non-trade customers. The Saturday afternoon patio-building brigade have long felt that they have been treated as second-class customers at trade outlets and, what is worse, have been forced to pay over the odds for this dubious privilege. How much more convivial to shop at a place where the prices are actually displayed, even if they aren't particularly cheap, and where the staff probably know even less than you do — "'ere, Sharon, do we sell rawlplugs?" " I dunno, tell him to look in lighting."

As a rule the DIY sheds are not very competitive on heavyside, bulky materials but tend to be pretty good on the finishes, provided you are not looking for anything fancy.

The one exception I've found is Wickes, whose prices are keen right across the board. Wickes is a hybrid between a builder's merchant and a DIY shed; the prices are close to (and sometimes better than) a regular builder's merchant's trade prices but they are also on full display — a big advantage to rookie builders. Wickes are now a near-nationwide chain and, though they don't operate credit accounts like the trade outlets, they are well worth looking out for. In 1996, Wickes was embroiled in a financial scandal of its own making and for a while looked like disappearing altogether but it has successfully climbed out of that morass and continues to be good value.

## Specialists

The general builder's merchant is to the building trade what a convenience store is to the high street shopper. You can get just about anything you want there and the prices are reasonable. However, for the serious shopper, intent on sniffing out bargains, there are any number of specialist suppliers who can usually undercut the general merchants in their own areas. The trouble is they take some hunting out, and often they don't want to be bothered by small fry, one-off housebuilders, let alone amateurs. You could spend an awful lot of time tracking down specialist suppliers and not save more than a few hundred quid overall, and it may well be that you decide the convenience (and often helpfulness) of a local builder's merchant is worth hanging on to.

However, I would not be doing my duty if I weren't to make you aware of how the professionals do it. Where do they go shopping? Well you could do worse than let your fingers do the walking and look in the Yellow Pages; this is where you will find many of the best local contacts, and subcontractors too for that matter. The general builder's merchants do still get a look in. They are conspicuously strong when it comes to supplying cement, drains, timber, plastering materials and joinery, but they tend to be out-priced by specialists in most other areas. However, do bear in mind that whilst the general merchants are to some extent geared to wallies asking stupid questions, the specialists usually expect you to know what you are talking about. Ask a steel stockholder what you should use to reinforce your garage floor and you'll probably get told some awful mother-in-law joke.

### Sand and Aggregates

Straight from quarries or via specialist hauliers. Check Yellow Pages under Quarries.

### Cement, Lime

General merchants are usually the best place to buy.

### Bricks, Blocks, Pavings

Besides the general merchants there are a number of specialist brick wholesalers (or factors) who specialise in supplying full loads direct to site. Look out for Brickability, particularly good for sourcing block paving. Also check Yellow Pages under Brick Merchants.

### Building Stone

Either direct from quarries or via brick or stone merchants. Check Yellow Pages under Stone Merchants.

### Readymix Concrete

Direct from readymix outfits. Check Yellow Pages under Concrete — Ready Mixed.

### Drainage

General merchants do well, though there are some specialists who are worth checking out. John Davidson Pipes are good for Osma and Burdens are good all round groundworks suppliers.

### Joinery

Mass-produced joinery is usually best sought out via the general merchants. Magnet joinery, which is characterised by being "good value", is alone amongst the major producers in being only available from its own depots — and for not making any deliveries. For workshop joinery, look in the Yellow Pages under Joinery Mfrs.

### Timber and Timber Boards

General merchants tend to do well here though some are conspicuously better than others. There are some specialist timber merchants and these are the places to look for unusual species. Check Yellow Pages under Timber Merchants.

*Encon are a nationwide insulation specialist particularly well geared to the needs of small builders*

### Roof Trusses

Many timber merchants run up roof trusses as a side line and this is a good line of approach. There are specialists though they are few and far between. One with a good reputation and near nationwide coverage is Scotts of Thrapston.

### Insulation

There are many specialist suppliers in this field and they usually undercut the general merchants. Check Yellow Pages under Insulation materials. Don't overlook the Insulation Installers section; many of these offer very good value either for supply only or supply and fix.

### Roofing

Another area where specialists reign supreme both as suppliers and subcontractors. Most Yellow Pages have several pages of both Roofing Materials and Roofing Services.

### Guttering

Buy from general merchants unless you want something better than the industry standard uPVC fittings.

### Lintels

Again buy from general merchants.

### Steel Beams, Reinforcing

Usually the steel stockholders offer the best value. They have their own Yellow Pages section.

### Glass

Again the specialists usually offer the best value, certainly cheaper than buying your glass with your joinery. Check Yellow Pages under Glass Merchants and Glaziers. Norman & Underwood have a good reputation for sealed units and supply to most of S.England.

### Plumbing

Plumbers buy from specialist plumber's merchants who get their own Yellow Pages section.

### Electrics

Look in Yellow Pages under Electrical Supplies Wholesalers or Retailers.

### Kitchens

As the section on kitchens, hopefully, makes clear, your kitchen could come from any number of sources: joinery shops, general merchants, kitchen specialists, you name it. There are also worktop specialists, appliance wholesalers and over 1000 kitchen unit manufacturers, many supplying direct. Details of many of these suppliers are in the section Kitchens in Chapter 11, Room by Room.

### Plastering

General merchants pick up the great bulk of sales to plasterers. However the Yellow Pages, Plastering & screeding, is a good source of contacts for hiring plasterers and dry-liners.

### Paints, Stains

Decorators' Merchants get a listing in Yellow Pages but for many people a general merchant or even a DIY shed will be just as cheap and more convenient.

### Ironmongery

There are specialist stockists offering wholesale prices but a one-off housebuilder is still going to do better by buying the right amounts rather than chasing extra keen prices. General merchants discount heavily on bulk orders and do well here. Also check local Bolt and Nut stockists in Yellow Pages. One firm which sells all manner of lightside building materials, delivered direct to small sites throughout England and Wales is R&J Builder's Hardware. Another is Screwfix who specialise in mail order nails and screws. Note that at most general merchants, price breaks for screws very often don't start till you've purchased more than 1000, so if you need just nine screws of a particular size there really is little point buying a whole box of 200.

### Door Furniture

If you want anything unusual, check out Architectural Ironmongers in the Yellow Pages.

### Ceramic Tiles

Check under Tile Mfrs & Suppliers. United Tile are a nationwide supplier and a very good source for basic ceramics — many builder's merchants buy from them

### Garage Doors

Check under Garage Doors.

This list is by no means exhaustive but I hope you have gleaned that in many cases the Yellow Pages is an essential reference tool both for digging out materials and for finding subcontractors. For items like central vacuum cleaners, underfloor heating and heat recovery units, where there may well be no local agents, the obvious place to look is in the self-build magazines, where the nationwide businesses actively seeking work are likely to be advertising. The directory at the end of this chapter includes head office phone numbers for all contacts that I've mentioned.

### *Salvage*

One other important area I've not touched on are the salvage yards. Time was when salvage yards were a source of cheap building materials, but there has been a flight to quality in this market and these days you are much more likely to be sniffing around expensive architectural gems which you probably won't be able to afford. If you are seriously into using salvaged building materials, you would do well to identify as early as possible what exactly it is you are going to get because incorporating changes to materials specification during construction can be very costly. There are hundreds of reclaimed building materials yards all over the country, varying in size from a couple of sheds in a back garden to multi-acre sites better equipped than the average builder's merchant. If you want to look further afield than your local Yellow Pages area, contact Salvo who keep a good database of material recyclers all over the UK. They are also one of the very few organisations in this book to run a cool web page — http://www.salvo.co.uk

Tool and equipment hire is a rather specialised area which deserves a section to itself. As with most things in the field of project management, a little planning beforehand will reap dividends along the way. What equipment you need to hire (or buy) depends very much on how you plan to manage your build. For instance, if you are entrusting the whole shooting match to a main contractor, then you really shouldn't need anything at all. But if you are acting as the main contractor and hiring subcontractors to complete the various trades, you will need to discuss each subcontractor's requirements beforehand.

It can be a confusing area. For instance, some subcontractors — notably plumbers, electricians and most carpenters — tend to come fully fitted out with toolkits and access equipment: others, typically bricklayers, expect you to provide everything other than their trowels and their levels. With groundworks, you tend to hire the kit and the labour together as a single unit — thus when a JCB is quoted at £160 a day you are getting both a JCB and a driver for that price.

## Scaffolding

A specialised area of plant hire that is normally undertaken by either dedicated scaffolders or sometimes roofing gangs. A standard scaffolding contract would specify an agreed price for a hire period of eight or, perhaps, ten weeks; if the hire continues beyond the agreed period, a surcharge is levied — typically 8% of the original price per week. The original price would include for three or sometimes four visits from the scaffolders to erect the different levels (known as lifts) needed for the other trades to put up the house.

Single-storey houses (and detached garages) will typically need only one lift but its level will have to be adjusted between brickwork and roofing; a two storey house needs two lifts, each being adjusted in level at some point. Guide prices for scaffolding are £6 per metre run per lift and to calculate the relevant metre runs add 15% to the perimeter measurements of the buildings you wish to scaffold to get the scaffolder's lengths. A guide price for a four bedroomed house with detached garage would be around £800 for ten weeks hire, followed by a £64/week surcharge for longer hire periods. If you want to take control of the scaffolding process itself, there is a system called Kwikstage by Kwikform UK which just slots together, rather similar to erecting an aluminium tower scaffold, mak-

ing it particularly suitable for those who are taking a more hands-on approach and want to have scaffolding erected for much longer than the normal time span. Kwikform provide some training for people who have never used scaffolding before or, alternatively, can provide an erection service. Rental prices for a four bedroom house- sized project work out at around £50/week.

## Skips

Part of your build plan should involve a close look at how you plan to dispose of waste; for many small builders a skip is a practical and economical solution. The basic cost of a builder's standard sized skip has all but trebled since the introduction of Landfill tax in 1996. By April 2004, this tax will have risen to £14/tonne, equivalent to £112 per skip. Ouch. Who said stealth taxes were dead? The days of the £200 skip cannot be far off but even so it may still make sense to use one on tight sites if you wish to run a clean and efficient building site.

Skips come in three sizes:
- LARGE hold 6.2m³ ("8 yards"), = around 7 8 tons and will cost £150-180 for one week and £4 extra for each subsequent week
- MEDIUM hold 3m³ ("4 yards"), = around 5 tons and will cost £100 for one week
- MINI-SKIPS hold 1.5m³ ("2 yards"), = up to 2.5 tons and are usually only hired for two or three days max. at a cost of around £70.

The rental element is usually surprisingly small (typically £5/week) and so you don't save money by delaying the arrival of a skip — you simply end up having to handle your rubbish twice over. Given that all building sites produce copious quantities of rubbish, I think that having a skip on site (certainly during the latter stages of the build) is essential: if you disagree, then at least have some coherent alternative strategy worked out for waste disposal.

## Site Fencing

There are an increasing number of sites where some sort of perimeter fencing is advisable, if only to stop unwanted visitors clambering all over your building site and walking off with your tools. The CDM health and safety regulations have also meant that professional builders are being forced to examine their policies in these areas because of accidents occurring with children playing on sites. Though a self builder will be largely exempt from these regulations, that is no reason for ignoring their importance and if you are unable to provide round the clock supervision to a site, you should consider some form of fencing if your site is vulnerable.

You can hire steel fencing for about 50p/metre/week (less for long periods) but it is the province of the specialist. Check out SGB's Heras Readifence which is about six-foot high and is very easy to assemble yet surprisingly secure. If you need security fencing for

*Scaffolding contracts usually stipulate extra charges if the scaffolding is up for more than 10 weeks*

more than five months, it will probably pay you to buy it and resell when you have finished.

### Tool Hire Shops

If you want to stay ahead of the game, then make sure you have opened trading accounts with a couple of tool hire shops because you will save yourself an awful lot of faffing about. For many novice project managers, tool and plant hire is one of those things that you just stumble into once the project is up and running. But after you've been and hired three things and left £50 deposits which did or didn't get credited to your final bill and anyway you've gone and lost the paperwork which was in the front of the car but now you cant find it...you'll wish you had opened a trading account at the hire shop too. If you do, you will be able to take tools for as long as you want without having to pay any deposit. Deliveries and collections are also much easier to organise — most hire shops will deliver and pick-up for a small charge (around £5-£10). Generally, the hire charges are structured so that you pay the highest rate over the first 24 hours, then the daily rate falls significantly if you hire for longer periods. After about ten weeks you will have paid as much in hire charges as it would cost you to

buy, so hiring really only makes sense over shorter periods. The number of things you can hire never ceases to amaze me and rather than bore you with a long list, if you are interested get hold of a catalogue yourself — Hewden Stuart's is particularly good.

### Hiring v Buying

Which begs the questions: what should you hire and what should you buy? There are a few basic bits of kit that it would seem near essential to have with you permanently and therefore you should buy if you haven't already got them. I would include in this basic hand tools like a 5m tape measure, hammer, saw, screwdriver, 1.2m spirit level, the sort of thing you need to put up shelves or assemble flat-pack kitchen units. I would also place a good, beefy (£70plus) power drill, a good extension lead (£10) and a 6m ladder (£120) on my list of essentials; this equipment will be useful for ongoing maintenance not just for housebuilding.

How much else it is worth buying is really only a question you can answer. It depends on how quickly you plan to build, how much direct involvement you will have in the building process and whether or not your selected

subbies will have their own equipment. A brickie gang will, for instance, very often expect you not only to supply tea but also a cement mixer, and it may well make good sense to buy one that you can sell on at the job's end (though don't expect very much for a used mixer). If you work in the trade or have serious DIY pretensions, then you will probably have all of the above plus a lot more and you may view your project as a wonderful opportunity to expand your range of tools. But if you don't intend to carry on building after you've finished your house, then it is pointless to lay out thousands to buy tools which will only ever fill up your precious storage space and provide rich pickings for would-be thieves.

Whether you hire or buy, the proportion of your total bill going on either hiring or buying equipment is large (often around 2% of total build costs) and can be one major hidden cost to creep up on the unwary. Also note that selfbuilders are not able to reclaim VAT on tool purchases or tool and plant hire, including such items as scaffolding and fencing.

# Trucking

Moving materials around the country is expensive. A lorry with an off-loading crane (usually a HIAB, pronounced high-ab) and driver will cost around £150-£250 to make a trip of more than half a day — although this will be less with an ordinary flat-back truck without a crane. This sum will be the same whatever the load and so from the buyer's point of view it makes good sense to get as near to a full load as possible. The best economies come when ordering 20 tonnes, which is usually a full payload.

### What's in a Full Load?

A 20-tonne lorry can shift:
- about 8000 standard bricks
- or 7200 block pavers ( =144m²)
- or 1440 dense blocks ( =144m²)
- or 2400 clinker blocks (= 240m²).

Aerated blocks (like Thermalite) are so light that the capacity constraint on haulage tends to be volume rather than weight. 20 tonnes of super-lightweight blocks would be about 6000 blocks, which would be 36 double packs.

There are no industry standards as to how masonry materials should be packed, although there is a tendency to use shrink-wrapped plastic (which keeps watertight) and to pack in weights and quantities that fit on to a pallet. A forklift can handle over two tonnes and a common pack size is around 1 tonne (which allows two packs to be lifted at once). When ordering direct loads, you'll have to accept the nearest pack size quantity so if, for instance, you wanted 8000 bricks and your selected brick is packed in 410s (many are), you would have to settle for either 19 packs (19x410 = 7790) or 20 packs (20x410 = 8200).

Packs will either come palletted or with fork holes for forklift off-loading. The chances are a fully laden 20-tonner will not be able to get off the road, so hire of a rough-terrain forklift may be the best solution for unloading. A rough-terrain forklift and driver should be available at around £100 for a half day and is usually money well spent if the site is big enough to warrant one. Bricks and blocks can (sometimes) be set around site, making labouring much quicker and easier. A JCB with forks can be used as an alternative to a rough-terrain forklift. AB Homes, the benchmark housebuilders, employ a full time fork-lift driver who is responsible for seeing everything is stacked in the right place.

### Plasterboard

The plasterboard manufacturers all pack in the same sizes. Better prices are usually negotiable on full packs. A 22-tonne direct load would be enough for three or four large timber frame houses — probably a bit too much for your average individual builder — however, by buying in full pack sizes you should be able to make savings.

- 1200 x 2400 x 9.5mm plasterboard comes in packs of 80 (1.76tonnes)
- 1200 x 2400 x 12.5mm plasterboard comes in packs of 60 (1.66 tonnes).

### Timber

Timber has to be purchased in 20m³ lots to take advantage of bulk discounts and 20m³ is an awful lot of timber. Furthermore, CLS studwork, which is perhaps the commonest size of timber used in timber frame buildings, has to be ordered in 40m³ lots. The average timber frame house uses around 1000m of CLS — a paltry 5m³! Full loads of timber can undercut merchants' best prices by as much as 30%, but you have to have some site going to justify such orders. By and large, you'd do better to try and concentrate on buying good rather than cheap timber.

### Pallets

Many builder's merchants now charge a £15 deposit on pallets supplied to site with tonne loads of cement or whatever. This can soon mount up to a substantial sum. Reclaiming the deposit is straightforward if your paper work is in order — i.e. you can't just take the pallets back, you need to prove that you ac-

*Above: a HIAB crane at work. Right: for many years, builder's merchants have charged a deposit on pallets. Take this pile back to Jewson's and you might hope to pick up about £2,500.*

tually paid a deposit before they will refund. This practice of charging a deposit on pallets does not yet appear to have extended to supplies direct from manufacturers so you may well end up with some pallets with a deposit on their heads whilst others are free spirits.

# Concrete

### Site Mix v Readymix

One person working with an electric or diesel mixer will mix 1m³ of wet concrete in about an hour. Making concrete on site in a mixer will cost between £40/m³ (Mats £28, Lab £12) and £60/m³ (M £46, L £14), largely dependant on how cheaply the aggregates (i.e. the sand and gravel) are bought, which itself depends on the quantity of aggregates bought. In largish (10 ton +) loads, they should be obtainable at around £6/tonne; in loads under 2 tonnes, this may rise to around £15/tonne. Another factor to consider is availability of mixers (usually hired at £10/day). As a rule, readymix will be cheaper when more than 2.5m³ is needed. Readymix loads are always going to be preferable where consistent concrete strength is important. Really, for anything other than laying the odd patio, it has to be site-delivered readymix concrete everytime.

### Strengths

Traditionally the design strengths of concrete have been expressed in ratios of volumes cement:sand:gravel (as in 1:3:6). However, things are stirring in the sleepy world of concrete and there are now at least three other labelling systems in operation. If you are mixing concrete on site, the old ratio system, as described, is fine and is actually very useful as you can use it to gauge how many shovels need to go into the mixer, although note that it is usually most convenient to have a sand and gravel mixture delivered to site — ask for "all-in ballast." If, however, you phone up for a readymix delivery you may do well just to explain what it is you want the concrete for and let them work out which mix it is you need:

- Foundation Mixes: 1:3:6 is traditional on site batched concrete. In readymix terms this is now known as a GEN 1 mix

- Floor Slab Mix: 1:2:4: is traditional volume way of looking at it — i.e. it's a bit stronger than the foundation mix. The readymix equivalent is usually referred to as a GEN 3. If you are screeding over your slab, you may be able to use a GEN 1 instead of a GEN 3. Basically, the lower the GEN number, the cheaper the mix. GEN 3 and GEN 4 are about 5-10% more expensive than GEN 1. There are lots of other more specialised mixes around. Reinforced work requires reinforced mixes, designated RC. Driveways and paths have their own mix known as PAV 1. If in doubt, ask the readymix rep.

When you add water to readymix, you weaken it. It often leaves the readymix yard in a perfect condition and is watered on site,

*Each of these is capable of holding 6m³ of readymixed concrete at an average cost of £250/truckload. The benchmark house used five loads.*

## Concrete Pumps

To hire a concrete pump, allow around £150-£200 per session. They pump a full load (6m³) in 20 minutes, about three times quicker than three men barrowing might do. Concrete pumps make financial sense on jobs with more than 30m³ of concrete to be poured but there are other reasons for using them, notably when speed is important or access is difficult. If using a pump be sure to let the readymix supplier know, because the mix design is wetter and the through-put of lorries is much faster than on a normal job. It's also a little more expensive.

## Foundation Flow

RMC have introduced a self-placing foundation concrete called Foundation Flow. It saves on having to barrow, dump or pump concrete around your foundation trenches. It sells for 10% premium but they reckon you can claw back the costs through labour and/or plant savings.

making a joke of its original spec. Watered concrete is the biggest single cause of concrete failure.

## Charging for Air

Readymix lorries mostly carry 6m³, though some are 5m³. Much of the cost involved with readymixed concrete is transport so the amount you pay depends very much on how far the truck has to travel so it pays to buy local. Prices for basic mixes like GEN 1 currently vary from around £45/m³ up to over £60/m³ in and around London. But be aware that on your first two truckloads you will be charged something for the empty carrying space on each lorry. So if you were to order 8m³ of GEN 1, for instance, you'd pay for 8m³ of concrete and 4m³ of unused capacity, often at around a third the price of the concrete itself. If you order over 12m³ (i.e. more than two loads) this charge is usually waived but be sure to find out beforehand how it is to be applied.

# Cement

The standard building cement, packed in 25kg bags, is known as OPC which stands for Ordinary Portland Cement and sometimes this is referred to as Portland Cement. The cement (and concrete) market is dominated by a small number of firms (RMC, Rugby, Blue Circle, Castle) and, being a mature industry, you'll find that there is remarkably little variation in cement prices — though cynics may have an alternative explanation for this. By all means shop around — current prices are hovering around £90/tonne (£2.30/bag) — but note that it is worth sticking with the same manufacturer once you've made your decision; cement colours vary and you can ruin face brickwork with a nasty change in mortar colours. Our benchmark house will have absorbed something like 4 tonnes of cement (excluding concrete) so, with a total value of under £400, cement purchase is never going to be a bank-breaker.

## Mix Designs

How strong do you want it? Strong mixes (1 part cement to 3 parts sand, henceforth 1:3) are used where the mortar must stand on its own (i.e. a floor screed) or is likely to get very wet (i.e. some underground work); for brick and blockwork and for wall renders, it is important not to get an over strong mix and also to get some plasticity into the mix. This is usually accomplished by using additives (such as FebMix or Cementone) or by substituting lime for some cement. Given the choice, most bricklayers would prefer to lay with lime in the mortar but it's not universally admired; it's bulky and easily wasted and transporting split bags is a pain. Also mixing has to be carried out more accurately as the addition of a third ingredient adds to the likelihood of changes in mortar colour.

## Masonry Cements

There are several other options available, all designed to make on-site gauging a little easier and a little more accurate. Wallcrete masonry cement is probably the best known; it consists of 85% OPC and 15% filler, usually crushed limestone. It's not as strong as OPC and doesn't behave as well as a sand:lime:cement mortar. This is because the modern, pure limes, when gauged, behave in

a way that makes the mix "fatty" and they help to cure the finished mortar, leaving it ever so slightly plastic enabling movement joints to close up. Wallcrete's fillers do not do this. A better alternative is a product from Buxton Lime Industries called Limebond which, as its name suggests, uses lime and not fillers and is, in effect, a pre-gauged package to which you just add sand. Note that Limebond is relatively new and many merchants have never even heard of it. Yet another option is to use a pre-mixed mortar (i.e. even the sand is mixed in for you)— RMC can supply these at around the £15-£20/tonne mark either in skips or tipped-off lorries.

## Idiot Proof Cements

All these masonry mortars are designed for low-strength applications like brickwork, blockwork and renders and their mistaken use in concrete mixes can present major structural problems. In contrast, Blue Circle's Mastercrete and Castle's MultiCem are designed to be completely idiot proof. They can be used in all the major cement applications (concrete, brick mortars, renders and

## 12a: Sand and Cement Estimating Guide

| | Soft Sand kg | Sharp Sand kg | O.P. Cement kg | Lime kg | Plast-iciser lt | Mortar Costs |
|---|---|---|---|---|---|---|
| **LIME MIXES (1 Cement: 1 Lime: 6 Sand)** | | | | | | |
| 1000 bricks (= 16.6m²) | 1000 | | 150 | 63 | | £ 37.80 |
| 1m² x Single Skin bricks | 60 | | 8.7 | 3.8 | | £ 2.30 |
| 1m² x100mm Blocks | 36 | | 5.2 | 2.3 | | £ 1.40 |
| 1m² x 12mm Render | | 24 | 3.5 | 1.5 | | £ 0.90 |
| **CEMENT/PLASTICISER MIXES (1 Cement: 6 Sand)** | | | | | | |
| 1000 bricks (= 16.6m²) | 1140 | | 166 | | 0.8 | £ 30.50 |
| 1m² x Single Skin bricks | 69 | | 10.1 | | 0.05 | £ 1.80 |
| 1m² x100mm Blocks | 41 | | 6 | | 0.03 | £ 1.10 |
| 1m² x 12mm Render | | 27 | 3.9 | | 0.02 | £ 0.72 |
| **SCREED MIXES (1 Cement: 3 Sand)** | | | | | | |
| 1m² x 50mm Screed | | 80 | 24 | | | £ 3.10 |
| 1m² x 65mm Screed | | 104 | 31 | | | £ 4.00 |

### Worked Example on Benchmark House

| | Amount in m² | Soft Sand kg | Sharp Sand kg | O.P. Cement kg | Lime kg | Plast-iciser lt | Mortar Costs |
|---|---|---|---|---|---|---|---|
| Brick Footings | 26 | 1794 | | 263 | | | £ 50 |
| Face Brickwork | 151 | 9060 | | 1314 | 574 | | £ 350 |
| 100mm Blockwork | 173 | 6228 | | 900 | 398 | | £ 240 |
| Render | NB. Internally, walls are dry lined | | | | | | |
| 65mm Screed | NB Ground floor finished with power floated slab | | | | | | |
| **TOTALS** | | **17,100** | **0** | **2,500** | **1,000** | **0** | **£ 600** |

screeds) and will go fatty enough in a mixer to be used without any additional additives. One brickie I know is very uncomplimentary about them, to the extent that if I was to print his comments, all you would see would be a whole bunch of asterisks.

## Lime

There is no compulsion to use cement for the construction of new buildings and there are many restoration projects where it would be advisable to avoid it altogether. The use of cement in housebuilding did not become widespread until the 1920s. Before that people used lime-only mortars which never set as hard as cement and one of the big advantages of lime mortars is that the mortar can be cleaned from the brick, making it possible for some bricks to be reused in other buildings. In contrast, cement mortars cannot be removed from bricks and cement-bedded bricks are good for nothing more than hardcore. Another advantage is that lime mortars remain slightly plastic and this pro-

vides a certain amount of flexibility to walls which helps to withstand subsidence and cracking. Whilst new builders would be best advised to stick with lime and cement mixtures for their above ground work, if you are restoring a pre-cement building then you should probably be using all lime mortar. Real lime mortar (known as lime putty) is not cheap because very little is produced nowadays but it is arguably a better way to build all round. If you wish to know more, phone the Lime Centre in Hampshire and go on one of their lime days.

## Quantities

I find it helpful to calculate how many cubic metres (m³) of mortar are needed in each application and this is how the accompanying table works. I have made some assumptions about just how far a m³ of mortar will go; if, for instance, you are laying a double-thick 215mm blockwall rather than the normal 100mm thick one, you would do well to adjust your quantities so that your coverage

is halved. The table is also complicated by the fact that there are several different mortar mixes commonly used on building sites; if you want to convert volumes (by which they are gauged) into weights (by which they are bought), look at the section called Crucial Measurements on page 233.

Another big imponderable is waste; just how do you go about allowing for it, how much will you waste? The answer is usually a surprisingly high amount though this figure varies substantially. My coverage rates are fairly conservative, allowing for between 15-30% of the m³ of mortar to end up somewhere other than you intend.

# Steel

Steel can be used in a wide variety of applications in new housebuilding and there are moves afoot to introduce steel framing as an alternative to timber framing. However, most housebuilders use it sparingly, preferring to use the traditional materials brick, concrete and timber wherever possible. Steel is the No.1 choice for standard fixings like nails and screws but elsewhere its use is restricted to a few specialised areas.

### Reinforcing

The commonest form of steel reinforcing used in housebuilding is A142 anti-crack mesh, which is often set in concrete floor slabs to add strength. The mesh costs between 75p and £1.20/m², depending on quantity needed but note that you'll need bolt croppers on site in order to cut it. It is usual (though by no means universal) to lay this in garage floor slabs. It needs to be located towards the bottom of the concrete layer in order to do its work properly. There are many other forms of steel reinforcing used in concrete but you are unlikely to come across them in housebuilding unless you are having to lay specialised foundations.

### Lintels

Though reinforced concrete is much cheaper, for many years now steel has been the preferred material for bridging the openings made by doorways and windows. The problem with concrete is that, in insulated new houses, it remains a large cold bridge through the wall which is bad news thermally and attracts condensation. Also, when viewed from outside, concrete lintels look crude and cheap. In contrast, steel can be insulated and the outer leaf support is hidden seamlessly over the top of the window or door. The market is dominated by two Welsh steel businesses, Catnic and IG, and designers usually specify their products. Alternative suppliers do exist and Dorman Long and Keystone can often be 10-15% cheaper. The most commonly used IG lintel is the L1/S, very suitable for bridging openings in cavity work with cavities up to 65mm. There is a heavy duty version, known as the L1/HD. They are made in lengths from 600mm to 4800mm and they increase in 150mm increments. The minimum end bearings must be 150mm so that an opening of 900 would need to be bridged by a lintel of 900 + 150 + 150 = 1200mm. Standard lintels tend to cost around £20-£25/lin.m. The benchmark house spend on lintels was just under £700 and £300 for steel beams used under the first floor bedroom walls.

In contrast, concrete lintels still tend to be the preferred choice to bridge internal doorways. Here the lintel is completely covered and the heat loss/condensation issue is irrelevant. The steel lintel manufacturers do produce an internal door lintel but it is not widely used. Timber framers tend use timber lintels, but note that where a brick skin is specified for the external wall, there are special steel lintels designed to do the job of just supporting the outer skin.

### Cavity Wall Ties

Where the facing material is brick, block or stone you need approx. 3.5 wall ties/m². If the inner skin of the cavity is timber frame rather than blockwork, the wall ties are a different shape and you need slightly more (about 4/m²). Look to pay between £8 and £20/100 for wall ties depending on type and quality. The benchmark house would have used around 500.

# Bricks & Blocks

Bricks remain the preferred material for external walls throughout England and Wales. They are reasonably cheap, they are well understood by the building trade, they can look attractive and, above all, they are durable. Not only should a brick wall not need any further care after construction, it should actually improve with age.

### Selecting the Right Brick

There are dozens of brick manufacturers and thousands of bricks to choose from. There is also a substantial business in reclaiming bricks from old buildings — though it only amounts to 1% of total brick sales, that's still 40 million bricks reclaimed each year. If you are limited by budget you will probably find your choice is rather narrow, but if you are prepared to pay more than £250/1000 (that's 25p/brick) then a whole world of choice opens up. Choosing a brick is quite an involved process and it is notoriously difficult to visualise what a brick wall will look like from a manufacturer's display board. Most British bricks are baked clay and these are the ones to go for if you are seeking out a character brick. There are other materials, notably concrete and sandlime, that get used to make bricks but the overall effect tends to be industrial looking and, crucially, there are no great price savings to be had — unlike in the world of roof tiles and block paving where concrete is invariably cheaper than clay.

There are two technical ratings for clay bricks to do with frost resistance and salt content. The frost rating is broken down into three categories being F (high), M (medium) and O (appalling), and the salt rating is split into just two categories, L (low) and N (normal). What does it matter? With frost, the problem is spalling, where the face of the brick starts crumbling away. Very soft bricks, rated O, would not be acceptable in any situation in the UK where they would be exposed to the elements — i.e. outside — but only severe frost areas (Scotland, the Welsh mountains and the English Lakes and Pennines) would require an F-rated brick. M-rated bricks are fine for almost all applications outside these areas, but note that in certain exposed applications (notably chimneys) you will be asked to add copings and overhanging courses if not using an F-rated brick.

The matter of low or normal salt content is not as important to housebuilders. In very wet areas (usually within sight of the Irish Sea) it is advisable to avoid bricks with an N rating as you may be asked to use sulphate-resisting cement. A merchant will be able to advise as to a brick's rating — but what if you're using second-hand bricks? You'll have to check your source and convince the building inspector that they are suitable for outdoor use. The building inspector will very probably have seen the brick before and will be able to assess its suitability. But do check before forking out. Take samples into the building control office if necessary.

### Engineering Bricks

These are particularly hard wearing and strong. Not only do they offer much greater structural support (and so they are a natural choice for supporting steel beams) but they are also extremely moisture-resistant. This second quality, combined with some very low prices (under £120/1000), has seen engineering bricks being widely used as a damp-proof course (DPC). The semi-gloss finish on the bricks (which are either blood red or slate blue) can be used to good effect in creating two-tone effect brickwork both at DPC level and elsewhere on brick elevations.

## Specials

This is the term given to bricks that aren't a standard rectangular box shape. These get used, typically, on details like cills and brick wall cappings where you want to stop rainwater pooling. Some of the more common specials are readily available but many have to be made to order which is a) expensive and b) time-consuming. If your chosen design incorporates specials then don't assume that they will just turn up with the rest of the bricks; you may have to wait another two months.

In response to these problems with procuring specials, there are now brick-bonding services which will cut and glue ordinary bricks into out-of-the-ordinary shapes. At between £3 and £4 per brick they are a little cheaper than unusual specials and with a turnaround of two weeks they are somewhat quicker. It's a particularly useful service if you are using a second-hand brick from which you could never otherwise hope to obtain specials. Try MC Brick Cutting Services.

## Brickies Rates

As of 2002, our local rate is up to £350/1000 face bricks laid, double what it was in 1995. In some cheaper areas it's still down around the £200/k mark whilst in London it's broken through £500/k. On typical British residential sites, a two-and-one gang (that's two brickies serviced by one labourer) will lay 1000 bricks a day — though normally they alternate between brick and blockwork. There are 60 bricks per square metre on single skin work. A rate such as this would normally include extra work like corners and reveals and fixing joinery and insulation, but not overly-fiddly details like dogs-toothing gables which would be negotiated separately. If paying brickies by the square metre, be clear whether or not your square metres are "solid" (i.e. include openings).

## Brick Factors

55% of British bricks go into new houses and the suppliers have developed specialised antennae for detecting new house building activity: note that if you phone up a merchant inquiring after bricks, the first thing you get asked is "Where is the site?" Why do they all want to know? Well, brick merchants get money for simply identifying (or "covering") a new site, even if they don't get the subsequent order. So the moment they inform the manufacturer that there is a new house going to be built in Pig Lane, they clock a commission, rising to near 20% if it turns into a sale. They also shut out competitors from this particular deal — only the initial contact gets offered the commission.

It would probably be better if you didn't know that. It's a cosy little relationship between manufacturers and merchants that reeks of Rip-off Britain. But would you get your bricks cheaper if it didn't happen? Maybe. The businesses which survive in this niche are called brick factors and the good factors have ever such long antennae. A factor will wave brick panels in front of you with gusto and the bricks will not be identifiable as Ibstocks or Hansons but have names like Mellow Red or Autumn Gold, renaming the bricks to make it harder for you to get alternative quotes. Don't get me wrong: dealing with brick factors can be fun and some of them do terrific deals, but there is more than a hint of the Middle Eastern souk about the whole process. As far as I can ascertain, this rigmarole is more or less restricted to bricks, although it is rumoured to occur with up-market roof tiles and pavings.

# Blocks

With blocks, there are two qualities that concern us: the first is strength and the second is how well it insulates. In many countries blocks are manufactured with feature finishes and are used extensively, instead of bricks or stone, as external wall finishes in their own right, but in Britain this hasn't proved to be a popular technique, except where cheaper substitutes for stone are sought. So when we look at building blocks we are analysing how well they perform structurally, not how good do they look.

## Block Strength

Block strength is calculated in Newton/mm$^2$, known in the trade as "Newtons" or just plain "N." Roughly speaking the more cement in the block, the higher the strength (or the more Newtons it is said to have). Most blocks qualify for the basic 3.5N strength, though some applications require 7N blocks (i.e. below ground and, some say, floor blocks). You will find a number of utility blocks on the market, often at a price less than £5.00/m$^2$, but their strength is not guaranteed.

## Block Types

There are many shapes and sizes of block made but there is an industry standard which is 440x215mm. This is the equivalent of six standard bricks and you need 10 of these blocks to build a m$^2$ of wall. They are usually 100mm thick, though some of the super-lightweight varieties are thicker in order to get their insulation values up to par.

### The Dense Block

Uncomfortably heavy to lift, they are usually used below ground, often at 7N strength. Cheap — full loads cost just around £5.00/m$^2$.

### Lightweight Clinker Blocks

Almost half the weight of a dense block, these are often used on the inner leaf of insulated cavities and in partition walls. They provide an excellent keying surface for plasters. They are also widely used in beam-and-block flooring; they are very similarly priced to dense blocks.

### Aerated Blocks

Introduced from Scandinavia, these blocks have become a huge hit in the UK market and more than 50% of new homes have been using them. There are four manufacturers, Celcon, Thermalite, Tarmac and Durox (though consolidation is likely soon which may reduce this number to just two). Their big plus was that they packed enough insulating properties to allow builders to carry on with empty cavities. They met all the thermal requirements thrown at them until 2002 when the newly revised Part L began calling for U values of 0.35. At this level, aerated blocks struggle without some additional insulation. You need 300mm wide blocks to get down to 0.35. Whether this will prove a big stumbling block for this type of block remains to be seen but Celcon have responded by launching a solid walling system called Jamera which they hope will catch on. It also uses thin-joint mortars, a type of glue based adhesive laid just 3mm thick instead of the normal 10mm cement mortars. Thin-joint systems are much quicker to lay but to date uptake has been a little slow in Britain.

## Fair-Faced Blockwork

As already mentioned, fair-faced blockwork is not a popular option in the UK. There are, however, a number of manufacturers, such as Forticrete, specialising in this type of finish, though the overall effect is usually hard and modern. One area where concrete blocks are commonly used in exterior applications is when people are looking for a cheap substitute for stone. Reconstituted stone blocks can look like a convincing imitation of real stone at a fraction of the cost. Check RMC Peakstone and Marshalls of Halifax.

## Trade Rates

An all-in rate of between £6 and £10/m$^2$ for laying blocks is OK, depending on area. All-in rate means that your brickies would fix wall ties, cavity wall insulation, joinery, lintels, airbricks, DPCs, etc. as they go. Also using an all-in rate saves the hassle of measuring non-standard runs like chimneys. A two-and-one gang should be able to lay between 30 and 40m$^2$/day.

# Timber & Joinery

You rarely see the price of timber advertised and you rarely see it on display in timber yards. This is because there is a wide range of prices charged for timber. The regular trade prices are usually around 33% less than those charged to casual in-off-the-street customers and large orders will get another 5-10% off the regular trade prices. The way to get good prices is invariably to send your (hopefully) large order in for quotation at least two weeks before you require it. By all means include second-fix items like skirting boards which you may not need for several months; it makes you look more like a serious customer.

## Carcassing

Most construction grade carcassing timber is spruce, usually referred to as carcassing, whitewood or deal — presumably because it's a good deal. It is relatively cheap and easy to work but it suffers from being one of the least durable timbers available. Of more interest to the builder is the strength of any particular piece of timber and there are several grading systems run by the timber trade for assessing this. The commonest form of grading at present is to see timber labelled as SC3 or SC4. SC4 timber is the stronger and the advantage of paying the 5% more for SC4 timber is that you are allowed to use them over longer spans. For instance the longest distance you can bridge with a 50x175mm section of timber is 3170mm in SC3, but this length rises to 3380mm in SC4. SC3 and SC4 are British Standards and moves are afoot to replace them with Euro gradings, C16 and C24 respectively.

## Kiln-Dried Timber

In 1995 it became compulsory to use low moisture timber in all internal structural applications — which means joists, studwork walls and roofs. Low moisture is defined as having a moisture content below 20% and in effect this means using kiln-dried timber. The advantage of kiln dried timber is that it is dimensionally stable — it will not twist or warp as cheaper timber will, especially if it's been treated — and that it is regularised, which means that it

has all been milled to an accuracy of 1mm. It is thus very much quicker and easier to put up accurate studwork and to fix flooring joists; non-regularised timber can sometimes vary in depth by 5mm or more and this is very noticeable when flooring is being laid over it. Having said that, there is a lot of supposedly regularised timber around which varies by plus or minus 5mm, sometimes even more, so the term is regularly abused.

## Timber Treatment

Spruce is not classified as a durable timber and this means that it is liable to rot if exposed to continuous damp. This has led to the increasingly widespread use of timber preservatives to add durability. These preservatives can be applied by brush on site but

more normally the timbers are immersed in a vacuum-pressure tank, which leads to them being referred to as having been "vacuum treated." There are two rival systems in regular use, Tanalising and Protimising. There is little to choose between them in price — they add around 10% to the cost of the raw timber — but they do perform rather differently. Tanalising is a water-based treatment which tends to dye the wood a light green colour although there is now a brown-dye version as well (useful if you plan to use brown or black stains); Protimising is spirit-based and usually leaves the wood uncoloured, although sometimes a red dye is added. You can usually tell if timber has been Protimised from the pungent, petrol-like smell. Generally tanalising is preferred in applications where

## 12b: Chippies Rates

| | TIME in MINS | Rate at £15/hr | | |
| --- | --- | --- | --- | --- |
| | | EACH | LIN.M | M² |
| Placing Joists | 10 | | £ 2.50 | |
| Joist Hangers | 10 | £ 2.50 | | |
| Joist Notching | 3 | £ 0.75 | | |
| Straps | 5 | £ 1.25 | | |
| Chipboard Floor | 15 | | | £ 3.75 |
| Plywood Floor | 25 | | | £ 6.25 |
| T&G Flooring | 40 | | | £ 10.00 |
| Wallplates | 15 | | £ 3.75 | |
| Standard Roof Trusses | 120 | £ 30.00 | | |
| Cut Roof/lin m | 15 | | £ 3.75 | |
| Cut Roof/m2 | 80 | | | £ 20.00 |
| Fascia | 15 | | £ 3.75 | |
| Soffit | 30 | | £ 7.50 | |
| Bargeboards | 15 | | £ 3.75 | |
| Studwork | 10 | | £ 2.50 | |
| Noggins | 10 | | £ 2.50 | |
| Studwork in m2 | 35 | | | £ 8.75 |
| Windowboard | 20 | £ 5.00 | | |
| Door Linings/Stop | 45 | £ 11.25 | | |
| External Doors | 250 | £ 62.50 | | |
| French Doors | 400 | £ 100.00 | | |
| Fitting Doorsets | 100 | £ 25.00 | | |
| Internal Doors | 120 | £ 30.00 | | |
| Architrave | 8 | | £ 2.00 | |
| Skirting - Nailed | 12 | | £ 3.00 | |
| Skirting - Screwed | 20 | | £ 5.00 | |
| Clapboard | 40 | | | £ 10.00 |
| Sheathing | 12 | | | £ 3.00 |
| Timber Panel Erection | 12 | | | £ 3.00 |

This table is, hopefully, self-explanatory. It covers most of the regular activities of the carpenter engaged in new housebuilding. However, it is a fairly basic summary and there are many complicated details which cannot be so easily summarised.

Prices include both hanging and furnishing doors

there is contact with the ground like fencing and protimising is preferred for structural timber (and joinery) because it is less likely to cause the timber to twist.

### Joinery Grade Redwood

The other commonly used wood in UK housebuilding is pine, or redwood as it is known. This is a denser and slightly more durable timber than spruce, and it is commonly used to manufacture windows and internal applications like skirting boards, floorboards and matchboard walling. It is more easily worked than spruce and it is most frequently seen in timber yards with a planed finish, usually referred to as Planed All Round (PAR) or Planed Square Edge (PSE). Scandinavia is the major supplier of redwoods.

You can use cheaper whitewoods for internal applications but they suffer from having what are called dead knots, which tend to work loose and fall out with time. Your mice may appreciate the odd dead knot in your skirting board but you will probably prefer to have timber with live knots which move with the timber as it expands and contracts.

### Buying Redwood 5ths

Scandinavian timber is quality graded into 6 groups, 1 being the highest and 6 being the lowest; 1 will be clear knot-tree timber, 6 will have large knots and possibly waney edges as well. Most planed timber sold in the UK is sold as "Best" and includes anything from grades 1-4, weeding out only grades 5 and 6. Increasingly we are seeing grade 5 coming on to the market — known as "5ths" — and it sells for 25% less than the normal, unsorted timber. Grade 5 timber is very much more knotty but most people find it perfectly adequate for their purposes. It is increasingly available for fascias, barge boards and skirtings. And whilst I'm on about skirtings, consider that there is another new development in this field and that is the use of MDF boarding to replace internal joinery items such as skirtings, architraves and windowboards (and soon door linings as well). MDF mouldings are about 15% more expensive than best redwood (therefore about 50% more than fifths); but it comes in lengths of 5.4m which can be a boon AND it comes undercoated ready for topcoat. If you are planning on a painted finish to your interior woodwork, then MDF is going to save you time and money.

### Specialist Softwoods

There are a number of more specialised softwoods available:

- Douglas Fir is particularly resinous and durable and it performs as well as many hardwoods. It is a favourite in high specification windows though one problem is that it doesn't hold paint well — wood stains are the solution.
- Hemlock is another North American speciality softwood which is mostly used in door construction.
- Cedar is particularly durable and really doesn't require any sort of onsite treatment at all. However, its use is very limited, tending to be restricted to external claddings such as garage doors, and roofing, where it is known as shingles.
- Parana Pine. This is a lovely looking South American timber, popular in several internal applications such as window boards and staircases. It is anything but durable and is very prone to buckling.

### Hardwoods

Generally, hardwoods are not an alternative to softwoods. Rather, they tend to get used in particular applications like flooring and kitchen worksurfaces where softwoods are not commonly used. Joinery is the obvious exception to this rule: see the section Windows in Chapter 7, Superstructure, where the pros and cons are examined. Also check Chapter 13, Green Issues, for the lowdown on tropical hardwoods.

## Joinery

The volume timber joinery business works very much on the principle of publishing list prices so that all and sundry can see, but then, in private, haggling over discounts obtainable off these list prices. Discounts are partially volume driven (i.e. the more you buy, the bigger the discounts) but they are also very sensitive to what the opposition are doing. To the novice builder this might appear to be a stumbling block because their design will more than probably specify a certain manufacturer's product and there may be only one supplier in the area. However, each manufacturer will almost certainly be producing a similar product which can be substituted. It's a complicated business because although the sizes and styles are often nearly identical, the reference codes are not.

### Discounts

Most small builders will expect to get 30% off the list prices shown in the catalogues as a matter of course and a selfbuilder should expect to get as much. The big boys will be looking to get 50% off, and if your order is big enough (say 15 windows or more) you ought to be able to negotiate a discount larger than 30%. Often the merchants will be more flexible than the direct outlets and they also often stock two or more manufacturers. Much of the uPVC market works in a slightly different way in that there are many more small suppliers who normally quote on your plans, rather than discounting off a list price.

### Service

A further consideration is the speed and quality of delivery. In my experience this can vary enormously; sometimes the wrong items turn up, sometimes stock is damaged or parts are missing, often they are supplied later than promised. Furthermore, there seems to be little consistency; a factory or depot can supply everything correctly on time for one order and make horrendous cock-ups two months later. A lot obviously depends on the staff at the dispatching end, and what state they are in one cannot know. Ordering and correct delivery of joinery is one of the most crucial elements in the managing of a construction project because its absence can throw the job programme out of the window (or should that be window opening); on the other hand its presence on site too early creates storage problems — joinery is prone to site damage, to warping if poorly stored and to theft. If you do negotiate some whammo deal, check to see if you have to take all the items in one delivery because that may well not be the smartest move.

### Delivery Times

Another frequent problem comes when ordering some of the more obscure items from the catalogues. Delivery times of six weeks are sometimes quoted — which in reality means they haven't got a clue how long it will take. Even slump conditions in the building trade don't help much because joinery factories are then prone to taking longish holidays — watch out for the extended August break. You can spend a long time and burn up your phone bill being shunted around from depot to depot trying to find out what has happened to your hardwood imperial French door frames. You'll get to talk to a lot of Geoffs, Steves, Daves, Sharons and Mandys but getting a fix on your missing order can prove virtually impossible. If speed is of the essence it will pay you to stick to readily available products: the catalogues make it clear which they are.

One way around the problem of coordinating joinery deliveries is to have the items delivered to your nearest depot (or builder's merchant) and then either pick the stuff up yourself or arrange a second delivery. Note that some suppliers will not do this (as it obviously adds considerably to their transport costs) but note also that Magnet have no site delivery service at all and that if you purchase from them they will be obliged to hold the stock for you until you want it (unless of course they sell it on to another customer!).

## Comparing Costs

Another problem is trying to evaluate the cost of finishing the joinery once it's installed in the building. Time was when it all arrived on site in the same condition; softwood frames with a single coat of primer on. Now things are a lot more complicated. The penchant for staining doors and windows instead of painting them has meant that the primer coat has been dropped in favour of a base coat of honey coloured wood stain which can be either painted over or stained. The new thermal buildings regs have also caused some big changes for joinery in that it now needs to meet certain minimum energy efficiency standards which generally means that factory glazing is going to become a lot more common. And of course, timber joinery is now facing stiff competition from other products, most notably uPVC, which tend to get delivered to site ready glazed and pre-finished. As a result you can now buy timber joinery pre-finished (if you don't mind waiting for it); it's also usually available in an in-between state with some extra coats of paint or stain applied in the factory, all designed to reduce your on site decorating costs. Whether these pre-finished or semi-finished options are worth paying extra for rather depends on how much time and money you are prepared to bestow on the naked versions of your joinery; the pricing of these pre-finished units is usually set to make it as cheap as paying someone to decorate them.

## 12c: Guide Prices for Sawn and Treated Timber

*Prices are per lin. metre*

|  | 25mm | | 38mm | | 47mm | | 75mm | |
|---|---|---|---|---|---|---|---|---|
|  | Raw | Treated | Raw | Treated | Raw | Treated | Raw | Treated |
| 19mm |  |  |  | £0.18 |  | £0.21 |  |  |
| 25mm |  |  |  | 0.21 |  |  |  |  |
| 38mm |  | 0.22 | 0.40 | 0.45 |  |  |  |  |
| 50mm |  | 0.30 | 0.50 | 0.55 | 0.50 | 0.55 |  |  |
| 75mm |  | 0.50 | 0.55 | 0.65 | 0.70 | 0.75 | 1.20 |  |
| 100mm | 0.55 | 0.60 | 0.80 |  | 0.90 | 1.05 | 1.60 |  |
| 125mm |  |  |  |  | 1.15 | 1.30 |  |  |
| 150mm | 0.80 | 0.90 | 1.20 |  | 1.40 | 1.60 | 2.20 |  |
| 175mm | 1.10 | 1.25 |  |  | 1.60 | 1.85 |  |  |
| 200mm | 1.30 |  | 1.65 |  | 1.80 | 2.15 | 3.50 |  |
| 225mm | 1.50 |  | 1.90 |  | 2.20 | 2.50 | 4.00 |  |

## 12d: Guide Prices for Planed Timber

*Prices are per lin. metre*

|  | 12.5mm | 16mm | 19mm | 25mm | 32mm | 38mm | 50mm | 75mm | 100mm |
|---|---|---|---|---|---|---|---|---|---|
| 25mm | £0.25 |  | £0.35 | £0.45 |  |  |  |  |  |
| 38mm | 0.35 | 0.45 | 0.50 | 0.60 |  | 0.60 |  |  |  |
| 50mm | 0.45 |  | 0.65 | 0.70 | 0.80 | 0.85 | 0.90 |  |  |
| 75mm |  |  | 0.75 | 0.80 | 0.90 | 1.00 | 1.20 | 2.00 |  |
| 100mm |  |  | 0.85 | 0.90 | 1.20 | 1.30 | 1.60 | 3.00 | 5.00 |
| 125mm |  |  | 1.00 | 1.05 | 1.30 | 1.60 | 2.00 |  |  |
| 150mm |  |  | 1.10 | 1.25 | 1.70 | 2.00 | 2.50 |  |  |
| 175mm |  |  |  | 1.50 | 2.30 |  | 3.00 |  |  |
| 200mm |  |  |  | 2.00 |  |  | 3.50 |  |  |
| 225mm |  |  |  | 2.50 |  |  | 4.00 |  |  |

## 12e: Guide Prices for Timber Board

*Prices are for individual sheets or boards*

|  | BOARD SIZE in mm | THICKNESS | | | |
|---|---|---|---|---|---|
|  |  | 9mm | 12mm | 18mm | 22/25mm |
| Standard Chipboard | 2440x1220 |  | £4.00 | £6.00 | £9.00 |
| T&G Green Chipboard | 2440x600 |  |  | 4.50 | 5.25 |
| Sterling Floor | 2400x600 |  |  | 6.00 |  |
| OSB/Sterling Board | 2440x1220 | 6.00 | 7.50 | 12.00 | 18.00 |
| Sheathing Ply | 2440x1220 | 8.00 | 12.00 | 16.00 |  |
| Premium Ply | 2440x1220 | 12.00 | 15.00 | 22.00 | 30.00 |
| Birch Plywood | 2440x1220 | 18.00 | 22.00 | 34.00 | 45.00 |
| Blockboard | 2440x1220 |  | 19.00 | 22.00 | 36.00 |
| MDF | 2440x1200 | 6.00 | 7.50 | 10.00 | 14.00 |

# Chapter 13
# Green Issues

Most of the interest in this field — and indeed, most of this chapter — is to do with saving energy. Interest in this subject really began during the 1974 oil crisis when people assumed — incorrectly — that we were facing a permanent fuel shortage and consequentially rocketing fuel prices. However, in more recent times, concern has grown that the ambient temperature of the entire planet Earth is gradually increasing, a phenomenon, known to us all now, as global warming. Why this should be is not yet understood but a very large finger of suspicion is pointing at us and, in particular, our habit of burning masses and masses of fossil fuels and thereby releasing carbon dioxide ($CO_2$) into the atmosphere. This may (or may not) be causing a greenhouse effect which, in turn, may (or may not) be causing temperatures to rise which, in turn, may (or may not) have

catastrophic effects on Mother Earth. It's only a theory; all that's known for certain is that a) there is much more $CO_2$ in the atmosphere than there was even 50 years ago and b) global temperatures have been rising. The crux of the problem is that we won't know how much of this theory is accurate for another 50 years by which time it could be too late to do much about it.

Reckoning that it is probably better to be safe than sorry, governments the world over have been signing (and, in the case of the Americans, ignoring) accords — most notably at Rio and Kyoto — to reduce levels of energy consumption though, as environmentalists point out, not by very much and sometimes by nothing at all. As private households contribute about a third of our national $CO_2$ emissions, the effect of these

undertakings is trickling down to the Building Regulations in the hope that stricter codes for new building will bring about some reduction. Hence many of the recent changes to the building regs are to do directly with reducing $CO_2$ emissions. What is interesting to the new housebuilder is that many of the energy (and therefore $CO_2$) saving features that can be built into a new home are also money saving features, and if you are concerned with ongoing running costs, then you can build energy saving into your home knowing that you will be saving money as well as possibly saving the planet. Energy saving is, however, not the be-all and end-all of environmental concerns and I'll start the chapter by taking a look at some of the other issues, including an assessment of how much energy is used in actually constructing a new house.

# Construction Audit

This book may be green-tinged but it is not what anyone would call an eco handbook. If you want to know more about green options then there are dozens of other titles available and I can especially recommend The Whole House Book by Pat Borer and Cindy Harris, which gives a good overview of the many different ways there are to build. Whatever your personal views on green issues, what can't be denied is that the green perspective has caused mainstream housebuilding to examine just what it does and to look at ways it could be improved. For most of the 20th century, housebuilding in Britain was driven by the desire to make houses cheaper and easier to construct. Now the agenda is subtly shifting so that at last we are beginning to worry about what it is that we are building. Is it any good? How much damage does it cause in order to get built? How long will it last? Can it be safely disposed of when we've finished with it? In a word, sustainability. How does the benchmark house stack up?

## Trade Balance

Materials going into our benchmark house weighed around 170 tonnes, the vast majority of which will have been produced within 200 miles of the house. Timber (5 tonnes) is the only significant import by weight, though copper (used extensively in plumbing and wiring) and kitchen appliances were also imported. Traditional housebuilding remains an overwhelmingly British business. It is low-tech and uses a lot of very bulky materials which are costly to transport. Even where foreign companies achieve market penetration in Britain, production is usually UK based.

As a rule, Britain runs a trade deficit in building materials. We are net exporters of steel, wallpapers, paints, sanitaryware and even a few bricks (mostly to Japan), whilst timber accounts for around 90% of our net imports with heating and plumbing gear being the only other significant contributor on this side of the account. Take out timber from the equation and everything else pretty much balances out.

## Embodied Energy

Energy use involved in building any house can be divided into three areas: material production, transport and construction. Broadly speaking, the less a material is processed, the less energy it takes to produce and the less distance a material travels the less energy is used in getting it there. Onsite energy use is remarkably low, unless heating and lighting are employed — unusual when doing spec.

housing. Table 13a summarises the energy used in constructing the benchmark house and it is based on the following figures:

- NATURAL MATERIALS take the least energy to produce. Sand, stone, slate and timber come into this group: production costs might be typically 100kWh/tonne.
- CEMENT-BASED PRODUCTS like concrete and render are low on energy use because they have a high proportion of natural sand or stone mixed in with the cement. They consume around 300kWh/tonne to produce.
- CLAY-BAKED products like bricks and clay roof tiles use around 800kWh/tonne. Also included in this group are plasters and plasterboard. Note that the manufacture of concrete products consumes just half the energy of their clay equivalents.
- GLASS: uses 9000kWh/tonne
- STEEL: uses 13,000kWh/tonne
- COPPER: uses 15,000kWh/tonne
- ALUMINIUM: uses 27,000kWh/tonne
- PLASTIC (inc. uPVC): uses 45,000kWh/tonne — but a tonne goes a long way.

## Transport

In addition to the manufacturing costs, there are energy costs involved in getting the materials to site. As previously mentioned, most of these materials are locally produced. The one big exception is timber which almost always is imported. Our joinery grade softwoods come mostly from Scandinavia, our carcassing from N. America, Scandinavia and Russia. Timber boards like plywood and chipboard can come from anywhere, though note that Sterling Board is produced in Scotland and most of our MDF comes from Ireland.

## Comparisons

The table breaks down the embodied energy that went into the benchmark house, which I calculate at around 90,000kWh. This is equivalent to the amount of energy the house will take to heat, light and cook during its first five years of occupation or, looked at another way, about eight years motoring in the family car doing 12,000miles/annum. The 2002 building codes mean that a new house is saving as much as 30,000kWh/annum over the average of what older housing stock would consume; that means that the energy consumed in production is recouped within three years. Arguably, many of the improvements built into new housing can be easily transferred into the existing housing stock, but on balance new housebuilding is still an

energy saving activity. It could of course be even better — hence the example of the German Passive House standard which represents the current best standard for low energy housing.

## Environmental Audit

### Extraction of Aggregates

Around 150 tonnes (over 90% by weight) of the benchmark house is composed of sands and gravels and clays, mostly bound together with cement. With 150,000 new houses being built in the UK each year, around three cubic miles of materials are being extracted annually to meet this demand. That's an awful lot of holes in the ground and it's one area where new house building is particularly greedy. Quarries pose no long-term health risks and, arguably, the scars of quarrying are actually healed remarkably quickly. However, that doesn't make quarries attractive to nearby residents and new quarrying proposals are always hotly disputed.

### Timber

The weight of timber used to construct houses is minute in comparison with masonry/concrete products. The benchmark house uses about 8m$^3$ (5 tonnes) of wood and wood-based products. Were it timber framed, this figure would rise to around 16m$^3$ (10 tonnes) and if the entire house were built from wood — cedar shingles on the roof, weatherboarded exterior and pine-panelled interiors — the volume of timber would still only be around 40m$^3$ (24 tonnes), less than a quarter of the equivalent weight if masonry products were used. On the face of it, building from a renewable resource like timber would seem to be very desirable but there are a few snags:

- Logging often has more in common with mineral extraction than agriculture; even so-called sustainable sources are often permanently damaged after the virgin crop is removed to be replaced by monotonous, species-thin plantations.
- Almost all structural timber has to be imported into Britain, making it the one major building component not to be sourced in the UK.
- Exterior timber and structural elements of timber frame housing have to be treated with preservatives, thus causing the manufacture of chemical nasties with all their associated health risks.

## 13a: Benchmark House Construction Audit
## Material Quantities and Energy Used to Construct House

| MATERIAL | ENERGY USED in MANUFACTURING (in kWh/tonne) | MATERIAL QUANTITY | WEIGHT (in tonnes) | ENERGY USED (in kWhs) |
|---|---|---|---|---|
| Concrete | 300 | 30 $m^3$ | 54 | 16,200 |
| Bricks | 800 | 9300 No | 23 | 18,400 |
| Lightweight Blocks | 300 | 260 $m^2$ | 22 | 6,600 |
| Concrete Floor Beams | 1,000 | 0 | 0 | 0 |
| Sand | 30 | 25 t | 25 | 800 |
| Cement | 1,500 | 4 t | 4 | 6,000 |
| Concrete Tiles | 300 | 134 $m^2$ | 6 | 1,800 |
| Concrete Paving | 300 | 25 $m^2$ | 3 | 900 |
| Hardcore and Gravel | 30 | 22 t | 22 | 700 |
| Timber | 100 | 8 $m^3$ | 5 | 500 |
| Chipboard/Plywood | 300 | 1 $m^3$ | 0.6 | 200 |
| Plasterboard | 800 | 540 $m^2$ | 5.2 | 4,200 |
| Steel | 13,000 | 1 t | 1 | 13,000 |
| Glass | 9,000 | 21 $m^2$ | 0.4 | 3,600 |
| Plastic/uPVC | 45,000 | 0.25 t | 0.25 | 11,300 |
| Sanitaryware | 5,000 | 0.2 t | 0.2 | 1,000 |
| Others Materials | 10,000 | | 0.2 | 2,000 |
| Timber Transport | 1 tonne uses 300kWh to travel 10,000km | | | 1,500 |
| Heavy Goods Transport | 1 tonne uses 0.3kWh to travel 1km | 15000 t x km | | 4,500 |
| **TOTAL** | | | **172** | **90,000** |

| COMPARISONS  Energy used/annum | kWh/annum |
|---|---|
| Benchmark House Built to 2002 standards | 20,000 |
| Benchmark House Built to Passive House standards | 5,000 |
| Benchmark House Built to 1975 standards | 70,000 |
| Family Car Doing 20,000km/annum | 20,000 |

## Tropical Hardwoods

The problem with using tropical hardwoods is to do with the way in which they are harvested (or plundered) with acres of virgin rainforest being destroyed often to fell just one particularly nice mahogany tree. By and large this land is then cleared and used for rather poor cattle grazing. This sort of wanton destruction is going on all over the tropics and, in truth, is as much to do with burgeoning population growth as it is with extracting hardwoods, but there is no doubt that the hardwood trade plays a significant part. The building trade is, as ever, very slow to pick up on the potential problems here and long after retailers have been selling furniture "Made from Renewable Resources", there is little sign of any green awareness from timber merchants, possibly because tropical hardwoods are a nice little earner.

However, the environmental problems resulting from using these hardwoods in new housebuilding should not be exaggerated because their use is rare precisely because of

their expense. Brazilian mahogany is specified as standard as a cill detail on timber door frames but otherwise you have to go looking for materials — chiefly joinery — made out of tropical hardwoods. Another area where you may stumble across them is as constituents of better grade plywoods (Far Eastern) and blockboards, but these are more commonly used for shelving than construction; MDF can be used as a cheaper substitute.

## Health Risks

### Formaldehyde

This glue is used to bind timber panel products, chiefly chipboards, MDF and plywoods. Some people are known to react badly to the fumes which are released very slowly over a period of months after manufacture, a process known as off-gassing. However, adverse reactions are rare and exact causes are difficult to pinpoint. Almost all volatile synthetic compounds (VOCs) have come under suspicion — including carpets and clothes — and it remains a complex and poorly understood

area. You can, of course, build and furnish a house from entirely natural materials but it is an expensive option.

### Solvents

Solvents are used in oil-based paints, stains and varnishes, as well as adhesives and mastics. Many people actually like the smell of solvents but long-term exposure to them has been linked with brain damage. Occasional users probably need not be alarmed, but be aware that solvents are likely to be far more damaging to young children than to adults; if youngsters (and pregnant women) are present then you would do well to consider using water-based paints and stains indoors.

### Wood Preservatives

One normally associates timber treatment with remedial work carried out on old houses, but a great deal of new timber gets pre-treated with either water-based tanalith or solvent-based protim. The tanalising treatments are based on the copper-chrome-arsenic compounds (CCAs) whilst the spirit-based systems use a cocktail of chemical nasties such as lindane, pentachlorophenol (PCPs) and tri-butyl-tin-oxide (TBTOs). They serve a dual purpose; one is to reduce risk of fungal infestations such as dry rot, the other is to reduce risk of insect attack such as woodworm and death watch beetle. The idea is that treated timber will taste so foul that insects and fungus will steer well clear: the danger is that these chemicals won't do us much good either.

External joinery is pre-treated as a matter of course and NHBC regulations require that timber in exposed walls is treated. There is a potential long term hazard, although this is rather along the lines of the formaldehyde and VOC threat — i.e. no one can say what it is — but there is also a more immediate danger to site carpenters who inevitably come into physical contact with treated timbers. Wearing gloves is not really an option for a chippie: the best precaution is to ensure that the timber is dried properly before it is worked — sometimes it arrives on site still dripping with the chemical preservatives, having just come out of the vacuum tank. Some commentators maintain that if the design detailing is good, then the timber does not need preserving but preservation is now an industry standard; note that timber frame kit houses tend to come with pre-treated timber specified everywhere, whether it's actually needed or not.

## Asbestos

In many ways, asbestos is a great product — lightweight, stable and with incredible fire resistance. But, and it's a big but, asbestos dust particles are a proven killer and great care should be taken when handling the product. Although asbestos is tending to be phased out, it is still present in a number of building products on sale today (cf. certain damp proof courses, artificial slates and other roofing products). However, you are at greater risk when removing asbestos products from old houses because this is where you are most likely to come into contact with the dust. Asbestos was extremely common in houses built from 1920-1980 and care should be taken if demolishing something from this era — watch out particularly for things like textured Artex ceilings. The risks of removing asbestos should not be underestimated and if you encounter it, or anything suspicious-looking dust forming material, you should look to call in specialist help — start with a call to your local Environmental Health Office.

## MDF

The problems related to formaldehyde have already been touched on and are not unique to MDF. However MDF is the board that gets worked most and it tends to produce the finest dust which sails through the average dust mask as if it's not there. This combination is reckoned (by some) to make MDF a hazard on a par with asbestos and moves are afoot to produce a similar board made with safer resins. Passive consumers of MDF products are unlikely to be at risk but you should look out if you work with a lot of MDF dust.

## Cement

Human skin does not react well with wet cement and concrete mixes; there is no instant sign that burning is taking place and many people assume that it is therefore harmless. It's not; prolonged exposure will cause very nasty burns.

## Fibreglass

Fibreglass insulation, together with the closely related mineral wool, are unpleasantly itchy on skin, and eyes like it even less. Thought by some to be similar to asbestos in effect, others claim that the fibres are generally too large to cause lethal irritation. Whoever proves to be correct, it makes sense not to be macho about it. Wear gloves and a mask when insulating.

## uPVC

The use of uPVC has been growing steadily in housebuilding. You will find it in plastic guttering and drainage pipes, in electric cable and, of course, uPVC windows and doors. However there is a growing campaign (led in this country by Greenpeace) against the use of uPVC, principally on the grounds that its production is a dirty, polluting business leading to the release of dioxins, not to mention the dumping of chlorine. What is not clear is whether uPVC manufacture is any worse than the rest of the chemicals/plastics industry.

## Site Safety

See section on Running a Site, in Chapter 5, Project Management.

## Eco Homes

In an attempt to introduce some objectivity to a subject which, in the eyes of many observers, is reeling with subjectivity, Britain's premier building science body, the Building Research Establishment or BRE published two booklets in 2000 called 1) Eco Homes and 2) The Green Guide to Housing Specification. Together they look at the impact on the environment and human health and they develop some criteria which allow you to rate housing development from the point of view of overall sustainability, not merely energy saving. You end up with a score in, wait for it, sunflowers. One sunflower is a PASS, four sunflowers, the maximum, indicates a development "which demonstrates exemplary environmental performance across the full range of issues."

So what makes a home an EcoHome? This is decided by an EcoHome Rating system which marks many aspects of your house design and performance. The maximum number of marks obtainable is 207. Energy efficiency measures only account for 40 points; you get almost as many for water efficiency measures (max 30 points) or specifying sustainable materials (max 31 points). Other point scoring features include being within 500m of a bus stop or railway station (4 points) and improving the ecological value of the site (up to 16 points). To get the top EcoHomes award (four sunflowers) you need to amass 145 points.

I put our decidedly pale green house, 1992 vintage, through the checklist and had scored 56 points (just over pass) when somewhere in the penultimate section I stopped understanding the questions. I couldn't decide whether or not we'd made "effective use of our footprint." No guidance appeared in either publication on what they could possibly mean by this though I have a hunch that they'd like us to have built a room-in-the-roof or a basement — we didn't do either — but that's not the way the question was phrased, so at that point I gave up.

The assessment is not meant to be a DIY affair in any event: rather the BRE are licensing organisations to carry out EcoHome ratings, in a similar manner to the energy rating schemes which have existed for some time. This may explain why the checklist is not at all easy to fathom — you need to be trained to understand it. Added to this, the two publications are being sold for a combined cost of £60 (exactly a pound per page) which clearly marks them out as not being aimed at the casual user. More's the pity because every wanna-be eco-home builder needs to go through an evaluation process like this before they can be sure that their ideas of what is environmentally-friendly chimes in with everybody else's.

### Contacts

The Whole House Book is £29.95 plus p&p from Centre for Alternative Technology Bookshop 01654 702948

The Green Guide to Housing Specification £35.00; Eco Homes £25.00. Both these are available rom CRC 0207 505 6622

As far as building regulations are concerned, green issues begin and end with energy saving. Energy saving measures first became part of the British homebuilding scene in the 1976 and they have been progressively tightened four times since then. The latest set of changes came into effect throughout the UK in 2002. The key points were as follows:
- More insulation is needed in order to meet the new U value requirements
- Windows and doors must be energy-rated and meet specific U value requirements. For the first time, this applies to replacement windows in existing dwellings. Doesn't apply yet in Scotland.
- Likewise, boilers must be energy-rated and meet certain standards. Again this applies to replacement boilers for the first time. In addition to this, new heating systems must be switched by more sophisticated controls. Likewise, these boiler requirements don't apply yet in Scotland.
- Energy saving lightbulbs will have to be used, though not exclusively or even extensively.
- A new method of rating energy performance, called the Carbon Index, has been introduced. Previous methods have concentrated on heating costs; this one looks at CO2 emissions.

Some of the details of the new requirements are looked at in their relevant sections. Thus boilers and controls are back in Chapter 8 and windows and doors are adrift somewhere in Chapter 7. And the lightbulb bit follows shortly (look under Energy Efficient Lighting). It would be a waste of valuable paper to repeat them here. But the U value requirements, arguably the most important bit of the exercise, has only been skirted around and alluded to till now so it's time to get to grips

## Section through a Brick and Block Cavity Wall, showing the R values of each element

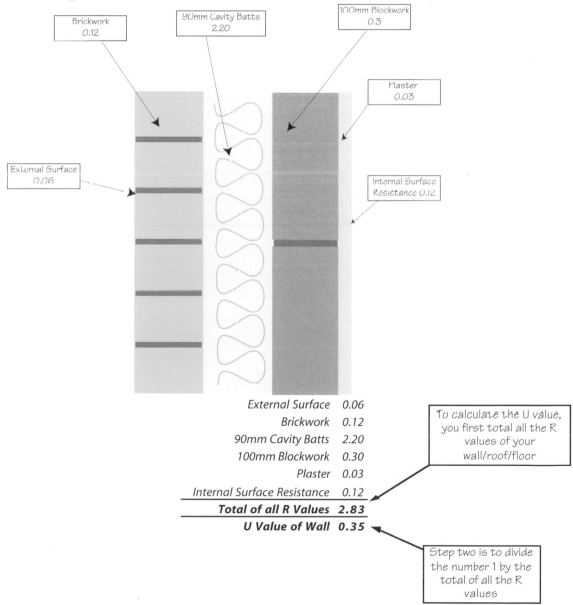

| | |
|---|---|
| External Surface | 0.06 |
| Brickwork | 0.12 |
| 90mm Cavity Batts | 2.20 |
| 100mm Blockwork | 0.30 |
| Plaster | 0.03 |
| Internal Surface Resistance | 0.12 |
| **Total of all R Values** | **2.83** |
| **U Value of Wall** | **0.35** |

To calculate the U value, you first total all the R values of your wall/roof/floor

Step two is to divide the number 1 by the total of all the R values

## 13b  R values of Common Building Materials

| INSULATION | | | | | BLOCKS | | | |
|---|---|---|---|---|---|---|---|---|
| Fibreglass/Mineral Wool | | | | | Clinker Blocks | 0.57 | 100 | 0.18 |
| Loose Quilt | 0.04 | 100 | 2.50 | | Aerated (Celcon) | 0.18 | 100 | 0.56 |
| | 0.04 | 150 | 3.75 | | Concrete Blocks | 1.9 | 100 | 0.05 |
| | 0.04 | 200 | 5.00 | | Granite | 2.9 | 100 | 0.03 |
| Cavity Batts | 0.038 | 50 | 1.32 | | Limestone | 1.7 | 100 | 0.06 |
| | 0.038 | 65 | 1.71 | | Sandstone | 2.3 | 100 | 0.04 |
| Timber Frame Batts | 0.038 | 90 | 2.37 | | Clay Tile | 1.0 | 10 | 0.01 |
| | 0.038 | 140 | 3.68 | | Concrete Tile | 1.5 | 12 | 0.01 |
| Expanded Polystyrene | 0.04 | 25 | 0.63 | | Roofing Felt | 0.2 | 2 | 0.01 |
| | 0.04 | 50 | 1.25 | | 50mm Screed | 0.4 | 50 | 0.13 |
| Extruded Polystyrene | 0.03 | 25 | 0.83 | | 65mm Screed | 0.4 | 65 | 0.16 |
| | 0.03 | 50 | 1.67 | | 100mm Concrete Slab | 1.3 | 100 | 0.08 |
| Polyurethane | 0.025 | 25 | 1.00 | | 150mm Concrete Slab | 1.3 | 150 | 0.12 |
| | 0.025 | 38 | 1.52 | | Render | 0.57 | 12 | 0.02 |
| | 0.025 | 50 | 2.00 | | Finish Plasters | 0.57 | 3 | 0.01 |
| Vermiculite | 0.075 | 100 | 1.33 | | **AIR GAPS** | | | |
| **OTHER MATERIALS** | | | | | Cavity 25mm plus | | | 0.20 |
| Softwood | 0.13 | 25 | 0.19 | | 10mm or less | | | 0.10 |
| | 0.13 | 50 | 0.38 | | Ventilated Loft Space | | | 0.20 |
| Hardwood | 0.18 | 25 | 0.14 | | **SURFACE RESISTANCE** | | | |
| | 0.18 | 50 | 0.28 | | External | | | 0.05 |
| Plywood/Chipboard | 0.13 | 9 | 0.07 | | Internal | | | 0.10 |
| | 0.13 | 18 | 0.14 | | | | | |
| | 0.13 | 22 | 0.17 | | | | | |
| Plasterboard | 0.25 | 9.5 | 0.04 | | | | | |
| | 0.25 | 12.5 | 0.05 | | | | | |
| add for Foil Backing | | | 0.20 | | | | | |
| uPVC | 0.4 | 2 | 0.01 | | | | | |
| Clay Brick | 0.77 | 102 | 0.13 | | | | | |

## 13c Additional R values for Ground Floors

Ground floor heat-loss calculations are a special case (see previous page). Edge:Area ratio is calculated by dividing the GF perimter length in metres by the GF area in m²

| EDGE:AREA RATIO | R VALUE | U VALUE |
|---|---|---|
| 0.2 | 2.8 | 0.36 |
| 0.3 | 2.0 | 0.5 |
| 0.4 | 1.6 | 0.6 |
| 0.5 | 1.4 | 0.7 |
| 0.6 | 1.2 | 0.8 |
| 0.7 | 1.1 | 0.9 |
| 0.8 | 1.0 | 1.0 |

If you want to improve on these 'as built' U values, you need to add insulation. To recalcluate the new U value add the edge:area R value to the R value of your chosen insulation , then calculate the U value

with it now. First an explanation of what a U value is. It's fairly dry, academic stuff but it's not without its moments.

Like most of the other values in our society, U values are declining; however, in this case, declining values are broadly welcomed. You see, a U value is a measure of heat loss and a material with a low U value loses less heat than one with a high U value. Low U value materials are said to be thermally efficient and, therefore, green. In many ways, that's all you need to know. However, a U value is not like a moral value which you either have or haven't got; it's actually a scientifically derived measurement and knowing your U values will help you make a whole lot more sense of your decisions about how to build and how to heat your house.

## Definitions

A U value is a measurement of the heat flow (measured in watts) through a square metre ($m^2$) of a building element for every 1°C temperature difference between the inside and the outside. That reads like the horrible sort of definition you had to learn for Science A-levels, which is why you never did one. It's actually got three different bits to it and in an algebra lesson they'd call them a, b, and c and make it even more unintelligible. However the point that it's trying to make is dead simple: some things are better at retaining heat than others. It's something you know instinctively without ever having to ascribe a value to it — after all you know just how many clothes you need to wear to feel comfortable. The U value is just some poor sod's attempt at quantifying this fact.

In fact the U value of just about everything you could ever think of using to construct a house has been worked out under laboratory conditions. What they do is establish how quickly heat leaks out of any given material — the boffins call this thermal conductivity. The answer is expressed as a value, known as the lambda value, which is in fact the same as the U value for a one metre thick slab of this material. The better the insulator, the lower the leakage rate. Our best insulators, things like polyurethane foams, have a lambda value of 0.025watts whilst a poor insulator like granite has a value of 2.9watts. From which you can deduce that polyurethane is around 100 times better than granite as an insulator or, put another way, a 1mm strip of polyurethane would keep you as warm as a 100mm wide granite brick. The final U value of a material is found by dividing the lambda value of the material by its actual width in metres. Thus 50mm (or 0.05m) of polyurethane foam (lambda value 0.025 remember) has a U value of 0.025 ÷ 0.05 = 0.5.

Now that's all fine and dandy but there is a mathematical problem to be faced here. A wall is conventionally made up of maybe four or five different elements. Each one has it's own U value, each contributes in some way to the insulating capabilities of that wall. Now in order to work out the cumulative U value of the wall you need some method of combining these values. You just can't add the U values together or subtract them from one another; you get a nonsensical answer. The trick is done by switching U values into R values, resistance values. R values are a mirror image of U values — the higher they go, the more they resist the passage of heat. To switch between U values and R values you always divide the number you are working with into 1. So a U value of 0.5 is an R value of 2.0 (i.e. 1 ÷ 0.5 = 2). And an R value of 4 is the same as a U value of 0.25 (i.e. 1 ÷ 4 = 0.25). Unlike U values, you can add R values together and get a coherent answer. When you've added all the R values together to give you a cumulative R value figure, you can then convert this total back to U values. It's not that difficult. I just explained it to my 11 year old son Adam who understood it but added "it wasn't exactly easy."

Interestingly, the Americans prefer to work everything in R values and you rarely see them refer to U values. Note however that if you get hold of some US building literature and you think their R values look amazingly high, it's not because they only build eco-cabins but because they use imperial measurements. A metric R value is worth 5.68 Imperial ones. R values are arguably a simpler concept to understand than U values — the higher the better — but U values are more useful because you can use them to carry out whole house heat calculations.

## Commentary

Table 13b covers most of the regular building elements that you might meet in constructing a new house. You can use it to roughly work out your own construction's U values by adding all the R values together and dividing 1 by the result. I have used the most regular thicknesses, but if you are not using one of these, remember that R values can be scaled up or down directly in proportion to the thickness of the material so that you can readily calculate your own. And also bear in mind that in more complex layers, such as a timber stud wall where the voids are filled with insulation, you have to work out the average R value based on the proportions of the area which are timber and insulation — typically 20% is timber and 80% is insulation.

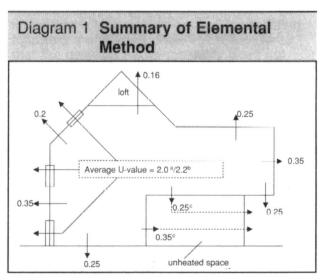

<sup>a</sup> if windows have wood or PVC frames
<sup>b</sup> if windows have metal frames
<sup>c</sup> includes the effect of the unheated space (see paragraph 0.8)

*Lifted from Approved Document Part L, this diagram shows the U values required for new homes since 2002*

Eagle-eyed readers will be asking "Where's the glass?" and the answer is back in the Glazing section in Chapter 7, Superstructure. Glass is a special case; when it's sunny, it gains heat — indeed it's specified as a heat source in passive solar designs.

## Ground Floors

U values for ground floors are also a special case and the process for calculating them is quite different, largely because heat has difficulty travelling in a downwards direction. However the cold bridging effect around the edges of the floors is pronounced and so the key calculation is concerned not with the R values of all the bits of the floor but in establishing a ratio of the edge or perimeter of the floor with the area of the floor. You measure the length of the perimeter walls (heated area only) in metres and divide the result by the area of the floor (heated area only) in square metres. It makes no difference if your ground floor is suspended or ground bearing, timber or concrete. On the benchmark house the calculation looks like this.

- Perimeter walls are 34m long; ground floor is 61m². 34 ÷ 61 = 0.56.

This ratio has to be looked up on a table (see Table 13c) from which the R value and the U value can be read off — remember the U value = 1 ÷ R value. Deconstruct the table and you can see that the bigger and squarer the building, the less heat it loses through the ground floor. A relatively small footprint like the benchmark house has a U value of around 0.75 without the addition of any underfloor

insulation. This was acceptable practice until the 2002 thermal regs came into effect. Now it is virtually compulsory to have some dedicated floor insulation in order to get the U values down to around 0.25.

## Radiant Barriers

One other problem with all these measurements is that they are very good at measuring conduction through building materials but much less good at spotting the two other methods of heat transfer, convection and radiation. There are a number of new products around, noticeably the reflective barriers (mentioned in Chapter 7) which simply don't work in conventional laboratory tests used to establish thermal conductivity. In order to prove their effectiveness, they have to be trialed side by side with equivalent products, a procedure known as witness testing. Having once been rather sceptical about these products, I am slowly becoming convinced that they do work as advertised (well it does rather depend on how they are advertised). It goes to show, partly, how little we actually understand about just how buildings work.

## U values in 2002

Within a generation we have gone from building homes with little or no insulation to building warmly cocooned shells which leak remarkably little heat. I was involved in some wacky eco home schemes back in 1980 when we were thought to be downright weird for putting 100mm of expanded polystyrene insulation around an external wall. Maybe I was. 100mm was off the scale back then. Now it's just about what you need to meet the 2002

regs. The worm has turned. Darker greens than me still complain that our current regs are inadequate and they look wistfully at what happens in Sweden and Canada where U values are around half our levels. And they dream of houses that require no heating systems at all. We are about three quarters of the way there now from when we started on this insulation process in 1976 but the final quarter is the most difficult and the most expensive to achieve so it may never become encoded in our building regs.

The basic 2002 U value standards are clear enough to comprehend from the accompanying diagram. In Scotland, the wall U value is slightly lower than England & Wales — it's 0.3 rather than 0.35. In the Irish Republic it seems it will be lower still at 0.27.

You don't have to build to these U values slavishly. There is a little leeway and a little trading-off available. You may, for instance, be able to use less insulation in exchange for a more efficient boiler. And if you are renovating a listed building you may well be exempted from some of the measures, notably the requirement for energy efficient glazing. "No way!" say English Heritage.

# Heat Calcs & Energy Ratings

To get a feel for what U values can do for you I have run some simplified heat calculations through the spreadsheet (shown as Table 13d) showing how it's all done. The measurements are taken from the benchmark house but the U values and the ventilation rates are adjusted with some licence. I have used three versions of the benchmark house.

- The 1975 house reflects how we built homes then, with little or no insulation. As you might suspect, it leaks heat.

- The 2002 house is built to the standards now in place in England and Wales.

- The Passive House is an example of an ultra-low energy dwelling which requires almost no heating. There are in fact many examples of what are sometimes called zero heat homes across the world but the Passive House standard is one of the best known. It hails from Germany — there it is called Passiv Haus — and there are about a thousand in existence there. The principles are always the same. Increase the insulation levels to such a degree that lightbulbs, appliances and body heat (the so-called *incidentals*) cover the entire heat loss for the house right down to your designed for minimum external temperature.

The calculations work as follows.

1. You start with measuring the areas of the different parts of the house fabric — i.e. walls, roof, floors, joinery. NB The walls and roof figure should exclude the area taken up by the joinery.

2. You then attribute a U value to each of these areas. The 2002 house shows the U values required to meet the current regs.

3. You multiply each area by its U value. The result is the specific heat loss (SHL) for each area. Thus a wall area of 120m² with a U value

## 13d Heat Loss Calcs for Benchmark House

**Built to three different standards**

| | | AREA or VOLUME | | U VALUE | | 1975 HOUSE | 2002 HOUSE | PASSIVE HOUSE |
|---|---|---|---|---|---|---|---|---|
| **A** | **ROOF** | 81 | m² | | | | | |
| | 1975 - little or no insulation | | | x | 0.8 | = 65 w | | |
| | 2002 standards 140mm Pu | | | x | 0.20 | | = 16 w | |
| | Passive House standard | | | x | 0.10 | | | = 8 w |
| **B** | **EXTERNAL WALLS** | 162 | m² | | | | | |
| | 1975 - no insulation | | | x | 1.5 | = 242 w | | |
| | 2002 standards | | | x | 0.35 | | = 57 w | |
| | Passive House standard | | | x | 0.10 | | | = 16 w |
| **C** | **WINDOWS** | 22 | m² | | | | | |
| | Single Glazing | | | x | 5.0 | = 111 w | | |
| | Double Glazing to 2002 standards | | | x | 2.0 | | = 44 w | |
| | Passive House standard | | | x | 0.8 | | | = 18 w |
| **D** | **EXTERNAL DOORS** | 9 | m² | | | | | |
| | 44mm Timber | | | x | 3.0 | = 28 w | | |
| | 2002 standards | | | x | 2.0 | | = 19 w | |
| | Passive House standard | | | x | 0.8 | | | = 7 w |
| **E** | **GROUND FLOOR** | 61 | m² | | | | | |
| | No Insulation | | | x | 0.7 | = 45 w | | |
| | 2002 standards | | | x | 0.25 | | = 13 w | |
| | Passive House standard | | | x | 0.10 | | | = 6 w |
| **F** | **VENTILATION** | 355 | m³ | | | | | |
| | **Specific Heat of Air** | 0.33 | w/m³ | | | | | |
| | Heat required for 1 air change/hr | 117 | w | | | | | |
| | 2 air changes/hr(1975) | | 2.0 | | | = 234 w | | |
| | 2002 standard (0.8 air changes/hr) | | 0.6 | | | | = 70 w | |
| | Passive House standard (with MVHR) | | 0.3 | | | | | = 35 w |

*Likely number of air changes per hour*

### WHOLE HOUSE HEAT LOSS

| | | | 1975 HOUSE | 2002 HOUSE | PASSIVE HOUSE |
|---|---|---|---|---|---|
| **SHL** | **Specific Heat Loss** | A+B+C+D+E+F | 725 w | 221 w | 91 w |
| | Heat load required for 20°C uplift | **SHL** x 20 ÷1000 | 14.50 kW | 4.43 kW | 1.81 kW |
| | 20° uplift/m³ | Heat load ÷ volume | 41 w | 12 w | 5 w |

of 0.5 will have a specific heat loss of 60watts/1°C temperature difference between inside and outside.

4. You then work out the specific heat loss for the ventilation. To do this you need to know the volume of the heated air space in the house in cubic metres. And you need to factor in the number of air changes per hour. It can vary from around two to well under a half. If you are building a new home you could probably hazard a guess that you would get to around the half air change per hour mark. Multiply the air changes per hour by the volume and you get the volume of new air passing through the house every hour. Multiply this figure by 0.33watts, the specific heat of

air (or the heat required to lift 1m³ of air through 1°C) and you have a specific heat figure for your ventilation requirements.

5. You then add all these figures together to give you a specific heat loss for the whole house. This is the amount of heat, in watts, that it takes to lift the entire house through 1°C. This is the crucial figure. The specific heat loss. It's sort of a sum of all the U values. The lower the SHL, the better insulated the structure is. As it's a measurements in watts, you can easily apply a multiplier to it to find out how much heat you need to keep the house warm on the coldest day. Normally we work to a design temperature of -1°C in England and Wales and -4°C in Scotland. Though

you are under no obligation to stick to them, the industry standards for desired temperature in each room are as follows:

| | |
|---|---|
| Living rooms/kitchen | 21°C |
| Bedrooms | 18°C |
| Hall/stairs | 16°C |
| Bathrooms | 22°C |

To make the calculations a bit simpler, you can even all these temperatures to get an average temperature of around 18°C, maybe 19°C if you're a bit of a wuss. In order to keep our homes say 18°C warmer than the minimum design temperatures you would multiply the SHL by 19°C in England & Wales and 22°C in Scotland. The results are always sur-

## 13e: Energy ratings for 3 standards of housebuilding

| | | | 1975 House | 2002 House | Passive House |
|---|---|---|---|---|---|
| A | Specific Heat Loss (1°C temp diff) | kw | 0.72 kW | 0.22 kW | 0.09 kW |
| B | Incidentals Heat Gains(body heat, electrics) | kW | 1.5 kW | 1.3 kW | 1.1 kW |
| C | Incidentals ÷ SHL | B÷A | 2.07 °C | 5.87 °C | 12.13 °C |
| D | Degree days of heating | | 2,500 dd | 2,500 dd | 2,500 dd |
| E | Reduction due to incidentals (200/1°C) | 200 x C | 410 dd | 1,170 dd | 2,430 dd |
| F | Adjusted degree days | D-E | 2,090 dd | 1,330 dd | 70 dd |
| G | Annual space heating demand | Fx24xA | 36,400 kWh | 7,100 kWh | 200 kWh |
| | Add for Domestic Hot water | | | | |
| Ha | say 4 people at 1000kWh ea/annum | | 4,000 kWh | 4,000 kWh | 4,000 kWh |
| Hb | Passive House uses solar panels (50% off) | | | | 2,000 kWh |
| H | Net use for DHW | Ha-Hb | 4,000 kWh | 4,000 kWh | 2,000 kWh |
| I | Combined total for space heating and DHW | G+H | 40,400 kWh | 11,100 kWh | 2,200 kWh |
| | **Gas** | | | | |
| J | Allowance for boiler efficiency | | 68% | 78% | 90% |
| K | kWh actually consumed | I÷J | 59,400 kWh | 14,200 kWh | 2,400 kWh |
| L | Unit cost of gas/kWh (in pence) | 1.49 | | | |
| M | Annual cost (exc standing orders) | | £ 885 | £ 212 | £ 36 |
| N | Carbon emmissions for gas | 0.19 | kg/kWh | | |
| P | Carbon emmissions in kg/annum | | 11300 kg | 2700 kg | 500 kg |
| Q | Carbon emmissions per square metre | 162 | 70 | 17 | 3 |
| R | Adjust by adding 45m2 to floor area | 207 | 55 | 13 | 2 |
| | Carbon Index Score | | 2.0 | 7.7 | 10.0 |
| | **Oil** | | | | |
| J | Allowance for boiler efficiency | | 70% | 85% | 95% |
| K | kWh actually consumed | I÷J | 57,700 kWh | 13,100 kWh | 2,300 kWh |
| L | Unit cost of oil/kWh (in pence) | 1.6 | | | |
| M | Annual cost (exc standing orders) | | £ 923 | £ 210 | £ 37 |
| N | Carbon emmissions for oil | 0.27 | kg/kWh | | |
| P | Carbon emmissions in kg/annum | | 15600 | 3500 | 600 |
| Q | Carbon emmissions per square metre | 162 | 96 | 22 | 4 |
| R | Adjust by adding 45m2 to floor area | 207 | 75 | 17 | 3 |
| | Carbon Index Score | | 0.8 | 6.6 | 10.0 |
| | **Dirty Electricity** | | | | |
| J | Allowance for efficiency | | 100% | 100% | 100% |
| K | kWh actually consumed | I÷J | 40,400 kWh | 11,100 kWh | 2,200 kWh |
| L | Unit cost of electricity/kWh (in pence) | 3.5 | | | |
| M | Annual cost (exc standing orders) | | £ 1,414 | £ 389 | £ 77 |
| N | Carbon emmissions for elelctricity | 0.41 | kg/kWh | | |
| P | Carbon emmissions in kg/annum | | 16600 | 4600 | 900 |
| Q | Carbon emmissions per square metre | 162 | 102 | 28 | 6 |
| R | Adjust by adding 45m2 to floor area | 207 | 80 | 22 | 4 |
| | Carbon Index Score | | 0.6 | 5.6 | 10.0 |

prisingly small. Try and persuade your plumber that you only need a 5kW boiler in your five bedroom house!

## Energy ratings

Energy ratings take the heat loss calcs one stage further and attempt to speculate about how much energy you will actually burn in your home each year. A full blown energy rating on a house is a complex beast involving many different interlinked calculations. The standard one used by the powers that be is the SAP Rating. It's full title is the Government's Standard Assessment Procedure for Energy Rating Dwellings and it's forever being tweaked here and there as new products come onto the market. The 2001 edition consists of 106 separate measurements and calculations looking in great detail at things like the orientation of your windows, your likely draughts and the amount of heat you will lose in your hot water pipes. From these figures it's possible to make a stab at your probable energy usage per annum expressed in units of energy, financial cost and $CO_2$ emissions.

It's very easy to pull holes in energy ratings, if you want to. Much of it is incredibly detailed to an altogether anal degree. Yet other bits use broad brush assumptions that can only ever approximate real energy use. For instance, hot water use is estimated to rise in proportion to the house floor area. Anyone can see that it's actually more likely to be affected by the number of people living in the house but a dumb spreadsheet can't speculate about that, can it? So in order to be able to compare one house with another, floor area is used a lot. Yet energy ratings are a useful exercise if only to help us understand just how houses work and how they do and do not burn energy.

Rather than go through SAP 2001 step by step, I have built a very dumbed down version on table 13e which shows the basics. The big variables are the Specific Heat Loss (already worked out for three different standards in Table 13d), the fuel used and the boiler efficiencies. Common sense really. The Carbon Index is now the preferred way of ranking new homes energy-wise: if you manage to match or beat 8.0 on the carbon index then your home is deemed to have passed the 2002 thermal requirements, however it is built.

Here are a few notes on the table to help make sense of it.

- A. Specific Heat Loss (SHL). This is calculated on table 13d. It the basis of the energy rating. Normally it's expressed in watts (as this is what U values are) but here I've divided the watts by 1000 to make it kilowatts because it makes better sense

later on it the table.
- B. Incidentals. This is the heat that you pump inadvertently into the house by way of lights, appliances, solar gains from sunshine, all those standby lights on computers and TVs and of course body heat. A person at rest gives off just over 100 watts, whilst moderate physical exercise gives off around 400watts. In all incidentals probably contribute between 1000w (1kW) and 1500w (1.5kW) to a typical household. Like much in the world of energy rating, incidentals are very variable and so a vague approximate figure is used. At times (during parties, for instance) the incidentals could amount several kW of heat being produced. And at other times (whilst your away skiing perhaps) they could amount to nothing at all.
- C. Incidentals divided by the Specific Heat Loss. Why? The SHL represents the rate of heat loss from the house for every 1°C temperature difference between inside and outside. If you wish to keep the inside of the house 20°C warmer than the outside, then you will require twenty times more heat than the SHL to achieve this. But if your incidentals are already providing some of this heat, then you need to subtract this amount from your overall heating requirement. So this figure tells you how many SHL units are accounted for by your incidentals. And the answer can be expressed in degrees Celsius because each SHL unit is 1°C. Neat, isn't it?
- D. Degree Days. Nothing to do with your daughter's impending graduation from the University of Wensleydale where she just squeezed a 3rd in Cheesemaking. Degree days are in fact a measurement of how cold each place gets in winter. Everyday it gets one degree below an agreed base temperature (I thinks it's around 15°C) counts as one degree day. If it gets to zero, then that day would count as a 15 degree day. Total it up for the whole year and you get an annual degree days total. In Britain it varies from 1800 DD at Land's End to 3000 at John O'Groats. The figure of 2500 DD is taken here, just above average. Just think, one of the benefits of global warming is that the typical DD figures will actually be falling year on year.
- E. Reduction due to Incidentals. Now here's a tweak and a half. Read this one carefully. If your incidentals can be expressed in degrees of heating (see above), then it follows that they can be subtracted from the number of degree days you need to cover. In effect, they lower your 15°C base temperature. Each degree less heat required because of your incidentals amounts to roughly 200 degree days less

## 13f: The Carbon Index

| Carbon factor(CF) kg/m² | Carbon Index CI |
|---|---|
| 7.17 or less | 10 |
| 8 | 9.6 |
| 9 | 9.1 |
| 10 | 8.7 |
| 11 | 8.3 |
| 12 | 6 |
| 13 | 7.7 |
| 14 | 7.4 |
| 15 | 7.1 |
| 16 | 6.9 |
| 17 | 6.6 |
| 18 | 6.4 |
| 19 | 6.2 |
| 20 | 6 |
| 22 | 5.6 |
| 24 | 5.3 |
| 26 | 5 |
| 28 | 4.7 |
| 30 | 4.4 |
| 32 | 4.2 |
| 34 | 3.9 |
| 36 | 3.7 |
| 38 | 3.5 |
| 40 | 3.3 |
| 45 | 2.8 |
| 50 | 2.4 |
| 55 | 2 |
| 60 | 1.7 |
| 65 | 1.4 |
| 70 | 1.1 |
| 75 | 0.8 |
| 80 | 0.6 |
| 85 | 0.3 |
| 90 | 0.1 |
| 92 or more | 0 |

over the whole year - in fact the relationship isn't directly proportional but then this is a dumbed down table — what did you expect?

• G. Having done this calculation, you can then have a healthy stab at how much heat you will actually need in your home to keep it warm throughout the heating season. You take the adjusted degree days (figure F), you multiply by 24 because there are 24 hours in every day and then you multiply this by your SHL figure. Voila. You have an answer in kilowatt hours (kWh) used per annum.

What is fascinating here is to momentarily reflect on the role of incidental heating in all this. Although the actual amount of incidental heat doesn't alter a great deal between the three different houses I have examined, the reduction in degree days rises dramatically as you increase the insulation levels, thereby reducing the SHL. In the extremely well insulated Passive House, you need just over 1kW of incidental heat to cover the anticipated heating requirements for the whole

house whereas in the 1975 house the same amount of incidental heat is (I can't resist it) virtually incidental.

Back to the task in hand.

• H. Domestic Hot Water (DHW) requirements. As already discussed, this part of the calculation is largely guesswork. But 4,000kWh is enough for 180lts of hot water every day of the year, about 2.5 bathfulls. That's probably what four people would use. I have given the Passive House some credit (2,000kWh) for having half their hot water being supplied by solar panels — it's the sort of thing Passive House people would do.

• I. Combine space heating and DHW and you have an estimate of annual energy demand (in kWh).

• J and K. Boiler efficiency. Now boilers are not 100% efficient — see Chapter 8, Boilers. They have been getting more efficient and the latest, state of the art, condensing boilers have broken through the 90% efficiency barrier, but you still need to factor the boiler efficiency into the

calculations.

• L and M. Fuel costs. Now we have a figure for consumption, we can calculate a fuel cost.

• N to R. Carbon emissions. Each fuel had a carbon emission factor. From this you can readily work out the total carbon dioxide release for each house type, by fuel type. And divide by the floor area to get a kg of carbon dioxide per square metre, the basis of the Carbon Index. In fact there is one more little tweak that goes in here, one that I don't begin to understand but need to point out. In the SAP worksheet, they ask you to add 45m$^2$ to your floor area before you divide your carbon emissions by it. Why 45m$^2$? It tends to give a better result to smaller homes (obvious when you think about it) so it may be a subtle drive by the government to stop us building big houses. Maybe not. The fact is if you don't indulge in this tweak, you end up with Carbon Index figures which don't tally. The conversion of carbon emissions to Carbon Index is given in table 13l.

## 13g: Benchmark House: Likely Fuel Bills

*Figures for 160m$^2$ house built to 2002 regs*

|  | kWh | % | cost | % |
|---|---|---|---|---|
| Central Heating | 9100 | 45% | £140 | 25% |
| Water Heating | 5100 | 26% | 80 | 14% |
| Gas Cooking | 1000 | 5% | 15 | 3% |
| Appliances | 3200 | 16% | 200 | 36% |
| Lights | 1600 | 8% | 100 | 18% |
| Standard Electricity Standing Charge | 0 | 0% | 25 | 4% |
| ANNUAL FUEL BILLS | | | £ 560 | |

*COSTS INCLUDE VAT @ 5%*

# 20 Energy Saving Tips

The benchmark house was not designed as a "green" house which would have fantastically low running costs, and yet it is interesting to note that the combined bills for space heating, water heating come to just 50% of the total fuel bills. And this was as built before the 2002 thermal regs came into effect. This proportion would drop to around 35% were the house to have been built now. Much of the literature and advertising you see aimed at selfbuilders and professionals alike goes on and on about thermal-efficiency this and energy-saving that and how you must have this gizmo to have low heating bills and save the planet; but a balanced view of all this will show you that you already have low heating bills in a new house and that if you want to lower over all fuel bills then it is best to concentrate on other areas.

Table 13h summarises twenty one commonly considered measures that can be taken by the householder wanting a low energy consuming house with low fuel bills. Details on most of these measures are looked at in greater depth in their relevant sections in other parts of the book, but here they are grouped together for easier comparison. The results I find rather extraordinary; the most cost effective measures are generally the least talked about and the least advertised and, conversely, the products which tend to get "sold" to us as being ultra-green are often of very doubtful value.

## Do without an Aga

It's not just Agas. Any cast iron stove will suck in power like Saddam Hussein. And belt out heat like it's Basra in August. They are fine in pre-1975 housing but you will cook faster than your dinner if you put one in a post-2002 house. If you must have one, think seriously about having a swimming pool as well. Then you'll have somewhere useful to put all that surplus heat.

## Open Fires

Arguably single most effective energy saving measure a new housebuilder can take is to do away with any thoughts of an open fire at the design stage, as indeed AB Homes have done in the benchmark house. Fires are a costly feature to build, they are inefficient in terms of heat output and, when not in use, the chimney sucks up warm air like a vacuum cleaner. Despite this, people (otherwise known as the market) love real fires and they are unlikely to go out of fashion for a while to come. Using an enclosed stove doubles the heating efficiency of an open fire but halves

the enjoyment value. See the sections Fires and Chimneys (Chapter 7, Superstructure) and Alternative Heating (Chapter 8, Services).

## Passive Solar Design

Sounds very grand but all it means is orienting your dayrooms so that they face south. Usually the possibility of doing this is dictated by the site and, given the choice, most people would opt for it instinctively. A good passive solar design will save around £30/annum in fuel bills.

## Off-Peak Electricity

Switch to an Economy 7 meter and, for an additional standing charge of around £20/annum, you get 7 hours night-time electricity at under 40% of peak-rate cost. Buy appliances with timers (or buy separate timers for £20) and run appliances at off-peak rates. Potential saving: £50/annum.

This is saving you money but isn't, strictly speaking, saving energy. Night-time electricity use is no different to daytime use in this respect. However the reason night-time electricity is cheap is that there is comparatively little demand for electricity at night and yet they can't shut down all the power stations — especially the nuclear ones — at the flick of a switch. So using electricity at night is saving energy indirectly because it would otherwise probably be wasted.

## Gas Tumble Dryers

Buying a gas-fired tumble dryer will pay for itself within three years. One for gas customers only. See following section, Kitchen and Laundry.

## Gas Cooking

Gas cooking is much cheaper than electric. Gas hobs are priced the same as electric ones but gas ovens are rather more expensive. Doesn't suit everyone— gas cookers are less controllable than electric ones. See following section, Kitchen and Laundry.

## Fuel Choices

Oil and mains gas are currently the two cheapest fuels. Most people gravitate to these if possible. Electric heating is expensive in comparison though note the growing interest in ground to water heat pumps. Expensive to install but very cheap to run.

## Draught Proofing

Paying proper attention to draught proofing is well worthwhile and not expensive. See also Ventilation section in Chapter 8, Services.

Unplanned ventilation, as it is sometimes known, is likely to be a much bigger problem in complex shaped homes with lots of junctions.

## Condensing Boilers

A gas-fired heating system run off a condensing boiler will cost an extra £200 to install and but should save £30/annum on heating and hot water costs. Really alone of the high-tech green gizmos, the condensing boiler is genuinely cost effective. Oil-fired condensers are very much more expensive and, therefore, only rate *moderate*. See section on Boilers in Chapter 8.

## Efficient Appliances

Washing machines, electric tumble dryers, dishwashers, each cost around £40/annum in electricity to run. Fridges and freezers cost around £25 each. Specify "low energy" models when buying new and you could save 25% on these annual costs. See following section, Kitchen and Laundry.

## Floor Insulation

The 2002 standards require significant levels of insulation under the ground floor. Typically either 50mm of polyurethane or 100mm of polystyrene. Upping the spec from this standard has very little impact on energy saving. See Flooring in Chapter 7, Superstructure.

## Extra Cavity Wall Insulation

Adding extra insulation in the external walls helps a bit but the building regs have already gone past the point of simple economic return.

## Extra Loft Insulation

Similar arguments apply here as to cavity walls. You may well be surprised by what the new standards for roof insulation are. A U value of 0.16 in the floor of the loft requires no less than 250mm of fibreglass quilt, to be laid in two rolls one between the joists and one above. Adding another 50mm of insulation to this blanket will still just about pay for itself in a few years but above 300mm the return falls away.

## Heating Controls

Almost all central heating controls are cost effective, though the savings are hard to quantify. Generally speaking, it is worth spending money on good controls though some of the more advanced controls, like boiler managers and zone control, are not appropriate to every situation. Thermostatic

## 13h: 20 Energy Saving Ideas Costed

| | | EXTRA COST | LIKELY ANNUAL SAVING |
|---|---|---|---|
| **EXCELLENT** | Do without an Aga | Save £5000 | £300 |
| | Do without Open Fire and Chimney | Save £2000 | £50 |
| | Passive Solar design | No cost | £30 |
| | Run Appliances on Off-Peak Electricity | £20/annum | £70 |
| | Use a Gas Tumble Dryer | £50 | £25 |
| | Cook by Gas instead of Electricity | £150 | £50 |
| | Choose the Right Fuel | zero-£400 | £120 |
| | Fastidious Draught Proofing | £200 | £30 |
| | Fit a Gas-fired Condensing Boiler | £200 | £30 |
| | Buy Efficient Electrical Appliances | £200 | £40 |
| **MODERATE** | Switch to Timber Frame Construction | £0-£3000 | £50 |
| | Add an extra 25mm of Ground Floor Insulation | £60 | £5 |
| | Add 25mm Extra Cavity Wall Insulation | £150 | £20 |
| | Put 100mm of Extra Insulation in the Roofspace | £40 | £5 |
| | Fit Better Space Heating Controls | £200 | £20 |
| | Design an Energy Saving Lighting Scheme | £500 | £45 |
| | Fit a Super-lagged, Quick Recovery Cylinder | £50 | £5 |
| **POOR** | Fit High Performance Windows | £800 | £20 |
| | Fit Solar Hot Water Panels | £3000 | £40 |
| | Fit PV solar electric cells | £10000 | £150 |
| | Fit a Heat Recovery System | £1500 | £0 |

radiator valves (TRVs) cost about £8 per radiator; system managers are available for an extra £100. See section on Heating Controls in Chapter 8.

### Low-Energy Lighting

Annual electricity bill for lighting a four-bedroom house is likely to be around £130: compact fluorescent "energy saving" bulbs are cost effective, but are not suitable in every situation. A well designed lighting scheme might save £45/annum in running costs but is likely to cost £500+ to install. Note that new houses are now required to have some energy efficient bulbs. See following section, Energy Efficient Lighting.

### Better Hot Water Cylinders

All new cylinders are pre-lagged to reduce heat loss to a minimum, though some are better than others: look for one with 50mm of polyurethane insulation. A "quick recovery" cylinder will cost an extra £50 to buy but will save £5/annum in making better use of boiler output. See section on Domestic Hot Water in Chapter 8.

### Switching to Timber Frame

This always used to be a sure-fire energy saver because a standard 90mm timber frame, stuffed with fibreglass or Rockwool, easily outshone most masonry walls in terms of insulation. But the new requirement for wall U values of 0.35 means that this method of insulating timber frame is no longer enough (it used to get a U value of around 0.4). There are several different ways of making up the difference, all considerably more expensive. It's probably rather fatuous to try and reduce this complex matter to a simple money in to money saved equation but I've done it, to make you think if nothing else. I still hold that for most people (maybe not the Scots) timber frame is slightly more expensive and yet it's still going to tend to give better energy performance than block work. See Inner Skin section in Chapter 7, Superstructure.

### Solar Panels

Don't be tempted by solar panels unless they cost less than £300, not on cost grounds at any rate. Annual savings are likely to be less than £40. See Alternative Heating section in Chapter 8, Services.

### High Performance Windows

What were referred to as High Performance windows in the last edition of this book are now Bog Standard windows — cf. Jeld Wen's Stormsure range. Again, the new thermal regs are behind this change. Low performance windows no longer cut the mustard. However you can still easily out spec Jeld Wen windows. There are many people making very high performance windows, notably a lot of Scandinavian triple glazed ones with U values down at 1.3 (as compared to 2.0 needed to pass the regs). The savings are unlikely to be more than £20 a year. See Windows section in Chapter 7, Superstructure.

### Heat Recovery Systems

These are justifiable in terms of energy savings but not in terms of financial savings. They cost a great deal (£1500+) and many of them cost more to run than they could possibly save. Even a system which saves three times the amount of energy it consumes may still end up costing you, because the energy saved costs around 2p/kWh whilst the energy used to run the thing costs over 6p/kWh (i.e. peak-rate electricity). See Ventilation section in Chapter 8 for a more information about MVHR (as it gets referred to) and also passive stack ventilation, a non-mechanical alternative which is greener because it uses no power. Worth mentioning also that most of these MVHR systems do not sell themselves principally on their energy saving capabilities; rather they emphasise the benefits of controlled ventilation and filtered air.

# Low Energy Lighting

Slipped into the 2002 thermal building regs was a little stipulation about lighting. For the first time, you are required to pay attention to the watts you burn through your lights. It's not terribly draconian but it is there — many people will find that offensive enough. There is a remorseless logic about it all of which more in a minute but first a look at what Part L requires of you if you are building a home or even just an extension. It asks you to install at least one fluorescent or compact fluorescent bulb for every three rooms you create. Hall, stairs and landings count as one room. Garages, lofts and outhouses don't. En suite bathrooms and utility rooms — it doesn't say, leaving plenty of room to argue. So the benchmark house has approximately 12 rooms so it would be required to fit four CF bulbs (or tubes). No problem, you say. Stick a few bulbs in and replace them with something that looks nicer when the building inspector has finalled the project. Not so fast. They have thought of that one. They are stipulating that you have to use fittings that will only take a fluorescent tube or a CF bulb. At the time of writing, no one appears to make such a fitting but what the hell — I'm sure they can knock them out in Taiwan for next to nothing given enough warning. It doesn't stipulate where you should fit these lights but you are expected to go for somewhere where you would expect to get reasonably heavy use, like halls and stairs or living rooms and kitchens.

There's more. The regs extend to external lighting. This is a first too. You are no longer allowed to rig up permanent lighting without it being energy efficient. You can fulfil this requirement either by using CF bulbs or by installing it with daylight and movement sensors — i.e. so it's only on occasionally.

So what effect will it have and what of this remorseless logic? Lighting is energy intensive relatively expensive because a) it is inefficient (95% of the energy coming out of a standard GLS light bulb is heat) and b) it is using peak-rate electricity at around four times the price of oil or gas. The benchmark house has 22 lights fitted and in normal usage patterns about a third of these will be heavily used, a third will be lightly used and a third rarely used. On occupation it is likely to gain a few more lamps with the furniture and could be expected to have around 35 lamps to burn when occupied.

A typical usage pattern would look something like this:

12 lamps @ 60w, ea. 2000hrs/annum
1500kWh used, cost £110
12 lamps @ 60w, ea. 500hrs/annum
350kWh used, cost £25
10 lamps @ 60w, ea. 50hrs/annum
30kWh used, cost £2.

Now if four of these heavily used lights are replaced by energy efficient lightbulbs, then you could anticipate savings of 45w per bulb or 360kWh per annum. That's 20% of the overall lighting bill. In terms of kWhs burned the lights amount to no more than 8% of the total burnt but because electricity is so much more expensive than gas, this mounts up to nearly 20% of the overall fuel bill. So it does appear quite logical for the building regs to concern themselves with lighting efficiency.

There is no reason why you have to stop at the building regs minimum. You could probably half the power used to light your home, if you set your mind to it. How?

Concentrate on the areas of heavy usage, which are generally kitchens, living rooms, hallways, stairwells and studies; the areas of light use (typically bedroom and bathroom lighting) are unlikely to produce any significant savings. You could simply substitute your 12 most heavily used GLS bulbs with compact fluorescent, energy saving bulbs.

The problem is that energy saving light bulbs are not always particularly suitable as direct replacements for GLS bulbs; they cannot be easily dimmed, the light quality tends to be a bit too cold for most people's taste, and they are generally not compatible with standard lampshades. Substituting fluorescent light for tungsten light makes for subtle changes in atmosphere, and ill-planned installation can end up putting people off energy-saving light bulbs for good. Energy efficient lighting doesn't have to be bad lighting but for too many people this is exactly what it becomes when they swap over to a compact fluorescent bulb. However technology has moved on since the early days of CF bulbs and the current crop are smaller, more efficient and give better light quality. A Which? report (October 99) rated the Sylvania Mini Lynx Professional range: not only was light quality good

but the bulbs are small enough to be exchangeable with GLS bulbs in standard light fittings.

## Kitchens

Fluorescent lighting can work well in the kitchen — specialised lights can be used for both task and background lighting.

## Living Areas

In contrast, fluorescent lighting will not work well in living rooms and dining rooms. Low-voltage downlighting is an option (they use roughly half the power of a GLS bulb but twice the power of a fluorescent) but because of the tightly focused nature of the beams, you will end up using twice as many fittings which neatly cancels out their 50% efficiency rating over GLS bulbs. Low-voltage does not have to be confined to downlighters and a well-designed scheme could achieve adequate lighting from half the number of lamps by using mini-spots and/or uplighters.

## Hallways and Stairs

The other areas of heavy use tend to be in hallways and stairwells. Arguably light quality is not so important here and there are numerous compact fluorescent (CF) fittings which will fit the task. Whilst you may struggle to get a CF bulb to look good in a lampshade, the small 9w bulbs do fit into most uplighters and there are an increasing number of specialised low-energy light fittings becoming available: downlighters, glazed ceiling fittings and wall lights. They tend to cost around £30 where the conventional fittings might be had for under a tenner and so they need to be heavily used to justify the extra expense.

## External

If you plan on external lights the 2002 regs require that you either control them with timed passive infra-red (PIR) switches or, if you want them on permanently, use low-energy fittings. As for utility rooms and garages, fluorescent lights are commonly used here in any event and they can't readily be improved on.

## Intelligent Switches

Don't overlook the fact that one of the best ways to save lighting bills is to turn lights off when they are not being used. However, if you've got a house full of stroppy teenagers this may not be quite as easy as it sounds. You can, of course, fit time switches in hallways and stairwells but they tend to be a bit institutional. We are now quite used to seeing PIR switching used for external security but its use indoors to control lighting is still rare, but no more expensive than external PIRs (prices from around £25). Home Automation produce an informative price list which includes such things, as well as dimmer switches for low-voltage and compact fluorescent lighting.

## Summary

A low-energy lighting scheme needs to be carefully designed to be successful. With potential extra savings of £50/annum, it is worth spending money on too — which you will have to. There is precious little professional advice available on the subject — many lighting consultants will specify lots of low-voltage halogen fittings that will cost you much money but which won't save on running costs. Many architects know next to nothing about lighting design and electricians are taught only the rudiments of good lighting practice. How much you spend on energy saving features is entirely up to you but if your budget extends much past £500 on a four-bedroom house like the benchmark house, then you are unlikely to get cost effective savings.

# Kitchen & Laundry

Together with lighting, household appliances are the great unseen energy consumers. An examination of the fuel costs for a new home reveal that, even without specifying superinsulation levels and condensing boilers, fuel bills are actually higher for cooking, kitchen appliances and lighting than they are for space and hot water heating. Yet with a little application it should be possible to reduce running costs by nearly half.

Table 13j includes a breakdown of estimated fuel costs for cooking and household appliances in the benchmark house using the standard arrangements and comparing them with the cheapest alternative. The "normal" arrangement assumes all electric appliances using peak rate power: the "cheapest" assumes a mains gas supply is available. These are very much notional average bills; a "dinky" household, without children, might well run up bills less than half this amount whilst a large family could easily double the sums.

## Cooking

Gas cooking is way cheaper than using electricity; cooking by gas costs almost a quarter of what costs to cook using peak-rate electricity. Many people prefer cooking on a gas hob (and most developer's packages offer them as an alternative at no extra cost) but gas ovens have an undeservedly poor reputation and they are now few and far between, particularly in the built-in market. Electric controls and electronic ignition have greatly improved the traditional gas oven and if you use a main oven or grill more than one hour a week, it will be worth paying the extra £150 to install a gas oven. Stoves, Canon, Parkinson Cowan, New World still produce them; British Gas showrooms (now called Energy Centres) display them although they are not cheap places to shop. MFI has a number of cheaply priced gas ovens (made for them by

Philips and Stoves). If mains gas is not available, then LPG models will still produce 50% savings on electric cooking.

If electric cooking is the only sensible option, there is currently very little one can do to reduce costs. Energy efficiency has yet to make any significant impact on this area, but note that microwaves are very efficient at cooking small quantities. Microwaves are quick and work at much lower power than conventional electric cookers: on the other hand, food bought ready for microwaving is expensive. It all depends on how you use them. The induction hob, described in Chapter 11 Kitchen Appliances, would also seem to offer efficiencies over an ordinary ceramic hob. Note that cast-iron stoves — and Agas in particular — are very heavy users of fuel. A gas- or oil-fired Aga kept on all year would cost over £300/annum to run.

## Tumble Dryers

If mains gas is available, then go for a gas-fired tumble dryer. Canon and Crosslee White Knight both produce reasonably priced gas tumble dryers. Expect to pay £220plus which is 50% more than the cheapest electric versions, and allow for gas plumbing, but they are very much cheaper to run — payback period is around five years.

## Off-Peak Electricity

If you are unable to get mains gas, then fit an Economy 7 meter and you can take advantage of electricity at around 40% of the peak rate by arranging to use your appliances during the off-peak hours. If you don't lead a nocturnal lifestyle, then buy equipment with delay timers (Bosch dishwashers, some expensive Hotpoint and Creda tumble dryers, some Hoover and Hotpoint washing machines) or make sure that you can easily access the sockets and fit separate delay timers

(cost £15-20). Despite the large savings to be had, delay timers still hardly feature as a sales aid: you have to go looking for them.

Off-peak electricity charges are complex to understand; each supply company (REC) sets its own charges.

• All of them increase the standing charge (tariff) for letting you buy cheap rate supplies. These increased tariffs vary from

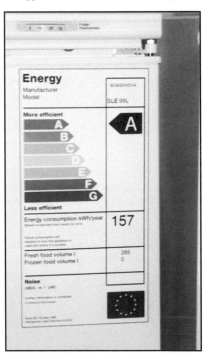

*If you've been shopping for white goods recently, you'll be familiar with Energy Labelling. It gets displayed on nearly all fridges, freezers, dishwashers and tumble dryers. In fact, so successful has this scheme been that it's spread to boilers and is soon to be adopted by some of our window manufacturers.*

£15 to £25/annum extra).
- All of them have an off-peak rate of around 2.5p/kWh (compared with peak rates of 7p/kWh or higher) at which you will be charged for all electricity supplies for seven hours each night.

The economies to be gained from using an off-peak tariff will vary from area to area, but if properly managed it should result in a reduction in electricity bills of 15%, perhaps more.

## Hot and Cold Fill

Look for dishwashers and washing machines which can be filled from your hot water pipes rather than heating their own water. This is now standard on new washing machines but is still rare on dishwashers (though Ariston make one). If using machines on delayed night-time switching, then separate H&C fill is of little benefit as the disparity between the costs of off-peak electrically heated water and boiler heated water is much reduced.

## Energy Efficient?

Many manufacturers are jumping on the bandwagon in claiming to produce machines which save on electricity, water and detergents. This is a complicated area and many of the claims are at best marginal and depend on the user understanding just what is expected of them. To help spread a little light into this murky area, fridges, freezers and washing machines are now routinely energy labelled to help the customer make an informed decision about how much power they use. A visit to my local Curry's revealed a wide range of scores: a Bosch Economic fridge freezer scored A and reckoned to use just 120kWh/annum (cost £8) whilst a giant Hotpoint power guzzler scored G, estimated to use 544kWh/annum (cost £38). Whilst the accuracy of energy labelling (which is carried out by the manufacturers) has been called into question (Which? Jun.96), the fact that there is now a comparative yardstick available on a range of white goods is a big boon.

Although these savings may not look individually very large, careful purchasing should be able to save £50 or more per annum of peak rate power and metered water. Water saving washing machines actually save remarkably little in cash terms and yet it is this feature which tends to be the strongest selling point on "Green" appliances.

For most buyers, there will be a number of other factors which will determine which machines they purchase — notably servicing costs and standards, reliability record, easy-to-use controls or perhaps it just all

came with the kitchen — and you may well be right to base your decision on these criteria, but don't be afraid to ask about water and electricity use. It is worth paying a little more for machines which perform well but, with the exception of cold storage, running the appliances during off-peak hours is by far the best option if you want to save on running costs. Don't be conned into paying out hundreds of pounds extra for "eco" products which bring minimal savings to you or the environment; instead, ask why it hasn't got a delay switch fitted.

## Use of Appliances

Considerable savings can be achieved by using your appliances efficiently. Really these are no more than common sense measures such as drying clothes on washing lines whenever possible, setting washing machine temperatures as low as possible and turning off lights when rooms are empty. If you've a

genuine interest in energy conservation — or just don't like paying bills — then at least part of the solution is in your hands.

## Summary

Energy-efficient appliances — or more particularly energy-efficient use of appliances — can be planned into a new house. The presence of gas on site makes for large cost savings but, even on remoter sites where gas is not available, there are numerous actions you can take to increase fuel efficiency. There is a cost penalty (though it is hard to quantify because there are so many variables) but there are also appreciable savings to be made. However, unlike installing insulation or efficient heating systems, saving energy in the kitchen requires you to interact intelligently with your machines and for many people this is just too much hassle.

## 13j: Running Costs of Household Appliances

|  | USE | NORMAL | CHEAPEST |
|---|---|---|---|
| Cooking | 400hrs/annum | £90 | £25 |
| Fridge/Freezer | Constant | £35 | £15 |
| Washing Machine | 300 times/annum | £45 | £20 |
| Dishwasher | 350 times/annum | £55 | £20 |
| Tumble Dryer | 200hrs/annum | £35 | £8 |
| TV/Video | 1500hrs/annum | £15 | £14 |
| Other Appliances |  | £20 | £18 |
| Electricity Standing Charge |  | £44 | £65 |
| **TOTAL** |  | **£ 339** | **£ 185** |

## 13k: Energy Efficient Appliances

|  | AVERAGE | BEST | ANNUAL COST SAVING |
|---|---|---|---|
| Washing Machine: Electricity Use | 2kW | 1.5kW | £12 |
| Washing Machine: Water Use | 90lts | 70lts | £4 |
| Dishwasher: Electricity Use | 2kW | 1.5kW | £12 |
| Dishwasher: Water Use | 35lts | 25lts | £2 |
| Electric Tumble Dryers | 2.5kW | 2kW | £10 |
| Fridge/Freezers per annum | 500kWh | 150kWh | £25 |

# Saving Water

Although 95% of UK property is still charged for water and sewage by a rating system, newly constructed housing in England & Wales is invariably metered (not so in Scotland and N. Ireland). Living with a metered water supply is a novel experience for most of us and it takes some getting used to. If you are connecting your drains into the main drains as well as tapping into the local water supplies, your bills will be broken down into four sections:

- Standing charge for water supply
  - Volume charge for water supply
- Standing charge for sewage disposal
  - Volume charge for sewage disposal.

Properties that dispose of waste by other means (usually septic tanks) will have other costs to pay instead of sewage charges — see section on Drains, Chapter 6, Groundworks.

## Water Charges

Unlike fuel prices, water supply charges have been going up. The average charge levied in England and Wales has doubled since 1989 and is only now beginning to level off. Average charge for water by volume is 70p/m³, although this can vary from 40p to over £1.00. In addition standing charges average £25/annum.

## Sewage Disposal Charges

Average charge is 90p/m³, but this also varies from 40p to £1.50/m³ in the South West. Welsh and Anglian also charge well above average. Annual standing charges payable for sewage disposal vary from £10 to £60 with an average of just over £30. As a rule,

*1000lts of water = 1m³ = 220 gallons = 12 baths = 120 flushing loos. When metered, this much water costs between £1.50 and £2.50 to use and pour away.*

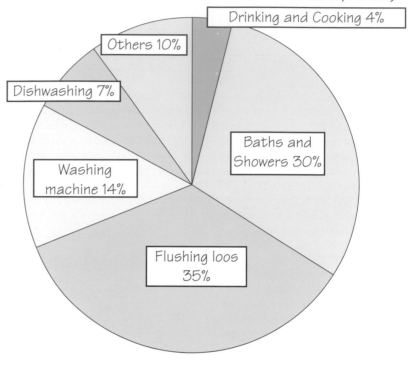

Drinking and Cooking 4%

Others 10%

Dishwashing 7%

Baths and Showers 30%

Washing machine 14%

Flushing loos 35%

companies with high standing charges have low volume charges and vice versa, so it does tend to even out.

## Metering: how it works

Only the water supply is metered. The volume of discharge you pour back down the drains is worked out from the amounts of water you consume: some companies reckon it to be 100%, some 95% and some 90%. If yours works on a 95% figure then, if you were to consume 100m³ of water, you would be charged for 95m³ of sewage.

A four-person household will typically use and discharge 185m³ of water/annum (equivalent to 2300 baths, that's just over six baths a day). This is likely to cost them between £300 and £450/annum depending on how much their water company charges. This 185m³ figure is very much an average and a new house with lots of thirsty appliances like dishwashers and power showers, not to mention children, could easily use 50% more. (Incidentally our household of five has all these thirsty appliances and we consistently consume 230m³ of water per annum). Heavy demand from swimming pools, garden sprinklers and the like would be in addition to these figures.

## Comparisons

The charges for average water usage are larger than the anticipated heating bills for a new home. Assuming the average 185m³/annum is consumed by our notional four-person household, the average bill, including standing charges, will be just over £300/annum. However, in some high charging areas such as the South West this could rise to over £450

### 13l: Water Appliance Consumption

| | |
|---|---|
| Av. Consumption/head | 150lts/day |
| Flushing a Loo | 7-10lts |
| Taking a Bath | 80lts |
| Ordinary Shower | 10lts/min |
| Power Shower | 30lts/min |
| Washing Machines | 70-100lts/wash |
| Dishwashers | 25-50lts/wash |
| Garden Hose/Sprinkler | 10lts/min |
| Tap Dripping Once a Second | 5lts/hr |

## 13m: Water Charges for New Dwellings

| | | ANNUAL CHARGES/ m³ | | |
|---|---|---|---|---|
| | | WATER | SEWAGE | COMBINED |
| Average Standing Charges | | £25 | £40 | £65 |
| Average Volume Charges | | £ 0.70 | £ 0.90 | £ 1.60 |
| **WATER USED BY 4-PERSON HOUSEHOLD** | | **ANNUAL VOLUME CHARGES** | | |
| ACTIVITY | Litres/day | As % | WATER | SEWAGE | COMBINED |
| Drinking/Cooking | 20 | 4% | £ 5 | £ 7 | £12 |
| Baths/Showers | 150 | 30% | £ 38 | £ 49 | £87 |
| Flushing Loos | 175 | 35% | £ 45 | £ 57 | £102 |
| Washing Machine | 70 | 14% | £ 18 | £ 23 | £41 |
| Dishwasher | 35 | 7% | £ 9 | £ 11 | £20 |
| Others | 50 | 10% | £ 13 | £ 16 | £29 |
| TOTAL | 500 | 100% | £ 128 | £ 164 | £292 |
| **STANDING CHARGES + VOLUME CHARGES** | | | **£153** | **£204** | **£357** |

| VARIATIONS | |
|---|---|
| 4-person household, Highest charging area (South West) | £490 |
| 4 -person household, Lowest charging area (Northumbria) | £290 |
| Average for 3-person household | £280 |
| Average for 2-person household | £210 |
| Average for 1-person household | £140 |

for the same volume of water. In comparison, the estimated space and water heating costs for the benchmark house are just £212 — including 5% VAT which is not levied on water and sewage services. With so much attention focused on saving energy, let us try to redress the balance and look at reducing water consumption. The pie chart illustrates how we consume our water.

What immediately stands out about these figures is how little water actually passes into our bodies (4%) compared to how much is consumed largely to keep us and our homes clean and hygienic. Part of the justification for higher water prices is the cost of maintaining drinking water standards but, on reflection, it seems extraordinary that we should go to such trouble to purify our water supplies in order to pour 95% back down the drains. In theory, at least, there is ample scope to use non-potable water and ample savings to be made by avoiding relatively expensive metered supplies.

### Use Less

Before delving into esoteric water-saving schemes, there are a number of common sense ways that water consumption can be reduced without making you smell:

• Wash yourself under showers, not in baths (impractical with small children)
• Don't fit a power shower
• Fit the smallest WC cisterns possible — the industry standard is now down to 6lt. per flush, thanks to a recent change in the water bylaws, but you may be able to source even smaller cisterns
• Don't run washing machines and dishwashers unless they are full
• Don't water lawns; water plants in the evening to avoid evaporation
• Use water butts (though attractive ones are hard to find)
• Don't build a swimming pool
• Pee anywhere except in the loo — easier for some sexes than others.

### Water Saving

Water-saving schemes are sommat else. They can be divided into two areas: rainwater collection which replaces water you'd normally buy through your water meter and grey water collection which recycles some of the water you have already used.

### Rainwater Collection

Even in dry lowland England (average rainfall = 750mm/annum) a four-bedroom house plus detached garage will get around 100m³ of rain falling on to it during the course of a year. Add in a paved yard and a drive and potentially you could collect your entire 185m³ annual consumption from the skies overhead. In wetter areas to the north and west this figure could easily double as rainfall levels are so much higher. The potential is there; the problem is that rainfall is not only unpredictable but sporadic whereas household usage is basically quite constant. You need to build a reservoir capable of holding enough rainwater to supply basic household needs, which is exactly what your own water company does on a much larger scale. Starting your very own water supply business may be an appealing prospect for some but it is likely to prove expensive to build and time-consuming to run. The bigger your reservoir, the more effective your own supplies will be in replacing your metered supply, but the more problems you are likely to have with construction and maintenance.

Rainwater harvesting has become quite trendy in no time at all and a surprising number of quite regular selfbuild homes are fitting tanks, filters and pumps so that they can reuse at least some of their free rainfall in a similar fashion. The Germans have been doing it on a domestic scale for twenty years and three of their systems — IRM, Wisy and KSB — are now available in the UK. Prices quoted are between £1,000 and £2,000: for this you get underground storage tanks (either plastic or concrete), filters to take out most of the leaves and twigs and a pump to lift the water back up to the house. Most people use it just for flushing loos, installing a second plumbing system supplying the cisterns from the storage tanks. You can rig it up so that the storage tanks never empty — the mains water cuts in when the level falls too low. More sophisticated arrangements allow rainwater to be used as drinking water but this requires on site treatment which is a complex affair.

## Grey Water

Only a water recycling scheme will cut down both supply and discharge. Grey water is the term given to waste which is reusable, notably the waste from baths, showers and wash basins. There is potential to recycle this water in the garden and especially for flushing loos. Because the waste from baths and washing is much more regular than rainfall, the storage facilities do not have to be nearly as large to be effective. A large bath-sized tank will be enough to flush ten loos and should get refilled most days.

As with rainwater harvesting, there has been a small explosion of interest in grey water recycling and there are now proprietary systems available using pumps and a small holding tank which can be placed in the loft. The grey water is treated with cleaning agents and passed through a carbon filter. Water Dynamics are producing grey water units for less than £1000. Grey water, requires much less storage than rainwater harvesting to be effective but there are potential problems with contamination which need to be addressed. Trials are underway at present to see just how effective grey water is — if it is as effective as claimed, it will pay for itself in around ten years in a four-person metered household.

## Potential

By combining rain-saving and grey water systems, the potential is there to reduce water demand in new housing by over 50%. Whilst the legislation dealing with carbon dioxide emissions (our thermal building regs) has grown steadily more onerous on the housebuilder, water saving has yet to be seriously considered. Yet the harmful effect of $CO_2$ — the so-called greenhouse effect — remains an unproven hypothesis (albeit with potentially catastrophic consequences), whilst the effects on the environment caused by reservoir building are all too tangible. The best that can be hoped for is that the whole area could be given a much needed boost by exempting developments incorporating water saving schemes from the perilous infrastructure charge — see Chapter 3, Pitfalls.

## Paying for Leaks

Whilst the problem of a dripping tap is well known (and costly for metered households), it palls into insignificance compared to the potential nightmare of an underground leak. You, the householder, are responsible for all water consumption downstream from the water meter — which is conventionally located outside, close to the plot boundary. Spring a leak underground between the meter and your internal stop tap and you may know nothing about it until a massive water bill arrives on your doorstep (as much as six months later); if you are lucky, the water company will let you off paying the sewage charge, but even so a bad leak might lose as much as 20m³ of water a day which would cost £1500 by the time you get your water bill. Be warned that sloppy installation (and loose connections) of water mains can be very expensive once you are on metered supplies.

## Boreholes

There is another way of avoiding water company charges — and infrastructure charges — and that is to sink your own borehole and draw your own water supply up from under the ground. It's where most of the water comes from in SE England and in many other areas besides and, whereas your local water company has a monopoly on piped supplies, there is nothing to stop you tapping into the enormous natural groundwater reservoir directly. That's an oversimplification; there is the small matter of installation costs which vary from £1000 and £10,000, depending on such matters as the depth of the borehole and the water pressure. For most people, that makes it an extremely expensive way of going about getting water and sends them straight back into the arms of their local water company.

If you are one of the small number who plan to draw their own water supply from under the ground, then you will be responsible for your own water quality. That's not to say that you won't have to submit your water for analysis to the local Environmental Health Inspector: indeed most councils will be around testing you every couple of years or so. Simple bacteria tests tend to be done in local hospitals and cost around £30; however tests for pollution are more expensive — I was quoted £100 for a nitrate test. The Environmental Health Inspector has the power to condemn your supply but this rarely happens because almost everything can be filtered out — at a cost. My local inspector reckoned that ground water pollution was something of an overstated problem and that when he did come across it, it was very often the house itself that was the cause of the pollution; he advised not to use ground water supplies in conjunction with a septic tank. Obvious when you think about it.

*The IRM Rainwater Harvesting system. The water is stored in the big underground tank and pumped back up into the house*

There are two very distinct processes here. You soften (or condition) water in an attempt to prolong the life of your domestic appliances, whereas you filter water in an attempt to prolong your own life. Both techniques are surrounded by a veil of mystery and intrigue which is hard to penetrate, and the whole subject is so rife with claim and counterclaim that it makes the job of the humble commentator akin to negotiating a minefield. Wish me luck as I go in.

## Softening and Conditioning

If you live in a soft water area (which includes most of Britain above a line drawn between the Humber and the Severn) then this section is one to miss. If in doubt, phone your water company to get figures on local conditions. Even if you live in a hard water area there is no need to panic. Households have been known to function quite adequately for years without so much as a hint of any water softeners about. However, many sane people swear by water softeners and insist that they produce tangible benefits — even if it's only to reduce the amount of soap powder they use in their washing machines

## Traditional Softeners

Permutit are the best known name here though there are a number of other manufacturers. For between £400 and £1000 you get a big box into which you add salt – you need around three 25kg bags of salt per person per annum, so this alone will cost you £30 each every year. Softeners work by separating out the hard bits in the water, exchanging them for softer sodium bits. The box needs an electrical supply and a drain-off point. The long-term benefits include reduced water heating bills and savings on soap powders (combined unlikely to be worth more than about £25/annum). Evidence that water softeners increase the lifespan of hot water appliances is — careful now — inconclusive but almost everyone who has one reckons they do make the water feel softer and the laundry appears cleaner.

As these boxes actually chemically change the water supply, their output should not be drunk or cooked with. Design your plumbing system so that the kitchen tap, at least, comes directly from the mains.

## Phosphate Conditioners

These are a sort of junior version of the big water softeners. They are designed to stop hot water appliances from scaling up and they are usually sold in conjunction with combination boilers and/or mains pressure hot water cylinders. You will see them in plumber's merchants — look for names like Combimate and Combicare. They work by adding phosphate solution to the incoming water, which inhibits scale formation — they don't "soften" the water as such but they are reckoned to prolong the life of water-heating equipment in hard water areas.

They cost around £80 and they don't need power or drainage facilities but the phosphate cartridges need replacing every year (cost £15 a time). Again the treated water is not ideal for drinking but these conditioners are normally only fitted to water heating devices.

## Inhibitors

Unlike the two preceding methods — which are chemical treatments — inhibitors act by passing a magnetic or an electrical charge through the water which — it is claimed — prevents the hard bits in the water from sticking to the pipes. They are relatively cheap (£30-£60), easy to install and need no maintenance. Also they do not affect drinking water qualities. Some need electrical power, most operate without. But do they work?

You may figure they are so cheap that there is nothing to lose in trying and you may well be right. But how will you know that your investment does the biz? Another thing to ponder on during those long dark nights. During 1995, Which? carried out a survey on this very issue and reported back with a wide range of reactions from "very pleased" to "a complete waste of time and money." If there was any conclusion at all it was that they work in some areas but not in others. Not really very helpful. Leading names are Salamander and Culligan, who both produce magnetic versions and electrolytic versions. If you want to know what the difference is (or what reverse osmosis is) then you sound like you're interested enough to make your own enquiries; start your investigations at the plumber's merchant.

## Filtering

In the last few years, there has been an enormous growth of interest in the subject of tap water quality. Whereas the Victorians basked in the glory of the technical achievement of providing clean drinking water to all homes, we have now become blasé about this and tend to worry that much of this water runs through lead pipes and, in any event, doesn't taste very good. Added to which there are fears (in lowland England at least) that we are now getting nitrate and pesticide residues in our tap water.

There is now a huge choice of water filters available, ranging from the free standing plastic jug affairs which can be picked up in Boots for a few quid to expensive, in-line purifiers. There are no British Standards for water purifiers ("tap water's just fine, old boy") and there is little concrete evidence on the effectiveness of the various methods. There is also concern that many filters may themselves be health hazards, providing spawning grounds for micro-bacteria. Nevertheless, interest in water filters continues to grow and one of the more innovative companies working in this field is Culligans who supply the whole range of water treatment gizmos from softeners and scale reducers to filters and ultra-violet disinfection units. If you want to find out more, get hold of their Practical Guide to Water Conditioning.

*A phosphate conditioner plumbed into the feeder main to a mains pressure cylinder*

# Eco Houses

I looked at the two predominant schools of house architecture back in the Design chapter. Traditional is of course just that but modern design is getting a bit long in the tooth itself. Modernism first appeared in the 1920s and by the 1950s it had evolved as far as it was going. American architect Phillip Johnson famously built a rectangular glass box house for himself in 1949 and that was it really. After that, all glass box houses have been variations on an established theme and modern simply became the name of another school of architecture like Georgian or Arts & Crafts. In the commercial world trends have moved on, but in housing there has been very little new happening stylistically since then — almost everything has been harking back to popular styles of the past.

## Eco History Lesson

But in the past few years a new style has begun to emerge, the Eco House. I think almost everybody is aware of the term Eco House but it's maddeningly difficult to define what an Eco House actually is. The concept first appeared in the 1970s shortly after the oil crisis begun to concentrate minds on the need to conserve energy — long before anyone had ever heard of global warming. Architect couple Robert and Brenda Vale are generally held up to be the pioneers behind it, at least as far as Britain is concerned. Back then they were called self-sufficient houses and the Vales lived in one and wrote books about how to do it. The Vales would be the first to admit that what they were building was hardly great architecture; it was more an example of environmental engineering. Yet the interest in what they were doing never went away and their influence has steadily grown. The Centre for Alternative Technology (CAT), based in a quarry in North Wales, also started in the 1970s and they began a programme (which continues to this day) of building ground breaking structures, moving away from simple energy saving to embrace a whole plethora of different techniques and materials. CAT is open to the public and each year thousands visit and this way slowly the seed has spread out through the community.

## A Style is Born

In the past few years the number of Eco Houses being built has mushroomed. Society generally seems to be slowly greening and the younger generation in particular is more aware of environmental issues and seems to be prepared to put their money where their mouths are. But what has also emerged is an Eco House style, a sort of organic cottagey look, which is quite unlike any form of housing we've had in Britain before. The Eco House has moved on from the early pioneering days and has begun to develop a language all its own. The key elements are the use of loads of natural materials, preferably as unprocessed as possible. Timber and slate are in, concrete and plastic out. The house needs to be engineered so that it has a minimal environmental footprint; this translates as being not only super energy-efficient but also water-efficient as well — water recycling is becoming de rigeur. Internally, the styling tends towards the aesthetic — white walls, wood or stone floors, little ornamentation, ethnic furnishings. Surprisingly, an awful lot of the kitchens still come from IKEA.

There is a strong echo here of the Arts & Crafts movement which flourished in Edwardian times. That too was an upmarket affair — principles are expensive — but whereas the champions of that movement were highbrow art lovers, the Eco House builders are self-consciously looking to build a better world, rejecting the values of trashy consumerism. It's as though the hippie movement has grown up and got rich and translated their core values onto that ultimate bourgeois status symbol, the detached four bedroomed house. Enough of these contradictions.

I realised that the Eco House had gone mainstream when I visited Vikki Martin in 1999 in her newly built Green House in Cambs. Till then, I had never come across an Eco House that hadn't been the brain child and baby of the owner/builder. Vikki was different: she had been persuaded to build green by her architect. "Previously I hadn't really known anything about it" she told me. "But Bill Miller thought it was a good idea and the more he talked about it the more I became convinced. The ideas seem so sensible." The Green House is cutting edge techno green: it has photovoltaic solar cells on the roof and the electricity they generate is sold to Eastern Electricity via a two-way meter — it's one of the first homes in the UK to do this. Unusual yes, but it's been built and it doesn't look like any other house in the village.

Eco houses are not yet the complete consumer item. But all it takes is a client who is prepared to spend a little more money, to take a longer view on how the building will work and what effect it will have on the environment and suddenly another one is underway. My estimates are that around 100 a year are now getting built in Britain and that this is increasing year on year at a steady pace. There are now dozens of architects and builders specialising in Eco Building — a very good place to find out about them all is the Association of Environment Conscious Builders (AECB) which publishes annual lists of practitioners as well as a useful magazine.

Besides the individual selfbuilders, there is growing interest from larger housing organisations, especially housing associations. We are also seeing a few green housing estates and even a few green villages popping up; the best known is probably the Beddington Zero Energy Village (or BedZed), brainchild of architect Bill Dunster which is emerging from out of an old sewage farm in South London — you can't get much more organic than that.

*Earth sheltered housing is a fascinating sub-set of eco housing. Such houses are warm in winter, naturally cool in summer and look like nothing else. This one was taking shape in Lincolnshire during 2002..*

# Chapter 14
# Apocrypha

*The Aprocrypha was written at the same time as the Holy Bible but was felt by the editors not to be quite up to the mark, so they published it separately. This Bible's Apocrypha consist of a few odds and ends that simply don't fit into the rest of the book. Analysing housebuilding as an activity is a bit like trying to figure out where every strand of spaghetti begins and ends. Some are easy to spot, some take some figuring out and some you just can't do, no matter what. So these are the bits to go into the Aprocrypha. All essential stuff, just doesn't fit neatly into the jigsaw. Note that the book website at www.housebuildersbible.co.uk also has a section called Aprocrypha and here you will find more misfit articles.*

# Security & Safety

The average private dwelling currently suffers an attempted break-in every 12 years and over half of these attempts are successful. Furthermore, the amount of burglary has nearly doubled since 1983 and if the crime rate continues to grow at this sort of pace, then by 2025 it will have risen to one attempted break-in at every home every other year.

Whether this Doomsday scenario ever comes about is open to doubt because it would involve an army of a quarter of a million burglars each breaking into a house every week. Whatever the future holds, burglary is not a problem that is likely to go away and anyone considering building a new house would be foolish not to consider the matter very carefully. Some inner city areas already suffer appallingly high burglary rates, making house contents insurance extremely expensive and sometimes even impossible to obtain.

## The Burglar

As you might suspect, the typical burglar is a young male but you might be surprised to learn that he is not part of a well-organised gang but usually a lone wolf whose break-in is often done almost on the spur-of-the-moment, when he sees the opportunity arise. There is really no reason to adopt a fatalistic attitude because, although it's entirely true that if someone really wants to get into a house they can, 90% of the time they won't bother if you go to the trouble of making life difficult for them. Our young burglar's main concern is not to get caught in the act and to this end he values being able to get in, and out, quickly and preferably unseen. Another surprising statistic thrown up is that as many as 20% of burglaries take place while the home is occupied. You'd think this would be amazingly risky for our burglar but it only takes a few seconds to come in through an open door and walk out again with something like a radio or a camera and you may not even realise that you've been burgled. If you are worried about this sort of thing happening, get a dog.

With regards to new housebuilding, current thinking focuses on the following areas:
• Site layout
• Preventing access to the rear of the house
• Decent locks fitted to ground floor windows and doors
• Burglar alarms where risk is high
• Security lighting.

## Site Layout

Though this area has more relevance to estates than to single dwellings, it's worth mentioning what they are on about. Dark corners and unlit alleyways should be avoided and houses should be sited where their neighbours can see who is coming and going. There is often little the individual housebuilder can do about this, though it is possible that consideration can be given to the issue when there are two or more houses to be sited near each other.

One obvious point that the professionals have tended to overlook is to locate the most widely used room in the house — usually the kitchen — at the front of the house, so that the occupants can see who is coming and going out on the street. However, this arrangement remains an extremely unpopular layout in this country; we still prefer our kitchens to be by the back door.

## Restricting Access

The rear of the house is the preferred area of entry for burglars. This is largely because the back of the house is almost always more private and is often very well screened from neighbours. A burglary often starts with a casual casing of the front of the house; if it looks as though there is no one at home, the second stage will be to go round the back and take a closer look. Only when they're convinced the coast is clear will the break-in proceed. If access to the back of the house is impeded, then the would-be burglar may abort the job at this early stage in the hope of there being easier pickings further up the road. A 2m fence and a stout gate — even without a bolt — will provide a considerable measure of defence against unwanted prowling. Back gardens can be protected, to a lesser extent, by walling or hedging them in. Plan in any obstructions that will at least slow down the progress of a potential burglar. However bear in mind that a fully enclosed garden, once breached, makes an ideal spot for our burglar to force an unseen rear entry so if your garden is going to be enclosed for security reasons, you need to do it well.

## Robust Locks

It is now an NHBC standard to have 5-lever locks on all external doors and to have window locks as well. At least one exit — usually the front door — must be protected by a night latch (Yale-type locks) which can be opened from the inside without a key; this is to aid escape in case of fire. The idea is to lock the door on the night latch when the house is occupied and to use the 5-lever mortise lock when the house is empty. Window locks are now fitted as standard on most volume joinery, so all new houses will — or should — be built to these security standards now and there is no further action that need be taken at the design stage.

## French and Patio Doors

It is marginally easier to force a door inwards than to prise it out but it is likely to be rather noisy. Most front doors open inwards. However, note that double-doors (french doors) are particularly easy to force in or prise outwards; most french doors open outwards and if you fit them be sure to fit decent sliding bolts to the top and bottom of both doors. For extra security, make these lockable bolts. Sliding patio doors are generally a much more secure (and draughtproof) alternative (though not half as elegant); however, many break-ins have occurred where the patio door frame has been levered out of its seating, having only ever been held in by six short screws or, sometimes, nothing more than mastic sealant.

## Glass

The current building regulations will ensure that you have to fit double-glazed sealed units and the safety standards on glazing insist that safety glass is fitted to all doors, windows next to doors and all glazing less than 800mm above the internal floor level. Safety glass is expensive, costing nearly twice as much as ordinary float glass. It comes in two varieties, toughened or laminated and they perform slightly differently. Toughened is harder to break but when it breaks it collapses into small nodules, whereas laminated glass has a sheet of plastic sandwiched between two layers of ordinary glass; this makes it harder to break through (from the burglar's point of view) and is therefore slightly more secure. The police are big fans of laminated glass, suggesting that it should be fitted wherever there is glass next to an accessible lock, but as this includes virtually every ground floor opening window it would be an expensive option.

## New Security Standards

Factory-glazed windows are available which meet a new British security standard, BS 7950. Rather than just testing the individual locks or the glass, BS 7950 tests the whole window assembly in situ. Typically such a window will have laminated glass on the external face and shootbolt espagnolette locking mechanisms. To get windows to this standard, they really need to have been factory glazed but this doesn't mean they have to be plastic — most of the big timber joinery manufactures now produce BS 5750 windows.

## Burglar Alarms

There are huge variety of different alarm systems out there and it's not easy deciding what to fit. It is usually cheaper to install a wired system which is particularly well suited to new housing as the wiring can be concealed during first-fix stage. Installation quotes for a four-bedroom house are likely to vary from £500 for a basic system based on a mixture of internal infra-red detectors and contact points to over £1000 for an external vibration detectors which are triggered by interference with doors and windows. Should you not want to go to the expense of installing an alarm, as an alternative, the wiring can be first fixed-in a day for between £100 and £200, so that the intruder detectors can be fitted at a later date without disruption to the decorations. Burglar alarms are eligible for zero-rating of VAT when building a new home.

Fixing a burglar alarm should not be beyond the capabilities of a competent DIYer and there are a number of systems designed for just this. DIY alarms usually consist of a control panel, the detectors and an external siren. The wired systems are the most reliable and are probably best suited to new builds. However, wireless alarms have their advocates and are easily fitted as an afterthought. The standard wireless systems still need mains connections for both the control panel and the siren but the latest generation work entirely on radio signalling; the siren and the control panels are solar powered and you activate the alarm by using a remote control. Response Alarms produce a totally solar powered alarm called the Sola costing just over £100 but it's fairly basic in its capabilities.

More features tend to add to the cost but it is still possible to get a well featured wireless system for under £200, such as Yale's High Security Alarm System which can handle up to 24 zones. Zones are the areas covered by individual detectors and most burglar alarms allow you to arm or disarm any of your zones individually. This is useful if you have pets or if you want only the downstairs armed when you are upstairs at night. Better systems have a capability of checking that all component parts are working — a feature sometimes referred to as a 24 hour zone..

## Detectors

The detectors on which burglar alarms are based come in a number of guises. The two commonest are the passive infrared (PIR) detector, which is triggered by movement across its path, and the door- or window-opening detector which is set off when a magnetic contact is broken. You can also get detectors based on pressure pads — typically these would be under a doormat and would be triggered when someone unexpected treads on it. You can give great thought to just which detector to put where and still get it all wrong. Many a break-in now occurs via an upstairs window: the thieves never go downstairs because they reckon it will be alarmed, so they just ransack the bedrooms before leaving the same way they came in. So maybe it pays to have lots of detection zones but possibly only if you are very confident in your ability to operate the system.

If you've never lived with a burglar alarm, you might be forgiven for thinking that they are the last word in home security. However, the consequences of fitting an alarm can be fairly tortuous for the householder and their neighbours. All systems are set to make a loud noise for a few minutes; false alarms will make you very unpopular and false alarms do happen, so a burglar alarm is not without its problems. A recent police estimate reckoned that no less than nine out of ten ringing alarms are actually false alarms and the police in some areas are now refusing to respond to ringing alarms, particularly if the alarm in question is known to be a repeat offender.

## Monitored Alarms

If you have a very remote site or are not entirely happy about a 105-decibel alarm ringing when a mouse crosses the floor, the next step up the security ladder is to get a monitored alarm. These link your house via the phone lines either to the local police or to a security firm. If you want the police to monitor your alarm, then the system must be installed by a company approved by one of two bodies; NACOSS (National Approval Council of Security Systems) or SSAIB (Security Systems and Alarm Inspection Board). Needless to say NACOSS or SSAIB approved systems cost rather more than unapproved ones. Or as one wag put it, it's daylight robbery what these guys get away with. Monitored systems also carry an annual charge which is likely to be in excess of £150; they are only available if two key holders besides the occupants live close by and are prepared to be called out in the middle of the night.

## Movement Sensors

Alarm systems don't have to just concern themselves with making loud noises or sending messages off to police stations. You can also rig up detector beams running across the front and the back of your house which set off a buzzer inside when they are crossed. They vary in sophistication from simple passive infrared beams like the ones used to trip lights to multi-height beams running between two concealed posts which aim to be cat and fox proof. The well designed systems will give you fairly reliable intruder alerts: a poor system, tripping out every time a bird flies by, will just make you paranoid.

Why bother with a movement sensor? Well, I would have tended to ask the same question until my mum had one installed a few years back. She loves it; she has one out the front and one out the back and she can tell the difference between the postman and the paperboy by the time they take to cross the beam. At night, it's switched from buzzer to warning light in the bedroom and once it's picked up a prowler round the back and enabled her to alert a neighbour before any damage was done.

## Car Parking

Both integral and detached garages can be included in whole house intruder alarm systems, but this tends to be very inconvenient; the car has to be left outside whilst the alarm is deactivated (usually inside the house). It rather defeats the purpose of these remote control devices for garage doors.

## Other Measures

Door chains (from £3) and viewers (from £4) are becoming more common, and are recommended by the police. Surely the most cheeky is the fake "Protected by Burglar Alarm" bell casing which you screw on to your outside wall. Available at around £8 from DIY sheds.

## Security Lighting

Passive Infra-Red (PIR) detectors, similar to the ones used on internal movement sensors in burglar alarms, are also used on external lighting. These can be very useful around dark entrances although the halogen bulbs (sometimes 500w) can be so bright that you dazzle passers-by and tend to make them think you live in a high-security prison. Installation of a good PIR security light will cost around £80 (Mats £40, Lab £40). There are some very cheap versions on the market (at around £10-£15) which are best avoided; at around £30 you start to get ones where it is possible to change the bulb. Better forms of external lighting exist which can be wired to PIR switches, as well as manual override switches, which give pleasant external illumination as well as some form of security (see Chapter 9).

There are also a number of products which can be used to give the effect of occupation when the house is empty. For around £20, you can buy a gizmo which fits in between a light-bulb and its lamp holder which acts as a light-sensitive switch, useful for simulating occupation when you are away.

### Shutter Protection

To fit security roll-down shutters to every opening on the benchmark house would cost over £6000 so no way is this a cheap and cheerful option. Indeed it looks pretty severe as well, but if you are away a lot and have particular reason to fear intruders, then shutters are very secure. They don't work well with outward opening windows (think about it) and are best designed around either sliding sash style or tilt and turn windows.

### Safes

Home safes are available from £150 for a wall fitting one and from £200 for one bolted to the floor. Placing a safe in an existing house can be awkward but in a new house it's a doddle — if you've planned ahead for it.

## Fire Safety

The fire brigades get called out to around 60,000 house fires every year and around 500 people die each year in house fires in this country. And many of these deaths could be easily prevented with a few basic precautions. Fortunately, most of these have been encoded in our building regs so if you are undertaking a newbuild or a major renovation, you will have to build them in.

The purpose of the fire safety regulations is not to stop buildings burning down but rather to allow the occupants time enough to escape from them when they do start burning down. One of the long held prejudices against timber-frame building is that people think it will be more likely to catch on fire but this really is not so as the timber elements are almost always enclosed in a layer of inert plasterboard which is enough to delay the onset of fire by half an hour. The real danger in house fires is caused when soft furnishings catch fire and the smoke quickly engulfs the occupants. Whilst there has been a steady introduction of non-flammable materials into the home furnishing market, the biggest step forward in the world of housebuilding came in 1992 when smoke detectors became mandatory. Since then, all new homes have been required to have smoke detectors not just fitted but mains-operated with a battery backup as a failsafe. Smoke detectors cost around £20 and can be wired into the house lighting circuit. Electricians are by now au fait with what's required. The regs are that there should be smoke alarms on each storey and that they shouldn't be further than 3m from any bedroom door, so that some larger designs will require two or more on the upstairs landing. The benchmark house has one unit on each of its three floors.

What the regs don't go into is the different types of smoke detector you can choose. The cheapest and commonest are the ionisation detectors which are very sensitive to small particles of smoke produced by flaming fires, such as chip pans, and will detect this type of fire before the smoke gets too thick. But you can also specify optical ones as well which are more effective at detecting larger particles of smoke produced by slow-burning fires, such as smouldering foam-filled upholstery and overheated PVC wiring. Optical detectors are more prone to going off in error; either the mirror gets dirty or thunderflies get in. A third and possibly more useful type is the heat sensor which gets triggered when temps reach around 55°C — fit it in the kitchen but not too near the cooker. Whatever you choose, it makes sense to have them all interconnectable so that when one is triggered, they all go into action. Some smoke alarms also have additional capabilities, such as emergency lights and silence buttons to override false alarms.

Other safety features you might choose to look at are the provision of fire blankets in the kitchen (around £30) and extinguishers in garages and near open fires (£70-£100). Your best bet is to stick with local firms which offer maintenance; look in Yellow Pages under Fire Extinguishing Eqpt.

### Three-storey Houses

Provided every room opens onto a hallway or corridor, a two storey house is not going to have any problems meeting fire safety regulations. But there is a critical safety level, defined as having a floor 4.5m above ground level, when it becomes necessary to beef up your escape procedures. One of the principal requirements relates to how your main staircase runs through the house. Ideally, the staircase should lead directly to the front entrance door within an enclosed hallway: what is frowned upon are open-plan arrangements, particularly when the staircase exits via the kitchen (reckoned to be the highest risk area).

You also need to consider how to protect the stairwell from encroaching fire. There are two options. The first is to make the entire stairwell what is called a fully protected enclosure; this means that the walls around the landing and stairwell must be rated at 30 minutes fire resistance and the doors opening onto the landing must be rated at 20 minutes. The second option doesn't insist on fire doors but instead requires that you design at least one window in the top floor as an escape window, allowing the fire brigade to get a ladder safely under it. You also need to consider the floor construction which also needs to meet the 30 minute fire rating. If you are undertaking a new build or a major renovation, it's not difficult to meet these standards; in fact in terms of walls and floors it's quite difficult not to meet them. The only place where you are likely to come unstuck is on the doors. Not only do you need a thicker door — most fire doors are 44mm thick, the same as external doors, but you will also be required to fit them with door-closers. The least obtrusive solution here is the Perko door-closer which is fitted into the hinge side of each door and connects to a plate fixed to the door frame. They are cheap to buy (around £7 each) and a pain to fit and adjust — at least I find them painful — but they do they job. Fire doors are also much more expensive than regular doors: Premdor Crosby are a good source for fire check doors. If you are converting an existing house, there are fireproof (or intumescent) paints that you can apply to doors to upgrade them; check out Environmental Seals.

Sound proofing. This is, without doubt, the most difficult section in the book. For me to write, for you to understand. I have beavered away at sound proofing several times over the past few years and never really got to grips with it. It's a very slippery subject. Just when you think you've got it licked, up pops another aspect you hadn't thought of before. You can't reduce it down to a matter of decibels and sound absorption. Experience has shown that walls or floors built with materials which should, in theory, sail through any acoustic tests often fail miserably. All I can venture to do is to give you a few pointers and hope you don't get overwhelmed by the subject. The sound regs — Part E in England & Wales, Part H in Scotland — are currently undergoing a complete overhaul and the new ones should be implemented in 2003. There are hundreds of pages of proposals. Completely over the top, you'd think, until you get down to examining the detail and then you realise what an amazing mishmash of conflicting theories it all is. The sound boffins want to introduce a regime involving acoustic testing on finished dwellings. They are convinced that this is the only genuine way to improve standards because the recommended details have failed so often in the past. The house builders are fighting this move tooth and claw because they see big problems in implementing pre-completion testing — and horrible costs if the structure should fail the tests. Acoustic testing may or may not come into force when part E is finally agreed and implemented; if it does, it won't affect people building individual homes but it could be required on all attached properties and flats, including conversions of exiting large houses into flats. It'll be expensive and it'll be even more expensive if your property fails.

## The principles

Sound is said to travel around buildings in three distinct ways, being

- Airborne sound — voices, radios, TVs, sound systems, traffic noises, embarrassing farting and bonking noises.
- Impact sound — footsteps and banging, amplified by the current fashion for hardwood and ceramic floor covers. Impact sound travels through the structure.
- Flanking sound — odd mechanical sounds (often connected with the plumbing) that also travel through the structure of the building via some devious and unexpected routes. Some say that flanking sound is just a specialised type of impact sound. Maybe it is, maybe it isn't. I have

barely started and already I am losing my grip!

There are basically three things you can do to ensure that none of these sounds is a problem.

1) provide enough mass to absorb the sound
2) build in some separation within the wall or floor structure
3) ensure the walls and floors are airtight.

If 3) seems a bit pernickety, consider this. If you build a solid masonry wall between two rooms, you'd be hoping to get a sound reduction in the order of 45dB (decibels). Now if you were to leave a small hole in this wall (say 25mm x 25mm) or a series of small holes amounting to a similar area, the sound reduction would fall to around 30db. At 45db reduction, you would probably be aware that a conversation was taking place in the next room but you wouldn't be able to hear what was being said. At 30db you could probably hear every word clearly. So ensuring the walls and the floors are airtight is vitally important if you don't want your neighbours to know what you are up to.

One of the axioms trotted out by fans of masonry construction is that it's much better at sound absorption. It's true, mostly. Mass is the easiest concept to understand in all this. The heavier your wall or your floor, the more it will tend to absorb sound. Thus a dense concrete block wall tends to perform well. Lightweight aircrete blocks (cf. Celcon or Thermalite) not as well. And hollow walls or floors made of wood or steel even less well. But it doesn't follow that a heavy block wall will *always* perform well. It may have those tell-tale holes in the mortar; if you want to be 100% sure, you probably need to apply a wet plastered finish in order to ensure air tightness. And heavy concrete beam and block floors have developed an unenviable reputation for poor sound performance. It's not altogether clear why but it seems it may have a lot do with the fact that the infill blocks never fit as tightly as they should and that they are sometimes removed to run pipes, ducts and cables. It is strongly rumoured that when the revised Part E is finally published that beam and block intermediate floors will no longer appear as a recommended detail. Instead the more expensive hollow core concrete floor planks (which can't be tampered with once installed) look set to take their place. Mass is fine, provided it's not compromised by holes.

Which leaves us with No 2) on that list, separation. This is another line of defence altogether. Build in a separate wall or a false ceiling and you dramatically enhance sound insulation. The same principle is at work on glazing where double glazing makes a big improvement on single glazing. Incidentally the best gap between panes for thermal efficiency is 20mm, the best gap for sound insulation is 100mm. There are a number of windows around (mostly made in Sweden but readily available in the UK) which are triple glazed with a double glazed sealed unit combined with a third pane encased in a single glazed opening casement, specifically designed to be both energy efficient and quiet. They are usually known as 2+1 windows.

I digress. This separation principle applies to walls and floors and it's generally how the lightweight materials like timber and steel achieve adequate acoustic standards. If you build a party wall between flats, then you'll have to have two separate walls unless you use a very dense concrete block with a wet plaster finish. Floors are more complicated still. A false ceiling is ideal but not always practical. Instead there are number products out there from a number of different manufacturers (mostly makers of insulation) which allow you to build up a floor with different layers. Rockwool produce some the best know systems. Typically these designs add a bit of mass (in Rockwool's case RW2, a dense form of their mineral wool, known as *sound deadening quilt*) into the voids between the joists, adding a little more mass to the ceiling below (by doubling up or even trebling the thickness of plasterboard) and additionally laying a separating acoustic layer above the floor which completely isolates the final floor cover from the rest of the structure of the house — this hopefully does for impact sound and flanking sound transmission. Of course none of this stuff is cheap so it's normally only used on separating floors between flats.

## Miracle products?

Well there of course are no miracle products. But there are a couple that you should be aware of. One is a very neat product for floors called Acoustilay which I came across in 1998. Here's an extract from an article I wrote about it then in Building Homes.

Tony Harrison is converting a block of listed buildings into flats in Camberwell, South London. Being listed, he had to respect the layout and false ceilings were not allowed. The work he carried out to sound proof the intermediate timber floors was in accordance with the standards set out in Part E of the Building Regulations: it involved building in an acoustic floor system, laying sound deadening quilt in chicken mesh in the floor voids and placing acoustic strip insulation along the top of the joists. However it was not enough. The day the first residents moved in upstairs, there were complaints about noise from the neighbours below. Harrison thought they were being unreasonable and was at first inclined to dismiss them. However, as the scheme filled, other residents began to complain and when one of the downstairs residents repeated verbatim a conversation he had just had with a subcontractor in an upstairs flat, he knew he had a big problem. The large living rooms in particular seemed to amplify both airborne and impact noise and they took the advice of a sound insulation specialist who recommended Acoustilay, a new acoustic flooring underlay.

They fitted the thickest section available, Acoustilay 15, which costs around £20/m$^2$, and immediately noticed a marked difference. Harrison remarked: "Basically it has cured the problem for us. Our specialist reckons it increases the decibel absorption by around 20%. First we fitted it into the unoccupied flats to see whether it worked and that was so successful that we then persuaded the upstairs occupants to let us lay Acoustilay under their carpets. Really I can't think of any other product that we would have been able to fit in this situation. It's been a godsend." Being a flexible material, an Acoustilaid floor is slightly spongy to walk on, not dissimilar to other floating floors. You can't lay vinyl on it but it will take hardwood flooring.

The company that makes Acoustilay is Sound Reduction Systems and they reckon they have the best product on the market for upgrading timber floors. Director Eddie Williams says: "Most of our orders are no greater than 50 or 100m$^2$ which means it's largely going to people doing one or two flats. But we are now getting larger orders coming through as well, notably a few from people who've fitted beam and block upper floors and find that they're still getting problems with impact noise." Unlike other acoustic floor systems, Acoustilay doesn't require any building in as it just lays on top of the floor exactly as a carpet underlay would do. It is laid in a staggered pattern across the floor and needs to be tightly butted together. It can be cut with a trimming knife and the edge details can be fixed with carpet strip. But it's still not a miracle product. If you want to limit impact sound, nothing beats a nice plush carpet. If you must have hardwood flooring (OK you must), Acoustilay under the flooring, coupled with a sound absorbing wall board is a good second best.

Which beings me on to non-miracle product No 2. Fermacell wall board. It's an alternative to plasterboard and, unlike Acoustilay, it's already had a mention in the section on Plastering in Chapter 10. It's much heavier than plasterboard — so it's got that mass thing sorted — and it's enormously popular in Germany where it's made. It's designed with the DIY market in mind in that, having fixed it, you just glue between the joints and then paint, so it's a very simple, unskilled operation compared to wet plastering or taping and jointing. And by substituting Fermacell board for conventional plasterboard on a room dividing wall, you add around 10db of sound absorbency. That's enough to beef up a stud wall to something close to a wet plastered block wall. You can get the same effect by using a heavier plasterboard and doubling it up but it's not quite as elegant a solution. There are some other benefits to using Fermacell but I've said enough — I'll let the Fermacell sales team take it on from here!

## Summary

If you are building flats or terracing, you will have to pay close attention to soundproofing between the units. Just meeting the new regs may prove to be quite a challenge. If you are just working with a single house, there is very little in the regs which requires your attention though for the first time it looks as though the long standing NHBC requirement to provide some additional soundproofing to studwork walls around bathrooms may become part of the regs and, in addition, it may be extended to bedrooms as well. But this can be met simply by placing some insulation within the void of a stud wall, or by beefing up the board used. If the location where you are building is particularly noisy, then consider triple glazing and consider using mechanical ventilation rather than trickle vents on all the windows — they let in the noise as well as fresh air. And if you are building in timber frame, consider using a heavy board like Fermacell on walls and ceilings to deaden the sound between rooms.

Provision for disabled access in housing became part of the building regulations for the first time in October 1999. The bit of the regulations which covers access issues in England and Wales is called Part M (Part Q in Scotland) and the changes have been greeted with enthusiasm by disability campaigners but have had a lukewarm reaction from both the housebuilders and the general public who feel that this is political correctness run riot. Personally, I'm torn between the extremes. The little Tory in me reacts negatively to having meddlesome legislation shoved across my soon-to-be-levelled doorstep; then I find myself talking with a builder whose wife is confined to a wheelchair and, as he describes the struggles they both have in coping with her disability, I suddenly chide myself for being so mean spirited and wish that the regulations went much further than they do. These changes were in fact first mooted by the Tories in the early 90s — they may appear to be very New Labour but they have been welcomed by politicians of all persuasions as a way of increasing the independence of both disabled and elderly people. Although Part M has been phrased in such a way as to make you think they are designed solely for wheelchair users, the groups who are expected to benefit from the changes is far reaching, including the blind and partially sighted and families with pre-school children

Part of the problem is that there are actually very few severely long-term disabled people around so making every new house conform to a rigid set of standards in order to meet their requirements seems both expensive and illogical. Perhaps. Perhaps not. It actually costs very little extra to build a Part M compliant house — in contrast it's always frighteningly expensive to retrofit such measures into an existing house. We are building homes which may well have a life expectancy stretching well into the 22nd century and during this lifespan there is every chance that several occupants will come to appreciate some of the 1999 Part M changes. Whatever your feelings about it all, Part M in housing is here and we are going to have to learn to live with it.

### What's in Part M?

To comply with Part M:
- Each house will have to have one level threshold — ideally, but not necessarily, the front door. This doorway should be a minimum clearance of 775mm between frame and opened door, which translates as having to use an 838mm door (the old imperial 2'9" size). A level threshold is defined as one which has a bump of no more than 15mm under the door.
- This entrance should be easily approachable from the outside. In practise this means there should be no steps and no incline of more than 1:20
- Every home must have a downstairs toilet. This room doesn't have to be big enough to accommodate a wheelchair. It's just the door has to be wide enough to get a wheelchair through (2'9" or 838mm again).
- Ground floor corridors and doorways must be wide enough to allow wheelchair users easy access. There is a trade-off here; wider corridors can have narrower doors but the rule of thumb which seems to be developing is to have all ground floor doors 838mm wide and to have corridors at least 1050 wide.
- Power sockets and switches must be placed no lower than 450mm and no higher than 1200mm above finished floor level throughout the house.

### Level thresholds

This is the feature that is giving designers and housebuilders the most sleepless nights. The standard (pre-1999) British front door involved stepping up from the ground into the house — indeed the internal floor level is typically 150mm (that's two brick courses) higher than the external ground level. Like many standards, this front step had never been a regulation but was simply a detail that had evolved, primarily as a way of keeping water from flowing in under the door. The level threshold changes all. It requires the doorstep to be re-engineered. Many builders will chose to provide a ramped access up to the level threshold but in situations where this is not possible, it will be necessary to sink the entire house by two brick courses. Don't shout it out too loudly but there is actually a small potential cost saving here.

Detailing a level threshold so that it is watertight is in itself a challenge. One of the authors of the new Part M, Dr. Andrew Burke, admitted in a seminar I attended that there were no designs which were totally foolproof: I find that worrying. You need to pay attention to rainwater ingress and to rising damp — the damp proof course around the door needs careful attention, as does thermal cold bridging and, in some cases, radon and methane penetration into the surrounding cavity. It's easy to install waterproof barriers underneath the front door only for the carpet fitters to come and rip them off later when they find that they can't actually open the door once the carpet has been fitted. This is another problem to be faced. If you pay close attention to your front door detailing, you will probably be fine but, traditionally, it's been a part of housebuilding design which has usually been sorted out on site. Traditionally front doors open inwards and traditionally floor covers have not been an issue because of the step. But level thresholds force you to consider carefully how you will finish the floor internally. Consider it carefully. A sunken matwell seems to be a good solution for many. This covers the area where the door opens and you can start your floor cover on the inside of the matwell.

In fact, we have already accumulated a wealth of experience in building level thresholds, mostly in the social housing sector. Habinteg is a housing association which has been specialising in special needs designs since 1970. They have fitted level thresholds to around 2000 properties and have not experienced any notable problems. Occasionally, they have to fit a gully across the threshold to collect rainwater but this can normally be avoided by creating a small (1 in 40) slope away from the door.

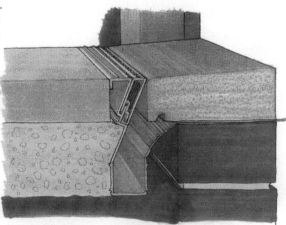

*Hepworth's Threshold Drain is the most ingenious solution yet to the problem of marrying level thresholds with maintaining a damp proof course under the door cill.*

Habinteg's standard detail satisfies the requirements for waterproofing, draught proofing and thermal bridging as well as level access. Instead of a timber cill, they use a precast concrete threshold, chamfered on the leading edge so that water runs off. Unlike a conventional timber cill, this concrete threshold sits below the damp proof course — the damp proof membrane is lapped up the inside face of the threshold. The cold bridge is stopped by a 20mm strip of insulation placed against the inside face of this threshold: this is in turn bridged by quarry tiles.

The waterbar and draught proofing details are provided by Caradon Wintun's Low Cill Sealbar. This comes in two sections, one which screws into the concrete threshold, the other is attached to the bottom of the door. When open the bar sits just 12mm proud of the finished floor level: when closed it provides two separate draught-proof barriers, arguably a rather better detail than that commonly in use today. To finish, Wintun produce a clip-on weatherbar, called the Colourclip, which is available in a range of finishes. The Low Cill Sealbar costs between £22 and £25/door, depending on the width, whilst the Colourclip is an additional £9.

## Other measures

The last edition of the Housebuilders Bible went to press just as Part M came into effect. Since then AB Homes have gone on and developed another estate using the same house types. The only difference between the two versions of the benchmark house was the need to incorporate Part M into the designs. Andy Allen, the designer/builder of these homes, found Part M reasonably easy to configure. The level thresholds were no problem, the new light switch and socket heights had been used throughout the house, the wider doorways were welcomed. He had even managed to do what I had written was impossible — fit a Part M-compliant loo under the stairs.

OK, they had packed out beside the stairs a little to make the loo wide enough for wheelchair access, and they had angled off the top of a 2'9" door to make it fit under the string, but he had done it. None of the new home buyers has passed comment on any aspect of the disabled access arrangements.

However there was one aspect of Part M that both Andy and his brother Roger really disliked; the ramp outside the front door. They felt it was really ugly and they also worried that it could in itself present a danger, an obstacle to be tripped over or fallen off. "Whilst it will help wheelchair users, I can see it being a hindrance to the blind," said Andy. He wondered why the ramps have to be permanent. In the longer term, I believe designers will become more confident about detailing sloped entrances where it's not even apparent there is a ramp. It would certainly be much preferable to the bolt-on ramps used to make pre-1999 house types comply with Part M.

Nothing else in Part M involves anything new or unusual. The regulations about ramp gradients and corridor widths are spelled out in the approved document and house designers should soon be up to speed on how these measures should or should not be incorporated into the home.

What is less clear is just how and where exceptions are to be made. Officially, Part M excludes only extensions and alterations to existing dwellings. All new dwellings in England and Wales are meant to comply with Part M access whether they be new builds or conversions. However, there are a number of cases where there may be opportunity to waive at least some of the obligations. Most prominent amongst these is the issue of people building flats: there is no requirement to provide lift access to the upper stories, so effectively the disabled will be no better off.

There is also expected to be some provision for steeply sloping sites which otherwise might not be developable without recourse to using stepped access. What is less clear is what will happen to people wanting to build upside-down houses or townhouse designs where the main living accommodation will be on the first floor.

## Lifetime Homes

From the point of view of the disabled, Part M is very tame. It concentrates on making new homes 'visitable' but it does little to make them more 'usable.' Disability campaigners would like to see Part M extended in scope to include further measures, building what are usually called Lifetime Homes (after an influential report by the Joseph Rowntree Foundation). What would turn a Part M compliant home into a Lifetime Home?

• Attention is paid to car parking: you need a space at least 3.3m wide to enable wheelchair users easy access to cars
• Thresholds should be illuminated as well as level; the main entrance should be covered
• The upper storeys should be potentially visitable as well; to do this, space should be left where a lift could be fitted in the future.
• All the house controls should be within reach, not just sockets and light switches; this includes things like window catches and trickle vents and central heating controls
• Drainage should be provided for floor showers in bathrooms and WCs and baths should be capable of being adapted to take handrails.

## Open Building

The open building movement is the ultimate stage on this road. It proposes that homes are built like office buildings with maximum flexibility in mind. You start by building a shell and then you fit it out to the occupants wishes. You don't start with an interior design fixed, just a very flexible construction which allows you to a number of possibilities. If you sell up and move out, the next occupant can easily dissemble what is there and fit it out the way they want it. So room partitions can be moved and services re-routed. Disabled access is built into the shell so it doesn't have to be thought of in any special way.

To date open building in the UK only happens in the commercial sector. The Dutch and the Japanese have done a fair amount of open residential building but their housing markets are pretty different to ours — typically they see it as a way of customising apartments (which is what they mostly build). Still it's food for thought.

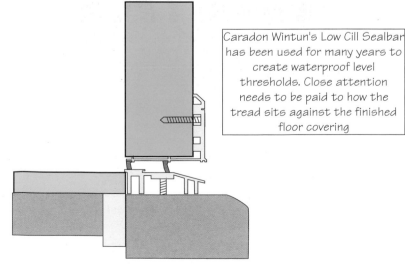

Caradon Wintun's Low Cill Sealbar has been used for many years to create waterproof level thresholds. Close attention needs to be paid to how the tread sits against the finished floor covering

# Future Proofing

Accessibility is often thought of as a way of building in measures to help the disabled. But there is another side of the coin and that is just how we access all the services we place inside a new house. It's something which modern building techniques have made increasingly difficult and there is a tendency to hide everything in walls and floors and to use materials like chipboard and plasterboard which make future access difficult. As the number of wires and pipes running around our homes multiplies, we are actually making it harder and harder to get at them, quite the opposite of what we might anticipate. It's certainly a long way from the idea of Open Building which, in it's purest form, is all about being able to easily rear range not just the services but the very structure of the house so that, for instance, rooms can be open plan or subdivided. But for many people it's more a question of being able to access cable and pipe runs, a way of leaving your future options open.

The trouble is open access to services is difficult to achieve and surprisingly expensive. Most houses can accommodate a major service run duct from, say, ground floor up into the loft space. The problems come when you want to get to the actual sockets. Both floors and walls tend to be pretty unremovable: you can adapt them but it is not easy. For instance, you can lay floor ducting into screeds which is fine if you cover the floor with carpet but not so useful if you put tiles or hardwood floors down: these can be taken up but not without a good deal of grief. Similarly you can build boxed-out skirting boards which can double up as cable ducts but this still leaves you with the problem of how to get to the back of the sockets and also presents problems at door openings.

Of course these problems have all been addressed in the office environment where all the cabling gets hidden in false ceilings and behind removable perimeter trunking. Though you can use such systems in the home, it does tend to look pretty industrial: people go to great lengths to conceal such things as waste pipes and soil stacks and this makes it seem somewhat retrogressive to start surface-mounting plastic trunkings. But it is an option. If you were prepared to say definitely just where the workspace in each room should be located, you could easily equip each room with a short section of trunking which would allow you the flexibility of later fitting data terminals, phone sockets, TV outlets or even good old mains sockets, bearing in mind that mains power is best kept a short distance away from data cables as you can get interference between the two. With a little forethought you should be able to plan access panels, ducting and cable runs into your home at the design stage.

Perimeter trunking can be made on site if you fancy your hand at second-fix carpentry. Alternatively, you can buy preassembled trunking from Centaur, Mita or any of the electrical wholesalers listed in your Yellow Pages. Trunking tends to come in 3m lengths and costs from around £15/m upwards depending on depth and finish specified. And to be readily accessible you have to sort out the vertical drops as well so that, ideally, you can lay new cable without disturbing any of the fittings in the house. In fact, both Centaur and Mita produce vertical columns designed to run from floor to ceiling (called Powerpoles) through which you can easily feed new cable and add as many outlets as you require.

The downside with this approach is that again you have to make some prediction about just how you are going to use the house in years to come. Will you want a TV or a computer or a phone in every bedroom? Will there be problems if you install them in some rooms but not others? And just where in each room should the outlets be?

In the meantime, at least pay attention to the idea of a wiring closet (see Chapter 9, TV, phones and cables, for an explanation). Whereas your electrician might persuade you to fit your fusebox under the stairs, if you have more room it is a good idea to set aside some wall space to take more complex gear in years to come. And provide some ducting between the floor beneath and the outside world.

## Secret plumbing

Exactly the same issues occur with plumbing. Indeed future accessibility is arguably more important because plumbing can leak. Piped water runs are often placed under the floor but this can be difficult if, as in the benchmark house, you have a power floated slab which goes down at the beginning of the construction process. If you lay a screed on your floor then you can fit ducting: check out Pendock Profiles who produce a range of galvanised steel channels which can accommodate water pipes and have a screwed plywood covering. They are designed to fit into either a 50mm or a 70mm screed: I estimate that fitting Pendock Profiles to the ground floor of the benchmark house would cost around £200 in materials: this would have been enough to take all the radiator pipes around the radiators downstairs. Whatever you do you should be aware that they are at their most useful when the ground floor gets a carpeting. Tiling of any description and tongued and grooved timber floors cannot be taken up without a good deal of disruption and it will be impossible to replace them as before.

*My 98/99 benchmark house was built with removable ducting laid into the floor. Very few builders now go to such trouble.*

# Barn Conversions

Many people reading this book start out with a dream of living in the countryside in a house built to their own designs. It's a widely shared aspiration but, for the majority, it will never become more than an aspiration. Britain has some of the tightest rural planning rules in the world and it's simply not possible to pitch up in Chipping Butty and build a house in Farmer Giles's meadow. What building plots that do come up are more likely to be the back garden of an existing house which may not be quite what you had in mind.

But there is a chink in the planning armour. Whilst the planners won't countenance building from scratch, they are keen to see existing rural buildings get a new lease of life. There are several hundred thousand farms dotted around the British countryside. Virtually everyone has outbuildings used to store cattle or grain or for various farmy type things and a huge number of these are now lying empty and unused. Now conservation bodies love these old barns and want to see them survive in some form but there is simply no call for them with modern farming. Such is the demand for rural building plots that people are willing to pay enormous sums to convert these barns into homes. In doing so, they have created an entirely new form of housing that seems to be unique to Britain. It is both ancient and modern. Ancient in that it involves restoring centuries old structures often using traditional techniques. Modern in that the space being created is often far more like an urban loft apartment than a traditional home as served up to us by the mass market developers.

The world of converting redundant buildings is very different to new housebuilding. You have to be prepared to have things imposed on you which you might think are unreasonable and unfair. The very fact that we are allowed to convert redundant buildings rather than just pulling them down demonstrates that we are engaging with the British obsession with preserving the past, and the planners have a number of ways of making sure that certain rules are adhered to in exchange for the right to create a home in a place you otherwise would not be able to. Chief amongst these is the idea that what you build should continue to look like what was there before. And not in anyway look like a conventional house. This goes for conversions of nearly all redundant buildings with some degree of historic interest; chapels, schools and pubs to name but three. But the bulk of single home conversions are going on in rural barns as these are by far the commonest rural structure up for conversion.

## The Rules

• reuse existing doorways, even if they were designed for carts
• don't block up existing openings
• no masonry chimneys — stainless steel flues acceptable only if kept away from the ridge
• as few new windows as possible — and any new windows should as plain as possible.
• no changes to the roof. Certainly no dormers and preferably no rooflights. If rooflights, preferably on the side no one sees.

• repair the original material wherever possible. If replaced, use something similar. If it's timber, it must be timber that matches the old style.

What a lot of barn designers end up doing is building in a large glazed screen area where once stood the main barn door. This is often inset into the structure — this borrows a little extra light for the rooms opening off the hallway behind the glazed screen. No matter that what you end up with doesn't look a bit like a farm building, it does make a very attractive structure. In fact the barn conversion, particularly the timber barn conversion, has rapidly attained iconic status as a fashion item in their own right. Whilst the history of the original barns has been documented by the likes of RW Brunskill, the history of barn conversions has yet to be written.

Barns tend to come in two distinct flavours, timber and stone. Timber predominates in the south and east where they tended to be built for threshing and storing corn. Stone barns are more common in the north and the west — the Scots refer to them as steadings — where they were most often used as cattle sheds. As cattle don't like going up stairs, the stone barns tend to be single storey, the timber ones are routinely two storey or, more accurately, high enough to accommodate a second storey. There are of course masses of exceptions to this rule of thumb and there are also masses of sheds and barns built of other interesting materials like cob and clay lump. After a penal brick tax was removed in 1857, you start to see a lot of brick barns being built which are also now ripe for conversion. I have even seen steel framed agricultural buildings (you can hardly call them barns) dating from the 1950s getting the modern barn conversion treatment, complete with stained weatherboard exterior. Another example of planning gone mad, perhaps. But why not?

If you see a barn on the market with planning permission for conversion, the chances are that it has already been subject to a thorough examination in order to have obtained that permission. Unlike virgin building plots, you can't obtain Outline permission on a barn conversion — it has to be Detailed which means that the design is closely scrutinised by the planners before any approval is granted. The planners would ideally like to see redundant farm buildings given over to some commercial use with the hope of creating some rural employment. In fact there are grants of 30% or more available for con-

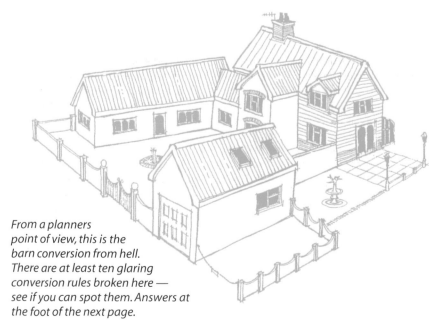

*From a planners point of view, this is the barn conversion from hell. There are at least ten glaring conversion rules broken here — see if you can spot them. Answers at the foot of the next page.*

version if you can find a viable business use for the building — this can include farm shops, workshops or even holiday lets. Diversification, that's the name of the game. Trouble is that for a huge number of barns there simply isn't any viable option other than residential conversion for resale (for which there is currently seems to be an insatiable demand). However in order to prove this, you have to carry out a business viability survey, assessing likely income from the converted building. Brian Belton, a surveyor with Durrant & Sons, based in Diss in Norfolk, handles a large number of these applications every year and he commented: "I've yet to find a barn in my patch, the Waveney valley, where the economics of a commercial conversion stack up. You need to show a return of 14 or 15% before banks will be willing to finance and you only ever seem to get around 7 or 8% returns showing through on the surveys, even with the grant money thrown in."

Only by showing a commercial conversion is unviable do you open the door to a residential conversion. But before such permission is forthcoming, a detailed structural survey also needs to be undertaken to see whether the barn is "permanent and substantial." In Durrant's practice, this involves measuring every timber and inspecting all the joints. Most timber barns are in need of a large amount of restoration but very few are unsalvageable. The rule seems to be if it's standing, it's salvageable. Typically the timber along the bottom edge — the sole plate — has rotted and sometimes twisted, causing the base of the barn to move outwards, but the sole plate can be replaced and the plinth can be reset. The very fact that a barn has stood for so long is usually a testament to how well built it was in the first place but sometimes decay can be rapid, especially if the roof cover has been removed or has blown off. On occasion, conversion has to be carried out in double quick time in order to save the building. If it collapses beyond repair, there will be no hope of obtaining permission to rebuild.

This raises another intriguing problem: insurance. Redundant buildings are intrinsically liabilities, not assets. What's of value here is the development potential, not the structure itself. But the development potential hangs on the structure continuing to at least exist. There a danger of buying a barn for conversion and losing everything when it burns down or gets blown over before you've started work. This insurance risk is at least recognised and specialist selfbuild brokers such as Holbrook offer cover for this. But do bear in mind always that most planning consents for barns conversions specifically state

*Before and during. The above shot, taken in Feb 2000, shows a timber barn on it's last legs. By June 2000, you'd quite easily think it was a new house taking shape. Basically it is. Only the original posts and beams remain.*

that the consent will become invalid if more alterations or repairs are carried out than were agreed — hence the need for a good survey and plenty of shoring up

## Timber Barns

With a little luck, your barn survives long enough for you to make a start on the conversion. What needs to be done? Start with the foundations. Rarely will any of these buildings have what we now call foundations in any shape or form. Stone or brick plinth walls just tended to spread a little below ground; there were never any attempts to dig down a metre of so onto hard bearing ground. However the barns have stood the test of time so the principle to be observed is that, if you don't change any of the loadings, there really shouldn't be any need to alter what exists. Given that the alternative is underpinning and that underpinning tends to cost a minimum of £500 per linear metre (likely to work out at over £20,000 for a barn), then it's well worth avoiding new foundations if possible. So if you wish to build in an upper storey, you have to find a way of keeping the added load

*Most of the timber barns coming onto the market in SE England were built to thresh and store corn. They were designed to take a horse and fully laden cart in through one door and out empty on the other side — occasionally this is reflected by having a high door on one side and a low one on the other but more often you get two similar sized barn doors facing each other. Despite every barn being seemingly different, there are some surprising similarities. They are routinely made up of bays, defined by the principal posts and trusses. The roof pitch often gives a clue to the age of the barn; the older the barn, the steeper the pitch. Thatch - widely used in parts of England in Tudor times - requires a pitch of more than 50° whereas pantiles and the like work with pitches of 35-40° and when slate arrived in the 19th century the pitch could be dropped to 30°.*

of this new floor off the existing walls. The solution lies in building a platform inside barn; this can be achieved with stud walls underneath or, more commonly, using a series of beefy posts which themselves get bedded on new concrete pads.

Then consider the ground floor. The condition of these varies from compacted earth through to level concrete in good condition. Concrete sounds like an advantage but bear in mind that in order to meet the latest U value requirement for floors you will almost certainly have to put insulation on top of it and consequently you may be losing significant height; sometimes it is better to dig out an existing floor and put in a new one. There are two additional points to consider here. You don't want to go down so deep that you expose the base of the walls otherwise you will suddenly find yourself in an underpinning situation — a couple of exploratory test digs should reveal how far down your walls go under the ground. On the other hand, if you are planning on building an upper deck, you may find that you have to negotiate a tie beam, tieing the roof trusses together. Ideally you want your finished ground floor level to be at least 4.5 metres below any tie beams otherwise you will be having to go on hands and knees to get under the tie beams. Incidentally, there is no minimum height for rooms or doorways encoded in our building regs, but realistically you need 1.8m clearance on doors to make them comfortable to pass through. If you haven't got a reasonable clearance there may be ways around the problem by gaining access to the different bays from half landings or maybe installing a second staircase. Physically, you may be able to lower the floor a little or you may even be able to jack the entire building up a little — though for God sake keep quiet about this, the planners would have a fit!

Actually, it is perfectly acceptable to jack a timber structure up when carrying out restoration work. Expected even. The procedure

is to strip away everything that you don't intend to keep. Often this means reducing the barn to nothing more than a timber skeleton. You then build an internal scaffold cage and then place pins under the header plates at the top of the walls which take the weight of the roof. The whole structure then gets lifted gently off the supporting walls at the bottom and this then allows you to get to work restoring these walls and go about replacing the sole plates. If all the bottom joints between the sole plate and the wall studs have rotted, it is standard practice to cut the wall studs shorter and fix a new sole plate (usually green oak) in a slightly higher position than the old one. If other pieces of the original frame are missing or damaged, now is the time that the replacements are made. You will then have to add a couple of courses of brick or stone onto the plinth wall underneath to make up the difference. At this point you would be expected to let the structure down again to sit on the repaired plinth.

From here on in, the timber barn conversion becomes a new build. The walls will normally get covered in plywood or something similar and a detail will be on hand to add insulation to the structure — in this respect a converted barn must perform to the same standards as a new house. In timber barns, most people want to see as much as possible of the original timbers and therefore the tendency is to find insulation systems which wrap around the exterior. The reflective foil insulations like Actis are gaining ground in these markets as they take up so little space. Normally a timber barn will get a new weatherboarded exterior.

## Stone Barns

Stone barns pose rather different problems. There will certainly be no jacking up of the structure, rather there may have to be a painstaking repair of what is there. And the requirement for good insulation levels means that one face, usually the inside, will have to be covered over. You may need to underpin, especially where new openings are formed and the wall loadings are altered — it very much depends on the ground conditions beneath.

An additional problem is making the structure watertight, something which it was doubtless never designed to be in the first place. A typical stone barn consists of two skins of sorted stone separated by a rubble filled cavity. The existing walls will often as much as 450mm thick so, on most barns, it's quite impractical to build another skin on the inside. So you have to work with what is there. It's difficult to install an effective damp proof course and it can be difficult to stop rain pen-

etration through the walls as well. The planners are unlikely to accept a waterproof render being applied to the outside face, the best you can realistically hope to do is to point up the gaps between the stones. And accept, perhaps, that you are not living in a new build and that you may have to put up with the odd damp patch from time to time.

## Cost

Barn conversions cost rather more than new housing on a square metre basis. On a like-for-like basis, the unit area rate works out at between 30% and 50% more than undertaking new builds. Durrants are currently budgeting around £900/m$^2$ for converting timber barns and of course this figure does not include the purchase price. An upper deck will be slightly cheaper to construct on a square metre basis making two floor barns cheaper than single storey ones. But the saving is not great. Stone barns will tend to be a little more expensive because stone is always time consuming and therefore expensive to work with. Modern (brick) barns will be cheaper because the structure is usually in better condition. The more exceptional the barn, the more it is likely to cost to convert. Most barns are not listed unless they happen to be in the grounds (or the curtilage, in planning speak) of a listed farm in which case there may well be extra features to consider (thatch?). Generally speaking, most barn conversions are undertaken by selfbuilders. Spec. builders tend to shy away from them because they don't like unpredictability though one or two plucky ones will go as far as importing barns from France in order to get the right feel.

Despite the costs and the risks involved, barn conversion opportunities don't hang around. As Brian Belton commented: *If somebody wants a home deep in the country, there often isn't that much choice so when barns for conversion come onto the market they are currently snapped up, usually within two weeks, four weeks maximum. And most of the people buying barns are doing it for their own occupation.*

*Ten broken rules? 1 Masonry chimney 2 With TV Aerial 3 Dormer window on main house 4 Casement windows on main house 5 Extension onto main house 6 Brick arches on extension windows 7 Swept head windows on annexe 8 Garage door 9 Garage rooflights 10 Fencing all wrong. And isn't that a conservatory behind the main house? And the fountains?*

# Beware Building Costs

You may have a very good idea of what you can afford but, unless you are an experienced developer, you are unlikely to have much idea of how much and what sort of house that money will build. The going rate for new homebuilding varies of course as you travel around the land — currently the magazine Homebuilding & Renovating publishes a useful table showing average build costs across the country which vary from over £1000/m² for a top notch job in the London area down to under £400/m² for a basic job with lots of DIY input somewhere cheap. Novice builders often make the mistake of clutching at building costs like these and assume that they should divide their budget by the going rate and the answer is the size of house they should build. For instance, if your building budget is £80,000, then — by dividing £80,000 by say £500/m² — you could build a 160m² house. You may be very happy with this outcome, but it is also just possible that a 120m² house built to a much higher specification would have suited you better. You don't judge cars by their size and you shouldn't judge houses that way either.

Trouble is that all of these figures which are casually bandied about — none more so than unit area build costs expressed either as £/m² or £/ft² — are themselves very casually defined. There is no British Standard number to define what a building cost actually is and there isn't really such a thing as an industry standard either. Neither is there complete agreement on just how floor areas of houses should be measured. Different businesses use different methods and this makes a minefield out of the task of comparing costs and setting budgets.

## Measuring Floor Areas

You might at first think that how you go about measuring a floor area is a little bit academic. It is, if you aren't basing your budget and/or designs on some cost/unit area, but the evidence is that a huge number of builders do just that. And for those contemplating buying a timber frame kit, the floor area measurements are habitually used to compare one supplier's product with another, despite the fact that there is every chance you will not be comparing like with like.

The most widely used floor area measurement in Britain is the one which refers to the internal floor area of the house. It expressly excludes the area of the external walls, although (largely for convenience when carrying out the measurements) the area taken up by the internal partition walls is included. This measurement is also known as the net floor area.

## Gross v Net

There is another floor area measurement commonly in use, the gross floor area, which includes the area of the external walls. The effect of including the external wall areas in the calculation is to increase the apparent size of the building by up to 15% as external walls are, these days, usually constructed at thicknesses of 240-300mm. On the continent, it's the gross floor area that people usually refer to and many of the kit home suppliers use gross floor areas in their sales literature without being explicit about the fact and there is often no way of telling which area they are talking about other than by measuring it up yourself with a ruler. Using a gross floor area will appear to reduce unit area costs by 15% — an illusion.

## Garages

Garages should not be regarded as living space, even when they are integral to the rest of the house. Again, there is no check other than you and your ruler and you need to be very careful when evaluating sales literature to see that any integral garage is not included in the overall floor area. In contrast, detached garages are unlikely to be included as part of the floor area of a house in such literature, but here the trick is to exclude their building costs from any overall budget calculations. As a garage will typically cost between £5000 and £8000 to build (which may be as much as 20% of the total building cost), either its inclusion in floor areas or its exclusion from building costs will have a dramatic (and wholly misleading) effect on apparent unit area cost.

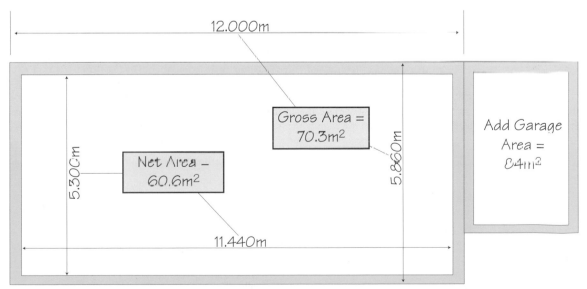

*One bungalow, three different ways of measuring the floor area. The net area — I think this is the correct one — shows a floor area at 60.6m². The gross area adds the external walls and comes out at 70.3m². Whilst the third way adds the attached garage, making the floor area total nearly 40% more than the net area.*

Added to possible confusion over net and gross floor areas, the lack of a consistent benchmark for measuring floor areas of houses means that a four-bedroom house with an integral garage could be said to be 150m$^2$ by one method and as much as 200m$^2$ by another.

## Grey Areas

There are a number of other features worth examining. When you get into the swing of measuring house sizes off plan, you will undoubtedly come across features which are not clear cut. Again there are no hard and fast rules but I would suggest the following assumptions are fair.

Cupboard Space: storage space such as under-eaves cupboards which are common when your upper storey is built into the roofspace, should be excluded from internal floor area. However, built-in full height wardrobes should be included as normal living space.

Utility Areas: normally these would be included as part of the living space. Sometimes it is hard to judge where a utility/storage area ends and a garage begins; if you're in this position don't worry too much because at least you understand what the issues are.

Internal Walls: conventionally, these are measured straight through and they are included as part of the internal area.

Stairwells: normally measured straight through on both floors and therefore included as internal floor area as if it was regular circulation space. The exception comes when you have a large open plan arrangement, not often seen in new houses but common in barn conversions where large openings have to be preserved. How do you decide when your ordinary stairwell becomes extraordinary? The rule is that if the upper floor opening is restricted to just the functioning stairwell, then measure straight through on both floors; if the open area extends beyond the immediate staircase, then you must exclude the entire stairwell area from the upper floor area.

## Building Costs

So much for defining the internal floor area. The "building costs" are even harder to define. There is no official standard but there is a sort of British way of defining building costs, as detailed in the accompanying Table. Making long lists and producing definitions is all very well, but what I am trying to get at is that building costs are really just a subgroup of development costs and that to concentrate on building costs to the exclusion of other costs is potentially disastrous. Like building costs, development costs can vary enormously and in this respect there is no greater variant than the price paid for your building plot. Some building plots are far more expensive to develop than others; problems can arise with bad ground, slopes, difficult service connections, difficult access, trees, legal covenants, intransigent planners — you name it! Now, the art of property developing is to be able to predict these problems and to negotiate a price on the land which reflects the cost of getting around them.

All housebuilders must pay close attention to these extra costs. One advantage a selfbuilder has over a professional is that they have more potential to control the project cashflow. For instance, you may not need to build a garage at all which could bring substantial savings. You can defer certain non-essential works such as landscaping for many years if cash is tight. You can substantially reduce your financial commitments by roughing it a little bit whilst the house is being built. And, of course, you can reduce costs by undertaking some of the work yourself. But all of this will pale into insignificance if you fail to budget the project correctly in the first place; to achieve significant savings, you need to buy and develop your plot appropriately, be very organised and be able to stick tightly to a budget.

## 14: Building Costs v Development Costs

| WHAT'S INCLUDED | WHAT'S EXCLUDED |
|---|---|
| House Superstructure | Building Plot |
| Electrics, Plumbing and Heating | Legal Fees |
| Kitchens and Bathrooms | Finance |
| Cooker and Hob | Insurance |
| Services Laid On | Design Fees |
| Working Drains | Planning Fees |
| Limited Paving | Building Regulation Fees |
| Garaging | Infrastructure Charge |
| Driveway | Service Connection Fees |
| Turfing | Floor Finishes |
| | Fitted Cupboards |
| | Laundry and Dishwasher |
| | Light Fittings |
| | Landscaping and Planting |
| | Curtains and Blinds |
| | Furnishings |

# Crucial Measurements

## Weight

1lb = 0.454kg
1kg = 2.2lbs
1cwt = 112lb = 50.9kg
1 ton = 20cwt = 1.016 tonne = 1016kg

## Length

1 millimetre (mm) = 0.039 inches
1 centimetre = 10mm = 0.394 inches
1 metre (m.) = 100cm = 1000mm = 39.4 inches
1 inch = 25.4mm
1ft = 305mm
1yard = 914mm = 0.914m

## Area

1 hectare = 10,000$m^2$ = 2.47 acres
1 acre = 4047$m^2$= an area 64m x 64m
1$m^2$ = 10.76$ft^2$ = 1.20$yd^2$
Area of a triangle = Half (Base x Height)

## Volume

1$m^3$ = 1.3$yd^3$
1$m^3$ = 1000lts = 220 gallons
1 gallon = 4.5lts

## Circles

Pi (,,) ‒ 3.14, r ‒ radius
Circumference ‒ 2,,r
Area of circle ‒ ,,$r^2$

## Heat

1kiloWatt = 3410 BTU (British Thermal Units)
1kiloWatt Hour (kWh) = 1kW burned for one hour
1 Joule ‒ 1 watt x 1 second
1 GJ = 278kWh
Specific heat of air = 0.33 watts/$m^3$/1°C

## Material densities

Sand : 1$m^3$ = 1.6 tonnes (20% more when wet)
All-in ballast: 1$m^3$ = 2 tonnes
OP Cement: 1$m^3$ = 1.4 tonnes
Hydrated lime: 1$m^3$ = 0.6 tonnes
Dense concrete blocks (+ paving): 1$m^3$ = 2 tonnes
Clinker blocks (lightweight): 1$m^3$ = 1.2 tonnes
Aerated blocks: 1$m^3$ = 0.65 tonnes
Super-lightweight blocks: 1$m^3$ = 0.48 tonnes
Face bricks: 1$m^3$ = 1.2 ‒ 1.6 tonnes
Softwood: 1$m^3$ = 0.6 tonnes

## What's in a Ton?

Conventionally when the word is written TON it refers to an imperial ton. When it's written TONNE, it's a metric ton(ne). The old imperial ton was 20cwt (hundredweight): the metric tonne is 1000 kilogrammes. The imperial ton is just 1.6% heavier than the metric tonne and therefore, to all intents and purposes you can ignore the difference.

Not so the differences between cubic metres and tonnes. Now quarries or merchants can sell by using either method. In fact many suppliers use both — volume up to 10 $m^3$ and tonnes above that level. The conversion on sand is 1$m^3$ ‒ 1.6tonnes but be warned that sand is much heavier when wet and so you'll be getting up to 20% less if you are buying by weight in wet weather. However, at £6 £10/ tonne for 10 tonne loads, it's cheap enough to not worry unduly over.

## Getting It Square

Only in a right-angled triangle is the square of the hypotenuse (the long side) equal to the square of the two shorter sides. This basic rule of geometry (*Pythagoras' Theorem*) allows us to get our corners dead square using nothing more than a tape measure. Most carpenters are taught this bit of geometry via the 3 4 5 rule which they use for squaring up frames but it is just as useful when setting out foundations. The classic 3-4-5 triangle calculation is demonstrated in the diagram but, of course, the calculation will work with any lengths, just as long as you can work out the squares — tip: get a calculator with a square root function.

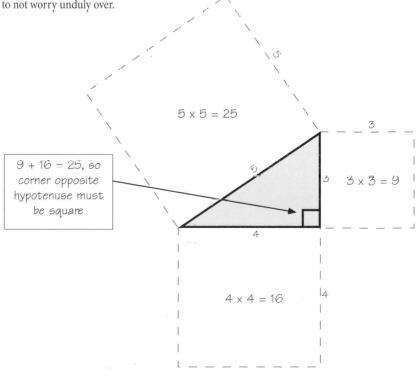

5 x 5 = 25

9 + 16 = 25, so corner opposite hypotenuse must be square

3 x 3 = 9

4 x 4 = 16

# Contacts

| Company | Phone | Website | Category |
|---|---|---|---|
| Abbey Pynford | 01923 211160 | www.abbeypynford.co.uk | Foundations |
| Actis | 01380 730195 | in french | Insulation |
| Advanced Showers | 01483 295930 | www.advanced-showers.com | Showers |
| AECB | 01559 370908 | www.aecb.net | Eco builders organisation |
| Aga Rayburn | 08457 125207 | www.aga-rayburn.co.uk | Cookers |
| Allied Manufacturing | 0208 205 4188 | www.kingswood-allied.co.uk | Kitchens |
| Altro Safety Floors | 01462 707600 | www.altro.co.uk | Floors |
| Amazon nails | 01706 814696 | www.strawbalefutures.org.uk | Straw bale housing |
| Amptec Boilers | 01256 363417 | www.electroheatuk.com | Electric boilers |
| Andersen Windows | 01283 511122 | www.andersenwindows.com | |
| Anki Chimneys | 01983 527997 | www.anki.co.uk | |
| Croydex H20 Showers | 01264 367224 | | Power showers |
| Architects Registration Board | 020 7580 5861 | www.arb.org.uk | |
| Arcon CAD software | 01420 520023 | www.3darchitect.co.uk | |
| Arrow | 01905 754200 | www.arrow-distributors.co.uk | Kitchen Appliances |
| B&Q | 0845 309 3099 | www.diy.com | DIY store |
| Basement Development Group | web site only | www.basements.org.uk | |
| Baxi Potterton | 08706 060623 | www.baxi.co.uk | Boilers |
| Beco Wallform | 01652 651641 | www.becowallform.co.uk | Polystyrene houses |
| BIAT | 020 7278 2206 | www.biat.org.uk | Architectural technologists |
| Bill Miller Architects | 01954 251426 | www.millerarchitects.co.uk | |
| Bio Bubble | 01243 370100 | www.bio-bubble.com | Off mains drainage |
| Blanc de Bierge | 01733 202566 | www.blancdebierges.com | Pavings |
| Border Oak | 01568 708752 | www.borderoak.com | Oak houses |
| BPAC | 01592 652017 | www.bpac.co.uk | SIPS houses |
| Brickability | 01656 645222 | no | Brick factors |
| British Fenestration Rating Council | 07000 780 971 | www.bfrc.org | |
| Buildstore Mortgages | 0800 018 5740 | www.buildstore.co.uk | |
| Buildstore's Plotsearch | 0870 870 9994 | www.buildstore.co.uk/plotsearch | Plot searches |
| Burdens | 0117 986 1766 | www.burdens.co.uk | Drainage |
| Buxton Lime Industries | 01298 768467 | | Limebond |
| Caradon Wintun | 0141 889 5969 | www.wintun.co.uk | Level thresholds |
| Carpenter Woodland Oak | 01225 743089 | www.carpenteroak.co.uk | Oak houses |
| CED Stone factors | 01708 867237 | www.ced.ltv.co.uk | |
| Celcon Jamera | 01732 886333 | www.celcon.co.uk | Block houses |
| Celotex | 01473 822093 | www.celotex.co.uk | Insulation |
| Centre for Earthen Architecture | 01752 233630 | checked 12/02/02 | |
| Chelmer Heating | 01245 471111 | www.chelmerheating.co.uk | Thermal stores |
| Classical Flagstones | 0117 9371960 | www.classical-flagstones.com | |
| Community Selfbuild Agency | 0207 415 7092 | www.communityselfbuildagency.org | |
| Conservation Engineering | 01359 268340 | www.conservation-engineering.co.uk | Heating design |
| Construction Resources | 0207 450 2211 | www.ecoconstruct.com | Green builders merchant |
| Cress Water | 01905 422707 | www.cresswater.co.uk | Reed beds |
| Crosslee Appliances | 01422 203585 | www.crosslee.co.uk | Gas tumble driers |
| Customs & Excise Advice Line | 08450 109000 | www.hmce.gov.uk | |
| British Earth Sheltered Housing Assoc | 01600 860359 | www.besa-uk.org | |
| Dale Joinery | 01706 350350 | www.dalejoinery.com | |
| DCD Heating Controllers | 01753 882028 | www.dcd.co.uk | |
| Design for Homes | | www.designforhomes.org | Find an architect |
| Devi ElectroHeat | 01359 242400 | www.devi.com | Electric underfloor heating |
| DMS Insurance | 01909 591652 | www.selfbuild.armor.co.uk | |
| DPS Heat | 01372 803675 | www.heatweb.com | Thermal stores |
| Durrant & Son | 01379 642233 | www.durrants.com | Suffolk Estate Agents |
| Ellis-Miller, Jonathan | 01223 359000 | www.ellis-miller.com | Architect |
| Encon | 01937 524200 | www.encon.co.uk | Insulation |
| Environment Agency | 08459 333111 | www.environment-agency.gov.uk | Services |
| Environmental Seals | 01304 842 555 | www.envirograf.com | Fire proofing paints |
| Esse | 01282 813235 | www.ouzledale.co.uk | Ranges |
| Excel Industries | 01495 350655 | www.warmcel.com | Insulation |

| | | | |
|---|---|---|---|
| F.P.Herting | 020 8606 7000 | www.fpherting.co.uk | Ironmongery shopping |
| Faral | 01342 317171 | www.faralradiators.co.uk | Radiators |
| Fenland Timber | 01733 350540 | | Flooring |
| Fermacell | 0870 6090306 | www.fermacell.co.uk | Wall boards |
| Fillcrete Tradis | | www.fillcrete.com | Breathing walls |
| Focus Do It All | 0800 436 436 | www.focusdoitall.co.uk | Kitchens |
| Hafele UK | 01788 542020 | www.hafele.co.uk | Kitchen ironmongery |
| Harris & Bailey | 020 8654 3181 | no | Stone factors |
| Harrison McCarthy | 0161 794 9021 | www.diyboilers.com | Plumbing supplies |
| Hewden Stuart | 0800 371565 | www.hewden.co.uk | Toll Hire |
| Holbrook Insurance | 01483 505932 | www.holbrook-insurance.co.uk | Insurance |
| Home Automation | 01249 443422 | www.homeautomation.co.uk | Intelligent switching |
| Hormann | 0800 0834639 | www.hormann.co.uk | Garage doors |
| Housebuilder XL | 01530 415600 | www.hbxl.co.uk | Project Management |
| Huf Haus | 01932 828502 | www.huf-haus.com | German prefab houses |
| Idrosplit | via Plumb Center | www.plumbcenter.co.uk | Chillers |
| IKEA | 020 8208 5600 | www.ikea.co.uk | Kitchens |
| IP Homenetworks | 0121 766 8460 | www.iphomenet.com | Structured cabling |
| IRM rainwater Harvesting | 01274 707050 | www.titanplastech.co.uk | |
| Isokern | 01202 861650 | www.isokern.co.uk | Chimneys |
| Jablite Roof Element | 0208 320 9100 | www.jablite.co.uk | SIPS Roofing |
| Jackson's Fencing | 01233 750393 | www.jacksons-fencing.co.uk | Fencing |
| Jeld Wen (John Carr) | 01302 394000 | www.jeld-wen.co.uk | Joinery |
| Jewson | 0800 539766 | www.jewson.co.uk | Large builders merchant |
| John Davidson Pipes | 01228 791503 | www.jdpipes.co.uk | Drainage |
| Johnson & Starley | 01604 762881 | www.johnsonandstarleyltd.co.uk | Warm air, passive stack |
| Keystone Lintels | | www.keystone-lintels.co.uk | |
| Kingspan | 01544 388601 | www.insulation.kingspan.co.uk | Insulation |
| Landbank Services | 0118 9626022 | www.landbank.co.uk | Plot search |
| Culligan (formerly Liff) | 01484 512537 | www.culligan.com | Water conditioning |
| Lindman | | www.lindman.co.uk | External doors |
| Machells | 0113 250 5043 | www.machells.co.uk | Salvage |
| Magnet | various | www.magnet.co.uk | Joinery |
| Marshall's Panablok | 01636 832000 | www.marshalls.co.uk | Panel housing |
| Mattick, Stephen | 01799 541695 | Superior house designer | |
| MFI | 0870 609 5555 | www.mfi.co.uk | Kitchens |
| Milbank Roofing | 01787 223931 | www.milbank.co.uk | Roofing, floors, basements |
| NHBC Solo | 01494 735363 | www.nhbc.co.uk | Warranties |
| Norman & Underwood | 0116 251 5000 | www.nandu.co.uk | Glass |
| Norwich & Peterborough | 0800 883322 | www.npbs.co.uk | Finance |
| OFFER | | www.open.gov.uk/offer | Electricity |
| OFWAT | 0121 625 1300 | www.ofwat.gov.uk | Water |
| QED Systemline | 01483 747474 | www.qed.co.uk | Audio |
| Osma | 01249 766600 | www.osma.co.uk | Drainage |
| Owens Corning | 0800 627465 | www.owenscorning.com | Insulation |
| Pendock Profiles | 01952 580590 | www.pendock.co.uk | Trunking |
| Plotfinder | 09065 575400 | www.plotfinder.net | Plot search |
| Potterton | 0870 606 0780 | www.potterton.co.uk | Boilers |
| Potton | 01480 401401 | www.potton.co.uk | Timber frame houses |
| Premdor | | www.pemdor.co.uk | Joinery |
| Project Builder | 020 7716 5050 | www.project-builder-insurance.com | Insurance, warranties |
| R&J Hardware | 01254 52525 | no | Ironmongery |
| Rackhams | 01924 455876 | www.housefloors.co.uk | Beam and block floors |
| Real Door Company | 01462 451230 | www.realdoor.co.uk | |
| Redbank | 01530 270333 | www.redbankmfg.co.uk | Flues, roofing |
| Redland Roofing | 08705 601000 | www.redland.co.uk | |
| Retrotec | 01453 836700 | www.retroteceurope.co.uk | Air pressure testing |
| RIAI | 016 761703 | www.riai.ie | Irish Architects |
| RIAS | 0131 229 7205 | www.rias.org.uk | Scottish Architects |
| RIBA Clients Advisory Service | 020 7307 3700 | www.architecture.com | English Architects |
| Tarmac Topfloor | 01223 837838 | www.tarmactopfloor.co.uk | Beam and block floors |
| RICS | 020 7222 7000 | www.rics.org | Surveyors |
| RMC Foundation Flow | 0800 667827 | www.rmc.co.uk | Concrete |
| Rockwool | 01656 862621 | www.rockwool.co.uk | Insulation |

| | | | |
|---|---|---|---|
| Roma Jay Kitchen Designs | 01702 715565 | | Kitchen Design |
| RSAW | 02920 874753 | www.architecture.com | Welsh Architects |
| RSUA | 02890 323760 | www.rsua.org.uk | Ulster Architects |
| Rytons | 01536 511874 | www.vents.co.uk | Ventilation |
| Salvo | | www.salvo.co.uk | Salvage directory |
| Scandia Hus | | www.scandia-hus.co.uk | Timber frame houses |
| Scottish Building Standards | | www.scotland.gov.uk/build_regs/ | |
| Scotts of Thrapston | 01832 732366 | www.scottsofthrapston.co.uk | Roof trusses |
| Seconds & Co | 01544 260501 | www.secondsandco.co.uk | Insulation |
| SEDBUK boiler ratings | web site only | www.boilers.org.uk | |
| Shackerley | 01257 273114 | www.shackerley.com | Glass blocks |
| Sheffield Insulation | | www.sheffins.co.uk | |
| SIPTEC | 01234 881551 | www.siptec.com | SIPS houses |
| Sound Reduction Systems | 01204 380074 | www.soundreduction.co.uk | Sound proofing |
| Space 4 | | www.space4.co.uk | SIPS houses |
| Spanish Slate Quarries | 020 8961 7725 | www.ssq.co.uk | Roofing |
| Spectus | 01625 420 400 | www.spectussystems.com | uPVC joinery |
| Star Curtains | 01638 666642 | no | Curtain makers |
| Sutherland Associates | 01737 370077 | www.sutherlandassociates.co.uk | Energy consultants |
| Taylor Lane | 01432 271912 | www.taylor-lane.co.uk | Timber frame houses |
| The Lime Centre | 01862 713636 | www.thelimecentre.co.uk | Lime consultants |
| Thermonex Basements | | www.thermonex.com | Prefab basements |
| TJ Crump Oakwrights | 01432 353353 | www.oakwrights.co.uk | Oak houses |
| TLC | 01293 565630 | www.tlc-direct.co.uk | Electrical wholesaler |
| Tudor Roof Tiles | 01797 320202 | www.tudorrooftiles.co.uk | |
| Unico Warm Air | 07785 985876 | www.unicosystem.com | Warm Air Heating |
| United Tile | 01384 480456 | www.unitedtile.co.uk | Tiling |
| VAT notices 708 and 0501 | 0845 0109000 | www.hmce.gov.uk | VAT |
| Velfac | 01223 897100 | www.velfac.co.uk | Composite windows |
| Velux | 0800 3169893 | www.velux.co.uk | Roof windows |
| Villavent | 01993 778481 | www.villavent.co.uk | Whole house ventilation |
| Walter Segal Trust | 01668 213544 | www.segalselfbuild.co.uk | Community selfbuild |
| Water Dynamics | 01622 873322 | www.waterdynamics.co.uk | Grey water recycling |
| Wickes | 0500 300 328 | www.wickes.co.uk | Builders merchant |
| Passivent | 0161 962 7113 | www.buildingproductdesign.com | Passive stack insurance |
| Woodalls | 0208 458 6434 | www.we-sell-it.co.uk | Kitchen Appliances |
| X10 | information on | www.kevinboone.com/x10 | Home Automation |
| Zurich Custombuild | 01252 387594 | no | Building warranties |

## Further Reading

| | | | |
|---|---|---|---|
| Blackberry Books | 01983 840310 | www.blackberry-books.co.uk | Selfbuild books |
| Building Bookshop | 0207 692 4040 | www.buildingcentre.co.uk | Bookshop |
| Build It | 020 7772 8300 | www.insidecom.co.uk | Self build magazine |
| Building Your Own Home | 01909 591652 | www.selfbuild.armor.co.uk | Books and insurance |
| CRC Bookshop | 0207 505 6622 | www.brebookshop.com | BRE Bookshop |
| EPA Press | 01799 541207 | no | The Electricians Guide |
| Homebuilding & Renovating | 01527 834406 | www.homebuilding.co.uk | Selfbuild magazine |
| How to Find and Buy a Building Plot | | 020 7772 8479 | Self build books |
| Selfbuild & Design | 01283 742970 | www.selfbuildanddesign.com | Selfbuild magazine |